ROUTLEDGE HANDBOOK OF ENVIRONMENTAL ANTHROPOLOGY

Environmental anthropology studies historic and present human–environment interactions. This volume illustrates the ways in which today's environmental anthropologists are constructing new paradigms for understanding the multiplicity of players, pressures, and ecologies in every environment, and the value of cultural knowledge of landscapes.

This Handbook provides a comprehensive survey of contemporary topics in environmental anthropology and thorough discussions on the current state and prospective future of the field in seven key sections. As the contributions to this volume demonstrate, the sub-field of environmental anthropology is responding to cultural adaptations and responses to environmental changes in multiple and complex ways. Operating in a discipline concerned primarily with human–environment interaction, environmental anthropologists recognize that they are now working within a pressure cooker of rapid environmental damage that is forcing behavioural and often cultural changes around the world. As we see in the breadth of topics presented in this volume, these environmental challenges have inspired both renewed foci on traditional topics such as food procurement, ethnobiology, and spiritual ecology; and a broad new range of subjects, such as resilience, non-human rights, architectural anthropology, industrialism, and education. This volume offers scholars and students quick access to both established and trending environmental anthropological explorations into theory, methodology, and practice.

Helen Kopnina is assistant professor of environmental anthropology at the Institute of Cultural Anthropology and Development Sociology at Leiden University, the Netherlands. She is also a coordinator and lecturer within the Sustainable Business Program and researcher in the fields of environmental education and environmental social sciences at The Hague University of Applied Sciences, the Netherlands.

Eleanor Shoreman-Ouimet is an environmental anthropologist and currently teaches in the Anthropology Department at the University of Connecticut, USA. Her research focuses on human–environment interactions, cross-cultural conservation practices, community response to natural hazards, and the effects of climate change.

ROUTLEDGE HANDBOOK OF ENVIRONMENTAL ANTHROPOLOGY

*Edited by Helen Kopnina and
Eleanor Shoreman-Ouimet*

Routledge
Taylor & Francis Group

LONDON AND NEW YORK

earthscan
from Routledge

First published 2017 by Routledge

2 Park Square, Milton Park, Abingdon, Oxfordshire OX14 4RN
711 Third Avenue, New York, NY 10017

Routledge is an imprint of the Taylor & Francis Group, an informa business

First issued in paperback 2018

British Library Cataloguing in Publication Data
A catalogue record for this book is available from the British Library.

Library of Congress Cataloging-in-Publication Data
Names: Kopnina, Helen, editor. | Shoreman-Ouimet, Eleanor, editor.
Title: Routledge handbook of environmental anthropology/
edited by Helen Kopnina and Eleanor Shoreman-Ouimet.
Description: New York, NY: Routledge, 2016. |
Includes bibliographical references and index.
Identifiers: LCCN 2016000785 | ISBN 9781138782877
(hardback) | ISBN 9781315768946 (ebook)
Subjects: LCSH: Human ecology—Handbooks, manuals, etc.
Classification: LCC GF41 .R678 2016 | DDC 304.2—dc23
LC record available at http://lccn.loc.gov/2016000785

ISBN: 978-1-138-78287-7 (hbk)
ISBN: 978-0-367-02703-2 (pbk)

Typeset in Bembo
by Keystroke, Neville Lodge, Tettenhall, Wolverhampton

CONTENTS

Contents

FIGURES

TABLES

CONTRIBUTORS

Editors:

Helen Kopnina

Helen Kopnina (PhD University of Cambridge, 2002) is a researcher in the fields of environmental education and environmental social sciences. Helen is currently employed at both Leiden University and at The Hague University of Applied Sciences (HHS) in the Netherlands. At the Leiden Institute of Cultural Anthropology and Development Sociology she is Assistant Professor of Environmental Anthropology. At the HHS, she is a coordinator and lecturer within the Sustainable Business Program. Helen is the author of more than 60 peer-reviewed articles and co-author and co-editor of 12 books, including *Sustainability: Key Issues* (2015) and *Culture and Conservation: Beyond Anthropocentrism* (2015).

Affiliation: Leiden University, Institute of Cultural Anthropology and Development Sociology and The Hague University of Applied Sciences, the Netherlands.

Eleanor Shoreman-Ouimet is Assistant Professor in Residence at the University of Connecticut. Her research focuses on human–environment interactions, cross-cultural conservation practices, community response to natural hazards and the effects of climate change, and the links between culture, history, economics, environmental ethics, and resource management. Her recent publications also address the study of environmental repair, the influence of anthropocentrism in the social sciences, and facilitating cooperative efforts between anthropologists and conservation groups. She is the co-author and co-editor of five books, including *Culture and Conservation: Beyond Anthropocentrism* (2015), and *Sustainability: Key Issues* (2015).

Affiliation: University of Connecticut, USA.

Contributors:

Ryan T. Adams is Assistant Professor of Anthropology at Lycoming College, in Williamsport, Pennsylvania, following three years at Indiana University–Purdue University Indianapolis (IUPUI). His research interests include economic and environmental anthropology, farming, elites, and the anthropology of food. He has been conducting fieldwork in the Brazilian Amazon since 2003; and in Brooklyn, New York since 2011. He has ongoing, long-term research interests studying up with large-scale landowners in Santarém, Pará State, Brazil, and working with food reformers in Brooklyn, New York. Past projects include an analysis of El Niño-related drought events in the Brazilian Amazon; a study of organic farming in Bloomington, Indiana; and collaboration on a number of research projects at the Anthropological Center for Training and Research on Global Environmental Change (ACT) at Indiana University.

Affiliation: Sociology/Anthropology Department, Lycoming College, Williamsport, PA, USA.

E. N. Anderson is Professor of Anthropology, Emeritus, at the University of California, Riverside, and Affiliate Professor at the University of Washington, Seattle. He received his PhD in Anthropology from the University of California, Berkeley, in 1967. He has done research on ethnobiology, cultural ecology, political ecology, and medical anthropology, in several areas, especially Hong Kong, British Columbia, California, and the Yucatán Peninsula of Mexico. His books include *The Food of China* (Yale University Press, 1988), *Ecologies of the Heart* (Oxford University Press, 1996), *Political Ecology in a Yucatec Maya Community* (University of Arizona Press, 2005), and *The Pursuit of Ecotopia* (Praeger, 2010). He has five children and five grandchildren. He lives in Riverside, California, with his wife Barbara Anderson and three large dogs.

Affiliation: Department of Anthropology, University of California, Riverside, USA; Department of Anthropology, University of Washington, Seattle, USA.

Mary K. Anglin is Associate Professor in the Department of Anthropology at the University of Kentucky, where she recently completed a term as department chair. Through long-term ethnographic research, based in urban Northern California, she has examined breast cancer as a public health problem and a social crisis, with attention to the role of social activism in challenging biomedical views of "risk" as well as approaches to treatment. Future plans include a return to ethnographic work on issues of environmental contamination in Appalachia, with attention to their impact on communities, health, and well-being. The theme that unites these various projects is an abiding interest in social justice and the potential uses of a critically applied anthropology.

Affiliation: Department of Anthropology, University of Kentucky, Lexington, USA.

Lauren Baker is the John D. Montgomery Post-Doctoral Fellow at the Pacific Basin Research Center at Soka University of America, Orange County, California. She has a PhD and a Master's of Environmental Management from the Yale School of Forestry & Environmental Studies. Her research examines indigenous social movements and identity politics in response to oil operations in the northeast Peruvian Amazon.

Affiliation: Soka University of America, California, USA.

Alan R. Beals is Professor Emeritus in Anthropology at the University of California, Riverside. He received his PhD in 1954 from the University of California, Berkeley. He has carried out field projects in a small town in Northern California, with an Air Force bomber crew, with the United States Army, and in Mexico. Most of his fieldwork has been in Karnatak State in South

India. His major interests are in cultural change, ecology, conflict, and demography. Selected publications: *Gopalpur: A South Indian Village* (1980); *Culture in Process* (1979, with George D. Spindler and Louise S. Spindler); *An Introduction to Anthropology* (1977, with R. L. Beals and H. Hoijer); *Village Life in South India* (1974); and *Divisiveness and Social Conflict* (1966, with B. J. Siegel).

Affiliation: Department of Anthropology, University of California, Riverside, USA.

Brenda R. Beckwith is a researcher, educator, and practitioner in ethnobotany and ethno-ecology. She is most interested in producing meaningful, relevant scholarship with direct benefit to Indigenous communities. Brenda works to cultivate the myriad connections of people and plants across the landscape, and practice community-engaged and collaborative methods of applied ethnoecology to embed these interdisciplinary approaches into the fields of conservation, land management, ecological restoration, and environmental education. In addition to working as a consultant (Principal, Beckwith Ecologies), she teaches courses that mix theory with application as an instructor in the School of Environment and Geomatics, Selkirk College; and as sessional instructor and adjunct professor in the School of Environmental Studies, University of Victoria, British Columbia.

Affiliation: Beckwith Ecologies; School of Environment and Geomatics, Selkirk College, Castlegar, British Columbia; School of Environmental Studies, University of Victoria, British Columbia, Canada.

Carol Black is an independent writer, researcher, and filmmaker. Her most recent film is *Schooling the World*, about the impacts of modern institutional education on small-scale land-based societies.

Eduardo Brondízio is Professor of Anthropology, co-director of the Center for the Analysis of Social-Ecological Landscapes (CASEL), and a member of the Advisory Board of the Ostrom Workshop in Political Theory and Policy Analysis at Indiana University Bloomington. He is also a member of the faculty of the Environment and Society Program at the University of Campinas (Universidade Estadual de Campinas; UNICAMP), Brazil. Brondízio's research in the field of environmental anthropology combines long-term, longitudinal studies of the transformation of rural and urban populations and landscapes in the Amazon with research on global environmental change. Brondízio is a member of the Science Committee of the international research initiative *Future Earth* and was a member of the Science Committee of the International Geosphere–Biosphere Programme (IGBP) from 2011 to 2015. He is co-editor-in-chief of Elsevier's *Current Opinion in Environmental Sustainability*.

Affiliation: Department of Anthropology, Center for the Analysis of Social-Ecological Landscapes (CASEL), and the Ostrom Workshop in Political Theory and Policy Analysis, Indiana University Bloomington, USA.

David G. Casagrande is Associate Professor of Anthropology at Lehigh University. He has studied how humans interact with their natural environments in Latin America and the United States with support from the U.S. National Science Foundation, National Sea Grant College Program, and National Institutes of Health. He earned a PhD in Ecological Anthropology from the University of Georgia, a Master's degree in Ecology and Policy from the Yale School of

Forestry & Environmental Studies, and a Bachelor's degree in Geography from Southern Connecticut State University. He lives on a small farm in rural Pennsylvania where he experiments with how to live sustainably.

Affiliation: Department of Anthropology, Lehigh University, Pennsylvania, USA.

C. Anne Claus is Assistant Professor of Anthropology at American University in Washington, DC. She has published work on the socio-economic impacts of environmental policies on coastal communities, the political ecology of disasters, and conservation social science. Her current research projects address the transformation of international conservation in Okinawa, Japan, and the development of alternative food provisioning systems in post-disaster spaces.

Affiliation: American University, Washington, DC, USA.

Mark Coeckelbergh is Professor of Philosophy of Media and Technology in the Department of Philosophy at the University of Vienna, and (part-time) Professor of Technology and Social Responsibility at De Montfort University, UK. He has also been managing director of the 3TU Centre for Ethics and Technology in the Netherlands. His publications include *Growing Moral Relations* (2012), *Human Being @ Risk* (2013), *Environmental Skill* (2015), *Money Machines* (2015), and numerous articles in the area of philosophy of technology, in particular the ethics of robotics and ICTs. He also has a keen interest in environmental philosophy.

Affiliation: Department of Philosophy, University of Vienna, Austria.

Lauren Dodaro is a cultural anthropologist researching Indigenous communities in the Ecuadorian Amazon. Originally from New York, she is pursuing her PhD at Tulane University in New Orleans.

Affiliation: Department of Anthropology, Tulane University, New Orleans, USA.

Michael R. Dove is the Margaret K. Musser Professor of Social Ecology, School of Forestry & Environmental Studies; curator, Peabody Museum of Natural History; Professor, Department of Anthropology; director, Council on Southeast Asia Studies; and co-coordinator of the joint doctoral program in Anthropology and Environmental Studies, Yale University. His most recent books are: *The Anthropology of Climate Change* (Wiley–Blackwell, 2014); *Climate Cultures* (co-editor J. Barnes; Yale University Press, 2015), and *Science, Society, and Environment* (co-author D. M. Kammen; Routledge, 2015). His current research takes a comparative, post-humanist approach to views of the environment in South and Southeast Asia.

Affiliation: Yale University, Connecticut, USA.

Rob Efird is Associate Professor of Anthropology and Asian Studies at Seattle University, Washington. His research focuses on environmental education in mainland China and the United States. Professor Efird is a member of the National Committee on US–China Relations' Public Intellectual Program and a former Fulbright Senior Research Fellow for China.

Affiliation: Department of Anthropology, Sociology, and Social Work, Seattle University, Washington, USA.

Stefano Fiorini is a social and cultural anthropologist with a background in the natural sciences. His work has involved multidisciplinary collaborations with biologists, ecologists, sociologists, and political scientists, in projects that often included an applied dimension. Most recently he has collaborated with institutional researchers, faculties, and administrators for the benefit of Indiana University, engaging with the emerging field of Learning Analytics and receiving recognition from the Association of Institutional Research (AIR). He has published in various journals, among them *American Anthropologist*, the *Journal of Applied Ecology,* and *Human Organization*. Stefano is Lead Research Management Analyst with Bloomington Assessment and Research and an adjunct faculty member in the Department of Anthropology at Indiana University Bloomington.

Affiliation: Indiana University Bloomington, USA.

Tania Halber is a learning theorist, curriculum development specialist, and ethnoecologist whose research integrates the fields of education, sociology, and ecology with anthropology and psychology, among others. She is interested in transformative learning, particularly in a multi-cultural context, and traditional knowledge systems in the Canadian and American Pacific Northwest, Cuba, and Europe. Since her PhD work, Tania has focused on applying and deepening her knowledge as a freelance education consultant. In addition to the program she developed for state officials and tribal leaders in Washington, Tania continues to develop various transformative nature-based programs including an International Transformative Nature Program for the early years, and a special program for mothers. She continues to explore the role of technology in integrated transformative nature-based learning through various eLearning projects.

Affiliation: Freelance education consultant (formerly Faculty of Education and School of Environmental Studies, University of Victoria, British Columbia, Canada.)

Chris Hebdon is a PhD candidate in Anthropology and Forestry & Environmental Studies at Yale University. His research examines the politics of energy transitions and concepts of energy in Ecuador.

Affiliation: Yale University, Connecticut, USA.

Susanna M. Hoffman (PhD, University of California, Berkeley) is a disaster anthropologist, author, co-author and editor of ten books, two ethnographic films, and more than 40 articles and columns. Among her books are *Catastrophe and Culture* (SAR Press, 2002) and *The Angry Earth* (Routledge, 1999; 2nd edn. forthcoming), both co-edited with Anthony Oliver-Smith. Ethnographic films include the award-winning *Kypseli: Women and Men Apart* and the Emmy-winning *The Nature of Culture*. She was the first recipient of the Fulbright Foundation's Aegean Initiative between Greece and Turkey. Recently she launched the Disaster Interest Group at the Society for Applied Anthropology, now home to many interdisciplinary researchers on disaster and featuring over 130 presentations yearly. Susanna has worked in Aceh, Sumatra; Uzbekistan; Kazakhstan; El Salvador; India; and within the United States on Hurricane Katrina, the Deepwater Horizon oil spill, the Oakland firestorm, and more. She helped write the United Nations report *Environmental Management and the Mitigation of Natural Disasters: A Gender Perspective*. She served as a board member of Project Concern International, an NGO dealing with risk reduction and disaster recovery in 13 countries and has advised the Red Cross, the Red Crescent, Northwest Medical Teams, and other organizations. Susanna consults and gives talks nationally and internationally and appears frequently on television and radio.

Affiliation: Hoffman Consulting, www.susannahoffman.com

Cindy Isenhour is Assistant Professor of Anthropology and cooperating faculty member in the School of Economics, The Climate Change Institute, and the Senator George J. Mitchell Center for Sustainability Solutions at the University of Maine. Her research in ecological and economic anthropology focuses on the materials economy, consumer culture, climate change, and environmental policy. She has published in *American Ethnologist, City & Society, Environment and Society, Local Environment, Conservation and Society*, and the *Journal of Cleaner Production*.

Affiliation: Department of Anthropology, University of Maine, USA.

Alder Keleman is a doctoral candidate in the combined degree program hosted by the Yale School of Forestry & Environmental Studies, the Yale Department of Anthropology, and the New York Botanical Gardens. Her research explores the contributions made by agrobiodiversity (or native and traditional crops) to household food security and food culture in Cochabamba, Bolivia. Previously, she worked in applied agricultural development research at the International Maize and Wheat Improvement Center (CIMMYT) in Mexico, and the United Nations Food and Agriculture Organization (FAO) in Rome, Italy.

Affiliation: Yale University, Connecticut, USA.

David W. Kidner worked as a process design engineer in the petroleum industry before turning to social science with a PhD in Psychology from the University of London. Having taught critical social science and environmental philosophy in the UK and the USA for three decades, he has recently retired from full-time academic teaching, and now lives in southwest France. His most recent book is *Nature and Experience in the Culture of Delusion* (Palgrave Macmillan, 2012).

Affiliation: Estampures, France.

Peter Wynn Kirby is an environmental specialist and ethnographer in the School of Geography and the Environment, University of Oxford. He holds a PhD in Social Anthropology from the University of Cambridge. Peter focuses on toxic waste and nuclear risk in Japan and China – notably in the irradiated aftermath of the 2011 tsunami disaster in Tohoku – and scrutinizes the cultural underpinnings of environmental attitudes, from popular culture to conceptions of purity and pollution. His most recent book is *Troubled Natures: Waste, Environment, Japan* (University of Hawai'i Press, 2011), and he has also published opinion pieces on a variety of topics in *The New York Times, The Japan Times, The Guardian*, and elsewhere.

Affiliation: School of Geography and the Environment, University of Oxford, UK.

Kimberly Kirner, PhD, is Associate Professor of Cultural Anthropology at California State University, Northridge, specializing in environmental anthropology, applied cognitive anthropology, and medical anthropology. She is interested in understanding interrelationships between cognition, emotion, and decision-making; construction of identity and community; and the way informal knowledge systems interact with policy to impact human behavior. Her research focuses on the political ecology of American West urban–rural interfaces, particularly in the face of climate change and water scarcity; cultural modeling of health-related beliefs and behavior; and the relationship between ritual, belief, and sustainable behaviors in contemporary Pagan traditions. Kimberly has also worked as an applied anthropologist in program design, evaluation, and fund development for the non-profit and government sectors.

Affiliation: California State University, Northridge, USA.

Stasja Koot, PhD, has been working with Bushmen people in Namibia since the late 1990s, when he did fieldwork for his MA in Anthropology. Between 2002 and 2007, he worked at the Treesleeper Camp, Tsintsabis; and in 2013 he wrote his PhD dissertation on "Dwelling in Tourism: Power and Myth amongst Bushmen in Southern Africa." He then worked for two years as a postdoctoral fellow at the International Institute of Social Studies, Erasmus University Rotterdam, where he also started research into the political economy of conservation in online and southern African environments. In 2015, he moved to Wageningen University, where he now works as a lecturer and a postdoctoral fellow.

Affiliation: Social Sciences Department, Wageningen University, the Netherlands.

Angela Kreutz is Lecturer in Architecture at Deakin University, Geelong, Australia. She received her architectural training from the University of Stuttgart, Germany, completed her PhD studies with the Aboriginal Environments Research Centre at the University of Queensland, Australia, and was the recipient of a German Academic Exchange Service (DAAD) postdoctoral fellowship with the Program in Environmental Design at the University of Colorado, Boulder, USA. Her research interests span across architecture, anthropology, and environmental psychology. She has researched, collaborated, and consulted with various communities, including their children, in Australia, Europe, and the United States. Her recent book is *Children and the Environment in an Australian Indigenous Community* (Routledge, 2015).

Affiliation: School of Architecture and Built Environment, Deakin University, Geelong, Australia.

José E. Martínez-Reyes is Associate Professor in the Department of Anthropology and School for the Environment and director of the Environmental Anthropology Program at the University of Massachusetts Boston. He has previously taught at the University of Puerto Rico Mayagüez and the University of Quintana Roo, Mexico and has been a Visiting Fellow at Yale University's Agrarian Studies Program. He specializes in political ecology, environmental anthropology, biocultural diversity conservation, and social theory. Recent publications include a co-edited special issue on biodiversity conservation in Mexico in *Conservation and Society* [12(2), 2014], with Nora Haenn, Liz Olson, and Leticia Durand. He is author of *Moral Ecology of a Forest: Nature Industry and Mayan Post-Conservation* (University of Arizona Press, fall 2016).

Affiliation: Department of Anthropology and School for the Environment, University of Massachusetts Boston, USA.

Hillary Mason is a PhD candidate in the School of Education and Human Development at the University of Colorado Denver. Her research focuses primarily on environmental identity at the nexus of environmental science education and discourse. In this context, she uses identity theory as a framework to explore the formative experiences and mental models individuals attribute to the way they view and teach about human–environment relationships. She is active in the global environmental education community, and has contributed to several journal publications, including the *Journal of College Science Teaching* and the *Journal of Research in Science Teaching*.

Affiliation: School of Education and Human Development, University of Colorado Denver, USA.

Paul Memmott is an anthropologist/architect and director of the Aboriginal Environments Research Centre (AERC), a research and resource centre based in the University of Queensland's School of Architecture, with staffing and logistical support from the university's Institute for Social Science Research (ISSR). The AERC has been constructed within the theoretical framework of behaviour–environment studies and environmental psychology that emerged in the 1960s and 1970s. Paul's major research interests are in architectural anthropology and material culture, Aboriginal housing and institutional architecture, Indigenous homelessness and public-place dwelling, Indigenous family violence and suicide, and Indigenous geography of place and cultural landscape.

Affiliation: School of Architecture and Institute for Social Science Research, University of Queensland, Australia.

Mark Nuttall is Professor and Henry Marshall Tory Chair of Anthropology at the University of Alberta. He also holds a visiting position as Professor of Climate and Society at the University of Greenland and the Greenland Climate Research Centre/Greenland Institute of Natural Resources, where he directs the Climate and Society Research Group. He has carried out extensive research and fieldwork in Greenland, Canada, Alaska, Finland, and Scotland. His current research focuses on climate change and extractive industries in Greenland and Canada. He is co-principal investigator for the EU project ICE–ARC (Ice, Climate, Economics–Arctic Research on Change), and co-principal investigator of a Norwegian Research Council-funded project on oil development in the Arctic. His latest book is *The Scramble for the Poles: The Geopolitics of the Arctic and Antarctic* (co-authored with Klaus Dodds; Polity Press, 2015) and he is currently writing a monograph on his research in Greenland.

Affiliation: Department of Anthropology, University of Alberta, Edmonton, Canada.

Anthony Oliver-Smith is Professor Emeritus of Anthropology at the University of Florida. He is also affiliated with the Center for Latin American Studies and the School of Natural Resources and Environment at that institution. He held the Munich Re Foundation Chair on Social Vulnerability at the United Nations University Institute for Environment and Human Security in Bonn, Germany (2007) and visiting professorships at la Universidad Complutense de Madrid (1982) and Tulane University (2007). He was awarded the Bronislaw Malinowski Award of the Society for Applied Anthropology for 2013 for his lifetime achievement and work in disaster studies and resettlement research. He has done anthropological research and consultation on issues relating to disasters as well as development-forced involuntary resettlement in Peru, Honduras, India, Brazil, Jamaica, Mexico, Panama, Japan, and the United States. Most recently he has focused on displacement and resettlement associated with climate change in Panama.

He has served on the executive boards of the National Association for the Practice of Anthropology and the Society for Applied Anthropology in the United States. He also served on the Global Climate Change Task Force of the American Anthropological Association. He is currently a member of the scientific committee on Integrated Research on Disaster Risk of the International Council for Science, and is chair of the Forensic Investigation of Disaster (FORIN) Working Group of that organization. His work on disasters has focused on issues of vulnerability analysis, post-disaster aid and reconstruction, consensus and conflict, and reconstruction. His work on involuntary resettlement has focused on the impacts of displacement, place attachment, resistance movements, adaptation, and resettlement project analysis. He has authored, edited, or co-edited eight books and more than 75 journal articles and book chapters.

Affiliation: Department of Anthropology, University of Florida, USA.

Bob Pokrant is Adjunct Professor of Anthropology, Department of Social Sciences and International Studies at Curtin University in Perth, Western Australia. He received his doctorate from the University of Cambridge in 1982 and has done ethnographic fieldwork in Nigeria, India, and Bangladesh. He has taught at university level in the United Kingdom, the United States, Canada, Sweden, Nigeria, Bangladesh, and Australia. His current research interest, in collaboration with Bangladeshi colleagues at the Center for Natural Resource Studies (CNRS), is adaptation to climate change among coastal communities in Bangladesh. He can be contacted at: B.Pokrant@curtin.edu.au

Affiliation: Department of Social Sciences and International Studies at Curtin University, Perth, Australia.

Sayd Randle is a PhD candidate in Environmental Anthropology at Yale University. Her research focuses on the politics of ecosystem services and water infrastructure in Southern California.

Affiliation: Yale University, Connecticut, USA.

Dustin Reuther is a PhD candidate at Tulane University in New Orleans, with interests in the intersection between traditional ecological knowledge and cultural resurgence amongst Arawak-speaking indigenous peoples in southwest Amazônia.

Affiliation: Tulane University, New Orleans, USA.

Melanie Rock is Associate Professor at the University of Calgary. She earned a Master's degree in Social Work (University of Toronto) and a PhD in Anthropology (McGill University). She then undertook a postdoctoral fellowship in public health (Université de Montréal). Her research program examines the societal and cultural dimensions of health, with an emphasis on social policies and community services that promote human–animal companionship, but also those that mitigate threats and nuisances associated with non-human animals (see www. ucalgary.ca/mrock). Since 2004, her research program has been continuously funded by the Canadian Government through successive awards from the Social Sciences and Humanities Research Council of Canada and the Canadian Institutes of Health Research.

Affiliation: Department of Community Health Sciences, Cumming School of Medicine, O'Brien Institute for Public Health, University of Calgary, Canada.

Holmes Rolston III is University Distinguished Professor and Professor of Philosophy Emeritus at Colorado State University. Some of his books are: *Three Big Bangs: Matter-Energy, Life, Mind* (2010); *Genes, Genesis and God* (1999); *Philosophy Gone Wild* (1989); *Science and Religion: A Critical Survey* (1987); and *Environmental Ethics* (1987). A more recent book is: *A*

New Environmental Ethics: The Next Millennium for Life on Earth (2011). Rolston was laureate for the 2003 Templeton Prize in Religion, gave the Gifford Lectures, University of Edinburgh, 1997–1998, and has lectured on all seven continents.

Affiliation: Colorado State University, USA.

Ronald A. Simkins received his PhD from Harvard University in 1990 in Near Eastern Languages and Civilizations and is presently Professor of Theology and Classical and Near Eastern Studies at Creighton University. His research is in the areas of the political economy of ancient Israel, creation myths, religion and the environment, and gender studies. He has published widely in these areas. He is director of the Kripke Center for the Study of Religion and Society at Creighton University, and is the general editor of the center's journal, the *Journal of Religion & Society* (www.moses.creighton.edu/jrs).

Affiliation: Department of Classical and Near Eastern Studies, and Kripke Center for the Study of Religion and Society, Creighton University, Omaha, Nebraska, USA.

Merrill Singer, PhD, a medical and cultural anthropologist, is Professor in the departments of Anthropology and Community Medicine at the University of Connecticut. The central issues in his work are the social determinants of health inequality, the biosocial nature of health, and environmental health. Over his career, his research and writing have addressed HIV/AIDS in highly vulnerable and disadvantaged populations, illicit drug use and drinking behavior, community and structural violence, and the political ecology of health including the health consequences of climate change. His current research focuses on community health impacts of climate change and infectious disease. Professor Singer has published more than 275 articles and book chapters and has authored or edited 29 books. He is a recipient of the Rudolf Virchow Professional Prize, the George Foster Memorial Award for Practicing Anthropology, the AIDS and Anthropology Paper Prize, the SANA Prize for Distinguished Achievement in the Critical Study of North America, the Solon T. Kimball Award for Public and Applied Anthropology from the American Anthropological Association, and the AIDS and Anthropology Research Group's Distinguished Service Award.

Affiliation: Department of Anthropology, University of Connecticut, USA.

J. Kenneth Smail is Professor of Anthropology Emeritus in the Department of Anthropology at Kenyon College, Ohio. He retired in 2004. He did his undergraduate work at DePauw University, holds Master's degrees from Pittsburgh, Indiana, and Yale universities, and earned his PhD (Yale 1976) in an interdisciplinary program in Primate and Human Paleobiology. While his primary academic focus over the past several decades has been directed toward undergraduate teaching, he has maintained scholarly interests in a number of areas: human evolutionary biology, both anatomical and behavioral; complexity theory in the bio-social sciences; the interface between science and religion; articulating a distinctive and non-violent approach to deterrence, peace-making, and confidence building; and calling attention to the rapidly growing global crisis posed by excessive human numbers in an ecologically finite world. His published work has focused primarily on the last two areas.

Affiliation: Department of Anthropology, Kenyon College, Ohio, USA.

Leslie E. Sponsel earned his BA in Geology from Indiana University (1965), and his MA (1973) and PhD (1981) in Biological and Cultural Anthropology from Cornell University. Over the last four decades he has taught at seven universities in four countries (two as a Fulbright Fellow). In 1981, he joined the Anthropology faculty at the University of Hawai'i to develop and direct the Ecological Anthropology Program.

From 1974 to 1981, Sponsel conducted several trips to the Venezuelan Amazon to research human ecology with the Yanomami and other indigenous societies. Almost yearly since 1986, Sponsel has made research trips to Thailand to study various aspects of Buddhist ecology and environmentalism, and in recent years has focused on sacred caves. His latest book is *Spiritual Ecology: A Quiet Revolution* (Praeger, 2012) (http://spiritualecology.info).

Affiliation: Department of Anthropology, University of Hawai'i.

Veronica Strang is the executive director of Durham University's interdisciplinary Institute of Advanced Study. An environmental anthropologist, she has conducted research in Australia, the UK, and New Zealand. Her work focuses on human–environmental relations, cultural landscapes and, in particular, societies' engagements with water. Since completing a DPhil at the University of Oxford in 1995, she has held teaching and research positions at the University of Oxford, the University of Wales, Goldsmiths, University of London, and the University of Auckland. In 2000, she was awarded a Royal Anthropological Institute Urgent Anthropology Fellowship; and in 2007, was named as one of UNESCO's *Les Lumières de L'Eau* [Water's Leading Lights]. Key publications include *The Meaning of Water* (Berg, 2004); *Gardening the World: Agency, Identity and the Ownership of Water* (Berghahn, 2009); *Ownership and Appropriation* (Berg, 2010); and *Water: Nature and Culture* (Reaktion Books and Chicago University Press, 2015). In 2013, she was elected as chair of the Association of Social Anthropologists of the UK and Commonwealth.

Affiliation: Institute of Advanced Study, Durham University, UK.

Sian Sullivan is Professor of Environment and Culture at Bath Spa University. Her research focuses on cultural ontologies of nature, the political ecology of biodiversity conservation, the financialisation of nature, and biodiversity offsetting. Currently she is leading a cross-disciplinary research project entitled Future Pasts (www.futurepasts.net) funded by the UK's Arts and Humanities Research Council (ref. AH/K005871/2) to explore culturally-inflected understandings of sustainability in Namibia, where she has long-term field experience. Her work on the intersections of culture, nature, and capitalism is available at http://siansullivan.net.

Affiliation: Field of Culture and Environment, College of Liberal Arts, Bath Spa University, UK.

Nancy J. Turner is Distinguished Professor, Hakai Professor in Ethnoecology, and P. E. Trudeau Fellow at the School of Environmental Studies, University of Victoria, British Columbia. An ethnobotanist and ethnoecologist whose research integrates the fields of botany and ecology with anthropology, geography, and linguistics, among others, she is interested in the traditional knowledge systems and traditional land and resource management systems of

Indigenous Peoples, particularly in western Canada. Nancy has worked with First Nations Elders and cultural specialists in northwestern North America for over 45 years, collaborating with Indigenous communities to help document, retain, and promote their traditional knowledge of plants and habitats, (including Indigenous foods, materials, and medicines), as well as language and vocabulary relating to plants and environments. Her interests also include the roles of plants and animals in narratives, ceremonies, language, and belief systems. Her courses in ethnobotany and ethnoecology at the University of Victoria, BC, have always included experiential learning opportunities.

Affiliation: School of Environmental Studies, University of Victoria, British Columbia, Canada.

Pauline von Hellermann is Lecturer in Anthropology at Goldsmiths, University of London. She has conducted research on environmental governance and landscape change in Nigeria and Tanzania. She is co-editor of *Multi-Sited Ethnography: Problems and Possibilities in the Translocation of Research Methods* (with Simon Coleman; Routledge, 2011) and author of *Things Fall Apart? The Political Ecology of Forest Governance in Southern Nigeria* (Berghahn, 2013).

Affiliation: Department of Anthropology, Goldsmiths, University of London, UK.

Bryan Wee is Associate Professor of Environmental Education and Director of the Sustainability Minor at the University of Colorado Denver. He holds a joint faculty appointment in Geography and Environmental Sciences and the School of Education. His scholarship is visual and emancipatory in nature. Using drawings, photographs, and interviews, he seeks out and validates children's environmental views to nurture equitable practices in research, teaching, and learning. In order to emphasize the role of culture/s in human–environment relationships, his work has taken him to different countries and into diverse settings. Most recently, he completed research in Sweden where he is an affiliated professor at Stockholm University.

Affiliation: University of Colorado Denver, USA; Stockholm University, Sweden.

Bernard Daley Zaleha is a PhD candidate at the University of California, Santa Cruz, currently researching in the areas of environmental and political sociology, sociology of religion, religious studies generally, and environmental law, presently emphasizing pantheism and nature-venerating religion in the United States, and the anti-environmental backlash within conservative American Christianity. He earned an MA in Sociology at the University of California, Santa Cruz in 2011, and his MA in Religion and Nature at the University of Florida in 2008, writing his thesis on American pantheism from Thoreau to the present. He received his Juris Doctor from Lewis & Clark Law School in 1987 and was an environmental litigator for 17 years. He has been an activist with the Sierra Club for more than three decades, serving in local, state, and national positions, serving as its national vice president from 2004 to 2006.

His articles include "Why Conservative Christians Don't Believe in Climate Change" (2015) in the *Bulletin of the Atomic Scientists* and "Keep Christianity Brown! Climate Denial on the Christian Right in the United States" (2014) (co-authored with Andrew Szasz); "Nature and

Nature Religion" and "Environment and Ecology in American Religion since the Mid-Nineteenth Century" in the *Encyclopedia of Religion in America* (2010); "'Our Only Heaven': Nature Veneration, Quest Religion, and Pro-Environment Behavior" and "James Nash as Christian Deep Ecologist: Forging a New Eco-theology for the Third Millennium" (2009) in the *Journal for the Study of Religion, Nature and Culture*. He has presented papers on pantheism at the meetings of the International Society for the Study of Religion, Nature and Culture in 2006, 2009, and 2012 in Gainesville, Amsterdam, and Malibu respectively; and on anti-environmental movements within conservative American Christianity at the annual meetings of the American Academy of Religion (2014) and the Association of Environmental Studies and Sciences (2012).

Affiliation: Department of Sociology, University of California, Santa Cruz, USA.

PART I

The development of environmental anthropology

1

AN INTRODUCTION TO ENVIRONMENTAL ANTHROPOLOGY

Helen Kopnina and Eleanor Shoreman-Ouimet

As so many of us are all too aware, we have entered the Anthropocene, marked by the large and active imprint that humans have made on the global environment. Environmental social sciences, and environmental anthropology in particular, have long focused on the interaction between human societies, cultures, and complex environments – both in physical and symbolic terms. Yet, as the world changes in response to the expansion of human presence and influence, a number of analytical frameworks, as well as ideologies, have been developed to address culture and nature in the era of human-dominated environments. As the contributions to this Handbook demonstrate, the sub-field of environmental anthropology is responding to cultural adaptations and responses to environmental changes in multiple and complex ways. Operating within a discipline concerned primarily with human–environment interaction, environmental anthropologists recognize that they are now working within a pressure cooker of rapid environmental damage that is forcing behavioural and often cultural changes around the world. As we see in the breadth of topics presented in this volume, these environmental challenges have inspired both renewed foci on traditional topics such as food procurement, ethnobiology, and spiritual ecology; and a broad new range of subjects, such as resilience, non-human rights, architectural anthropology, industrialism, and education. These studies are illustrated by intensive ethnographic case studies supported by 'traditional' anthropological as well as innovative and transdisciplinary methodologies in pursuit of a more ecologically holistic understanding of the human–environment relationship and perhaps even solutions to environmental degradation.

The field of anthropology is broken into four sub-fields: physical/biological anthropology, social/cultural anthropology, linguistic anthropology, and archaeology; as well as applied (sometimes called engaged or participatory) anthropology. Environmental or ecological anthropology is a specialization within cultural anthropology that studies historic and present human–environment interactions. Although the terms, 'environmental anthropology' and 'ecological anthropology' are often used interchangeably, environmental anthropology is considered by some to be the applied dimension of ecological anthropology which encompasses the broad topics of primate ecology, palaeoecology, cultural ecology, ethno-ecology, ethno-ornithology, historical ecology, political ecology, spiritual ecology, human behavioral ecology, and evolutionary ecology. It has been argued that the new ecological anthropology, or what is often referred to in this volume as environmental anthropology, mirrors more general changes in the discipline: the shift from research focusing on a single community or unique culture

> to recognizing pervasive linkages and concomitant flows of people, technology, images, and information, and to acknowledging the impact of differential power and status in the postmodern world on local entities. In the new ecological anthropology, everything is on a larger scale.
>
> *(Kottak 1999: 25)*

This Handbook takes as its point of departure today's pressing environmental challenges, ranging from climate change to biodiversity loss, and from pollution to the depletion of natural resources, with contributors acknowledging and discussing a number of areas of tension embodied in these challenges. Such tensions exist between local livelihoods and international conservation efforts, between communities and wildlife, and finally between traditional ways of living and 'modernity'. While traditional ways of living used to be characterized by a relatively moderate effect on habitats due to low population densities and inherently sustainable subsistence practices, advanced neoliberal capitalism is characterized by the commodification of nature and its elements. This volume is thus premised on the idea that while these tensions cannot be easily resolved, they can be better understood by considering both social and ecological effects, in equal measure.

Some anthropologists whose work is presented in this Handbook work towards global sustainability at a time when efforts to conserve biodiversity and reduce carbon emissions that cause climate change correspond with land grabs by large corporations, food insecurity, and human displacement. While they seek to reconcile more-than-human relations and responsibilities in the Anthropocene, they also struggle to accommodate social justice and the seemingly global desire for economic development. One could argue that the expansion of human influence is responsible for the destruction of natural systems, including the current threats to biodiversity, disruption of the planet's climate, and the large-scale pollution of land, water, and air. Many critical social scientists argue that the discipline of anthropology has not been adequately attentive to these destructive trends, particularly to the expansion of human populations and consumption habits in the context of industrial and economic development. It has also been argued that anthropologists too often discount pressing environmental problems and their causes while focusing on 'traditional' anthropological subjects such as the cultural mediation of meaning, and symbolic interaction with nature and its elements. These arguments are reflected in different sections throughout this Handbook, and help to highlight where and how anthropological expertise – attention to cultural specificity and the micro-analysis of human–environmental interaction – can be integrated into a broader locus of environmental change.

Other contributors are more specifically concerned with the continuation and renewal of anthropological interest in what environment, broadly defined, means for people – in material, social, and culturally symbolic terms – and with injustices suffered as a consequence of environmental destruction. Much of this work focuses specifically on the vulnerability of structurally weaker and marginal communities, including many indigenous groups during the appropriation of natural resources by industrial developers, as well as on the effects of climate change, natural hazards, and the increasingly frequent incidence of migration induced by climate change. Largely as a result of the juxtaposition of issues such as cultural and ecological preservation and/or rights, we have begun to see tensions develop between the anthropology of development, or anthropology that focuses on indigenous rights to use and/or profit from nature, and more conservation-minded efforts to protect fragile habitats. While once anthropologists addressed development as something to be avoided based on its sociocultural impacts, it seems to have taken a place among the anthropological sub-disciplines as an essential part of human life. As many of the contributors to this volume so aptly demonstrate, however, environmental anthropology is moving towards a stronger recognition of the combined social and environmental consequences of an expanding humanity whose existence is dramatically marked by destruction due to the 'progress' of development.

In 2013, Clive Hamilton argued that the dramatic impacts of climate change could mark the end of the social sciences. Hamilton (2013: para. 5) contended that the Kantian dualism of humans and the environment, on which so much social science rests its analyses, "can no longer be sustained, that the natural and the human are mixed up, and their influences cannot be neatly distinguished". The advent of the Anthropocene, Hamilton warns,

> shatters the self-contained world of social analysis that is the terrain of modern social science, and explains why those intellectuals who remain within it find it impossible to "analyze" the politics, sociology or philosophy of climate change in a way that is true to the science. They end up floundering in the old categories, unable to see that something epochal has occurred, a rupture on the scale of the Industrial Revolution or the emergence of civilization itself.
>
> *(Hamilton 2013: para. 12)*

No longer is environmental preservation the exclusive domain of ecosystem scientists and ecologists; rather, conservation and environmental protection must be addressed by scholars and practitioners in their analyses of palaeo-environments, habitats, fisheries, industries, rural communities, urban settings, and any locale across the earth where expanding numbers of humans remain both reliant and an active force on the environment. Environmental anthropologists are thus specifically called upon to recognize and pay careful attention to the multiplicity of players in every environment, the variety and origin of conservation ethics around the world, and the value of cultural knowledge of landscapes and environmental change. Just as we have learned that no one formula for conservation will be universally applicable in diverse environments, so too are environmental anthropologists demonstrating that no solution to the worldwide environmental crisis can ignore the human element in every habitat.

Environmental anthropology: a sub-field with a goal

Like ecological and other anthropological sub-fields, environmental anthropology addresses both the similarities and differences between human cultures. For many environmental anthropologists, one of the aims of their research is largely to find solutions to environmental damage, and issues associated with environmental justice, migration, scarcity, and health. To this end, over a decade ago, one of the sub-field's most environmentally enlightened authors, Kay Milton (1993, 1996, 2002) suggested three main ways in which anthropological knowledge might contribute to the environmentalist cause:

1   The study of human–environment relations, or anthropology as human ecology.
2   Anthropologists as 'trans-cultural' interpreters of environmental knowledge and practice.
3   The study of environmentalism itself as a cultural practice, treated as an object of analysis.

Milton argues (1993: 80) that an anthropologist's engagement should include an "active involvement in the discourse of environmentalism, in the process of defining and implementing environmental responsibilities". This volume presents the myriad ways that environmental anthropologists are responding to such calls for environmental engagement, study, and advocacy. The following chapters have been organized to demonstrate this dynamism and the pertinence of this ever-evolving study of human–environment interaction. They include examples of interdisciplinary, environmentally focused projects that are bringing anthropology to the forefront of community conservation projects, climate adaptation and mitigation, environmental health studies, and policy initiatives. The contributors to this volume take into account a range of environmental and social issues around the world and present various examples of environmental degradation, ethics, and knowledge, as well as instances of environmental conservation efforts and learning. They furthermore provide valuable methods of accessing such knowledge and insightful theoretical frameworks for assessing and synthesizing cultural and environmental data. The authors seek to demonstrate how environmental anthropologists are contributing to the world's understanding of how human beings have diversely occupied, interacted with, damaged, and sustained the environment over time; and how environmental anthropology can serve as a policy tool and an applied science to help all of humanity adapt to and remedy current environmental crises.

Introducing the sections

This Handbook is broken into seven parts written by accomplished academics as well as young scholars from anthropology and related disciplines, and demonstrates the range of work currently being conducted within the sub-field, as well as those issues and ideas that the authors believe will, and/or perhaps should, characterize the future of the study. It is our hope that this collection will enable scholars to quickly and easily access both established and trending environmental anthropological explorations into theory, methodology, and practice; and provide students with the opportunity to learn more about the topics that its most prominent researchers consider pertinent to the field and its service to peoples and environments around the world.

Part I introduces us to the development of environmental anthropology as a distinct sub-field and its central theoretical issues; and provides extensive intellectual histories and commentary by the contributors. As these chapters discuss, a number of key developments in the history of environmental anthropology can be identified. First, there is a move from the studies of communities as self-enclosed entities towards recognizing them as part of wider political-ecological systems and questioning their 'boundedness'. Second, there has been a move away from synchronic and towards diachronic approaches, as well as a general shift in the field away from assumptions of equilibrium towards assumptions of disequilibrium. Third, environmental anthropology is not just becoming more involved with politics, but is starting to become more political itself. Fourth, environmental anthropology has become increasingly influenced by post-structural theory. Finally, environmental anthropology is becoming increasingly interdisciplinary, freely crossing the boundaries between the natural and social sciences, as well as the humanities.

In addition to providing thorough examinations of environmental anthropology in distant and more recent history, this section also presents specific examinations of subjects, such as ethnobiology and ethnoclassification systems, further demonstrating the development of not only the field as a whole, but the ways in which the branches of environmental anthropology have developed in conjunction with scientific and ethnographic inquiry.

Part II presents further investigations into the sub-fields of environmental anthropology and provides a wide breadth of lenses through which to view the human–environmental relationship. It brings together works on a range of topics including material culture studies, agency, architectural anthropology, as well as putting forth recommendations for moving past anthropocentric and ecocentric divides and towards reconciliation between social and/or ecological justice. While examining these specific sub-fields, this part also provides examples of innovative ethnographic subjects and methodologies to demonstrate the ways in which anthropologists can utilize traditional and novel lenses to explore the range of ways in which humans dwell in, identify, and modify the environment.

Part III delves into the connections between knowledge, belief, and sustainability, and the rich repository of ethical history and practical knowledge that can inform current sustainability efforts. Because sustainability is a global cause with all cultures, peoples, creeds, and nationalities at stake, the contributors to this section have been chosen for their particular attention to cultural attempts at sustainability, defined in environmental, social, and broad conceptual terms. In addition, several of the authors included in this section provide invaluable critiques of the enterprise of sustainable development and address the myriad ways in which the recent combining of sustainability initiatives with economic interests carries neoliberal and neocolonial undertones that makes many question whether the goal of such efforts is human-environmental well-being or economic control. The chapters in this section speak to the many instances of cultural beliefs that espouse unity with nature and the powerful connection between spirituality and sustainability. Also included are chapters speaking more specifically to the nature of environmental knowledge, the origins and language of unsustainability, and how anthropology as a discipline engages with and contributes to discourses on sustainability and energy. In anthropological efforts to understand and investigate sustainable initiatives and get to the heart of motivation and foreseeable outcomes, the authors included here demonstrate that the future of environmental anthropology may need to be more focused on finding the universals that underlie human differences and understanding how these universals can best be put to use to end environmental damage.

In Part IV, contributors address the urgent issues related to resilience and vulnerability to natural hazards, disasters, and the rippling effects of climate change. It is not surprising that anthropologists are intimately involved in the study of how communities are affected by and respond to the effects of climate change and natural disasters. The authors of these chapters, themselves, have been particularly instrumental in describing the history of community response to disaster as well as how we must be prepared to assess vulnerability and resilience in the future. They demonstrate that understanding the effects that climate change and natural disasters have on human communities depends on developing appropriate conceptual tools that can adequately frame the sociocultural construction of risks and effects and the impacts of those effects.

Part V comprises chapters on the equally pressing and related issues of justice, ethics, and governance. Here, authors explore recent developments in the relationship between anthropology and the environment from the perspective of justice. The recent shift towards the interdisciplinary study of the human–environment relationship is largely driven by environmental justice debates. Today, researchers debate the primacy of four different types of environmental justice, linking them to questions of neoliberalism and altruism. This part highlights all sides of the debate over environmental and ecological justice – representing those who fight for cultural rights over environmental prioritization, those who believe that discrimination against non-human species is equivalent to racism and sexism, as well as those seeking to strike a balance and establish a more stringent code of environmental ethics in anthropological research. This part also presents the investigation of ethics, power, environmental governance and policy and is intended to marry the previous section on climate change with research in political ecology and political science on how necessary policy changes are being and will be considered, established, implemented, and regulated. This includes historically anthropological issues of common property regimes/managing the commons; as well as recent work on issues like 'co-management'; and the construction of subjectivities.

Part VI grapples with the important intersections of health, population, and the environment, combining insights from different sub-disciplines related to anthropology that deal with both health and environmental topics, such as medical anthropology, ecological sociology, and environmental health; as well as food production and cultural food movements. This section emphasizes the importance of understanding food, health, and disease as biosocial processes that often require us to consider the intersection of values and species' lifeways, as well as socioeconomics, industrialization, and the threats posed to humans and non-humans by human-induced environmental changes. Many of these changes have been caused by the sheer volume of people on this planet, and given the rapid continuation of human population growth, it is likely that the evolutionary, ecological, and sociocultural impacts of our presence will only deepen. Thus, this part of the book takes on difficult questions about how humans are choosing to nourish, care for, and protect themselves as individuals while simultaneously threatening their own and all other species' existence by their sum total.

Part VII, the final section of this Handbook, underlines the urgency of the world's environmental crisis through the study of education and the impact of globalization and industrialization, as well as the power of local environmental knowledge and experience around the world. These chapters give us a glimpse into how children see the environment, speak of the environment and their capacity to care for it. They demonstrate the loss of nature contact that so many children suffer through didactic forms of institutionalized educa-tion and decreasing exposure to the natural environment. Yet the chapters also give several examples of how we can improve upon this reality. These examples include methodologies for engaging young people in environments and traditional ways of taking from and giving back to the natural world. The chapters in this section discuss important philosophies for anthropologists on the role that we can and must play in converting our knowledge of human relationships with nature into a support system for fostering environmentally sound and protective relationships in the future.

As the chapters in this Handbook demonstrate, environmental anthropologists have unique access, as well as tools, theories, and skill sets for understanding the relationship between human cultures and the environment. Not only can these methodologies help to illuminate the basis for culturally diverse perceptions of the environment and environmental damage around the world, but they can help to dissolve cultural barriers to conservation and be used to determine motivational triggers, communicate the benefits of conservation, and inform environmental education efforts. Throughout this book, authors address the underlying importance of utilizing the strengths of anthropological knowledge. In highlighting motivation, cultural norms, values, and beliefs as well as logistical and ideological barriers in relation to environmental action, anthropologists improve our understanding of the world around us and the diversity of ways of existing on this planet.

References

Hamilton, C. 2013. Climate change signals the end of social sciences. *The Conversation*, posted 25 January. http://theconversation.com/climate-change-signals-the-end-of-the-social-sciences-11722 (accessed 2 February 2016).

Kottak, C. P. 1999. The new ecological anthropology. *American Anthropologist* 101(1): 23–35.

Milton, K. 1993. Introduction. In K. Milton (ed.) *Environmentalism: The View from Anthropology*. New York: Routledge, pp. 73–84.

Milton, K. 1996. *Environmentalism and Cultural Theory: Exploring the Role of Anthropology in Environmental Discourse*. New York: Routledge.

Milton, K. 2002. *Loving Nature: Toward an Ecology of Emotion*. New York: Routledge.

2

HISTORY AND SCOPE OF ENVIRONMENTAL ANTHROPOLOGY

Eduardo Brondízio, Ryan T. Adams, and Stefano Fiorini

Introduction

Environmental Anthropology is the general designation for the anthropological investigation of human–environment relationships. This area of research consists of a wide range of interests at various levels of analysis ranging from adaptation and resource management to environmental values and religion; from cognition and perception to global climate change; from conservation initiatives and their impacts upon populations to urban environments; from human rights and social justice to international agreements, and the list goes on. This rainbow of foci is the product of discussion, debate, and interdisciplinary cross-fertilization over the last 100 years, in the course of which paradigms have risen and fallen while the social, economic, and cultural context has shifted with respect to both the practice of anthropology and the nature of human–environment relationships.

The aim of this chapter is to introduce and propose a historical chronology of the development of Environmental Anthropology. We start with a brief discussion about the evolution of terminology as applied to Environmental Anthropology and fields of specialization within it. We then highlight how different specialties developed – one dominated by an ecosystem-oriented approach, one by a political-economy-oriented approach, one by a historical-landscape approach, and another by a symbolic-oriented approach. We then discuss how these approaches developed with different degrees of overlap into the various specialties that comprise contemporary Environmental Anthropology. In doing so, we overview the history of Cultural Ecology, Ecological Anthropology, Political Ecology, Symbolic Ecology, Historical Ecology, and Ethnobiology.[1] We conclude by reflecting on the continuous challenge to overcome intellectual differences among these specialties, moving the discipline towards a new synthesis commensurable with the complexity of human–environment interactions in a world of accelerated and interconnected changes.

Historical view of Environmental Anthropology

As mentioned above, what we call Environmental Anthropology today is a product of research and cross-fertilization taking place since the beginning of the twentieth century (Figure 2.1). During this period, the nature of questions and problems has changed, specialized disciplinary communities have emerged, and with that new theoretical and methodological toolkits (Vaccaro *et al.* 2010). Environmental Anthropology as a term only gained popularity during the 1990s, providing a more inclusive umbrella to a diverse community of anthropologists at a time when heated and often unproductive debates dominated the field. Initially used in the United States, the term has since gained international usage. It is often used as a broader term when compared to Ecological Anthropology, although the latter is sometimes used as a proxy for Environmental Anthropology (Kottak 1999). In Europe, the term Anthropology of Nature continues to be used as a general designation for anthropological works on environmental issues. In the same way that Environmental Anthropology has served as an umbrella within Anthropology, Human Ecology has served this role for a larger interdisciplinary community, and it is still widely used to designate areas of research and also academic programmes, including some in Anthropology (Sponsel 2004). Similarly, Cultural Ecology is sometimes used in Anthropology as a general reference to human–environment studies and is a term some authors have suggested should not be abandoned (Netting 1968; Sutton and Anderson 2004).[2] Recognizing the ambiguities among these terms, this chapter unfolds the storyline of Environmental Anthropology. As Figure 2.1 indicates, we take as our starting point the formative period of the field within US Anthropology in the early twentieth century. Debates and theoretical-methodological developments during this period led to the evolution of Cultural Ecology in the 1950s. Subsequently, adding to the trends already recognized by Benjamin Orlove (1980) – i.e. ecosystem-oriented approach (neofunctionalist[3]) and political-economy-oriented approach

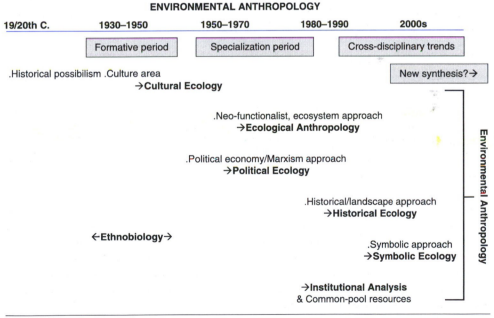

Figure 2.1 Historical timeline summarizing human–environment research in Anthropology and the emergence of Environmental Anthropology. As a term, Environmental Anthropology appears during the 1990s.

(Marxian) – we introduce trends that emphasize historical-landscape, symbolic-cosmological, ethnobiological, and institutional approaches.

Orlove identified intersections between the 1960s and the 1980s for a growing research community of anthropologists interested in human–environment research and those working within other disciplines on research that shared common methodologies or theoretical concerns, including Geography, Sociology, Ecology, Political Science, and so forth. From these intersections, Ecological Anthropology and Political Ecology emerged as research fields in their own rights. During the late 1980s, Symbolic Ecology and Historical Ecology appeared, bringing complementary perspectives to an expanding set of research questions and problems related to human–environmental issues. The former emphasized interpretive symbolic approaches and cosmological analysis, while the latter emphasized deeper timeframes and landscape-level analysis. Since the 1950s, however, Ethnobiology and related fields have evolved somewhat independently from anthropological debates related to the fields above. The same is true, albeit later (1980s) for the interdisciplinary field of Institutional Analysis and common-pool resources, which although independent, are increasingly important within Environmental Anthropology. In proposing this organization, however, we recognize the limitations of our interpretation to account for the development of fields such as Primate Ecology, Human Behavioural and Evolutionary Ecology, Spiritual Ecology, the Ecology of Conflict, and several others not covered here.

Cultural Ecology

The field of Cultural Ecology is formally defined by Julian Steward's seminal book *Theory of Culture Change* (1955), although the term dates to his 1938 *Basin Plateau Aboriginal Sociopolitical Groups*. The history of the field, however, is rooted in debates dating back to the formative period of anthropology. Emerging as a discipline, the anthropology that nurtured Cultural Ecology was characterized by theoretical discussions among proponents of 'cultural evolutionism' in Europe and 'historical possibilism' in the United States. Cultural factors were deemed to determine the possibilities of human action in the latter approach. The works of US anthropologists Franz Boas (e.g. 1911) and Alfred Kroeber (e.g. 1939), including the analysis of cultural elements, traits, and the delineation of 'cultural areas' as organizing cultural-environmental units became the basis from which Cultural Ecology developed. The Boasian 'cultural possibilism' approach was, in part, a reaction against earlier evolutionary approaches (Morgan 1965 [1877]) and environmental determinism (Ratzel 1896), which postulated that the physical environment was conducive to, or limiting of, the development of culture and socio-political complexity. An emphasis on environmental determinism rendered the environment as a structuring and static constraint to humans' livelihood. In contrast, the 'culture area' was a cultural unit defined in relation to a biome (or environmental compartment) and described by a set of cultural and social elements associated with the material culture and forms of livelihood of different groups.

The collection of cultural characteristics observed and described by anthropologists allowed for comparisons of different cultural areas. This approach was furthered by Kroeber's work, *Cultural and Natural Areas of Native North America* (1939), and Steward's efforts with the *Handbook of South American Indians* (1939–1946). Among the elements needed for cross-cultural comparisons and applied to describe cultural groups and the landscapes of different parts of the Americas were habitat characteristics and population densities. This approach provided a rich collection of comparative ethnographic records on indigenous populations throughout the continent. Historical particularism and the 'culture area' approach stressed history and diffusion as forces of change (Harris 1968).

This emphasis on culture areas was later advanced and challenged by two new evolutionary approaches: the unilinear evolution model of Leslie White and the multilinear evolution of Julian Steward (Nash 2014). White saw energy use and technology as the mechanism of cultural evolution (Bernard 2000); in this, change afforded increased ability to harness energy (White 1943, 1949). White's concern with energy re-emerged later in Ecological Anthropology in the attention that the 'ecosystem approach' paid to energy flow in ecosystems and caloric intake among indigenous groups and peasants. Steward's approach, avoiding both the extremes of Boasian historical particularism and White's unilinear evolutionism, provided the basis for much of what developed later in human–environment studies in Anthropology.

Steward focused his attention on cultural adaptation to the environment, identifying both functional, synchronic formulations of observed cultural features, and diachronic regularities in the ways people organize themselves, adapt to their environment, and use technology (Murphy 1981; Sponsel 1997; Kern 2003). The priority was to understand how localized forms of social organization relate to resource utilization processes (Moran 1990). He conceptualized a 'culture core' consisting of social and cultural features with more direct functional interrelationships with the local environment. He also recognized that these localized forms of social organization and adaptation are part of and influenced by higher levels of sociocultural integration (Steward 1955). For Steward, a multilinear framework rather than the unilinear evolutionary frameworks of his predecessors and contemporaries was better suited to the understanding of social and cultural change. A multilinear framework also allowed, more explicitly than Boasian cultural relativism and historical particularism, for understanding parallels of form and function in social-cultural change. Empirical at its core, Steward's Cultural Ecology focused on "conditions determining phenomena of limited occurrence" stressing that no cultural phenomenon is universal. This approach was intended to foster scientific investigations, hypothesis testing, and comparative analysis of cultural phenomena. Steward's Cultural Ecology has influenced a wide array of research questions and applications, contributing to generations of scholars examining human–environment interactions.

Ecological Anthropology

Ecological Anthropology emerges during the mid-1960s (Vayda and Rappaport 1968), built upon Steward's Cultural Ecology, White's energy model, and the rise of the ecosystem approach. Moving away from the strong attention paid to culture, Ecological Anthropology includes a stronger engagement with ecosystem ecology and systems analysis with more meaningful attention to human communities functioning as a 'population' within a biophysical environment. The focus on ecosystem and population allowed Ecological Anthropology to open a dialogue with the biological sciences and systems theory based on shared terms and concepts, including the use of niche, ecosystem, natural disasters, adaptation, primary production, limiting factors, and energy and information flows in the works of many anthropologists.

Concepts related to ecosystem functioning became more widely adopted thanks to the work of Clifford Geertz, John Bennett, and Roy Rappaport along with Gregory Bateson. In particular, Bateson's influential collection of papers, *Steps to an Ecology of Mind* (1972), borrowed concepts from the scientific study of ecosystems, cybernetics, and general system theory, and were widely read, helping to establish the ecosystem concept in anthropology. In Geertz's (1963) *Agricultural Involution*, the ecosystem concept provided an organizing structure to analyse the role of historical and political factors to explain forms of agricultural change in different parts of Indonesia. Bennett's *Northern Plainsmen* (1969) drew the attention to the importance of regional studies and emphasized the role of socio-political and institutional adaptation, a theme he developed further in his classic *The Ecological Transition* (2005 [1976]), planting the seeds of what later became Historical Ecology. Along with the elements articulated in a seminal article by Vayda and Rappaport (1968), Rappaport's *Pigs for the Ancestors* (1968) marked (definitively and somewhat controversially) the assimilation of the ecosystem approach into Anthropology, and the full emergence of Ecological Anthropology. Rappaport achieved this by showing how a local population maintained homeostatic equilibrium with the environment through a ritual system that facilitated control of the pig population.

The criticism levelled at Rappaport and others for assuming conditions of homeostasis, equilibrium, and stability along with their strong bioenergetic emphasis characterized this period of the history of environmental studies in Anthropology. In Anthropology, critics focused on the misuse of equilibrium and carrying capacity assumptions and the limitations of the anthropological application of the ecosystem concept (Orlove 1980; Ellen 1982). Because this approach adopted scaled-down models based on a macro-level understanding of ecosystem functions that portrayed the ecosystem more as a biological unit decontextualized from social and political units rather than as a dynamic structure of relationships, it was limited in its ability to account for simultaneous cultural and environmental change.

Donald Hardesty's discussion of the ecosystem concept in *Ecological Anthropology* (1977), Emilio Moran's in *Human Adaptability* (see editions 1979, 2007), and Roy Ellen's in *Environment, Subsistence, and System* (1982) represented solid efforts among anthropologists to demonstrate the epistemological value of the application of ecosystem analysis in Ecological Anthropology and address the concerns noted above. Moran's and Ellen's views, in particular, reflected a general consensus that many of the tools provided by the ecosystem approach had tremendous utility despite the potential problems. They proposed separating ecosystem analysis from homeostatic models, and criticized energy flow models and ahistorical ecological analyses. The potential of an ecosystem approach without theoretical reductionism and which positioned anthropology within a wider interdisciplinary research agenda was still strong (Ellen 1982; Moran 1990; Rappaport 1990; Wilk 1991; Bates and Lees 1997). Examples of these criticisms and revision of the concept in anthropology can be followed in *The Ecosystem Approach in Anthropology* (Moran 1984, 1990).

Following this revision, the emergence of a wider research agenda on the human dimensions of global environmental change led Anthropology, Geography, Ecology, and other fields to work together on new methodologies. The availability of new tools, such as satellite remote sensing, Geographic Information Systems (GIS), and modelling environments (e.g. agent-based modelling) resulted in new opportunities to integrate temporal and spatial scales (Brondízio and Van Holt 2014). Ethnographic approaches and survey instruments were combined with tools for spatial and temporal analysis to interpret changing local, regional, and global environments (Behrens 1994; Moran and Brondízio 2001; Castro *et al.* 2002). This made it possible to aggregate site-specific data, incorporate these data into a larger set of data from other scales, and observe the dynamics of ecological variables on multiple scales.

Ecological Anthropology has expanded considerably during the last three decades drawing from all sub-fields of Anthropology (Sponsel 2004). As Biersack's "new ecologies" (1999) put it, the field has evolved (and matured), including a greater concern with symbolism and stronger emphasis on the historical, political, and economic contexts; bringing together interest in environmental values and religion, cultural construction of the environment

14

(space and place), globalization and consumerism, tourism, gender and ethnicity, and human rights, as well as the human dimensions of global environmental change. Several research approaches illustrate these developments and their applications to different problems; for example, to the study of market impact on indigenous populations (Godoy *et al.* 2005), tropical deforestation and land use (Sponsel and Headland 1996; Nyerges and Green 2000; Brondízio 2006; Moran 2006), and climate anthropology (Nelson and Finan 2000; Orlove *et al.* 2000; Galvin *et al.* 2001; Magistro *et al.* 2001), among others. As Ecological Anthropology moved away from an overly deterministic and localized framework, political and historical approaches began to emerge in order to accurately frame explanations of the trajectories and outcomes of human–environment interactions.

Political Ecology

Interest in connecting local human–environment processes to the wider political economy paved the way for the emergence of Political Ecology, a term popularized by Wolf (1972). These linkages, however, started to be explored much earlier, for instance as part of the ambitious research programme led by Steward, *The People of Puerto Rico* project, or as part of the above cited work of Geertz in Indonesia. *The People of Puerto Rico* project, in particular, contributed to the expansion of research foci in space and time, as represented, for instance, in the works of Steward's students Eric Wolf and Sidney Mintz (among others) originating from the project. The project was an attempt to understand the Cultural Ecology of complex societies by building on the framework that was developed and tested on small-scale social groups. Wolf (1999: 44) described the shortcomings of the Cultural Ecology in *The People of Puerto Rico* (Steward 1956) as follows: "I would say that what Steward was primarily interested in was the social relations of work, to the considerable neglect of what Marxists call the social relations of production." This change in perspective called for understanding the use of resources in terms of the complex economic and social dynamics resulting from historical processes and global interconnections (see e.g. Wolf 1966, 1982; Cole and Wolf 1974; Mintz 1985).

Political Ecology tends to offer explanations in terms of the competing alliances of actors and accompanying structures as causes of the problems in environmental conditions and social justice (Little 1999). This approach has proven very flexible by adding political and institutional investigations to ecological studies in various contexts, but especially situations in which environmentalist interventions are prominent. Researchers sought to play down the role of ecological constraints to human adaptation over the primacy of political or economic forces in affecting the environment or changes in production systems. However, as some critics have pointed out (Vayda and Walters 1999), in many cases, this approach has led to a fairly typical storyline of capitalist forces usurping control of local resources, which leads to a decline in environmental quality and local prosperity.

Greenberg and Park (1994) in their introductory article for the first issue of the *Journal of Political Ecology*[4] perceived the roots of Political Ecology to lie in the Cultural Ecology of Julian Steward in combination with broader scholarship related to ecosystem ecology and political economy, in particular dependency theory and world systems theory. Nora Haenn (1997) has described how in actual practice, Political Ecology approaches tended to follow the powerful core to determine the actions of the weak periphery as delineated in Immanuel Wallerstein's (1974) World Systems Theory. In one of the seminal Political Ecology studies, Schmink and Wood showed how competing social actors (such as 'The Military', 'Colonists', 'Miners' and 'The Kayapó') battled over the control of resources in Southern Pará, Brazil.

Their analysis was a careful examination of the multidimensional bases of power – physical, economic, political, ideological – and the strategies adopted by participants in specific conflicts constructed upon these bases of power.

> [T]he constitutive aspect of social process stresses the idea that both peasants and ranchers, in negotiating the contests that involved them and in the process of mobilizing the various sources of power at their disposal, continually reconstructed their respective interests, amending their strategies, bonds, and alliances accordingly.
>
> *(Schmink and Wood 1992: 17)*

Political Ecology and Institutional Analysis share some common interests and problems, but have evolved somewhat distinctively in their theoretical focus and methodological approach to examining those interests. While Political Ecology examines political explanations for behaviours that have an impact on the environment, Institutional Analysis is fundamentally concerned with factors affecting collective action, such as those related to the management of common-pool resources (Agrawal 2003; Acheson 2006). The field of Institutional Analysis emerged in reaction to an oversimplification of common-pool resources in an extremely influential paper by Hardin published in 1968 in the journal *Science*, entitled 'The tragedy of the commons'. Hardin (1968) claimed that the unsustainable exploitation of natural resources and environmental services, caused by an increase in population and maximization of per capita consumption in the absence of rules of use, could be controlled only through privatization or centralized government (Ostrom *et al.* 1999; Dietz *et al.* 2003).

Institutional analysis of empirical case studies based on ethnographic work carried out by anthropologists soon uncovered the existence of a variety of successful institutional arrangements for the management of natural resources (McCay and Acheson 1987; Ostrom 1990). This analysis not only revealed that humans were not inherently destructive of their environment or required to be subjected to external control, but able to engender forms of collective action to successfully manage common and public goods (see Ostrom 1990). Attention to common-pool resources occurred parallel to and in connection with the rise of indigenous and local social movements for the reclamation of access to resources. Building upon the now classic work of political scientist Elinor Ostrom and the Bloomington School of Political Economy (Ostrom 1990; Acheson 2011), this field has developed with a rare combination of theoretical concern (e.g. collective action, game theory) and applied contributions (Poteete *et al.* 2010). Several recent examples illustrate the productive engagement of Anthropology with institutional research; for example, around conservation conflicts (Petursson and Vedeld 2015), fisheries and markets (Acheson 2003; McCay *et al.* 2014), co-management systems (Castro and McGraph 2003), and commodity markets (Tucker 2008), among others.

Vayda and Walters (1999) took the field of Political Ecology to task for being biased in favour of political explanations even when that was not the primary cause of an ecological event. They suggested that ecological events be given the central position in an analysis and that the true causes should then be pursued through progressive contextualization, a position Vayda had previously espoused (1983). Interestingly, some political ecologists now cite this article as presenting ecological causation as part of an expanding string of factors to be addressed in Political Ecology studies (Vasquez-Leon and Liverman 2004). This flexibility and receptivity to critiques perhaps originated from frustration with the bitter materialist/ post-modernist debates that took place during most of the 1990s in the United States. As a consequence, the field of Political Ecology seemed to expand its areas and factors of investigation rather than engaging in contrasting debates with new approaches (Biersack and

Greenberg 2006). Several new perspectives have emerged to broaden the scope of Political Ecology (Robbins 2012) to include cultured environmental perceptions (as described in Bryant 1998), local agency (Peluso 1991; Haenn 2002), emotions and beliefs (Anderson 1996), gender (Gezon 2002), discourse (Escobar 1996, 1999; Adger *et al.* 2001), event analysis (Penna-Firme 2012), and feminist perspectives (Rocheleau *et al.* 1997).[5] The intellectual challenge for Political Ecology is whether concern with the ecological context, political economy, social justice, and global environmental change can all be contained under a single rubric.

Symbolic Ecology and Environmentalism

In different ways, Strathern (1981), Ingold (1986, 2000), Descola (1994 [1986], 2013), Descola and Pálsson (1996), Latour (1993), Ellen and Fukui (1996) and Scoones (1999), among others, critiqued the materialistic thinking of Ecological Anthropology and Political Ecology, and cautioned against Ethnobiology's reproduction of Western concepts and taxonomies of nature, and the absence of ideational power relations in Institutional Analysis. Their critiques called attention to the social construction of the environment, for some grounded in colonialist frameworks for science and Western perspectives on the environment. In contesting the culture/nature dichotomy, they called attention to alternative interpretations and ontologies of the environment. These debates have affected, albeit differently, each of the fields listed here. As suggested above, European Anthropology – as represented by Strathern, Ingold, Descola, Pálsson, Latour, Ellen, and Scoones, among others – played a central and fundamental role in the process, but this movement eventually found fertile ground in the United States as well (e.g. Biersack 1999).

The re-conceptualization of Symbolic Ecology (Descola and Pálsson 1996) from its earlier traditions in Anthropology (for instance in Rappaport's *Pigs for the Ancestors*, 1968) occurred during a period of renewed interest and conceptual innovation in the study of human–environmental relationships. This period is marked by both a relativist concern with situated knowledge and contextualized cosmologies and a comparativist concern with forms of cognition and interactions with the environment (Descola 1996). Furthermore, as Philippe Descola puts it (1996: 18), "Rethinking the nature-society interface means rethinking Ecological Anthropology, in particular its notion of the relation between person and environment." The broader outcomes of these discussions, however, are aimed at developing a brand of Anthropology that refutes culture/nature and other dichotomist divides (Latour 1993; Descola and Pálsson 1996).

Revisiting the culture/nature dichotomy and its implications for a comparative understanding of human–environment relationships set the stage for rethinking Ecological Anthropology at a time when the discipline as a whole was engaged in debates about postmodernism. Thus, it provided a timely and influential contribution to the development of a more inclusive Environmental Anthropology such as we describe in this chapter. In many ways, it offered a nexus to disparate perspectives of human–environment analyses: materialist perspectives on the one side, Symbolic Anthropology and structuralism on the other. Both approaches, but Descola's model in particular, lead to provocative interpretations of the conservation movement and anticipated some key issues for the study of environmentalism, as discussed below. As Descola puts it:

> Fetishing nature as a transcendental object, the control of which would be displaced
> from predatory capitalism to the rational management of modern ecological science,

the conservationist movement, far from questioning the foundation of Western cosmology, tends rather to perpetuate the ontological dualism typical of modern ideology.

(Descola 1996: 97)

Another important contribution to this debate during the 1990s was the volume organized by Ellen and Fukui (1996), bringing together perspectives from Cognitive Anthropology and Ecological Anthropology, Biology, and general Ethnology. As Moran did in the 1980s (1990 [1984]) with a revision of the ecosystem concept, Ellen and Fukui (1996: 1) proposed a revision of "the concept of nature as an analytical device, and the way it features in anthropological explanation". They recognized that beyond accepting and understanding the cultural construction of nature, once a concept is deconstructed, the problem of how to move forward remains. As Ellen's comprehensive introduction puts it, "the real challenge is to examine the implications of such epistemological relativity for the objective practices of scientists of all kinds, and for those who attempt to build on these to implement change in the lives of people outside Academy" (1996: 1–2). Ellen recognizes that the culture/nature dichotomy is deeply embedded in anthropological history and that the disciplinary wars around the topic ended up reinforcing this dichotomy, saying (1996: 18): "Every social anthropologist who asserts that there is no need to take heed of biological explanation is re-asserting the nature–culture opposition, even if the terms are not used."

Ellen's concern is about the process of overcoming these divides rather than reinforcing them. He cites Robert Norgaard in noting that "it is always a synergy of the utilitarian and the aesthetics, the pragmatics and the symbolic, and knowledge of it can never be independent of relations with it" (Norgaard 1987: 118, cited in Ellen 1996: 12). In other words, and here he draws on Stephen Gould (1991), dichotomies may serve as an analytical framework where oppositions complement each other and as such can be useful or misleading, rather than true or false.

During this period, synergistically related to these developments in ontology and Cognitive Anthropology and connected to Political Ecology, one sees a rise in anthropological studies of environmentalism. Kay Milton (1996) suggested that a focus on how culture shapes the social structure of human environmental values might lead to a better understanding of human–environment interaction. In particular, she calls for revealing how environmental values underlie decisions about the physical and economic organization of human activity and conservation efforts.

It is not simply technology that determines the human impact on the environment, but a combination of technology with economic values, ethical standards, political ideologies, religious conventions, practical knowledge, the assumptions on which all these things are based and the activities that are generated by them.

(Milton 1996: 6)

Others have taken this general approach to analysing the social context of environmentalism, such as Walsh's ecotourism ethnography of local perceptions of Western models of environmentalism in Madagascar (Walsh 2005) and Harper's (2005) study of the environmental movement in Hungary. On a larger scale, Kempton *et al.* (1995) studied the ways that cultural models of nature lead to different perceptions of environmental problems in the United States. They combined survey and ethnographic approaches to examine broad patterns of environmental values and to understand current environmental problems.

The intersection between environmentalism and indigenous/rural social movements has impacted research and policies in numerous ways during the past two decades. Anthropologists such as Charles Hale (2002, 2006) relate these interactions to a process they call 'neoliberal multiculturalism' (see also Brockington *et al.* 2008). Whether a result of global political dynamics, as these authors put it, or a convergence of historically independent regional social changes, the 1990s witnessed the global boom in conservation areas, indigenous reserves, and the spread of eco-cultural tourism based on the value of indigeneity and traditionality bestowed on different places and groups. These issues are well represented in the review articles by West *et al.* (2006) and Dove (2006), focusing on people and parks and indigenous knowledge, respectively, as akin to globalization, both of which are related to the construction, popularization, and political appropriation of concepts such as biodiversity, traditionality, and sustainability. Elsewhere scholars have expanded on Foucault's concept of 'governmentality' (1991) to conceptualize 'environmentality' (Agrawal 2005), as when analysing and criticizing the use of market-based conservation practices (Fletcher 2010; Buscher *et al.* 2012; Haenn *et al.* 2014; Adams 2015).

Productive new lines are emerging between Political and Symbolic Ecology as scholars examine interactions between practices associated with a Political Economy approach, with an examination of value systems, cultural constructions of meaning, and shifting narratives of development. For instance, Jeffrey Hoelle (2011, 2015) blends a political-economic analysis with a study of the cultural constructions of 'rainforest cowboy' identities to understand the growth and impact of cattle ranching on deforestation rates in Acre, Brazil.

Historical Ecology

The inclusion of historical perspectives in Ecological Anthropology started in the 1970s and 1980s (Bennett 1976; Netting 1981) and provided opportunities for intra-disciplinary and interdisciplinary exchanges, alongside an engagement with contemporary debates about resource management and global change (Crumley 1994; Balée 2006).[6] In the early 1970s, Netting's study of a village in the Swiss Alps provided a long-term historical population record in a bounded geographic area (1981). These data and research conditions allowed for an accurate and diachronic linkage of population and landscape variables to test for the existence of long-term homeostatic equilibrium, as well as a connection between institutional arrangements and property systems interactions with biophysical conditions across landscapes. Although not always recognized as such, *Balancing on an Alp* (1981) represented a precursor to what was later called Historical Ecology – the historical analysis of the relationship between population and environment through the focus on landscapes (Crumley 1994; Headland 1997; Balée 1998, 2006).

In the edited volume, *Historical Ecology*, Crumley (1994) and the contributing authors intended to develop a "multiscalar temporal and spatial frame, with an explicit focus on the role of human cognition in the human-environment dialectic" (Crumley 1994: 5). The goal was to be obtained through the integration of documents, ethnographies, historical records, archaeological records, remote sensing and GIS. Historical Ecology emerged as a distinct "research program" focusing on deeper timeframes with the landscape as the organizing principle and unit of analysis. The landscape is seen as the material manifestation of the human–environment dialectical relationship (Crumley 1994; see also Winterhalder 1994).

The initial phases of this trend were supported by William Balée's work in the Amazon. He debunked a long-standing environmentally deterministic position in the debate about human–environment relations in the region with a well-constructed argument about the anthropogenic history of Amazonian forests and their biodiversity (Balée 1989). His definition of Historical Ecology has some contrasts with that used in the Crumley volume, in that it is more centred on humans than on landscapes, and on human action in historical sequences: "historical, not evolutionary, events are responsible for the principal changes in relationships between human societies and their immediate environments" (Balée 1998: 13). This view of Historical Ecology takes Balée close to the Boasians' and Goldenweiser's views of humans as makers of their own environment (Moran 2007). Balée's (1994, 2006) perspective takes the impact of human action and history on the environment as underwriting the landscape concept, and as such, finds synchrony with developments in Ethnobiology, Political Ecology, and Symbolic Ecology.

Balée and Crumley both agree, however, that 'landscape' can help to bridge the gap between social and life sciences concerned with human–environment interactions (Balée 1998). Landscape approaches have allowed researchers to examine important aspects of human–environment interaction by looking at the relationship between the environment and the way people draw meaning from it. In *The Anthropology of Landscape*, Hirsch and O'Hanlon (1995) suggested that the concept of landscape might be useful in understanding how cultural processes shaped the ways that people related to socially constructed images of spaces with internally constructed and localized representations of places. For instance, in the Brazilian Amazon, as new landscapes related to the large-scale production of soybeans replace a mosaic of ranches and small-scale farms, the experience and representation of the new landscape, mediated with technology, creates social conditions that may reduce the sensitivity of landowners to local environmental changes (Adams 2008). The act of 'placemaking' was seen as a way in which spaces were rendered as meaningful through material and non-material experiences, such as perception and narration (Gow 1995; Hirsch and O'Hanlon 1995; Schama 1995), not unlike the concept of 'dwelling' and 'skills' proposed by Tim Ingold to discuss the social construction of landscapes (2000).

In addition to landscape, deeper timeframes have helped to define Historical Ecology. As Charles Redman (1999: xiii) suggests, "I see the contemporary political and economic situation as being the end product of thousands of years of a slowly changing, fundamentally similar set of human-environmental interactions." This point resonates with the prehistoric work in Kirch and Hunt's edited volume (1997). William Denevan's article 'The pristine myth – the landscape of the Americas in 1492' illustrates that human populations everywhere have manipulated their environments with diverse outcomes, and that an unmanaged environment is not necessarily synonymous with ecological health (Denevan 1992; Redman 1999).

The research within Environmental History carried out by Alfred Crosby (1986) and William Cronon (1983) explored the importance of changing landscapes (for example, the changing context of weeds and diseases) as primers of European expansion and social change. Environmental History has also continued to receive the renewed attention of anthropologists, as illustrated in the work of Alf Hornborg et al. (2007). Their work, *Rethinking Environmental History: World-system History and Global Environmental Change*, explores the rich theoretical territory at the intersection of Environmental History and Political Economy. Historical ecological frameworks with a focus on population (e.g. Viazzo 1989) have also represented fertile ground for contributing to biocultural approaches to the study of ethnic groups, providing, for example, a critical outlook to population units adopted in bio-anthropological investigations (Fiorini et al. 2007).

The methodological integration found in the Historical Ecology trend contributes to the ability of Environmental Anthropology to address holistically the study of human societies, cultures, and environments, including the analysis of current land-use change (Brondízio 2006). The macroscopic conceptual frame to our understanding of human–environment relationships adds essential historical depth to observed changes in those relationships and the multi-layered systems of meaning and value that can underlie the human relationships with specific landscapes.

Ethnobiology and related fields

Ethnobiology has been an intrinsic part of many of the paradigms discussed above for the last half century. While already practised in some way at least since the 1920s, Ethnobiology evolved particularly since the 1950s by combining the analysis of language structure, lexicon, perception and conception (cognitive environment) with the analysis of resource management (behavioural environment) (e.g. Frake 1962). Ethnobiology and related fields developed relatively independently from, but nonetheless closely associated with, Cultural Ecology (Conklin 1954; Johnson 1974). For instance, Harold Conklin's studies of the ethnoecology of shifting cultivators (1961) provided much of the basis for studies on agricultural production systems.

The earliest root to Ethnobiology comes from Ethnobotany, which encompassed the study of people–plant relationships. The term was utilized to describe the use of plants (largely in an archaeological context) by indigenous people at the end of the nineteenth century and was already an active field during the first half of the twentieth century (see Ford 1978; Schultes and Von Reis 1995). The confluence and overlap of terminology (Ethnobiology, Ethnoecology, Ethnobotany, Ethnozoology, etc.) continues to the present day. For this reason, and unless specified, we have selected Ethnobiology as a general term to represent this field.

During the 1960s, controversies and criticism emerged relating to the insufficiency of links between the cognitive domain and behaviour in ethnobiological data; that is, how people behave in relationship to what they say (Burling 1964). However, with the development of more complex methods, both in terms of systematic observations and linguistic analysis (Frake 1962; Sturtevant 1964), Ethnobiology became an important method for those practising Cultural Ecology.

At this point, it is useful to distinguish three complementary trends that developed in the field: universalism, particularism, and applied Ethnobiology (see also Ellen 2006 who uses a different terminology). During the 1960s, while most of the field continued in a particularist tradition concerned with assessment of knowledge systems, resource management, and material culture of specific groups and environments, some started to focus attention on the study of generalized systems of cognition and classificatory universals (Berlin *et al.* 1968). In the late 1960s and 1970s, important work in folk systematics and taxonomies contributed to understanding the general principles of cognitive models and folk classification relative to formal biological taxonomies (Berlin *et al.* 1973; Berlin *et al.* 1966, 1974; Johnson 1971, 1972), setting the stage for Ethnoecology beyond descriptions of folk classification systems in its explanation of cognitive patterns of biological classification and behavioural practices.

Applied Ethnobiology emerges during the 1980s and 1990s with a focus on various aspects of resource management systems and economic development, particularly contesting and proposing alternatives to development (Posey *et al.* 1984; Posey and Overal 1990; Escobar 1998) and calling attention to issues of intellectual property rights (Posey 1990; Brush and Stabinsky 1997), cultural memory, and biodiversity conservation (Nazarea 2006). Building upon a long-term research programme, the seminal work of Brent Berlin – *Ethnobiological*

Classification (1992) – provided a generalizable conceptual framework for the field by presenting a formal interpretation of classification principles in traditional societies parallel to scientific taxonomic principles (Hunn 2007).

Ethnobiology and related fields were concerned with contributing to new alternatives for resource management (e.g. alternatives to deforestation) and informing debates about agricultural development issues (e.g. local production systems), with anthropologists contributing to studies of biodiversity and agrodiversity (Orlove and Brush 1996; Nazarea 1998; Maffi 2001). The abundance of work in the tropics created a new framework and environmental discourse for indigenous communities to propose a sustainable development perspective to those engaged in debates about resource management and to advocate for the potential benefits in opening new markets for non-timber forest products (Balick 1987; Denevan and Padoch 1987; Posey *et al.* 1984; Prance *et al.* 1984; Bennett 1992). Following on Conklin's tradition, this line of work has been important within the agricultural intensification debate (Boserup 1965) and the analysis of agricultural cycle, thus providing a new appreciation for the productivity of indigenous and local production systems (Brondízio and Siqueira 1997).

As illustrated by Balée's *Footprints in the Forest* (1994), Ethnobiology and related fields have fulfilled an important role by bridging environmental approaches within and beyond Anthropology and have provided many conceptual and methodological tools essential to Ecological Anthropology in general, and Historical Ecology in particular. Ethnobiology gave additional tools to Historical Ecology to move beyond the culture/nature dichotomy and adaptationist approaches. It has helped to overcome the deterministic role of the environment in Cultural Ecology models by presenting a more active role for human understanding and transformation of the environment.

The valorization of indigenous and local knowledge emphasized through Ethnobiology, as well as the way anthropologists became ethically and practically engaged as advocates, contributed to the establishment of an alliance between indigenous–rights advocates, indigenous communities, and the environmental movement around issues of deforestation and resource depletion (Posey *et al.* 1984, Conklin and Graham 1995; Dove 2006). This process facilitated a convergence between indigenous and peasant social movements fighting for land rights, and the environmental movement confronting development policies. Increasingly, however, local knowledge became idealized and romanticized. An expectation developed among some activists that indigenous and peasant people would behave in ways seen as environmentally responsible by environmentalists, as though they were disconnected from political and economic forces (Tsing 1999). This revival of the 'noble savage' image (Dove 2006; Hames 2007) and the formal designation of 'traditional populations' (Hanazaki *et al.* 2007) as a quasi-ethnic category (e.g. Brazil) served important political roles in pursuit of the peasant and indigenous communities' goals (e.g. land demarcation and rights to access resources), but it came at a cost of [mis]representation (Dove 2006).

During the 1990s and 2000s, the economic potential for bio-prospecting (sampling plant pharmaceutical compounds based on local practices of use) created a dilemma and led to criticism of Ethnobiology. Ethnobiologists (and anthropologists in general) often mediated the interaction of governments, communities, and pharmaceutical companies, despite the lack of cultural and legal frameworks for access to benefits and an equitable distribution of profits for local communities (Brush and Stabinsky 1997). The field became politically and legally sensitive due to pressures from social movements, the popular spread of the idea of 'bio-piracy', and legislation imposed to control access to local knowledge and biological resources, even though those within the ethnobiological research community were generally quite concerned about ensuring ethical research practices (e.g. Posey and Overal 1990). The overemphasis on the value of knowledge and the perception that biological resources are 'property' have contributed to an increase in competition for resource ownership, commodification of ethnicity, and monetarization within and between indigenous groups (Comaroff and Comaroff 2008). These experiences echo an earlier pattern we illustrated in regard to anthropological studies of environmentalism. Despite these concerns, Ethnobiology continues to evolve, with new areas of research addressing contemporary issues, including research among urbanized and industrialized populations (Viladrich 2006), a growing attention to cultural change, cognition, and cultural consensus analysis (Reyes-Garcia *et al.* 2003; Ross *et al.* 2003), inter-generational change and transmission of knowledge (Zarger and Stepp 2004), cultural memory (Nazarea 2006), globalization and markets (Brondízio 2008), and agrodiversity and social networks (Emperaire and Peroni 2007), among others.

Concluding remarks

The predominant inductive approach of Anthropology has represented a continuous challenge to the rise of dominating theoretical frameworks. Thus, whenever a paradigm emerged to facilitate the explanation of a certain relationship, the potential for new interpretations could arise in contestation (for example, the shifts following Steward's Puerto Rico project, or the challenge that political-historical factors provided to the ecosystem approach). Hence, tensions at the theoretical level arise regularly in relation to findings from empirical case studies. Environmental Anthropology, as an overarching term widely used today has arisen as a conceptual category above tensions between theoretical frameworks, and is indicative of a more inclusive field of study for diverse perspectives on human–environment interaction as well as various types of engagement with environmental and societal problems.

Environmental Anthropology has been shaped by debates about the relative balance of environmental, cultural, political, and historical factors in providing meaningful explanations to human–environment interaction without resorting to determinism. As a consequence, it has served to reconcile contrasting perspectives and accommodate diverse specialties within the discipline. On the other hand, it continues to face the challenge of integrating these approaches into a new synthesis able to provide a useful understanding of the growing complexity of human–environment interactions within an ever-changing world, thereby contributing to our understanding of alternative models of socio-economic development and environmental sustainability more broadly. The challenge ahead for environmental anthropologists is to continue to be inclusive and reflexive in order to contribute and learn from a broad and growing community interested in understanding the relationship between people and the environment. At the same time, the field must reunite its rich array of specialties into cohesive frameworks able to productively position Anthropology within the broader discussions of human–environment interactions and global change today and in the future.

Acknowledgements

We would like to thank our current and former home institutions: the Department of Anthropology, the Anthropological Center for Training and Research on Global Environmental Change (ACT) at Indiana University; the Department of Anthropology at Indiana University–Purdue University Indianapolis (IUPUI) and Lycoming College; and the James Hutton Institute (formerly The Macaulay Land Use Research Institute) in Aberdeen, Scotland for the support provided during several phases of writing this chapter. We also thank the Laboratoire d'anthropologie sociale at the Collège de France, particularly Philippe Descola for the opportunity to participate in the seminar 'Anthropologie de la Nature' which he presented with Florence Brunois, and for the support provided during the sabbatical (academic year 2008/2009) of Eduardo S. Brondízio when this chapter was revised. We would like to thank our colleagues Bill Slee, Andrea D. Siqueira, and Rodrigo P. F. Pedrosa for their comments on a previous version of the chapter; Vonnie Peischl, Barbara Fuqua, Matthew Amendolara, Amber Seibel, and Kelsey Scroggins for their administrative and editorial work. We would also like to thank Michael Hakin (editor for the Cultural Anthropology section of the UNESCO Encyclopedia of Life Support Systems [EOLSS]), two anonymous reviewers for their careful work and valuable suggestions, and the editors of the UNESCO EOLSS (www.eolss.net) for improving an earlier version of this chapter. We are solely responsible for the views expressed in this chapter.

Notes

1 In presenting these fields, we recognize that all of them extend and include wider interdisciplinary communities spanning many disciplines. Their inclusion as part of this review recognizes their roots and/or history within Anthropology and their current critical mass of scholarship in the discipline.
2 Cultural Ecology and Political Ecology are very active fields, particularly in Geography. Illustrative of the cross-fertilization between Anthropology and Geography, the Association of American Geographers offers an annual award in Cultural Ecology named after anthropologist Robert Netting.
3 Using Benjamin Orlove's definition of the term (1980: 240): "The term neo-functionalism is used because the followers of this approach see the social organization and culture of specific populations as functional adaptations which permit the populations to exploit their environments successfully without exceeding their carrying capacity."
4 While the *Journal of Political Ecology* is commonly referred to as the first academic publication dedicated to the field, an earlier and still active journal of similar name (*Revista Ecología Política*) has been published in Spain since 1991 (www.ecologiapolitica.info/ep/anteriores.htm).
5 Latour (2004) took issue with the culture/nature dichotomy perspective perpetuated in Political Ecology and argued for a Political Ecology closer to a philosophy of science and politics, although his use of the term Political Ecology seems to differ from that presented here (2004: 8).
6 William Balée (foreword of the 1998 volume *Advances in Historical Ecology*) refers to Carol Crumley's genealogy of the term, beginning with anthropologist Edward S. Deevey (University of Florida) in 1976 and later (1980) in an interdisciplinary collection entitled *Historical Ecology: Essays on Environmental and Social Change* organized by historian Lester J. Bilsky.

References

Acheson J. M. 2003. *Capturing the Commons: Devising Institutions to Manage the Maine Lobster Industry.* Hanover, NH: University Press of New England.
Acheson J. M. 2006. Institutional failure in resource management. *Annual Review of Anthropology* 35: 117–134.
Acheson J. 2011. Ostrom for anthropologists. *International Journal of the Commons* 5(2): 319–339.
Adams R. 2008. Large-scale mechanized soybean farmers in Amazônia: New ways of experiencing land. *Culture and Agriculture* 30(1&2): 32–37.
Adams R. 2015. Becoming 'environmentally responsible' soybean farmers: Neoliberal environmentality in Santarém. *Culture, Agriculture, Food, and Environment* (CAFE) 37(2): 63–78.
Adger W., Benjaminsen T., Brown K. and Svarstad H. 2001. Advancing a political ecology of global environmental discourses. *Development and Change* 32(4): 681–715.
Agrawal A. 2003. Sustainable governance of common-pool resources: Context, methods, and politics. *Annual Review of Anthropology* 32: 243–262.
Agrawal A. 2005. *Environmentality: Technologies of Government and the Making of Subjects.* Durham, NC: Duke University Press.

Anderson K. 1996. Place/culture/representation. *Annals of the Association of American Geographers* 86(1): 162–164.

Balée W. L. (1989). The culture of Amazônian forests. *Advances in Economic Botany* 7: 1–21.

Balée W. L. 1994. *Footprints in the Forest: Ka'apor Ethnobotany—The Historical Ecology of Plant Utilization by an Amazonian People*. New York: Columbia University Press.

Balée W. L. 1998. *Advances in Historical Ecology*. New York: Columbia University Press.

Balée W. L. 2006. The research program of historical ecology. *Annual Review of Anthropology* 35(1): 75–98.

Balick M. J. 1987. The economic utilization of the Babassu palm: A conservation strategy for sustaining tropical forest resources. *Journal of the Washington Academy of Sciences* 77(4): 215–223.

Bates D. G. and Lees S. H. (eds) 1997. *Case Studies in Human Ecology*. New York: Plenum.

Bateson G. 1972. *Steps to an Ecology of Mind: Collected Essays in Anthropology, Psychiatry, Evolution, and Epistemology*. Chicago, IL: University Of Chicago Press.

Behrens C. A. 1994. Recent advances in the regional analysis of indigenous land use and tropical deforestation. *Human Ecology* (Special issue), 22(3): 243–247.

Bennett A. J. 1992. Dynamics of forestry and agriculture at the forest edge. Paper presented at the Oxford Conference on Tropical Forests, Oxford, UK, 30 March–1 April.

Bennett J. W. 1969. *Northern Plainsmen: Adaptive Strategy and Agrarian Life*. Chicago, IL: Aldine Publishing Company.

Bennett J. W. 1976. Anticipation, adaptation and the concept of culture in anthropology. *Science* 192(4242): 847–853.

Bennett J. W. 2005 [1976]. *The Ecological Transition*. New Brunswick, NJ: Transaction Publishers.

Berlin B. 1992. *Ethnobiological Classification: Principles of Categorization of Plants and Animals in Traditional Societies*. Princeton, NJ: Princeton University Press.

Berlin B., Breedlove D. E. and Raven P. H. 1966. Folk taxonomies and biological classification. *Science* 154(3746): 273–275.

Berlin B., Breedlove D. E. and Raven P. H. 1968. Covert categories and folk taxonomies. *American Anthropologist* 70(2): 290–299.

Berlin B., Breedlove D. E. and Raven P. H. 1973. General principles of classification and nomenclature in folk biology. *American Anthropologist* 75(1): 214–242.

Berlin B., Breedlove D. E. and Raven P. H. 1974. *Principles of Tzeltal Plant Classification: An Introduction to the Botanical Ethnography of a Mayan-speaking People of Highland Chiapas*. New York: Academic Press.

Bernard H. R. 2000. *Social Research Methods: Qualitative and Quantitative Approaches*. Thousand Oaks, CA: Sage Publications.

Biersack A. 1999. Introduction: From the 'New Ecology' to the new ecologies. *American Anthropologist* 101(1): 5–18.

Biersack A. and Greenberg J. B. (eds) 2006. *Reimagining Political Ecology*. Durham, NC: Duke University Press.

Boas F. 1911. *The Mind of Primitive Man*. New York: Macmillan.

Boserup E. 1965. *The Conditions of Agricultural Growth: The Economics of Agrarian Change under Population Pressure*. Chicago, IL: Aldine Publishing Company.

Brockington D., Duffy R. and Igoe J. 2008. *Nature Unbound: Conservation, Capitalism and the Future of Protected Areas*. London and Sterling, VA: Earthscan.

Brondízio E. S. 2006. Landscapes of the past, footprints of the future: historical ecology and the analysis of land use change in the Amazon. In W. Balée and C. Erikson (eds) *Time and Complexity in Historical Ecology: Studies in the Neotropical Lowlands*. New York: Columbia University Press, pp. 365–405.

Brondízio E. S. 2008. *The Amazonian Caboclo and the Açaí Palm: Forest Farmers in the Global Market*. Bronx: New York Botanical Garden Press.

Brondízio E. S. and Siqueira A. D. 1997. From extractivists to forest farmers: Changing concepts of agricultural intensification and peasantry in the Amazon estuary. *Research in Economic Anthropology* 18: 233–279.

Brondízio E. S. and Van Holt T. 2014. Geospatial analysis in anthropology. In H. R. Bernard and C. L. Gravelee (eds) *Handbook of Methods in Cultural Anthropology*. Lanham, MD: AltaMira Press, pp. 601–629.

Brush S. and Stabinsky D. 1997. *Valuing Local Knowledge: Indigenous People and Intellectual Property Rights*. Washington, DC: Island Press.

Bryant R. L. 1998. Rethinking environmental management. *Progress in Human Geography* 22(3): 321–343.

Burling R. 1964. Cognition and componential analysis – God's truth or hocus-pocus? *American Anthropologist* 66(1): 20–28.

Buscher B., Sullivan S., Neves K., Igoe J. and Brockington D. 2012. Toward a synthesized critique of neoliberal biodiversity conservation. *Capitalism Nature Socialism* 23(2): 4–30.

Castro F. and McGraph D. 2003. Community-based management of lakes and sustainability of floodplain resources in the lower Amazon. *Human Organization* 62(2): 123–133.

Castro F., Silva-Forsberg M. C., Wilson W., Brondizio E. S. and Moran E. F. 2002. The use of remotely-sensed data in rapid rural assessment. *Field Methods* 14(3): 243–310.

Cole J. W. and Wolf E. R. 1974. *The Hidden Frontier: Ecology and Ethnicity in an Alpine Valley.* New York: Academic Press.

Comaroff J. and Comaroff J. 2008. Ethnicity, INC. *Indiana University David Skomp Distinguished Lecture in Anthropology Paper Series.* Bloomington: Department of Anthropology, Indiana University.

Conklin B. A. and Graham L. R. 1995. The shifting middle ground: Amazonian Indians and eco-politics. *American Anthropologist* 97(4): 695–710.

Conklin H. 1954. An ethnoecological approach to shifting agriculture. *Transactions of the New York Academy of Sciences* 17(2): 133–142.

Conklin H. C. 1961. The study of shifting cultivation. *Current Anthropology* 2(1): 27–61.

Cronon W. 1983. *Changes in the Land: Indians, Colonists, and the Ecology of New England.* New York: Hill and Wang.

Crosby A. W. 1986. *Ecological Imperialism: The Biological Expansion of Europe, 900–1900.* Cambridge, UK and New York: Cambridge University Press.

Crumley C. L. 1994. *Historical Ecology: Cultural Knowledge and Changing Landscapes.* 1st edn. Santa Fe, NM and Seattle, WA: School of American Research Press.

Denevan W. M. 1992. The pristine myth – the landscape of the Americas in 1492. *Annals of the Association of American Geographers* 82(3): 369–385.

Denevan W. M. and Padoch C. 1987. *Swidden-fallow Agroforestry in the Peruvian Amazon.* Bronx: New York Botanical Garden Press.

Descola P. 1986. *La Nature domestique: Symbolisme et praxis dans l'écologie des Achuar.* Charenton-le-Pont, France: Editions de la Maison des sciences de l'homme.

Descola P. 1994 [1986]. *In the Society of Nature: A Native Ecology in Amazônia* (originally published in French). Cambridge, UK: Cambridge University Press.

Descola P. 1996. Constructing natures. In P. Descola and G. Pálsson (eds) *Nature and Society: Anthropological Perspectives.* New York: Routledge, pp. 82–102.

Descola P. 2013. *Beyond Nature and Culture.* Chicago, IL: University of Chicago Press.

Descola P. and Pálsson G. (eds) 1996. *Nature and Society: Anthropological Perspectives.* London: Routledge.

Dietz T., Ostrom E. and Stern P. 2003. The struggle to govern the commons. *Science* 302(5652): 1907–1912.

Dove M. 2006. Indigenous people and environmental politics. *Annual Review of Anthropology* 35: 191–208.

Ellen R. F. 1982. *Environment, Subsistence, and System: The Ecology of Small-scale Social Formations.* Cambridge, UK and New York: Cambridge University Press.

Ellen R. F. 1996. Introduction. In R. F. Ellen and K. Fukui (eds) *Redefining Nature: Ecology, Culture, and Domestication.* Oxford and Washington, DC: Berg Publishers, pp. 1–36.

Ellen R. F. 2006. Ethnobiology: Introduction. *Journal of the Royal Anthropological Institute* 12(1): 1–22.

Ellen R. F. and Fukui K. 1996. *Redefining Nature: Ecology, Culture, and Domestication.* Oxford and Washington, DC: Berg Publishers.

Emperaire L. and Peroni N. 2007. Traditional management of agro biodiversity in Brazil: A case study of manioc. *Human Ecology* 35(6): 761–768.

Escobar A. 1996. Construction nature: Elements for a post-structuralist political ecology. *Futures* 28(4): 325–343.

Escobar A. 1998. Whose knowledge, whose nature? Biodiversity, conservation, and the political ecology of social movements. *Journal of Political Ecology* 5(1): 53–82.

Escobar A. 1999. After nature: Steps to an antiessentialist political ecology. *Current Anthropology* 40(1): 1–30.

Fiorini S., Tagarelli G., Boattini A., Luiselli D., Piro A., Tagarelli A. and Pettener D. 2007. Ethnicity and evolution of the biodemographic structure of Arbereshe and Italian populations of the Pollino area, Southern Italy (1820–1984). *American Anthropologist* 109: 734–746.

Fletcher R. 2010. Neoliberal environmentality: Towards a poststructuralist political ecology of the conservation debate. *Conservation and Society* 8(3): 171–181.

Ford R. 1978. The nature and status of ethnobotany. In R. I. Ford (ed.) *Anthropological Papers*, no. 67. Ann Arbor: University of Michigan Museum of Anthropology, pp. 33–49.

Foucault M. 1991. Governmentality. In G. Burchell, C. Gordon and P. Miller (eds) *The Foucault Effect: Studies in Governmentality*. Hemel Hempstead, UK: Harvester Wheatsheaf, pp. 87–104.

Frake C. O. 1962. Cultural ecology and ethnography. *American Anthropologist* 64(1): 53–59.

Galvin K. A., Boone R. B., Smith N. M. and Lynn S. J. 2001. Impacts of climate variability on east African pastoralists: Linking social science and remote sensing. *Climate Research* 19(1): 161–172.

Geertz C. 1963. *Agricultural Involution: The Process of Ecological Change in Indonesia*. Published for the Association of Asian Studies. Berkeley: University of California Press.

Gezon L. 2002. Marriage, kin, and compensation: A socio-political ecology of gender in Ankarana, Madagascar. *Anthropological Quarterly* 75(4): 675–706.

Godoy R., Reyes-Garcia V., Byron E., Leonard W. R. and Vadez V. 2005. The effect of market economies on the well-being of indigenous peoples and on their use of natural resources. *Annual Review of Anthropology* 34: 121–138.

Gould S. 1991. Exaptation: A crucial tool for an evolutionary psychology. *Journal of Social Issues* 47(3): 43–65.

Gow P. 1995. Land, people and paper in western Amazônia. In E. Hirsch and M. O'Hanlon (eds) *The Anthropology of Landscape: Perspectives on Place and Space*. Oxford: Oxford University Press, pp. 43–62.

Greenberg J. B. and Park T. K. 1994. Political ecology. *Political Ecology* 1(1): 1–12.

Haenn N. 1997 'The Government gave us the land': Political ecology and regional culture in Campeche, Mexico. Unpublished PhD thesis, Department of Anthropology, Indiana University, Bloomington.

Haenn N. 2002. Nature regimes in southern Mexico: A history of power and environment. *Ethnology* 41(1): 1–26.

Haenn N., Olson E., Martinez-Reyes J. and Durand L. 2014. Introduction: Between capitalism, the state, and the grassroots: Mexico's contribution to a global conservation debate. *Conservation and Society* 12(2): 111–119.

Hale C. 2002. Does multiculturalism menace? Governance, cultural rights and the politics of identity in Guatemala. *Journal of Latin American Studies* 34(3): 485–525.

Hale C. 2006. Activist research vs. cultural critique: Indigenous land rights and the contradictions of politically engaged anthropology. *Cultural Anthropology* 21(1): 96–120.

Hames R. 2007. The ecologically noble savage debate. *Annual Review of Anthropology* 36(1): 177–190.

Hanazaki, N., de Castro F., Oliveira V. G. and Peroni N. 2007. Between the sea and the land: The livelihood of estuarine people in southeastern Brazil. *Ambiente & Sociedade* 10(1): 121–136.

Hardesty D. L. 1977. *Ecological Anthropology*. New York: John Wiley.

Hardin G. 1968. The tragedy of the commons. *Science* 162(3859): 1243–1248.

Harper K. 2005. 'Wild capitalism' and 'ecocolonialism': A tale of two rivers. *American Anthropologist* 107(2): 221–233.

Harris, M. (1968). *The Rise of Anthropological Theory: A History of Theories of Culture*. New York: Crowell.

Headland T. 1997. Revisionism in ecological anthropology. *Current Anthropology* 38(4): 605–630.

Hirsch E. and O'Hanlon M. 1995. *The Anthropology of Landscape: Perspectives on Place and Space*. Oxford and New York: Clarendon Press/Oxford University Press.

Hoelle J. 2011. Convergence on cattle: Political ecology, social group perceptions, and socioeconomic relationships in Acre, Brazil. *Culture, Agriculture, Food and Environment (CAFE)* 33(2): 95–106.

Hoelle J. 2015. *Rainforest Cowboys: The Rise of Ranching and Cattle Culture in Western Amazonia*. Austin: University of Texas Press.

Hornborg A., McNeill J. and Martinez-Alier J. 2007. *Rethinking Environmental History: World-system History and Global Environmental Change*. Lanham, MD: AltaMira Press.

Hunn E. S. 2007. Ethnobiology in four phases. *Journal of Ethnobiology* 27(1): 1–10.

Ingold T. 1986. *The Appropriation of Nature: Essays on Human Ecology and Social Relations*. Manchester: Manchester University Press.

Ingold T. 2000. *The Perception of the Environment: Essays on Livelihood, Dwelling and Skill*. London: Routledge.

Johnson A. 1971. *Sharecroppers of the Sertão: Economics and Dependence on a Brazilian Plantation*. Stanford, CA: Stanford University Press.

Johnson A. 1972. Individuality and experimentation in traditional agriculture. *Human Ecology* 1(2): 149–159.

Johnson A. 1974. Ethnoecology and planting practices in a swidden agricultural system. *American Ethnologist* 1(1): 87–101.

Kempton W., Boster J. S. and Hartley J. A. 1995. *Environmental Values in American Culture*. Cambridge, MA: The MIT Press.

Kern S. 2003. *The Culture of Time and Space 1880–1918*. Cambridge, MA: Harvard University Press.

Kirch P. V. and Hunt T. L. (eds) 1997. *Historical Ecology in the Pacific Islands: Prehistoric Environmental and Landscape Change*. New Haven, CT: Yale University Press.

Kottak C. 1999. The new ecological anthropology. *American Anthropologist* 101(1): 23–35.

Kroeber A. L. 1939. *Cultural and Natural Areas of Native North America*. Berkeley: University of California Press.

Latour B. 1993. *We Have Never Been Modern*. Cambridge, MA: Harvard University Press.

Latour B. 2004. *Politics of Nature: How to Bring the Sciences into Democracy*. Cambridge, MA: Harvard University Press.

Little P. E. 1999. Environments and environmentalisms in anthropological research: Facing a new millennium. *Annual Review of Anthropology* 28(1): 253–284.

McCay B. J. and Acheson J. M. 1987. *The Question of the Commons: The Culture and Ecology of Communal Resources*. Tucson: University of Arizona Press.

McCay B. J., Micheli F., Ponce-Díaz G., Murray G., Shester G., Ramirez-Sanchez S. and Weisman W. 2014. Cooperatives, concessions, and co-management on the Pacific coast of Mexico. *Marine Policy* 44: 49–59.

Maffi L. (ed.) 2001. *On Biocultural Diversity: Linking Language, Knowledge, and the Environment*. Washington, DC: Smithsonian Institution Press.

Magistro J., Roncoli C. and Hulme M. 2001. Anthropological perspectives and policy implications of climate change research. Special issue of *Climate Research* 19: 91–178.

Milton K. 1996. *Environmentalism and Cultural Theory: Exploring the Role of Anthropology in Environmental Discourse*. London and New York: Routledge.

Mintz S. W. 1985. *Sweetness and Power: The Place of Sugar in Modern History*. New York: Penguin Books.

Moran E. F. 1979. *Human Adaptability: An Introduction to Ecological Anthropology*. North Scituate, MA: Duxbury Press.

Moran E. F. 1984. (ed.) *The Ecosystem Concept in Anthropology*. Boulder, CO: Westview Press.

Moran E. F. 1990 [1984]. Levels of analysis shifting and its implications for Amazonian research. In E. F. Moran (ed.) *The Ecosystem Concept in Anthropology*. Boulder, CO: Westview Press, pp. 279–308.

Moran E. F. 1990. *The Ecosystem Approach in Anthropology: From Concept to Practice*. Ann Arbor: University of Michigan Press.

Moran E. F. 2006. The human–environment nexus: Progress in the past decade in the integrated analysis of human and biophysical factors. In A. Hornborg and C. Crumley (eds) *The World System and the Earth System: Global Socioenvironmental Change and Sustainability since the Neolithic*. Walnut Creek, CA: Left Coast Press, pp. 231–242.

Moran E. F. 2007. *Human Adaptability: An Introduction to Ecological Anthropology*. 3rd edn. Boulder, CO: Westview Press.

Moran E. F. and Brondízio E. S. 2001. Human ecology from space: Ecological anthropology engages the study of global environmental change. In E. Messer and M. J. Lambek (eds) *Ecology and the Sacred: Engaging the Anthropology of Roy A. Rappaport*. Ann Arbor: University of Michigan Press, pp. 64–87

Morgan L. H. 1965 [1877]. *Ancient Society*. Cambridge, MA: The Belknap Press of Harvard University Press.

Murphy R. 1981. Julian Steward. In S. Silverman (ed.) *Totems and Teachers: Perspectives on the History of Anthropology*. New York: Columbia University Press, pp. 171–206.

Nash J. 2014. Reassessing the culture concept in the analysis of global social movements: An anthropological perspective. In B. Baumgarten, P. Daphi and P. Ullrich (eds) *Conceptualizing Culture in Social Movement Research*. Houndsmills, Basingstoke, UK: Palgrave Macmillan, pp. 67–91.

Nazarea V. 1998. *Cultural Memory and Biodiversity*. Tucson: University of Arizona Press.

Nazarea V. 2006. Local knowledge and memory in biodiversity conservation. *Annual Review of Anthropology* 35(1): 317–335.

Nelson D. and Finan T. 2000. The emergence of a climate anthropology in Northeast Brazil. *Practicing Anthropology* 22(4): 6–10.

Netting R. M. 1968. *Hill Farmers of Nigeria: Cultural Ecology of the Kofyar of the Jos Plateau*. Seattle: University of Washington Press.

Netting R. M. 1981. *Balancing on an Alp: Ecological Change and Continuity in a Swiss Mountain Community*. Cambridge, UK and New York: Cambridge University Press.

Norgaard, R. B. 1987. Economics as mechanics and the demise of biological diversity. *Ecological Modelling* 38: 107–121.

Nyerges E. A. and Green G. M. 2000. The ethnography of landscape: GIS and remote sensing in the study of forest change in West African Guinea Savana. *American Anthropologist* 102(2): 1–19.

Orlove B. S. 1980. Ecological anthropology. *Annual Review of Anthropology* 9: 235–273.

Orlove B. S. and Brush S. 1996. Anthropology and the conservation of biodiversity. *Annual Review of Anthropology* 25: 329–352.

Orlove B. S., Chiang J. H. and Cane M. A. 2000. Forecasting Andean rainfall and crop yield from the influence of El Niño on Pleiades visibility. *Nature* 403: 68–71.

Ostrom E. 1990. *Governing the Commons: The Evolution of Institutions for Collective Action.* Cambridge, UK and New York: Cambridge University Press.

Ostrom E., Burger, J., Field C. B., Norgaard R. B. and Policansky D. 1999. Sustainability – revisiting the commons: Local lessons, global challenges. *Science* 284(5412): 278–282.

Peluso N. L. 1991. Case Study One, rattan industries in East Kalimantan, Indonesia. In J. Y. Campbell (ed.) *Case Studies in Forest-based Small Scale Enterprises in Asia.* Bangkok: Community Forestry Case Study 4, Food and Agriculture Organization of the United Nations, pp. 5–28.

Penna-Firme R. P. 2012. Political and event ecology: Critiques and opportunities for collaboration. *Journal of Political Ecology* 20: 199–216.

Petursson J. G. and Vedeld P. 2015. The 'nine lives' of protected areas. A historical-institutional analysis from the transboundary Mt Elgon, Uganda and Kenya. *Land Use Policy* 42: 251–263.

Posey D. A. 1990. Intellectual property rights: What is the position of ethnobiology? *Journal of Ethnobiology* 10(1): 93–98.

Posey D. A. and Overal W. L. (eds) 1990. *Ethnobiology: Implications and Applications.* Proceedings of the First International Congress of Ethnobiology. Belém, Brazil: Museu Goeldi.

Posey D. A., Frechione J., Eddins J., DaSilva L. F., Myers D., Case D. and Macbeth P. 1984. Ethnoecology as applied anthropology in Amazonian development. *Human Organization* 43(2): 95–107.

Poteete A. R., Janssen M. A. and Ostrom E. (eds) 2010. *Working Together: Collective Action, the Commons, and Multiple Methods in Practice.* Princeton, NJ: Princeton University Press.

Prance G. T., Kallunki J. A. and New York Botanical Garden 1984. *Ethnobotany in the Neotropics: Proceedings.* Bronx: New York Botanical Garden Press.

Rappaport R. A. 1968. *Pigs for the Ancestors: Ritual in the Ecology of a New Guinea People.* New Haven, CT: Yale University Press.

Rappaport R. A. 1990. Ecosystems, populations, and people. In E. F. Moran (ed.) *The Ecosystem Approach in Anthropology: From Concept to Practice.* Ann Arbor: University of Michigan Press, pp. 41–74.

Ratzel F. 1896. *The History of Mankind* (trans. A. J. Butler). London: Macmillan.

Redman C. L. 1999. *Human Impact on Ancient Environments.* Tucson:

University of Arizona Press.Reyes-Garcia V., Godoy R., Vadez V., Apaza L., Byron E., Huanca T., Leonard W. R., Pérez E. and Wilkie D. 2003. Ethnobotanical knowledge shared widely among Tsimane' Amerindians, Bolivia. *Science* 299(5613): 1707.

Robbins P. 2012. *Political Ecology: A Critical Introduction.* 2nd edn. Cambridge, MA: Blackwell.

Rocheleau D. E., Thomas-Slayter B. and Wangari E. (eds) 1997. *Feminist Political Ecology: Global Perspectives and Local Experience.* New York: Routledge.

Ross N., Medin D., Coley J. D. and Atran S. 2003. Cultural and experiential differences in the development of folkbiological induction. *Cognitive Development* 18(1): 25–47.

Schama S. 1995. *Landscape and Memory.* London and New York: HarperCollins.

Schmink M. and Wood C. H. 1992. *Contested Frontiers in Amazonia.* New York: Columbia University Press.

Schultes R. and Von Reis S. 1995. *Ethnobotany: Evolution of a Discipline.* Portland, OR: Timber Press.

Scoones I. 1999. New ecology and the social sciences: What prospects for a fruitful engagement? *Annual Review of Anthropology* 28: 479–507.

Sponsel L. E. 1997. Julian Steward. In T. Barfield (ed.) *The Dictionary of Anthropology.* Oxford: Blackwell Publishers, pp. 448–450.

Sponsel L. 2004. Contemporary ecological anthropology: Survey, analysis, and commentary on its academic characteristics and resources. Unpublished manuscript.

Sponsel L. E. and Headland T. N. 1996. *Tropical Deforestation: The Human Dimension.* New York: Columbia University Press.

Steward, J. H. (1938). *Basin-Plateau Aboriginal Sociopolitical Groups.* Washington, DC: U.S. Government Printing Office.

Steward, J. H. 1939–1946. *Handbook of South American Indians.* Washington, DC: U.S. Government Printing Office.

Steward J. H. 1955. *Theory of Culture Change: The Methodology of Multilinear Evolution*. Urbana: University of Illinois Press.

Steward J. H. 1956. *The People of Puerto Rico, A Study in Social Anthropology*. Urbana: University of Illinois Press.

Strathern M. 1981. No nature, no culture: The Hagen case. In C. MacCormack and M. Strathern (eds) *Nature, Culture, and Gender*. Cambridge, UK: Cambridge University Press, pp. 174–222.

Sturtevant W. C. 1964. Studies in ethnoscience. *American Anthropologist* 66(3): 99–131.

Sutton M. and Anderson E. N. 2004. *An Introduction to Cultural Ecology*. Lanham, MD: AltaMira Press.

Tsing A. L. 1999. Becoming a tribal elder, and other green development fantasies. In T. Li (ed.) *Transforming the Indonesian Uplands: Studies in Environmental Anthropology*. New York: Routledge, pp. 157–199.

Tucker C. 2008. *Changing Forests: Collective Action, Common Property, and Coffee in Honduras*. Dordrecht, the Netherlands: Springer.

Vaccaro I., Smith E. A. and Aswani S. (eds) 2010. *Environmental Social Sciences: Methods and Research Design*. Cambridge, UK: Cambridge University Press.

Vasquez-Leon M. and Liverman D. 2004. The political ecology of land-use change: Affluent ranchers and destitute farmers in the Mexican Municipio of Alamos. *Human Organization* 63(1): 21–33.

Vayda A. P. 1983. Progressive contextualization: Methods for research in human ecology. *Human Ecology* 11(3): 265–281.

Vayda A. P. and Rappaport R. 1968. Ecology, cultural and noncultural. In J. A. Clifton (ed.) *Introduction to Cultural Anthropology: Essays in the Scope and Methods of the Science of Man*. Boston, MA: Houghton Mifflin, pp. 476–498.

Vayda A. P. and Walters B. 1999. Against political ecology. *Human Ecology* 27(1): 167–180.

Viazzo P. P. 1989. *Upland Communities: Environment, Population, and Social Structure in the Alps since the Sixteenth Century*. Cambridge, UK and New York: Cambridge University Press.

Viladrich A. 2006. Botánicas in America's backyard: Uncovering the world of Latino healers' herbal healing practices in New York City. *Human Organization* 65(4): 407–419.

Wallerstein I. M. 1974. *The Modern World-System*. New York: Academic Press.

Walsh A. 2005. The obvious aspects of ecological underprivilege in Ankarana, Northern Madagascar. *American Anthropologist* 107(4): 654–665.

West P., Igoe J. and Brockington D. 2006. Parks and peoples: The social impact of protected areas. *Annual Review of Anthropology* 25: 251–277.

White L. 1943. Energy and the evolution of culture. *American Anthropologist* 45: 335–356.

White L. 1949. *The Science of Culture*. New York: Free Books.

Wilk R. 1991. *Household Ecology: Economic Change and Domestic Life Among the Kekchi Maya in Belize*. Tucson: University of Arizona Press.

Winterhalder B. 1994. Concepts in historical ecology. In C. L. Crumley (ed.) *Historical Ecology: Cultural Knowledge and Changing Landscapes*. Santa Fe, NM and Seattle, WA: School of American Research Press, pp. 17–41.

Wolf E. R. 1966. *Peasants*. Englewood Cliffs, NJ: Prentice-Hall.

Wolf E. R. 1972. Ownership and political ecology. *Anthropological Quarterly* 45(3): 201–205.

Wolf E. R. 1982. *Europe and the People without History*. Berkeley: University of California Press.

Wolf E. R. 1999. *Envisioning Power: Ideologies of Dominance and Crisis*. Berkeley: University of California Press.

Zarger R. K. and Stepp J. R. 2004. Persistence of botanical knowledge among Tzeltal Maya children. *Current Anthropology* 45(3): 413–418.

3

ETHNOBIOLOGY AND THE NEW ENVIRONMENTAL ANTHROPOLOGY

E. N. Anderson

Introduction

Ethnobiology has moved through several stages: descriptive, cognitive-analytic, ecological, widely inclusive, and multidisciplinary. The field has rapidly evolved from one concerned with the ancient traditions of small-scale societies to one concerned with all aspects of environmental knowledge and wisdom. It has thus expanded to investigate cosmology, worldview, and ontology, and has tended to merge with or blend into political ecology, environmental science, natural history, and psychology.

Eugene Hunn (2007) has divided the history of ethnobiology into four stages. First came a long period of recording names and uses. A second phase began with the application of cognitive, linguistic, and cultural theories to plant and animal knowledge, in the "ethnoscience" movement of the 1950s (see e.g. Conklin 1957; Sturtevant 1964). A third period came with the expansion of ethnoscience to include ethnoecology, and the subsequent fusion of ethnoscientific and ecological anthropology; a pioneer in this effort was Victor Toledo (1992). A fourth period emerged from all the above, in which Indigenous peoples are writing their own ethnobiological texts (Bernard and Salinas Pedraza 1989; Saem Majnep 2007; Saem Majnep and Bulmer 1977) or cooperating with academics in coauthored works (Anderson and Medina Tzuc 2005; Hunn and Selam 1990; Turner *et al.* 1990 and other works).

None of the later stages replaced earlier ones. They simply added new tasks and inquiries. The vast majority of ethnobiological accounts today remain documentations of names and uses. However, much of the interest in the field has shifted to the later concerns. The present chapter is structured according to Hunn's useful divisions.

Collecting knowledge

Ethnobiology began with the first detailed recordings of biological knowledge. Early scholars had to draw heavily on folk wisdom for their material. Marja Eloheimo (2013) refers to this as a stage of a specificity paradigm, and of "appropriation," because it was largely a matter of learning useful knowledge from other cultures. In the colonial period, this became exploitative in more than a few cases. Useful plants were adopted without compensation or permission.

Even in the earliest recorded history of ethnobotany, the Indigenous voice has never been totally absent. Theophrastus' ancient Greek botany (Theophrastus 1916, originally written c. 300 BC) was already using and citing local knowledge systems, including such matters as the different values of trees for firewood and timber. Pedanius Dioscorides, composing his herbal in the second century, drew on his enormous and detailed knowledge gathered from local communities around the Mediterranean (Riddle 1985); this herbal was to become the most influential medical botany of all time, inspiring two millennia of studies that steadily increased the number of herbs and the details recorded about their medical uses (Collins 2000).

The early Chinese were less candid about their sources, but it seems clear that such works as the *Shen Nong Herbal* (Yang 1998), China's equivalent of Dioscorides, drew heavily on folk knowledge. This herbal was named after the ox-headed god of agriculture, Shen Nong ("Divine Farmer"), who supposedly lived in the twenty-eighth century BC. The herbal was actually written around 100 AD, then edited and updated by the great Chinese polymath Tao Hongjing in the sixth century.

Later Greek, Arab, Chinese, and Indian science drew heavily on folk knowledge, sometimes acknowledged. A vast literature pursuant to Theophrastus and Dioscorides grew up in the Near East and later in Europe. In China, a similarly huge literature followed the early *bencao* ("basic herbal") works. An early ethnobotany is the *Nanfang Caomu Zhuang*, a description of useful and valuable Southeast Asian plants written in 304 AD (though updated subsequently; Li 1979).

An encyclopedia of Near Eastern medicine, the *Huihui Yaofang,* was compiled for the Chinese under the Mongol Empire. The greatest herbal in Chinese imperial times, the *Bencao Gangmu* of Li Shizhen, appeared in 1593, and remains standard to this day in Chinese medicine (Li 2003).

At the same time that the Mongols were bringing Near Eastern medicine to China, European scholars were bringing it to Europe, translating the great medical texts. More significant in terms of actual ethnobiological exploration was the Spanish effort in Mexico, which involved working with Native American consultants, artists, and writers. Hernández (1959 [1577]) and Sahagún (1956, 1950–1969) drew heavily on Native advisors. Ruiz de Alarcón (1982, original c. 1600) transcribed Indigenous texts that include valuable ethnobiological material. One Indigenous Mexican, the Nahua writer Martin de la Cruz, produced a great ethnobotany (1964, from a sixteenth-century manuscript). In Peru, Garcilaso de la Vega (1987, original c. 1600) and other writers of Inca descent produced works with considerable ethnobiological content.

Toward the end of the nineteenth century, scholars discovered traditional small-scale cultures. John Harshberger coined the term "ethnobotany" in 1895 (Ford 2011). The other "ethno-" terms were coined later, following Harshberger's usage. Both ethnographers and archeologists recorded data (Ford 2011; Pearsall 2001), with rapidly growing research on ancient Egypt (see e.g. Manniche 1989), Mesopotamia, China, Greece, and other ancient civilizations. Nor have alcoholic drinks been neglected (McGovern 2009). .

In the "Golden Age" of ethnography, the early twentieth century, vast compilations of local lore included varying, but usually considerable, amounts of material on ethnobiology. Bronislaw Malinowski included much data in his general works, and wrote an entire, thorough, excellent work on gardening and related activities in the Trobriand Islands (Malinowski 1935).

Many colonial and settler voices reduced Indigenous people to the category of "survivals" of "the primitive." However, even at the dawn of modern anthropology, this was not a universal approach. As early as the 1870s, Frank Cushing contrasted his attempts to capture Indigenous systems of knowledge in their entirety with the sort of ethnobotany that consisted solely of recording names and uses without indigenous systems and cosmologies (see Cushing 1920). Several Native American ethnographers worked during this period; notable for ethnobiological recording was Francis La Flesche, an Omaha anthropologist (Fletcher and La Flesche 1906; La Flesche 1921–1930).

Franz Boas recorded thousands of pages of texts and encouraged Native American consultants to record thousands more (e.g. Boas and Hunt 1902–1905, 1906). The most industrious of his students was Edward Sapir, who died rather young, leaving much material. His most forthcoming Indigenous consultant and coauthor, Tom Sayach'apis of the Nuu-chah-nulth, now has a great-granddaughter, Charlotte Coté, teaching Native American Studies at the University of Washington (see Coté 2010; Sapir 1922). Not only Boas, but also J. Wesley Powell, head of the Bureau of American Ethnology, trained Native American ethnobiologists, and the great Greenlander ethnographer and ethnobiologist Knud Rasmussen was trained by the Danish anthropologist Kai Birket-Smith (Rasmussen 1931, 1932, 1999 [1927]). This turned out to be basic to the rising discipline, since it thoroughly introduced the next generation to truly Indigenous worldviews. It was left to Marjorie Halpin (1978) to rescue from the shadows the Tsimshian chief William Beynon, who now emerges as a monumental ethnographer and ethnobiologist (e.g. Barbeau and Beynon 1987).

Ethnoscience

Ethnoscience crystallized after World War II. The first work was actually on the navigation systems of the Micronesians (Gladwin 1995; Goodenough 1953). These were followed by studies of botany, zoology, and other matters, including path-breaking studies by Harold Conklin (1957, 2007) and Charles Frake (1980). The group coined the term "ethnoscience" for the subject of their work. Eloheimo (2013) sees this as a phase of studying classification, with a systemic paradigm informing it. The systemic paradigm dominated ecology during this period also, with enormous attention devoted to defining and modeling ecosystems—a new concept at the time. Eloheimo defines a structural paradigm, more related to ethnoecology in her thinking, but applicable here as well, since the early ethnoscientists were highly informed by structural linguistics, cognitive psychology (which emphasized structures of thought at the time), and structural anthropology (see Lévi-Strauss 1962, 1963 [1958]).

Much of the interest at this time was in finding "native categories": the full meanings, or at least the full denotational meanings, of terms in local languages and their classification systems. At the time, cognitive psychology was developing, and influencing linguistics. The "cognitive revolution" (Gardner 1985) was taking place at this point, with enormous paradigm-shifting impacts on psychology, information science, and anthropology. Ethnoscientists felt they were getting at structures of thought, or at least of language.

Claude Lévi-Strauss's related structuralist program reduced thought to the rational oppositions and orderings which Immanuel Kant (1978 [1798]) identified when he invented anthropology as a field. Critics, however, showed that human thought structures can be more or less transient results of an often chaotic process of change, interaction, negotiation, and ambiguity (Bourdieu 1977, 1990). Historical and linguistic research by Cecil Brown (1986), Hunn (1982), and other scholars proved that folk classification systems do emerge from negotiation and debate, but they can be stable for long periods of time.

Ethnoscience was criticized at the time for attention to arcane matters, especially by Marvin Harris (1968). Harris cited the study by Duane Metzger and G. Williams (1966) of

Tzeltal Maya firewood knowledge. Harris was apparently unaware that firewood gathering occupied hours per week, and sometimes hours per day, of Maya time. On a worldwide scale, firewood, then as now, was the leading use of wood—well ahead of papermaking or construction. A more humorous example of classification that made a difference occurred in a trial in New York in 1818 (Burnett 2007). The trial concerned whether a whale was a fish or a mammal. Whale oil was a major commodity at the time, and fish oil was taxed in New York, while mammal fat was not. It will surprise no one to learn that, in spite of the best zoological testimony, the state held and the court ruled that whales were fish.

One problem with ethnoscience, as with most anthropology at that time, was its tendency to treat local societies as if they were isolated, self-contained units, slow to change, living in functionalist harmony. We now see human ecology and ethnobiology as fields for conflict, power, and debate (Anderson 1972). Because of such realizations, the field of political ecology appeared at this time, invented by Eric Wolf in 1972.

The importance of biology to ethnoscience reached a whole new level with the work of Richard Evans Schultes at Harvard in the 1950s to 1980s. Schultes had worked in the Amazon, and become interested in medical and psychotropic plants. He trained a whole generation of ethnobotanists who are now leaders in the field, including Michael Balick, Robert Bye, Paul Cox, Wade Davis, and Mark Plotkin, to say nothing of alternative medicine advocate Andrew Weil. The book by Schultes and Von Reis Altschul, *Ethnobotany: Evolution of a Discipline* (1995) gives a fascinating and idiosyncratic view of this era. Balick and Cox (1996) provide an excellent introduction to ethnobotany from this tradition. (See also Amadeo Rea [1983, 1997, 1998, 2007], for a different biological tradition). The journal *Economic Botany*, formerly a practical journal of agriculural and horticultural exploration and experimentation, has become an ethnobotany journal. A peak in the search for medicinal plants (bioprospecting) followed, with high hopes of major medical breakthroughs (see e.g. Plotkin 1993, 2000).

The major legacy of the ethnoscience phase or period in ethnobiological research lies in methodology. All respectable studies of traditional environmental knowledge now make serious attempts to use the methodology developed by the ethnoscience pioneers: get the meanings of the words right, using frame elicitation and similar methodology. The technique of using repeated field walks over designated routes is now also standard practice. Most studies go on to develop some idea of local classification systems, cosmological systems, and knowledge systems in general. These are added to more traditional social-science methods such as focus groups, field checking, and traditional participant observation; and to essential biological methods, notably collection of voucher specimens (for plants and insects) or photographs, or comparable field data (for larger animals).

More formal studies add techniques like pile sorts and Likert scales; more humanistic ones add textual and discourse analysis, depth interviewing, and interpretation in the tradition of Geertz, Ingold (2011), and other phenomenological anthropologists (Anderson *et al.* 2011; Bernard 2006; Frake 1980).

Ethnoecology

Ethnoecology grew naturally from ethnobiology, adding ecology to the list of things studied. Ethnobiologists now look at how people classify environmental features: soil types, weather and climate, and other ecological subjects (Johnson and Davidson 2011; Johnson and Hunn 2010). Ethnoecology merged with a wider concern with places and landscapes, which stems from Carl Sauer's brilliant work in the early twentieth century (Sauer 1963;

Tuan 1969). Landscapes are taken to be human-influenced environments, in which the cultural and social production of space (and sometimes time) is a critically important question to study. How people see the landscape is determined by both social and ecological factors. Management becomes a very complicated matter of integrating perception, cognition, and action.

Earthquakes happen whether one believes they are due to continental drift, to the earth expanding or shrinking (as many geologists used to believe), or to a giant underground animal moving about (as many traditional cultures teach). The assumed cause may not matter. On the other hand, it does matter if one believes that trees have powerful good spirits within them, rather than seeing them as mere timber or mere clutter on the landscape. The former idea was instrumental in keeping Southeast Asia 90 percent forested until the late twentieth century; the latter led to the eastern United States being 90 percent deforested by European settlers by 1920. (The population densities were similar; wealth differences were not overwhelming.)

An issue of interest has been the striking difference in the ways that traditional people perceive the land as opposed to the ways that new settlers or visitors from outside perceive it. This literature usually contrasts Indigenous and settler societies, as in Veronica Strang's classic *Uncommon Ground* (1997) and Paul Nadasdy's *Hunters and Bureaucrats* (2004), but rural and urban white Americans can be almost as distant and uncomprehending of each other (Breslow 2011; Brugger 2009). Landscape research has led to major regional syntheses of traditional or pre-modern resource management (e.g. M. K. Anderson 2005; and the three-volume series Denevan 2001, Doolittle 2000, Whitmore and Turner 2001). Interesting and important findings include the extreme complexity of mental maps that local people can have for their environment (Istomin and Dwyer 2009).

Many studies highlight the non-meeting of minds between urban biologists and local people. Typically, these contrast the biologists' book-learning (without field experience) with the local people's field experience (without book-learning). As one would, sadly, expect, Indigenous knowledge is most often devalued and even held in contempt (e.g. Nadasdy 2004, 2007). However, Indigenous people are not alone. It turns out that even educated white males often have their field knowledge subjected to disrespect and disapproval by urban biologists. Several excellent recent studies report this (Argandoña 2012 and unpublished research; Breslow 2011; Hedrick 2007). It appears that being a member of a privileged class is little help when a newly-minted MA in environmental studies is dismissing several generations of "mere" field experience because it wasn't in the textbook.

The views of "savages" as wasteful wreckers, or as "ecologically noble" and "in harmony with nature," are equally wrong. Some groups are model conservers (Pinkaew 2001; Wang 2013), some are totally indifferent to conservation (Alvard 1995; Alvard *et al.* 1997; Kay and Simmons 2002), and most are somewhere in between (Anderson 2014; Beckerman *et al.* 2002). Pioneer settlers in particular are destructive, not knowing the local system and not having an obvious need to save it; this is true from ancient Polynesia to nineteenth-century America and twenty-first-century Amazonia (Anderson 2014).

Another concern involves environmental justice (Anderson 2010). Conservationists have often displaced local communities (Brockington *et al.* 2008; West *et al.* 2006). Usually, these are Indigenous or impoverished groups that can ill afford the loss of their lands. However, well-to-do whites are far from safe. They too may be summarily displaced for bureaucratic reasons (Brugger 2009). In Australia, white settlers first stopped the Aboriginal people from burning the environment, then they found that healthy plant growth depended on fire, and healthy animal populations depended on the plant growth (see e.g. Bliege Bird and Bird 2008; Bliege Bird *et al.* 2012). Aboriginal burning has been restored in some areas

(Anderson 2014). The same basic facts about fire prevention hold for California (M. K. Anderson 2005; Minnich 2008), but controlled burns remain rare.

In East Africa, displacing the Maasai led to deterioration of the lands they had kept open, causing loss of African hunting dogs and other wildlife (Brockington *et al.* 2008; Igoe, ongoing research). The Maasai do not hunt except to kill predators that take their stock; and Maasai burning and grazing open the fields for the vast herbivore herds so familiar to tourists. Without such activity, the savannahs grow up to brush and the herbivores decline. Just as we are now aware of "nature's services" (Daily 1997), we need to be aware of "culture's services."

Indigenous involvement

Today ethnobiologists regularly coauthor books with field consultants. There are also countless Indigenous people from all parts of the world who are full-fledged PhDs—often without losing their traditional culture or their role in it. Examples range from the Akha minority anthropologist Jianhua Wang in China (Wang 2013) to the Tsimshian environmental social scientist Charles Menzies in British Columbia (Menzies 2006). Nancy Turner of the University of Victoria in British Columbia has produced a literal 5-foot shelf of ethnobotanies, all done with acknowledgement and most done with actual coauthorship of Indigenous experts (e.g. Turner *et al.* 1990). Eugene Hunn and Yakama Nation leader James Selam published a detailed study of Yakama ethnoscience (Hunn and Selam 1990).

Ethnobiologists also work with Indigenous individuals to publish their own academic books. Russell Bernard's Mezquital Valley consultant Jesús Salinas Pedraza (Bernard and Salinas Pedraza 1989) produced a superb ethnography, and Bulmer's friend and field collaborator Saem Majnep, of highland Papua New Guinea, produced books on mammal and bird knowledge (Saem Majnep 2007; Saem Majnep and Bulmer 1977).

All this exemplifies a developing paradigm that Eloheimo (2013) calls "relational"; it involves real relationships between people working across cultures and across social and linguistic lines, taking account of Indigenous paradigms and scientific theories. Native American zoologist Ray Pierotti not only brings Native American knowledge into the mainstream; he uses it to inform biological science (e.g. Pierotti 2011). The Nuu-chah-nulth anthropologists Richard Atleo (2004, 2011), Earl Maquinna George (2003), and Ki-Ke-In provide detailed accounts of the Nuu-chah-nulth worldview, which is heavily involved with the animal world.

Many "outsider" writers on local knowledge draw on Indigenous accounts. Paige West (2006, 2012) has produced excellent, trenchant studies of local ecological knowledge and practice. West says:

> My worry is that environmental anthropology in the guise of political ecology—in its rush to show how external structures affect local socioecological lives—has begun to translate local environmental understandings and actions in ways that generify them and that fail to show them to be aesthetic, poetic, and deeply social.
>
> *(West 2005: 639)*

Many Western scholars have turned to their own roots in rural American, British, European or other societies. For instance, Joshua Lockyer and James Veteto have studied Appalachian America and modern ecological action there (Lockyer and Veteto 2013).

Many now go far beyond plant name lists and into Indigenous ontology, epistemology, and metaphysics. Most early anthropologists would have dismissed the thought that non-Western small-scale societies could have such abstract philosophy, though early scholars such as Paul Radin (1916, 1927, 1957) realized it. *Worldview* normally suggests a general, rather informal, set of everyday perceptions, beliefs, and understandings of the world (Kearney 1984). *Cosmology* refers to beliefs about the wider environment—heavens and earth, origins and fates thereof, and basic principles behind all.

Recently, much attention has been given to *ontology*: the study of what is, what is not, and what might be. Western scientific ontology holds that real things are made up of quarks, electrons, photons, and other "particles," the quarks being bound up into baryons. The Shuar ontology recorded by Kohn (2013) includes jaguar spirits, dog dreams that foretell the future, and visionary snakes. Neither are close to the hard-headed ontology of Aristotle, with its small nearby stars, solid rocks, and Prime Mover. The research of the Colombian anthropologist Gerardo Reichel-Dolmatoff (1971, 1976, 1996) was path-breaking. Far more radical is the work on Indigenous ontologies by recent writers such as Eduardo Viveiros de Castro (2015), Mario Blaser (2009, 2010), and Eduardo Kohn (2013). Other noteworthy work includes that of Deborah Rose in Australia (2000, 2005) and Rane Willerslev in Siberia (2007). Arturo Escobar (2008) has synthesized many approaches in masterful work on local agency, power disparities, and on-the-ground wisdom and difference in Colombia. Like West, he stresses the agency and adaptability of local cultures, and decries the common reduction to "mere victims" in literature on international aid, development, and politics.

Many societies use words broadly translated as "respect" to construct their moral relation-ship with non-human realms. Atleo (2004) discusses the Nuu-chah-nulth word *isaak* in this regard: basically it means "respect." The Mongol *shuteekh* and *khundlekh* are similar in force and usage (personal research in Mongolia; email from Marissa Smith, 8 July 2013; Kenin-Lopsan 1997; Metzo 2005). The Akha of Southeast Asia use the word *taqheeq-e,* also meaning "respect," for this purpose (Wang 2013 and personal communication). The focal meaning of all these words is respect for one's elders and for one's social world; it is extended to the non-human world because the latter is considered to be part of society. Mongol *shuteekh* even extends to rocks; a young Mongolian friend of mine felt guilty about collecting pretty rocks because moving rocks for no good reason is disrespectful.

Among the deepest lessons from traditional society are those that teach us how to look at the natural world. Indigenous writers clearly have the advantage: they know and under-stand these deep lessons, from their early experience. Indigenous ontology is often religion, in the Durkheimian sense of community cooperation growing into cultural knowledge and from that into ethical behavior (Durkheim 1995 [1912]). This realization has led many to study religion and its role in constructing and managing the non-human realms. From political ecology, Fikret Berkes has constructed *Sacred Ecology* (2008) and Leslie Sponsel *Spiritual Ecology* (2012; see also Anderson 2010; West 2012).

This reinforces the need for a united *biocultural* field: cultural documentation and inter-pretation, with biological grounding. This type of fusion has been done since the field began, and is now exemplified by such scholars as Nancy Turner, Gary Nabhan (e.g. 1985), and many others, in model studies. Collaboration of biologists, anthropologists, and Indigenous people (who are often biologists or anthropologists themselves) is routine. The opposition of "humanistic" and "scientistic" anthropology is fatal to such understanding. One can easily imagine the benefit accruing as scholars interface studies such as Beckerman and Lizarralde's relatively biology-oriented study of the Barí of Colombia (2013) with Kohn's more human-istic study of the ecologically similar Shuar of Peru (2013).

A challenge

One challenge to ethnobiological research is the problem of intellectual property rights. In a world of patenting and corporate control of patents, any Indigenous and local knowledge is subject to predatory appropriation (Brown 1998, 2003; Shiva 1997). This "biopiracy" has been blocked by desperate and expensive action of the Indian Government in at least two cases: attempts to patent neem oil (used universally for thousands of years in India) and to patent the name "basmati" for a rice that was not even a real basmati (Aoki 2008; Muchit and Thompson 2007; Shiva 1997).

In an earlier case, Mexico lost the income from the birth control pill, developed from a Mexican yam and now possibly the most profitable drug in the world; this was not outright biopiracy, since Mexico had essentially signed off, through a series of ill-considered agreements (Soto Laveaga 2009). In consequence of that and other cases, Mexico has shut down bioprospecting entirely (Hayden 2003).

Problems of biopiracy are compounded by the lack of licensing within anthropology, such that anyone can call him- or herself an "anthropologist." Many self-appointed or untrained anthropologists inflict annoyance, tactless behavior, and even biopiracy on a community. And legitimate scholars often fail to publish their results. Now that the vast majority of people worldwide are literate, and most have some access to the Internet, there is no excuse for not making data available. Many traditional societies have their own rules for use and sharing of knowledge. Pacific Northwest Coast societies in Canada and the United States have elaborate ownership systems for songs, dances, ceremonies, designs, and displays. These are structured along kinship lines. The Yucatec Maya have varying degrees of protected knowledge, taught only to apprentices. Highly structured systems like these can provide sources for improvements to modern patent laws.

In many areas, individuals and institutions, including the Missouri Botanical Garden and the University of Hawaii, have worked out accommodations with local people. However, these agreements may not always be legally enforceable, in the corrupt and cut-throat worlds of international patent law and drug development.

What next?

Anthropology was launched by Immanuel Kant, whose *Anthropology from a Pragmatic Point of View* (1978 [1798]) basically invented the field. The vision that has truly made anthropology came from another Enlightenment German: Johann Gottfried Herder (Herder 2002). He was the first person to maintain, unflinchingly and without qualifications, that all cultures and folk traditions are achievements of the human spirit, and deserve respect, recognition, and admiration because of that. To my knowledge, all statements to that effect—not only cultural relativity (Brown 2008), but modern multiculturalism and celebration of diversity—go directly back to Herder.

Anthropology has today become so concerned with power and politics that it has often fallen into the trap of turning its subjects into mere victims. We often find ourselves dealing with modern horrors that are far from the admirable small traditions that Herder valorized. There is nothing worthy, nothing of the Herderian human spirit, about genocide, or denying medical care, or starving people to death as a point of policy (Sen 1982, 1992). Yet people remain truly creative. The complex, intricate, perfectly tuned landscape management systems of the Yucatec Maya (E. N. Anderson 2005), the Akha (Wang 2013), and the California Indians (M. K. Anderson 2005) are as amazing and, in their way, as beautiful as Chartres

Cathedral or the Vatican. This is not mere imposed romanticism. The people that create them are sensitive to the beauty of their well-managed landscapes. In the words of an old African-American spiritual, their legacy "outshines the sun."

Acknowledgements

Thanks to Helen Kopnina and Eleanor (Elle) Shoreman-Ouimet for excellent editing.

References

Alvard, Michael. 1995. "Interspecific Prey Choice by Amazonian Hunters." *Current Anthropology* 36(5): 789–818.

Alvard, Michael, John G. Robinson, Kent H. Redford and Hillard Kaplan. 1997. "The Sustainability of Subsistence Hunting in the Neotropics." *Conservation Biology* 11(4): 977–982.

Anderson, E. N. 1972. "The Life and Culture of Ecotopia." In Dell Hymes (ed.) *Reinventing Anthropology*. New York: Pantheon Press, pp. 264–283.

—— 2005. *Political Ecology of a Yucatec Maya Community*. Tucson: University of Arizona Press.

—— 2010. *The Pursuit of Utopia*. Santa Barbara, CA: AltaMira Press.

—— 2014. *Caring for Place*. Walnut Creek, CA: Left Coast Press.

Anderson, E. N. and Felix Medina Tzuc. 2005. *Animals and the Maya in Southeast Mexico*. Tucson: University of Arizona Press.

Anderson, E. N., Deborah M. Pearsall, Eugene S. Hunn and Nancy J. Turner (eds) 2011. *Ethnobiology*. Hoboken, NJ: Wiley–Blackwell.

Anderson, M. Kat. 2005. *Tending the Wild: Native American Knowledge and the Management of California's Natural Resources*. Berkeley: University of California Press.

Aoki, Keith. 2008. *Seed Wars: Controversies and Cases on Plant Genetic Resources and Intellectual Property*. Durham, NC: Carolina Academic Press.

Argandoña, Monica. 2012. Every Square Inch: The Fight for the California Desert. PhD thesis, Department of Anthropology, University of California, Riverside [publicly available via University Microfilms].

Atleo, E. Richard. 2004. *Tsawalk: A Nuu-Chah-Nulth Worldview*. Vancouver: University of British Columbia Press.

—— 2011. *Principles of Tsawalk: An Indigenous Approach to Global Crisis*. Vancouver: University of British Columbia Press.

Balick, Michael J. and Paul A. Cox. 1996. *Plants, People, and Culture: The Science of Ethnobotany*. New York: Scientific American Library.

Barbeau, Marius and William Beynon. 1987. *Tsimshian Narratives* (edited by John Cove and George MacDonald). 2 volumes. Ottawa, ON: Canadian Museum of Civilisation.

Beckerman, Stephen and Roberto Lizarralde. 2013. *The Ecology of the Barí: Rainforest Horticulturalists of South America*. Austin: University of Texas Press.

Beckerman, Stephen, Paul Valentine and Elise Eller. 2002. "Conservation and Native Amazonians: Why Some Do and Some Don't." *Antropologica* 96: 31–51.

Berkes, Fikret. 2008. *Sacred Ecology*. 2nd edn. New York: Routledge.

Bernard, H. Russell. 2006. *Research Methods in Anthropology*. Lanham, MD: AltaMira (Rowman & Littlefield).

Bernard, H. Russell and Jesús Salinas Pedraza. 1989. *Native Ethnography: A Mexican Indian Describes his Culture*. Newbury Park, CA: Sage.

Blaser, Mario. 2009. "The Threat of the Yrmo: The Political Ontology of a Sustainable Hunting Program." *American Anthropologist* 111(1): 10–20.

—— 2010. *Storytelling Globalization from the Chaco and Beyond*. Durham, NC: Duke University Press.

Bliege Bird, Rebecca and Douglas W. Bird. 2008. "Why Women Hunt: Risk and Contemporary Foraging in a Western Desert Aboriginal Community." *Current Anthropology* 49(4): 655–694.

Bliege Bird, Rebecca, Brian Codding, Peter Kauhanen and Douglas W. Bird. 2012. "Aboriginal Hunting Buffers Climate-Driven Fire-Size Variability in Australia's Spinifex Grasslands." *Proceedings of the American Academy of Sciences* 109(26): 10287–10292. doi 10.1073/pnas.1204585109

Boas, Franz and George Hunt. 1902–1905. *Kwakiutl Texts*. Memoir V, American Museum of Natural History. New York: American Museum of Natural History.

—— 1906. *Kwakiutl Texts, Second Series*. Memoir XIV, American Museum of Natural History. New York: American Museum of Natural History.

Bourdieu, Pierre. 1977. *Outline of a Theory of Practice* (transl. by Richard Nice). New York: Cambridge University Press.

——1990. *The Logic of Practice* (transl. by Richard Nice). Stanford, CA: Stanford University Press.

Breslow, Sara Jo. 2011. Salmon Habitat Restoration, Farmland Preservation, and Environmental Drama in the Skagit River Valley. PhD dissertation, Department of Anthropology, University of Washington, Seattle [publicly available via University Microfilms].

Brockington, Dan, Rosaleen Duff and Jim Igoe. 2008. *Nature Unbound: Conservation, Capitalism and the Future of Protected Areas*. London: Earthscan.

Brown, Cecil. 1986. "The Growth of Ethnobiological Nomenclature." *Current Anthropology* 27(1): 1–18.

Brown, Michael. 1998. "Can Culture Be Copyrighted?" *Current Anthropology* 39(2): 193–222.

——2003. *Who Owns Native Culture?* Cambridge, MA: Harvard University Press.

——2008. *"Cultural Relativism 2.0."* *Current Anthropology* 49(3): 363–383.

Brugger, Julie. 2009. Public Land and American Democratic Imaginaries: A Case Study of Conflict over the Management of Grand Staircase-Escalante National Monument. PhD dissertation, Department of Anthropology, University of Washington [publicly available via University Microfilms].

Burnett, D. Graham. 2007. *Trying Leviathan*. Princeton, NJ: Princeton University Press.

Collins, Minta. 2000. *Medieval Herbals: The Illustrative Tradition*. London: British Museum.

Conklin, Harold. 1957. *Hanunoo Agriculture*. Rome: FAO.

—— 2007. *Fine Description* (edited by Joel Kuipers and Ray McDermott). Monograph 56. New Haven, CT: Council on Yale Southeast Asia Studies.

Coté, Charlotte. 2010. *Spirits of our Whaling Ancestors: Revitalizing Makah and Nuu-chah-nulth Traditions*. Seattle: University of Washington Press.

Cushing, Frank. l920. *Zuni Breadstuffs*. Indian Notes and Monographs, VII. New York: Museum of the American Indian (Heye Foundation), pp. 7–642.

Daily, Gretchen (ed.). 1997. *Nature's Services: Societal Dependence on Natural Ecosystems*. Washington, DC: Island.

de la Cruz, M. 1964. *Libellus de Medicinalibus Indorum Herbis* (edited by E. C. del Pozo; original 1552). México: IMSS.

de la Vega, Garcilaso. 1987. *Royal Commentaries of the Incas and General History of Peru* (transl. by Harold Livermore; original seventeenth century). Austin: University of Texas Press.

Denevan, William M. 2001. *Cultivated Landscapes of Native Amazonia and the Andes*. New York: Oxford University Press.

Doolittle, William. 2000. *Cultivated Landscapes of Native North America*. New York: Oxford University Press.

Durkheim, Émile. 1995 [1912]. *The Elementary Forms of Religious Life* (transl. by Karen E. Fields). New York: Free Press.

Eloheimo, Marja. 2013. Fostering Sustainable Healthcare through Community-Based Herbalism. PhD thesis, Department of Anthropology, University of Washington, Seattle [publicly available via University Microfilms].

Escobar, Arturo. 2008. *Territories of Difference: Place, Movements, Life, Redes*. Durham, NC: Duke University Press.

Fletcher, Alice and Francis La Flesche. 1906. *The Omaha Tribe*. Annual Report XXVII. Washington, DC: Bureau of American Ethnology, pp. 17–654.

Ford, Richard. 2011. "History of Ethnobiology." In E. N. Anderson, Deborah Pearsall, Eugene S. Hunn and Nancy Turner (eds) *Ethnobiology*. Hoboken, NJ: Wiley–Blackwell, pp. 15–26.

Frake, Charles. 1980. *Language and Cultural Description* (edited by Anwar S. Dil). Stanford, CA: Stanford University Press.

Gardner, Howard. 1985. *The Mind's New Science: A History of the Cognitive Revolution*. New York: Basic Books.

George, Earl Maquinna. 2003. *Living on the Edge: Nuu-Chah-Nulth History from an Ahousaht Chief's Perspective*. Winlaw, BC: Sono Nis Press.

Gladwin, Thomas. 1995. *East is a Big Bird*. Cambridge, MA: Harvard University Press.

Goodenough, Ward. l953. *Native Astronomy in the Central Carolines*. Philadelphia: University Museum, University of Pennsylvania.

Halpin, Marjorie. 1978. "William Beynon, Ethnographer, Tsimshian, 1888–1958." In Margot Liberty (ed.) *American Indian Intellectuals*. St. Paul, MN: West Publishing Co. pp. 140–156.

Harris, Marvin. 1968. *The Rise of Anthropological Theory*. New York: Thomas Crowell.

Hayden, Cori. 2003. *When Nature Goes Public: The Making and Unmaking of Bioprospecting in Mexico*. Princeton, NJ: Princeton University Press.

Hedrick, Kimberly. 2007. Our Way of Life: Identity, Landscape, and Conflict. PhD thesis, Department of Anthropology, University of California, Riverside [publicly available via University Microfilms].

Herder, Johann Gottfried. 2002. *Philosophical Writings* (edited and transl. by Michael N. Forster). Cambridge, UK: Cambridge University Press.

Hernández, F. 1959 [1577]. *Historia natural de la Nueva España*. 2 volumes. México: Universidad Nacional Autónoma de México.

Hunn, Eugene. 1982. "The Utilitarian Factor in Folk Biological Classification." *American Anthropologist* 84(4): 830–847.

——2007. "Ethnobiology in Four Phases." *Journal of Ethnobiology* 27:1–10.

Hunn, Eugene with James Selam. 1990. *N'Chi-Wana, the Big River*. Seattle: University of Washington Press.

Ingold, Tim. 2011. *The Perception of the Environment: Essays in Livelihood, Dwelling and Skill*. 2nd edn. London: Routledge.

Istomin, Kirill V. and Mark J. Dwyer. 2009. "Finding the Way: A Critical Discussion of Anthropological Theories of Human Spatial Orientation with Reference to Reindeer Herders of Northeastern Europe and Western Siberia." *Current Anthropology* 50(1): 29–50.

Johnson, Leslie M. and Eugene S. Hunn (eds). 2010. *Landscape Ethnoecology: Concepts of Biotic and Physical Space*. New York: Berghahn Books.

Johnson, Leslie M. and Iain Davidson. 2011. "Ethnoecology and Landscapes." In E. N. Anderson, Deborah M. Pearsall, Eugene S. Hunn and Nancy J. Turner (eds) *Ethnobiology*. Hoboken, NJ: Wiley–Blackwell, pp. 267–284.

Kant, Immanuel. 1978 [1798]. *Anthropology from a Pragmatic Point of View* (transl. by Victor L. Dowdell). Carbondale: Southern Illinois University Press.

Kay, Charles E. and Randy T. Simmons (eds). 2002. *Wilderness and Political Ecology: Aboriginal Influences and the Original State of Nature*. Salt Lake City: University of Utah Press.

Kearney, Michael. 1984. *Worldview*. Novato, CA: Chandler and Sharp.

Kenin-Lopsan, Mongush B. 1997. *Shamanic Songs and Myths of Tuva* (edited by Mihaly Hoppal with Christiana Buckbee). Budapest: Akademiai Kiado.

Kohn, Eduardo. 2013. *How Forests Think: Toward an Anthropology beyond the Human*. Berkeley: University of California Press.

La Flesche, Francis. 1921–1930. *The Osage Tribe*. Annual Report XXXVI, pp. 35–604; XXXIX, pp. 31–630; XLIII, pp. 3–164: XLV, pp. 529–833. Washington, DC: Bureau of American Ethnology.

Lévi-Strauss, Claude. 1962. *La pensée sauvage*. Paris: Plon.

—— 1963 [1958]. *Structural Anthropology* (transl. by Claire Jacobson and Brooke Grundfest Schoepf). New York: Basic Books.

Li, Hui-lin. 1979. *Nan-fang Ts'ao-mu Chuang: A Fourth Century Flora of Southeast Asia*. Hong Kong: Chinese University of Hong Kong.

Li, Shizhen. 2003. *Compendium of Materia Medica (Bencao Gangmu)* (transl. by Xiao Xiaoming, Li Zhenguo and committee; Chinese original 1593). Beijing: Foreign Languages Press.

Lockyer, Joshua and James R. Veteto. 2013. *Environmental Anthropology Engaging Ecotopia: Bioregionalism, Permaculture, and Ecovillages*. New York: Berghahn Books.

McGovern, Patrick. 2009. *Uncorking the Past: The Quest for Wine, Beer, and Other Alcoholic Beverages*. Berkeley: University of California Press.

Malinowski, Bronislaw. 1935. *Coral Gardens and their Magic*. New York: American Book Company.

Manniche, Lise. 1989. *An Ancient Egyptian Herbal*. London: British Museum.

Menzies, Charles (ed.). 2006. *Traditional Ecological Knowledge and Natural Resource Management*. Lincoln: University of Nebraska Press.

Metzger, Duane and Gerald Williams. 1966. "Some Procedures and Results in the Study of Native Categories: Tzeltal 'Firewood'." *American Anthropologist* 68(2): 389–407.

Metzo, Katherine R. 2005. "Articulating a Baikal Environmental Ethic." *Anthropology and Humanism* 30(1): 39–54.

Minnich, Richard. 2008. *California's Fading Wildflowers: Lost Legacy and Biological Invasions*. Berkeley: University of California Press.

Muchit, Andrew and Carol Thompson. 2007. *Biopiracy of Biodiversity: Global Exchange as Enclosure*. Trenton, NJ and Asmara, Eritrea: Africa World Press.

Nabhan, Gary. 1985. *Gathering the Desert*. Tucson: University of Arizona Press.

Nadasdy, Paul. 2004. *Hunters and Bureaucrats: Power, Knowledge, and Aboriginal–State Relations in the Southwest Yukon*. Vancouver: University of British Columbia Press.

—— 2007. "The Gift of the Animals: The Ontology of Hunting and Human–Animal Sociality." *American Ethnologist* 34: 25–47.

Pearsall, D. 2001. *Paleoethnobotany*. 2nd edn. New York: Academic Press.

Pierotti, Raymond. 2011. *Indigenous Knowledge, Ecology, and Evolutionary Biology*. New York: Routledge.

Pinkaew, Laungaramsri. 2001. *Redefining Nature: Karen Ecological Knowledge and the Challenge to the Modern Conservation Paradigm*. Chennai, India: Earthworm Books.

Plotkin, Mark. 1993. *Tales of a Shaman's Apprentice*. New York: Viking Penguin.

—— 2000. *Medicine Quest: In Search of Nature's Healing Secrets*. New York: Viking.

Radin, Paul. 1916. *The Winnebago Tribe*. Annual Report XXXVII. Washington, DC: Bureau of American Ethnology, pp. 33–550.

—— 1927. *Primitive Man as Philosopher*. New York: Appleton.

—— 1957. *Primitive Religion* (originally published 1937; this has a new preface). New York: Dover.

Rasmussen, Knud. 1999 [1927]. *Across Arctic America: The Narrative of the Fifth Thule Expedition*. Fairbanks: University of Alaska Press.

—— 1931. *The Netsilik Eskimos*. Reports of the Fifth Thule Expedition, Vol. 8. Copenhagen: Gyldendal Boghandel, Nordisk Forlag.

—— 1932. *Intellectual Culture of the Copper Eskimos*. Reports of the Fifth Thule Expedition, Vol. 9. Copenhagen: Gyldendal Boghandel, Nordisk Forlag.

Rea, Amadeo. 1983. *Once a River: Bird Life and Habitat Changes on the Middle Gila*. Tucson: University of Arizona Press.

—— 1997. *At the Desert's Green Edge: An Ethnobotany of the Gila River Pima*. Tucson: University of Arizona Press.

—— 1998. *Folk Mammalogy of the Northern Pimans*. Tucson: University of Arizona Press.

—— 2007. *Wings in the Desert: A Folk Ornithology of the Northern Pimans*. Tucson: University of Arizona Press.

Reichel-Dolmatoff, G. 1971. *Amazonian Cosmos: The Sexual and Religious Symbolism of the Tukano Indians*. Chicago, IL: University of Chicago Press.

—— 1976. "Cosmology as Ecological Analysis: A View from the Rain Forest." *Man* 11(3): 307–316.

—— 1996. *The Forest Within: The World-View of the Tukano Amazonian Indians*. Dartington, UK: Themis, imprint of Green Books.

Riddle, John M. 1985. *Dioscorides on Pharmacy and Medicine*. Austin: University of Texas Press.

Rose, Deborah. 2000. *Dingo Makes us Human: Life and Land in an Australian Aboriginal Culture*. New York: Cambridge University Press.

—— 2005. "An Indigenous Philosophical Ecology." *Australian Journal of Anthropology* 16(3): 294–305.

Ruiz de Alarcón, Hernando. 1982. *Aztec Sorcerers in Seventeenth Century Mexico: The Treatise on Superstitions by Hernando Ruiz de Alarcón* (original c. 1600). Albany: Institute for Mesoamerican Studies, State University of New York at Albany.

Saem Majnep, Ian. 2007. *Animals the Ancestors Hunted*. Adelaide, South Australia: Crawford House.

Saem Majnep, I. and R. N. H. Bulmer. 1977. *Mn'mon Yad Kalam Yakt. Birds of my Kalam Country*. Auckland, New Zealand: Auckland University Press and Oxford University Press.

Sahagún, Berndardino de. 1956. *Historia general de las cosas de la Nueva España* (edited by A. M. Garibay; original 1793 from a manuscript c. 1577). México: Porrua.

—— 1950–1969. *Florentine Codex. General History of the Things of New Spain* (edited and transl. by C. E. Dibble and A. J. O. Anderson). 12 volumes. Salt Lake City: University of Utah Press.

Sapir, Edward. 1922. "Sayach'apis, a Nootka Trader." In Elsie Clews Parsons (ed.) *American Indian Life*. New York: B. W. Heubsch, pp. 297–323.

Sauer, Carl. 1963. *Land and Life, a Selection from the Writings of Carl Ortwin Sauer* (edited by John Leighly). Berkeley: University of California Press.

Schultes, Richard E. and Siri Von Reis Altschul (eds). 1995. *Ethnobotany: Evolution of a Discipline*. Portland, OR: Timber Press.

Sen, Amartya. 1982. *Poverty and Famines: An Essay on Entitlement and Deprivation*. Oxford: Oxford University Press.

—— 1992. *Inequality Reconsidered*. Cambridge, MA: Harvard University Press and Russell Sage Foundation.

Shiva, Vandana. 1997. *Biopiracy: The Plunder of Nature and Knowledge*. Boston, MA: South End Press.

Soto Laveaga, Gabriela. 2009. *Jungle Laboratories: Mexican Peasants, National Projects, and the Making of the Pill*. Durham, NC: Duke University Press.

Sponsel, Leslie E. 2012. *Spiritual Ecology: A Quiet Revolution*. Santa Barbara, CA: Praeger.

Strang, Veronica. 1997. *Uncommon Ground: Cultural Landscapes and Environmental Values*. Oxford: Berg.

Sturtevant, W. C. 1964. "Studies in Ethnoscience." *American Anthropologist* 66(3): 99–113.

Theophrastus. 1916. *Inquiry into Plants* (transl. by Arthur Hort; ancient Greek original c. 300 BC). 2 volumes. Cambridge, MA: Harvard University Press, Loeb Classical Library.

Toledo, V. M. 1992. "What Is Ethnoecology? Origins, Scope and Implications of a Rising Discipline." *Etnoecológica* 1: 5–21.

Tuan, Yi-Fu. 1969. *China*. Chicago, IL: Aldine Publishing Company.

Turner, Nancy, Laurence C. Thompson, M. Terry Thompson and Annie Z. York. 1990. *Thompson Ethnobotany: Knowledge and Usage of Plants by the Thompson Indians of British Columbia*. Memoir 3. Victoria: Royal British Columbia Museum. Viveiros de Castro, Eduardo. 2015. *The Relative Native: Essays on Indigenous Conceptual Worlds*. Chicago, IL: HAU Press.

Wang, Jianhua. 2013. Sacred and Contested Landscapes. PhD dissertation, Department of Anthropology, University of California, Riverside [publicly available via University Microfilms].

West, Paige. 2005. "Translation, Value, and Space: Theorizing an Ethnographic and Engaged Environmental Anthropology." *American Anthropologist* 107(4): 632–642.

—— 2006. *Conservation is our Government Now: The Politics of Ecology in Papua New Guinea*. Durham, NC: Duke University Press.

—— 2012. *From Modern Production to Imagined Primitive: The Social World of Coffee from Papua New Guinea*. Durham, NC: Duke University Press.

West, Paige, James Igoe and Dan Brockington. 2006. "Parks and Peoples: The Social Impact of Protected Areas." *Annual Review of Anthropology* 35(1): 251–277.

Whitmore, Thomas M. and B. L. Turner II. 2001. *Cultivated Landscapes of Middle America on the Eve of Conquest*. New York: Oxford University Press.

Willerslev, Rane. 2007. *Soul Hunters: Hunting, Animism and Personhood Among the Siberian Yukaghirs*. Berkeley: University of California Press.

Wolf, Eric. 1972. "Ownership and Political Ecology." *Anthropological Quarterly* 45(3): 201–205.

Yang, Shou-Zhong. 1998. *The Divine Farmer's Materia Medica: A Translation of the Shen Nong Ben Cao Jing*. Boulder, CO: Blue Poppy Press.

4

ANTHROPOLOGY AND THE ENVIRONMENT

Beginnings

Alan R. Beals

The knowledge of man's course of life, from the remote past to the present, will not only help us to forecast the future, but may guide us in our duty of leaving the world better than we found it.

(Tylor 1871: 439–440)

Introduction

Human beings and their activities have long been perceived as parts of complex interactive systems forming a cosmos, a single ecological whole. Father Sky and Mother Earth have dominated our thinking for millennia. This chapter traces ideas about environmental and cultural systems from the time of the European Enlightenment and the first calls for the scientific study of humankind to the end of the nineteenth century. If we think of anthropology as the study of human beings and their surroundings, anthropology is as old as humanity. In *Primitive Culture*, for example, Edward B. Tylor (1889: 4–5) justifies the scientific study of human behavior by arguing that every human being must examine his or her natural and social surroundings and reach conclusions about how to behave properly within them. The individual's study of his or her own culture and surroundings, his or her personal theory of culture and the nature of things, constitutes a primitive form of ethnography. It was only after the Enlightenment that anthropology began to emerge as a serious scientific discipline involving complex relationships between the environment and human beings.

Ethnology, the science of culture, involves the comparison of ethnographic accounts in order to reach understandings of the nature of culture. With the systematic collection of ethnographic data concerning the environment and the human beings in it, ethnology began its course of development during the nineteenth century. Individuals study and learn how to behave correctly within particular cultures, but most have no idea what culture is, thinking that their ways of behaving are simply the commands of the ancestors, the words of the deity, the product of some kind of genetic inheritance, or something that has always been. Throughout history some have recognized culture and even taken it upon themselves to revise and reform customary practices. As people learn particular ways of behaving or otherwise discover what to do when things happen, some realize that the games were designed by human beings and passed along from ancestor to descendant or from neighbor to neighbor without too much regard for supernatural protocol or geographical impact.

Again, a more general knowledge of the existence of culture as a human artifact began to develop during the eighteenth and nineteenth centuries. As they say in South India, "Our forefathers planted this banana tree, and we must all hang from it."

The eighteenth century

In the 1780s, Johann Gottfried Herder (1966 [1784]: v), following Kant's somewhat different vision, demanded creation of a formal field of scientific investigation to be called anthropology. Herder saw the importance of a science of man and bewailed the absence of the data required to construct such a science. Herder might well be considered the forefather of ecological anthropology because he seems to be the first relatively modern person to have actually grasped the interactive complexities of environments and ecosystems. Herder's interest in anthropological science stems almost certainly from his contacts with Georg Forster (1777). Forster's scientifically trained father took his teenage son with him when he sailed around the world with Captain Cook. The young Forster wrote an influential account of Cook's voyage. An ardent supporter of the French Revolution, he had contacts with both Herder and Alexander von Humboldt. Whereas Lewis Henry Morgan (1877) placed Tahitians at the lower levels of savagery, Forster believed that the Tahitian way of life was far superior to that of the British sailors on Cook's ship. This surely fed into Herder's view that other ways of life had desirable features that should be perpetuated.

Herder rejected the doctrine of the separate creation of human races then used as a justification for colonialism and slavery. He argued that geography and tradition, not biological race, accounted for the differences among the varieties of mankind. Sidestepping the issue of divine interference, Herder chose "Nature" as the force that causes groups of human beings to develop in particular ways with each tribe or nation striving for perfection within the limits set by the rivers and mountain ranges that defined their territory. Anticipating Darwin, he allowed for the possibility that one tribe or nation might push aside another in a kind of natural selection, but it was his strong feeling that each tribe and nation should be allowed to develop in its own way. He anticipated the "Prime Directive" (never interfere with other cultures) found in *Star Trek*, an American television series.

At the time Herder wrote, many Europeans would have agreed with Morgan's assertion (1877), nearly a hundred years later, that human development was the result of a unilinear evolution, that caused all peoples to develop from the state of savagery, to barbarism, and, finally, to civilization equal to that of the Europeans and Americans. Such a unilinear view of human evolutionary process, from hunter–gatherer to cosmopolitan civilization, fits with a unitary human history focused on similarities between peoples and a worldwide pattern of technological change. The theory doesn't work so well when it is applied to specific regions. Despite Morgan, it doesn't do well when applied to forms of social organization and worldview. Early on, William H. Dall (Dall and Gibbs 1877; Dall *et al.* 1898) was surprised to discover that the stages of evolution on the Aleutian Islands in Alaska were quite different from those proposed by Morgan. From an environmental standpoint, if progress consists of a simple set of stages, it follows that the role of environment in the development of culture is limited. The importance of anything to be learned from peoples considered savage (forest-dwelling) or barbarian (farmers and herders) was negligible since they were simply going through stages through which the "more advanced" peoples had already passed. A good story never dies, and many people still support the doctrines of unilinear evolution. In any event, ecological and anthropological considerations were not of much interest to European writers, representing a civilization that "had been there and done that."

In Herder's day, scholars who chose to write about the history of mankind would have had little access to truthful information about other peoples. They wrote their accounts, such as they were, from the parochial viewpoint of a Europe that had not begun to understand the variety of human cultures. Herder was exceptional in placing his "History of Man" in a future where concrete evidence was available (if not in the nineteenth century, at least by the millennium). In his critique of unilinear evolution, Herder concluded that Nature would not have an interest in creating large numbers of identical peoples passing through the same dreary evolutionary stages. The game was not to be better than everyone else, but to be the best you can be within the limits imposed by your own natural environment. With amazing discernment, he chooses California as an example of a place where the living is easy and little adaptation is required. Nature's plan was for each tribe and nation to achieve adaptation to a unique environment, not to become American, English, French, or German.

Herder and his contemporaries were born into a world in which a failure to acknowledge the works of God could result in severe and even deadly consequences. The founding myth of the scientific revolution was acceptance of a remote deity who sets the world in motion, but then leaves human beings to deal with it as they will. The natural science developing in the nineteenth century was designed to discover the intentions of God, Herder's "Nature", by reading the testament provided by the natural environment. To discover Natural law was to discover the intentions of the Prime Mover. "Natural law" assumes ecology since everything has to be well planned and well connected.

Herder's (1966 [1784]: 64) demand for the study of nature as a complex whole including mankind was attended to by a variety of travelers and naturalists in France, Germany, England, and the United States, many of them inspired by the stunning voyages of Captain Cook. As the nineteenth century unfolded, naturalists, missionaries, and other travelers would amass ever more detailed data concerning the peoples of the world. As Herder says in the preface to his *Outlines of a Philosophy of the History of Man* (1966 [1784]: vii): "All these questions must be investigated, they must be unraveled through the wild whirl of ages and governments, before a general result for mankind at large can be produced." Herder's desire that mankind be investigated by the methods of science required the amassing of vast amounts of data.

Humboldtian science: the nineteenth century

A few decades after Herder, Alexander von Humboldt, possibly working with his brother, Wilhelm, who was concerned with linguistics and the intellectual history of man, used his extensive travels, especially in Latin America, as a basis for the formation of an empirical science dedicated to the study of nature as a whole. Von Humboldt (Humboldt and Williams 1814) examined New World monuments and a few New World peoples as a first attempt to lay out the anthropological part of his new science. Unfortunately, von Humboldt's approach was marred by a failure to consider the actual behavior of the many people he befriended on his travels. Perhaps influenced by his brother, his concept of the intellectual history of humankind and of humans' place in nature consisted of detailed descriptions of monuments and art objects. His attempts at descriptions of actual people are superficial.

Through most of the nineteenth century, greater importance seems to have been given to human interpretations of the environment and to human use of the environment than to human interactions within it, a point of view that still persists. Perhaps it was thought that Nature's intentions would be revealed by the study of human worldviews. Several writers explicitly interpreted mythology as a variety of attempts to understand the cosmos. In *Cosmos*

(2010 [1845–1862]), von Humboldt actively seeks for a human connection to the complex ecology of nature, but his approach is through an analysis of art works, many depicting and glorifying nature. Such an analysis might be considered a good beginning, but it is hardly the be all and end all of attempts to include human beings within organic nature. The nineteenth century dealt with humanity and environment on a tribal and national scale, rather than at the level of group and community. Under the domination of theories of unilinear evolution, it was hard to come to grips with Robert H. Lowie's (1920: 427) "mottled diversity" of cultures and organizations, each having its own peculiar environmental adaptations.

Steeped in the primitive evolutionism of his times, von Humboldt still manages to downplay the differences between human races. On his travels he had noticed that the more "advanced" people were, the more they were racially mixed. This was certainly an unexpected finding considering the prevailing tendency to attribute the higher levels of civilization to particular races. His studies of arts and monuments in relation to nature are cross-cultural in intent, ranging across the globe. In collecting information, von Humboldt, along with Sir Joseph Banks, the sponsor of Cook's voyages, and many others, wove together a network of natural historians and scientists dedicated to the objective description of nature. Henry Sumner Maine (1861), lecturing in Calcutta, presented "Science" as a field in which all men were equal, regardless of race or country of origin. The followers of "Humboldtian Science" collected the detailed information upon which an anthropological science could be constructed. Von Humboldt played a key role in developing biological approaches to ecology, but he lacked the tools needed to create an ecological science—a science of the whole—that would include human beings and their cultures. We are still not quite there.

Classical scholars considered reality to be so complicated and confusing as to be useless as a source of information about the universe. Plato's ideal types were believed to undergo major distortions as they descended from the higher realm. Great truths were to be established by means of rational deduction from established principles. For example, planetary orbits could be considered circular since the circle was the perfect geometric form. No need for telescopes. Regrettably, social philosophers and some economists, apparently driven by divine inspiration, still manufacture the dogmas that currently rule the world. The founders of anthropology, Morgan, Tylor, von Humboldt, John Wesley Powell, and many others, though devotees of natural science, did not completely escape the heavy hand of traditional deductive approaches. Powell wanted to replace inductive and deductive approaches with "the method of multiple working hypotheses" as suggested by his colleague Chamberlain (Manning 1967: 91–92), but he did not apply the method successfully. Even with the most determined attachment to observed facts, it is difficult to demand in every case, as did Franz Boas (1940), that generalizations about humanity be supported by actual evidence: that done, there was still the problem of figuring out how to observe and organize things.

In the nineteenth century, statistics and genetics were in their early stages. Herder, von Humboldt and, later, Powell and Otis Tufton Mason grasped the concept of a holistic cosmos, but they had little idea of what the complex system they envisioned would actually be like. Morgan's "systems" (1870) involved a limited number of kinship terms, and Morgan mistakenly deduced that those systems of nomenclature reflected the actual practice of marriage and descent. Insofar as people thought of systems at all, they thought of cause-and-effect relationships in which the arrows all pointed one way from determinants to the things determined. The environment, considered god-given, had impacts upon human beings and human beings had impacts on it, but there was no concept of interaction. The environment was there to be ruled and pillaged along with the "subject" peoples who inhabited it.

The "Arts of Life" were simply ways in which human beings exploited an environment that had been put there for their use. Lewis and Clark, Henry Rowe Schoolcraft, von Humboldt, Forster, Powell, and the other scientific explorers were more concerned with ways of using the environment than with ways of protecting and conserving it. Before the beginning of the present era, Hindus, Buddhists, and Jains expressed deep concern about ethical relationships to the environment, but the scientific study of ethical relationships receives little notice before Edvard Westermarck (1911).

The systematic collection of detailed evidence, following Cook's voyage around the world, made the discoveries of Darwin and Tylor possible, even inevitable. Darwin's *On the Origin of Species* (1988 [1859]) uses the methods outlined by von Humboldt to develop ideas of natural selection put forward by Herder and Malthus, among others. Darwin's findings firmly place humanity within the natural order, and so create a position in the hierarchy of academic departments requiring the presence of Herder's anthropological science. Six years after Darwin, Tylor completed his own work of Humboldtian science, *Researches into the Early History of Mankind and the Development of Civilization* (1865). This is possibly the first anthropological research study that uses Humboldtian science to test a particular hypothesis. Morgan's *Systems of Consanguinity and Affinity of the Human Family,* another expression of Humboldtian science, would be published by Powell at the Smithsonian Institution in 1870. It was accepted for publication in 1868. Because they used ethnographic data to demonstrate their conclusions, Morgan and Tylor can justly be considered the "fathers" of scientific research in anthropology.

Darwin, Morgan, and Tylor created their respective fields of endeavor by collecting such vast quantities of data that it was impossible to overlook the importance of their discoveries. In *Researches in the Early History of Mankind* (1865), Tylor examines a vast range of data, from sign language to religion and from all over the world, in order to test the hypothesis that all human beings think in much the same way. In sign language, a great many signs are virtually universal, others are widespread, and some are idiosyncratic. Everywhere, on every continent and among every people there is evidence that culture elements are independently invented with some frequency and that they are spread from group to group by diffusion. The universality of independent invention and diffusion is unassailable evidence that the working of men's minds is everywhere the same. Today, Tylor's proof of the similarity of people's minds is so widely accepted that it is difficult to realize that in Tylor's day, many people believed that the different groups of human beings were separately created with very different mental capacities. Some were believed to be little better than brutes and could be treated as such. In demonstrating that "all men are brothers," Tylor removed hunter-gatherers and, for that matter, peasants and slum dwellers, from the realm of the sub-human and placed them squarely within the human species.

Six years after Darwin's publication, Tylor (1865) provided a systematic definition of culture and began the work of developing a four-field academic discipline around it. His emphasis was upon culture seen as all of the objects and ideas acquired through transmission from other members of society and created by other members of society. The realization that cultures are systems and that human beings create them is a remarkable and influential discovery that is not fully appreciated even today.

In founding anthropology as a four-field discipline along the lines suggested by Herder, Tylor had to deal with highly regarded but conflicting theories. There was the prevailing religious theory that existing forms of humanity were formed by the degeneration of individual cultures after the end of the Golden Age, sometimes because they occupied unfavorable environments. Many others believed that geographical factors were direct and exclusive determinants of the differences among human beings. Within anthropology, Morgan and many of his predecessors believed that human evolution was based upon a planned series of steps through which each race and culture had to pass in order to reach civilization. Tylor identified with this pattern of unilinear evolution, but he left himself a great deal of "wiggle room" in case it turned out not to be correct. Always cautious, Tylor makes it plain that the stages of evolution can get out of order and that a great deal needed to be learned before commonly accepted interpretations of culture, race, and geography could be accepted. Tylor's data demonstrated that progress was the most general form of human evolution, but he accepted the possibility of degeneration even in the most "advanced" societies. The prevention of degeneration and the weeding out of surviving characteristics of "savagery" and "barbarism" was an important role that anthropology would play in the future. Here, Tylor specifically targets slavery, colonialism, and other practices characteristic of savage and barbarian peoples, and establishes the position of anthropology as a reformist or revolutionary discipline that would point out primitive survivals so that they could be eliminated. Later, in his 1881 textbook, *Anthropology*, Tylor accepts a version of "scientific" racism.

Somewhat like von Humboldt, Tylor's thoughts about explaining the cosmos turned to the fields of cognition and religion. In deducing that animism was the earliest and most universal stage of religious evolution, Tylor's faith in inductive science wavered, and his beliefs were soon to be questioned by his student and later colleague, Robert R. Marett (1912). Another generation would pass, and several brilliant ethnographies would be published, but in the 1920s, Bronislaw Malinowski would formalize the process of writing a holistic ethnography bringing consideration of the environment into the description of cultural systems. Malinowski's small Trobriand cosmos (1922) was a fully fleshed version of the larger universal cosmos envisioned by von Humboldt.

In producing the first great work on kinship, Morgan (1870) also drifted away from the path of true science, for he came to believe that kinship nomenclature represented actual kinship practice. *Ancient Society*, Morgan's attempt (1877) to encapsulate the history of mankind, suffers from what seems to be a casual attitude toward ethnographic data. Many groups simply can't be placed in the hierarchy of cultures where Morgan puts them. Morgan's ideas were enthusiastically adopted by a growing band of American anthropologists brought together by Powell, another admirer of von Humboldt. A Civil War hero, who lost an arm in the Battle of Shiloh (1862), Powell concluded that a muddy river like the Colorado would wear down all obstacles and so be relatively free of waterfalls. After his well-publicized journey down the Colorado River, made possible by a comparative absence of waterfalls, Powell could obtain almost anything he wanted. What he wanted was to establish a Bureau of American Ethnology (in 1879) within the Smithsonian Institution, and a Geological Survey of Western North America. As director of both institutions, Powell brought American anthropology out of the shadows, making the publications of the Bureau of American Ethnology a virtual compendium of the masterworks of early anthropology (Powell *et al.* 1881).

A devout follower of Alexander von Humboldt, Powell founded the Cosmos Club in his living room in 1878, bringing together representatives of science, literature, and the arts in Washington, DC. In addition, he held receptions every Sunday morning for members of the Geological Survey and the Bureau of American Ethnology. He was a founding member of the Anthropological Society of Washington and the American Anthropological Association. He was associated with anthropological societies in both Paris and Berlin.

Powell organized the study of American Indian languages and, working with the Geological Survey, he played a major role in planning for the utilization of the arid lands of the United States. It was Powell who forced Congress to create democratic water districts under the theory that local citizens should have complete control of local water. As a sideline, while navigating the Grand Canyon, Powell carried out extensive ethnographic studies of the local populations. He was one of the first to carry out ethnography in the language of the people being described (Albritton 1969). Powell was the chief architect of governmental plans to explore and occupy the arid western regions of the United States. He planned for utopian communities of small farmers as originally conceived by Thomas Jefferson. Powell's scheme was soon overwhelmed by public demands for free land even in places where agriculture could not be practiced. Even so, Powell's plans for the arid lands must be counted as a major achievement of applied environmental anthropology,

Powell also attempted to complete the task of describing the cosmos that von Humboldt had set himself, but his attempts to explain the history of man are beyond confusing. They are bewildering, and they may be the reason that Powell is not often listed as a forefather of anthropology. Another unlisted forefather of anthropology, Mason, who was the keeper of the United States National Museum, depicted Tylor's "Arts of Life," in connection with the environments in which they were found. At first, Mason, like Pitt Rivers in England, arranged artifacts for display in terms of type without regard for the environments in which they were found. Later, at the urging of Boas, he began arranging them in terms of cultural and environmental areas (Mason 1895, 1899, 1914). Boas felt that culture traits should be interpreted and compared in terms of context and not on the basis of superficial resemblance, and he was very outspoken. Mason (1875) pays tribute to the human "inventing animal" and traces the origin of our conceptions of cosmos to the hard work done by our ancestors:

> After centuries of cultivating acquaintance with discrete phenomena around him, he has now striven to coordinate them, to make them organic, to read system into them. He has learned by degrees to comprehend all things as parts of a single mechanism.
>
> *(Mason 1875: 403–404)*

In his discussions of "technogeography" (1894), Mason begins by stressing the role of the environment in the shaping of human behavior and enthusiastically embraces the concept of a cosmic organism, specifically the earth goddess: "in every respect we are justified in speaking of it as an organism, a being, a creature, a body of living forces, a congeries of intelligent resources" (1894: 147). Finally, nineteenth-century triumphalism takes over and he contemplates a worldwide *Oikoumene* (inhabited earth) dominated by a single advanced civilization intent on destroying every natural feature, plant, animal, or culture that fails to meet the tests of progress. In present-day terms, after another century of, dare we say it, "progress," this seems a dark vision of the Anthropocene, although perhaps not an unrealistic one.

Overall, the picture of the universe, the cosmos, as a unified whole, as a system, remained strong even as the focus of anthropology shifted from understanding the divine plan to an understanding of the role of human beings within a fabric of complicated and interacting natural systems. Nineteenth-century anthropologists had a clear grip on a kind of basic ecology, but they did not have the kind of understandings of systems and complex interactions that would begin to develop after World War II. Although most anthropologists expressed a certain skepticism about racial differences, it was also the case that most nineteenth-century anthropological researchers were trained in physical or biological sciences where the concept of race was dominant and unobjectionable. The outright rejection of the significance of human races, under the leadership of Boas, took place gradually, and the concept of race disappears from anthropology in the 1950s, but not entirely from the medical and biological sciences.

Julian Haynes Steward's concept of multilineal evolution (1955, 1977) was derived from the work of Clark Wissler (1923, 1926) and Alfred L. Kroeber (1939) on cultural and natural areas, and was implicit in Boas's Eskimo studies. There seems to be a direct line of descent from Herder to Boas, Mason, and Kroeber, and onward to Kroeber's students, Steward and Cyril Daryll Forde (1934), who are sometimes considered originators of anthropological ecology in the United States and England respectively.

Trained as a physicist and a statistician, Boas brought a strong current of Humboldtian Science into anthropology. His (1895) study of the distribution of myths on the Northwest Coast of North America demonstrated empirically that the myths spread from one group to another—despite geographical, racial, and linguistic differences between different groups. If the myths had been independently invented according to stages of culture, the different myths would have been distributed in a random pattern across the region. In fact, distributions were continuous, proving that culture could spread independently of race, language, and stage of development (Boas *et al.* 2002).

Scientific racism, which had become prevalent after the abolition of slavery in the United States, was the next victim of Boas's empiricism. He published studies showing that immigrants to the United States responded to the new environment by developing physical characteristics quite different from those of their ancestors. Boas (1940) showed that the cephalic index, which was being used to measure the intellectual capacity of different races, was actually determined by environmental factors such as the hardness of the baby's mattress. Overall, following Herder and von Humboldt, Boas showed that physical variation within human groups was greater than the variation between human groups. The removal of "race" as a determinant of human behavior greatly simplifies the task of developing an ecological anthropology.

Boas's study (1888) of the Central Eskimo (now Inuit) is oriented toward the study of the location of Inuit groups and the influence of local environments in the choice of settlement locations. Connections between settlements by established routes and by marriage are also emphasized. Still, the rocks, glaciers, seals, and other geographical circumstances are basically just there and the only actors depicted are the Inuit. For that matter, it would appear that the Inuit had a better grip on environmental dynamics than did Boas. Still, it is noteworthy that the Inuit are not considered as a racial, national, or linguistic group, but as a collection of interconnected settlements, each one having unique social and environmental relationships.

Conclusion

Anthropologists and proto-anthropologists of the eighteenth and nineteenth centuries had no maps to the cognitive territory that they were invading. They took wrong turns and they perpetuated some unfortunate misconceptions. Laboriously, slowly, and imperfectly, they overcame the parochial mythology of their largely European heritage and created an anthropological science. In this review, I have mentioned only a sample of the work of the pioneers who mapped the territory across which twentieth-century anthropology would steadily progress. Because there is always somebody who reached some particular destination long before others reached it, it is probably unwise to speculate about what anthropologists knew or did not know about environmental matters at the dawn of the twentieth century, but I shall do it anyhow.

Well into the middle of the twentieth century, there was a disconnection between anthropological studies of culture and understandings of the environment; ecological concepts remained weak. The atomic bomb, dropped on Hiroshima in 1946, ended my own faith in progress and probably that of many other people as well. For most anthropologists, the environment remained a static and passive presence, never reaching the status of the vibrant goddess portrayed by Herder, von Humboldt, and Mason. The concept of complex interrelated systems of relationship was well developed, but it was difficult to get past the idea that the environment was simply uninhabited land awaiting exploitation.

Morgan's systems were closed and static, consisting of a relatively small number of kin relationships. Tylor thought that cultural systems were interactive, but he does nothing with the concept. Years later, perhaps with tongue in cheek, Max Gluckman (1964) spoke of "closed systems" and "open minds," suggesting a reluctance to consider "open systems." The cultural system itself, at least in the beginning, was seen as consisting of territory, language, and race coming together to create ethnic groups or nations. As a rule, anthropologists had difficulty thinking about cultural units that involved negotiation, internal contradictions, and decision making. It was difficult to visualize apparently separate cultures as nodes within complex networks linking groups to each other and to the environment. Over all stands the terrifying fact that the "system" is not closed at all, but as open to every wind as the early summer tent of the Inuit.

Back in the day, Arjuna, one of the heroes of the great Indian epic, the *Mahabharata*, was terrified by his first sight of the actual living body of Krishna, his divine charioteer representing the cosmos, seen as a complex open system. Nineteenth-century scientists still had God, albeit a remote god, to provide them with some confidence that there was a purpose to the endless complexity. By the end of the century, God and his miracles had virtually disappeared from anthropology to be replaced by a triumphant industrial man working his way into the dismal future foreseen by Herder. Morgan, known to be a friend of the Iroquois, believed that the only effective way to save them from extinction was to assimilate them, to civilize them. Progress along a single unilinear channel was inevitable. In Mason's view, the environment and the people, plants, and animals living in it were not to be saved or conserved, but used up and transformed. Cultural and natural diversity were valued by some, but very few nineteenth-century anthropologists, especially outside North America, worried about the possibility that other peoples would become extinct or that the natural environment would be radically altered before what they considered to be the inexorable advance of civilization.

Through the twentieth century, the concepts of progress and unilinear evolution were gradually supplemented or replaced by ecological approaches that attempted to deal with the awesome complexity of cultural and natural systems. Still in the process of development, truly ecological approaches do not really begin to develop until the mid-twentieth century when the appearance of the computer triggers a host of new and complicated mathematical approaches to the study of reality. Closed and static systems, while still valued for some purposes, have gradually given way to open systems existing in complicated interaction with each other. The concept of human dominion over a universe constructed exclusively for human use is slowly giving way to a more nuanced and complicated view. For example, early agriculture has ceased to be the exclusive product of human ingenuity, but a pattern of complex interaction among human beings, plants, and animals. The human animal itself has come to be a complicated environment inhabited by enormous numbers of microorganisms.

Now, as the consequences of previous human activity are unfolding, science is being asked to predict the relationships between environment and humanity in the year 2100.

Electronic means of data analysis and vastly more sophisticated understandings of computation are most likely at the heart of the revolution in Humboldtian Science that has made possible the emergence of at least the beginnings of an ecological anthropology capable of dealing with the complexity and connectedness of all things.

References

Albritton, C. 1969. "John Wesley Powell and the Anthropology of the Canyon Country. Don D. Fowler, Robert C. Euler, and Catherine S. Fowler. U.S. Geological Survey, Washington, D.C., 1969 (available from the U.S. Government Printing Office, Washington). v 30 Pp., Illus. Paper, 50. USGS Professional Paper 670." *Science* 166(3913): 1611–1612.

Boas, Franz. 1888. *The Central Eskimo (Introduction by Henry B. Collins)*. Washington, DC: Smithsonian Institution, Bureau of American Ethnology.

Boas, Franz. 1895. Indianische sagen von der nord-pacifischen Küste Amerikas. Berlin: A. Asher & Co.

Boas, Franz. 1940. *Race, Language and Culture*. New York: Macmillan.

Boas, Franz, Randy Bouchard, Dorothy I. D. Kennedy and Dietrich Bertz. 2002. *Indian Myths & Legends from the North Pacific Coast of America: A Translation of Franz Boas' 1895 Edition of Indianische Sagen Von Der Nord-Pacifischen Küste Amerikas*. Vancouver, BC: Talon.

Dall, William H. and George Gibbs. 1877. *Tribes of the Extreme Northwest/by W. H. Dall. Tribes of Western Washington and Northwestern Oregon/by Geo. Gibbs*. Washington, DC: Government Printing Office.

Dall, William H., George M.Dawson and William Ogilvie. 1898. *The Yukon Territory the Narrative of W.H. Dall, Leader of the Expedition to Alaska in 1866–1868; the Narrative of an Exploration Made in 1887 in the Yukon District by George M. Dawson, D.S., F.G.S.; Extracts from the Report of an Exploration Made in 1896–1897 by Wm. Ogilvie, D.L.S., F.R.G.S.* London: Downey.

Darwin, Charles. 1988 [1859]. *On the Origin of Species, 1859*. Vol. 15 in *The Works of Charles Darwin* (edited by P. H. Barrett and R. B. Freeman). New York: New York University Press.

Forde, Cyril D. 1934. *Habitat, Economy and Society: A Geographical Introduction to Ethnology*. London: Methuen.

Forster, Georg. 1777. *A Voyage Round the World: In His Britannic Majesty's Sloop, Resolution, Commanded by Capt. James Cook, During the Years 1772, 3, 4, and 5. By George Forster. In Two Volumes.* London: B. White.

Gluckman, Max. 1964. *Closed Systems and Open Minds: The Limits of Naivety in Social Anthropology*. Chicago, IL: Aldine Publishing Company.

Herder, Johann Gottfried. 1966 [1784]. *Outlines of a Philosophy of the History of Man*. New York: Bergman.

Humboldt, Alexander von and Williams, Helen M. 1814. *Researches Concerning the Institutions & Monuments of the Ancient Inhabitants of America: With Descriptions & Views of Some of the Most Striking Scenes in the Cordilleras!* London: Longman, Hurst, Rees, Orme & Brown, J. Murray & H. Colburn.

Humboldt, Alexander von, Edward Sabine and Elizabeth J. Sabine. 2010 [1845–1862]. *Cosmos: Sketch of a Physical Description of the Universe*. Cambridge, UK: Cambridge University Press.

Kroeber, Alfred L. 1939. *Cultural and Natural Areas of Native North America*. Berkeley: University of California Press.

Lowie, Robert H. 1920. *Primitive Society*. New York: Boni and Liveright.

Maine, Henry Sumner. 1861. *Ancient Law: Its Connection with the Early History of Society, and its Relation to Modern Ideas*. London: John Murray.

Maine, Henry Sumner. 1872. *Village-Communities in the East and West. Six Lectures Delivered at Oxford*. London: John Murray.

Malinowski, Bronislaw. 1922. *Argonauts of the Western Pacific: An Account of Native Enterprise and Adventure in the Archipelagoes of Melanesian New Guinea*. London: G. Routledge & Sons.

Manning, Thomas G. 1967. *Government in Science. The U.S. Geological Survey, 1867–1894*. Lexington: University of Kentucky Press.

Marett, Robert R. 1912. *Anthropology*. New York: H. Holt.

Mason, Otis T. 1875. *Ethnological Directions Relative to the Indian Tribes of the United States*. Washington, DC: U.S. Government Printing Office.

Mason, Otis T. 1894. "Technogeography or the Relation of the Earth to the Industries of Mankind." *American Anthropologist* 7(2): 137–161.

Mason, Otis T. 1895. *Migration and the Food Quest: A Study in the Peopling of America*. Washington, DC: Smithsonian Institution.

Mason, Otis T. 1899. *The Man's Knife among the North American Indians: A Study in the Collections of the U.S. National Museum.* Washington, DC: Government Printing Office.

Mason, Otis T. 1914. *Woman's Share in Primitive Culture.* New York: D. Appleton.

Morgan, Lewis Henry. 1870. *Systems of Consanguinity and Affinity of the Human Family.* Washington, DC: Smithsonian Institution.

Morgan, Lewis Henry. 1877. *Ancient Society.* London: Macmillan.

Powell, John Wesley, H. C. Yarrow, Edward S. Holden, Charles C. Royce, Garrick Mallery, James C. Pilling, James O. Dorsey, Albert S. Gatschet and Stephen R. Riggs. 1881. *First Annual Report of the Bureau of Ethnology to the Secretary of the Smithsonian Institution, 1879–80.* Washington, DC: Government Printing Office.

Steward, Julian Haynes. 1955. *Theory of Culture Change: The Methodology of Multilinear Evolution.* Urbana: University of Illinois.

Steward, Julian Haynes. 1977. *Evolution and Ecology: Essays on Social Transformation.* Urbana: University of Illinois.

Tylor, Edward B. 1865. *Researches into the Early History of Mankind and the Development of Civilization.* London: J. Murray.

Tylor, Edward B. 1871. *Primitive Culture: Researches into the Development of Mythology, Philosophy, Religion, Art, and Custom.* London: J. Murray.

Tylor, Edward B. 1881. *Anthropology: An Introduction to the Study of Man and Civilization.* New York: D. Appleton.

Tylor, Edward B. 1889. *Primitive Culture: Researches into the Development of Mythology, Philosophy, Religion, Language, Art, and Custom.* New York: Holt.

Westermarck, Edvard. 1911. *The History of Human Marriage.* London: Macmillan.

Wissler, Clark. 1923. *Man and Culture.* New York: Thomas Y. Crowell.

Wissler, Clark. 1926. *The Relation of Nature to Man in Aboriginal America.* New York: Oxford University Press.

5

ETHNOSCIENTIFIC IMPLICATIONS OF CLASSIFICATION AS A SOCIO-CULTURAL PROCESS

David G. Casagrande

Introduction

My research into how the Tzeltal Maya of Chiapas, Mexico, use medicinal plants required me to walk mountain trails between houses and villages with my Tzeltal collaborators. We often encountered other Tzeltal who were surprised to see a stranger like me in the woods and would usually ask my collaborator, "What's he doing here?" I would reply in my best Tzeltal, "I'm studying medicinal plants." Quite often the response would be something like, "Medicinal plants? Well, do you know *yakan k'ulub wamal*?" I would reply that I knew this plant was used often to treat diarrhea. The stranger might then quiz me on a few other plants. If I passed the quiz, we might start talking about more esoteric plant treatments like those known only to him or his family. Conversations like this occurred frequently and were remarkable for a few reasons. They always started with *yakan k'ulub wamal* (*Verbena litoralis*). They then proceeded to a core group of three or four other well-known plants. Only after these commonly known plants were used to establish a discourse frame could we move on to more in-depth conversation. If I had not known the most typical medicinal plants, the conversation would have quickly moved on to other topics. Instead, we engaged in a dialogue drawing on Tzeltal and modern plant and illness classification systems. In this chapter, I make suggestions for studying how the way that people classify and name biological items integrates with discourse, cultural transmission, and cultural adaptation, with special attention to what ethnoscientists call "prototypicality."

Ethnoscience is a subfield of anthropology in which we attempt to bridge cultural epistemologies in order to understand how people organize knowledge, reason, and communicate about their world. Ethnobiology is primarily concerned with the relationship of people with their local biota. In this chapter, I will focus most on ethnobotany, ethnoecology, and ethnomedicine because these are my areas of research and are relevant to the environmental focus of this volume. However, my review of theory and methods can be applied to other subfields of ethnoscience.

'Classification' refers both to the cognitive process of arranging environmental stimuli into categories based on similarities or differences and to linguistic naming systems (nomenclatures) used to label categories and items within them. Early linguistic analyses—later supported by brain imaging—showed that human thought and communication organize environmental stimuli in semantic domains like kinship, color, plants, illnesses, or animals. The early mission of ethnoscience was to look for structure in these domains using "componential analysis" (Goodenough 1964; Lounsbury 1964). For example, any kinship classification can be reduced to components by which kin are compared and contrasted, such as gender, generation, proximity to ego, and marriage.

Ethnobiologists began looking for the components used to classify plants in the early 1960s, which required documenting all the names for items included in the domain. Ethnobotanists also identified plants that were named in the local language using the modern biological (Linnaean) system as a way of glossing lexical items and to allow comparison of nomenclatures across cultures—what Hunn (1975: 309) called an "etic grid." Conklin's (1954) work among the Hanunóo in the Philippines was the first to document a complete botanical nomenclature and relate it to modern botanical classification. The Tzeltal Maya classification of nature is the most comprehensively documented, with complete nomenclatures and their modern scientific correlates identified for plants (Berlin *et al.* 1974), animals (Hunn 1977), illnesses (Berlin and Berlin 1996; Maffi 1994), mushrooms (Lampman 2007), and even firewood classification (Metzger and Williams 1966). Conklin, Berlin, Hunn, and others documented rigorous knowledge systems with highly sophisticated classifications that challenged the ethnocentric view that indigenous knowledge was less rigorous than modern science.

Ethnobiological research continues to be published in *Economic Botany*, the *Journal of Ethnopharmacology*, and many journals not specifically dedicated to ethnoscientific subfields. Since the founding of the *Journal of Ethnobiology* in 1981, there has been a steady increase in peer-reviewed journals dedicated to ethnobiology. These include the *Journal of Ethnobiology and Ethnomedicine*, the *Journal of Ethnobiology and Conservation*, *Ethnobiology Letters*, and *Ethnobotany Research and Applications*. Many papers published in these journals are descriptive reports with lists of biological items used by indigenous peoples. This is important, but I agree with Albuquerque and Muniz de Medeiros (2012) that more researchers could concern themselves with theoretical and methodological development. My opening vignette is intended to highlight the untapped potential for integrating naming and use of biological items into socio-cultural processes.

Drawing on Ellen's (1993) view that classification is a social process, not an end result, and Ross and Revilla-Minaya's (2011) observation that knowledge content cannot be separated from processing of information, I suggest that classifications provide only snapshots of distributed cognition and cultural transmission embedded in ever-changing natural and social environments. Prototypicality grounds discourse and behavior amidst this social change. Our methods should reflect these types of processes. This perspective also follows Wallace (1972), one of the founders of ethnoscience, who wrote that componential analysis generates rules for categorization, but these must be situated in ethnography to reveal rules for behavior. I advocate that our cognitive methodologies could be better integrated with participant observation, discourse analysis, and new methods like social network analysis to yield insights.

In the next section, I briefly review some theoretical foundations of classification within ethnoscience with a focus on ethnobiology. The breadth and depth of ethnobiology is too vast to possibly cover in one chapter, so I have selected a few issues that both define the field and have the greatest relevance for future research. After that, I describe some common methods used to operationalize these theoretical issues, highlight new and exciting methodological developments, and discuss potential future directions of research. I conclude by discussing some broader implications of treating classification as a socio-cultural process.

Theoretical and empirical foundations of classification

Humans have an innate propensity to name and categorize items in their environment in order to create order (Lévi-Strauss 1966: 9–10), form epistemologies (Atran 1990), and communicate (Ellen 1999). The systems of classification that result from categorizing and naming provide opportunities for cross-cultural comparison. Ethnobiologists have found both universal patterns and cultural particulars when comparing classification systems around the world.

Humans cannot help but notice that a robin is different from a sparrow or a dog. Because we might see more than one robin at once, we assume there are many independent items (robins) that share some essence that makes them different from other items like sparrows (Atran 1998; Gelman and Hirschfeld 1999). Experimental research by Rosch (1978) showed that the human mind attends to clusters and discontinuities in sets of item attributes. Because attributes like feathers and the ability to fly tend to co-occur, subjects are likely to form categories of items that display those attributes (Hunn 1977: 46). We form *basic-level* categories that maximize information with the least cognitive effort based on discontinuities presented by nature (Rosch 1978). Berlin (1992: 19) refers to these categories as "folk generics." These categories tend to be named with simple lexemes (oak), as opposed to complex lexemes (red oak), and include by far the greatest number of names in any classification system (Berlin 1992: 34). It appears that cognitive economy is maximized at the contrastive level of folk generics (Hunn 1977: 46). This is why we see the greatest correlation of categories across cultures at the folk generic level of contrast (Atran 1998; Hunn 1975), which conforms nearly identically to the modern scientific concept of genus (Berlin 1992: 34). Cross-cultural correlation of classification works remarkably well for biological domains like plants, animals, and even mushrooms (Lampman 2007), but less so for soils (Furbee 1989), landscapes (Casagrande 2004a; Molnár 2012), and other domains.

Most classification systems aggregate folk generics into life-form categories (e.g. 'plants' as opposed to 'animals'). Cross-cultural analyses show that classification systems rarely include names for all local plants and animals. They are usually limited to about 500 names within a particular life-form (Berlin 1992: 96; Hunn 1994). Classification systems aggregate folk generics into intermediate categories within life-forms and divide folk generics like 'oak' into subcategories like 'red oak' and 'white oak' (i.e. species or varieties). How this is done is subject to cultural interpretations (Ellen 1986; Hunn 1982). For example, Bulmer (1967) described how the Kalam of New Guinea did not classify the cassowary, a large flightless bird, with other birds. Instead they placed the cassowary closer to humans due to symbolic interpretation. Also, some societies have names for intermediate groups like the Tzeltal word *mut*, which connotes 'birds' in general, while others do not name such categories (Randall and Hunn 1984). Binomials (e.g. 'white oak,' or *Quercus alba*) and differentiation within binomials are believed to indicate cultural importance. Conklin (1954) documented what is perhaps the greatest differentiation of folk genera with Hanunóo names for varieties of rice. Brown (1984) and Berlin (1972) proposed an evolutionary scheme in which the need to differentiate and name sub-specific varieties increases with a change from foraging to agriculture.

Ethnobiologists have debated whether hierarchical, mutually exclusive taxonomies like the Linnaean system are universal (Atran 1998; Berlin 1992: 31) as opposed to fuzzy, context-specific, flexible classifications (Bulmer 1967; Ellen 1986; Hunn and French 1984). Although there are exceptions, folk biological categories tend to be broadly hierarchical and mutually exclusive (Berlin, 1992: 22). Sparrows and robins are types of birds, and therefore, cannot be types of plants. But the boundaries of categories and attributes used to form them are variable. Componential analysis holds up well across cultures for domains like kinship, but universal components used to categorize biological items within life-forms remain elusive. A fundamental question is whether categories are defined using attributes all members must share, or are formed around items that typify the category because they best display the most attributes.

Many students of human cognition believe that people organize information in their minds by relying on *prototypicality* (MacLaurey 1991). People create subsets of the vast array of items encountered in the world by recognizing attributes shared by some items and not by others (Rosch 1978). Items that best express the suite of attributes that signify the category (the prototype) represent category typicality. People tend to focus on items that typify categories during childhood learning, when performing memory recall, or attempting to communicate about categories (Kempton 1982; Markman 1989; Winters 1990). Ask several Americans to recall all of the birds they know and they will mention robins or sparrows much more often, and sooner, than penguins (Boster 1988). Tzeltal Maya freelisting clearly shows that *Verbena litoralis* best represents medicinal plant category typicality (Figure 5.1, p. 61). This is also the plant that was used to begin the trail conversation I described at the beginning of this chapter. Indeed, most conversations I had about medicinal plants included mention of *V. litoralis*. Below, I suggest that category typicality has implications for communication, cultural transmission, and cultural adaptation.

To summarize, we recognize discontinuities in patterns of nature as kinds of plants, birds, animals, illnesses, or landscapes, and we name them. Ethnobiologists generally agree about universal principles of classification like basic-level categorization and prototypicality, but do not agree about the structure of taxonomies. Next, I describe what we know about how people use classification to reason about relationships between items, categories, and ecological processes.

Scott Atran (1999) conducted comparative experiments with Michigan University students and Itza´ Maya. These included sorting tasks to determine taxonomic relationships and induction experiments to determine the role of taxonomy in inductive reasoning (e.g. "If this item has a disease can these other items get it?"). The Michigan students relied more on taxonomic relationships to reason about abstract biological processes. They believed that if more distantly related items share a property, it was more likely that all items will share that property. The Itza´ Maya were more likely to search for causal explanations (e.g. diseases are transmitted among animals that all live in trees). Coley *et al.* (1999) found that Americans who lacked direct experience with ecological processes used taxonomic relationships for inductive reasoning, whereas Americans with experience used ecological models like the Itza´. This is consistent with my findings that direct experience with medicinal plants overrode the tendency of Tzeltal subjects to assume that closely related taxa shared medicinal properties (Casagrande 2002). Various research projects suggest that we use taxonomic relationships for reasoning, but mostly when direct experience with ecological context is lacking. Research on inductive reasoning also suggests that we use cognitive processes of classification differently from cultural models (Ross and Revilla-Minaya 2011).

Cultural models are cognitive frameworks used to reason and communicate about topics of importance in a culture (D'Andrade 2005). Researchers identify propositions, metaphors, or other components of cultural models by analyzing narratives or conversations to work out the important ways people reason about a topic (Quinn 2005). Kempton *et al.* (1996) used this method to describe an American cultural model of 'nature' in which the earth is a closed system upon which humans depend, different parts of nature are interdependent and altering one can harm another, and humans cannot predict these effects and should not interfere with nature. Contrasting this with the inductive reasoning by Americans elucidated by Atran

(1999) shows how different methodologies within ethnoecology—one beginning with classification and the other with linguistics—lead to different results. More recently, Atran and Medin (2008) made a vital contribution to ethnoscience by integrating category-based induction with cultural models, behavior, social networks, and cultural transmission among Maya and Ladinos in Guatemala. Their work highlights how classification is as much a socially-distributed process as it is a function of individual cognition.

Ethnobiologists are interested in how and why classification varies within cultural groups (e.g. Ellen 1993), and have found patterns of variation based on age, kinship, sexual division of labor, and post-marital residence (Boster 1985, 1986; Casagrande 2002; Gollin 2001; Hays 1974; Hopkins *et al.* 2015). As social complexity increases, so does the information load of communication (Tainter 1988). Roy Ellen (1999) provides an example of how cultures respond to increasing specialization. He compared foraging and cultivating people of the Southeast Asian rainforest to test the notion that binomialization (the proliferation of complex terms like 'red oak') is a response to the need for an expanded ethnobiological repertoire. He distinguishes substantive knowledge (knowledge about items) from formal knowledge (the lexicon). Substantive knowledge among foragers is more experiential and is less necessary to encode as formal knowledge. Increasing specialization, sedentation, and social complexity necessitate the formalization of substantive knowledge. Gatewood (1983: 385) suggests that, "In very complex societies, it is more important to know how to talk about something than it is to know what one is talking about."

We use classification not only to make sense of the world, but also to talk about it (Edwards 1991). Classifying and naming items is necessary for cultural transmission among adults and from adults to children (Stross 1973; Waxman 1999; Zarger 2011). But it isn't necessary, or even possible, for individuals to carry exact replicas of each other's classifications in their heads or reproduce them in discourse. The informational and cognitive load of conversation and learning are reduced significantly by establishing discourse frames using category typicality (Casagrande 2000, 2002: 238–242). This is what was happening during my trail encounters with the Tzeltal. A plant that best represents the category (*V. litoralis*) was used to efficiently instantiate a discourse frame—a tacit understanding that we all have some knowledge in common that makes any subsequent meaningful exchange possible (Fillmore 1982). Wallace (1970: 35) suggested that humans share basic cognitive frameworks, but fill them with idiosyncratic details to allow for more social complexity than any one individual can have in his or her head. I suggest that as societies become more complex, the need for discursive efficiency increases and so does the importance of category typicality.[1]

The social and natural environments in which human societies are embedded are always changing. Societies that don't adapt to changing environments become extinct. Cultural adaptation requires variation of knowledge and ideas, similar to the genetic variation needed for biological species to adapt. Social distribution of knowledge, individual experimentation, social complexity, and specialization all increase cultural variation. But it's not enough for *individuals* to have different knowledge. In order to adapt as a society, we must also be able to share information with others in an effective and efficient manner. Societies fail to adapt to environmental and social change if critical information cannot flow efficiently (Casagrande and Peters 2013), possibly even leading to social collapse (Tainter 1988). Some level of consensus is required for information flow. This is why, in any cultural domain, we will find a pattern of 'consensus within diversity' (Barrett 1995; Casagrande 2004b; Ferreira Júnior and Albuquerque 2015). Shared item typicality is one way in which consensus is established (Casagrande 2000). It is possible that as variation of knowledge within a domain increases, the saliency of the prototypical item will also increase.

I propose that category typicality is necessary for cultural transmission and is a foundation for the consensus within variation needed for cultural adaptation. I consider some methodological implications of this proposal within the following general discussion of classification research methods.

Methodological implications of classification as a socio-cultural process

Two methods ethnobiologists have used most often to study classification are to ask research subjects to recall items in a domain (freelisting) and to show subjects items and ask them to name and/or categorize them.[2] I began studying medicinal plants with the Tzeltal in a typical way. I elicited freelists by asking 42 men and women who lived in the Chiapas Highlands to name all the medicinal plants they could recall. Then I took Tzeltal assistants into the field to collect specimens of the plants that were mentioned, as well as plants we encountered that had not been mentioned, but my assistants knew were medicinal. We pressed and dried a collection of 130 medicinal plant species. I interviewed 14 men and 14 women, showing them each dried specimen one at a time and asking them for the plant's name, what illness it cured, where it grew, how they learned it, and whether its humoral property was hot or cold.[3] In other words, I was asking them to classify the plant collection in five different ways. I replicated these methods in newly founded lowland Tzeltal communities to understand how prototyping and cultural models of curing had influenced knowledge acquisition as the Tzeltal migrated from high elevations to new communities in the tropical lowlands (Casagrande 2002).

In another project, I asked Tzeltal informants to name birds and tell me what habitats they occupied, using pictures cut out of a field guide (Casagrande 2004a). Identifying pressed plants and pictures of birds proved difficult for some interviewees. Sometimes people who had identified a plant or bird when we were in the field could not identify the same item as a specimen or picture. This is because we use cues in our natural environment to fill in much of the information we don't need to keep in our head—a process called "distributed cognition" (Hazlehurst 2011; Hutchins 1995). Identifying and categorizing items out of their natural context is a skill that must be learned, which brings us to the issue of "psychological reality" (D'Andrade 1995: 101).

Many classification systems lack names for categories between folk generics and life-forms. Berlin used sorting experiments to elicit "covert" intermediate categories (i.e. unnamed but psychologically valid categories; Berlin *et al.* 1981). Do such categories really exist in the minds of informants, or are they merely produced when asked for? If we accepted the distributed nature of cognition, as opposed to assuming that it is all "in our heads," we could escape this conundrum by designing methods that mimic natural and social interactions. Random trail conversations and spontaneous conversations I overheard while the Tzeltal were actively engaged in treating illnesses were crucial for understanding the limitations of my systematic methods and interpreting their significance. There is no substitute for participant observation.

Eliciting and analyzing category typicality

Category typicality is easily revealed by measuring item saliency in freelists of cultural domains. When asking research subjects to recall names of items in a domain, prototypical items tend to be mentioned earliest and most often (Rosch *et al.* 1976). Smith's Index measures saliency by accounting for both order and frequency of items in freelists (Borgatti 1996: 21). My Tzeltal freelist results clearly show that *V. litoralis* best represents the medicinal plant domain (Figure 5.1).

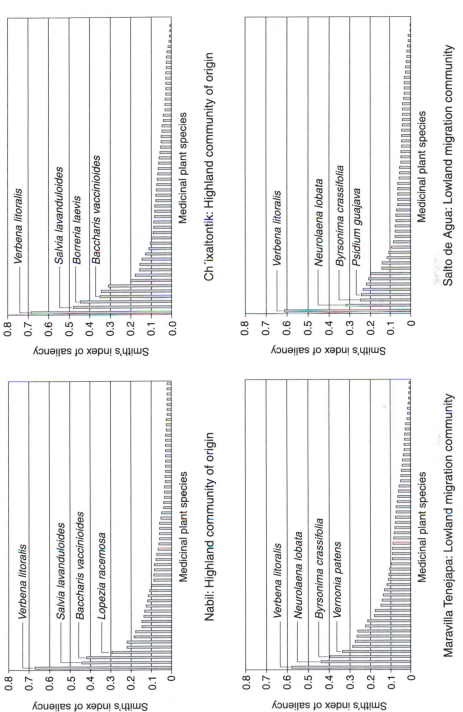

Figure 5.1 Medicinal plant saliency from two highland Tzeltal communities of origin and two lowland Tzeltal migrant communities. *Verbena litoralis* remains prototypical in the tropical lowlands even though it is less common —suggesting that category typicality provides consensus within variation amidst the extreme social change of migration.

Explaining why an item is prototypical is more challenging. Does the item best represent attributes used to define a category, or are there other explanations? I statistically correlated item saliency with frequency of use, plant abundance, knowledge distribution, strength ratings of taste, efficacy ratings, and agreement about hot or cold qualities. I also observed and participated in household curing events, and coded transcriptions of 21 hours of discourse for themes related to saliency. The only important attribute for inclusion in the domain of medicinal plants was whether a plant cured. Subjects believed that *V. litoralis* was a highly effective treatment for diarrhea, but *Salvia lavanduloides* (the next most salient plant in the highlands) was most effective for curing cough. Why is *V. litoralis* most salient? Participant observation revealed that the Tzeltal use *V. litoralis* very often because it conveniently grows near houses and parasitic diarrhea has become very common as sanitation has not kept pace with recent population growth. Thus, my combination of methods indicated that *V. litoralis* was salient because it is effective, easily accessible, and is used frequently to treat common illnesses that are a major factor in child mortality (Casagrande 2002: 181). It is one of the first medicinal plants a Tzeltal child learns. *V. litoralis* is less abundant in the tropical lowlands. Nevertheless, it remained the most salient plant for those who had migrated to the lowlands (Figure 5.1). These findings suggest the importance of item saliency in social processes like communication, cultural transmission, and ecological adaptation.

Cultural consensus and multidimensional categories

Cultural Consensus Analysis (CCA) is a statistical technique that compares variation in respondents' answers to questions in order to determine how they agree about a culturally shared concept (Weller 2007). It has been used widely in classification studies. CCA is a form of factor analysis in which different factors may explain variation among answers. If a domain of knowledge is shared by respondents, one factor should explain the variation much better than any other factor. This technique is highly useful for determining the 'culturally correct' names of plants or animals shown to respondents.

CCA could be used to test my suggestion that as variation in knowledge increases, so must consensus within the domain, consensus in another domain, or item saliency. If variation in answers increases, but the first factor explains most of it, we could argue that consensus within variation is higher. Dressler *et al.* (2015) proposed a different way to use CCA to look at cultural adaptation by showing how the second factor can represent cultural change. This is important because any classification system we observe is only a snapshot of a process of continuing cultural evolution.

Complex domains like 'medicinal plants' are also multidimensional, which means items within them can be categorized more than one way (Alcántara-Salinas *et al.* 2013). The Tzeltal will categorize medicinal plants based on what illnesses they cure, where they grow, how they taste or smell, whether they are hot or cold, and so on. The dimension in use at any given time depends on the context of the event or conversation (Mathews 1983) or one's learned predisposition—what (Ellen 1993: 229) terms "prehension." Garro (1986) suggested that the different ways Tarascan healers in west-central Mexico categorized illnesses are the building blocks (or features) of a shared cultural model. I also argued that the plants used to cure illnesses and the various ways they can be classified are part of a shared cultural model of curing for the Tzeltal (Casagrande 2002). CCA of my data showed consensus was highest for names of plants, less so for illnesses cured by plants, and even lower for hot and cold properties (Table 5.1). These dimensions conform to Gatewood's (2011) distinction between "knowledge of," "knowledge about," and "knowledge how."

Table 5.1 Tzeltal medicinal plant knowledge Cultural Consensus Analysis results for Gatewood's (2011) distinction between *knowledge of*, *knowledge about*, and *knowledge how*. *Knowledge of* provides a foundation for other dimensions within a cultural model of curing.

Type of knowledge	Eigen value of the 1st factor	Percent of variance explained by 1st factor	Average respondent knowledge
Names of plants (knowledge of)	13.5	68% (n = 22)	0.82 (SD = 0.08)
Medicinal use of plants (knowledge about)	6.7	34% (n = 22)	0.57 (SD = 0.11)
Hot/cold property (knowledge of how they cure)	4.4	24% (n = 18)	0.48 (SD = 0.11)

The results suggest that naming (or "knowledge of") is a foundation for the other dimensions within a cultural model of curing.

More work remains to be done to reconcile cognitive approaches to classification and linguistic approaches to cultural models. CCA is a powerful technique for measuring agreement, but ethnoscientists must keep in mind that classification can be multidimensional, in flux, and different people will use classification differently in different contexts.

Cultural transmission and social networks

Understanding the role of classification and knowledge in cultural transmission and socially distributed cognition requires us to understand how social relationships and institutions shape information flow (Atran *et al.* 2002; Boster 1986; Ellen 1993). Similar to Boster's work with manioc in the Amazon (1986), I found variation in Tzeltal medicinal plant classification to cluster by household and gender (Casagrande 2002: 220), but with an additional twist. The knowledge of young married women was more similar to that of their in-laws than that of the households they grew up in, and their cultural competence measured with CCA increased rapidly in the years after they married. The Tzeltal practice patrilocal post-marital residence. The obvious explanation is that after they marry and have children, their need to learn new plants increases and they learn them from the women in their new household. This again points to the importance of ethnographic context. It also shows how an abrupt shift in cultural transmission from parents to children to intra-generational transmission is accompanied by an abrupt change in social networks.

Social network analysis is a relatively recent modeling technique in which networks are represented as ties between nodes (Borgatti *et al.* 2013). If the nodes represent people, the ties between them can represent strength of friendship, frequency of contact, or other attributes of relationships. Social network analysis allows one to see the structure of networks and people's positions within them. Scholars have begun integrating methods like CCA with social network analysis to understand the distribution of folk knowledge as a function of social relationships. Hopkins *et al.* (2015) found that subjects who had higher competence in herbal remedies measured with CCA tended to be older and more centrally located in herbal remedy networks. Atran and Medin (2008: 210) show that the structures of social networks of three neighboring groups in Guatemala (Itza´, Ladino, Q´eqchi´) influenced the distribution of taxonomic and ecological knowledge within each group. I propose that adding linguistic analysis would also reveal how prototypes and cultural models provide discourse frames to allow information flow between networks.

Prior to 1990, most ethnobiologists assumed that each culture had one shared classification system and deviations from that system were generally ignored. Now, variation in types of classification within a cultural domain and variation in knowledge among members of cultures are central areas of research. We have also seen progress in methodological approaches for integrating individual cognition with social processes.

Conclusion: some general implications of classification as social process

I have described how classifications are distributed socially and how category typicality provides a foundation for cultural transmission and the consensus within variation needed for cultural adaptation. I have called for more integration of cognitive approaches to classification with social network analysis, linguistic approaches to cultural models, and ethnography (in particular, participant observation). As my Tzeltal trail encounters illustrate, prototyping is important for facilitating communication between social groups. There are probably many other communicative aspects of classification waiting to be discovered, some of which are unique to biological classification and some of which may or may not be culturally universal. Comparative research is therefore still important, but more so for studying effects of social organization and adaptation, not just classifications in and of themselves.

Barsh (1997) suggested we study people as they move into new ecological contexts to see how they learn about plants. Migration provides excellent opportunities to study classification within social change (Albuquerque and Muniz de Medeiros 2012). I found the gap between Tzeltal who knew many medicinal plants and those who knew few was much greater in lowland migrant communities compared to the highlands of origin (Casagrande 2005). This resulted from global capitalist reorganization of social relations and had negative implications for health.

Migration provides an opportunity to study category typicality and consensus within variation during extreme social change. Even though *V. litoralis* is less abundant in the tropical lowlands of Chiapas, it remained a prototypical core as the pharmacopoeia around it was transformed (Figure 5.1) and reciprocity between people was replaced by capital (Casagrande 2005). Atran has argued that nature-based domains provide a superior foundation for cognition and induction (Atran and Medin 2008). Following this logic, I suggest that natural prototypes play a unique role in assuaging social disruption because they symbolically, cognitively, and linguistically integrate human social relations, traditional ecological knowledge, and natural landscapes. This provides yet another justification for maintaining *in situ* biocultural diversity (Maffi 1999).

Early studies of classification helped legitimize indigenous knowledge in the West, but I agree with Anderson (2011) that the tendency to treat traditional knowledge as something that can be documented and filed away for posterity represents an unfortunate failure to appreciate the value of ongoing biocultural evolution and the lessons we can learn from each other about social relationships integrated with nature (Albuquerque and Muniz de Medeiros 2013). Since Dougherty (1978) first turned the ethnobiological gaze back toward Western culture, we have been cognizant of our own biocultural devolution and its negative impacts on our cognitive potential (Atran and Medin 2008) and general well-being (e.g. Louv 2008). Random encounters with curious Tzeltal on the mountainous trails of Chiapas taught me how classification is a social process embedded in human and natural ecosystems that brings value and meaning to people's lives—a benefit of nature that too many in the world are losing.

Notes

1 Zipf (1949) proposed that interlocutors don't want to work any harder than necessary to achieve consensus. This results in a pattern of word frequency in general language use that is strikingly similar to item typicality elicited from freelists.

2 Gary Martin's (2004) ethnobotany methods manual is the essential source for ethnobotany field methods, many of which can be applied to other domains. The introductory chapter of Ellen (1993) is a good source for ethnozoological methods. Bernard (2006) describes many of the techniques used to analyze ethnobiological field data.

3 The Tzeltal classify plants and illnesses as hot or cold (Berlin and Berlin 1996: 61), which is true of many cultures (Anderson 1987).

References

Albuquerque U P and Muniz de Medeiros P 2012. Systematic reviews and meta-analysis applied to ethnobiological research. *Ethnobiology and Conservation* 1: 6.

Albuquerque U P and Muniz de Medeiros P 2013. What is evolutionary ethnobiology? *Ethnobiology and Conservation* 2: 6.

Alcántara-Salinas G, Ellen R F, Valiñas-Coalla L, Caballero J and Argueta-Villamar A 2013. Alternative ways of representing Zapotec and Cuicatec folk classification of birds: A multidimensional model and its implications for culturally-informed conservation in Oaxaca, México. *Journal of Ethnobiology and Ethnomedicine* 9: 81.

Anderson E N 1987. Why is humoral medicine so popular? *Social Science & Medicine* 25(4): 331–337.

Anderson E N 2011. Ethnobiology: Overview of a growing field. In E N Anderson, D Pearsall, E Hunn and N Turner (eds) *Ethnobiology*. Hoboken, NJ: Wiley–Blackwell, pp. 1–14.

Atran S 1990. *Cognitive foundations of natural history: Towards an anthropology of science*. New York: Cambridge University Press.

Atran S 1998. Folk biology and the anthropology of science: Cognitive universals and cultural particulars. *Behavioral and Brain Sciences* 21(4): 547–609.

Atran S 1999. Itzaj Maya folkbiological taxonomy: Cognitive universals and cultural particulars. In D L Medin and S Atran (eds) *Folkbiology*. Cambridge, MA: The MIT Press, pp. 119–203.

Atran S and Medin D 2008. *The native mind and the cultural construction of nature*. Cambridge, MA: The MIT Press.

Atran S, Medin D, Ross N, Lynch E, Vapnarsky V, Ek' E U, Coley J, Timura C and Baran M 2002. Folkecology, cultural epidemiology, and the spirit of the commons: A garden experiment in the Maya lowlands, 1991–2001. *Current Anthropology* 43(3): 421–450.

Barrett B 1995. Herbal knowledge on Nicaragua's Atlantic coast: Consensus within diversity. *Journal of Community Health* 20(5): 403–421.

Barsh R 1997. The epistemology of traditional healing systems. *Human Organization* 56(1): 28–37.

Berlin B 1972. Speculations on the growth of ethnobotanical nomenclature. *Language in Society* 1(1): 51–86.

Berlin B 1992. *Ethnobiological classification: Principles of categorization of plants and animals in traditional societies*. Princeton, NJ: Princeton University Press.

Berlin E A and Berlin B 1996. *Medical ethnobiology of the Highland Maya of Chiapas, Mexico: The gastrointestinal diseases*. Princeton, NJ: Princeton University Press.

Berlin B, Breedlove D E and Raven P H 1974. *Principles of Tzeltal plant classification*. New York: Academic Press.

Berlin B, Boster J and O'Neill J 1981. The perceptual basis of ethnobiological classification. *Journal of Ethnobiology* 1(1): 95–108.

Bernard H R 2006. *Research methods in anthropology: Qualitative and quantitative approaches*. Walnut Creek, CA: AltaMira Press.

Borgatti S P 1996. *ANTHROPAC 4.0 reference manual*. Natick, MA: Analytic Technologies.

Borgatti S P, Everett M G and Johnson J C 2013. *Analyzing social networks*. Thousand Oaks, CA: Sage.

Boster J S 1985. "Requiem for the omniscient informant": There's life in the old girl yet. In J W D Dougherty (ed.) *Directions in cognitive anthropology*. Urbana: University of Illinois Press, pp. 177–197.

Boster J S 1986. Exchange of varieties and information between Aguaruna manioc cultivators. *American Anthropologist* 88(2): 428–436.

Boster J S 1988. Natural sources of internal category structure: Typicality, familiarity, and similarity of birds. *Memory and Cognition* 16(3): 258–270.

Brown C H 1984. *Language and living things: Uniformities in folk classification and naming*. New Brunswick, NJ: Rutgers University Press.

Bulmer R 1967. Why is the cassowary not a bird? A problem of zoological taxonomy among the Karam of the New Guinea Highlands. *Man* 2(1): 5–25.

Casagrande D G 2000. Human taste and cognition in Tzeltal Maya medicinal plant use. *Journal of Ecological Anthropology* 4: 57–69.

Casagrande D G 2002. Ecology, cognition, and cultural transmission of Tzeltal Maya medicinal plant knowledge. PhD dissertation, Department of Anthropology, University of Georgia, Athens.

Casagrande D G 2004a. Conceptions of primary forest in a Tzeltal Maya community: Implications for conservation. *Human Organization* 63(2): 189–202.

Casagrande D G 2004b. Ethnobiology lives! Theory, collaboration, and possibilities for the study of folk biologies. *Reviews in Anthropology* 33(4): 351–370.

Casagrande D G 2005. Globalization, migration, and indigenous commodification of medicinal plants in Chiapas, Mexico. In G Guest (ed.) *Globalization, health, and the environment: An integrated perspective*. Lanham, MD: AltaMira Press, pp. 83–106.

Casagrande D G and Peters C 2013. Ecomyopia meets the *longue durée*: An information ecology of the increasingly arid Southwestern United States. In H Kopnina and E Shoreman-Ouimet (eds) *Environmental anthropology: Future directions*. New York: Routledge, pp. 97–144.

Coley J D, Medin D L, Proffitt J B, Lynch E and Atran S 1999. Inductive reasoning in folkbiological thought. In D L Medin and S Atran (eds) *Folkbiology*. Cambridge, MA: The MIT Press, pp. 206–232.

Conklin H C 1954. The relation of Hanunóo culture to the plant world. PhD dissertation, Yale University, New Haven, CT.

D'Andrade R 1995. *The development of cognitive anthropology*. Cambridge, UK: Cambridge University Press.

D'Andrade R 2005. Some methods for studying cultural cognitive structures. In N Quinn (ed.) *Finding culture in talk: A collection of methods*. New York: Palgrave Macmillan, pp. 83–104.

Dougherty J W D 1978. Salience and relativity in classification. *American Ethnologist* 5(1): 66–79.

Dressler W W, Balieiro M C and Ernesto de Santos J E 2015. Finding culture change in the second factor: Stability and change in cultural consensus and residual agreement. *Field Methods* 27: 22–38.

Edwards D 1991. Categories are for talking: On the cognitive and discursive bases of categorization. *Theory and Psychology* 1(4): 515–542.

Ellen R F 1986. Ethnobiology, cognition and the structure of prehension: Some general theoretical notes. *Journal of Ethnobiology* 6(1): 83–98.

Ellen R F 1993. *The cultural relations of classification: An analysis of Nuaulu animal categories from central Seram*. Cambridge, UK: Cambridge University Press.

Ellen R 1999. Modes of subsistence and ethnobiological knowledge: Between extraction and cultivation in Southeast Asia. In D L Medin and S Atran (eds) *Folkbiology*. Cambridge, MA: The MIT Press, pp. 91–117.

Ferreira Júnior W S and Albuquerque U P 2015. "Consensus within Diversity": An evolutionary perspective on local medical systems. *Biological Theory* 10(4): 363–368.

Fillmore C J 1982. Frame semantics. In Linguistic Society of Korea (ed.) *Linguistics in the morning calm*. Seoul, S. Korea: Hanshin, pp. 111–138.

Furbee L 1989. A folk expert system: Soils classification in the Colca Valley, Peru. *Anthropological Quarterly* 62(2): 83–102.

Garro L C 1986. Intracultural variation in folk medical knowledge: A comparison between curers and noncurers. *American Anthropologist* 88(2): 351–370.

Gatewood J B 1983. Loose talk: Linguistic competence and recognition ability. *American Anthropologist* 85(2): 378–387.

Gatewood J B 2011. Personal knowledge and collective representations. In D Kronenfeld, G Bennardo, V de Munck and M D Fischer (eds) *A companion to cognitive anthropology*. Chichester, UK: Wiley–Blackwell, pp. 102–114.

Gelman S and Hirschfeld L A 1999. How biological is essentialism? In D L Medin and S Atran (eds) *Folkbiology*. Cambridge, MA: The MIT Press, pp. 403–446.

Gollin L 2001. The taste and smell of Taban Kenyah (Kenyah medicine): An exploration of chemo-sensory selection criteria for medicinal plants among the Kenyah Leppo´ Ke of East Kalimantan, Borneo, Indonesia. PhD dissertation, University of Hawai‘i.

Goodenough W H 1964. Componential analysis of Könkämä lapp kinship terminology. In W H Goodenough (ed.) *Explorations in cultural anthropology*. New York: McGraw-Hill, pp. 221–238.

Hays T E 1974. Mauna: Explorations in Ndumba ethnobotany. PhD dissertation, University of Washington, Seattle.

Hazlehurst B 2011. The distributed cognition model of the mind. In D Kronenfeld, G Bennardo, V de Munck and M D Fischer (eds) *A companion to cognitive anthropology*. Chichester, UK: Wiley–Blackwell, pp. 471–488.

Hopkins A, Stepp J, McCarty C and Gordon J 2015. Herbal remedy knowledge acquisition and transmission among the Yucatec Maya in Tabi, Mexico: A cross-sectional study. *Journal of Ethnobiology and Ethnomedicine* 11(1): 33.

Hunn E 1975. A measure of the degree of correspondence of folk to scientific biological classification. *American Ethnologist* 2(2): 309–327.

Hunn E S 1977. *Tzeltal folk zoology: The classification of discontinuities in nature*. New York: Academic Press.

Hunn E 1982. The utilitarian factor in folk biological classification. *American Anthropologist* 84(4): 830–847.

Hunn E 1994. Place-names, population density, and the magic number 500. *Current Anthropology* 35(1): 81–85.

Hunn E and French D H 1984. Alternative to taxonomic hierarchy: The Sahaptin case. *Journal of Ethnobiology* 4(1): 73–92.

Hutchins E 1995. *Cognition in the wild*. Cambridge, MA: The MIT Press.

Kempton W 1982. *The folk classification of ceramics: A study of cognitive prototypes*. New York: Academic Press.

Kempton W, Boster J S and Hartley J A 1996. *Environmental values in American culture*. Cambridge, MA: The MIT Press.

Lampman A M 2007. General principles of ethnomycological classification among the Tzeltal Maya of Chiapas, Mexico. *Journal of Ethnobiology* 27(1): 11–27.

Lévi-Strauss C 1966. *The savage mind*. Chicago, IL: University of Chicago Press.

Lounsbury F G 1964. A formal account of the crow- and Omaha-type kinship terminologies. In W H Goodenough (ed.) *Explorations in cultural anthropology*. New York: McGraw-Hill, pp. 351–393.

Louv R 2008. *Last child in the woods: Saving our children from nature-deficit disorder*. New York: Algonquin Books.

MacLaurey R E 1991. Prototypes revisited. *Annual Review of Anthropology* 20: 55–74.

Maffi L 1994. A linguistic analysis of Tzeltal Maya ethnosymptomatology. PhD dissertation, University of California, Berkeley.

Maffi L 1999. Linguistic diversity. In D A Posey (ed.) *Cultural and spiritual values of biodiversity*. London: Intermediate Technology Publications, pp. 19–35.

Markman E M 1989. *Categorization and naming in children*. Cambridge, MA: The MIT Press.

Martin G J 2004. *Ethnobotany: A methods manual*. New York: Chapman & Hall.

Mathews H F 1983. Context-specific variation in humoral classification. *American Anthropologist* 85(4): 826–847.

Metzger D G and Williams G E 1966. Some procedures and results in the study of native categories: Tzeltal "firewood." *American Anthropologist* 68(2): 389–407.

Molnár Z 2012. Classification of pasture habitats by Hungarian herders in a steppe landscape (Hungary). *Journal of Ethnobiology and Ethnomedicine* 8: 28.

Quinn N 2005. How to reconstruct schemas people share from what they say. In N Quinn (ed.) *Finding culture in talk: A collection of methods*. New York: Palgrave Macmillan, pp. 35–81.

Randall R A and Hunn E S 1984. Do life-forms evolve or do uses for life? Some doubts about Brown's universals hypothesis. *American Ethnologist* 11: 329–349.

Rosch E 1978. Principles of categorization. In E Rosch and B Lloyd (eds) *Cognition and categorization*. Hillsdale, NJ: Lawrence Erlbaum Associates, pp. 28–49.

Rosch E, Simpson C and Miller R S 1976. Structural bases of typicality effects. *Journal of Experimental Psychology: Human Perception and Performance* 2(4): 491–502.

Ross N and Revilla–Minaya C 2011. Cognitive studies in ethnobiology: What can we learn about mind as well as human environmental interaction? In E N Anderson, D Pearsall, E Hunn and N Turner (eds) *Ethnobiology*. Hoboken, NJ: Wiley–Blackwell, pp. 335–349.

Stross B 1973. Acquisition of botanical terminology by Tzeltal children. In M S Edmonson (ed.) *Meaning in Mayan languages*. The Hague, the Netherlands: Mouton, pp. 107–141.

Tainter J A 1988. *The collapse of complex societies*. Cambridge, UK: Cambridge University Press.

Wallace A F C 1970. *Culture and personality*. New York: Random House.

Wallace A F C 1972. Culture and cognition. In J P Spradley (ed.) *Culture and cognition: Rules, maps, and plans*. San Francisco, CA: Chandler, pp. 111–126.

Waxman S 1999. The dubbing ceremony revisited: Object naming and categorization in infancy and early childhood. In D L Medin and S Atran (eds) *Folkbiology*. Cambridge, MA: The MIT Press, pp. 233–284.

Weller S C 2007. Cultural consensus theory: Applications and frequently asked questions. *Field Methods* 19(4): 339–368.

Winters M E 1990. Toward a theory of syntactic prototypes. In S L Tsohatzidis (ed.) *Meanings and prototypes: Studies in linguistic categorization*. London: Routledge, pp. 285–306.

Zarger R 2011. Learning ethnobiology: Creating knowledge and skills about the living world. In E N Anderson, D Pearsall, E Hunn and N Turner (eds) *Ethnobiology*. Hoboken, NJ: Wiley–Blackwell, pp. 371–387.

Zipf G K 1949. *Human behavior and the principle of least effort*. Cambridge, MA: Addison–Wesley.

PART II

Investigations in sub-fields of environmental anthropology

6

ENVIROMATERIALITY

Exploring the links between political ecology and material culture studies

José E. Martínez-Reyes

Introduction

In a review article comparing ecological anthropology and material culture studies, Tim Ingold wonders why both fields have always dealt with materials and material culture, yet their practitioners 'are speaking past one another in largely incommensurate theoretical languages' (Ingold 2012: 427). While the field of material culture studies focuses upon how 'persons and things are bound in relational networks', ecological anthropology emphasizes how 'human beings and other organisms are bound in webs of life' (Ingold 2012: 428). His solution for solving the impasse between both is that they should 'focus on the active materials that compose the lifeworld' (Ingold 2012: 429). While I agree with some of the main arguments that Ingold espouses above, I am left wondering – what about political ecology? Here I refer to political ecology as a part of environmental anthropology with a particular focus on power and conflicts over access to and use of resources. As I discuss below, the field of material culture studies has effectively incorporated a critical political *economy* of consumption and materiality, but has neglected environmental resource conflicts. On the other hand, political ecology (with few exceptions) has neglected materiality as an important dimension of human–environmental relations.

Using the linkage between a tree species, Honduran mahogany (*Swietenia macrophylla*) and its transformation into an artefact (a Gibson Les Paul guitar), and based on fieldwork in a Mayan agro-forest community in Quintana Roo, Mexico, I propose and illustrate a framework for analysing material culture with political ecology. I call it 'enviromateriality'. I argue that this perspective enhances environmental anthropology by shedding light on the complex chain of production and transformations of mahogany into guitars and how the perceived properties of the material are used to market them. This examination also sheds light on how forest communities, guitar builders, and players are entangled in a meshwork of power relations, mediated by the making and the playing of the electric guitar.

Materials, materiality, enviromateriality

Although there is a wide and sophisticated literature on material culture studies, I was drawn into a debate between Ingold (2007) and Daniel Miller (2007) over the role of materials, their properties, and their consumption. This debate was initiated by Ingold, who challenged the field of material culture studies to pay more attention to the properties of 'materials' (Ingold 2012). This re-focus on materials by Ingold was a provocative response to materiality studies which, on his account, 'have hardly anything to say about *materials*' (2007: 1, his emphasis) because of their overwhelming focus on the consumption of objects that are finished products; for example, food, clothing, electronic devices, etc. For Ingold, materials are not fixed, but relational, because of how they are caught up in what he calls lifeworlds (i.e. people's everyday engagement with their environment).

In addition to the re-focus on the properties of materials, he also suggests that anthropologists should look at the process of making and transforming those materials (i.e. artisan labour) as an important and intimate aspect of human–environmental relations and materiality (Ingold 2013). In a chapter titled 'The Textility of Making', Ingold, following Deleuze and Guattari (1987), states that his aim is to overthrow the Aristotelian model of creation between form and matter by replacing it with 'an ontology that assigns primacy to the process of formation as against their final products' and to the 'flows and transformations of materials as against states of matter' (2011: 210). Ingold gives primacy to the interaction between the individual and the environment and the processes of transforming materials into things. In other words, he emphasizes the production process instead of consumption, as in his example of basket making and the plant material used. However, in many cases, these materials and processes are separated. For example, the mahogany agro-foresters and the guitar makers are not the same people. While Ingold importantly began the debate by suggesting a turn to the essence and properties of the 'material' (2007), I contend that this perspective offers too narrow an explanation and fails to account for larger, global processes and the material consequences for the use of a particular matter.

Responding in the same (2007) issue of *Archaeological Dialogues*, Miller contends that Ingold is wrong in his approach because today people deal with fully-produced commercial artefacts. For this reason, he argues, material culture studies focus on artefacts that are

> far removed from any claim to be natural substances. So the material processes we have to understand and whose qualities and consequences we document involve the life histories of not wood and stone but mobile phones, washing machines, tractors and sushi.
>
> *(Miller 2007: 26)*

To Miller, it is about the consumption of materials as objects and its ethnography, not pheno-menological contemplations about the materials, as Ingold seems to suggest. Miller says in the same response that materials are what Ingold, or anyone, 'wants them to be' (2007: 26). For instance, he states, 'I write books about the sari, not the silkworm', because if he had to write about the silkworm, 'it would have to include the impact of the life cycle of this worm on the political economy of silk production' (2007: 26). Miller negates the latter as not important because he thinks that the reason people are interested in silk is because of its vast consumption and dismisses both pre-product labour and the relations and knowledge of humans with their environs. In essence, commodity fetishism trumps the material. For Miller, it seems that the only meaning-making or relations of power of importance are from the consumption of the finished commodity.

So what about an object such as the Gibson Les Paul guitar? This instrument is an obvious commodity which is made with materials that do matter to builders and players and it helps exemplify what is missing in the Ingold–Miller debate. The material, mahogany, is important because it is entangled in the commodity that has been created and marketed by the guitar industry for its consumption. While I agree with Miller about the enormous significance that the political economy of consumption plays, I believe it comes up short. At the same time, bringing the argument back to the material, as Ingold does, is imperative as well, but also limited. There is an element of truth in both arguments.

At this juncture, Christopher Tilley (2007) tries to bridge this gap. He agrees with some aspects of Ingold's position, mainly the materiality of affordances that 'things' provide, as well as the phenomenological perspective in relation to materiality, finding 'that the sensuous world of material things has effects on the way people think and behave' (2007: 19). Nevertheless, he is not ready to take the extreme position that materials are more influential than materiality as Ingold suggests. Tilley's perspective on materials and materiality is based on the principle that '[a]ll materials have their properties which may be described but only *some* of these materials and their properties are significant to people' (Tilley 2007: 17, my emphasis). This raises questions for Tilley as to 'why some properties of things rather than others come to have significance' (2007: 20); 'what do these properties mean in different social and historical contexts', 'how they are experienced' (2007: 18); and finally, 'how they affect human conduct, both enabling and empowering people's lives and constraining them' (2007: 19). According to Tilley, *some* materials and their properties are more significant than others. This middle ground is not as extreme as Ingold on one side, and Miller on the other.

However, I believe there is still something missing in the analysis. I suggest that the missing piece is the ecology of the materials, and the extent to which the process of production and its consumption as a finished commodity are contributing to environmental degradation. I understand that this may not apply to all materials, as not all threaten local and global environments. However, in this case, and surely other cases can be found, the political ecology of the main material, Honduran mahogany, plays an important role. In my study, I ask if the use of mahogany is solely about its properties and its tonal qualities? Does it matter where it is grown, or who grows it, or what the labour relations are for the producers? Or what the environmental consequences are for mahogany and for forest communities that depend on it?

From production to consumption there are several moments of transformations, processes of becoming, from material to materiality that constitute in practice the expressions of a global political ecology and power relations that are not properly treated in the Ingold–Miller debate. It is in order to explain these moments that I developed the concept of 'enviromateriality', a perspective that articulates the phenomenological perspective of Ingold, the insights of material culture and materiality studies (Miller 2005; Tilley 2007) and global political ecology (Peet *et al.* 2011) to overcome the overemphasis on either the material or materiality and provide a richer analysis that takes into account the political ecology of materials.

Enviromateriality perspective

One of the ways to transcend this stalemate between Ingold and Miller is to be specific about what material or to what kind of artefact we are referring. As we know, not all artefacts share the same characteristics, or uses, and this plays a key role in how humans relate to them. Miller is thinking of cell phones while Ingold is talking about stones and artefacts made of wood. However, neither all trees nor all wood are the same or have the same meanings to people despite the fact that they are all trees and, if cut, wood. For example, some trees take 50 years or more to mature while others take much less time. Additionally, processed materials are not immaterial. While for some commodities, the material becomes part of the materiality – that is, it becomes an essential component – this is not to say that processed materials are immaterial. In the case of musical instruments, and more specifically, the electric guitar, mahogany becomes one of the 'some' to which Tilley refers whose material properties are important to people. Certainly, one can follow the plastic or other materials that make up a cell phone. This should not deter us from including a political ecology of plastics when conducting a study about them as the chemical industry contributes to health risks and environmental pollution.

A central component of the enviromateriality model is the perspective of political ecology. Political ecology is an established framework that incorporates the concerns of political economy, exploitation, and underdevelopment as a way to explain environmental degradation as a consequence of capitalism and conflicts over access to resources (e.g. Escobar 1999; Martínez-Alier 2002; Peet *et al.* 2011) and its cultural manifestations (Biersack 2006) in diverse biological and cultural regions of the world. Political ecology ethnographies have shown that forests, which are rich in biodiversity, are highly contested areas (e.g. Tsing 2005; Escobar 2008). Political ecology has documented and highlighted the sophisticated and diverse traditional ecological knowledge as well as the symbolic meanings of trees for forest dwellers. It has also countered the nature/culture ontological divide in modern theories (Ingold 2000; Descola 2006), and illuminated the importance of attachment to place for environmental social movements (Escobar 2008; Blaser 2010). As sustainable development and modern conservation strategies such as biosphere reserves began to have an impact on forest-dependent communities, political ecology scholars problematized biodiversity conservation (Brockington *et al.* 2008) and wood certification (Klooster 2010) as well as the role of corporations in forest conservation (Hardin 2011). In essence, political ecology provides a foundation to understand global wood and forest politics.

One limitation of political ecology is that it has never adequately tackled the question of materiality. There have been some efforts in the analysis of global natural resources or food crops, like coffee for instance, that raise questions about consumption and materiality (Dove 2011; West 2012), but they often do not explicitly take up material culture theory. Jane Bennett, a political theorist, has taken a first step. In her (2010) book, *Vibrant Matter: A Political Ecology of Things*, she engages philosophers' understanding of the concept of assemblages – particularly Spinoza, Deleuze, and Guattari – and, finally, Latour's (2006) actor–network theory (ANT). Her objective is to create 'a more horizontal representation of the relation between human and nonhuman actants' (2010: 98). She argues that materials are not inert, but rather 'act as quasi agents or forces with trajectories, propensities, or tendencies of their own' (2010: viii). In this case, political ecology is used more to engage environmentalism in the West and her plea is for changing environmentalism's rhetoric to 'vital materiality' by acknowledging that the vital materiality of animals and things, as part of horizontal assemblages, will challenge human hierarchies and human dominance of non-humans, and the resulting awareness will shift public opinion towards conservation. There are aspects that seem incongruous, as when she argues that '[v]arious materialities do not exercise exactly the same kind of agency, but neither is it easy to arrange them into a hierarchy' (2010: 98). I disagree with this statement, especially the latter part on hierarchy because as with other assemblages, it depends on the situation. For example, a Mayan farmer, who labours cutting mahogany, getting paid very little, and entering quasi debt-peonage relations with the mahogany exporters can be placed into a hierarchy.

Another problem with Bennett's 'political ecology of things' (and with Latour's ANT for that matter) is the overemphasis on the question of agency. I agree with Ingold who, like

Bennett, shares the idea that 'materials are inherently lively' (Ingold 2013: 96), but obsessing whether non-humans possess X or Y form of agency seems unproductive. Humans and non-humans are entangled in complex and dynamic relations because of such vitality of materials. Therefore, Ingold argues that 'we need a theory not of agency but of life' (2013: 97) . . . 'that allows matter its due as an active participant of the world's becoming' (Barad 2003, cited in Ingold 2013: 97). I would add that such a theory needs to pay attention and be sensitive to power relations between humans, as well as human–non-human relations, because they are at the heart of environmental problems such as deforestation.

Here I integrate political ecology and the importance of materiality through three phases. It goes from the materials and materiality and back again, in which materials turn into objects that produce a certain materiality. These phases are not mutually exclusive and are conceptual in nature. The first phase considers the material in question. This prompts several questions that are not exhaustive, but give an idea of the kind of power relations that are involved. What are its properties? What is its historical geography? In other words, in what ways has the material (mahogany) been entangled with people and how have they mutually influenced each other? What kind of division of labour is enacted? Who has access to the resources? Do the people own or have legal entitlements to the land, or are the people landless and engaging in illegal activities in order to maintain their livelihoods? What is the system of land tenure and how does it impact access to resources? What roles do gender, race, or ethnicity play? In addition to the political economy inquiry, materiality entanglements come to the surface. A particular materiality develops between people and resources in this phase and this needs exploration.

The second phase is the building and making. This phase acts as a sort of liminality in which the raw material is transformed into something else. This process of transition is a process of becoming. In the case of instrument making, instruments relied heavily on the process of enskillment (Ingold 2000). Today, it is an in-between transition that relies heavily on technologies and factories for mass production. However, this does not mean that luthier skills are not needed. In the case of guitars, machines can nowadays rough cut the basic shapes of the guitar as well as other hardware, but nevertheless, there is still a large amount of human skill involved in the fine details from sanding and finishing to adjusting all the hardware to make it playable. The division of labour is also present in the case of wage earners. Another important aspect is to understand the market forces that are behind the production of the commodity. There is a wide range of production of guitars from small independent luthiers to employees of large factories such as Gibson. Here, too, there is an experience of materiality between the wood in transformation and the builders comparable to the relation of the work of art and the artist (Dudley 2014).

The third phase is the consumption of the finished commodity. This is one of the main areas of the field of materiality studies, which has tackled issues of consumption in modern society, the materiality of body senses (including smells, taste, touch, vision, sounds), commodity exchange, and identity (Tilley 2007). The early work of Miller was influential in consumption studies because his work countered the anti-materialist assumption that all consumption is the expression of capitalism. His later work contributed to the materiality of everyday life (Miller 2005, 2010). Therefore, the experience of the fetishism of commodities is important as materiality studies have shown. In the case of the guitar, the aesthetics and feel of the instrument as material are important, but as a sounded instrument, it is the tonalities that emanate from the coupling of the player and the instrument that create its materiality. In the following section, I will elaborate on the three phases of the enviromateriality model as it pertains to mahogany and the artefact, the Gibson Les Paul guitar.

The material: Honduran mahogany

As a stringed instrument maker, Gibson has relied on what is commonly known in the guitar world as 'tonewoods'. These woods are selected to be used in instruments based on their characteristics of being a wood that is easy to work with using hand tools, has good resonance in the finished products, and in some cases, has a desired aesthetic appeal (colour consistency and grain patterns). Based on these elements, mahogany became an important source for the construction of mandolins and early acoustic guitars at the turn of the twentieth century. In the 1950s, when companies like Fender and Gibson, both pioneers of the electric guitar, came up with their designs, one of the defining features was that it had to have a solid body construction to prevent feedback when amplified. Mahogany became the main wood for the body and neck of Gibson Les Pauls in 1952.

Prior to its use in guitars, the global and material life of mahogany begins in the Americas. Honduran mahogany (*Swietenia macrophylla*) is considered to be the wood from trees of the botanical genus *Swietenia*, which is native to the Americas. Honduran mahogany grows naturally from the lowlands of the Yucatán peninsula, across Central America, to the north-western Amazon rainforest in South America. As a tree native to Mesoamerica, mahogany has had important use for its native inhabitants. It was used for building houses and other structures, for the construction of a musical instrument called the *tunkul*, a hollowed-out trunk used as a drum, and also for canoes. The 'natural' stands that exist today, while native, are not without human relations. The Maya helped to reproduce the species in the forest because mahogany benefits from the 'disturbance' caused by swidden agriculture (Atran 1993; Gomez-Pompa 1987; Steinberg 2005), as well as natural disturbances such as hurricanes (Snook 2003).

Trade and exploitation of Honduran mahogany began in Honduras and Belize by the British in the 1800s when Cuban mahogany (*Swietenia mahogani*), grown in the West Indies in the 1700s, declined (Bowett 1996). The main reason for its decline was its massive use for furniture and cabinetmaking in early Colonial America (Anderson 2012). This exploitation extended south to the north coast of Honduras and to the north of British Honduras to the Mayan territory of the eastern Yucatán (the area where I conducted my research), where the Maya were rebelling against Mexican elites in the Caste War of the Yucatán from 1847 to 1901.

Over the years, new challenges emerged to test Maya resilience and management of their environment amid capitalism-based development projects sponsored by the Mexican Government. The Government granted itself a 25-year concession from 1957 to 1982 in which it held exclusive rights to mahogany and other timber products. After the concession ended, and with the dire situation in which mahogany found itself, the Plan Piloto Forestal was implemented in order to guarantee the sustainability and regeneration of mahogany. The plan was seen as a success early on, and by the early 1990s, the Rainforest Alliance began their 'SmartWood' certification (predecessor to the Forest Stewardship Council), the programme through which Gibson sources its wood for guitars and which continues to the present day. In the next section, I briefly cover some of the dynamics of mahogany harvest in Southern Mexico in the Maya Forest, as well as Gibson's entry into the 'sustainable' mahogany trade.

One important facet of mahogany production is the labour and knowledge that go into growing and harvesting in order to supply the timber to the market. The amount of physical labour and the risk of serious injuries became evident to me while I was doing fieldwork. The community where I conducted research has been supplying mahogany to corporate concessions since its founding in the early 1900s, after the Mexican Government took control of the region. One elder of the community whose father worked harvesting mahogany told me, 'Imagine when my father worked in the *ka'ax* [forest in Maya], there were no electric saws like today . . . all work by hand and with donkeys to pull the *kanak che'* [mahogany]'. And he continued, 'You had to stay several days in there [forest], sawing, sleeping in hammocks, then bring it little by little to the main road. No trucks like today!' Although it does seem that it was intense labour in those days, that doesn't mean it doesn't continue to be. Working in the dense tropical bug-filled forest is still no easy feat.

Since the launch of the SmartWood series, Gibson has been employing 'green' rhetoric by arguing that countries should have a certification system so that the market can pay premium prices for the wood and thus combat the causes of deforestation. According to my source, Gibson pays mahogany growers in Central America $7 per neck blank (which makes two necks) and $5 for a body blank. The body and the neck are the foundation of the guitar. These will end up in guitars that will retail between $1,000 on the lower end to $7,500 for Custom Shop on the higher end, with some limited production artist replicas costing over $10,000. That is a vast amount of profit. The notion that communities that grow mahogany should get paid better is something that I heard them say repeatedly. In Mexico, mahogany can be harvested at a minimum of 25 years, although experts agree that proper quality mahogany should be over 50 years old to reach the optimum size.

Once the wood is exported out of Mexico, it reaches the factory to continue its process of becoming and transforming. Unlike traditional luthiery, in which the instrument maker works on every aspect of the production of the instrument from beginning to end, the Gibson Les Paul is mass-produced in a factory facilitated by special machinery and a division of labour between the different stages of production in an assembly line. The cutting of the bodies and necks, glueing, applying binding and inlays, installing and levelling frets, sanding, applying colour and finish, installing electronics, stringing the instrument, and setting up for optimum playability by adjusting neck and intonation are all done by different work groups.

What is the materiality of 'mahogany guitar' for people that work in the factories? For builders it is a livelihood, but working with the materials that end up in the guitar has its own materiality. If we go back to Ingold (above), we remember that his project is to assign primacy to the *process of formation* over final products. That means that in this case, he would have given primacy to each individual worker as they engage with their specific tasks with the material. He argues that when the carpenter works, there is more than meets the eye in terms of the dynamic between the wood and her (or him): 'no two strokes of the saw are quite alike' (Ingold 2011: 216). While I agree this is true, there is more to the story, but Ingold doesn't continue. Factory employees who spend all day sanding necks, which is a task that needs a particular skill and feel for the wood and shape, are there as wage earners. Giving primacy of production to an independent luthier is different than giving it to a wage earner who produces one or two tasks in a factory.

Although Ingold is inspired by the work of Deleuze and Guattari because of their insistence on the vital material assemblages of people and materials, there is one aspect that he neglects. This is the 'apparatus of capture', which refers to appropriation of land and labour by capitalists and the unequal exchange that develops from unequal relations, which forms *another kind of assemblage*. This assemblage gives rise to flows of money, labour, and property (Deleuze and Guattari 1987: 449), which are correlate to the apparatus of capture, socially and geographically extending not only to Europe and North America, but also parts of the so-called Third World. The enviromateriality perspective incorporates the capital–labour dynamic as an essential component of the material–materiality assemblage.

In this case, the Gibson company is the one that controls this aspect of the flow of capital in the mahogany–Les Paul vital constellation. The flow of the Gibson production produces 400 guitars per day. The Les Paul model is by far its most popular. It also represents all other elements of contemporary capitalist practices including wage-labour and fetishism of commodities. In the end, whatever object-commodity they produce on a daily basis has its own hidden histories and has become without question one of the most powerful symbols in popular culture and popular music in the last six decades, the Gibson Les Paul.

The Les Paul: material and materiality

The electric guitar has been truly revolutionary in Western popular music since its creation. It took the guitar from the background of musical groups into the forefront, not only as a symbol, but as the new amplified sounds took over emerging sounds (Attali 1985), particularly for rock'n'roll. The influence that particular instruments give to forms of music is unquestionable. As Jacques Attali reminds us:

> Music should be a reminder to others that if *Incontri* was not written for a symphony orchestra, or the *Lamentations* for the electric guitar, it is because each instrument, each tool, theoretical or concrete, implies a sound field, a field of knowledge, an imaginable and explorable universe.
>
> *(Attali 1985: 133)*

In effect, the electric guitar created a new, distinct element in the music world. An element that turned this object into an instrument of desire that influenced several domains of society: youth, gender, race, and class (Waksman 1999).

Of the solid body guitars, the Gibson Les Paul is one of the most iconic. Paradoxically, Gibson phased out the Les Paul in 1960 – until a new wave of British and American musicians rediscovered the Les Paul, influencing with their music a new generation of guitar players (Bacon 2008). It sparked interest in the discontinued guitar and, little by little, it became one of the most sought-after instruments. There were approximately 1,700 made between 1958 and 1960. Today they are valued between $100,000 and $250,000 depending on the condition and history.

Apart from the availability, what is it about these mass-produced guitars that makes them so popular? Dan Erlewine, a renowned luthier and author of many books on building and repairing guitars, wrote an article (1998), 'Majesty in Mahogany: What Makes a Vintage Les Paul Tick' in *Guitar Player* magazine discussing what it is about the Les Paul that makes many players desire to own one. As the title suggests, one of the keys to the sound is the material foundation.

> Tonewood selection is part of Gibson's heritage, and they have always offered guitars built, at least in part, from select Honduras mahogany. Honduras [sic] is stable, good-looking, great sounding, and reasonably lightweight. It produces the warm, sweet, midrangy tone for which many Gibson guitars—both electric and acoustic— are famous.
>
> *(Erlewine 1998: 113)*

The guitar is the result of the combination of several materials: wood, metals, electronics, and plastic. Each contributes to the artefact's totality and with the help of a talented player can produce a wide range of sounds. But not all materials are the same or project the same sound. This is why Ingold's argument about going back to the material is well founded.

Additionally, the commoditization and fetishism associated with it matter. Gibson restarted mass production of the Les Paul in the early 1970s. By then, there was new management and the new Les Pauls were not quite the same as the 1950s models. In the 1980s, Les Pauls fell temporarily out of fashion, only to have an economic revival among younger players but also with 'amateur boomer guitarists' (Ryan and Peterson 2001) who grew up listening to the guitar heroes of their youth and who had more money to spend on guitars. Some became performers, others gave up, still others were content with being 'bedroom' players. Other players collect vintage Les Pauls that again go for over $100,000, or the reproductions that Gibson began to produce in the early 1990s. One trend that began to develop is the practice of 'relic-ing'; that is, of building and selling new guitars with signs of use and wear, as if they were relics or vintage instruments. This is somewhat similar to what Miller observes in his denim project about jeans being stonewashed to make them feel already aged and worn (2012: 94). Replicas are artificially aged, their steel hardware is distressed, nicks and dings are added to make the guitar look like a vintage instrument of 30+ years. This supports Miller's claim of the importance of materiality, and yet the wood materials continue to matter to the consumer.

Conclusion

The primary purpose of this chapter was to put forward the perspective of enviromateriality as a framework of analysis that links material culture studies with political ecology. The material–materiality debate sparked by Ingold and Miller has provided a good platform to rethink the strengths and limitations of each perspective. In this case, their debate has allowed me to illustrate enviromateriality and provide an overview of the material–materiality nexus using the Gibson Les Paul guitar and its main material, mahogany, historically as well as in different stages of production and consumption. I argued that enviromateriality enables us to break the impasse between material and materiality. The idea of objects having their histories in relation to others underscores the fact that they are not static. Such conditions reinforce the fact that guitar playing, and music in general, are important in shaping identities and imagined communities of guitar players and consumers of music. However, we must not forget what lies within global commodities. Marx initiated the critique with the discussion of commodity fetishism and capitalism's power to transform materials into commodities while hiding their real value, but as Carrier (2010) reminds us, it goes beyond that. It is also about abstracting people, processes, places, whether material or not.

References

Anderson, J (2012) *Mahogany: The Cost of Luxury in Early America*. Cambridge, MA: Harvard University Press.

Attali, J (1985) *Noise: The Political Economy of Music*. Minneapolis: University of Minnesota Press.

Atran, S (1993) Itzá Maya Tropical Agroforestry. *Current Anthropology* 14(5): 633–700.

Bacon, T (2008) *Million Dollar Les Paul: In Search of the Most Valuable Guitar in the World*. London: Jawbone Press.

Bennett, J (2010) *Vibrant Matter: A Political Ecology of Things*. Durham, NC: Duke University Press.

Biersack, A (2006) Reimagining Political Ecology: Culture/Power/History/Nature. In A Biersack and J Greenberg (eds) *Reimagining Political Ecology*. Durham, NC: Duke University Press, pp. 3–40.

Blaser, M (2010) *Storytelling Globalization*. Durham, NC: Duke University Press.

Bowett, A (1996) The English Mahogany Trade. PhD dissertation, Brunel University.

Brockington, D, R Duffy and J Igoe (2008) *Nature Unbound: Conservation, Capitalism, and the Future of Protected Areas*. London: Earthscan.

Carrier, J (2010) Protecting the Environment the Natural Way: Ethical Consumption and Commodity Fetishism. *Antipode* 42(3): 672–689.

Deleuze, G and F Guattari (1987) *A Thousand Plateaus*. Minneapolis: University of Minnesota Press.

Descola, P (2006) Beyond Nature and Culture. *Proceedings of the British Academy* 139: 137–155.

Dove, M (2011) *The Banana Tree at the Gate: A History of Marginal Peoples and Global Markets in Borneo*. New Haven, CT: Yale University Press.

Dudley, K (2014) Guitar Makers: The Endurance of Artisanal Values in North America. Chicago, IL: University of Chicago Press.

Erlewine, D (1998) Majesty in Mahogany: What Makes a Vintage Les Paul Tick. *Guitar Player*, December, p. 113.

Escobar, A (1999) After Nature: Elements for a Post Structuralist Political Ecology. *Current Anthropology* 40(1): 1–30.

Escobar, A (2008) *Territories of Difference*. Durham, NC: Duke University Press.

Gomez-Pompa, A (1987) On Maya Silviculture. *Mexican Studies/Estudios Mexicanos* 3(1): 1–17.

Hardin, R (2011) Concessionary Politics: Property, Patronage, and Political Rivalry in Central African Forest Management. *Current Anthropology* 52(3): S113–S125.

Ingold, T (2000) *Perception of the Environment*. London: Routledge.

Ingold, T (2007) Materials against Materiality. *Archaeological Dialogues* 14(1): 1–16.

Ingold, T (2011) *Being Alive: Essays in Knowledge, Movement, and Description*. London: Routledge.

Ingold, T (2012) Toward an Ecology of Materials. *Annual Review of Anthropology* 41: 427–442.

Ingold, T (2013) *Making*. London: Routledge.

Klooster, D (2010) Standardizing Sustainable Development? The Forest Stewardship Council's Plantation Policy Review Process as Neoliberal Environmental Governance. *Geoforum* 41(1): 117–129.

Latour, B (2006) *Reassembling the Social: An Introduction to Actor–Network Theory*. Oxford: Oxford University Press.

Martínez–Alier, J (2002) *The Environmentalism of the Poor: A Study of Environmental Conflict and Valuation*. Cheltenham, UK: Edward Elgar.

Miller, D (2005) Materiality: An Introduction. In D Miller (ed.) *Materiality*. Durham, NC: Duke University Press, pp. 1–50.

Miller, D (2007) Stone Age or Plastic Age? *Archaeological Dialogues* 14(1): 23–27.

Miller, D (2010) *Stuff*. Cambridge, UK: Polity Press.

Miller, D (2012) *Consumption and its Discontents*. Cambridge, UK: Polity Press.

Peet, R, P Robbins and M Watts (eds) (2011) *Global Political Ecology*. London: Routledge.

Ryan, J and Peterson, R A (2001) The Guitar as Artifact and Icon: Identity Formation in the Babyboom Generation. In A Bennett and K Dawe (eds) *Guitar Culture*. Oxford: Berg, pp. 89–116.

Snook, L (2003) Regeneration, Growth, and Sustainability of Mahogany in Mexico's Yucatán Forests. In A Lugo, P Figueroa and M Alayón (eds) *Big-leaf Mahogany: Genetics, Ecology, and Management*. New York: Springer, pp. 169–192.

Steinberg, M (2005) Mahogany (*Swietenia Macrophylla*) in the Maya Lowlands: Implications for Past Land Use and Environmental Change? *Journal of Latin American Geography* 4(1): 127–134.

Tilley, C (2007) Materiality in Materials. *Archaeological Dialogues* 14(1): 16–20.

Tsing, A (2005) *Friction: An Ethnography of Global Connection*. Princeton, NJ: Princeton University Press.

Waksman, S (1999) *Instruments of Desire: The Electric Guitar and the Shaping of Musical Experience*. Cambridge, MA: Harvard University Press.

West, P (2012) *From Modern Production to Imagined Primitive: The Social World of Coffee from Papua New Guinea*. Durham, NC: Duke University Press.

7

HISTORICAL ECOLOGY

Agency in human–environment interaction

Lauren Dodaro and Dustin Reuther

Introduction: what is historical ecology?

In anthropology, *historical ecology* focuses on human–environment interactions throughout time as well as the outcomes that those interactions have had and may have both locally and globally (Balée 2006; Crumley 1994; Szabó 2014). Historical ecology is a *research program*, meaning it is composed of proposed interdependent and fundamental principles with which some, but not necessarily all, members of the scientific community agree (Balée 2006; Lakatos 1980). Like much of anthropology, historical ecology is interdisciplinary, relying on a wide variety of data from archival sources to the natural sciences (Szabó 2014). The four fundamental principles (Balée 2006) of historical ecology are:

1   nearly all of Earth's environments have been affected by humans;
2   humans are not inherently harmful or helpful to the environment;
3   different societies impact landscapes to varying degrees and in different ways depending on socioeconomic, political, and cultural factors;
4   a wide variety of human–environment interactions differing in both historical and ecological contexts may be studied as a total phenomenon.

Historical ecology differs from the concept of *cultural ecology* in environmental anthropological theory in that historical ecology is not deterministic. Cultural ecologists, such as Julian Steward (1948, 1949) view the environment as a determining factor in the culture of the people dwelling therein. Unlike cultural ecology, historical ecology holds instead that while the environment plays a role in shaping human culture, it does not determine human culture. Thus, historical ecology considers the *agency* of people. Agency is one's ability to make decisions that make an impact; it is one's power, influence, and instrumentality. Historical ecology acknowledges people's agency to make choices that are not predetermined by the environment; instead, the environment is a factor that both impacts and is impacted by people.

Historical ecologists utilize a number of terms to talk about the reciprocal impact between humans and the environment. These interactions between humans, other biological agents, and the physical environment coalesce to create a *landscape*. Historical ecologists are especially interested in the effects of the interactions over various temporal scales, or in other words, how landscapes change over time. Species diversity is often used as a primary means of measuring changes within landscapes. *Alpha diversity* refers to species' diversity within a specific, confined, locale. *Beta diversity* looks at diversity across an environmental gradient. Finally, *gamma diversity* looks at diversity across a region that comprises multiple environments (e.g. the Amazon). Shifts in species diversity either come about through *primary landscape transformations*, in which there is a complete turnover in species diversity (e.g. clearcutting a forest and building a parking lot over the top), or *secondary landscape transformations*, in which there is only partial turnover in species diversity (e.g. making small clearings in a larger forest to cultivate plants) (Balée 2013). These transformations beget *contingent diversity*, the case in which a locale's diversity is (or has been) contingent on human activity (Balée 2013).

Scholars such as Crutzen and Stoermer (2000) posit that the rate and magnitude of human impact on Earth has escalated enough to call the geological period that we live in the Anthropocene, or the age of humans. Other scholars such as Ruddiman (2013) debate the details of when the Anthropocene began, depending on how one quantifies domesticated landscapes over time. Regardless of its start date, human activity has had an extreme impact on the current state of the climate, the landscape, the oceans, etc., in the form of either primary or secondary landscape transformation. This impact is so extreme that even areas of the planet that scholars had once deemed "untouched" by humans are now being brought into question. For example, only recently have scholars realized the pivotal role that humans have played in creating the biodiversity makeup, the soil, and the landscape features of some forests in Amazonia, Malesia, and western sub-Saharan Africa (Fairhead and Leach 1996; Ruddiman 2013); these anthropogenic landscapes are known as cultural forests—forests that have been used and modified by people—and their human-influenced history is not always readily apparent, instead requiring deep investigation.

Human-impacted landscapes are not always created intentionally. Therefore, a combination of humans' intentional and unintentional environmental transformation toward a productive landscape for the use of humans (and other species) creates a *domesticated landscape*, or an environment that has been impacted by humans (Erickson 2002). These transformations revolve around "resource creation and management," with a focus on "diversity, distribution, and availability of species" (Erickson 2002: 158) for increased usefulness to humans. Clement (2002: 165) defines landscape domestication as a "human manipulation of the landscape" that leads to "changes in landscape ecology" as well as the flora and fauna demographics, "resulting in a landscape more productive and congenial for humans."

Historical ecology contests the concept that it is possible for an environment in which people live to be pristine (Wolf 1982), such as the Amazon basin (Balée 1989, 2006; Denevan 1992). This is linked to notions of a distinct difference between the "natural" and the "human" world that have skewed understanding of Amazonia's history. According to such notions, humans exist in contrast to "wild" and "pristine" Amazonian forests (see Crist 2004). Modern-day economic extractive activities confounded scholars' view of the human impact on Amazonia: the agriculture, cattle farming, logging, mining, and city-building of the twentieth century have degraded Amazonia's environment to an extreme and lead people to conclude that any widespread human activity would do the same; prehistory, however, shows us otherwise (Erickson 2002). Furthermore, in the human/nature dichotomy, problematic Rousseauian ideals have created an image of the indigenous Amazonian as a noble savage, frozen in time and part of the nature side of this constructed dichotomy (Hames 2007). This is incorrect and has clouded people's view of human impact in Amazonia. The landscape of

Amazonia exists in part as the result of indigenous knowledge of resource creation/management and land use (Erickson 2002: 158).

Case studies: the Amazon basin

The model of the environment limiting human culture is challenged by the lives of pre-Columbian Amazonians who participated in a number of activities and practices (species encouragement and transplanting, forest management, burning, settlement, agriculture, fertility management, etc.) in which they demonstrated control over the environment. Amazonia covers a vast area of South America and therefore the undocumented history of pre-contact Amazonians probably included a variety of human culture throughout that area. While the pre-contact history of Amazonia is a highly contested issue (see Balée 2013; Barlow *et al.* 2011; McMichael *et al.* 2012), research has uncovered some cases in which it is evident that some pre-Columbian Amazonians altered the landscape to increase its usefulness and even sustainability to humans.

Case study: Amazonian dark earth

Highly productive, anthropogenic soils, called Amazonian dark earths (henceforth referred to as ADE), are one of the key features informing scholars today that pre-Columbian peoples did not simply adapt to the minimally productive soil of the Amazon, but rather improved and managed the soil for subsistence production (Erickson 2002). Other monikers include "Indian black earth" or "*terra preta do indio.*" Amazonian dark earth is an ancient, human-produced soil found in an estimated 0.1 to 10 percent (6,000 to 600,000 km²) of the Amazon basin (Erickson 2002: 71). The natural soil of the Amazon basin is generally unproductive and unable to sustain agricultural growth for large populations of humans, lacking essential nutrients, such as carbon and phosphorous (Meggers 1996). People overcame this limitation with ADE. The ability of ADE to support a large number of people is suggested by the multitude of archeological sites found to have ADE (Woods and McCann 1999). These sites range in size from as small as < 1 hectare to as large as 200 hectares (Erickson 2002: 71). Initially, ADE was probably unintentionally created in the refuse piles outside people's dwellings. However, it could not have taken long for people to realize the value of the soil and they eventually began to deliberately produce ADE for increased growth of useful plants.

Amazonian dark earths achieve their high productivity from admixtures combined with Amazonian soils. The added components represent items typically associated with refuse created from human habitation, such as plant matter, animal remains, and pottery fragments (which are found in nearly all ADE soils), resulting in a soil that is high in carbon, calcium, zinc, manganese, and phosphorus, and less acidic than surrounding, non-anthropogenic soils (Tsai *et al.* 2009). This compost-heavy sediment also acts as an incubator for an extremely rich array of microbial content. In fact, ADEs have been shown to actually "grow" through their microbial activity (Neves *et al.* 2004; Smith 1980).

It is this later property, the ability to grow, that contributes to the more interesting form of anthropogenic soils in the region, called *terra mulata*. *Terra mulata* lacks much of the archeological content common in other ADEs. Instead, it is thought that people primed future agricultural fields by first doing a "cool burn," or low-heat incomplete combustion, of existing forest, before possibly adding microbes by transplanting ADE soils (Balée 2010). In fact, some researchers argue

---

that *terra mulata* allowed for the growth of the more nutrient-intensive bitter manioc, leading to a massive population explosion in the Amazon around 1500 BP (Arroyo-Kalin 2010), though evidence for other ADE first shows up around 4700 BP in the southwest Amazon (Neves and Peterson 2006).

According to Erickson (2002), ADE's primary purposes probably ranged from settlement, to house gardens, and also permanent fields (as opposed to today's more common swidden agriculture). Its presence is important as it provides evidence that some pre-Columbian Amazonian people were able to grow much more of their sustenance than the regular soil of the area would allow. We now know that at least some pre-Columbian Amazonian people overcame the limitation of the natural soil by employing their agency via landscape transformation. However, the exact process by which ADE is created remains speculative today; knowledge of the intricacies of the process as it existed in pre-Columbian times was lost with along with 90 percent of the indigenous population after the arrival of Europeans (Hecht 2004).

Case study: Llanos de Mojos

While people transformed sections of forest into garden plots with ADEs, other areas of the Amazon show vast modifications of entire regions by human hands. This is especially visible in the Llanos de Mojos area of northern Bolivia. The environment of the region is characterized by "pampas," which are seasonally inundated savannahs. Extreme environmental fluctuations between wet-season flooding and dry-season droughts make the establishment of tropical forests, as well as agricultural sites, difficult. Yet, archeologically this region demonstrates strong evidence for large pre-Columbian populations (Denevan 1992; Erickson 2010).

The landscape of the Llanos de Mojos is a "palimpsest" of past human activity, made legible through multidisciplinary approaches that embrace the shared concept of historical ecology (Erickson and Balée 2006). Inhabitants of the region burned, and continue to burn, vast swaths of the savannah, removing old growth to make the region more attractive for animals (Erickson 2006). Repeated burnings over centuries nurtured an environmental regime acclimated to continuous burnings and favorable for hunting conditions. On this savannah, humans erected more than 35,000 raised fields, starting around 2400 BP (Denevan 2001). These fields have sustained many of their major agriculture crops, such as manioc, by keeping them out of seasonal floodwaters. Even today, these fields are still visible due to environmental reinforcing systems, such as termites, which deposit organic matter on the mounds (McKey *et al.* 2010). These fields supplied agricultural products for a population that lived in and around an estimated 10,000 anthropogenic earthen mounds, some of which covered over nine hectares (Erickson and Balée 2006; Lee 1995, as cited in Erickson 2006). Along with these earthworks were scattered an assortment of causeways, canals, fish weirs, and ring ditch sites which regulated human traffic as well as water flow. The mounds, and the forests around them, also support a rich array of biodiversity. Though the savannah normally lacks forest cover, with seasonal weather extremes making it difficult for trees to establish themselves, mounds, causeways, and surrounding areas are more conducive as habitats and typically harbor trees (Erickson 2006). Two forest inventories, one done on a mound and another done in a nearby forest on the savannah, demonstrate a surprising amount of fruit trees in both inventories, as well as a large amount of trees considered useful to humans in general, with the inventory on the mound containing slightly more of the latter (Erickson and Balée 2006). The biodiversity of plant life on and around the mounds is indicative of past human activity, and contributed a valuable resource to past populations, especially as it stands in contrast to the dearth of tree species typically found on the savannah in general.

Historical ecology approaches combine methods from disciplines such as geography, archeology, and ecology, evincing a clear case for conceptualizing the Llanos de Mojos as a domesticated landscape. The sheer amount of earthmoving involved in the landscape modifications would have required a sizable population, one that was able to maintain a presence in the region for thousands of years, up until contact with Europeans (Mann 2008). Despite the fact that savannah habitats are often viewed as marginal in regard to agricultural potential due to extreme seasonality, human settlements flourished in this region. This is due to the fact that anthropogenic hydrological manipulation, at the scale of the landscape, created a mosaic of ecotones, helping to augment biodiversity, especially in regard to plants holding high utilitarian value to human populations (Balée and Erickson 2006; Erickson 2010; Levis *et al.* 2012; Mayle *et al.* 2007; Plotkin 2011). Effort focused on the landscape as a whole, instead of toward a small number of individual crop species. In turn, this effort produced a landscape more productive for humans, and richer in biodiversity than one without human influences.

Historical ecology and cognitive anthropology

Historical ecology is also a useful lens through which to research contemporary peoples' relationships with their local environments. It is a helpful tool in understanding how people conceptualize their environment. Indigenous peoples, for example, have a long historical, practical connection to specific locales, and often acutely perceive ecological processes as a result of this connection. This knowledge of their local environment may encode information about human activity (Berlin 1992; Posey 2002). For instance, the utility that people recognize in a plant (such as medicinal properties) informs how they interact with that plant. More theoretically, re-examining the local environmental elements that people perceive helps to determine intentionality in landscape modifications (i.e. people do not intentionally alter something that they do not recognize as a *thing*).

Case study: freelisting and the Ka'apor

Freelisting is one of the ethnographic tools that historical ecologists use to analyze these perceptions people have of their environment—how they conceive their local environment. In freelisting, a researcher asks informants to supply a list of names within particular domains (e.g. "List all the tree names you know."). Freelists can be analyzed for a wide variety of information (Bernard 2011). Most commonly, they are utilized to determine the salience of items to informants, working from the premise that people list psychologically salient items first. The salience of an item reflects its importance to the individual and group (Balée 2013). For example, US students often list cats or dogs first when responding to freelists asking them for animal names. People also tend to clump items together in loose sub-domains; for example, North American students tend to list zoo animals or farm animals together in the same animal-name freelists (Borgatti 1996). Thus, freelists can also examine how people relate items within a domain (e.g. animals) to each other, hinting at sub-domains that aren't always explicitly labeled (Posey 2002). Differences in responses among members of a study population can further be analyzed in terms of cultural consensus; that is, recognizing answers with a strong consensus as a cultural "truth" (Borgatti 1996). Answers that differ from such a consensus reflect a lack of cultural knowledge within a particular domain. Freelists then, give themselves to a wide range of analytical tools

William Balée (2013) has employed freelists in his research with the Ka'apor, an eastern Amazonian Tupi-Guarani-speaking indigenous group, to better discern their role in the historical ecology of the region. Balée compared the tree and vine composition of eight 1-hectare forest inventories with freelist data. He did four of these inventories in "old fallow" forests—that is, at some time between 80 and 200 years ago, they were used by the Ka'apor as swidden agriculture fields. Conversely, four plots were in "high forest"—that is, they had been unaffected by significant human modification for at least 200 years, and probably longer (Balée 1994). The two forest types only shared roughly 11 percent of the same species, with old fallow forests containing a greater number of palms and fruit trees.

Interestingly, when asked to freelist tree names, the most salient tree (*Handroanthus impetiginosus*) was one found almost exclusively within old fallow forests (Balée 2013). While Ka'apor labeled old fallow and high forests with different terms, researchers also wanted to know if they thought about them in terms of differing species composition. For example, perhaps they were classified differently because of historical associations. Researchers asked Ka'apor to list trees of *anthropogenic forests*. They compared this list to the 20 most ecologically important trees (calculated by relative density, frequency, and dominance) of old fallows and high forests. Nine of the top 20 most salient anthropogenic trees corresponded to trees in the top twenty most ecologically important for old fallows, while only three of the most salient corresponded with trees in the top 20 most ecologically important for high forests (with one tree shared between lists for top ecological importance between the two). Thus, not only are anthropogenic disturbance-contingent trees highly salient for the Ka'apor (e.g. *Handroanthus impetiginosus*), but the Ka'apor evidently distinguish species composition of the inventoried plots as human activity-related. With this information, researchers have a better grasp of how the Ka'apor think about their own historical ecology in the region, as well as the Ka'apor's contribution to it.

Applied historical ecology

Today, the scholarly discussion of human agency within human–environment interactions is more timely and pressing than ever. Applied historical ecology, also known as restoration ecology (Balée 2006), allows scholars not only to examine critical topics such as sustainability and resilience (Petty *et al.* 2014), but also to apply that examination to solving real-world problems. In a time when human activity poses a major threat to the environment, historical ecology is an invaluable tool to be applied to problem-solving and policy-making related to social-ecological systems (SES).

Case study: aboriginal fire management

Petty *et al.* (2014) discuss the critical role that applied historical ecology has played in fire management in northern Australia's tropical savannah Kakadu National Park. The park is prone to fires during the dry season. Before the arrival of humans to the area, these fires were caused only by lightning—particularly toward the end of the season when the landscape was the driest—and though the fires were less numerous than when people were present, they were much grander in scale and more destructive. Historically, aboriginal land management practices included small, controlled burnings organized by family units responsible for the land, helping to regulate the fires throughout the dry season and minimize their damage; however, European settlement in the area disrupted these practices in the late nineteenth century.

With significant decreases in aboriginal land management practices in the area, the proportion of fires during the late dry season over the early dry season had clearly increased by the mid-twentieth century (Russell-Smith and Edwards 2006). Not only a safety concern, these numerous late dry-season fires destroyed plant species that had once been protected by the anthropogenic fires. Examination of the area's ethnohistory made clear to contemporary policy-makers the once widespread aboriginal land management practices that had thrived at the core of a successful social-ecological system. Thus, by the 1990s, the Australian government implemented a controlled burn program inspired by the aboriginal methods (Petty *et al.* 2014).

Due to the present sociocultural context of Kakadu National Park, there are some major differences between the current government-mandated burn program and the aboriginal method. For example, the logistical constraints of carrying out the burns by foot led to the decision to control the burns from helicopters. Also, rather than spreading out the fires relatively evenly throughout the season, the program involves more fires early on so as to avoid the potentially most destructive late dry-season fires. The contemporary fire management practice does reduce the number of massive and widely dangerous fires in the area, though it is still unclear whether or not it has made an impact in reviving the plant diversity (Petty *et al.* 2014).

Conclusion

Historical ecology is an invaluable research tool, both in scholarly research and applied research, as in policy-making. Central concepts associated with historical ecology, such as the domesticated landscape and the significance of human agency, allow researchers to frame human–environment interactions in its dynamic reality. As demonstrated in this chapter, historical ecology has been instrumental in reshaping scholarly understanding of the past, particularly in locales lacking in extensive historic documentation, like pre-Columbian Amazonia. Lessons that scholars have learned from examining the past through the lens of historical ecology have been numerous. Just in this chapter, we have looked at ADEs, the anthropogenic soils of Amazonia that allowed past populations to thrive beyond the limitations of the region's natural soil; the Llanos de Mojos, where a significant amount of human labor effort is evident on the landscape today; and the once widespread aboriginal fire management practices of northern Australia, that have been re-employed to solve contemporary fire management issues.

Indeed, in the context of extreme worldwide human-mediated disturbance (Balée 2013), or the Anthropocene, understanding social-ecological systems (SES) is a critical part of social research today; the outcomes of past human–environment interactions have implications for future outcomes. Through disciplines such as archeology, ethnohistory, ethnobiology, geology, and geography, scholars can understand the past as an environmental reference; however, applying that referential knowledge today requires the additional understanding of the current setting (social, political, economic, etc.), different from the setting of the past, and how that affects the choices around and outcomes of applied historical ecology.

References

Arroyo-Kalin M 2010. The Amazonian Formative: Crop Domestication and Anthropogenic Soils. *Diversity* 2(4): 473–504.

Balée W 1989. The Culture of Amazonian Forests. In D A Posey and W Balée (eds) *Resource Management in Amazonia: Indigenous and Folk Strategies*. Advances in Economic Botany, Vol. 7. Bronx, NY: New York Botanical Garden Press, pp. 1–21.

Balée W 1994. *Footprints of the Forest : Ka'apor Ethnobotany—the Historical Ecology of Plant Utilization by an Amazonian People*. New York: Columbia University Press.

Balée W 2006. The Research Program of Historical Ecology. *Annual Review of Anthropology* 35(1): 75–98.

Balée W 2010. Amazonian Dark Earths. Review of J Lehmann, D C Kern, B Glaser and W I Woods (eds) *Amazonian Dark Earths: Origins, Properties, Management*; B Glaser and W I Woods (eds) *Amazonian Dark Earths: Explorations in Space and Time*; and W I Woods, W G Teixeira, J Lehmann, C Steiner, A M G A WinklerPrins and L Rebellato (eds) *Amazonian Dark Earths: Wim Sombroek's Vision. Tipití: Journal of the Society for the Anthropology of Lowland South America* 8(1): Article 3.

Balée W 2013. *Cultural Forests of the Amazon: A Historical Ecology of People and their Landscape*. Tuscaloosa: The University of Alabama Press.

Balée W and Erickson C L (eds) 2006. *Time and Complexity in Historical Ecology: Studies in the Neotropical Lowlands*. New York: Columbia University Press.

Barlow J, Gardner T A, Lees A C, Parry L and Peres C A 2011. How Pristine are Tropical Forests? An Ecological Perspective on the Pre-Columbian Human Footprint in Amazonia and Implications for Contemporary Conservation. *Biological Conservation* 151(1): 1–5.

Berlin B 1992. *Ethnobiological Classification : Principles of Categorization of Plants and Animals in Traditional Societies*. Princeton, NJ: Princeton University Press.

Bernard H R 2011. *Research Methods in Anthropology: Qualitative and Quantitative Approaches*. Lanham, MD: AltaMira.

Borgatti S 1996. *ANTHROPAC 4 Methods Guide*. Natick, MA: Analytic Technologies.

Clement C R 2002. Fruit Trees and the Transition to Food Production in Amazonia. In W Balée and C L Erickson (eds) *Time and Complexity in Historical Ecology: Studies in the Neotropical Lowlands*. New York: Columbia University Press, pp. 165–186.

Crist E 2004. Against the Social Construction of Nature and Wilderness. *Environmental Ethics* 26(1): 5–23.

Crumley C L (ed.) 1994. *Historical Ecology: Cultural Knowledge and Changing Landscapes*. Santa Fe, NM: School of American Research Press.

Crutzen P J and Stoermer E F 2000. The "Anthropocene." *IGBP Global Newsletter* 41: 12–14.

Denevan W M 1992. The Pristine Myth: The Landscape of the Americas in 1492. *Annals of the Association of American Geographers* 82(3): 369–385.

Denevan W M 2001. *Cultivated Landscapes of Native Amazonia and the Andes: Triumph over the Soil*. New York: Oxford University Press.

Erickson C L 2002. Amazonia: The Historical Ecology of a Domesticated Landscape. In H Silverman and W H Isbell (eds) *Handbook of South American Archaeology*. New York: Springer, pp. 157–183.

Erickson C L 2006. The Domesticated Landscape of the Bolivian Amazon. In W Balée and C L Erickson (eds) *Time and Complexity in Historical Ecology: Studies in the Neotropical Lowlands*. New York: Columbia University Press, pp. 235–278.

Erickson C L 2010. The Transformation of Environment into Landscape: The Historical Ecology of Monumental Earthwork Construction in the Bolivian Amazon. *Diversity* 2(4): 618–652.

Erickson C L and Balée W 2006. The Historical Ecology of a Complex Landscape in Bolivia. In W Balée and C L Erickson (eds) *Time and Complexity in Historical Ecology: Studies in the Neotropical Lowlands*. New York: Columbia University Press, pp. 1–20.

Fairhead J and Leach M 1996. Enriching the Landscape: Social History and the Management of Transition Ecology in the Forest–Savanna Mosaic of the Republic of Guinea. *Africa* 66(1): 14–36.

Hames R 2007. The Ecologically Noble Savage Debate. *The Annual Review of Anthropology* 36(1): 177–190.

Hecht S B 2004. Indigenous Soil Management and the Creation of Amazonian Dark Earths: Implications of Kayapó Practices. In J Lehmann, D C Kern, B Glaser and W I Woods (eds) *Amazonian Dark Earths: Origins, Properties, Management*. Dordrecht, the Netherlands: Kluwer Academic Publishers, pp. 355–372.

Lakatos I 1980. *The Methodology of Scientific Research Programmes*. Cambridge, UK: Cambridge University Press.

Lee K 1995. Apuntes sobre las obras hidráulicas prehispánicas de las llanuras de Moxos: Una opción ecológica inédita. Unpublished manuscript, Trinidad, Bolivia.

Levis C, Figueira de Souza P, Schietti J, Emilio T, Purri da Veiga Pinto J L, Clement C R and Costa F R C 2012. Historical Human Footprint on Modern Tree Species Composition in the Purus-Madeira Interfluve, Central Amazonia. *PloS ONE* 7(11) [online publication only].

McKey D, Rostain S, Iriarte J, Glaser B, Birk J J, Holst I and Renard D 2010. Pre-Columbian Agricultural Landscapes, Ecosystem Engineers, and Self-organized Patchiness in Amazonia. *Proceedings of the National Academy of Sciences of the United States of America* 107(17): 7823–7828.

McMichael C H, Piperno D R, Bush M B, Silman M R, Zimmerman A R, Raczka M F and Lobato L C 2012. Sparse Pre-Columbian Human Habitation in Western Amazonia. *Science* 336(6087): 1429–1431.

Mann C C 2008. Ancient Earthmovers of the Amazon. *Science* 321(5893): 1148–1152.

Mayle F E, Langstroth R P, Fisher R A and Meir P 2007. Long-term Forest-savannah Dynamics in the Bolivian Amazon: Implications for Conservation. *Philosophical Transactions of the Royal Society B: Biological Sciences* 362(1478): 291–307.

Meggers B J 1996. *Amazonia: Men and Culture in a Counterfeit Paradise*. 2nd edn. Washington, DC: The Smithsonian Institute.

Neves E G and Petersen J B 2006. Political Economy and Pre-Columbian Landscape Transformations in Central Amazonia. In W Balée and C Erickson (eds) *Time and Complexity in Historical Ecology: Studies in the Neotropical Lowlands*. New York: Columbia University Press, pp. 279–310,

Neves E G, Petersen J B, Bartone R N and Heckenberger M J 2004. The Timing of Terra Preta Formations in the Central Amazon: Archaeological Data from Three Sites. In B Glaser and W I Woods (eds) *Amazonian Dark Earths: Explorations in Space and Time*. Berlin, Heidelberg and New York: Springer-Verlag, pp. 125–134.

Petty A M, Isendahl C, Brenkert-Smith H, Goldstein D J, Rhemtulla J M, Ajijur Rahman S A and Kumasi T K 2014. Applying Historical Ecology to Natural Resource Management Institutions: Lessons from Two Case Studies of Landscape Fire Management. *Global Environmental Change* 31: 1–10.

Plotkin R L 2011. Biogeography of the Llanos de Moxos: Natural and Anthropogenic Determinants. *Geographica Helvetica* 66(3): 183–192.

Posey D A 2002. Hierarchy and Utility in a Folk Biological Taxonomic System: Patterns in Classification of Arthropods by the Kayapó Indians of Brazil. In K Plenderleith (ed.) *Kayapó Ethnoecology and Culture*. New York: Routledge, pp. 93–111.

Ruddiman W F 2013. The Anthropocene. *The Annual Review of Earth and Planetary Sciences* 41(1): 45–68.

Russell-Smith J and Edwards A 2006. Seasonality and Fire Severity in Savanna Landscapes of Monsoonal Northern Australia. *International Journal of Wildland Fire* 15: 541–550.

Smith N 1980. Anthrosols and Human Carrying Capacity in Amazonia. *Annals of the Association of American Geographers* 70(4): 553–566.

Steward J H (ed.) 1948. *The Tropical Forest Tales. Handbook of South American Indians, Volume 3*. Bulletin 143. Washington, DC: Bureau of American Ethnology, Smithsonian Institute.

Steward J H 1949. The Native Population of South America. In J H Steward (ed.) *The Comparative Ethnology of South American Indians. Handbook of South American Indians, Volume 5*. Bulletin 143. Washington, DC: Bureau of American Ethnology, Smithsonian Institute, pp. 655–668.

Szabó P 2014. Historical Ecology: Past, Present, and Future. *Biological Reviews* 90(4): 997–1014.

Tsai S M, O'Neill B, Cannavan F S, Saito D, Falcao N P S, Kern D C, Grossman J and Thies J 2009. The Microbial World of Terra Preta. In W I Woods, W G Teixeira, J Lehmann, C Steiner, A M G A WinklerPrins and L Rebellato (eds) *Amazonian Dark Earths: Wim Sombroek's Vision*. New York: Springer Science and Business Media B.V., pp. 299–308.

Wolf E R 1982. *Europe and the People without History*. Los Angeles: University of California Press.

Woods W I and McCann J M 1999. The Anthropogenic Origins and Persistence of Amazonian Dark Earths. *Yearbook Conference of Latin Americanist Geographers* 25: 7–14.

8

ARCHITECTURAL ANTHROPOLOGY

Developing a methodological framework for Indigenous wellbeing

Angela Kreutz and Paul Memmott

Architectural anthropology considers the inseparable relationships between people, culture, and the built environment. Drawing on social and cultural anthropology and environment–behaviour studies in architecture, architectural anthropology not only seeks to produce theoretical outcomes, but also applied research findings to assist people to evolve, adapt, and change (or resist change) in their environments. In this chapter, we argue that a transactional focus in architectural anthropology provides a developing methodological framework for addressing Indigenous wellbeing. 'Wellbeing' is a term with both many meanings and without any one universal meaning, but within the context of this chapter, it generally suggests a good (or at least satisfactory) condition of existence. In our view, a transactional approach guides research that seeks to improve the degree of congruence between Indigenous people and their built environment. People–environment congruence is a prerequisite for achieving wellbeing and for architects, planners, and policy makers it involves striving for an inclusive community design. Inclusive community design is about meeting the needs of all people in society and their environment and reconciling cross-cultural conflicts of values about environmental properties and uses.

The transactional methodological framework is founded on a transactional people–environment relations model that captures the evolving, mutually influential relations between people and their surrounding environments. It focuses on the degree of congruency, or 'good fit', between culturally distinct values, behaviours, and practices and the designed environment and governance policies in given local contexts. We propose that this people–environment approach is useful for analysing contemporary Indigenous problems arising from the colonial imposition of cultural change. In order to understand how Indigenous people might be responding to environmental change, it is useful to view architecture from a synthesized anthropological, environment–behaviour studies, and ethnographic perspective. We suggest that finding solutions that improve environmental congruence and wellbeing contributes to a form of culturally sustainable architecture; an architecture that responds to a culture-specific context, history, genius loci, and human need. We therefore suggest that a transactional perspective provides an alternative window through which to analyse contemporary social problems in Aboriginal communities, and we offer a methodological framework for achieving greater environmental congruence and thus Indigenous well-being. Two exemplary Australian Indigenous case studies in architectural anthropology will be presented that illustrate how transactionally-oriented research can lead to greater environmental congruence and Indigenous wellbeing.

Anthropology of architecture

Architectural anthropology is an emerging sub-discipline of anthropology that has many shared approaches and applications to environmental anthropology. Alongside the contemporary perspectives of environmental anthropology, architectural anthropology questions the conventional Western nature–culture dichotomy and recognizes that cultural beliefs and practices and the material and built environment are always mutually defining and not readily separable (Dove and Carpenter 2008: 2). From this standpoint, architectural anthropology takes an active role in examining the complex relationships between people, culture, and the built environment over time. There has been much primary research on the traditional architectures of the world and their transformation within wider processes of cultural change for people and their architecture under the impacts of colonialism and globalization (Egenter 2001; Rapoport 2001; Asquith and Vellinga 2006). These studies contribute to analysing the extent of congruency between culturally distinct behaviours and the built environment.

We purposefully and strategically frame architectural anthropology from an environment–behaviour studies perspective. The goal of the environment–behaviour studies field is to seek solutions towards problems involving human–environmental transactions and to create, manage, protect, and restore environments that promote socially preferred behaviours for a better quality of life. The anthropological study of the spatial dimension of environmental behaviours, values, and beliefs within households, institutional settings, factories, recreational buildings, and more broadly throughout all spaces and places is in many ways an ethnography of human–built environment relationships. The ethnographic method is significant not only to anthropology but also to architecture in overlapping ways. Anthropologists engage in comparative studies of societies and cultures in order to capture the patterns of their distinct thoughts, beliefs, rules, and customs; while designers, especially architects and planners, are required to understand the patterns of needs, beliefs, and behaviours of the users in relation to their environments and buildings (Otto and Smith 2013). Architectural anthropology can expand the explanatory power of architectural theories and improve problem-solving capacities for practitioners of both environmental design and social planning in several important ways.

First, mainstream architecture too often continues to focus on architectural functionalism (forms are generated by activities and functions). This approach addresses human needs through form-based rather than experienced-based approaches (Groat and Wang 2002). The anthropologist Tim Ingold and his colleagues argue that this static, rigid, and object-focused approach leads to a disconnection between people and their environments (Anusas and Ingold 2013; Gatt and Ingold 2013). Environmental alienation through excessive use of smooth walls and surfaces makes it difficult for people to follow or connect with their material traces and environmental impacts, including soil, burrows, roots, water, sewage, energy, and telecommunications, which are all hidden away from everyday perception (Anusas and Ingold 2013). Instead, Tim Ingold and his co-authors argue that design can prioritize understandings of human perception and connection to the environment and spatial movement, acknowledging that the reciprocal nature of people–environment transactions necessitates problem-solving interventions and design improvements that are of mutual benefit to people and their environments.

Second, the definition of architecture within the context of architectural anthropology is much broader than its mainstream definition and thereby relevant to a wider range of settlement contexts. The term anthropology of architecture is inclusive of all cultural groups and their built environments, no matter how modest or ephemeral, including all vernacular buildings and environments (Vellinga *et al.* 2007: 3). This structural definition of architecture takes into account temporary and minimal architectural features often found among Indigenous peoples, such as the spinifex grass shelters used throughout inland Australia, as well as permanent buildings found in most global urban contexts. From his analysis of the shelters and camps of Australian Aboriginal people, Memmott defines architecture as:

> a selected, arranged and constructed configuration of environmental properties, both natural and artificial, in and around one or more activity spaces or behavioural settings, all within a cultural landscape, and combined with patterns of behavioural rules and meanings as well as incorporating cultural constructs of space and time, to result in human comfort and quality of lifestyle.
>
> *(Memmott 2007: 300)*

This definition takes into account human behaviours within physical aspects of the environment, and their fluid inter-relationships through time. Architecture in this context is understood as a process of socio-cultural appropriation involving physical setting, configurative choices, and selection of functions and meanings before any overlay of supporting physical structure and material. The last comes at the end of this more initial fundamental, broader process of selection, design, and place-making. Taking a broader definition of 'architecture' is especially important when attempting to understand how design can respond to the life world of peoples from non-Western backgrounds.

Transactional life world

The 'life world' can be defined as the constant life process of one's consciousness of movement through never-ending spaces with or without other persons, and the accompanying mental perceptions, thoughts, reactions, interpreted meanings, and accompanying resurgent memories. The life worlds of many Aboriginal people draw on the traditional Australian Indigenous epistemology which provides an intuitive way of knowing that is based on the religious belief system of The Dreaming (The Law), and which has been passed on from generation to generation by storytelling, ritual practice, and other acculturative means. Simplified, this is a belief that humans, animals, and the environment are embedded in a distant past epoch that continuously asserts its spiritual controls, powers, and energies in the contemporaneous life world (Memmott 2013). Despite changes to their worldview, this belief greatly influences the way in which many Indigenous people continue to transact with other peoples and their environments.

Let us introduce an example here. When Memmott undertook his doctoral case study on the concept of 'place' amongst the Lardil, a coastal Aboriginal tribal group on Mornington Island in the north of Australia (Figure 8.1), he discovered some striking cultural contrasts between Lardil models of people–environment relations and those of Western science (Memmott 1979). For example, the Lardil believe that their coastal land systems were shaped and installed with food, water, and material resources by their ancestral heroes *Maarnbil*, *Jirn-jirn* and *Diwal-diwal* during the early epoch of The Dreaming. The explanation of Western science is in terms of coastal geomorphology, and does not involve the influence

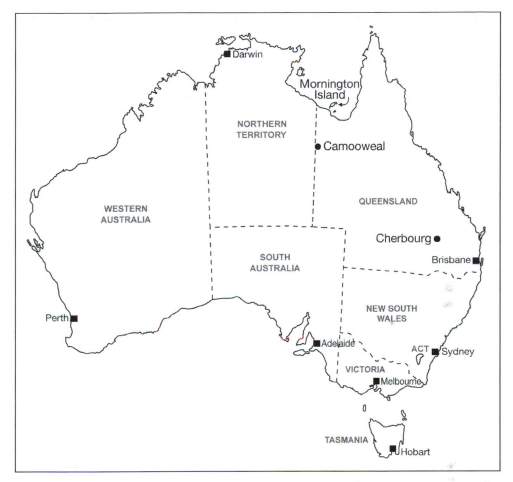

Figure 8.1 Map of Australia showing Aboriginal communities mentioned in the text: Cherbourg, Camooweal, and Mornington Island.

of people. In the Aboriginal explanation, the 'outside' country along the relatively fertile coast was constructed by people; in the Western one, by nature. The Lardil also believe that they can influence the weather and the reproductivity of animals and plants with special songs and actions at special coastal places (sacred sites) – whereas Western science provides bio-ecological explanations which, again, do not involve the human influence. A third example is that of totemism, of identifying with coastal places and the special energies said to be contained in those places that belong to or are derived from animal and plant species. Such identity is so strong that Aboriginal people believe that they contain some place energy within them, and that special places contain a part of their own energies – a sharing of being. Such systems of belief illustrate the necessity to never assume person–environment relations to be a simple dichotomy. The Lardil cultural identity was clearly expressed by the Elder Larry Lanley in 1978: 'If our Dreaming and our laws and languages and our way of living die then that will be the end of Aboriginal people' (*The Advertiser* 1978).

However, since this earlier case study (1970s), Aboriginal Australians have progressively engaged with Anglo–Australian and indeed global constructs, ideologies, beliefs, and practices in cultural change processes that result in individuals and groups adopting an intercultural character to their behaviour and practices. In understanding how particular groups acquire their intercultural values which draw on both their traditional and new systems of thought, architectural anthropology provides a further capacity to supply explanatory models based on theories of cultural change (Memmott 2013). The concept of the 'intercultural' pertains to the idea that within processes of cultural change, Aboriginal people are taking on identities that move between both the relational and the possessive constructs of self and synthesize them in particular contexts (Hinkson and Smith 2005; Moran 2010). An intercultural view accommodates a mix of bi-cultural, mainstream, and culturally specific aspects working in unison, which in turn can support flexible policies and practices that are culturally respectful (Milligan *et al.* 2007).

Much Western thought classifies people as independent of their environment, but from a transactional viewpoint, which is less tied to Western ideals, 'people' and 'environment' do not comprise mutually exclusive categories either for classification or analysis. A transactional people–environment congruence approach captures these mutually adaptive relations between people and their natural and built environments, and examines a wide set of Indigenous behaviours and experiences in a variety of places. A more transactional, complete understanding of contemporary Indigenous life worlds and their processes of cultural change can in turn help (too often ethnocentric) policy makers more appropriately analyse a range of Indigenous social problems. These recur despite the constant bureaucratic agenda of housing procurement and management, addressing crowding, and homelessness, and constant top-down service delivery over the last 45 years in Australia.

Environmental congruence and culture

In architectural anthropology, culture is central to understanding life ways and world-views and more specifically, in understanding the degree of congruence between culturally distinct behaviours and values in specific places. Environmental congruence, or environment–behaviour congruence, is the degree to which the environment meets the needs, goals, and desires of its occupants (Stokols 1979: 44). While people's experiences can be considered at a highly detailed and multi-perceptive set of levels within a wider phenomenological analysis, when framed within a transactional perspective, experiential aspects are inevitably tied up with the more stimulating physical properties of the environment. This perspective helps researchers focus on the ways in which environmental design can improve the degree of congruence between people's beliefs, behaviours, and their local setting (Stokols and Shumaker 1981). A fundamental assumption is that congruent design will not only improve wellbeing, but it will inevitably encourage sustainable behaviours and superior environmental management decisions.

This environment–behaviour studies construct assists in the understanding of the quality of environment–behaviour transactions. When congruence between the built environment and human behaviour is poor, due to inappropriate design, there is wear and tear on both people and their environment. People are under greater degrees of stress if their built environment does not respond to their vital immediate and long-term goals and the built environment, including its surrounding natural features, may suffer neglect, vandalism, complete destruction, or abandonment from its users. A further level of complexity enters the analysis when there are competing uses of the built environment by different cultural groups in a society, and political decision-making favours one group over another. Religious, government, and corporate agencies have continually adapted and reshaped the environment to suit their needs and desires, yet this has not necessarily contributed to the betterment of wellbeing and quality of life of all citizens. Marginal groups, including the young, the elderly, and in Australia, many Indigenous communities, have little influence over the design and construction decisions in their living environments which are officially sanctioned and empowered by governments and other institutionalized bodies of the state.

The importance of recognizing the extent of environmental congruency is especially valuable in countries like Australia where culturally distinct behaviours and experiences of Indigenous peoples in their environment are often unrecognized. For example, it is rarely understood that Indigenous issues are inseparable from local religious-based beliefs, and that environmental sites, territories, and spiritual entities shape individual and group identities, which in turn shape behavioural values and practices (Memmott 2013). For many traditionally-oriented Aboriginal householders, living in a rental suburban house entails 'a loss of control over one's social environment . . . with little choice over his [or her] neighbours, and the general social and physical organisation of space' (Reser 1979: 68). There are multiple ways in which design ideas require policy supports, and the examination of the congruency between culturally distinct values, behaviours, and practices can positively influence policies and regulations and assist in resolving competing priorities of usage. These in turn can encourage design approaches that can accommodate the needs of minority groups with distinctive cultural traits.

Environment–behaviour congruence is dynamic. Beliefs, values, and behavioural practices are changing during one's life along various time scales, while at the same time many elements of the object, built, and natural worlds are also changing at a multitude of time scales. While person–environment congruence may be present for a period of one's life, it can be swiftly disrupted by these changing phenomena. Certain customs and beliefs remain, despite environmental change, yet others may have transformed or disappeared (Hume 2000). Memmott *et al.* (2015) argue that many customs, beliefs, and practices have inherent meaning and value to Indigenous people, and not only are being retained, but can provide elements for solutions to social problems through syncretistic processes of adaptation to contemporary contexts. In Australia, Indigenous communities have continuously adapted and changed their environment to suit their own needs and desires through self-constructed architecture such as humpies (huts), wind-breaks, lean-tos, and outdoor kitchens. These vernacular enclosures, platforms, roofs, and screens create a greater openness to environmental conditions and the spiritual landscape at large. The majority of these creative design changes are positive in that they increase environmental congruence.

Working across disciplines

The many phenomena considered in addressing people–environment congruence clearly indicate that a range of scholarly disciplines is needed to study it. Transdisciplinary approaches offer a novel reflection of dialogue across disciplines, across professions, and across practices. Architectural anthropologists need to work across various social science, engineering, and environmental disciplines, observing, interviewing, and often engaging residents in participatory design processes, in order to address real-life challenges through culturally appropriate design solutions (Grant 2014; Kreutz 2015; Moran *et al.* 2014). They seek higher intellectual and practical involvement between disciplines to challenge each of their basic assumptions, theories, and methodologies (Lawrence and Despres 2004: 399).

An example of this, most pertinent to our proposition, is the *interactionalist* perspective, which has been dominant in the disciplines of sociology, psychology, and anthropology.

From an interactionalist point of view, the individual and the environment are treated as interacting, yet independent from one another. This inevitably means that culture plays a causal rather than a phenomenological role in understanding human–environment relationships (Heft 2013). An alternative view, the *transactional* perspective, focuses on the trans- rather than the inter-*action* and captures the evolving, mutually influential relations between people, culture, and their surrounding environment.

The transactional-oriented approach and methodology are important to architectural anthropology because they presume that people's psycho-biological behavioural components and the physical components of a situation in the environment are involved in a continuous neural structure (loop, net, or matrix), whereby an individual is continuously assimilating and interpreting stimuli and events in the environment (Werner *et al.* 2002; Memmott 2013; Kreutz 2015). Rather than designing 'intuitively', architectural anthropology encourages architects to consider the shared cultural and environmental perceptions and values of the users that result from these psychological processes within a society or social group. This approach moves beyond identifying singular environmental features or isolated individual perceptions and behaviours to include a wider set of people's overall relationships to their environment (Moser 2009). A transactional view suits an environmental congruence approach to wellbeing because it takes into account the various aspects of a place and situation.

Transactional perspective in people–environment studies

Transactionalism arose in the early to mid-twentieth century as a reaction against much of the dualistic thinking in Western academic discourses (Boisvert 1998). The forerunners of transactional thinking were the educationalist John Dewey and the philosopher Arthur Bentley (1949) who argued that the multifactorial influences on a situation are difficult to anticipate and suggested that an enquiry into everyday life should not come from pre-figured answers to problems. This is especially valuable in cross-cultural research where findings tend to emerge during the research process. The transactional perspective in people–environment studies holds valuable insights for people living with, and in, built spaces. Here there is an understanding that design research considers social order and social goals, and hence societal health and wellbeing. It is useful for researchers attempting to examine the 'whole' situation, to take into account both stability and change, as well as multiple scales of understandings from the micro to the macro.

The transactional view opposes the basic differentiation of subject versus object, soul versus body, and mind versus matter. Integral to this perspective is the presumption that individuality and human experience can only exist within the context of others and the environment. People are constantly having an impact on their social, natural, and built environment, and the environment is always impacting on people's behaviour and experiences (Werner and Altman 2000: 21). This proposition takes into account the various influences of culture – people's behaviour is shaped by their environment and the environment is shaped by people's behaviour, design, and building techniques. While cultural anthropology effectively builds upon constructs of culture, material culture, social behaviour, cultural change process, and constructs of 'person' and 'self', this discipline tends to place a lens of 'culture' over the top of a situation under study to differentiate life ways and worldviews. In contrast, a transactional perspective views 'culture' as inherent to people and the environment; the precept being that the cultural domain is deeply and longitudinally embedded in both the person and the environment (Heft 2013).

Many anthropologists recognize the social, cultural, and historical aspects of relationships, but they often overlook the physical environmental features, materials, and symbolic artefacts to focus more narrowly on cognitive processes and socially prescribed rules and ideals. Architectural anthropologists, however, recognize, as do most environmental anthropologists, that this can lead to a fragmented and incomplete description of people's lives and experiences. Rather than presenting the environment from a strictly social or cultural perspective, people–environment relations are described as a set of transactional processes that situate people both physically and culturally in their built environment. From a transactional perspective, human behaviour and experience are not solely understood in terms of psychological processes and the immediate socio-cultural environment, but are considered to be inseparable from the broader physical setting in which people are actively involved (Altman and Rogoff 1987). Human wellbeing depends upon multiple factors that are biological, environmental, and spiritual. In order to capture these holistic relationships, transactional research borrows concepts, models, and theories from people–environment research; yet, for the most part, it does not tie itself exclusively to Western precepts and methodologies.

A transactional methodological framework

A transactionally-oriented methodology does not prescribe, but rather guides a research investigation that is suited to the phenomenon under study. As a collectivistic, holistic, participatory, and non-measurement-based transactional approach to design and planning, it avoids an over-reliance on Western ideals, values, and solutions that do not always match up with Indigenous perceptions and knowledge (Tunstall 2013). The former are often perceived as individual, controlling, depowering, compartmental, measurement-focused, and non-Aboriginal (Marshall and Batten 2004). Western design generates 'innovation', but architectural anthropology, and design anthropology more broadly, are more about improvisation than innovation (Gatt and Ingold 2013). Innovative design is founded on creatively calculated solutions to perceived problems, whereas design improvisation focuses on the continuous and incremental adaptation of inhabitants to the ever-changing circumstances of their lives (Gatt and Ingold 2013: 145). The transactional perspective supports the development of a research methodology that is appropriate to other cultures and the process of cultural change. Practically-oriented design research that focuses on the physical articulation of spaces and how they are culturally constructed benefits from a transactional orientation that captures the interconnections among the cultural and architectural components of a place.

A transactional methodological framework is less encumbered by specific theoretical postulates and associated procedures or measures, and provides a sound theoretical basis for research plans that are flexible and open to uncertainty. It opposes the exclusive objectivism of the behaviourist tradition and the privileged subjectivism of individualistic perspectives (Kreutz 2013). Rather, it combines observational and physical measurement techniques with interview and psychological perspectives in order to characterize an environment and its people. The open-endedness and intellectual rigour of this transactional methodological framework is in many ways similar to a grounded theory or ethno-methodological approach in that it encourages the research focus to emerge out of initial empirical explorations. The methodology tends to be holistic, flexible, and reflective, which lends itself to qualitative research and encourages the use of multiple viewpoints and mixed methods. Studies on an unfolding person–environment relationship are often carried out in situ where researchers consider the holistic transactions between people, experiences, and behaviours and their built environment.

The holistic, adaptive, and flexible nature of the transactional approach means that research, especially fieldwork, can appear cumbersome. Some guiding principles on transactionally-oriented research include, first, a clear aim to establish a well-defined research focus; second, an ongoing process of reflexivity; third, the use of multiple methods and the collection of multiple viewpoints; fourth, continuous data triangulation throughout the data collection process; and finally, a focus shift from pure academic description to community action (see also Cutchin and Dickie 2013; Werner *et al.* 2002). In what follows, the authors relate two exemplary case studies that utilized a transactionally-oriented methodology and display architectural anthropology in the light of achieving Indigenous wellbeing through environmental congruence.

Australian Indigenous case studies

Ethnographic study of Australian Aboriginal children

The transactional perspective was used by Kreutz who undertook an ethnographic study of children's experience of place in the Australian Aboriginal community Cherbourg, Queensland (Figure 8.1). Cherbourg is a discrete, relatively closed Aboriginal community that was formerly a government reserve settlement administered as an institution where remnant tribal groups were taken from all over Queensland in the early twentieth century. Today it is the third largest Aboriginal community in Queensland with a total population of around 1,200 residents. More than 97 per cent of residents are Indigenous, and of these, over one-third are under 15 years of age (Australian Bureau of Statistics 2011).

The study sought to discover where local children go, what they do, and how they feel (Kreutz 2015). The methodological flexibility that evolved out of a transactional approach supported emergent, in situ, and participant-specific approaches and insights. Research access into the community was gained through the Cherbourg Aboriginal Council and Cherbourg State School. Fieldwork involved regular visits to the primary school, during which time the researcher built a rapport with children, made contact with their extended families, and got to know staff at the school and various community agencies. This encouraged research participation from children and their parents, guardians, and several non-residents employed at the local school and other service institutions around the community.

A total of 24 children (12 girls and 12 boys) volunteered to participate in this study. They were aged between 9 and 12 years and came from a diverse group of families in the community. They each participated in multiple methods that captured their behaviours and experiences in their community. These included self-directed photography, free-hand mapping, weekly activity diaries, place expeditions, semi-structured interviews, and behavioural observations recorded in a field notebook. Some 38 adult residents and non-residents employed at the school and other local government, health, and welfare organizations participated in a semi-structured interview.

This ethnographic study collected rich qualitative material using multiple methods. Rather than a mere collection or patchwork of methods, however, the sequencing in which the methods were implemented maximized their distinctive advantage and value. The initial implementation of the self-directed photography, free-hand mapping, place expeditions, and activity diary tasks provided a means to gain the children's trust and learn about their unique socio-cultural surroundings. This helped the children gain a deeper understanding of the research focus and concerns and circumvented problems relating to Indigenous cultural norms, such as conspicuousness and shame. The subsequent development of more structured analytical and verbal methods, such as the one-on-one semi-structured interview, provided deeper and more detailed descriptions of the physical, cultural, and social aspects of the children's environment.

The flexibility and adaptability of the transactional approach was conducive to this research in that it supported initial exploration of the lives of children, bringing to light unanticipated community issues. This in turn encouraged the development of culturally appropriate research and helped frame specific research questions with regard to children's local place transactions. The study could thus focus on the 'whole child' and supported a flexible methodology that captured children's place use and experiences – ecologically through observations of children's behaviour in the environment; and phenomenologically through self-report responses about their experiences. The free-hand mapping and place expeditions recorded children's mobility; adult interviews and behaviour observations documented children's place use; and children's self-directed photography and the semi-structured interviews with children and adults captured place attachments. The triangulation of observations and reported experiences resulted in more complete descriptions of children's lives.

Combining participant observations with visual methods and interviews allowed for the study of what children do in their environment alongside what they say they do and why they do it (Figure 8.2). Focusing on children's immediate psychological needs and experience domain, the

Figure 8.2 Child-led walks to discover children's perceptions and use of their community environment at Cherbourg, 2008.

Source: Angela Kreutz.

research took on a fluid participant observation approach and methodology, supported by interviews and other convergent, multi-method procedures. These methods and procedures uncovered environmental features and properties that frustrated, rather than facilitated, Aboriginal children's needs and desires in their local community environment. Those features that frustrated children included, but were not limited to, playgrounds and sports facilities situated on the outskirts of the community; few retail outlets; monotonous suburban layout; insufficient shade and shelter; and high fences, bolts, bars, and locks that ostracized them from many public buildings. These and other poorly designed features caused children to suffer from boredom, crowding, privacy issues, and a sense that they lacked control (for a detailed description of findings, see Kreutz 2014, 2015).

The discovery of frustrating planning and design features led to a set of recommendations that sought to improve the degree of congruence between children and their local community. Intensive community engagement, including participant observation, ensured that these recommendations were specific to the needs of the residents and children of this culturally distinct community. The design recommendations were flexible and adaptable to the ever-changing circumstances of community life, suggesting environmental modifications and features that increased the number of behaviour and experience opportunities. These included relocating isolated playgrounds to the community centre, increasing the number of commercial and food outlets, and providing community meeting spaces by modifying and opening the gates to existing public venues and facilities, thus making numerous active and passive recreation activities more widely available to the community. Such design and planning suggestions can help guide the design decisions of planners and architects who are commissioned to improve housing and settlement design for Aboriginal families and their children in this specific community.

The Dugalunji Camp at Camooweal

This is a case study employing the principles outlined previously of a transactional methodology to examine and evaluate a design approach that achieves cross-cultural design congruence through an integrated set of what could be called Aboriginal behaviour settings in a remote Australian context (Memmott 2010). A modern construction camp (the Dugalunji Camp) was established for the Indjilandji-Dhidhanu people of the Georgina River in 2001 within the Town Common of the remote Australian township of Camooweal (see Figure 8.1).

The Indjilandji-Dhidhanu company, the Myuma Pty Ltd, runs an enterprise operation and also employs and delivers accredited pre-vocational training programmes to young Aboriginal people in civil and mining construction and related support services, including training as Land Rangers, hospitality, and catering. At the time of writing, the number of workers ranged between 60 and 80, depending on shifting project demands and numbers of trainees; at peak staff levels, over 90 per cent were Aboriginal. Myuma purposefully engaged people from the neighbouring Traditional Owner Aboriginal groups in all projects.

Senior Myuma staff act as informal social workers or counsellors to maintain the harmony and wellbeing in the Dugalunji Camp. Above all, the Dugalunji Camp provides workers and trainees with a calm residential setting, relatively free of problems or chaos, where people can feel at home in the world, where relatedness is constructed for many with their fellows in the camp and with their aesthetic and spiritual environment in the Georgina River Valley where the regional cultural landscape is believed to contain perpetual energies implanted into its many sacred sites during 'The Dreaming'. Camp harmony results from intra-group harmony which in turn results from the requirements of a strong personal moral code conveyed through the camp rules and the authoritative guidance of Indjilandji leader Colin Saltmere as camp boss.

The Myuma pre-vocational training programme has encouraged the development of career narratives and purpose in life. It has opened a window to alternate life ways and career pathways that may not have been apparent or available in the home communities of the trainees. The Dugalunji Camp can be considered to be a system of 'Aboriginal behavioural settings', with recurring behaviour patterns in physical settings, such that there is a synomorphic relation or 'fit' between the human behaviour episodes that occur and the physical and temporal environments of the settings. It is largely controlled by Aboriginal people, and is designed by Aboriginal leaders in collaboration with an architect to be comfortable for Aboriginal residents. This is achieved through a combination of behavioural patterns and environmental (landscaping) features, artefactual features (built and loose structures, objects), and behaviour setting controls which are designed to be relatively comfortable, predictable, secure, and conducive for Aboriginal people to use. There is also a sense of identity with and even ownership of such a system of settings by Aboriginal people.

In terms of designing the environmental, artefactual, and temporal character of the camp, the group leader Colin Saltmere has stated that he based the idea of the design on a traditional camp, first by setting it up on his country (traditional land) and drawing in as many of his family who were available and willing to participate. This established a clear role for the senior members of his family as Traditional Owners within the precepts of traditional Aboriginal law. Second, Colin controls and runs the camp like a traditional multi-tribal camp. For planning, he drew on a number of socio-spatial elements deriving from traditional Aboriginal camps, which were in turn utilized in the pastoral stockcamps in which he, along with other Aboriginal stockmen, worked and lived in their younger years. Such elements include separate nocturnal sleeping areas for married couples, single men, and single women; the capacity for separation of older single men and younger single men; provision for an externally-oriented lifestyle (verandas, open-walled roofed structures), with enclosed shelter mostly utilized for nocturnal sleeping; and a capacity for camp leaders to maintain from a central position visual surveillance (and thus setting control) of all the workers and those approaching the camp (Figure 8.3). With the assistance of the trainees, a variety of shade roofs and wind-break walls have been built throughout the camp using natural foliage materials such as spinifex grass as well as other landscaping features (lawn, shade and fruit trees). However, at night, the trainees each have a private room, which for a good number of them is the first fully private space they have ever lived in and personalized.

Another aspect of the Dugalunji Camp which is reminiscent of the pastoral stockcamps of Colin's earlier adulthood is the structure of time (time is a cultural topic that represents a specialist anthropological study in itself; e.g. Munn 1992). The Myuma day starts early with the breakfast bell sounding at 6.30 a.m. A cooked breakfast is consumed and then workers who are travelling away from the camp prepare their own lunches. Management staff attend a 'pre-start' meeting, followed by a Workers' meeting to organize tasks in the camp as well as off-site. As the working day progresses, there is thus a strong sense of order in the Dugalunji Camp, reminiscent of a mission institution in the sense of having a defined set of rules and a fixed timetable, but one that is not forcibly imposed (because individuals are free to leave); rather, one in which there is a voluntary engagement. Nevertheless, individuals are instructed that they must accept the consequences of their actions if they break the camp rules. Colin Saltmere is working aspects of his Aboriginal and colonial upbringing into a camp that functions in the present. In establishing the desired Aboriginal

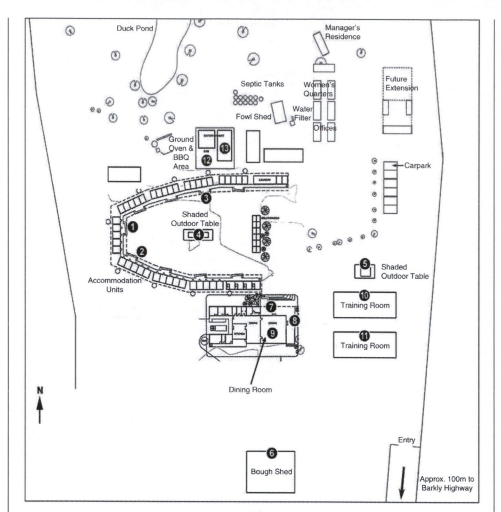

Figure 8.3 The Dugalunji Camp of Myuma Pty Ltd at Camooweal, 2015, showing the system of Indigenous behaviour settings accommodating 60–80 workers of whom some 90 per cent are Aboriginal.

behaviour patterns with minimal behavioural deviancy or dysfunction, he also believes that the conformity to the training regime and the successful completion rate are partly due to there being sufficient trainees for a critical mass to generate a peer-group pressure over individual behaviour, albeit within an Aboriginal value system. The Dugalunji Camp can be seen as a positive Aboriginal behaviour-setting system supporting social, physical, mental, and spiritual wellbeing, and based on intuitively improvised, but transactionally sensitive design knowledge to achieve cultural congruency and a degree of Indigenous people–environment congruence.

Conclusion

A quality of life can only be sustained if there is congruence between people and their environment. There are various aspects that contribute to environmental congruence including environmental design, environment behaviour, cultural values and practices, and local management. Such an anthropological view towards architecture recognizes that the latter both reflects and influences cultural thought, expression, and behaviour. In other words, architecture shapes culture and is in turn being shaped by it. The transactional methodological framework is suited to architectural anthropology, and environmental anthropology for that matter, because it acknowledges the inseparable relationship between people and place, while recognizing that culture is embedded between both. Australian Government policy continuously fails to recognize the nature of Indigenous relational beliefs and values and the responsibilities that people of a certain kinship hold to one another and to their environment. A transactional view with a focus on congruence is open to the nature of Australian Indigenous relational beliefs and values. This makes it useful for analysing Indigenous problems and finding responsive solutions that ultimately strive to improve Indigenous wellbeing.

References

The Advertiser 1978. 12 September. Report on address by Larry Lanley to the UNESCO Seminar in Adelaide.

Altman I and Rogoff B 1987. World view in psychology: Trait, interactional, organismic, and transactional perspectives. In D Stokols and I Altman (eds) *Handbook of environmental psychology*. New York: Wiley, pp. 1–40.

Anusas M and Ingold T 2013. Design environmental relations: From opacity to textility. *Design Issues* 29(4): 58–68.

Asquith L and Vellinga L (eds) 2006. *Vernacular architecture in the twenty-first century: Theory, education and practice*. London: Taylor & Francis.

Australian Bureau of Statistics 2011. *Census of population and housing 2006*. Canberra, ACT: Australian Bureau of Statistics.

Boisvert R 1998. *John Dewey: Rethinking our time*. New York: State University of New York Press.

Cutchin M and Dickie V (eds) 2013. *Transactional perspectives on occupation*. New York: Springer.

Dewey J and Bentley A 1949. *Knowing and the known*. Boston, MA: Beacon Press.

Dove M and Carpenter C (eds) 2008. *Environmental anthropology: A historical reader*. Malden, MA: Blackwell.

Egenter N 2001. The deep structure of architecture: Constructivity and human evolution. In M Amerlinck (ed.) *Architectural anthropology*. Westport, CT: Bergin & Garvey, pp. 43–81.

Gatt C and Ingold T 2013. From description to correspondence: Anthropology in real time. In W Gunn, T Otto and R C Smith (eds) *Design anthropology: Theory and practice*. London: Bloomsbury, pp. 139–158.

Grant E 2014. Special feature: Architecture for Aboriginal and Torres Strait Islander children. *Place: Architecture, Design and Placemaking South Australia* 45: 21–24.

Groat L and Wang D 2002. *Architectural research methods*. Toronto, ON: John Wiley & Sons.

Heft H 2013. Environment, cognition, and culture: Reconsidering the cognitive map. *Journal of Environmental Psychology* 33: 14–25.

Hinkson M and Smith B 2005. Introduction: Conceptual moves towards an intercultural analysis. *Oceania* 75(3): 157–166.

Hume L 2000. The Dreaming in contemporary Aboriginal Australia. In G Harvey (ed.) *Indigenous religions: A companion*. London: Cassell, pp. 125–138.

Kreutz A 2013. Munu gukooreree: Aboriginal children's use and experience of space and place in Cherbourg. Unpublished PhD thesis, Department of Architecture, University of Queensland.

Kreutz A 2014. Lack of child–environment congruence in Cherbourg, Australia: Obstacles to well-being in an Indigenous community. *Children, Youth and Environments* 24(1): 53–81.

Kreutz A 2015. *Children and the environment in an Australian Indigenous community: A psychological approach.* London: Routledge.

Lawrence R and Despres C 2004. Futures of transdisciplinarity. *Futures* 36(4): 397–405.

Marshall A and Batten S 2004. Researching across cultures: Issues of ethics and power. *Qualitative Social Research* 5(3): article 39. Retrieved 8 February 2016 from www.qualitative-research.net/index.php/fqs/article/view/572/1241

Memmott P 1979. Lardil properties of place, an ethnographical study in man–environment systems. Unpublished thesis, Department of Architecture, University of Queensland.

Memmott P 2007. *Gunyah, Goondie + Wurley: The aboriginal architecture of Australia.* St Lucia: University of Queensland Press.

Memmott P 2010. Demand-responsive services and culturally sustainable enterprise in remote Aboriginal settings: A case study of the Myuma Group, Desert Knowledge Cooperative Research Centre, Alice Springs. Report No. 63. Retrieved 8 February 2016 from www.nintione.com.au/resource/dkcrc-report-63-demand-responsive-service-the-myuma-group.pdf

Memmott P 2013. Integrating transactional people–environment studies into architectural anthropology: A case for useful theory building. Paper presented at the 30th Annual Conference of the Society of Architectural Historians, Australia and New Zealand, Gold Coast, Queensland.

Memmott P, Nash D and Passi C 2015. Cultural relativism and indigenous family violence. In A Day and E Fernandez (eds) *Preventing violence in Australia: Policy, practice and solutions.* Leichhardt, NSW: The Federation Press, pp. 164–185.

Milligan V, Phillips R, Easthope H, Liu E and Memmott P 2007. *Urban Social Housing for Aboriginal People and Torres Strait Islanders: Respecting Culture and Adapting Services.* AHURI Final Report No. 172. Melbourne, VIC: Australian Housing and Urban Research Institute.

Moran M 2010. The intercultural practice of local governance in an Aboriginal settlement in Australia. *Human Organization* 69(1): 65–74.

Moran M, Memmott P, Birdsall-Jones C and Nash D 2014. Case study rationale and location scoping study. Melbourne, VIC: Australian Housing and Urban Research Institute.

Moser G 2009. Quality of life and sustainability: Toward person–environment congruity. *Journal of Environmental Psychology* 29(3): 351–357.

Munn N 1992. The cultural anthropology of time: A critical essay. *Annual Review of Anthropology* 21: 93–123.

Otto T and Smith R C 2013. Design anthropology: A distinct style of knowing. In W Gunn, T Otto and R C Smith (eds) *Design anthropology: Theory and practice.* London: Bloomsbury.

Rapoport A 2001. Architectural anthropology or environnment–behaviour studies? In M Amerlinck (ed.) *Architectural Anthropology.* Westport, CT: Bergin & Garvey, pp. 27–41.

Reser J A 1979. A matter of control: Aboriginal housing circumstances in remote communities and settlements. In M Heppell (ed.) *A black reality: Aboriginal camps and housing in remote Australia.* Canberra, ACT: Australian Institute of Aboriginal Studies, pp. 65–96.

Stokols D 1979. A congruence analysis of human stress. In I G Sarason and C D Spielberger (eds) *Stress and anxiety. Vol. 6.* New York: John Wiley, pp. 35–64.

Stokols D and Shumaker S 1981. People in places: A transactional view of settings. In J Harvey (ed.) *Cognition, social behaviour, and the environment.* Hillsdale, NJ: Lawrence Erlbaum Associates, pp. 441–488.

Tunstall E 2013. Decolonising design innovation: Design anthropology, critical anthropology, and Indigenous knowledge. In W Gunn, T Otto and R C Smith (eds) *Design anthropology: Theory and practice.* London: Bloomsbury, pp. 232–250.

Vellinga M, Oliver P and Bridge A 2007. *Atlas of vernacular architecture of the world.* London: Routledge.

Werner C and Altman I 2000. Human and nature: Insights from a transactional view. In S Wapner, J Demick, T Yamamoto and F Minami (eds) *Theoretical perspectives in environment-behaviour research: Underlying assumptions, research problems, and methodologies.* New York: Plenum Press, pp. 21–37.

Werner C, Brown B and Altman I 2002. Planning and doing transactionally-oriented research: Examples and strategies. In R Bechtel and A Churchman (eds) *Handbook of environmental psychology.* New York: John Wiley & Sons, pp. 203–221.

9

BEYOND "NATURE"

Towards more engaged and care-full ways of relating to the environment

Mark Coeckelbergh

Introduction

In modernity the environment is usually perceived as "nature": either it is seen from an objectivist–technoscientific point of view, or it is experienced in subjectivist–romantic terms – both of which are entangled with how we act. This chapter uses philosophical reflection and argument to show that both modes of seeing and treating the environment present a distorted view of the basic, existential relation between humans and their environment – and indeed a distorted view of the human – and undesirably limit the range of possibilities we have for relating to our environment. Influenced by Heideggerian phenomenology and contemporary anthropology, it explores how we might conceptualize a less dualistic and less alienated relation to the environment, and makes us pay attention to the role of technology and the moral significance of the language we use to talk about the environment. It uses the terms "engagement" and "care" to articulate different relational possibilities, and suggests a conception of the human–environment relation which deconstructs not only the technoscientific–romantic dialectic but also goes beyond the anthropocentrism–ecocentrism duality.

Whereas in the 1970s and the 1980s, political and ethical concern for the environment was perceived as new, radical, and somewhat marginal, today it is mainstream. There is a sense in which we are all "green" now – or at least think of ourselves as such. Most educated people in the Western world would claim that they care about the environment. Many of us want to be closer to "nature" and live in a more "natural" way. Moreover, during the past decades, environmental values have been anchored in policies at the local, regional, national, and international level. Most political parties have absorbed discourse about the value of "nature" and the environment (even if their policies and conceptions of the environment differ considerably), and we now find terms such as "sustainability", "ecosystem services" and "ecological structure" in policy documents and in academic discourse. Yet in spite of this proclaimed concern for "nature" and belief in "sustainability", and in spite of the accompanying "environmental turn" in philosophy (Rolston 2012: 1–2), relatively little change has happened in the ways we live our lives, produce goods, and conduct politics. We still produce and consume unsustainable products, we still use fossil fuels, we still use natural "resources" and treat animals in ways that threaten wildlife and biodiversity. Why does this still happen? How is it possible that there is such a gap between our discourse and our action?

There are various mundane explanations for this gap; for example, the pressure on politicians to prioritize human interests (especially in times of financial and economic crisis), the (short-term) interests large multi-national corporations have in continuing unsustainable activities, and our personal addiction to a consumerist lifestyle, including industrially produced food.[1] In this chapter, however, I would like to relate the problem to (the discourse about) a deeper, cultural–philosophical pattern that is usually indicated by the term "modernity". I will show that the ways we think about the environment today, including the very *concepts* we use to talk about the environment, are still very "modern". I will argue that these modern ways of thinking are problematic and explore an alternative conception of the relation between humans and their environment which is less modern and less romantic.[2] Moreover, I will also argue that this conception does not only enable us to critically address what has been called the anthropocentric bias and the emphasis on mastery and control in much contemporary thinking about the environment,[3] but also helps us to offer a critique of the anthropocentrism–ecocentrism dichotomy itself, at least as far as this dichotomy is framed in terms of a human–nature or culture–nature opposition.

First I will describe and criticize two modern ways of perceiving and seeing the environment: an objectivist–technoscientific one and a subjectivist–romantic one, which may be understood as standing in a dialectic relation. Whereas the first is well known and has been sufficiently criticized in the past century, the second has received a lot less attention, but is, so I will argue, at least as important if we care to understand the roots and meaning of contemporary environmentalism as a *modern* phenomenon. After presenting this brief analysis of the dialectic of modern environmentalism, I will then explore a route towards a less modern, less dualistic way of thinking about the environment, which also deconstructs the anthropocentrism–ecocentrism duality. This part will also be inspired by the phenomenological tradition in philosophical thinking (especially the works of Heidegger), but will also refer to contemporary anthropology (in particular Ingold's interpretation of anthropological studies). I will end with a brief reflection on the possibility of environmental change; that is, positive change to the way(s) we perceive and treat the environment.

Two modern ways of thinking about the environment

Today there are at least two dominant ways of perceiving – and therefore treating – the environment. The first I call "objectivist–technoscientific". Since early modern thinking and since the Enlightenment, we want to understand and control nature. The normative part of this way of seeing and doing is strongly anthropocentric: what counts is our, that is *human* aims and values, and "nature" is a collection of resources we can use for our purposes. It is, to use Heidegger's words, a "standing reserve" (Heidegger 1977); it stands by for our purposes and has no value of its own, no intrinsic value. It is supposed to stand ready for us as a container of resources, products, and services for our use; we can take whatever and how much we need from it. The non-human world is there to be used for our benefit and advantage. We can extract energy from it, we can make food out of it, we can transform the whole planet into "spaceship earth".[4] The tools for doing this are science and technology, which help us to understand nature, to force nature to reveal its laws and workings, and use this knowledge to dominate it, subject it, bring it to submission. My use of "master" imagery and perhaps phallocentric metaphors is intended: there is indeed what the feminist environmental philosopher Plumwood (1993) calls a "dream of power" in modern thinking. Considering ourselves as masters of nature, we use instrumental rationality to get what we want out of our environment in order to reach our (human) aims.

Today we can discern this way of seeing the environment in the discourse about natural "resources", "natural capital", and "ecosystem services". Let me take the latter as an example. The idea of "ecosystem services" is that the environment consists of ecosystems that supply resources and processes from which humanity benefits. In other words, the environment provides *services* to humankind. Similarly, one can say that it provides *goods*. For example, it provides "products" such as water, food, and energy, and it has processes that decompose waste, purify water, take care of crop pollination, etc. It also provides possibilities for recreation. Now seeing the environment as a provider of services or goods is a clear case of the objectivist–technoscientific way of thinking, which sees the environment as a "standing reserve". It is only viewed in terms of our, human, purposes, and is treated as such.

In spite of the widespread use of this kind of concept in policy and in the environmental literature, this way of thinking is very suspect, to say the least, from the point of view of modernity criticism. Indeed, in the humanities and the social sciences there has been sufficient criticism of the objectivist–technoscientific dimension of modern thinking. Consider, for instance, work inspired by Marx, Weber, and Heidegger. Moreover, even without modernity criticism many people recognize that using the natural environment as a mere means for human purposes has had devastating *consequences* for the natural environment. The criticism can thus be analysed into two types of objection. The first type concerns objections to this way of thinking in itself: the desire for total control and the "violence" that is present in the objectification of nature and non-human beings – and indeed human beings, which are also seen as objects; for example, machines. The second type of objection consists of arguments that point to the empirical consequences of this way of thinking: consequences for nature (e.g. destruction of biodiversity) and consequences for human beings. What we wanted to do was make human lives better by using science and technology, so the latter argument goes, but by destroying and threatening nature we have made things worse for humans, and now our very existence is threatened by those things that were meant to improve it. Although these critiques are one-sided (science and technology have also benefited us, as Latour [1993] has argued, science in practice is more non-modern than we think, and I also made a caricature[5] of them in order to clearly and briefly articulate the modern attitude), there is truth in them and in a less radical form they are embraced by many people. In particular, among people who are concerned about the environment, it has been widely recognized that we have somehow "alienated" ourselves from "nature".

This brings me to a second way of perceiving the environment, which I call "subjectivist–romantic". Historically and conceptually, an important response to the "objectivist–technoscientific" perception is and has been a romantic and nostalgic one. Against the objectivist orientation of science, the romantic thinker emphasizes subjective feeling. Against the domination of nature, the romantic poet expresses her love of nature. Against the "artificial" world of the "machine" and the "system", "artificial" society, and the destruction of the "natural", the romantic wants to promote harmony, naturalness, and authenticity. Some people are nostalgic about a "state of nature" (e.g. Rousseau), an original state when things were still "natural" and "good", when people could still live in an "authentic" way. Some think that this "natural" state is the wilderness, untouched by human hands and human tools. Others think the "original" state is a pastoral one, or one in which there was subsistence agriculture. Thus, here too, "nature" is used, but here "nature" has acquired a very different meaning. It is no longer a container of resources, but a mirror for our subjective feelings, a recipient of our love, a paradise lost, a place of harmony and goodness.

Today we can see this way of thinking in the desire many people have for "natural" products, for "authentic" travels, for going "outdoor" into "nature" rather than staying in in "artificial" environments. Romanticism has become so much part of how we think about the environment that we no longer notice it. Moreover, the objectivist–technoscientific current, which was supposed to be completely different from romanticism, has successfully absorbed, colonized, and "processed" our romantic desires. The eco-tourism industry and the outdoor equipment industry produce goods and provide services that respond to our romantic cravings. In the commercialization of "nature", romanticism meets objectivist production. The "natural" and the "authentic" have become commodified. In this way, the two faces of modernity meet. The objectivist rationalist and the subjectivist romantic find one another in a ghastly and sorrowful, yet so far rather successful, embrace.

Moreover, the romantic face is as anthropocentric as the technoscientific one: what counts is our *human* feeling, our desire for harmony. The environment tends to become a screen onto which we project our feelings, a resource for our romantic fantasies, a background to our self-absorbed attempts to be "authentic". It turns out that both are and remain strongly anthropocentric. In so far as they are romantic, those who embrace the "wild"[6] are not ecocentric at all; what they really care about and hope to find "outdoor" is the "nature", the "wilderness", and "authenticity", and the freedom in and of themselves. Real engagement with their environment is accidental or instrumental.

This leads me to a further deconstruction of the technoscientific–romantic dialectic. The romantic was supposed to be the antithesis of the technoscientific (with our current, somewhat odd modern mixture of both being the ugly, if not comic, synthesis of the two). But in fact the technoscientific and the romantic face of modernity share more than they would admit.[7] In particular, they share the same conception of the environment and the same conception of the human–environment relation. They conceptualize the environment as "nature", and although they give different meanings to the term, *both* use the term "nature" to construct the environment as something that is external to the human, something "out there" which either has to be forced into submission and transformed, or has to be left alone and function as a paradise lost to which we hope to return.[8] Thus, in both views, the relation between humans and their environment is an external one, there is a fundamental ontological *distance* and separation between them. It is only when we see the environment as something external to us that we can seek to become its master; that we can enslave it and treat it as an object that can be transformed or as a provider of goods and services. It is only when we view the environment as something external to us that we can treat it as a lost world and as a projection screen of our inner feelings. It is only when we see the human as fundamentally separated from its environment that we can think of the human as having to do with "subject" as opposed to "object"; "mind" or "spirit" (German: *Geist*) as different from "matter" and "flesh"; "culture" as distinct from "nature".

In addition, it is only when we see the human–environment relation in this way that we can set up an opposition between "anthropocentric" and "ecocentric" at all.[9] If the "human" is separated from "nature" and conceptually entirely distinct from it, then it seems that in our descriptive and normative orientations we have to *choose* between one of them. This is the modern dilemma. But it need not be ours. In the next pages, I will explore a route towards a less dualistic, less modern way of thinking about the human–environment relation. My main idea is that we are always already "environmental" by nature (pun intended) and that the environment can only appear as part of our "world"; that is, as perceived by us and as worked upon/transformed by us.

Towards a less dualistic understanding of the human–environment relation

Searching for different ways of thinking means searching for a different language, which is always connected to searching for different habits, different technologies, and indeed for different ways of life, for what Wittgenstein (2009) calls different *forms of life*. For this purpose, we have to attend to non-modern cultures: pre-modern cultures (as far as we can know them at all) or, if contemporary, *less* modern cultures, since most if not all living cultures have been transformed by modernity. Let me sketch a route for non-modern, or at least *less* modern thinking about the environment by using Heidegger (especially Zimmerman's interpretation; 1990) and Ingold (who is also influenced by Heidegger). My aim here is not to adopt Heidegger's history of being or his view of modern technology, but rather to discern in Heideggerian thinking a route, or perhaps only some stepping stones and signposts, towards (understanding) non-modern thinking and living.

Heidegger tried to think differently by playing with ancient Greek language. Although he partly thought in romantic terms – he is interested in the "authentic" – his Greek-German prose offers some suggestions for how we might re-frame the human–environment relation in a less modern way. Indeed, one alternative to the objectivist–technoscientific domination of the environment is a human–environment relation, which comes close to Heidegger's interpretation of the Greek word *techne*. In his essay 'The Question Concerning Technology' (Heidegger 1977), he criticizes modern technology and finds in the ancient Greek term *techne* a mode of knowing, doing, and making that is about skill, craft, and art, rather than scientific knowing and domination of nature. Now usually making things is seen as "human" or "cultural" and thus different from "nature"; this is why we do not associate "technology" with "nature". But Heidegger points to what he thinks is the original meaning of *techne* and makes a link between *techne* and *physis* (nature), and in this way tries to avoid the meaning of control, calculation, and domination. Let me explain this.

Heidegger's alternative to modern control is what he calls "bringing-forth" (*poiesis*), which happens in nature (*physis*) as well as in craft and art: both have "the bursting open belonging to bringing-forth, e.g., the bursting of a blossom into bloom" or the bringing-forth in the craftsman or artist (Heidegger 1977: 10–11). This is different from what Heidegger thinks modern technology does. Modern technology forces nature, "challenges" nature, *demands* from nature something (e.g. energy). Heidegger writes (1977: 17): "Everywhere everything is ordered to stand by, to be immediately at hand, indeed to stand there just so that it may be on call for a further ordering. . . . We call it the standing-reserve (*Bestand*)."

He also gives the examples of "human resources" and "the supply of patients for a clinic" (1977: 18) – something that is still surprisingly relevant to today's problems. Heidegger's point is that in so far as our current practices and our current technological actions are *modern*, they turn everything – including "nature" – into a standing-reserve. "Bursting open", by contrast, is a very different way of perceiving both humans and the environment. It suggests a different relation to the environment: one that is similar to what the craftsperson and the artist do, and one that has less to do with control and more with letting-be, with letting the revealing and the bringing-forth *happen* somehow. Yet as far as humans are concerned, this letting-be should not be understood as passivity. It is about doing things in a different way. Rather, it also has to do with an active *caring* and being-concerned-with – with oneself and with one's natural and social environment. As Zimmerman helpfully interprets Heidegger:

> Authentic producing, *techne*, then is not a matter of an "agent" using "force" to push material together into a specific form. Rather, it is a disclosure of entities for their own sakes. This conception of *techne* is consistent with Heidegger's contention that the very being of human *Dasein* is "care." To exist authentically means to care

for oneself, for others, and for things in an appropriate way. . . . The great work of art, especially poetry, is the *techne* which enables people to be at home with things.

(Zimmerman 1990: 230)

However, in Heidegger it is not very clear what exactly this *techne*, this art, this "letting-be", this "care", and this "being at home with things" means, let alone what this means for shaping our relation to the environment. It is clear that it is a non-modern way of perceiving and doing, and we may also conclude that it is a non-romantic way of perceiving and doing. As I have suggested, the romantic perception of the environment as "nature" is remarkably similar to that other modern mode of seeing and doing, the objectivist–technoscientific one. In a sense, *both* objectify the environment and instrumentalize it, albeit for different purposes. Heidegger presents an alternative here, and it is interesting, for example, that he does not see an opposition between care for oneself and care for things (say the not-self, if we must use dualistic language). With regard to the environment, it suggests the possibility that care for humans and care for the environment can coincide. But what exactly does this "care" relation mean when it comes to the environment? What does it mean to relate to the environment in a more *care-full* way, and in a way that lets things be? And how does it overcome alienation from the environment?

Perhaps we can get a clearer picture by looking at "non-modern" cultures and reflecting on their forms of life. It is clear that hunting-gathering, for example, offers a more engaged way of relating to the environment than sitting in an office and doing computer-mediated work five or six days a week. The problem with the latter is not that it is less "natural" and more "artificial", but that – at least so it seems[10] – the engagement with one's environment is rather limited, has low intensity. There is no direct relation between on the one hand the environment, and on the other hand what most of us do and (literally) making a living (including looking for food, building, etc.). The underlying problem, however, is not so much "more" or "less" environment, but rather *how* we perceive our environment and *how* we deal with it. Again this can be reflected upon by looking at non-modern, or (today) at least *less* modern cultures. Judged on the basis of descriptions quoted and discussed by the contemporary anthropologist Tim Ingold (2000), hunter-gatherers have clearly a less modern or non-modern form of life. The hunter does not view the animal as a standing-reserve of food and clothing, and the food is not "produced" – at least not in an industrial way; at most, it is "brought-forth" by the hunt and by related practices. And as Ingold suggests (see also below), the animal has to reveal itself, has to "give itself" somehow to the hunter. He quotes a study which found that the Cree people of north-eastern Canada think that they can only catch an animal when it is "given" to them and that only respectful activity can enhance the readiness with which the animals give themselves (Ingold 2000: 48). Thus, the animal cannot be *demanded* and it cannot be controlled. What is needed is respect, waiting, attention. If there is killing, it is only when it is necessary, and proper rituals should be observed to avoid wasting of meat (2000: 67). Moreover, a kind of conservation is required, but one that is different from the *management* of natural "resources". Ingold puts it as follows:

> [T]he environmental conservation practices by hunter-gatherers, if such it is, differs fundamentally from the so-called "scientific" conservation advocated by Western wild-life protection agencies. Scientific conservation is firmly rooted in the doctrine . . . that the world of nature is separate from, and subordinate to, the world of humanity. . . . Scientific conservation operates, then, by sealing off portions of wilderness and their animal inhabitants, and by restricting or banning human intervention.

(Ingold 2000: 68)

Hunter-gatherers, by contrast, care for their environment "through a direct engagement with the constituents of the environment, not through a detached, hands-off approach" (2000: 68). Care for the environment, in this view, is a relational matter: "it requires a deep, personal and affectionate involvement".[11] This makes it possible to see a hunt not as an act of control or violence, but rather as "proof of amicable relations between the hunter and the animal" (2000: 69). The model for this kind of human–environment and human–animal relationship is the human–human relation; indeed, Ingold's interpretation suggests that there is no *fundamental* difference here between human–human and human–animal relations (2000: 69); there is one social–natural world.

This way of experiencing and treating one's environment seems close to what Heidegger means with letting-be and care/concern (German: *Sorge*). Ingold describes (2000: 76) hunter-gatherer cultures and practices as living "a history of human *concern* with animals, insofar as this notion conveys a caring, attentive regard, a 'being with'." Again, such a description of our dealings with the environment and with the non-humans we encounter in it suggests that we can learn from anthropology about more care-full, engaged forms of life. It becomes clearer what less control and more care and letting-be, perhaps also letting-appear and letting-blossom, mean in practice.

However, there is a danger that we frame those ways of life in a romantic way, especially when we present such "primitive" (in history) or "indigenous" (today) people as being somehow "closer to nature", as more "natural" than we are. Although the myth of the noble savage has been criticized in philosophy and anthropology, it remains both tempting and highly problematic. What the romantic–nostalgic view gets right, I think, is the intuition that less modern people are or have been less alienated from their environment. What it gets wrong, however, is that it frames this intuition in terms of an opposition between "nature" and "culture", between "natural" and "artificial", between "authentic" and "non-authentic". It is true that they are more engaged with their environment, but to put this in terms of "nature" is to deny the very ground that makes such engagement possible. To think in terms of the nature–culture duality is itself part of *our* alienation. And our culture is as much "natural" or "authentic" as theirs. Let me further explain and develop this thought by deconstructing the nature–culture duality, which is what I take Ingold to be doing in *The Perception of the Environment* (2000).

Drawing on ethnographic observation of people who make their living by means of hunting and gathering, Ingold seeks to "replace the dichotomy of nature and culture with the synergy of organism and environment" (Ingold 2000: 9). People's involvement with their environment – also *our* involvement with our environment – is as much "natural" as it is "cultural". Ingold shows that "hunter-gatherers' perception of the environment is embedded in practices of engagement" rather than being the result of a social–cultural construction of "naturally given realities" (2000: 10). It is not the case that first there is a "nature" which then gets transformed in our perception into a "cultural" construction. Rather, knowledge is grounded in experience, in our active engagement with and in our environment. Finding a new relation to our environment is indeed about wanting to *be* at home, as Heidegger suggests; it is also about actively *making* oneself at home, in perception and action – which are intrinsically related. It is about home-making, about – to use a Heideggerian term that Ingold also uses – dwelling. "Experience", Ingold writes (2000: 11), "does not mediate between mind and nature, since these are not separate in the first place. It is rather intrinsic to the process of 'being alive to the world'." This view and these studies therefore do not only show that there are more engaged, perhaps more "direct" ways of relating to our environment; they also reveal a more basic, existential kind of engagement that we tend to forget about in the West and that is the very foundation of knowledge – in pre-modern or less modern cultures as well as in our culture: the basic, existential engagement all of us *always* have with our environment. We are indeed environmental beings. With Ingold (who is also influenced by Heidegger), we must thus reject both the dualism of objectivist science *and* the dualism of romanticism. The latter was a reversal of the former, but turning things upside down is not enough; we need to go beyond modern dualism, also concerning the subject–object dichotomy and the modern philosophy of mind and philosophy of perception that informs the dominant ways of seeing and treating the environment.

Indeed, from this Heideggerian, anthropological, more *integral* and certainly less dualistic point of view, it becomes also more clear what Zimmerman says about Heidegger's view of the relation between "earth" and "world"; that is, between the environment and the human, that earth and world should not be separated, but instead are internally related: "Rightly understood, *physis* names both the earthly and the worldly dimension of things. . . . *Physis* brings forth the humans necessary to disclose what *physis* brings forth." (Zimmerman 1990: 234).

Thus, there is not "nature" apart from human subjectivity and (I would add) human activity, which lets the environment appear – lets it appear at all, and in particular ways – and which transforms it: again, this can be done in various ways, modern ways and others. There is not on the one hand an "environment" and on the other hand "the human". There are humans, but these humans are already "natural" and are always already *in* their environment as they experience, know, and act. There is an environment, but as we speak, think, and interact with it, it is always already a perceived environment,[12] an experienced environment, a *lived environment* and an environment that is worked on by humans, which is as much "earth" as it is "world", non-human and human, natural and cultural. In the lived environment, there is a bringing-forth which is at the same time "natural" and "artificial", which is *physis* in the richer sense suggested by Heidegger and Zimmerman.

For thinking about the environment, this means that the modern ways of viewing the environment as "nature" are fundamentally wrong about the relation between humans and the environment, and that both anthropocentrism and ecocentrism (and those who frame the descriptive and normative discussion about the environment in these terms) get it wrong, at least in so far as they miss the point that (1) humans are always already "natural" and "environmental", indeed *environmental by nature*; and that (2) our environment is always an environment already perceived, known, experienced, and acted upon by humans. Even ecocentrism maintains the "human" versus "nature" duality; it is a mere reversal. Moreover, by framing the environment as "nature", these modern ways of seeing close off other possibilities to relate to nature, such as those suggested by Heidegger and by Ingold. We *can* interact with our environment in a different, more care-full, and less controlling way. There is that possibility – although it may be very difficult to actualize it under present conditions, that is, as far as we are still modern, as far as we still *live* modernity. Let me further reflect on this.

Closing and opening

In this chapter, I have articulated and distinguished two modern ways of perceiving (and treating) the environment – both of which revolve around the term "nature" and both of which are problematic in similar ways. It seems that we need a change here towards more intense and direct engagement with our environment, which must start from the recognition that our modern framing of the human–environment relation is highly problematic, and which can take inspiration from thinkers who explore non-modern ways of talking about the environment by studying and discussing past or present non-modern (or less modern) forms of life.

However, we cannot simply escape modern ways of perceiving and treating our environment. It seems entirely reasonable that, based on the insights presented in this chapter, we want to move towards a more engaged and care-full form of life, informed by a more relational and non-dualistic understanding of the environment and of the human–environment relation. As I argued in *Growing Moral Relations* (2012),[13] moral change is dependent on a number of related conditions of possibility, including language, culture, and technology. As this chapter suggests, how we think about the environment depends partly on what language we use. For example, I have shown that talking about "nature" is problematic and is connected to an entire (modern) culture, including ways of thinking and ways of doing. How we conceive of our relations to animals, for example, depends on the language we use to describe them (e.g. as "livestock" that stands reserve versus a particular animal as a "companion" or "friend" with a name) and also on the existing relations we have with them, relations that are embedded within an entire form of life. If we use the terms "wilderness" and "conservation management", this is also not morally neutral but presupposes modern thinking about, and a modern relation to, the environment. And the concept of "ecosystem services" is clearly illustrative of the modern, controlling, and demanding attitude, which Heidegger described as aiming to turn everything into a standing-reserve, a resource that we can use for our human purposes. I have also argued that even a concept such as "ecocentrism" is in danger of maintaining the modern status quo; in particular, the assumption that there is a "nature" versus a "culture", that the environment is only externally connected to human subjectivity and human sociality and human life. Unless we can change all this, we are still living under the spell of a way of thinking and doing that does not only destroy non-human environments and non-human beings, but that also denies, disrespects, and thus in a sense *violates* the environmental nature of humanity.

If we want a less dualistic and less alienated relation to the environment, then one thing we can do is attend to the moral significance of the language we use to talk about the environment. For example, in this chapter I have suggested that by using terms "engagement" and "care" we can try to articulate different relational possibilities. We need a conception of the human–environment relation which deconstructs not only the technoscientific–romantic dialectic, but also goes beyond the anthropocentrism–ecocentrism duality. This can give us a new framework from within which to think about the environment. It may also support experimenting with, and learning from, less modern attitudes and relations to the environment.

Does this mean environmental change is just around the corner? Such a view would be misleading. Of course we can tinker with our moral language and with our moral relations in order to try to make a change, indeed craft a change. I think this is what Heidegger did and what Ingold does. I also hope to have made a small contribution to this here. But perhaps this tinkering can only be done "in the margin", "marginally", slowly, and while accepting that there are limits to what we can do with words and that there is something that Heidegger calls a "destiny". We have already turned the earth into a "spaceship earth" that is managed, controlled, used, and sold. Under these conditions, and keeping in mind the dangers of modern thinking (Heidegger would say: "technological" thinking), it is a bad idea to respond to our predicament with a voluntarist call for action and for change, with a management plan, a call for revolution, or another modern device. Of course we can conclude from this discussion that we must change our moral–environmental language, we must change our moral–environmental relations, we must change our lives. But we will also need some letting-be, what Heidegger calls *Gelassenheit* (Heidegger 1966). If our care-full handling of, more intense engagement with, and respectful relating to the environment has that quality of bringing-forth, then new blossoms might burst into bloom; then we give a different, less modern environmental poetics a chance to unfold and reveal itself.

Notes

1 There are also other explanations. Empirical research in environmental psychology and education also point to various "internal" barriers to pro-environmental action such as problems related to motivation (for an overview, see Kollmuss and Agyeman 2002) and lack of direct experience and emotional attachment (Milton 2002). The latter – especially direct experience – is related to the argument of this chapter: what is needed is more engagement with nature, rather than romantic consumption of nature as an external good.

2 Note that I further develop my argument against a romantic environmental ethics elsewhere (Coeckelbergh 2015).

3 Some authors have also argued that there is such a bias in anthropology (e.g. Kopnina 2012) and philosophy (e.g. Plumwood 1993).

4 The term was first used in the 1960s by Adlai Stevenson, Barbara Ward, Kenneth Boulding, and Buckminster Fuller, and today it is often used to express concern about limited resources and unsustainable ways of living. Here I use it for illustrating our modern approach to the earth: a spaceship is something you manage, something you (want to) control. It is an instrument in your hands; it does not have intrinsic value. What matters is the survival and well-being of the crew.

5 In contrast to the received view, I hold that caricature, exaggeration, etc. can play a positive role in philosophical argument, provided one is aware of using it and provided it helps to bring out more clearly, to bring into the open, a particular view.

6 The qualification "in so far as they are romantic" is important in this sentence. Many contemporary writers might well be less modern and less romantic about the wilderness than suggested here, and in contemporary environmental philosophy, there has been a significant amount of critical discussion about the wilderness and wild nature. For example, Callicott has argued that the wilderness concept "perpetuates the pre-Darwinian Western metaphysical dichotomy between 'man' and nature", encouraging getting in contact with the radical non-human "other" (Callicott 1991: 348). Against Callicott, Rolston has argued that there are radical discontinuities between culture and nature (1991: 371). And in more recent work (2012: 179), he discusses the view that "wild nature, out there independently of humans does not exist. . . . The only nature we have from here onward is a nature to which humans have put their hands." Yet romanticism continues to heavily influence the common view of "nature" and "the wild" in environmentalism, and while the concepts of nature and wilderness have received much attention, their romantic heritage remains largely hidden.

7 Thus, romanticism can and must be seen as a mere *inversion* or *reversal* of technoscientific rationalism. And reversal means always that dualism is not overcome. To use Plumwood's metaphor:

> In feminist and liberation theory, the misty, forbidden passes of the Mountains of Dualism have swallowed many an unwary traveller in their mazes and chasms. In these mountains, a well-trodden path leads through a steep defile to the Cavern of Reversal, where travellers fall into an upside-down world which strangely resembles the one they seek to escape. Trapped Romantics wander here, lamenting their exile, as do various tribes of Arcadians, Earth Mothers, Noble Savages and Working-Class heroes whose identities are defined by reversing the valuations of the dominant culture.
>
> *(Plumwood 1993: 3)*

8 Note that the religious connotation here is not accidental – however, I will not further discuss this here.

9 See for example the Wikipedia definition of ecocentrism: it is defined as a term used "to denote a nature-centred, as opposed to human-centred system of values". This clearly reveals the term as being part of dualistic "nature"–"human" thinking.

10 My position on information technology and the way it shapes our contemporary form of life is more nuanced ("environment" also includes the "digital", "virtual", or "online" environment, and our activities include more than those mediated by electronic technologies), but let me for the sake of argument assume that, at least in general, there is today in our (work) lives less direct engagement with the environment, and that information technology plays *a* role in that; otherwise it is hard to explain our feeling of alienation and our romantic urge to escape and go into "nature".

11 See also Kay Milton's discussion (2002) of how we develop emotional commitments to nature.

12 By saying this, I do not mean that nature is a mere construct. It is a construct, but not a *mere* construct. We only have access to it through human language, culture, and technology. But on the other hand, it does not only exist in our imagination and our language. It is real and it is not entirely and not necessarily dependent on humans for its existence. But we cannot get to "it" except via human culture. It may have some degree of "otherness", but this otherness is never absolute and is always experienced through the lens of human subjectivity and human transformation of nature. Thus, I agree for example with Horigan (1988), who criticizes the Enlightenment opposition between nature and culture, and I partly agree with constructivist approaches to the environment. There is always perception of the environment: we always know it through the glasses of human subjectivity and culture, and this perception is also connected to social realities and values; it is never neutral. But I disagree if "constructed" means "only existing in language and human reality". (This is a long-standing debate in philosophy, of course: discussions about signs and representation, the question whether there is something independent of the perceiver, etc.)

13 More precisely, the book's focus was on changes to moral status, but its main arguments can be applied to moral change in general.

References

Callicott J B 1991. The wilderness idea revisited: The sustainable development alternative. *The Environmental Professional* 13: 235–247.

Coeckelbergh M 2012. *Growing moral relations: Critique of moral status ascription.* Basingstoke, UK and New York: Palgrave Macmillan.

Coeckelbergh M 2015. *Environmental skill: Motivation, knowledge, and the possibility of a non-romantic environmental ethics.* New York: Routledge.

Heidegger M 1966. *Discourse on thinking* (transl. J M Anderson and E H Freund). New York: Harper & Row.

Heidegger M 1977. *The question concerning technology and other essays* (transl. W Lovitt). New York: Harper & Row.

Horigan S 1988. *Nature and culture in Western discourses.* London and New York: Routledge.

Ingold T 2000. *The perception of the environment: Essays in livelihood, dwelling and skill.* London: Routledge.

Kollmuss A and Agyeman J 2002. Mind the gap: Why do people act environmentally and what are the barriers to pro-environmental behavior? *Environmental Education Research* 8(3): 239–260.

Kopnina H 2012. Toward conservational anthropology: Addressing anthropocentric bias in anthropology. *Dialectical Anthropology* 36(1): 127–146.

Latour B 1993. *We have never been modern* (transl. C Porter). Cambridge, MA: Harvard University Press.

Milton K 2002. *Loving nature: Towards an ecology of emotion.* New York: Routledge.

Plumwood V 1993. *Feminism and the mastery of nature.* London: Routledge.

Rolston III H 1991. The wilderness idea reaffirmed. *The Environmental Professional* 13: 370–377.

Rolston III H 2012. *A new environmental ethics: The next millennium for life on earth.* New York: Routledge.

Wittgenstein L 2009. *Philosophical investigations* (transl. G E M Anscombe, P M S Hacker and J Schulte). Revised 4th edn. Malden, MA and Oxford: Wiley–Blackwell.

Zimmerman M E 1990. *Heidegger's confrontation with modernity: Technology, politics, art.* Bloomington: Indiana University Press.

PART III

Ecological knowledge, belief, and sustainability

10

AN ANTHROPOLOGY OF NATURE – OR AN INDUSTRIALIST ANTHROPOLOGY?

David W. Kidner

Introduction

The alienation from nature that is foundational to so much of the industrialised world has also left its imprint on academic thought; and this trend has become even more firmly established since the mid-1980s. Today, the suggestion that evolutionary or ecological factors are primary influences on human life is distinctly out of fashion among anthropologists. The association of evolutionary perspectives with the eugenic movement, racist ideologies, and the sometimes simplistic notions of evolutionary psychology has led to a retreat into the paralysing embrace of a defensive relativist ideology which regards human being simply as the malleable product of cultural factors (Bloch 2005). This trend has been reinforced by reactions to the inadequacy of some early anthropologists' attempts to generalise about 'human nature'. But rejecting simplistic accounts of our rootedness within the natural world need not entail a wholesale denial of its significance; and in denying nature we risk being drawn into the same assumptive framework as industrialism, viewing humanity as anchored within a context that is defined solely by technological, 'cultural', and economic considerations. In this chapter, I will sketch out some of the ways that anthropology may sometimes unwittingly legitimate industrialism's destruction of the natural world, redefining humanity according to an industrial template and framing nature as the formless raw material out of which industrial products are manufactured.

Academic knowledge about 'human life in the world' tends to be polarised between a culture-free natural science and a culturally focused social science which pays only lip-service to nature. Today, for example, determined efforts are being made to rewrite natural history as if it was a solely *human* history (see e.g. Balée 2006). Even when nature is recognised, it is often merely as background to the human drama which is played out in a diversity of ways in different societies. Critiquing this backgrounding of the natural world, Tim Ingold has pointed out that even when indigenous peoples claim that their lives and practices are embedded in and follow from the character of their natural environment, anthropologists tend to invert this relationship so that the natural world in effect becomes an offshoot of the social (Ingold 2000: 54). As Douglas Medin and Scott Atran (1999: 6) remark, "at times within anthropology, the methodological point that anthropological observations are socially constructed has been elevated to a form of self-immolation that threatens to destroy the science part of anthropology as a social science and move it squarely into literature." Any adequate anthropology of nature has to start from the realist recognition that we participate in human life as embodied creatures who have evolved to possess certain basic tendencies and characteristics; and that although we have some leeway to define, interpret, and modify natural processes according to our needs and our cultural frames, ultimately we have to recognise them as the bedrock of our existence. Attempts to reverse this ontological primacy simply align anthropology with the industrialist enterprise and collude with it in its march towards oblivion.

The value difference ascribed to the human and the non-human realms is a central ideological component of industrialism, and the critique of anthropocentrism has an important place within the broader critique of industrialism's impact on the natural world. However, to the extent that theory focuses on this value difference, we overshadow the more politically incendiary realisation that industrialism also impoverishes the overwhelming majority of the *human* population (Kidner 2014). This impoverishment is often material (Manno 2000; Nadeau 2003), but especially undermines those social, cultural, and spiritual aspects of life that cannot be expressed monetarily (Lane 2000). The emergent principles of capital expansion are incompatible with the organic structures of the natural order, including those aspects of human being that are grounded in nature; and only those humans who can afford to insulate themselves from the degraded natural context can to some extent avoid the negative consequences of ecological degradation. Increasingly, industrialism benefits only itself, together with a small minority of the rich and powerful (McMurtry 2002); and to represent it as benefitting humanity more widely requires a vast and sophisticated propaganda network.

Environmental anthropology, therefore, faces some troubling challenges, which I will explore in this chapter. Do we continue to follow the industrialist mainstream in regarding nature as a subservient and secondary realm that is, supposedly, 'constructed' by cultural life; or do we recognise that humanity must ultimately be consistent with the natural order if it is to survive? Can we, for example, accept that notions such as sociality or intelligence, which have been used to prise humanity apart from the rest of the natural world, equally apply to many non-human species (Tsing 2013)? Can we recognise that attempts to maintain a radical distinction between the human and non-human realms ignore the important semiotic continuities between them (Hoffmeyer 2009; Kohn 2013)? And do our intellectual habits and theoretical preconceptions sometimes foster an unwitting convergence with industrial structures, so that anthropology becomes covertly hostile to the natural order?

The issues I have identified above, among many related ones, all revolve around a single underlying question that is central to the fate of life on this planet. This is the question of whether human life can be reoriented to be part of a healthy natural order, or whether nature is viewed simply as the raw material out of which we forge a technological and industrialist future. If anthropology is to contribute to this crucial debate, it cannot be rooted in the same assumptions as the industrial economy, nor can it simply view the current state of 'the postmodern world' as a taken-for-granted backdrop to research. I will begin to explore this point by outlining how the meaning of the term 'culture' has slid towards consistency with industrialist understandings.

The fragmentation of culture

The meaning of the term 'culture' has, since the mid-1960s, shed its earlier connotations of social integration and moral and conceptual progress, as well as the idea of "uniformity in the words, acts, and artifacts of human groups" (Kroeber and Kluckhohn 1952: 182). Rather than signifying the ability of a society to transform individual experiences and affects into socially coherent events, the term is often used today to indicate a descriptive taxonomy devoid of depth or meaning, simply referring to the behaviours and beliefs characteristic of almost any group from Manchester United fans to cocaine addicts. As Russell Jacoby (1999: 38) remarks, when "culture is defined as 'an ensemble of tools, codes, rituals, and behaviours', not simply every people, but every group and subgroup has a 'culture'", so that we lose sight of the larger organising principles of society. By tacitly assuming and legitimating the ongoing fragmentation of social structures, social scientific terminology therefore serves to camouflage actual changes in lived experience. In a similar way, current political and academic rhetoric is often liberally sprinkled with the term 'community' in order to give the impression that communities continue in good health, so that the survival of this label conceals the fading of the reality to which it refers. As Eric Hobsbawm put it, "never was the word 'community' used more indiscriminately and emptily than in the decades when communities in the sociological sense became hard to find in real life" (quoted by Bauman 2001: 151). What we see, then, is a fragmentation and an individualisation of social life, creating a homogeneous pool of mobile, needy, and freely available 'workers' and 'consumers'. This leaves an experiential vacuum where the integrative cultural forms that result from the coalescence of groups and individuals might be found – one that at an organisational level is filled by administrative and economic structures, and at the individual level, by consumerism and the productions of the leisure industry (Kasser 2003). Thus symbolic references to lost or desired aspects of social life are used to gloss over and disguise changes that might otherwise be recognised and challenged, facilitating our passive assimilation into the industrial economy.

Anthropological terminology has largely accepted these changes without comment or critique, marching in step to them, and therefore legitimating them. For example, Akhil Gupta and James Ferguson (1997: 1–3) argue that "the idea of 'a culture' as forming a system of meaning", requiring "description and analysis as an integrated totality", has become untenable, so that "the anthropological gaze" has instead turned "in the direction of social and economic processes that connected even the most isolated of local settings within a wider world". In place of "separate, integrated cultural systems", we now have a "polyphony" of "many different voices" within a "contested, contingent political field, the battlefield in an ongoing 'war of position'" (Gupta and Ferguson 1997: 3–5). As a *description* of a contemporary world dominated by competitive marketeering and military adventurism, this bellicose characterisation seems apt; but the point is that this splintered, conflictual social landscape needs to be critically examined rather than passively incorporated into ethnography. What are the underlying forces that fragment cultures into a homogeneous melting-pot of 'human resources'? What do they have in common with the forces that dissolve ecosystems into disparate stockpiles of 'raw materials'? What are their implications for human well-being? For example, if deforestation and the annexation of small landholdings in South America fractures communities and drives peasants to seek work in the cities, is this simply an opportunity to study the 'new forms of identity' that follow from these changes? If anthropology just accepts developments such as these as defining the stage on which research takes place, does the discipline not simply become an adjunct of the industrialist system, marching to the same drummer, and deriving its fundamental assumptions from it?

To summarise, a series of dissociations splits the human from the non-human, individuals from communities, and lived experience from representation. At the same time, however, there is a covert centripetal undertow in which these various fragments of a previously whole world are reconstituted and commodified to take their place within the new industrialist

121

forms of organisation. One of the functions of representing these split-off realms as intrinsically separate seems to be to conceal this uniformity of industrial effects, and to give the impression that industrialism is simply an expression of human enterprise that works for the human good, albeit by dominating other species. In maintaining these dichotomies, there is a danger that anthropology and other disciplines are unwittingly acting as 'fronts' for industrialist ideology in much the same way that public relations companies sanitise the actions of multinational corporations.

The fragmentation of ecosystems

In a close parallel to the social and experiential fragmentation that occurs within industrial and industrialising societies, contemporary understandings of the natural world frequently define individuals and small groups in terms of their own *intrinsic* characteristics rather than through their roles and relations within an ecosystem. As Ingold (2000: 217) puts it, "living things are classified and compared . . . in terms of intrinsic properties that they are deemed to possess by virtue of genealogical connection, *irrespective of their positioning in relation to one another in an environment*" (my italics). Just as cultures are viewed as collections of subcultures or individuals, so, within ecosystems, "difference is rendered as diversity" (Ingold 2000: 217), and the original notion of an 'ecosystem' as more than the sum of its parts has faded as ecosystems have come to be regarded, in Hull and Robertson's terms (2000: 106), as "transitory assemblages of biotic and abiotic elements that exist (or could exist) contingent upon accidents of environmental history, evolutionary chance, human management, and the theoretical perspective one applies to define the boundaries". This has practical consequences for their preservation, as Gary Nabhan argues:

> [T]he focus of efforts to conserve biodiversity has often been primarily on species rather than on their interactions. In many cases, ignorance of biotic interactions has led to the decline of a particular plant or animal species that has lost its mutualists, even though it occurs within a formally protected area such as a national park or forest.
>
> *(Nabhan 2001: 147)*

Furthermore, just as the integrative character of ecosystems often escapes biological science, so, as Nabhan shows, the indigenous knowledge that is continuous with and derived from this ecosystemic awareness is also often disregarded. However, the explicit prioritisation of industrial assumptions over those of non-industrial peoples is unfashionable in the post-colonial world; so while 'traditional ecological knowledge' (TEK) is frequently 'taken into account' by agencies and researchers, this often signifies merely that the style of assimilation to industrialism is less overt than before. As Paul Nadasdy (1999) shows, the integration of TEK into policy often requires that it undergo a process of 'distillation', so that only those aspects of TEK that are compatible with current scientific and administrative practice are recognised.

For example, while the Yukon Territorial Government Committee designated to make recommendations for the management of Dall sheep populations included First Nations representatives, the views of these representatives were subtly discounted through a process of data selection:

> [When] Kluane First Nation members expressed concern over the current practice of restricting hunters to shooting only full curl [fully mature] rams, [arguing that] these

animals are especially important to the overall sheep population because . . . it is from these mature rams that the younger rams learn proper mating and rutting behavior as well as more general survival strategies . . . the scientists and resource managers present at the meetings neither dismissed nor refuted this argument. They simply ignored it.

(Nadasdy 1999: 8)

Furthermore, understanding "how animals think and behave is every bit as important to [First Nations representatives] as the numbers sought by biologists; yet scientific resource managers are unable to accommodate this kind of information" (Nadasdy 1999: 8).

Multiple reductions of natural structure are occurring here. First, non-human beings, which have been widely regarded by many indigenous groups as intelligent and sentient, are reduced to biological automata that are qualitatively distinct from humankind. Second, Ingold (1996: 26) has pointed out that while the hunting behaviour of humans is invariably viewed as consciously planned, the often indistinguishable behaviour of non-human animals is frequently considered to have been "worked out for them in advance, by the evolutionary force of natural selection". And in addition to the 'filtering' process described above, Nadasdy shows that 'ecological knowledge' is often considered in isolation from social and cultural beliefs and practices, although Kluane people consider themselves to be "part of the land, part of the water", so that "the very idea of separating ecological from non-ecological knowledge becomes nonsensical" (Nadasdy 1999: 4). An environmental anthropology that allows itself to be drawn into these ideological slants is, therefore, not about *nature* at all, but rather about *industrialist representations* of nature. Conrad Kottak's (1999: 33) claim that "ecological anthropology must put anthropology ahead of ecology" is the anthropological echo of the industrialist imperative to separate humans from nature and to place us above it, denying the possibility of a culture that is *integrated with* ecology. Such assumptions, by implicitly incorporating the fundamentals of industrial ideology, undermine a supposed anthropology of nature from the start. Just as the loss of culture reduces us to individual 'consumers' and 'workers', so the representation of nature as a split-off 'resource' leads us to see it, as Steven Vogel (2002: 32) puts it, simply as an infinitely transformable "substrate that exists prior to our actions".

Industrialism is here operating in two ways: first, by directly fragmenting ecological and cultural systems; and second, by representing these systems as *essentially* and *already* fragmented. Like animals in a zoo or plants in a garden, we are viewed as individuals within an assumed context that remains largely mysterious and unrecognised; and because of our lack of systemic awareness, industrialism – under cover of misleadingly constant representations – can be slid into place of the natural order with minimal protest. For example, although the differences between contemporary economic realities and a village market are clear, terms such as 'market', 'value', and 'trading' give the impression that little has changed.

To the extent that anthropology naturalises and assumes this fragmentation of cultures and ecosystems, it demonstrates its assimilation by industrialism. For example, Daniel Gade's (1999: 6) argument that "even wilderness has become a human creation through our management of it and ultimately through the conscious societal decisions to preserve it as such" exemplifies the slippage between ecological reality and the way it is represented, allowing nature to be discursively – and later physically – assimilated to industrialist needs. Gade argues that to differentiate between domesticated and wild nature is "to set up a dichotomy between humans and 'wild nature' [therefore reinforcing] a false view of life on earth" (Gade 1999: 6). However, the crucial distinction is not between *humans* and wild nature, but between *industrialism* and wild nature. Many, mostly indigenous, humans have lived as part of the nature in which they were immersed without damaging or even, to varying degrees, 'managing' it (Nabhan 1982; Atran 2001); and cultural practices and beliefs may be rather directly rooted, as Laura Rival (1993: 649) suggests, in "a non-mediated perceptual knowledge which orders social relations between people, and between people and other living organisms". Furthermore, if nature is being assimilated and destroyed by an entirely alien and hostile form such as industrialism, then it is realistic, not dualistic, to draw a critical comparison between these foundational systems within which our lives exist. The assumption underlying Gade's statement is that 'human' equals 'industrial'; and while this equation is increasingly accurate as humanity becomes more fully colonised by industrialist assumptions, it is still far from universal.

Symbolic evasions

In understanding the interlinked fragmentation of social and natural systems, we have to appreciate the role played by humanity's great symbolic capacity, and by the media industry that exploits this symbolic capacity to advance industrial activity. This contrasts with the situation in less industrialised societies, in which forms of symbolism unamplified by digital technologies remain to varying degrees consistent with the natural order (see Kohn 2013). Indeed, people's survival is dependent on the accuracy of such articulations, since any divergence from natural processes is likely to have dire and immediate consequences. As Hugh Brody (2000: 117) remarks, for hunter-gatherers, "well being depends on knowing, rather than changing, the environment".

In the 'developed' world, a public relations industry has grown up to reframe, conceal, and justify casually destructive industrial operations, so that terms such as 'green', 'sustainable', 'smart', and 'eco-friendly' are invariably applied to practices that are none of these. For example, David Casagrande and Charles Peters (2013) demonstrate how a combination of propaganda disseminated by special interest groups, "self-limiting psychological practices and groupthink" (2013: 138), and the facile media repetition of metaphors such as 'the oasis in the desert' to cities such as Phoenix, Arizona undermine people's ability realistically to recognise and plan for water shortages in the coming years. Thus the 'construction of reality' is not a widely applicable description of a culturally universal process, but is rather an industrialist fantasy peculiar to those societies which have advanced propaganda apparatuses.

Likewise, while some anthropological writing has articulated the extent to which identity is necessarily embedded within its natural context, there has also been an influential tendency to portray it as created only within an abstract discursive universe (Ingold 2000: 54), so reproducing and normalising the rupture between people and their ancestral land that is all too often part of lived reality. Ethnographies such as Colin Turnbull's (1980) account of the disastrous outcome of the Ik's displacement from their mountain hunting grounds, or Cisco Lassiter's (1987) description of the psychological consequences of the forced removal of Navaho herders from their traditional lands, are deeply unwelcome in some anthropological circles since they insist that landscape is not a trivial or dispensable contributor to identity and culture. This reluctance to acknowledge landscape's contribution to identity may be partly derived from an unspoken awareness that spurious 'ancestral' claims have been used to justify the occupation and colonisation of others' land; but the occasional distortion of historical relation must be addressed by rejecting the distortion, not the relation. For example, despite plentiful examples that illustrate the crucial links between identity and land (e.g. Lassiter 1987; Feldman 2006), one writer regards "presumptions (never more than myth-ological) of the . . . 'natural' relationships between territories and culturally unitary groups

[as] increasingly ludicrous and unsupportable". "Palestinian refugee identity, *as other social identities*", he adds, is "the unstable contingent reflection of a dialogic process in which a number . . . of voices are raised" (Bisharat 1997: 203–204; my italics). In viewing humans as thus mobile and unattached, we take as our model the rats, lice, and other r-selected species – mobile, opportunistic, and omnivorous scavengers – that displace other species that have a more enduring relationship with a particular landscape.

Furthermore, this instability and contingency are arguably due to the forced removal of peoples from their lands, rather than being an intrinsic quality of identity. Were it allowed to evolve undisturbed through multi-generational interaction within a particular landscape, identity might well be more permanent, stable, and grounded. Thus while identity may be *distorted* by political and military turmoil, to argue that it simply *reflects* these factors is like suggesting that industrially degraded wilderness should be the basis of our understanding of wilderness ecology. The forces which distort current forms of identity cannot also be allowed uncritically to shape anthropological theory, but should themselves be identified and critiqued. Likewise, an adequate environmental anthropology cannot just study peoples' relation – or lack of relation – to the land *as both are currently constituted*, but should also retain a longer-term notion of what constitutes a *healthy* relation. As we will see in the next section, however, industrialism operates precisely by suppressing this historical awareness.

Affirming an industrialist subjectivity

Ecosocial systems also have *temporal* rhythms and patterns, and these too may become assimilated to an industrialist present. Industrialism operates by sucking the past into the present and borrowing from ('discounting') the future; and its objectives are generally based around short- or medium-term profitability (Nadeau 2003). For example, cultural traditions and ancient churches are reborn as tourist attractions, wilderness becomes a source of 'raw materials', and genetic manipulation threatens to scramble evolutionary timescales. Our children are likely to inherit a world in which the relatively orderly processes of evolution have been replaced by an all-consuming explosion of instant need fulfilment in which everything, in effect, becomes defined by its economic value in the present. Oblivious to these changes, consciousness instead orients itself through them, so that accepted norms and practices are based only on current ideology. The present sweeps away rather than builds on the past, and what cannot be commodified becomes merely obsolete. Individual artefacts are presented as history-less, and history is rewritten as a prelude to capitalism, which is made to seem inevitable, the only possible way of life. As Paul Connerton, following Lukács, argues:

> [T]he capitalist system of production was constituted by the loss of its memory of the very process through which it is produced. As an organised structure of misrecognition, it blocked access to recollection of the past processes which erected it and maintained it in being.
>
> *(Connerton 2009: 43)*

Importantly, this 'structure of misrecognition' extends the notion of forgetting "from something an individual might do . . . to something societies, or indeed civilisations, might do" (Connerton 2009: 47). Memory, and its organisation, become a function of technologies and systems that are *outside* the individual (Donald 2001: 276–277), and so are subject to the interests and priorities of these external organisations, moulding consciousness towards an unquestioning assumption that capitalism is inevitable, rational, and even 'natural'. Likewise, conscience and empathy appear to be diminishing as surveillance is becoming widespread (Konrath *et al.* 2011); and awareness of the natural world is receding (Atran and Medin 2008) at the same time as the digital representation of wild nature on TV and in glossy magazines and calendars is becoming more widespread. Thus there is a technology of consciousness within industrial society that influences what is remembered and what is forgotten, raising questions about the degree of agency that is actually allowable within supposedly 'democratic' societies. It is ironic that at a time when concepts of 'individual choice' and 'democracy' within the 'free world' have been used to distinguish the character of industrial life from that in (sometimes, in some respects) less 'free' societies, individuality is simultaneously being dissolved into bureaucratic, governmental, and corporate structures.

The social sciences have often faithfully reproduced these trends, seeing the past simply as a precursor to the present, shorn of any characteristics that importantly distinguish the two eras. As Alf Hornborg (2001: 234) remarks, it "is ironic that the image of the spiritual, ecological native, though widely disseminated by earlier generations of anthropologists, is now being systematically dismissed as romanticism". Correspondingly, the early existence of wild nature that was relatively unchanged by large-scale human action is nowadays also dismissed as a 'romantic fantasy'. Wilderness, we are told, is not only absent today; it never existed at all (e.g. Mann 2000), so that its destruction by industrialism must also be a fantasy!

This manipulation of subjectivity is essential in detaching human consciousness from the natural order so that it becomes consistent with industrialism's focus on short-term profitability. While it is true, as Edward Sampson (1981: 735–736) remarks, that existing "arrangements of power and domination within a society are served when people accept a change in their subjective experience as a substitute for changes in their objective reality", it is equally true, as I pointed out above, that the same arrangements of power and domination are served when real and malign changes are concealed by a manipulated *constancy* of subjective experience. Television nature programmes portray apparently wild and undamaged landscapes – sometimes authentically, but increasingly through contrived representations in studios, zoos, and game parks (Vivanco 2002); and the use of terms such as 'forest', 'wilderness', 'nature' to apply to ever more impoverished wildlands gives a misleading impression of ecological constancy. The constructionist metaphor which is so prevalent in anthropology is quite inadequate to address this issue, since it views subjectivity as a product of the *existing* 'social' context, implicitly denying the possibility – or the reality – of a disjunction between the two. An adequate theorisation of life in the industrialised world needs to recognise and express the increasing tension between the vestiges of our evolutionary past within the natural order and a social and economic context that is indifferent to humanity, so that important elements of human being are allowed to survive only in the interstices of industrial organisation. In this respect, the predicament of humans is much the same as that of non-human creatures such as the captured wild horses described in Cormac McCarthy's (2002: 107) novel *All the Pretty Horses*, "coming to reckon slowly with the remorselessness of this rendering of their fluid and collective selves into that condition of separate and helpless paralysis which seemed to be among them like a creeping plague".

The effects of this condition on human beings represent a curious theoretical lacuna which has seldom been explored. Could it be that the multiple social, environmental, and psychological pathologies we are witnessing today are due not to the working out of vulnerabilities that are intrinsic to humankind, but instead to our colonisation and imprisonment within an ideology that undermines not only ecological structure, but every other aspect of being, including human being? As John Rodman (1977: 102) suggests, "the 'wild beast' that we have so long caged within us is nasty, violent, and insatiable, not because it is wild, but because it has been caged". Thus the reformulation of human being operates in synchrony with the physical restructuring of the earth, and both are facets of the overall industrialist project. History, memory, and understanding must also be brought into line with the industrialist narrative, and alternatives are to be dismissed as 'flawed', 'romantic', and 'nostalgic', "edenic narratives . . . of origins and purity" (Braun and Castree 1998: 23). These are fundamental – indeed, epoch-defining – changes in the character of the earth and its inhabitants; and an adequate environmental anthropology cannot avoid engaging with them.

Regrettably, an unresisting acceptance of the industrial context as 'reality' has become increasingly common in anthropological writing, the accepted wisdom being succinctly summarised by a leading anthropological text of the 1980s: "to invoke another culture . . . is to locate it in a time and space contemporaneous with our own, and thus to see it as part of our world, rather than as a mirror or alternative to ourselves" (Marcus and Fischer 1986: 134). By de-emphasising the "exotic other", we are told, anthropology can turn its attention to "more important" issues at home, such as "providing ethnographic data for administrative policy" (Marcus and Fischer 1986: 113). Thus "our world" becomes the only possible world, and as Hornborg (2001: 235) sardonically puts it, we "have always been capitalists".

Nature as industrially manufactured

Consistent with this, the notion that nature is 'socially constructed' has become influential in anthropological writing; and I will argue that this is a profoundly incoherent viewpoint that has sown confusion amongst anthropologists. Since I have critiqued constructionism elsewhere (Kidner 2000), I will here consider only one of its implications – that nature does not have its own structure, but is rather a sort of raw material that takes whatever form we humans care to give it. Thus Vogel claims that when

> appeals are made to 'what nature requires' or assertions of knowledge made regarding nature's true 'essence' or 'telos', all that happens . . . is that particular socially mediated conceptions get projected onto a supposedly pre-social world and then [are] illegitimately claimed to have been grounded there.
>
> *(Vogel 2002: 34–35)*

Here the 'social' is actually a sort of alias for 'industrial', as Braun and Castree (1998: 4) imply in their claim that "global nature is increasingly remade in the image of the commodity". In this perspective, then, nature has been fully dissolved into industrialism; and to the extent that anthropology adopts the constructionist metaphor, it is clear that it is floating on the same ideological tide as the entire industrialist project.

However, to argue that nature is 'remade' in the image of the commodity begs the question of how nature was made in the first place; and this – together with the whole process of its subsequent dissolution into the 'raw materials' of industrial production – is what is ignored by the constructionist thesis. For constructionists, nature (the raw material sort) is simply the shadowy and formless matter out of which nature (the humanly constructed sort) is forged. In effect, then, there are two natures, one consisting of the 'raw materials' and the other the results of human action on this 'raw material' (Ingold 2000: 40–43). This curiously schizoid view is often implicit in anthropological writing, but occasionally becomes explicit, as in the argument that "the process by which nature is constructed is preceded, presumably, by the experience of it in an unconstructed or differently constructed condition and this presupposes that the natural world is experienced in two quite separate moments" (Franklin 2002: 51). More commonly, however, anthropologists vacillate about whether nature stands outside cultural existence, or whether it is a product of it. For example, Keith Basso explains that for White River Apache,

> the past lies embedded in features of the earth – in canyons and lakes, mountains and arroyos, rocks and vacant fields – which together endow their lands with multiple forms of significance that reach into their lives and shape the ways they think.
>
> *(Basso 1996: 34)*

Later, however, it becomes clear that this relation between the White River Apache and the land they inhabit is not really a relation at all, but rather a matter of solipsistic musing:

> [P]laces may seem to speak. But . . . such voices as places possess should not be mistaken for their own. Animated by the thoughts and feelings of persons who attend to them, places express only what their animators enable them to say . . . Human constructions par excellence, places consist in what gets made of them . . . and their disembodied voices, immanent though inaudible, are merely those of people speaking silently to themselves.
>
> *(Basso 1996: 108)*

There is an ironic truth here; for the academic claim that nature and personhood are 'socially constructed' is indeed becoming more accurate as the natural order is demolished and replaced by a fabricated 'nature'. But this is not just 'the way things are', to be taken for granted by anthropologists as providing an assumed background for their more detailed research into particular identities, subcultures, and social practices. It is, rather, the vital core of current political, cultural, and environmental change that anthropologists should be most intensively investigating. Both the view that nature consists of formless 'natural resources' which are processed to form saleable products, as well as the assertion that our ideas of and knowledge about nature are projections onto this formless 'substrate', are moments within a broader industrialist current that attempts to deny the underlying properties and tendencies of nature and to invert the necessary grounding of life within the evolutionarily-derived natural order. For an anthropology of nature to assume this inversion without critique or comment represents the most extraordinary and fundamental error; for, as Roy Bhaskar (1997: 22) points out, while knowledge may be socially constructed, it is about things that *aren't* socially constructed.

But what sort of social or cultural environment is it that supposedly constructs us? Given the alleged importance of society in constructing both us and our natural environment, one might think that a good deal of effort would be made to assess the character of this society. A search through the constructionist literature, however, reveals that extraordinarily little has been written about this vital question, and there is simply a tacit presumption that nature reflects 'social' structures and processes, harmoniously complementing the industrial system. This conveniently denies the reality that nature and industrial society are utterly opposed to each other, and that the latter is consuming and destroying the former. The vagueness of the term 'social' is employed in this context to disguise the fact that the underlying determinants of the changes that are taking place in the natural world are *economic*. On the other hand, the much more plausible possibility that our character, as well as that of the rest of the natural world, has been shaped not only by social processes, but also by multiple, evolving interactions within the totality of the natural order over evolutionary timescales, mostly in distinctly non-industrial environments, is generally dismissed as 'essentialist'.

The constructionist ideology therefore serves the purpose of uprooting us from the natural order and replanting us within an unexamined industrial context, providing a pseudo-explanation that works in four main ways. First, by denying the character of wild nature, it makes it seem invisible – a fantasy or myth rather than an experienced reality or, increasingly, a memory. Second, by naturalising the metaphor of industrial production, it normalises industrialism's destruction of nature by making it appear consistent with the ceaseless flow of natural change. Third, the 'social construction' of reality and personhood is invoked to 'explain' behaviour in much the same way that a mediaeval theologian might have ascribed events to 'God's will' or a behaviourist might refer to 'the contingencies of reinforcement'. In other words, by providing an 'explanation' that is both vague and apparently all-encompassing, it puts a stop to further thought about the reasons for our environmental debacle, thus heading off any challenge to industrialism's dominance. And fourth, the inoffensive term 'social', by making the processes involved seem to be just a natural part of everyday life, serves to mystify and disguise the *industrialist* drive to commodify, exploit, and replace the natural order. Anthropological theorising of this type therefore achieves the same objectives in the ideological sphere as corporate expansionism, military aggression, and the use of debt as an economic weapon achieve them in physical reality – to annul existing cultural and natural structures and to put in place alternatives consistent with industrialism.

Conclusion: an industrialist anthropology?

The influences that shape social science are often indirect and conceptually elusive, making anthropology's subtly industrialist slant difficult to perceive. These influences exist within a total context which seems numbingly 'real', enclosing both everyday life and academic thought within a deceptively consistent set of assumptions and underlying beliefs. This belief system is maintained by a relentless barrage of sophisticated propaganda from the corporate world, government, and the mass media, as well as the more subtle pressures of academic fashion, making divergence from assumed attitudes difficult, psychologically costly, and sometimes career-changing. Whether environmental anthropology chooses to passively incorporate this ideological frame, or alternatively to break out of the ideological prison and explore genuinely critical perspectives, will define the discipline for decades to come.

References

Atran, Scott, 2001. "The vanishing landscape of the Peten Maya lowlands". In Luisa Maffi (ed.), *On Biocultural Diversity: Linking Language, Knowledge, and the Environment*. Washington, DC: Smithsonian Institution Press.

Atran, Scott and Douglas Medin, 2008. *The Native Mind and the Cultural Construction of Nature*. Cambridge, MA: The MIT Press.

Balée, William L, 2006. "The research programme of historical ecology". *Annual Review of Anthropology* 35(1): 75–98.

Basso, Keith, 1996. *Wisdom Sits in Places*. Albuquerque: University of New Mexico Press.

Bauman, Zygmunt, 2001. *The Individualized Society*. Cambridge, UK: Polity Press.

Bhaskar, Roy, 1997. *A Realist Theory of Science*. London: Verso.

Bisharat, George E, 1997. "Exile to compatriot: Transformations in the social identity of Palestinian refugees in the West Bank". In Akhil Gupta and James Ferguson (eds), *Culture, Power, Place: Explorations in Critical Anthropology*. Durham, NC: Duke University Press, pp. 203–233.

Bloch, Maurice, 2005. "Where did anthropology go? Or, the need for 'human nature'". www.lse.ac.uk/PublicEvents/pdf/20050224-bloch-anthropology.pdf (accessed 13 January 2014).

Braun, Bruce and Noel Castree (eds), 1998. *Remaking Reality: Nature at the Millennium*. London: Routledge.

Brody, Hugh, 2000. *The Other Side of Eden: Hunter-Gatherers, Farmers, and the Shaping of the World*. Vancouver, BC: Douglas & McIntyre.

Casagrande, David and Charles Peters, 2013. "Ecomyopia meets the *longue durée*: Information ecology of the increasingly arid southwestern United States". In Helen Kopnina and Eleanor Shoreman-Ouimet (eds), *Environmental Anthropology: Future Directions*. London: Routledge, pp. 97–144.

Connerton, Paul, 2009. *How Modernity Forgets*. Cambridge, UK: Cambridge University Press.

Donald, Merlin, 2001. *A Mind So Rare*. New York: W. W. Norton & Company.

Feldman, Ilana, 2006. "Home as refrain: Remembering and living displacement in Gaza". *History and Memory* 18(2): 10–47.

Franklin, Adrian, 2002. *Nature and Social Theory*. London, Sage.

Gade, Daniel, 1999. *Nature and Culture in the Andes*. Madison: University of Wisconsin Press.

Gupta, Akhil and James Ferguson, 1997. "Culture, power, place: Ethnography at the end of an era". In Akhil Gupta and James Ferguson (eds), *Culture, Power, Place: Explorations in Critical Anthropology*. Durham, NC: Duke University Press, pp. 1–29.

Hoffmeyer, Jesper, 2009. *Biosemiotics: An Examination into the Life of Signs and the Signs of Life*. Chicago, IL: University of Chicago Press.

Hornborg, Alf, 2001. *The Power of the Machine: Global Inequalities of Power, Technology, and Environment*. Walnut Creek, CA: AltaMira Press.

Hull, R Bruce and David P Robertson, 2000. "The language of nature matters: We need a more public ecology". In Paul H Gobster and R Bruce Hull (eds), *Restoring Nature: Perspectives from the Social Sciences and Humanities*. Washington, DC: Island Press, pp. 97–118.

Ingold, Tim, 1996. "The optimal forager and economic man". In Philippe Descola and Gísli Pálsson (eds), *Nature and Society: Anthropological Perspectives*. London: Routledge.

Ingold, Tim, 2000. *The Perception of the Environment*. London: Routledge.

Jacoby, Russell, 1999. *The End of Utopia: Politics and Culture in an Age of Apathy*. New York: Basic Books.

Kasser, Tim, 2003. *The High Price of Materialism*. Cambridge, MA: The MIT Press.

Kidner, David, 2000. "Fabricating nature: A critique of the social construction of nature". *Environmental Ethics*, 22(4): 339–357.

Kidner, David, 2014. "Why 'anthropocentrism' is not anthropocentric". *Dialectical Anthropology* 38(4): 465–480.

Kohn, Eduardo, 2013. *How Forests Think: Toward an Anthropology Beyond the Human*. Berkeley: University of California Press.

Konrath, Sara H, Edward H O'Brien, and Courtney Hsing, 2011. "Changes in dispositional empathy in American college students over time: A meta-analysis". *Personality and Social Psychology Review* 15(2): 180–198.

Kottak, Conrad, 1999. "The new ecological anthropology". *American Anthropologist* 101(1): 23–35.

Kroeber, A L and Clyde Kluckhohn, 1952. *Culture: A Critical Review of Concepts and Definitions*. Cambridge, MA: Peabody Museum of American Archaeology and Ethnology, Harvard University.

Lane, Robert E, 2000. *The Loss of Happiness in Market Democracies*. New Haven, CT: Yale University Press.

Lassiter, Cisco, 1987. "Relocation and illness: the plight of the Navaho". In David M Levin (ed.), *Pathologies of the Modern Self: Postmodern Studies on Narcissism, Schizophrenia, and Depression*. New York: New York University Press.

McCarthy, Cormac, 2002. *All the Pretty Horses*. Volume 1 of *The Border Trilogy*. London: Paladin.

McMurtry, John, 2002. *Value Wars: The Global Market versus the Life Economy*. London: Pluto Press.

Mann, Charles, 2000. "Three trees: Inescapable blendings of the human and the natural". *Harvard Design Magazine*, Winter/Spring: 31–35.

Manno, Jack P, 2000. *Privileged Goods: Commoditization and its Impact on Environment and Society*. Boca Raton, FL: CRC Press.

Marcus, George and Michael M J Fischer, 1986. *Anthropology as Cultural Critique*. Chicago, IL: University of Chicago Press.

Medin, Douglas L and Scott Atran (eds), 1999. *Folkbiology*. Cambridge, MA: The MIT Press.

Nabhan, Gary P, 1982. *The Desert Smells like Rain*. Tucson: University of Arizona Press.

Nabhan, Gary P, 2001. "Cultural perceptions of ecological interactions". In Luisa Maffi (ed.), *On Biocultural Diversity: Linking Language, Knowledge, and the Environment*. Washington, DC: Smithsonian Institution Press.

Nadasdy, Paul, 1999. "The politics of TEK: Power and the 'integration' of knowledge". *Arctic Anthropology* 36(1–2): 1–18.

Nadeau, Robert L, 2003. *The Wealth of Nature: How Mainstream Economics Has Failed the Environment*. New York: Columbia University Press.

Rival, Laura, 1993. "The growth of family trees: Understanding Huaorani perceptions of the forest". *Man* 28(4): 635–652.

Rodman, John, 1977. "The liberation of nature?" *Inquiry* 20(1–4): 83–145.

Sampson, Edward, 1981. "Cognitive psychology as ideology". *American Psychologist* 36(7): 730–743.

Tsing, Anna, 2013. "More-than-human sociality: A call for critical description". In Kirsten Hastrup (ed.), *Anthropology and Nature*. New York: Routledge, pp. 27–42.

Turnbull, Colin, 1980. *The Mountain People*. London: Macmillan.

Vivanco, Luis A, 2002. "Seeing green: Knowing and saving the environment on film". *American Anthropologist* 104(4): 1195–1204.

Vogel, Steven, 2002. "Environmental philosophy after the end of nature". *Environmental Ethics* 24(1): 23–39.

11

SPIRITUAL ECOLOGY, SACRED PLACES, AND BIODIVERSITY CONSERVATION

Leslie E. Sponsel

Introduction

Many cultures have survived and adapted successfully for centuries or even millennia (Anderson 2010, 2014; International Union for the Conservation of Nature and Natural Resources 1997). Others have degraded their habitat and depleted the natural resources in it to the extent of undermining their economic and social viability (Sponsel 2012, 2013a). Among those that have proven to be sustainable, it can be hypothesized that spiritual ecology, and one of its manifestations through sacred places in nature, may be important in facilitating biodiversity conservation in many cases (cf. Grim 2001). Accumulating research from different scientific disciplines is progressively exploring and documenting the possibilities of connections between sacred places and biodiversity conservation around the world (Dudley *et al.* 2005; Lee and Wauchope 2003; Pungetti *et al.* 2012; Ramakrishnan *et al.* 1998; Schaaf and Lee 2006; Verschuuren *et al.* 2010). In such efforts, environmental anthropology has a strategic role to play in basic research, applied work, and advocacy (Orlove and Brush 1996, Sponsel 2007a).

Previously these three subjects of spiritual ecology, sacred places, and biodiversity conservation were treated separately and usually still are. Here the special focus is on their mutual relevance. This chapter explores each of these three in turn, and then demonstrates their interrelationships with the particular case of sacred groves.

Spiritual ecology

Spiritual ecology refers to the vast, complex, diverse, and dynamic arena at the interfaces of religions and spiritualities on the one hand; and on the other, environments, ecologies, and environmentalisms. The term spiritual ecology is used simply because it is more inclusive than religion, referring to individual as well as organizational ideas and actions in this arena. In addition, it parallels the designation of other approaches within environmental anthropology, such as cultural ecology, historical ecology, and political ecology (Sponsel 2007a). Each of these four approaches may be viewed as complementary rather than exclusionary, as simply a personal preference and because of the necessity of pursuing some focus. (For surveys of spiritual ecology, see Gottlieb 2006a, 2006b; Grim and Tucker 2014; Kinsley 1994; Sponsel 2012, 2014a; Taylor 2005, 2010; and Tucker 2006.)

Since the first Earth Day, on 22 April 1970, numerous and diverse secular approaches have contributed significantly toward resolving, or at least reducing, many particular environmental problems, such as some types of air and water pollution in certain areas. In addition, whole new fields of professional expertise, research, and teaching have developed, such as environmental sciences, studies, education, philosophy, ethics, history, economics, politics, policies, law, and regulations (Collett and Karakashian 1995). Nevertheless, a multitude of diverse environmental problems persist from the local to the global levels, new ones are being discovered, and many are even worsening. Moreover, a growing number of astute observers and deep thinkers are convinced that the situation worldwide is increasingly grave and urgent (e.g. Macy and Johnstone 2012). Their view is sustained by numerous international scientific investigations, such as the Millennium Ecosystem Assessment (United Nations Environmental Programme 2005). Thus, while secular approaches to environmental concerns are certainly necessary and have achieved significant progress, just as certainly so far they have proven insufficient in resolving many environmental problems. Most treat superficial symptoms of particular problems, rather than the deeper root causes as a whole.

Spiritual ecology may be pursued as a scientific or academic endeavor, a personal path of spirituality, and/or a form of environmental activism (e.g. Sponsel 2014b). Those who are variously engaged in spiritual ecology share the conviction that the worsening environmental crisis, including global climate change, can only be resolved by fundamental changes in the way humans relate to nature as individuals and as societies. This must involve far more sustainable and greener environmental worldviews, attitudes, values, behaviors, and institutions (Sponsel 2012). No single religion is considered to be either the cause of or the solution for environmental problems (cf. White 1967). Instead, among many other initiatives, the adherents to whatever religion or spiritual practice they prefer are encouraged to reconnect with nature and pursue introspection in order to develop much more environmentally friendly ideas and actions in the areas where they live and work (Hecking 2011).

Religion is an ancient cross-cultural universal. No society is known that does not have one or more religions, even though individuals within any society vary in the manner and degree of their religiosity and/or spirituality, if any (Blanes and Espirito Santo 2014; Strenski 2008). As a component of culture as a system, religion can be a most powerful influence on the worldviews, values, attitudes, motivations, decisions, and behaviors of individuals, groups, and societies, for better or worse, depending on the specific circumstance. This includes the ways that individuals interact with nature and deal with environmental problems (Anderson 2012a, 2012b, 2014; Selin 2003; Sponsel 2012).

Religions are alternative ways of affording nature various philosophical, cultural, moral, and spiritual meanings and significances. They may define the place of humans in nature, including how they should act toward non-human beings and other aspects of the environment. A religion may be grounded in the idea that nature as a whole is sacred, and/or particular places in nature are especially sacred, such as Mount Fuji in Japan, Uluru (Ayers Rock) in Australia, and Mount Kilimanjaro in Tanzania (Bernbaum 1990). Many scientists, as well as religious leaders and others, recognize that whatever someone regards as sacred or spiritual is much more likely to be revered and protected, although not always (e.g. Global Forum 1990).

Since the 1980s, one of the most interesting and promising developments has been the growing dialogue among people from different religions, as well as between representatives from religions and sciences, regarding the environment, this in spite of recurrent mutual antagonisms through the centuries (Clayton 2008; Kellert and Farnham 2002). Although there are many problems and issues that these parties find difficult, if not impossible, to confront constructively together, the worsening environmental situation in general has increasingly become a catalyst for dialogue, and more importantly, action, sometimes in collaboration (Grim and Tucker 2014; Sponsel 2012).

At the same time, there are degrees of religiosity among different individuals, from nominal to strict adherence, and there are non-believers as well. There are also serious discrepancies between the professed ideals and actual behaviors of individuals and organizations in religion, as in any other sector of society including science and academia. One example of such complications is the Ganges, the most sacred river in India for Hindus seeking ritual purification, yet simultaneously the most polluted physically (Alley 2002). It should be cautioned as well that particular religious beliefs and practices may be ecologically adaptive, maladaptive, or neutral (Tanner and Mitchell 2002). Thus, overgeneralization and oversimplification need to be avoided in considering the relationships between any religion and the environment. It is best to objectively, systematically, and holistically scrutinize with an open mind the specifics of the ecology of particular religious individuals and communities on a case-by-case basis.

In spite of many complications, difficulties, obstacles, and uncertainties, spiritual ecology, encompassing religious environmental action, might finally prove to be a turning point in alleviating many environmental problems. However, only coming decades will reveal the full extent of its success, although there have already been many achievements (Gottlieb 2006a; Grim and Tucker 2014; Sponsel 2012). Spiritual ecology can provide critiques and alternatives to the exclusively anthropocentric, dualistic, reductionist, materialistic, utilitarian, and economistic worldview that has contributed to environmental problems and crises (e.g. Macy and Johnstone 2012). Among other pivotal points, spiritual ecology challenges the fundamental fallacy infecting industrial capitalism, that unlimited growth is possible on a limited base. That base includes land, water, and natural resources as well as the capacity of environmental systems to absorb and process pollution (Meadows *et al.* 2004; Rees *et al.* 1998). Some see the impact of spiritual ecology as potentially revolutionary, albeit in a non-violent manner. However, those within the establishment who wish to maintain the status quo may view it as subversive and to be totally rejected (see Crosby 2002; Hawken 2007; Macy and Johnstone 2012; Nadeau 2013; Sponsel 2012; Taylor 2010; Uhl 2013).

Some vocal skeptics and critics exist who summarily dismiss spiritual ecology. One is Murray Bookchin (1995) in his social ecology indictment of mysticism and supposed anti-rationalism, but he is clearly biased by Marxism. Iain Provan's (2013) critique of what he refers to as the "questionable myth" of deep ecology, and Robert Whelan *et al.* (1996) in their spurious criticisms of so-called "radical environmentalism" provide other examples. Both of the last two books are obviously biased by the version of Christianity of the authors. Within environmental anthropology, Andrew P. Vayda stands out in opposing what he mistakenly views as spiritual ecology's privileging of religion (Sponsel 2014c; Vayda 2014). As indicated previously, spiritual ecology can be viewed as complementary with other approaches in environmental anthropology, each simply being a personal preference in response to the necessity of pursuing some focus, but not exclusionary. That does not signify a kind of totalitarianism that automatically rejects all other possible considerations, contrary to Vayda.

Substantial accomplishments have been accumulating in research, education, and action concerning the interrelationships between religions and nature (e.g. Dudley *et al.* 2005; Grim and Tucker 2014; Posey 1998; Tanner and Mitchell 2002; Taylor 2010; Tucker 2012). However, much more in-depth research needs to be done by scientists, academics, and others to objectively, systematically, and holistically examine the specific interrelationships between nature and individuals and groups from particular religions, in both theory and practice.

It is in the interest of the environmental sciences, environmental studies, environmentalism, nature conservation, human ecology, and environmental anthropology to seriously consider spiritual ecology (cf. Grim and Tucker 2014). Environmental anthropology often has tended to privilege anything else to the neglect of religion, perhaps reflecting a Marxist, materialist, and/or anti-religion bias on the part of many practitioners. However, science and scholarship progress with the mind open to pursuing any possibilities. (For literature reviews on spiritual ecology in environmental anthropology, see Sponsel 2001, 2007b, 2010, 2011, and 2013b).

Sacred places

One of the most concrete manifestations of the phenomena of spiritual ecology is sacred places in nature. Often places in the landscape are not only geological, biological, cultural, geographical, historic, and/or prehistoric, but deemed sacred and therefore also religious or spiritual. Billions of people throughout the world variously recognize and appreciate the special meanings and significances of certain sacred places in their own habitats and elsewhere. Many of these sites attract pilgrims and tourists, some sites with thousands or even millions of visitors annually, such as Lourdes in France or Mecca in Saudi Arabia. Moreover, curiously, individuals from many different ecological, cultural, religious, and national backgrounds may independently consider the same site to be sacred, like Mount Kailash in Tibet (Sponsel 2008; Swan 1990).

Sacred places are particular sites or areas that have one or more attributes which distinguish them as somehow extraordinary, usually in a religious or spiritual sense. Individuals may experience a sacred place in different ways as a site of awe, mystery, power, fascination, attraction, connectedness, oneness, danger, ordeal, healing, ritual, meaning, identity, revelation, and/or transformation. As Anderson (1996, 2010) and Milton (2002) affirm, emotion as well as reason can be important in human–environment interactions. (For studies of extraordinary experiences in nature, see Clayton and Opotow 2003; Marshall 2005; and Schauffler 2003.)

A wide range of "natural" phenomena are considered sacred by people in the some 7,000 extant cultures of the world. These may include particular mountains, volcanoes, hills, caves, rocks, dunes, soils, waterfalls, springs, rivers, streams, lakes, ponds, swamps, trees, groves, forests, plants, animals, wind, clouds, rain, rainbows, and so on. There are also coastal and marine phenomena that are believed to be sacred, such as parts of marshes, mangroves, estuaries, lagoons, beaches, islands, sea arches, sea grass beds, coral reefs, and tides. Some sacred places are connected with solar, lunar, and/or stellar cycles as well (Sponsel 2008). (For a case study of caves as sacred, see Sponsel 2015.)

A particular sacred place or area can encompass various individual sites and phenomena as integral parts of a whole, thereby comprising a sacred landscape. An example is Mount Shasta in Northern California with its waterfalls, springs, caves, and meadows considered sacred by the Wintu and several other Native American cultures in the area. Sites can be connected by a river, legends or stories, the histories of individuals or groups, and/or pilgrimage routes, like the centuries-old Way of Saint James to the Cathedral of Santiago de Compostela in Spain. In contrast, there are other sacred places where humans are excluded, or access is strictly limited to a special class of individuals, such as ritual specialists, healers, or elders. (For surveys of sacred places of the world, see Brockman 2011, Gray 2007, and National Geographic Society 2008. Also, see the documentary films by Feiler 2014 and McLeod 2013.)

Sacred places are complex phenomena that can be viewed for heuristic purposes as varying along several continua ranging from natural (or biophysical) to anthropogenic (or socio-cultural); prehistoric to historic, recent, or newly created; secret or private to public; single culture (or religion) to multicultural (or multi-religious); intrinsic to extrinsic in value; uncontested to contested; and protected to endangered. Particular sacred places tend to variously reflect one pole or another with some combination of these continua. It is also noteworthy that some sacred places have persisted for centuries or even millennia (Sponsel 2008).

The close interconnections of many sacred places with cultural and biological diversity mean that, if any one of these three is threatened or endangered, then the other two may be as well (McLeod 2013; Maffi 2001; Terralingua 2015). Many sacred places are contested by different interest groups, such as Mato Tipila (Devil's Tower) in Wyoming by rock climbers and local indigenous people. Sacred sites can be a focus of human rights advocacy and legal action as well as basic research and applied work (Burton 2002; Matthiessen 1984; McLeod 2013; Nabokov 2006).

Sacred places are a promising new frontier for multidisciplinary and interdisciplinary scientific and academic research on their own merits, as one kind of manifestation of the phenomena of spiritual ecology, and for their possible relevance in biodiversity conservation. The religious and/or cultural designation of an area as sacred, especially those that are relatively natural, may, either intentionally or coincidentally, promote the conservation of its associated biodiversity. Such sacred places may complement national parks and other "secular" protected areas established by governments (Sponsel *et al.* 1998).

Biodiversity

To be more specific, biodiversity may be defined as the variety of life at all levels from the genetic through those of the population, species, community, ecosystem, biome, and biosphere. Since the 1980s, Edward O. Wilson (1999) and other biologists have advanced biodiversity as a powerful conceptual catalyst for environmental research, education, and action. They do this with a profound sense of gravity and urgency regarding the plight of life on Earth as increasingly endangered because of habitat degradation, species extinction, and other factors (Sponsel 2013a; Wilson 2003). This concern has been reinforced by international scientific investigations, such as the aforementioned final report of the Millennium Ecosystem Assessment (United Nations Environmental Programme 2005). It warns that, if present patterns of biodiversity loss continue, then future generations of humanity may be at risk. It estimates that the current anthropogenic spasm of species extinction rates may be higher than it would normally be in nature by a thousand times or more. Estimates are that 12 percent of bird species and 23 percent of mammalian species are threatened with extinction (cf. International Union for the Conservation of Nature and Natural Resources 2014; Red List). Even some evolutionary and ecological processes may be jeopardized as well. Accordingly, the mass extinction crisis is one of the most critical challenges for the twenty-first century, and it is further compounded by the reality of global climate change. (For overviews on biodiversity, see Gaston and Spicer 2004; Levin 2013; and Pereira *et al.* 2012. See Orlove and Brush 1996 on the relevance of environmental anthropology for biodiversity.)

After extensive interviews with biologists, David Takacs observes that:

> Some biologists have found their own brand of religion, and it is based on biodiversity.
> The biologists portrayed here attach the label spiritual to deep, driving feelings they

cannot understand, but that give their lives meaning, impel their professional activities, and make them ardent conservationists.

(Takacs 1996: 270)

Furthermore, Takacs (1996: 256) concludes that: "If the value of biodiversity were felt not merely in the pocket or in the brain but in the soul, then the most effective, permanent conservation ethic imaginable might result."

Sacred groves

The interrelationships among spiritual ecology, sacred places, and biodiversity conservation can be illustrated by sacred groves. Basically, sacred groves are one manifestation of spiritual ecology and also they may facilitate biodiversity conservation. They are stands of trees, or patches of forest, that local communities reserve and protect primarily because of their religious importance. They may serve economic, nutritional, medicinal, social, cultural, and/or ecological functions as well. For example, some plant species in sacred groves may provide emergency foods during periods of drought, crop failure, or famine.

A variety of factors may promote the conservation of biodiversity in sacred groves, such as general or selective limits or prohibitions on the use of plant and animal species in them. In addition, sacred groves may help to protect watershed resources like streams and springs; soil retention, fertility, and moisture; and ecosystem processes such as nutrient cycling. However, this is not to claim that all sacred groves necessarily facilitate environmental and biodiversity conservation. They must be examined on a case-by-case basis, especially because they and their surrounding conditions are so variable.

In India, typically, sacred groves are associated with almost every village and temple. Today there are still some 150,000 sacred groves covering 33,000 hectares in total, according to Malhotra *et al.* (2001). They range in size from a fraction of a hectare to a few square kilometers. In India and elsewhere, sacred groves often appear to be – in effect, if not always also in intent – a very ancient, widespread, and important traditional system of environmental conservation. They are far older than Western strategies for protected areas, such as wildlife sanctuaries and national parks that are established by a central government rather than being community-based.

Sacred groves and other "traditional" systems that may perform a conservation role, whether actual or potential, and whether intentional or coincidental, may need to be strengthened or augmented by economic incentives for local communities; legal, governmental, and/or international environmental protection schemes; and the establishment and maintenance of buffer zones (Malhotra *et al.* 2001; cf. Smith and Wishnie 2000). Recognition and protection of sacred groves by scientific, environmental, conservation, governmental, and/or non-governmental organizations can simultaneously promote the protection of their associated biodiversity and culture(s), although in some circumstances, they may be detrimental to them (cf. West *et al.* 2006). (For a concise overview of sacred groves in many parts of the world, see Anderson 2014: 83–86; and for a particular case study in India, see Kent 2013.)

Some researchers are skeptical about the relevance of sacred groves for conservation. As one recent prominent example, Michael R. Dove and colleagues (2011: 6–10) make several generalizations by way of criticism of the sample of literature that they cite. However, the publications they cite are only a small sample of the far more substantial literature available that, taken as a whole, reveals much more variation, complexity, and sophistication in research on sacred groves than they appear to appreciate. They do not offer any analytical survey of the literature to prove that their generalizations as criticisms are any more than selective impressions, some of which might be inadvertently misleading.

Numerous examples from the substantial literature could be cited to challenge almost every one of the generalizations made by Dove *et al.* (2011). As just one specific example, Safia Aggarwal (2001) demonstrates empirically that in the Central Himalayas many local communities purposefully designate areas as sacred groves for conservation, but may later de-sanctify some of them in order to use more fully the natural resources therein, while they set aside other patches of forest as sacred. Thus, these sacred groves are a component of dynamic systems culturally as well as ecologically. They are not viewed as static isolates or "premodern" survivals in this case, in contrast to the generalization by Dove *et al.* (2011). Nor is this a simple matter of equilibrium versus disequilibrium, nature versus culture, or traditional versus modern. Aggarwal does not treat sacred groves as some kind of closed entity to the neglect of the wider context. (For a few other examples, see Byers *et al.* 2001; Fairhead and Leach 1996; Hakkenberg 2008; Keating 2012; Malhotra 1998; Malhotra *et al.* 2001; Ramakrishnan *et al.* 1998; Sheridan and Nyamweru 2008; Snodgrass and Tiedje 2008; Srivastana *et al.* 2007; Xiaoli *et al.* 2012.)

Sacred groves are dynamic systems, each with a historical ecology. They may persist through centuries or more as a relic of a natural and/or anthropogenic ecosystem, be revived with the renewal of some cultural or religious traditions, or be newly established, in some cases explicitly for the purpose of conservation. Sacred groves are dynamic systems as well because the species composition of any plant community naturally changes over time with ecological succession, and this happens even without natural perturbations or human disturbances, as when trees eventually die, for example. They may also serve as a seed source for an adjacent buffer zone and/or for the ecological restoration of degraded landscapes (Sponsel 2008, 2012: 1–5). Indeed, sacred groves, like many other types of sacred places in nature, often stand out as rich in biodiversity in contrast to their surroundings which are often degraded landscapes (cf. Gadgil and Guha 2013).

From an ecological perspective, sacred groves, sacred forests, and even lone sacred trees are an integral component of wider regional environmental systems. This stands in contrast to the assertion of Dove *et al.* (2011) that researchers always treat sacred groves as isolated entities. For instance, collectively through space and cumulatively over time, small sacred groves, and even lone sacred trees, may well add up to have some ecological and conservation significance (Sponsel 2012: 1–5; Sponsel *et al.* 1997). While in some cases, the designation of a tree, grove, or forest as sacred may be a response to surrounding deforestation, this does not necessarily lessen their actual or potential value for the conservation of biodiversity and ecological processes. Furthermore, not all sacred groves are "tiny" in size, as argued by Dove *et al.* (2011). Rather, some sacred groves extend over an area of several square kilometers or more. It is important as well to realize that, from the perspective of biological ecology, even small areas may have some significance in the case of fauna because invertebrates comprise by far most of biodiversity and biomass (Wilson 1999: 136). In addition, it should be recognized that, whether or not a sacred grove or sacred forest is intended for the purpose of conservation, or fits Western concepts of conservation, it may still, in effect, promote the protection of the associated biodiversity and ecological processes (Sponsel 2012: 1–5; cf. Smith and Wishnie 2000).

Systematic multidisciplinary and interdisciplinary research is needed on the variety of sacred places with respect to biological matters such as their size, age, species composition, biodiversity level, and degree of naturalness as well as any historical, social, cultural, religious, economic, political, tenure, and legal issues. In particular, there is a need for controlled comparisons between sacred places and adjacent secular ones of the same size and type of biotic community in order to describe and assess any differences that might arise because of sacred status. It is vital that hypotheses about the conservation efficacy of sacred localities be tested empirically and quantitatively, rather than relying only on assumptions and assertions. In such endeavors, multidisciplinary team research is ideal.

As specialists who bridge the natural and social sciences, and sometimes even the humanities, environmental anthropologists are especially well-positioned to help explore, document, and manage the connections among sacred places, cultures, religions, biodiversity, and conservation. A society's view of nature and interaction with it is largely culturally constructed and mediated. This principle applies not only to communities with ideas about the sacredness of particular localities in nature, but also to science and government with ideas about wilderness and biodiversity (Oelschlaeger 1991; Sarkar 2005; and Takacs 1996). In other words, there are different cultural meanings and approaches to conservation, just as there are to nature (Coates 1988; Glacken 1967; Selin 2003). Anthropologists and others have demonstrated that Western science, technology, and government have no monopoly on what is in effect environmental conservation (Posey 1998; Selin 2003; Sponsel *et al.* 1997). Some anthropologists also collaborate with members of local communities in promoting their practical concerns through applied or advocacy work, such as Christopher McLeod's Sacred Land Film Project at the Earth Island Institute (McLeod 2013; Sponsel 2014d). In addition, anthropologists are especially well situated to serve as mediators among individuals from different interest groups like environmental, conservation, government, community, and religious organizations.

Numerous and diverse sacred places in nature are associated with indigenous societies. Because anthropology has traditionally focused on indigenous societies, and certainly they remain a core commitment of the profession, it has a unique role to play in this arena through basic and applied research as well as through advocacy, in promoting community empowerment, and where appropriate, co-management schemes. Protecting sacred places can simultaneously help to protect cultures, religions, and rights as well as the associated biotic species, ecosystems, and ecological processes.

Conclusion

Many who study spiritual ecology, sacred places, and related subjects are convinced that there is a crucial need for considering the interrelationships among religion, spirituality, human ecology, environmentalism, and conservation (e.g. Uhl 2013). Furthermore, they affirm that the recognition and protection of sacred places in nature may well be needed more than ever before for the survival of biodiversity and accordingly that of humankind in the twenty-first century. Such concerns are reflected in an insightful statement by the Lakota historian, theologian, and lawyer, Vine Deloria, Jr (1994: 282):

> Sacred places are the foundation of all other beliefs and practices because they represent the presence of the sacred in our lives. They properly inform us that we are not larger than nature and that we have responsibilities to the rest of the natural world that transcend our own personal desires and wishes. This lesson must be learned by each generation; unfortunately the technology of industrial society always leads us in the other direction. Yet it is certain that as we permanently foul our planetary nest, we shall have to learn a most bitter lesson. There is probably not sufficient time for the

non-Indian population to understand the meaning of sacred lands and incorporate the idea into their lives and practices. We can but hope that some protection can be afforded these sacred places before the world becomes wholly secular and is destroyed.

(Deloria, Jr 1994: 282)

References

Note: All websites accessed on 9 February 2015.

Aggarwal, Safia, 2001. Supernatural Sanctions in Commons Management: Panchayat Forest Conservation in the Central Himalayas. PhD dissertation, Department of Geography, University of Hawai'i.

Alley, Kelly, 2002. *On the Banks of the Ganges: When Wastewater Meets a Sacred River*. Ann Arbor: University of Michigan Press.

Anderson, E. N., 1996. *Ecologies of the Heart: Emotion, Belief, and the Environment*. New York: Oxford University Press.

_____ 2010. *The Pursuit of Ecotopia: Lessons from Indigenous and Traditional Societies for the Human Ecology of Our Modern World*. Santa Barbara, CA: Praeger.

_____ 2012a. "Anthropology of Religion and Environment: A Skeletal History to 1970." *Journal for the Study of Religion, Nature and Culture* 6(1): 9–36.

_____ 2012b. "Religion in Conservation and Management: A Durkheimian View." *Journal for the Study of Religion, Nature and Culture* 6(4): 398–420.

_____ 2014. *Caring for Place: Ecology, Ideology, and Emotion in Traditional Landscape Management*. Walnut Creek, CA: Left Coast Press.

Bernbaum, Edwin, 1990. *Sacred Mountains of the World*. San Francisco, CA: Sierra Club Books.

Blanes, Ruy and Diana Espirito Santo (eds), 2014. *The Social Life of Spirits*. Chicago, IL: University of Chicago Press.

Bookchin, Murray, 1995. *Re-enchanting Humanity: A Defense of the Human Spirit against Anti-humanism, Misanthropy, Mysticism and Primitivism*. London: Cassell.

Brockman, Norbert C., 2011. *Encyclopedia of Sacred Places*. 2nd edn. Santa Barbara, CA: ABC-CLIO.

Burton, Lloyd, 2002. *Worship and Wilderness: Culture, Religion, and Law in Public Lands Management*. Madison: University of Wisconsin Press.

Byers, Bruce A., Robert N. Cunliffe and Andrew T. Hudak, 2001. "Linking the Conservation of Culture and Nature: A Case Study of Sacred Forests in Zimbabwe." *Human Ecology* 29(2): 187–218.

Clayton, Philip (ed.), 2008. *Oxford Handbook of Religion and Science*. New York: Oxford University Press.

Clayton, Susan and Susan Opotow, 2003. *Identity and the Natural Environment: The Psychological Significance of Nature*. Cambridge, MA: The MIT Press.

Coates, Peter, 1988. *Nature: Western Attitudes since Ancient Times*. Berkeley: University of California Press.

Collett, Jonathan and Stephen Karakashian (eds), 1995. Greening the College Curriculum. 2nd edn. Washington, DC: Island Press.

Crosby, Donald A., 2002. *A Religion of Nature*. Albany: State University of New York Press.

Deloria, Jr, Vine, 1994. *God Is Red: A Native View of Religion*. Golden, CO: Fulcrum.

Dove, Michael R., Percy E. Sajise and Amity A. Doolittle (eds), 2011. *Beyond the Sacred Forest: Complicating Conservation in Southeast Asia*. Durham, NC: Duke University Press.

Dudley, Nigel, Liza Higgins-Zogib and Stephanie Mansourian (eds), 2005. *Beyond Belief: Linking Faiths and Protected Areas to Support Biodiversity Conservation* (Gland, Switzerland/Manchester: World Wide Fund for Nature/Alliance of Religions and Conservation. www.arcworld.org/downloads/WWF%20 Beyond%20Belief.pdf

Fairhead, James and Melissa Leach, 1996. *Misreading the African Landscape: Society and Ecology in a Forest–Savanna Mosaic*. Cambridge, UK: Cambridge University Press.

Feiler, Bruce, 2014. *Sacred Journeys*. Arlington, VA: Corporation of Public Broadcasting.

Gadgil, Madhav and Ramachandra Guha, 2013. *This Fissured Land: An Ecological History of India*. 2nd edn. New York: Oxford University Press.

Gaston, Kevin J. and John I. Spicer, 2004. *Biodiversity: An Introduction*. 2nd edn. Malden, MA: Blackwell Publishing.

Glacken, Clarence J., 1967. *Traces on a Rhodian Shore: Nature and Culture in Western Thought from Ancient Times to the End of the Eighteenth Century*. Berkeley: University of California Press.

Global Forum, 1990. "Preserving and Cherishing the Earth: An Appeal for Joint Commitment in Science and Religion." Moscow: Global Forum. http://fore.research.yale.edu/publications/statements/preserve/

Gottlieb, Roger S., 2006a. *A Greener Faith: Religious Environmentalism and Our Planet's Future.* New York: Oxford University Press.

_____ (ed.), 2006b. *The Oxford Handbook of Religion and Ecology.* New York: Oxford University Press.

Gray, Martin, 2007. *Sacred Earth.* New York: Sterling Publishing Co., Inc.

Grim, John A. (ed.), 2001. *Indigenous Traditions and Ecology: The Interconnections of Cosmology and Community.* Cambridge, MA: Harvard University Press.

Grim, John and Mary E. Tucker, 2014. *Ecology and Religion.* Washington, DC: Island Press.

Hakkenberg, Christopher, 2008. "Biodiversity and Sacred Sites: Vernacular Conservation Practices in Northwest Yunnan, China." *Worldviews: Global Religions, Culture, Ecology* 12(1): 74–90.

Hawken, Paul, 2007. *Blessed Unrest: How the Largest Movement in the World Came into Being and Why No One Saw It Coming.* New York: Viking Penguin.

Hecking, Rebecca James, 2011. *The Sustainable Soul: Eco-spiritual Reflections and Practices.* Boston, MA: Skinner House Books.

International Union for the Conservation of Nature and Natural Resources, 1997. *Indigenous Peoples and Sustainability: Cases and Actions.* Utrecht, the Netherlands: International Books.

International Union for the Conservation of Nature and Natural Resources, 2014. *The IUCN Red List of Threatened Species.* Gland, Switzerland: IUCN. www.iucnredlist.org/

Keating, Neal, 2012. "From Spirit Forest to Rubber Plantations: The Accelerating Disaster of 'Development' in Cambodia." *ASIA Network Exchange* 19(2): 68–80.

Kellert, Stephen R. and Timothy J. Farnham (eds), 2002. *The Good in Nature and Humanity: Connecting Science, Religion, and Spirituality with the Natural World.* Washington, DC: Island Press.

Kent, Eliza F., 2013. *Sacred Groves and Local Gods: Religion and Environmentalism in South India.* New York: Oxford University Press.

Kinsley, David, 1994. *Ecology and Religion: Ecological Spirituality in Cross-cultural Perspective.* Englewood Cliffs, NJ: Prentice Hall.

Lee, Cathy and Samanatha Wauchope (eds), 2003. *The Importance of Sacred Natural Sites for Biodiversity Conservation.* Paris: UNESCO–MAB Programme.

Levin, Simon A. (ed.-in-chief), 2013. *Encyclopedia of Biodiversity.* Vols 1–7. Waltham, MA: Academic Press.

McLeod, Christopher, 2013. *Standing on Sacred Ground.* Sacred Land Film Project. Oley, PA: Bullfrog Films/Oakland. www.sacredland.org

Macy, Joanna and Chris Johnstone, 2012. *Active Hope: How to Face the Mess We're in without Going Crazy.* Novato, CA: New World Library.

Maffi, Luisa (ed.), 2001. *On Biocultural Diversity: Linking Language, Knowledge, and the Environment.* Washington, DC: Smithsonian Institution Press.

Malhotra, Kailash C., 1998. "Anthropological Dimensions of Sacred Groves in India: An Overview." In P. S. Ramakrishnan, K. G. Saxena and U. M. Chandrashekara (eds) *Conserving the Sacred for Biodiversity Management.* Enfield, CT: Science Publishers, Inc., pp. 423–438.

Malhotra, Kailash C., Yogesh Gokhale, Sudipto Chatterjee and Sanjeev Srivastava, 2001. *Cultural and Ecological Dimensions of Sacred Groves in India.* New Delhi/Bhopal: Indian National Science Academy/Indira Gandhi Rashtriya Manav Sangrahalaya.

Marshall, Paul, 2005. *Mystical Encounters with the Natural World: Experience and Explanations.* New York: Oxford University Press.

Matthiessen, Peter, 1984. *Indian Country.* New York: Penguin Books.

Meadows, Donella H., Jorgen Randers and Dennis Meadows, 2004. *Limits to Growth: The 30-year Update.* White River Junction, VT: Chelsea Green Publishing.

Milton, Kay, 2002. *Loving Nature: Towards an Ecology of Emotion.* New York: Routledge.

Nabokov, Peter, 2006. *Where the Lightning Strikes: The Lives of American Indian Sacred Places.* New York: Penguin.

Nadeau, Robert L., 2013. *Rebirth of the Sacred: Science, Religion, and the New Environmental Ethos.* New York: Oxford University Press.

National Geographic Society, 2008. *Sacred Places of a Lifetime: 500 of the World's Most Peaceful and Powerful Destinations.* Washington, DC: National Geographic Society.

Oelschlaeger, Max, 1991. *The Idea of Wilderness: From Prehistory to the Age of Ecology.* New Haven, CT: Yale University Press.

Orlove, Benjamin S. and Stephen B. Brush, 1996. "Anthropology and the Conservation of Biodiversity." *Annual Review of Anthropology* 25: 329–352.

Pereira, Henrique M., Laetita M. Navarro and Ines S. Martins, 2012. "Global Biodiversity Change: The Bad, the Good, and the Unknown." *Annual Review of Environment and Resources* 37(1): 25–50.

Posey, Darrell A. (ed.), 1998: *Cultural and Spiritual Values of Biodiversity*. Leiden, the Netherlands: Leiden University Press, Intermediate Technology Publications, and United Nations Environmental Programme.

Provan, Iain, 2013. *Convenient Myths: The Axial Age, Dark Green Religion, and the World that Never Was*. Waco, TX: Baylor University Press.

Pungetti, Gloria, Gonzalo Oviedo and Della Hooke (eds), 2012. *Sacred Species and Sites: Advances in Biocultural Conservation*. New York: Cambridge University Press.

Ramakrishnan, P.S., K.G. Saxena and U.M. Chandrashekara (eds), 1998. *Conserving the Sacred for Biodiversity*. Enfield, CT: Science Publishers, Inc.

Rees, William E., Mathis Wackernagel and Phil Testemale, 1998. *Our Ecological Footprint: Reducing Human Impact on the Earth*. Gabriola Island, BC: New Society Publishers.

Sarkar, Sahotra, 2005. *Biodiversity and Environmental Philosophy: An Introduction*. New York: Cambridge University Press.

Schaaf, Thomas and Cathy Lee, (eds), 2006. *Conserving Cultural and Biological Diversity: The Role of Sacred Natural Sites and Cultural Landscapes*. Paris: UNESCO–MAB Programme.

Schauffler, F. Marina, 2003. *Turning to Earth: Stories of Ecological Conversion*. Charlottesville: University of Virginia Press.

Selin, Helaine (ed.), 2003. *Nature across Cultures: Views of Nature and the Environment in Non-Western Cultures*. Boston, MA: Kluwer Academic Press.

Sheridan, Michael J. and Celia Nyamweru (eds), 2008. *African Sacred Groves: Ecological Dynamics of Social Change*. Oxford: James Currey.

Smith, Eric A. and Mark Wishnie, 2000. "Conservation and Subsistence in Small-scale Societies." *Annual Review of Anthropology* 29: 493–524.

Snodgrass, Jeffrey G. and Kristina Tiedje, 2008. "Indigenous Nature Reverence and Conservation: Seven Ways of Transcending an Unnecessary Dichotomy." *Journal for the Study of Religion, Nature and Culture* 2(1): 6–29.

Sponsel, Leslie E., 2001. "Do Anthropologists Need Religion, and Vice Versa? Adventures and Dangers in Spiritual Ecology." In Carole Crumley (ed.) *New Directions in Anthropology and Environment: Intersections*. Walnut Creek, CA: AltaMira Press, pp. 177–200.

_____ 2007a. "Ecological Anthropology." In Cutler J. Cleveland (founding ed.-in-chief) *The Encyclopedia of Earth*. Washington, DC: National Council for Science and the Environment, Environmental Information Coalition. www.eoearth.org/view/article/51cbed787896bb431f692653

_____ 2007b. "Spiritual Ecology: One Anthropologist's Reflections." *Journal for the Study of Religion, Nature and Culture* 1(3): 340–350.

_____ 2008. "Sacred Places and Biodiversity Conservation." In Cutler J. Cleveland (founding ed.-in-chief) *Encyclopedia of Earth*. Washington, DC: National Council for Science and the Environment, Environmental Information Coalition. www.eoearth.org/article/Sacred_places_and_biodiversity_conservation

_____ 2010. "Religion and Environment: Exploring Spiritual Ecology." In Simon Coleman and Ramon Sarro (eds) *Religion and Society: Advances in Research*, Volume 1. New York: Berghahn Books, pp. 131–145.

_____ 2011. "The Religion and Environment Interface: Spiritual Ecology in Ecological Anthropology." In Helen Kopnina and Eleanor Shoreman-Ouimet (eds) *Environmental Anthropology Today*. New York: Routledge, pp. 37–55.

_____ 2012. *Spiritual Ecology: A Quiet Revolution*. Santa Barbara, CA: Praeger. http://spiritualecology.info

_____ 2013a. "Human Impact on Biodiversity: Overview." In Simon A. Levin (ed.-in-chief) *Encyclopedia of Biodiversity*. 2nd edn., Volume 4. Waltham, MA: Academic Press, pp. 137–152.

_____ 2013b. "Leslie Sponsel on Spiritual Ecology, Connection, and Environmental Change." AAA Anthropology and Environment Society *Engagement* blog, posted 1 October. www.aaanet.org/sections/ae/index.php/leslie-sponsel-on-spiritual-ecology-connection-and-environmental-change/

_____ 2014a. "Bibliographic Essay – Spiritual Ecology: Is it the Ultimate Solution for the Environmental Crisis?" *CHOICE* 51(8): 1339–1342, 1344–1348.

_____ 2014b. "Spiritual Ecology as an International Environmental Movement." In Liam Leonard and Syra Buryn Kedzior (eds) *Occupy the Earth: Global Environmental Movements*. New York: Emerald Group Publishing pp. 275–293.

_____ 2014c. "Reply to Vayda's Review." *Human Ecology* 42(5): 801–802.

_____ 2014d. "Indigenous Sacred Places: Threats and Responses (Review of 'Standing on Sacred Ground')." *AAA Anthropology News/Society for the Anthropology of Religion Section* 54(3): 1–3.

_____ 2015. "Sacred Caves of the World: Illuminating Darkness." In Stanley D. Brunn (ed.) *The Changing World Religion Map: Sacred Places, Identities, Practices, and Politics*, Volume 1. New York: Springer, pp. 503–522.

Sponsel, Leslie E., Poranee Natadecha-Sponsel, Nukul Ruttanadakul and Somporn Juntadach, 1997. "Sacred and/or Secular Approaches to Biodiversity Conservation in Thailand." *Worldviews: Environment, Culture, Religion* 2(2): 155–167.

Srivastana, Sanjiv, Sudipto Chatterjee, Yogesh Gokhale and Kailash C. Malhotra, 2007. *Sacred Groves of India: An Overview*. New Delhi: Aryan Books International.

Strenski, Ivan, 2008. "The Spiritual Dimension." In Kenrika Kuklick (ed.) *A New History of Anthropology*. Malden, MA: Blackwell Publishing, pp. 113–127.

Swan, James A., 1990. *Sacred Places: How the Living Earth Seeks our Friendship*. Santa Fe, NM: Bear and Company.

Takacs, David, 1996. *The Idea of Biodiversity: Philosophies of Paradise*. Baltimore, MD: Johns Hopkins University Press.

Tanner, Ralph and Colin Mitchell, 2002. *Religion and the Environment*. New York: Palgrave Macmillan.

Taylor, Bron R. (ed.-in-chief), 2005. *The Encyclopedia of Religion and Nature*. New York: Thoemmes Continuum.

_____ 2010. *Dark Green Religion: Nature Spirituality and the Planetary Future*. Berkeley: University of California Press.

Terralingua, 2015. *Partnership for Linguistic and Biological Diversity*. www.terralingua.org/

Tucker, Catherine (ed.), 2012. *Nature, Science, and Religion: Intersections Shaping Society and Environment*. Santa Fe, NM: School for Advanced Research Press.

Tucker, Mary E., 2006. "Religion and Ecology: Survey of the Field." In Roger S. Gottlieb (ed.) *The Oxford Handbook of Religion and Ecology*. New York: Oxford University Press, pp. 398–418.

Uhl, Christopher, 2013. *Developing Ecological Consciousness: The End of Separation*. Lanham, MD: Rowman & Littlefield Publishers, Inc.

United Nations Environmental Programme, 2005. *Millennium Ecosystem Assessment*. Gland, Switzerland: UNEP. www.millenniumassessment.org/en/index.html

Vayda, Andrew P., 2014. "Review: Leslie E. Sponsel, Spiritual Ecology: A Quiet Revolution." *Human Ecology* 42(2): 347–348.

Verschuuren, Bas, Robert Wild, Jeffrey A. McNeely and Gonzalo Oviedo, (eds), 2010. *Sacred Natural Sites Conserving Nature and Culture*. Washington, DC: Earthscan.

West, Paige, Joe Igoe and Dan Brockington, 2006. "Parks and Peoples: The Social Impact of Protected Areas." *Annual Review of Anthropology* 35(1): 251–277.

Whelan, Robert, Joseph Kirwan and Paul Haffner, 1996. *The Cross and the Rainforest: A Critique of Radical Green Spirituality*. Grand Rapids, MI: Eerdmans.

White, Jr, Lynn, 1967. "The Historical Roots of Our Ecologic Crisis." *Science* 155(3767): 1203–1207.

Wilson, Edward O., 1999. *The Diversity of Life*. 2nd edn. New York: W. W. Norton & Company.

_____ 2003. *The Future of Life*. New York: Vintage.

Xiaoli, Shen, Zhi Lu, Shengzhi Li and Nyima Chen, 2012. "Tibetan Sacred Sites: Understanding the Traditional Management System and its Role in Modern Conservation." *Ecology and Society* 17(2): Article 13. www.ecologyandsociety.org/vol17/iss2/art13/

12

THE BIBLE, RELIGION, AND THE ENVIRONMENT

Ronald A. Simkins

Introduction

The Bible and religion have played an important role in contemporary discussion about the environment since the mid-1960s. In 1967, when Lynn White, Jr, in a brief yet seminal essay, "The Historic Roots of our Ecologic Crisis," traced the origins of modern Western science and technology to the medieval Christian worldview that was inspired by the biblical cosmology, he transformed the environmental crisis into a religious problem, with Western Christianity and the Bible bearing a huge burden of guilt. According to White, the biblical religion, with its idea of linear history and perpetual progress, robbed the natural world of its enchantment. Nature was transformed from a subject to be revered to an object to be used. White says (1967: 1205), "By destroying pagan animism, Christianity made it possible to exploit nature in a mood of indifference to the feelings of natural objects." Moreover, the biblical cosmology, in which humans are created in the image of God and given dominion over nature, separated humans from nature, enabling humans to share, in part, God's transcendence. From this cosmology, Western Christianity emerged as "the most anthropocentric religion the world has seen" (White 1967: 1205). Because, as White argued, modern science and technology developed out of and shared the axioms of this Christian matrix, the environmental crisis cannot be addressed simply with more science and technology. Instead, the problem is with religion: "What people do about their ecology depends on what they think about themselves in relation to things around them. Human ecology is deeply conditioned by beliefs about our nature and destiny—that is, by religion." (White 1967: 1205).

Although contested from many quarters, White's thesis that religion is decisive in the human treatment of the environment, and that Western Christianity's worldview in particular is culpable, has generated reams of scholarship and new academic fields. Biblical scholars have challenged White's reading of the Genesis creation stories (Trible 1971; Barr 1972; Anderson 1975; Hiers 1984; though cf. Harrison 1999), historians have questioned White's argument linking the rise of modern science with the Western Christian worldview (Sessions 1974; Whitney 1993), and other scholars have noted that Western Christian civilizations are not unique in their abuse and exploitation of the environment (Tuan 1970; Dubos 1972; Hughes 1975; cf. Glacken 1976). Nevertheless, White's essay was widely reprinted and quoted, and its thesis was embraced by environmental activists, especially by those for whom religion served as a convenient culprit for the growing environmental crisis (Derr 1975), and shaped the emerging academic fields of environmental ethics, and religion and the environment (Minteer and Manning 2005; Jenkins 2009).

Following White's lead, the interrelationship between religion and the environment seemed apparent and became the subject of scholarly research. As Jenkins (2011: 442) puts it, "Environmental studies and religious studies share research phenomena where human interaction with environmental systems is influenced by religious systems and where religious traditions or forms of experience themselves change in relation to changing environments." Numerous studies have been conducted to understand how religious affiliation, participation, and beliefs may affect environmental concern and activism (see e.g. Guth *et al.* 1995; Sherkat and Ellison 2007; Truelove and Joireman 2009; Djupe and Hunt 2009; Djupe and Gwiasda 2010; and the literature cited therein); and religion scholars, especially, have sought to reform and leverage religious traditions in addressing the environmental crisis (see the ten volumes edited by Tucker and Grim 1997–2004; Gottlieb 2007, 2009, 2010).

The relationship between religion and the environment, however, remains largely ideational. Although the correlation between religious beliefs and environmental concern is well documented, the material impact of religion on the environment, both positively and negatively, remains an open question (see also Whitney 1993). Many material factors contribute to human interaction with the environment—such as economic, sociological, and technological factors—so that benevolent environmental behavior and actions are not simply a matter of thinking and believing appropriately. Religious values may be frustrated by other concerns, and material issues may prevent the realization of ideational values. There is often a disjunction between belief and practice; the environmental crisis is not just a religious issue. Religion remains, nevertheless, an important component in environmental discussions. It offers a language of moral seriousness within a value-oriented context that is helpful in shaping institutional and individual behavior, and it provides models for humane and compassionate engagement that are useful for environmental activism (Gottlieb 2007).

For Christianity, in particular, the Bible plays a significant role in its relationship to the environment. As the sacred and authoritative scriptures for approximately two billion Christians globally, the Bible is a foundational source of Christian theology and provides ethical guidance within the context of the biblical worldview. The Bible's contribution to environmental discussions today, however, is complex and mixed at best (see Horrell 2010). On the one hand, the biblical writers' experience of the natural world was so very different from much of the contemporary experience. Whereas the vast majority of Israelites lived in small agrarian villages eking out their existence in a subsistence economy, the modern, especially Western, population is largely urban, technologically oriented, globally connected, and dependent on a surplus economy. As a result, the biblical values toward the natural world (Simkins 1994) do not easily translate into contemporary environmental ethics. On the other hand, the Bible's agrarian worldview offers a critique of and provides an alternative to the contemporary anthropocentric, materialistic, industrial worldview that has so often been destructive of the environment.

Unfortunately, the meaning of the Bible, as read in new, contemporary contexts, often reflects the worldview of its interpreters rather than its own socio-historical context, and thus the Bible may serve to reinforce the existing worldviews, ideologies, and behaviors of its interpreters (see Berry 1993). This is precisely the problem with the medieval appropriation of the biblical cosmology that White highlights in his essay. White argues that during the medieval period in the West, the human relationship to nature changed, in part due to technological innovations such as the introduction of a new type of plow. Humans began viewing themselves as distinct from and the masters of nature. Christianity, for its part, according to White, reinforced this new perception through its biblical cosmology. But the Bible was read in ways that were contrary to its original context. In order for the Bible to speak authentically in current environmental discussions, therefore, the Bible needs to be read critically within the socio-historical context out of which it emerged. In what follows, this chapter will focus on three contemporary readings of the Bible which have been deemed as problematic for its use in environmental discussions: the anthropocentrism of the biblical worldview; the role of work, law, and covenant; and the otherworldly orientation of eschatology. Each of these readings will be assessed critically and a new, nuanced interpretation will be offered that articulates how the Bible may contribute to environmental discussions.

Anthropocentrism and the Biblical worldview

Central to Lynn White's critique of Western Christianity is the claim that the Bible is anthropocentric and thus provides the conditions for human exploitation of the environment. Citing the creation story in Genesis 1, which culminates in God creating humans in his image and giving them dominion, White asserts, "God planned all of this explicitly for man's benefit and rule: no item in the physical creation had any purpose save to serve man's purposes" (White 1967: 1205). White is not wrong that the Bible, and Genesis 1 in particular, has been read anthropocentrically, and it is not difficult to find Christian expressions of anthropocentrism. Pope Benedict XVI, for example, in a talk encouraging care for the environment, nevertheless defends anthropocentrism against its alternatives:

> If the Church's magisterium expresses grave misgivings about notions of the environment inspired by ecocentrism and biocentrism, it is because such notions eliminate the difference of identity and worth between the human person and other living things . . . such notions end up abolishing the distinctiveness and superior role of human beings.
>
> *(Benedict XVI 2009: 13)*

The context of Benedict's defense of anthropocentrism raises the question of whether anthropocentrism is inherently deleterious to the environment. After all, Benedict's anthropocentrism also leads him to assert that humans have a responsibility "to protect earth, water and air as gifts of God the Creator meant for everyone" (Benedict XVI 2009: 12). Indeed, the meaning and breadth of anthropocentrism, and so its significance for the environment, have been debated (Norton 1984; Hargrove 1992; Midgley 1994; Spitler 1982; Grey 1998). Different degrees of anthropocentrism are possible. For White, the fundamental problem with anthropocentrism is its separation of humans from nature, and for this reason he puts forward the biocentrism of St Francis (Mizzoni 2008) as a remedy to Western Christianity's anthropocentrism. What White fails to recognize, however, is that St Francis's biocentrism and Western Christianity's anthropocentrism both find their support in the same biblical tradition. Whether or not a particular expression of Christianity is anthropocentric or biocentric is more dependent on the culture and worldview of its adherents than on the Bible itself. St Francis offered medieval Christianity a radically new vision of the relationship between humans and nature, and he read the biblical tradition through the lens of this worldview. The dominant Western Christian understanding of the biblical tradition, in contrast, has been shaped by a post-Cartesian worldview that distinguishes between mind and body, history and nature. Thus, in the modern anthropocentric reading of the Bible, humankind is often assumed to be separate and distinct from the natural world (see also Hoffman and Sandelands 2005: 149–155), but such a reading of the Bible reflects the cultural assumptions of its readers. The reading is imposed on the Bible rather than emerging from an understanding of the text in its own socio-historical context.

The Bible emerged out of the agrarian worldview of the ancient Near East in which there was no separation between humans and the rest of the natural world (Simkins 1994). The Bible does indeed give a great deal of attention to humans; it is, after all, a human text produced for and about humans. Nevertheless, humans in the Bible are everywhere embedded in the larger context of creation and especially in their relationship to God. The Bible presents a theocentric worldview in which both humans and the rest of the natural world have intrinsic value because they are the creation of God, who remains in relationship with it (Simkins 2014). God imputes value to the whole creation—humans, animals, land—and God the creator is the measure of all that is good and right in the world.

Genesis 1 is the hallmark text that is generally brought forward to illustrate the Bible's so-called anthropocentrism. On the sixth day, God creates the human couple in the image of God and tells them, "Be fruitful and multiply, and fill the earth and subdue it; and have dominion over the fish of the sea and over the birds of the air and over every living thing that moves upon the earth" (Genesis 1:28; New Revised Standard Version). According to the anthropocentric reading, as espoused by White and others, this text places humans at the pinnacle of creation, with all of nature given to them for their use. On closer inspection, however, the creation does not revolve around humans, nor does the creation exist for human exploitation. Subduing the earth probably entails no more than agriculture: tilling and sowing arable land, and perhaps removing rock and shrubs that hinder farming. It is unclear from the context of Genesis 1 what are the practical consequences of human dominion over the fish, birds, and animals. It clearly does not mean that humans can eat them, for they are given only plants to eat (Genesis 1:29). God permits humans to eat living creatures only after the flood. Human dominion is limited to the animal world—it does not encompass, for example, the climate, water resources, or natural processes (see also Kay 1989: 222). But even in this regard, human dominion is never fully realized; everywhere in the biblical tradition, *wild* animals remain beyond the scope of human rule.

The lofty language of Genesis 1 does attest to the distinctive status of humans among God's creatures; only humans are created in the image of God (see also Psalm 8). But such language does not signal an anthropocentric worldview. Rather, as the biblical tradition makes clear, humans remain dependent on and subordinate to God. A human couple may come together in sexual intercourse to procreate, but the woman will only bear a child when God opens the womb. Humans may subdue the earth by farming the land, but their work is dependent on God who brings the rain that softens the soil and causes the seed to germinate. Although God eventually permits humans to eat living creatures, God nevertheless restricts how they should be killed (i.e. the creatures should be drained of blood; Genesis 9:3–4) and which animals can be eaten (i.e. no unclean creature should be eaten; Leviticus 11).

Finally, God's instructions to the human couple in Genesis 1 are put in the context of blessing, and therefore human procreation, subduing the earth, and dominion over living creatures remain dependent on God's own activity (see also Kay 1989: 220). Blessing in the biblical tradition is the expression of God's creative activity. As God's blessing of humans, subduing and having dominion are therefore not inherent characteristics of humankind, nor a divine right given to humans, but rather the manner by which humans, created in the image of God, may participate in God's creative activity through their own work. In other words, Genesis 1 expresses a theocentric worldview in which human subduing of the earth and having dominion over other creatures is only made possible through God's blessing. Being in the image of God entails not only human similarity to God, but also human subordination to and dependence on God. Humans have a distinctive status and role within creation, but, contrary to some anthropocentric interpretations of Genesis 1, humans are neither the purpose nor the measure of creation. They are creatures of God blessed to participate as creative agents in God's creation.

Whereas Genesis 1 emphasizes the distinctive status of humankind, Psalm 104 undermines that status. Although a hymn praising God's sustaining role in the creation rather than a creation account, Psalm 104 shares so many similarities with Genesis 1 that many scholars have argued for the dependence of one text on the other, though which is primary is debated (see Levenson 1988: 54–65; Berlin 2005). The differences between the texts, however, are more significant for understanding the psalm. The distinctive status and role of humans so evident in Genesis 1 is virtually absent in Psalm 104; humans are not singled out in the psalm as either special or having a distinctive role (except perhaps in terms of their wickedness; see v. 35). Attention instead is given to the diverse world God created and sustains. No reference is made to humans being in the image of God or to having dominion over other living creatures. Instead, humans are but one of God's creatures, all of whom are dependent upon God for their food and subsistence.

Significantly, all the creatures referenced in the psalm are wild animals (with the possible exception of the "cattle" in verse 14), and they live and carry out their tasks independently of humankind and human dominion. Even the "cattle," which elsewhere includes the domestic species, live separately from humans and are taken care of by God. The great sea monster Leviathan, which elsewhere in the biblical tradition God defeated in a cosmogonic battle (Psalm 74:12–17), was never thought to be subject to human dominion. Indeed, its defeat or subjugation was thought to be necessary for creation to flourish (see Job 41:1–11). But in this psalm, Leviathan is simply one of God's creatures in which he delights. Thus, no creature, not even the "cattle" and especially not Leviathan, exists to serve humankind (see Harrelson 1975: 20). Moreover, all the animals are engaged in activities that resemble human tasks: drinking, eating, resting, sitting, having homes, going to work, returning home, and playing. The psalmist thinks of the animals and even Leviathan "as fellow creatures with whom he or she shared a common life" (Whitekettle 2011: 183).

The role of God in Psalm 104 corresponds to what the modern scientific worldview would identify as the forces of nature. Whereas the modern worldview would explain change in the world in terms of natural causality—physical, chemical, and biological causes—the biblical worldview of the psalmist understood the world in terms of personal causality. The biblical scribes attributed all change in the world, beyond individual agency, to God, and thus all life was understood to be dependent on God. According to the psalmist, it is God who brings out the sun to light and heat the day and to signal the work day and seasonal chores; it is God who controls the water that gushes forth from springs, fills river beds and the seas, or rains upon the land; it is God who causes the grass and the crops to grow and gives food to the lions. Life is only possible through God's creative and sustaining activity. The distinction between humans and animals that is highlighted elsewhere in the biblical tradition is insignificant in the context of God's ever-present activity in creation, which is praised in this psalm. For the psalmist, humans are as dependent upon God as all other creatures.

In the biblical tradition, Genesis 1 and Psalm 104 represent the polar extremes of the distinctive status of humankind in the world. In Genesis 1, humans are assigned a lofty position in the creation, but clearly one with limits; and at the other end of the continuum,

Psalm 104 treats humans as only one of God's many creatures (though with a unique propensity toward wickedness). Most of the biblical tradition falls between these two extremes. Nevertheless, both texts, and all those in between, express a theocentric worldview, in which the world belongs to God, who created and sustains it. Humans may have a distinctive role, but they are part and parcel of the creation, along with the rest of the natural world, and their role within the creation cannot separate them from the creation.

Work, law, and covenant

Although humans are not separated from nature in the biblical tradition, and so God relates to humans as part of the creation, humans are nevertheless given a pivotal role in the created world. According to the predominant traditions in the Bible (especially the Deuteronomic and Priestly traditions), the condition of the natural world is determined by the Israelites' own obedience to or observance of the laws of the Sinai covenant. If the Israelites follow the laws, then the natural world will flourish as the Israelites also do well; but if the Israelites disregard the laws, then both the Israelites and the natural world will suffer. This covenantal relationship between human actions and the condition of the natural world is expressed straightforwardly in Deuteronomy:

> If you [the Israelites] will only heed [God's] every commandment that I am commanding you today—loving the LORD your God, and serving him with all your heart and with all your soul—then he will give the rain for your land in its season, the early rain and the later rain, and you will gather in your grain, your wine, and your oil; and he will give grass in your field for your livestock, and you will eat your fill. Take care, or you will be seduced into turning away, serving other gods and worshiping them, for then the anger of the LORD will be kindled against you and he will shut up the heavens, so that there will be no rain and the land will yield no fruit; then you will perish quickly off the good land that the LORD is giving you.
>
> (*Deuteronomy 11:13–17*)

The covenant is a formal relationship between God and Israel, rooted in God's past actions on behalf of Israel and requiring in response Israel's observance of God's laws, which have the consequence of blessings or curses (McCarthy 1963; Hillers 1969; Baltzer 1971; Levenson 1985). The above text from Deuteronomy and other covenantal texts seem to suggest that God rewards Israel's observance of laws and punishes Israel's failures, but the covenantal worldview suggests that the blessings and curses have a more direct relationship to Israel's actions. The covenantal worldview holds that God established the structure of creation so that there is an inherent connection between human actions and their consequences. As Knight (1985: 150) puts it, "This act/consequence cosmogony envisions such pervasive order in the closed circuit of creation that whatever humans do, whether for good or for ill, will necessarily have repercussions in nature as easily as among people." Thus, when the Israelites follow the covenant and observe the laws, they live in accord with the created order, and the creation—Israel, its land and animals, and the rest of the natural world—flourishes as God intended. However, when the Israelites disregard the laws of the covenant, they corrupt the order of creation. Through their transgression of the covenant, the Israelites do objective damage to the order of creation, which responds accordingly. God's role in creation consists in setting in motion and bringing to completion those effects—blessings or curses—that God established in the created order (Koch 1983).

Whereas the Deuteronomic presentation of the covenant remains largely ethnocentric, based exclusively on Israel's historical relationship to God, the Priestly tradition universalizes the foundation of God's covenant with Israel by rooting it in God's creation of the world. In Genesis 1:1–2:3, the Priestly tradition presents the creation of the world in terms of God's work. In six days God works to create an ordered, differentiated, and inhabited world from what was originally formless and empty. Then, on the seventh day, God rests from his labors. When God creates humans in his image on the sixth day, God also assigns work to the humans—procreation, subduing the earth, and dominion over living creatures—but the significance of the work remains inchoate: the human work–rest cycle represented by the sabbath replicates God's own creative activity in the world. Only with the law is the significance of human work fully articulated when the Priestly tradition connects the sabbath with God's covenant at Sinai:

> You will keep my sabbaths, for this is a sign between me and you throughout your generations to know that I am the LORD who sanctifies you . . . and the Israelites shall keep the sabbath, observing the sabbath throughout their generations as an eternal covenant. It is a sign forever between me and the Israelites.
>
> *(Exodus 31:12–17)*

As a symbol of the covenant, the Israelites' observance of the sabbath becomes an indication of their faithfulness to God's covenant. By connecting the sabbath and God's covenant, the Priestly tradition clarifies the character of human work: human work that replicates God's creative activity is also in accord with God's covenant. Or to state the reverse, when human work violates God's covenant, it does damage to God's creation. Human work, for the Priestly tradition, either builds upon and sustains, or is contrary to and undermines, God's own creative activity, and such work is defined in relation to the requirements of the covenant (i.e. observing the law).

The covenantal worldview affirms that humans are embedded in the natural world and that human actions have consequences in the natural world. As such, this worldview may contribute to an environmental ethics. Few would argue with the assumption that the environmental crisis is ultimately rooted in human behavior, whether explicitly through pollution or implicitly through overpopulation and consumption, and this biblical worldview enables religious language, such as "sin," to be applied to human behavior that is contrary, or does violence, to the order and structure of the natural world (Gottlieb 2007). Nevertheless, this worldview is not without problems, especially when viewed anthropocentrically. Although human behavior has repercussions in the natural world, the condition of the natural world is not simply a barometer of human behavior; the world does not revolve around humans. This critique of the covenantal worldview is presented in the book of Job, which challenges not only an anthropocentric appropriation of the covenantal worldview, but also its deterministic link between human behavior and the condition of the natural world. Through Job's many speeches, and especially through the speech of God (Job 38–42), the book emphasizes that the natural world is not an unambiguous witness to the character of human behavior. Moreover, and perhaps more significantly, the book of Job puts humans in their place: the creation neither revolves around humans, nor was it created for human purposes. The creation and all that is in it belongs to God.

Eschatology and the end of nature

In his popular book, *The End of Nature* (1989), Bill McKibben describes in dreadful detail how humans have polluted and irreversibly altered the environment and the painful consequences that await the future. For McKibben, we have reached the end of nature because the idea of nature is no longer possible—that is, the non-human world is no longer independent of humans and their activity. Human fingerprints are everywhere. Humans have become like God—indeed, humans have replaced God—as the makers of the natural world. The role of a transcendent God in this scenario is ambiguous. At best, God remains silent as humans wrestle with the consequences of their actions. At worst, the end of nature means the death of God. In any case, humans are left on their own—to confront alone the problems they have wrought, to live in a world of their own making. McKibben's description of the end of nature may be scientifically accurate and present plausible scenarios, but it does little to instill hope that we may overcome our environmental problems, human-made though they are.

The biblical tradition also has a vision of a coming catastrophe, which is a consequence of the covenantal worldview. The prophetic tradition, in particular, prophesied Israel and Judah's destruction due to the people's rejection of God's laws, and more broadly, the destruction of the nations and even the collapse of the cosmos due to rampant human violence and injustice. The destruction will not only encompass the cities and people, but also the land, the plants and vegetation, the birds, fish, and animals, and in some contexts the creation as a whole (see e.g. Hosea 4:1–3; Zephaniah 1:2–3; Isaiah 24:4–6; Jeremiah 4:23–26; Jeremiah 9:10–11). In the biblical vision, humans are inseparable from the rest of the natural world so that the coming catastrophe will impact all creation. Although human actions are what precipitate the catastrophe, all creation suffers the consequences. But unlike McKibben's "eschatological" vision, the biblical vision also includes a redemption in which all creation will participate (see e.g. Amos 9:13–15; Hosea 2:18–23; Isaiah 11:6–9; Ezekiel 36:8–11).

The eschatological visions in the biblical tradition are problematic in regard to an environmental ethic or theology (Horrell 2010: 88–114). On the one hand, visions of catastrophe may undermine concern for the environment; there is little urgency to protect the environment, if catastrophe is inevitable. On the other hand, visions of redemption place the burden of redemption solely on God, leaving uncertain the human role. Indeed, when viewed on their own, these eschatological visions offer little help for environmental concern. When read in the context of the larger biblical tradition, however, such eschatological visions articulate the fundamental values of the tradition and may provide a religious framework for understanding one's relationship to the environment.

The story of God's activity in the Bible, from the creation of Adam and Eve, through the calling of Abraham, leading Moses and the Israelites from Egypt and making a covenant with them, anointing David as his chosen king, to calling the prophets who proclaimed God's message to the people, is often called "salvation history." It is viewed as the history of God's relationship with humans, and especially Israel; in this context, the prophets proclaimed God's coming redemption, which was understood primarily in historical, human terms. Indeed, the Bible tells the history of a humankind in need of redemption, for "the inclination of the human heart is evil from youth" (Genesis 8:21). Although humans (along with the rest of creation) are created as "very good" (Genesis 1:31) and are capable of heroic and merciful acts, more often than not, they go against God's desires, violate his laws, and suffer the consequences. Thus the Bible envisions a future re-creation of the human heart, which will be inclined to observe God's laws (Jeremiah 31:31–34; Ezekiel 36:22–32). The problem with this understanding, however, is that it is incomplete. God's activity encompasses the whole creation. God created an ordered and good habitable world in which humans and other living creatures may flourish. God sustains the world and blesses it with abundant life. God's relationship is with more than just humans, for humans are simply part of the creation, and so God's prophesied redemption includes the whole creation. Humans are in need of redemption because of their evil inclination and rebellion against God's covenant. But the rest of creation also needs to be redeemed, not because it is evil or against God, but because it has been corrupted by human sin (Rolston 1994).

In linking the environmental crisis to religion, Lynn White claimed that human ecology is conditioned by beliefs about nature and destiny (White 1967: 1205). Human "nature and destiny" is what the biblical eschatology is all about. The biblical ecology embeds humans in the natural world and links human destiny to that of the rest of the natural world. It is not certain that White is correct that people's thinking about ecological relationships shapes their behavior toward the environment. There is clearly evidence to the contrary; many other factors are involved. Nevertheless, religion *can* shape how people respond to environmental concerns. The Evangelical Climate Initiative (2006), for example, represents a political shift by many prominent Evangelical leaders to support initiatives fighting global warming. What is their rationale? The science supporting human-induced climate change is convincing *and* the Bible calls us to care for the creation. This much, at least, is encouraging.

The implications of the biblical eschatology for addressing the environmental crisis are complex. The claims of the biblical eschatology are neither scientific nor historical. We cannot simply take comfort in the hope that God will restore the earth at the end. Instead, the biblical eschatology presents a moral vision:

> The value of these texts lies not in their capacity to predict cosmic or human history in advance—that they cannot do—but in their capacity to *shape* our behavior now toward each other and the other denizens of the earthly ecosystem.
>
> *(Towner 1996: 31)*

The biblical eschatology tells us about God, God's character, and God's intention for the creation. It tells us about humans and human character, and our relationship to the rest of creation. It can provide hope and motivation in working toward a sustainable world.

Because humans are fully embedded in the creation, the biblical tradition cannot envision the redemption of humans apart from the redemption of the entire creation. The future of humans and the natural world are bound together. This means that environmental activism must also concern itself with issues of social justice, and social justice cannot achieve its goals until ecology is taken into account. From the perspective of the biblical tradition, both humans and the environment are in need of redemption, and only as both are addressed will healing and redemption come to the creation.

References

Anderson, Bernhard W. 1975. "Human Dominion over Nature." In M. Ward (ed.) *Biblical Studies in Contemporary Thought*. Somerville, MA: Greeno, Hadden, and Co., pp. 27–45.

Baltzer, Klaus. 1971. *The Covenant Formulary: In Old Testament, Jewish, and Early Christian Writings* (transl. by D. E. Green). Philadelphia, PA: Fortress.

Barr, James. 1972. "Man and Nature: The Ecological Controversy and the Old Testament." *Bulletin of the John Rylands Library* 51(1): 11–26.

Benedict XVI. 2009. "If you Want to Cultivate Peace, Protect Creation." Message for the 43rd World Day of Peace 2010 (text released 8 December 2009). www.vatican.va/holy_father/benedict_xvi/messages/peace/documents/hf_ben-xvi_mes_20091208_xliii-world-day-peace_en.html

Berlin, Adele. 2005. "The Wisdom of Creation in Psalm 104." In R. L. Troxel, K. G. Friebel, and D. R. Magary (eds) *Seeking Out the Wisdom of the Ancients: Essays Offered in Honor of Michael V. Fox on the Occasion of his Sixty-Fifth Birthday*. Winona Lake, IN: Eisenbrauns, pp. 71–83.

Berry, Wendell. 1993. "Christianity and the Survival of Creation." *Cross Currents* 43(2): 149–163.

Derr, Thomas S. 1975. "Religion's Responsibility for the Ecological Crisis: An Argument Run Amok." *Worldview* 18: 39–45.

Djupe, Paul A. and Patrick K.Hunt. 2009. "Beyond the Lynn White Thesis: Congregational Effects on Environmental Concern." *Journal for the Scientific Study of Religion* 48(4): 670–686.

Djupe, Paul A. and Gregory W. Gwiasda. 2010. "Evangelizing the Environment: Decision Process Effects in Political Persuasion." *Journal for the Scientific Study of Religion* 49(1): 73–86.

Dubos, René. 1972. *A God Within*. New York: Charles Scribner's Sons.

Evangelical Climate Initiative. 2006. "Climate Change: An Evangelical Call to Action." www.npr.org/documents/2006/feb/evangelical/calltoaction.pdf (accessed 15 February 2015).

Glacken, Clarence J. 1976. *Traces on the Rhodian Shore: Nature and Culture in Western Thought from Ancient Times to the End of the Eighteenth Century*. Berkeley: University of California Press.

Gottlieb, Roger S. 2007. "Religious Environmentalism: What it Is, Where it's Heading and Why we Should Be Going in the Same Direction." *Journal for the Study of Religion, Nature and Culture* 1(1): 81–91.

—— 2009. *A Greener Faith: Religious Environmentalism and our Planet's Future*. Oxford: Oxford University Press.

—— (ed.) 2010. *Religion and the Environment*. 4 Volumes. London: Routledge.

Grey, William. 1998. "Environmental Value and Anthropocentrism." *Ethics and the Environment* 3(1): 97–103.

Guth, James L., John C. Green, Lyman A. Kellstedt, and Corwin E. Smidt. 1995. "Faith and the Environment: Religious Beliefs and Attitudes on Environmental Policy." *American Journal of Political Science* 39(2): 364–382.

Hargrove, Eugene C. 1992. "Weak Anthropocentric Intrinsic Value." *The Monist* 75(2): 183–207.

Harrelson, Walter. 1975. "Of God's Care for the Earth: Psalm 104." *Currents in Theology and Mission* 2(1): 19–22.

Harrison, Peter. 1999. "Subduing the Earth: Genesis 1, Early Modern Science, and the Exploitation of Nature." *Journal of Religion* 79(1): 86–109.

Hiers, Richard H. 1984. "Ecology, Biblical Theology, and Methodology: Biblical Perspectives on the Environment." *Zygon* 19(1): 43–59.

Hillers, Delbert. 1969. *Covenant: The History of a Biblical Idea*. Baltimore, MD: The Johns Hopkins Press.

Hoffman, Andrew J. and Lloyd E. Sandelands. 2005. "Getting Right with Nature: Anthropocentrism, Ecocentrism, and Theocentrism." *Organization and Environment* 18(2): 141–162.

Horrell, David G. 2010. *The Bible and the Environment: Towards a Critical Ecological Biblical Theology*. London: Equinox.

Hughes, J. Donald. 1975. *Ecology in Ancient Civilizations*. Albuquerque: University of New Mexico Press.

Jenkins, Willis. 2009. "After Lynn White: Religious Ethics and Environmental Problems." *Journal of Religious Ethics* 37(2): 283–309.

—— 2011. "Religion and Environment." *Annual Review of Environment and Resources* 36: 441–463.

Kay, Jeanne. 1989. "Human Dominion over Nature in the Hebrew Bible." *Annals of the Association of American Geographers* 79(2): 214–232.

Knight, Douglas A. 1985. "Cosmogony and Order in the Hebrew Tradition." In R. W. Lovin and F. E. Reynolds (eds) *Cosmogony and Ethical Order: New Studies in Comparative Ethics*. Chicago, IL: University of Chicago Press, pp. 133–157.

Koch, Klaus. 1983. "Is There a Doctrine of Retribution in the Old Testament?" In J. L. Crenshaw (ed.) *Theodicy in the Old Testament*. Philadelphia, PA: Fortress, pp. 57–87.

Levenson, Jon D. 1985. *Sinai and Zion: An Entry into the Jewish Bible*. San Francisco, CA: Harper & Row.

—— 1988. *Creation and the Persistence of Evil: The Jewish Drama of Divine Omnipotence*. San Francisco, CA: Harper & Row.

McCarthy, Dennis J. 1963. *Treaty and Covenant: A Study in Form in the Ancient Oriental Documents and in the Old Testament*. Rome: Pontifical Biblical Institute.

McKibben, Bill. 1989. *The End of Nature*. New York: Random House.

Midgley, Mary. 1994. "The End of Anthropocentrism?" In Robin Attfield and Andrew Belsey (eds) *Philosophy and the Natural Environment*. Royal Institute of Philosophy Supplement 36. Cambridge, UK: Cambridge University Press, pp. 103–112.

Minteer, Ben A. and Robert E. Manning 2005. "An Appraisal of the Critique of Anthropocentrism and Three Lesser Known Themes in Lynn White's 'The Historical Roots of Our Ecologic Crisis'." *Organization and Environment* 15(2): 163–176.

Mizzoni, John. 2008. "Franciscan Biocentrism and the Franciscan Tradition." *Ethics and the Environment* 13(1): 121–134.

Norton, Bryan G. 1984. "Environmental Ethics and Weak Anthropocentrism." *Environmental Ethics* 6: 131–148.

Rolston, III, Holmes. 1994. "Does Nature Need to Be Redeemed?" *Zygon* 29(2): 205–229.

Sessions, George S. 1974. "Anthropocentrism and the Environmental Crisis." *Humboldt Journal of Social Relations* 2: 71–81.

Sherkat, Darren E. and Christopher G. Ellison. 2007. "Structuring the Religion–Environment Connection: Identifying Religious Influences on Environmental Concern and Activism." *Journal for the Scientific Study of Religion* 46(1): 71–85.

Simkins, Ronald A. 1994. *Creator and Creation: Nature in the Worldview of Ancient Israel*. Peabody, MA: Hendrickson.

—— 2014. "The Bible and Anthropocentrism: Putting Humans in Their Place." *Dialectical Anthropology* 38(4): 397–413. doi 10.1007/s10624-014-9348-z

Spitler, Gene. 1982. "Justifying a Respect for Nature." *Environmental Ethics* 4: 255–260.

Towner, W. Sibley. 1996. "The Future of Nature." *Interpretation* 50(1): 27–35.

Trible, Phyllis. 1971. "Ancient Priests and Modern Polluters." *Andover Newton Quarterly* 12(2): 74–79.

Truelove, Heather Barnes, and Jeff Joireman. 2009. "Understanding the Relationship between Christian Orthodoxy and Environmentalism: The Mediating Role of Perceived Environmental Consequences." *Environment and Behavior* 41(6): 806–820.

Tuan, Yi-Fu. 1970. "Our Treatment of the Environment in Ideal and Actuality." *American Scientist* 58(3): 244–249.

Tucker, Mary E. and John Grim (eds) 1997–2004. *Religions of the World and Ecology* (series). Cambridge, MA: Harvard University Press.

White, Jr, Lynn. 1967. "The Historical Roots of our Ecologic Crisis." *Science* 155(3767): 1203–1207.

Whitekettle, Richard. 2011. "A Communion of Subjects: Zoological Classification and Human/Animal Relations in Psalm 104." *Bulletin for Biblical Research* 21(2): 173–188.

Whitney, Elspeth. 1993. "Lynn White, Ecotheology, and History." *Environmental Ethics* 15: 151–169.

13

WHAT'S ONTOLOGY GOT TO DO WITH IT?

On the knowledge of nature and the nature of knowledge in environmental anthropology

Sian Sullivan

I don't know if you've ever had the . . . experience of having your life changed by a quite trivial incident. . . . It happened to me on that trip. I was on the *Southern Cross* – that's the mission boat – and there was a group of islanders there – recent converts. . . . And I thought I'd go through my usual routine, so I started asking questions. The first question was, what would you do with it if you earned or found a guinea? Would you share it, and if so who would you share it *with*? It gets their attention because to them it's a lot of money, and you can uncover all kinds of things about kinship structure and economic arrangements, and so on. Anyway, at the end of this – we were all sitting cross-legged on the deck, miles from anywhere – they decided they'd turn the tables on me, and ask me the same questions. Starting with: What would *I* do with a guinea? Who would I share it with? I explained I was unmarried and that I wouldn't necessarily feel obliged to share it with anybody. They were *incredulous*. How could anybody live *like that*? And so it went on, question after question. . . . They were rolling round the deck by the time I'd finished. And suddenly I realised that *anything* I told them would have got the same response. . . . And I suddenly saw that their reactions to my society were neither more nor less valid than mine to theirs. And do you know that was a moment of the most *amazing* freedom. . . . It was . . . the *Great White God* de-throned, I suppose. Because we did, we quite unselfconsciously *assumed* we were the measure of all things. That was how we approached them. And suddenly I saw not only that we weren't the measure of all things, but that *there was no measure*.

> (Anthropologist W. H. R. Rivers (1864–1922) who conducted
> ethnographic research amongst Torres Straits Islanders
> in the late 1800s, speaking in Barker [1991: 241–242].)

Introduction: ontological dimensions in environmental anthropology[1]

If there is anything normative about 'environmental anthropology' it is the intention to understand, as far as possible, the internal or emic logic of specific culturenature practices and values: all those culturally-inflected norms and actions that shape specific human relationships with more-than-human others. In this endeavour, the sub-discipline builds on the will in socio-cultural anthropology more broadly to understand observed cultural phenomena in the terms through which they are understood by their practitioners. For Malinowski (1922), writing of the birth of participant observation that became anthropology's methodological trademark, this meant understanding 'the native's point of view'. For Geertz (1973), writing several decades later, it meant reaching towards a 'thick description' of culturally-embedded practices and the worldview of 'the other': one that is deep, nuanced, and internally appropriate, as opposed to a 'thin' or superficial projection that says more about the values and assumptions of the observer than the reality of the observed. In recent years, and drawing on diverse cultural knowledges of the 'nature of nature' found globally, this fine-tuned attention to the realities of the other has emerged as an 'ontological turn' in anthropology, confirming a 'multiplicity of forms of existence enacted in concrete practices' (Holbraad *et al.* 2014: online; also Descola 2013).

Anthropology at its heart, then, affirms diversity in both cultural knowledges of the world, and in the very nature of the worlds that are culturally known. This diversity of knowledge-and-nature couplings shapes the varied forms of ethos and ethical praxes enacted culturally in the world (see also Bourdieu 1992). As alluded to in the fictionalised passage by anthropologist W. H. R. Rivers that opens this chapter, non-judgemental curiosity and openness regarding this diversity are virtues on which the practice of ethnography that is so critical to the discipline builds. Practitioners of anthropology may have their own normative views of what the most appropriate nature–knowledge relationship might be, views that might be shaped by ethnographic and other encounters with the world. But it is from curiosity and openness to empirical circumstances that ethnographic understanding can arise.

In environmental anthropology more explicitly, a move towards ontological considerations seems to have intensified as researchers have dug more deeply into divergences regarding the assumed nature of reality, as revealed by differences in how environmental phenomena are framed and thereby constructed culturally. Concentrating in the 1990s, detailed research by environmental anthropologists, particularly in African contexts, demonstrated that a range of 'received wisdoms' regarding environmental phenomena, in response to which development policies were being designed, could be understood instead as knowledge constructions built discursively with significant power-effects in terms of access to land and 'resources' (see, for example, Richards 1985; Homewood and Rodgers 1987; Fairhead and Leach 1996; Leach and Mearns 1996; Reij *et al.* 1996; Sullivan 2000). These studies demonstrated that powerful national and international discourses regarding environmental phenomena, which often tended to demonise the use and value practices of local people in the contexts researched, could be destabilised and deconstructed by bringing varied sources of data to bear on their key assertions. As such, these researchers assumed a *critical realist* approach to the acquisition of knowledge regarding the nature of environmental change(s). They affirmed an objective environment 'out there' that can be known through empirical research methodologies, while asserting that the deployment of methods and data to produce policy-relevant environmental knowledge also reflects 'regimes of truth' shaping prominent views of the world and associated powerful interests. Among environmental anthropologists, geographers, and political scientists alike, this Foucault-inspired orientation towards empirical understanding of the constructed nature of dominant environmental knowledges and discourses has been key to the emergence of the field of 'political ecology' (see e.g. Bryant and Bailey 1997; Stott and Sullivan 2000; Adger *et al.* 2001; Forsythe 2003; Robbins *et al.* 2010; the nexus of power/knowledge and the ideological functions served by science are emphasised in Foucault 1980, 1982).

Recently, and associated with a consolidated ontological turn in the social sciences and humanities more broadly (Smith 1981), anthropologists of culturenature relationships have increasingly emphasised how different cultures globally may understand the nature of the natures they both utilise and with which they co-exist. Building on earlier work by anthropologists such as Hallowell (1960), diverse understandings of relationships between humans and natures-beyond-the-human (after Kohn 2013) have been shown to frequently include assumptions challenging to a modern scientific worldview (see in-depth review in Descola 2013). Some of these understandings are considered below. But before thinking through what ontology has to do with the knowledge of nature and the nature of knowledge, let's explore the nature of ontology.

On 'ontology'

Ontology as a form of enquiry asks questions regarding the nature of being so as to make assertions regarding the known nature of reality and how this can be legitimately known. Ontological assumptions denote what entities can exist, into what categories they can be sorted, and by what practices and methods they can be known (i.e. epistemology). A cross-cultural perspective affirms that cultural and historical differences create the possibility for *plural ontologies*. It suggests the parallel existence of different ways of understanding how reality is constructed, how the world and its entities can be known, and what constitutes appropriate ethical praxis in relation to these entities. From an anthropological as well as a postcolonial perspective, Western assumptions regarding how nature is constituted, while universalising, are understood in fact to be highly *particular* (Chakrabarty 2000). They are embedded in and made possible by particular cultural and historical contexts that do not necessarily translate well into non-Western cultural experiences (Viveiros de Castro 2004; Descola 2013; Kohn 2013). Indeed, ontological plurality can be found in perhaps the unlikeliest of places. Even the hardest of sciences, namely physics, makes varied and contested observations regarding the foundational nature of being and the methods through which this can be known. The radical historical shift from Newtonian mechanism to quantum indeterminacy within the last hundred years, and the current variety of views regarding underlying universal phenomena (particles, strings, plasma, etc.), illustrate this diversity.

Of relevance at this moment of global environmental predicament is that we find ourselves living in the shadow of two thousand years of hierarchical value-ordering in Western thought regarding the relationships of different orders of being, as summarised in Table 13.1. This ordering became consolidated in the 'Cartesian moment' of the Enlightenment, when philosopher René Descartes famously asserted a dichotomy between mind and body, and simultaneously privileged a transcendent reasoning 'mind' over the brute, mechanistic matter of 'the body' (Descartes 1968 [1637]; Hall 2011; Marder 2013; also Abram 2010: 159–181). The translation of this dichotomy into an equally constructed split between culture and nature was additionally accompanied by a demotion of non-human entities into machine-like 'automata'. In 'Discourse 5' of Descartes' *Discourse on Method,* he writes of animals that:

> they do not have a mind, and . . . it is nature which acts in them according to the disposition of their organs, as one sees that a clock, which is made up of only wheels and springs, can count the hours and measure time more exactly than we can with all our art.[2]

> *(Descartes 1968 [1637]: 75–76)*

Table 13.1 Plato's and Aristotle's ontological value hierarchies of faculties of soul.

Plato		Aristotle	
spirited	enabling activity and volition	intellective	rational soul possessing mind/reason 'humans excellence'
rational	enabling intelligence and self-control	locomotive	mobility found in *humans and animals* but *not* plants
	associated with reason/mind/opinion and located in men who are thus able to rule	desiderative	able to desire, i.e. to have appetite, passion, wish – found in *humans and animals*
appetitive	associated with pleasure/pain/desire as well as passivity	perceptive	able to sense pleasure and pain – found in *humans and animals*
	located in the ruled – slaves, women, children and slaves	nutritive	mechanical ability to feed and reproduce.
	plants as fixed, rooted, passive		*plants* possess only this 'soul', i.e. otherwise rendered as passive

Source: Based on Hall (2011: 19–26) after Plumwood (2006).

Through this entrenched dichotomisation and hierarchisation, a reality has been constructed and normalised whereby only humans, and often only particular humans, possess intelligence and mind. At the other end of the hierarchy, plants, for example, are viewed merely as 'vegetables' – dispossessed of the capacities of agency, movement, perception, communication, and intentionality, and thus usefully backgrounded as existing only for the instrumental ends of humans. The accompanying 'naturalist' (Descola 2013) ontological production of a nature-beyond-the-human that is distant, stilled, and 'outside', has additionally created this nature as usefully amenable to objectification, instrumentalisation, and myriad associated violations.

In this hierarchical ontology, consolidated over the last few centuries of Western thought, a tendency has been for only the intelligence characteristic of (particular) human entities to confer moral consideration, since only this intelligence is understood as possessing scope for communication, purpose, and subjectivity. The ontological denial of these latter faculties in other kinds of embodied being including, historically, the bodies of the non-Western human 'other' (as conveyed in brutal detail for South American imperial contexts in Taussig 1987) has permitted the doing of harm without *recognition* that harm has been done. Although often it is more complex than this, in that the denial of capacities for communication, purpose, and subjectivity in 'non-human others' perhaps manifests more as *disavowal*: as the simultaneous acknowledgement of harms caused, accompanied by a strategy – an apparent solution – to seemingly mitigate this harm (after Freud 2009 [1938]). An early example of this, and of the pathology that such 'solutions' can embody, comes from the post-Cartesian vivisectionists. While operating in a Cartesian mode, i.e. construing animals as soulless automata, these scientists would also cut the vocal cords of their experimental subjects so that they would not be able to hear the ensuing cries of pain (Hornborg 2006: 24; after Evernden 1985: 17–21). Through this apparent 'solution', the scientists' embodied acknowledgement of the communicative and experiential capacities of animals was denied, so as to literally make the animals subject to their experiments into mute objects. Strategies of disavowal – of the simultaneous acknowledgement of, and turning away from, harms caused – abound today through the sale and purchase of various forms of tradeable 'offsets' for 'solving' problems of environmental harm. Purchase of environmental 'credits' (such as carbon or biodiversity offsets) generated in one place are thus considered to 'solve' damage effected somewhere else, although arguably such 'solutions' also entrench a disconnection (or splitting-off) from the continuation of damage-producing behaviours that such offsets require (Sullivan 2013b, drawing on Fletcher 2013).

Ethnography – the methodological attempt to understand in detail the makings of social reality in different cultural contexts, *without necessary recourse to 'the West' as the measure of all things* – can assist with illuminating the shape of different cultural ontologies regarding relationships between humans and other-than-human entities. For some environmental anthropologists this may involve a further normative dimension. This is because ethnographically-grounded elucidations of 'non-Western', 'amodern' and non-capitalist culturenatures can both clarify the ontological underpinnings justifying the more destructive dimensions of advanced and expansionary capitalist and industrial societies, while containing seeds of corrective and alternative possibilities.

In particular, it is hard not to notice that many indigenous communities globally – i.e. cultures who have retained some degree of long-term, continuous ancestral connection with land areas – are frequently also associated with localities now celebrated for their environmental health as 'biodiversity hotspots' (Gorenflo *et al.* 2012). Biodiversity hotspots, as framed by conservation biologists (Myers *et al.* 2000), are geographical areas characterised by high species diversity and the incidence of endemism and rarity, set within a broader context of environmental degradation that bears the hallmark of a global anthropogenic extinction event. Human cultural arrangements in these contexts have been associated with the maintenance of relationships with diverse natures-beyond-the-human, despite immense modern pressures to transform such cultural landscapes in the interests of economic growth. As Gorenflo *et al.* (2012: 8037) state, 'the tendency for both [biological and linguistic diversity] to be high in particular regions suggests that certain cultural systems and practices, represented by speakers of particular indigenous and nonmigrant languages, tend to be compatible with high biodiversity'.

Environmental anthropology has a critical role to play in generating nuanced understanding of the ontologies that have made it possible for human cultures in these contexts to maintain particular relational sustainabilities. The sub-discipline can thus assist with enhancing awareness regarding possibilities for living in more accommodating ethical relationships with many kinds of selves, only some of whom are human (Ingold 2000; Kohn 2013; Sullivan 2013a; Hannis and Sullivan forthcoming). In the next section I review some ontological themes that seem consistent among the cultures considered by Gorenflo *et al.* (2012) to be 'compatible with high biodiversity'.

Animist ontological tendencies

Remaining indigenous cultures living on the edges of an expansionary capitalist modernity in landscapes of high conservation priority often exhibit ontological assumptions and associated practices of use and appreciation that can be described using the signifier 'animism'. Put simply, animist ontologies assume the alive sentience of other-than-human natures, affirm the possibility of agency enacted by 'non-human' entities, and tend to adjust human relationships with these entities accordingly. The term 'animism' enfolds pagan cultures framed as 'mistaken primitives' positioned prior to the attainment of Enlightenment rationality by Edward Tylor in his theory of religion (Tylor 1913 [1871]) with postmodern 'eco-pagans' of the industrial West, for whom animism is a contemporary eco-ethical 'concern with knowing how to behave appropriately towards persons, not all of whom are human' (Harvey 2005: xi). As such, 'animism' is both 'a knowledge construct of the West' (Garuba 2012: 7), and a universalising term acknowledging a 'primacy of relationality' (see also Bird–David 1992; Ingold 2006) and a set of affirmative practices that privilege an expansionary intersubjectivity which resists the objectification of non-human others (Franke 2012: 4, 7). Below I summarise some key tendencies in both perception and practice that ethnographic study suggests are prominent in animist ontologies, drawing on diverse literatures as well as ethnographic field research in varied contexts over more than 20 years.

Primal time and the cultural kinship of beings

In the beginning, people and animals were related: not so much in terms of their shared biology, but in the sense that they shared language, culture, and kinship. Assertions of such a 'primal time' are key to understanding a range of indigenous/animist ontologies: from KhoeSān peoples of southern Africa (Solomon 1997; personal field notes) to Amerindian peoples of the Amazon (Viveiros de Castro 2004). Because people and animals were of the same order in the past they continue to exist in agential and reciprocal relationships in the present, with animals and other 'non-human' entities retaining communicative and subjective attributes that confer personhood (Hallowell 1960; Harvey 2005; Brightman *et al.* 2012). Humans can empathically experience and intuit the presence and experiences of animals, for example, and the possibility of one transforming into or lodging in the other remains.

Anthropologist Eduardo Viveiros de Castro (2004) thus speaks of the *multinatural* 'perspectivism' of cosmologies associated with peoples of the Amazon, positing this as the understanding that all beings share culture, kinship, and reciprocal relationships, their perspectives differing due to being seated in different bodily affects (or 'natures'). Key aspects of this proposition are as follows: an original culture disaggregated into different embodied perspectives; animals and plants conceived as subjects/persons sharing a spirited hypostases cloaked in different embodied perspectives; and all embodiments understood as sentient, alive, and able to act with intentionality. Ecological relations thus are social relations, with all *persons* able to share and exchange knowledge. Communication and even transformation between such different embodied perspectives is an intrinsic possibility and exists in contradistinction to the naturalism of modernity, which proposes a shared universal Nature from which human culture and Reason rise and become progressively separate (as critiqued in Gray 2002). The 'Amerindian' conception instead is that 'having been people [in the mythological past] animals and other species continue to be people behind their everyday appearance', endowed with the soul or spirit that personifies them (Viveiros de Castro 2004: 467; also cf. Biesele 1993 for Kalahari Ju | 'hoansi contexts). As such, 'non-humans', including ancestors and spirits, are attributed with 'the capacities of conscious intentionality and social agency' (Viveiros de Castro 2004: 467). They are understood as subjects with empathically knowable and communicable subject positions that complexify possibilities for social and moral action.

Agency beyond-the-human

Agency, shaped by the different bodily perspectives of actants, thus is present everywhere. This means that all activity – by animals, components of weather, plants, spirit-beings, ancestors, and so on – is simultaneously imbued with a moral, if relative and frequently ambiguous, dimension (Ingold 2000). Of particular relevance, and as emphasised by Eduardo Kohn, are the ethical perspectives and practices that may arise when people live as if other kinds of being can see 'us', so as to act as if the way(s) that 'they' see 'us' matter. As Kohn (2013) writes:

> How other kinds of beings see us matters. That other kinds of beings see us changes things. If jaguars also represent us – in ways that can matter vitally to us – then anthropology cannot limit itself just to exploring how people from different societies might happen to represent them as doing so. Such encounters with other kinds of being force us to recognize the fact that seeing, representing, and perhaps knowing, even thinking, are not exclusively human affairs.
>
> *(Kohn 2013: 1)*

In the west Namibian field context in which I conduct ethnographic research, for example, and although attenuated through displacement, acculturation, and the variously disruptive effects of modernity, various ≠Nūkhoen and ||Ubun *!haoti* (i.e. land and lineage groupings) have lived in a world of multiple, layered, and interacting agencies that have demanded appropriate practices and observations (Hannis and Sullivan forthcoming). Ancestral agencies associated with potent places are thus connected with through greeting and offering practices, through which ancestors (*kai khoen* – i.e. big or old people) in the realm of the spirits of the dead are requested to act in the present to open the road so that travellers can see the best way to go. They are asked for guidance regarding the most appropriate ways to do things, and their support is evidenced through the intuitions people receive in response to queries that may arise as they are travelling. They are also asked to mediate the activities of potentially dangerous animals such as lions, who are understood very much as other *ensouled* beings who assert their own agencies and intentionality (see below). Ontologically, the ancestors are spirits or souls that have left humans whose bodies have died. As these spirit beings they have ontological reality in the present: they are not simply people who lived in the past, nor are they entities that require worship or blood sacrifice (as occurs in other African contexts; cf. Lewis 2015). They are understood more as specific types of entities that, through pragmatic relationship practices, are called upon to intervene – to assert agency – in the present, so as to influence outcomes.

Sometimes this includes intervention in the agency of other non-human agents, such as lions, a species with which humans in this context continue to live in close contact, as they have done throughout the remembered past. Lions are a key and formidable predator, encounters with whom may result in the loss of human life, or the life of herded livestock. Nonetheless, people in the past sought them out in order to scavenge meat from their kills, and lions figure in peoples' realities as animals imbued with agency and intentionality. Just as Kohn (2013) describes for Runa interactions with jaguars, and Brightman *et al.* (2012: 8) review for cultural interactions with bears and jaguars in Siberian and Amazonian contexts respectively, lions are conceived as being able to see, recognise, and represent the people they encounter and interact with. The proximity of lions to humans is indicated by calling to lions as 'big brother', 'big head', or as a 'big dog' (since dogs are seen as also socially close to humans) – names which denote respect and proximity. In non-ordinary states of consciousness associated with healing, KhoeSān reality also embraces the perceptual possibility of shapeshifting between lions and humans (for discussion of conceptual and material mutability in KhoeSān thought, see Guenther 1999; Sullivan and Low 2014).

In this context, animals generally are considered to be cognate with humans not so much because of their biological and morphological similarities, as in natural history and evolutionary perspectives (although these are important), but because like humans they are animated by a soul that passes from them when they die, and that confers to individuals a sense of self. It is this soul that gives humans and animals their unique smell or 'wind', confers their abilities to move as well as to assert agency and intentionality, and also informs the qualities of action and behaviour from which humans learn how to act appropriately. In the West, by contrast, and as noted above, the conceptual removal of 'soul' from animals was achieved by Descartes' affirmation that they were merely 'soulless automata' (Descartes 1968 [1637]: 75–76), an ontological strategy that has arguably sanctioned ruthless instrumentalisation of animals by justifying moral indifference (Callicott 2013: 112; Sullivan in press). In the ||Khao-a Dama context, asking whether or not animals have a soul is responded to as a derisory question. Indeed, an indication of how radical Descartes' proposition was even in the European context of the 1600s, is the fact that this Enlightenment moment overlapped with centuries of so-called 'animal trials' which took place throughout Europe from the thirteenth to the eighteenth centuries (Cohen 1986). In these trials, non-human animals were attributed such subjectivity, intentionality, and personhood that they were treated as legal persons requiring professional representation (discussed further in Sullivan 2013a).

Agency and intentionality can be extended further still in west Namibia to include the actions of a particular class of plants referred to by the adjective *soxa* as well as to physical phenomena. Regarding the latter, for ||Khao-a Dama and other related KhoeSān peoples, it is the personified, supernatural force behind the phenomena of rain – known here as |*nanus* – that asserts agency in selecting those humans who become healers. Healers are thus known as |*nanu-aob* or |*nanu-aos* – meaning literally man or woman of the rain. When someone is called by |*nanus* they experience a psychological transformation precipitated by a loss of a sense of self. They go into the field (!*garob*) and wander around, lost to the normal world of everyday waking ego consciousness. On realising that they have disappeared, people of their community go looking for them singing the songs of healing dances called *arus*. It is when the nascent |*nanu-aob/s* hears the enchanting threads of the familiar songs of the *arus* that they are able to re-enter the normal social world, having been 'opened' by |*nanus* so that they can see sicknesses of the people. By virtue of their selection by |*nanus*, combined with ritualised practices of consumption of particular rain- and healing-associated substances – such as the *soxa* plant *tuhorabeb* ('*tu*' = rain; see also Schmidt 2014: 147) which assists with being able to see – healers are conferred certain powers of perception that permit them to see and cure sickness. These powers are independent of other forms of leadership, so are not necessarily consistent with any sort of political authority (see also Clastres 1988).

This final example takes us towards what might be conceived as the 'ontological edges' of modernity, to extend a currently lively seam of work in the humanities that explores and opens up some of these ontological edges. This includes work encouraging recognition of the biologically-grounded ontologies of being of non-human species towards more sensitive attunements with other-than-human presence (see e.g. Haraway 2008; Flusser 2011 [1987]; Marder 2013), as well as work that takes seriously the socio-ecological and ethical demands of materiality (see e.g. Bennett 2010; Jackson 2013). But for anthropologists and others working in variously 'non-modern' cultural contexts, there is a whole *other* ontological edge that demands to be taken seriously, as gestured towards in the examples above. This is the diverse world of both ancestors and spirits, which in many cultural contexts are known and encountered as agency-enacting entities with ontological reality. As Kohn (2013: 217, 216) writes, 'spirits are their own kind of real' emerging 'from a specifically human way of engaging with and relating to a living world that lies in part beyond the human', that is discounted in the ontological assumptions informing scientific endeavour (Chakrabarty 2000). Since the spirit realm has its own future-making logics and habits, Kohn remarks additionally that how this reality is treated 'is as important as recognizing it as such' (2013: 208, 216). An expanded relational and reciprocal ontology thus opens multiple vistas for consideration, with implications for ethical praxis and future flourishings.

Reciprocity and the moral economy of sharing

Animist ontologies and associated practices, as indicated in the descriptions above, illuminate how people might live in specific relational contexts with different kinds of agency-asserting entities, only some of whom are human. What seems clear from such contexts is the insistence on an expanded zone of agency that includes entities beyond-the-human (Sullivan 1999; Kohn 2013; Behrens 2014; Kelbessa 2014), as these are embedded and constituted in specific and dynamic relational settings (see also Whatmore 2002; Castree 2003). The attribution of agency to multiple beings beyond-the-human makes possible both an expanded sphere of moral agency and considerability, as well as relations of reciprocity with these other-than-human entities.

A great deal of ethnographic research regarding cultural relationships with natures-beyond-the-human confirms this open and extended reciprocity, and an associated moral economy of sharing that has the assumption and production of abundance at its core. Nurit Bird-David (1992), whose ethnographic work on 'animism' has been important for establishing key parameters in this sub-field, thus develops Marshall Sahlins' (1974) conception of 'the original affluent society' through considering so-called hunter-gatherer conceptions of the provisioning roles of other-than-human natures in such economies. Her ethnographies are of Nayaka of South India (also see Bird-David and Naveh 2008), Batek of Malaysia and Mbuti of Zaire. Their orientations to non-human natures are understood in terms of assuming 'the environment' *to give to* humans in a profound 'economy of sharing' that mediates human-with-human and nature-with-human provisioning. 'Non-human' natures are 'humanised' such that they are known as kin and as ancestral embodiments, as communicative agencies, and as friends. Landscape entities as well as non-human animal species are attributed with life and consciousness. An *order of goodness*, while at times ambivalent, in general is assumed. Such knowledges find expression in value practices oriented towards sung, spoken, and danced communication and multi-way gift-giving with non-human natures that are equivalently expressive (see below). All of these situate human persons as agents continually doing their part to maintain a moral and dynamically generative socio-ecological order of trust that implicitly is assumed to be both abundant and good. This assumption of abundance and the associated 'full-subject' (i.e. there are none of the 'gaps' associated with alienation; see Glynos 2012: 2379) mitigates against a need for excessive consumption or hoarding of possessions.

Specific cultural innovations assist with the maintenance of this sense and assumption of abundance. Ongoing work by anthropologist Jerome Lewis (2008) with Mbendjele Yaka of Congo-Brazzaville (Republic of Congo) thus emphasises the importance of appropriate sharing through the guiding concept of *ekila*. As Lewis (2008: 13) states, 'for Yaka, people should be successful in their activities because nature is abundant. If they are not, it is because they, or somebody else, has ruined their *ekila* by sharing inappropriately'. Significantly, '*ekila* regulates Yaka environmental relations by defining what constitutes proper sharing' (Lewis 2008: 13). *Ekila* is ruined by such actions as not sharing hunted meat, being excessively successful and thus engendering envy, by inappropriately sharing sexuality, or by sharing laughter in such a way that the forest will not rejoice. By regulating potency through appropriate sharing, dynamic abundance is maintained for all. As Lewis (2008: 13) writes, such culturenature ontologies and associated value practices have established a relationship with other-than-human-natures which has meant that Yaka people have 'experienced the forest as a place of abundance for the entirety of their cultural memory'. This is in rather stark contrast with modern discourses of resource scarcity and the associated competitive and accumulative urgency to capture 'values' in both extractive industry and conservation activity.

For ||Khao-a Dama elders of west Namibia, while soul animates animals at the top of the food chain, such as lions, it also confers vitality and agency to much smaller creatures such as insects. Social insects such as harvester ants who harvest seeds subsequently gathered by people, and bees from whom people harvest honey, are valued extremely highly, not only for how hard they work to gather important foods that are then shared with humans, but also for the *egalitarianism* with which they share both this work and the resulting foods. Great care is taken by people when gathering seeds or honey from harvester ants' nests and beehives respectively, so as to ensure productivity in future years. Human action reciprocally supports the harvesting work done by harvester ants, and neither seeds from harvester ants' nests (seen as the 'home' – *oms* – of the ants in a manner that is parallel to the homes or *omti* of humans) nor honey harvested from beehives, should be gathered in such a way as to leave nothing for the future sustenance of the ants or bees (Sullivan 1999).

These perceptions and practices mean that although humans are of course seeking to eat from the multiple kinds of selves with which they live, since these selves are conceived as variously able to also see, represent, and act, an expanded sense of reciprocity and relationality arguably informs these contexts (see also Kohn 2013; Hannis and Sullivan forthcoming). As Herman (2014: 141) asserts, 'the most sustainable self is the one that insists leasts on its own sovereignty'.

Knowing 'nature' through 'technologies of enchantment'

Humans, everywhere, are dependent through pragmatic consumptive relationships on the ecology of selves amongst which we live. Animist relationality, however, tends to extend radically beyond these pragmatic relationships into relational dimensions beyond-the-human that deploy what Lewis (2015; following Gell 1999) refers to as 'technologies of enchantment' (on enchantment, also see Curry 2016). Through making and experiencing intricate and intimate 'technologies' of song, music, rhythm, dance, stories, and costume, an array of affects are stimulated: aesthetic appreciation, senses of delight, wonder, and mystery, perceptual opening to the presence and forms of spirit-beings, and the experience of joy and connection with entities beyond-the-self.

As Lewis (2015) describes for the diverse array of 'spirit-plays' performed by the spectrum of BaYaka peoples who for millennia have inhabited the forested areas of central and west Africa:

> Each spirit-play contributes to an economy of joy – a system of distributing practices and knowledge that ensure particular euphoric states are repeatedly produced and available to all present. . . . Each spirit-play has its own characteristic style that creates a different quality of joyful experience. During the total darkness of no-moon *Malobe*, for instance, fires are put out and torches forbidden, participants huddle together in

the middle of camp with their legs resting on their neighbours', and their voices intertwine in a complex polyphony until tiny luminous dots float into camp producing a calm, wondrous and expansive joy. In the pitch black participants melt into one another and the forest.

(*Lewis 2015: 7*)

These varied rituals 'seduce non-physical entities (spirits) from the forest in order to establish something non-physical (spirit) in the sense of an uplifting or joyful atmosphere' that 'people, animals and the forest will feel' (Lewis 2015: 8). Skill and intention are deployed so as 'to enchant many senses', 'using strange sounds, stirring sights, beautiful songs and dance movements, humour and parody, touch and smell, emotions and desires, . . . trance and overlapping percussive rhythms' (Lewis 2015: 8). Through building enthusiasm among participants, 'the music takes on a life of its own' so as to reach 'astounding synchronicity' between singers, engendering euphoric experiences of beyond-self connections between people, spirits, and forest (Lewis 2015: 15).

In the healing dances of southern African San contexts, complex polyphonic songs sung predominantly by women and accompanied by driving syncopated clapped rhythms become similarly increasingly entrained, supporting the attainment of trance-states by healer-shamans in which they draw on information echoing from the primal/ancestral time of animal and human connections and are able to see and pull out sicknesses in the people (Biesele 1993; Low 2008, 2015; Sullivan and Low 2014; personal observation). For Amazonian shamans, technologies of enchantment arise through the singing of delicate spirit-songs (known widely as *icaros*) taught especially by plant spirits, which, in conjunction with potent psychoactive plant technologies, are sung so as to attain a focused perceptual openness in which forest spirit-beings can be seen and communicated with, and sicknesses can be seen and healed (personal observation). For ≠Nūkhoen (Damara) of west Namibia, |geis are songs sung alone or collectively sung and danced so as to appreciate and remember key events associated with particular places, animals, insects, and plants, and thus to stimulate 'happiness in one's heart'; while *arus* or healing songs and dances, frequently invoking the qualities perceived as associated with different animals, create the vibrant collective energies needed for a healer to see sicknesses and for healing to occur (personal observation).

These connecting and experiential practices of joy, enchantment, and participation in the agencies of beyond-human entities act to entwine human being, desire, and imagination with the interests of an ecology of selves-beyond-the-human. They are markedly different from a modern imaginary that fixes and instrumentalises nature and nature knowledge through surveys, measurements, maps, numerical models, economic values, and metrics. Some of the implications of this divergence will be considered briefly in the conclusion.

Conclusion

The above examples illustrate what might be thought of as ontological 'roughness' or diversity in animist praxis. This roughness can be seen in contradistinction to a modern impetus to reduce difference to seemingly commensurable and exchangeable units – as is privileged in the lingering mechanistic worldview guiding responses to contemporary environmental problems. In the latter, considerations of the specific agencies of different species and other non-human entities become swallowed, for example, in the desire to count forests in terms of units of carbon, for which a calculated unit is the same whether emitted from a coal-fired power station or stored in an Amazonian endemic tree. Similarly, a biodiversity offset unit is an exchangeable measure that potentially creates equivalence between different species, habitats, and ecosystem presents and futures. As with the islanders mentioned in the epigraph opening this chapter, many cultures would roll around laughing at such proposals with their weird grasp on 'reality'.

The contemporary offsetting practices mentioned here are based on an ontology that acts to discount the differences embodied and embedded in real bodies and places, so as to enable natures to be managed and controlled through decisions made from afar. The tendencies of animist ontologies described above instead value the ability to know and interact directly with the alive agencies of a world of multiplicitous selves, without prioritising systemic control over these agencies or a reduction of their diversity.

Sadly, we are living through a convulsion that threatens not only the biological richness of the species who are our companions here on earth, but also the cultural, linguistic, and ontological diversity through which these species have been known, encountered, utilised, and appreciated over millennia.[3] Environmental anthropology has a critical and exciting role to play in generating understanding of the possibility for mutually nourishing relationships between cultural and biological diversity; and in fostering appreciation of the sophisticated and poetic as well as utilitarian ways through which people have cohabited with diverse natures globally. As both discipline and method, environmental anthropology can thus assist with the generation of discourses regarding ontology and epistemology that affirm practical ways through which human beings can live well with a prolific ecology of different kinds of beings. Animist ontologies in particular provide important gestures towards the generation of such positive narratives.

Acknowledgements

I gratefully acknowledge support from the UK's Arts and Humanities Research Council (ref. AH/K005871/2) for the project *Future Pasts* (www.futurepasts.net), which has permitted some of the field research on which this chapter is based.

Notes

1 In this chapter I draw on work in various stages of publication, particularly Sullivan 2010, 2013a, 2016; Sullivan and Low 2014; Hannis and Sullivan forthcoming.
2 Other authors argue against the thesis that Descartes considered animals to be incapable of feeling, while affirming his insistence on animals as automata, possessing neither thought nor self-consciousness (Harrison 1992: 219–220).
3 See UNESCO's *Atlas of the World's Languages in Danger*. www.unesco.org/languages-atlas/

References

Abram, D. 2010. *Becoming Animal: An Earthly Cosmology*. New York: Pantheon Books.
Adger, W. N., Benjaminsen, T. A., Brown, K. and Svarstad, H. 2001. Advancing a political ecology of global environmental discourses. *Development and Change* 32(4): 681–715.
Barker, P. 1991. *Regeneration*. London: Penguin Books.
Behrens, K. G. 2014. An African relational environmentalism and moral considerability. *Environmental Ethics* 36(1): 63–82.
Bennett, J. 2010. *Vibrant Matter: A Political Ecology of Things*. Durham, NC: Duke University Press.
Biesele, M. 1993. *Women Like Meat: The Folklore and Foraging Ideology of the Kalahari Ju | 'hoan*. Johannesburg/ Bloomington and Indianapolis: Wits University Press/Indiana University Press.
Bird-David, N. 1992. Beyond 'the original affluent society': A culturalist reformulation. *Current Anthropology* 33(1): 26–34.

Bird-David, N. and Naveh, D. 2008. Relational epistemology, immediacy, and conservation: Or, what do the Nayaka try to conserve? *Journal for the Study of Religion, Nature and Culture* 2(1): 55–73.

Bourdieu, P. 1992. *The Logic of Practice*. Cambridge, UK: Polity Press.

Brightman, M., Grotti, V. E. and Ulturgasheva, O. 2012. Animism and invisible worlds: The place of non-humans in indigenous ontologies. In M. Brightman, V. E. Grotti and O. Ulturgasheva (eds) *Animism in Rainforest and Tundra: Personhood, Animals, Plants and Things in Contemporary Amazonia and Siberia*. Oxford: Berghahn Books, pp. 1–27.

Bryant, R. L. and Bailey, S. 1997. *Third World Political Ecology*. London, Routledge.

Callicott, J. B. 2013. Ecology and moral ontology. In D. Bergandi (ed.) *The Structural Links between Ecology, Evolution and Ethics: The Virtuous Epistemic Circle*. Boston Studies in the Philosophy of Science 296. New York: Springer, pp. 101–116.

Castree, N. 2003. A post-environmental ethics? *Ethics, Place and Environment* 6(1): 3–12.

Chakrabarty, D. 2000. *Provincialising Europe: Postcolonial Thought and Historical Difference*. Princeton, NJ: Princeton University Press.

Clastres, P. 1988. *Society against the State: Essays in Political Anthropology*. Cambridge, MA: The MIT Press.

Cohen, E. 1986. Law, folklore and animal lore. *Past and Present* 110(1): 6–37.

Curry, P. 2016. From Enlightenment to enchantment: Changing the question. In R. Pellicer-Thomas, V. de Lucia and S. Sullivan (eds) *Contributions to Law, Philosophy and Ecology: Exploring Re-Embodiments*. Routledge Law, Justice and Ecology Series. London: GlassHouse Books, pp. 106–118.

Descartes, R. 1968 [1637]. *Discourse on Method*. London: Penguin Books.

Descola, P. 2013. *Beyond Nature and Culture*. Chicago, IL: University of Chicago Press.

Evernden, N. 1985. *The Human Alien: Humankind and Environment*. Toronto, ON: University of Toronto Press.

Fairhead, J. and Leach, M. 1996. *Misreading the African Landscape: Society and Ecology in a Forest–Savanna Mosaic*. Cambridge, UK: Cambridge University Press.

Fletcher, R. 2013. How I learned to stop worrying and love the market: Virtualism, disavowal, and public secrecy in neoliberal environmental conservation. *Environment and Planning D: Society and Space* 31(5): 796–812.

Flusser, V. 2011 [1987]. *Vampyroteuthis infernalis*. New York: Atropos Press.

Forsyth, T. 2003. *Critical Political Ecology: The Politics of Environmental Science*. London: Routledge.

Foucault, M. 1980. *Power/knowledge: Selected Interviews and Other Writings, 1972–1977* (edited by C. Gordon). London: Harvester Wheatsheaf.

Foucault, M. 1982. The subject and power. *Critical Enquiry* 8(4): 777–795.

Franke, A. 2012. Animism: Notes on an exhibition. *E-flux* 36. Online. www.e-flux.com/journal/animism-notes-on-an-exhibition/ (accessed 2 January 2013).

Freud, S. 2009 [1938]. Splitting of the ego in the process of defence. In T. Bokanowski and S. Lewkovitz (eds) *On Freud's 'Splitting of the Ego in the Process of Defence'*. London: Karnac Books, pp. 3–6.

Garuba, H. 2012. On animism, modernity/colonialism, and the African order of knowledge: Provisional reflections. *E-flux* 36. Online. www.e-flux.com/journal/on-animism-modernitycolonialism-and-the-african-order-of-knowledge-provisional-reflections/ (accessed 23 February 2016).

Geertz, C. 1973. *The Interpretation of Cultures*. London: Fontana Press.

Gell, A. 1999. *The Art of Anthropology: Essays and Diagrams*. London: Bloomsbury.

Glynos, J. 2012. The place of fantasy in a critical political economy: The case of market boundaries. *Cardozo Law Review* 33(6): 2373–2411.

Gorenflo, L. J., Romaine, S., Mittermeier, R. A. and Walker-Painemilla, K. 2012. Co-occurrence of linguistic and biological diversity in biodiversity hotspots and high biodiversity wilderness areas. *Proceedings of the National Academy of Sciences of the United States of America* 109(21): 8032–8037.

Gray, J. 2002 *Straw Dogs: Thoughts on Humans and Other Animals*. London: Granta Books.

Guenther, M. 1999. *Tricksters and Trancers: Bushman Religion and Society*. Bloomington: Indiana University Press.

Hall, M. 2011. *Plants as Persons: A Philosophical Botany*. New York: State University of New York Press.

Hallowell, I. 1960. Ojibwa ontology, behavior and world view. In S. Diamond (ed.) *Culture in History: Essays in Honour of Paul Radin*. New York: Octagon Books, pp. 19–52.

Hannis, M. and Sullivan, S. forthcoming. Relationality, reciprocity and flourishing in an African landscape. In L. Hartmann (ed.) *Flourishing: Comparative Religious Environmental Ethics*. Oxford: Oxford University Press.

Haraway, D. 2008. *When Species Meet*. Minneapolis: University of Minnesota Press.

Harrison, P. 1992. Descartes on animals. *The Philosophical Quarterly* 42(169): 219–227.

Harvey, G. 2005. *Animism: Respecting the Living World.* London: Hurst and Co.

Herman, D. 2014. Narratology beyond the human. *Diagesis* 3(2): 131–143.

Holbraad, M., Pedersen, M. A. and Viveiros de Castro, E. 2014. The politics of ontology: Anthropological positions. *Cultural Anthropology.* Online. www.culanth.org/fieldsights/462-the-politics-of-ontology-anthropological-positions (accessed 13 January 2014).

Homewood, K. and Rodgers, A. 1987. Pastoralism, conservation and the overgrazing controversy. In D. Anderson and R. Grove (eds) *Conservation in Africa: People, Policies and Practice.* Cambridge, UK: Cambridge University Press, pp. 111–128.

Hornborg, A. 2006. Animism, fetishism, and objectivism as strategies for knowing (or not knowing) the world. *Ethnos: Journal of Anthropology* 71(1): 21–32.

Ingold, T. 2000. *The Perception of the Environment: Essays in Livelihood, Dwelling and Skill.* London: Routledge.

Ingold, T. 2006. Rethinking the animate, re-animating thought. *Ethnos* 71(1): 9–20.

Jackson, M. 2013. Plastic islands and processual grounds: Ethics, ontology, and the matter of decay. *Cultural Geographies* 20(2): 205–224.

Kelbessa, W. 2014. Can an African environmental ethics contribute to environmental policy in Africa? *Environmental Ethics* 36(1): 31–61.

Kohn, E. 2013. *How Forests Think: Towards an Anthropology of Nature beyond the Human.* Berkeley: University of California Press.

Leach, M. and Mearns, R. 1996. *The Lie of the Land: Challenging Received Wisdom on the African Environment.* Oxford: James Currey.

Lewis, J. 2008. Maintaining abundance, not chasing scarcity: The real challenge for the 21st century. *Radical Anthropology* 2: 11–18.

Lewis, J. 2015. Where goods are free but knowledge costs: Hunter-gatherer ritual economics in Western Central Africa. *Hunter Gatherer Research* 1(1). doi:10.3828/hgr.2015.2

Low, C. 2008. *Khoisan Medicine in History and Practice.* Köln: Rüdiger Köppe Verlag.

Low, C. 2015. The role of the body in Kalahari San healing dances. *Hunter Gatherer Research* 1(1): 27–58.

Malinowski, B. 1922. *Argonauts of the Western Pacific.* London: Routledge and Kegan Paul.

Marder, M. 2013. *Plant-Thinking: A Philosophy of Vegetal Life.* New York: Columbia University Press.

Myers, N., Mittermeier, R. A., Mittermeier, C. G., da Fonseca, G. A. B. and Kent, J. 2000. Biodiversity hotspots for conservation priorities. *Nature* 423(6772): 853–858.

Plumwood, V. 2006. *Feminism and the Mastery of Nature.* London: Routledge.

Reij, C., Scoones, I. and Toulmin, C. (eds) 1996. *Sustaining the Soil: Indigenous Soil and Water Conservation in Africa.* London: Routledge.

Richards, P. 1985. *Indigenous Agricultural Revolution.* London: HarperCollins.

Robbins, P., Hintz, J. and Moore, S. A. 2010. *Environment and Society: A Critical Introduction.* Chichester, UK: Wiley–Blackwell.

Sahlins, M. 1974. *Stone Age Economics.* Piscataway, NJ: Aldine Transaction.

Schmidt, S. 2014. Spirits: Some thoughts on ancient Damara folk belief. *Journal of the Namibian Scientific Society* 62: 133–160.

Smith, H. 1981. Four cultures: The ontological turn. *Syracuse Scholar (1979–1991)* 2(1): Article 13. Online. http://surface.syr.edu/suscholar/vol2/iss1/13 (accessed 23 February 2016).

Solomon, A. 1997. The myth of ritual origins? Ethnography, mythology and interpretation of San rock art. *South African Archaeological Bulletin* 52(165): 3–13

Stott, P. and Sullivan, S. (eds) 2000. *Political Ecology: Science, Myth and Power.* London: Edward Arnold.

Sullivan, S. 1999. Folk and formal, local and national: Damara cultural knowledge and community-based conservation in southern Kunene, Namibia. *Cimbebasia* 15: 1–28.

Sullivan, S. 2000. Getting the science right, or introducing science in the first place? Local 'facts', global discourse – 'desertification' in north-west Namibia.In P. Stott and S. Sullivan (eds) *Political Ecology: Science, Myth and Power.* London: Edward Arnold, pp. 15–44.

Sullivan, S. 2010. 'Ecosystem service commodities' – a new imperial ecology? Implications for animist immanent ecologies, with Deleuze and Guattari. *New Formations: A Journal of Culture/Theory/Politics* 69 (Special issue on Imperial Ecologies): 111–128.

Sullivan, S. 2013a. Nature on the move III: (Re)countenancing an animate nature. *New Proposals: Journal of Marxism and Interdisciplinary Enquiry* 6(1–2): 50–71.

Sullivan, S. 2013b. At the Edinburgh Forums on Natural Capital and Natural Commons: From disavowal to plutonomy, via 'natural capital'. http://siansullivan.net/2013/11/21/on-the-eve-of-the edinburgh-forums-on-natural-capital-and-natural-commons-notes-on-disavowal-biocultural-diversity-the-nature-of-natural-capital-and-plutonomy/

Sullivan, S. 2016. (Re-)embodying which body? Philosophical, cross-cultural and personal reflections on corporeality. In R. Thomas-Pellicer, V. de Lucia and S. Sullivan (eds) *Contributions to Law, Philosophy and Ecology: Exploring Re-Embodiments*. Routledge Law, Justice and Ecology Series. London: GlassHouse Books, pp. 119–138.

Sullivan, S. and Low, C. 2014. Shades of the rainbow serpent? A KhoeSān animal between myth and landscape in southern Africa – ethnographic contextualisations of rock art representations. *The Arts* 3(2) (Special Issue on World Rock Art): 215–244.

Taussig, M. 1987. *Shamanism, Colonialism and the Wild Man: A Study in Terror and Healing*. Chicago, IL: University of Chicago Press.

Tylor, E. 1913 [1871]. *Primitive Culture*. 2 Volumes. London: John Murray.

Viveiros de Castro, E. 2004. Exchanging perspectives: The transformation of objects into subjects in Amerindian ontologies. *Common Knowledge* 10(3): 463–484.

Whatmore, S. 2002. *Hybrid Geographies: Natures Cultures Spaces*. London: Sage.

14

UNSUSTAINABILITY IN ACTION

An ethnographic examination

Sayd Randle, Lauren Baker, C. Anne Claus,
Chris Hebdon, Alder Keleman, and Michael R. Dove

Introduction

The concept of sustainability went mainstream some time ago, and it has drawn some interesting and rather diverse bedfellows together in the name of its articulation. As the concept has gained currency, an attendant body of critical sustainability literature has accumulated, interrogating the diversity of meanings and uses that have congealed around the notion. Our contribution proceeds from the recognition that sustainability's ugly, dirty other—unsustainability—has received relatively little attention within this body of work. Our ethnographic research indicates that, on the ground, the notion of unsustainability is put to work in strange and sometimes surprising ways. In some cases, the "unsustainable" label is a weapon wielded by the state or ruling classes; in others, it is a tool of subaltern groups. It has been used to describe fossil fuel extraction in Peru, distributed energy production in Germany, and a coral festival in Okinawa. The sheer diversity within this small sample of "unsustainabilities" suggests the value in a deeper analysis, and raises the question: what is the concept doing in these contexts, for whom, and how (e.g. Kopnina and Shoreman–Ouimet 2015)?

Most accounts of sustainability, while acknowledging that the notion was in circulation for some time beforehand, cite the Brundtland Commission Report (World Commission on Environment and Development 1987) as a key moment of the concept's ascendance and legitimation among international institutions and governments. Defining sustainable development as that which "meets the needs of the present without compromising the ability of future generations to meet their own needs," (1987: 43) then framing it as development institutions' *raison d'être*, the Brundtland report centered notions of reproducibility and ecological support within the ongoing conceptualization of development's mission. Many have noted the crucial elision that Brundtland's sustainable development concept (and much of the sustainability talk that has followed) entails—namely, that robust capitalist development and environmental preservation are mutually constitutive, not conflicting aims. Drawing heavily on Foucauldian notions of discourse and power, some scholars argue that the push for sustainable development should be read as part of a broader process of making populations and landscapes across the global South newly visible to the metropole, allowing them to be operationalized, managed, and exploited more effectively (Escobar 1995). Others have traced the concept's ascension within the global North, particularly its imbrication with discourses of "ecological modernization" and its assumptions of a cleaner capitalism through technological innovation and carefully crafted market incentives (Hajer 1995; Harvey 1996; Mol and Sonnenfeld 2000). Some critiques have foregrounded the depoliticizing effects of the concept, framing it as a non-starter for anyone hoping to imagine a world outside neoliberal capitalism (Keil 2007; Swyngedouw 2007). Others have emphasized the extent to which a focus on attaining sustainability can obscure the uneven environmental effects of economic systems, minimizing issues of historic and ongoing environmental injustice (Agyeman *et al.* 2003). Recent analyses, while acknowledging these critiques, note that there are now multiple "sustainabilities" in circulation among practitioners, and that the discourse must be analyzed as multiple and tactically deployed, rather than as coherent and hegemonic (Krueger and Gibbs 2007; Greenberg 2013).

Examining unsustainability discourses in action foregrounds the complicated ways in which economic and environmental collapse are framed as co-constitutive, and how easily an unsustainable economy is equated with an unsustaining ecology. Contrary to the broadly damning "anti-political" critiques we cite above, however, cases from our recent field research suggest that the notion of unsustainability can be deployed to challenge dominant economic logics and entrenched power relations. Such instances complicate accounts which suggest that agitating in terms of sustainability (or lack thereof) precludes a radical politics (e.g. Swyngedouw 2010). To explore the politics of unsustainability, our first section presents a pair of case studies that illustrate ways in which claims about unsustainability function to either challenge or reproduce current power relations and political economies. In Peru, indigenous peoples point to the unsustainability of extractive industries and other state-sponsored projects in order to reinforce indigenous claims to resources and territories and to confront a development model that favors corporate interests over local ownership. In Okinawa, conservationists from mainland Japan criticize a coral festival as an unsustainable ritual, citing it as evidence of the lack of Okinawan environmental awareness—despite the fact that mainland Japanese are the main festival participants. In these cases, the charge of "unsustainability" is leveled to either subvert or reinforce local/extra-local power dynamics.

In our second section, we develop an account of unsustainability's assumed temporality. What time horizons and premises of futurity do discourses of unsustainability assume and mobilize? Sustainability seems to be timeless, by definition, but this is not so for unsustainability. Nothing is unsustainable in the moment. Unsustainability implies a time dimension; it implies the passage of time, and an "end-time" (Stewart and Harding 1999). Both sustainability and unsustainability are about end-times—times that are "not yet" catastrophic in the case of unsustainability, and "not yet" problematic in the case of sustainability. Unsustainability then is latent in all sustainabilities. Some critical literature on sustainability notes the implicit presence of catastrophic (or even apocalyptic) near-futures (Masco 2010)—but to call an ongoing process or system "unsustainable" necessarily raises the question of when and how this crash will come to pass. Anthropologists have been studying discourses of environmental degradation for several decades now, but their focus has been more on the empirical accuracy of the discourse, and perhaps its politics, than its temporality. Fabian (1983) and Derrida (1994), however, have alerted us to how time is used to both mark off and not mark off "other" peoples and eras; scholars like Cronon (1992) and Fairhead and Leach (1996) have drawn attention to the importance of how trajectories of environmental change are drawn; and there is recent work on the concept of the apocalypse in contemporary climate-change rhetoric (Masco 2010; Swyngedouw 2010), as well as the perceived temporal break of the "anthropocene" (Sayre 2012). Our examinations in Section II of swidden agriculture, German renewable energy policy, and childhood malnutrition in Bolivia trace the diversity of environmental and economic futures that can fit within rhetorics of "unsustainability."

Section I: Uses of "unsustainability"—politics and power dynamics

Case study A: Indigenous critiques of extractive industries in Peru

In Peru, extractive industries have been heavily promoted to the public as vital for national development (Arce 2014; Bebbington *et al.* 2014). Moreover, despite being strongly associated with social conflict and environmental contamination, government representatives routinely assert that modern iterations of extraction are both socially responsible and environmentally friendly, and as such constitute a legitimate form of sustainable development (García Pérez 2007; Bebbington 2009; de la Flor 2014). In response, indigenous leaders from zones of extraction have cast the same projects as destructive to local environments and economies, suggesting that they are neither "sustainable" nor "development" (e.g. Stetson 2012). Such claims about the unsustainability of both development projects and the economic models that underlie such projects serve to shore up indigenous rights' claims and the promotion of alternative conceptions of development.

In order to demonstrate this dynamic, we examine a stump speech delivered by a Peruvian indigenous leader, Alfonso Lopez, to more than 50 different Cocama indigenous communities between April and June 2011.[1] This sustained outreach to the communities that form his indigenous organization, known as the Cocama Association for Development and Conservation, San Pablo de Tipishca, was motivated by a pair of goals: to solidify the base of the organization and to gather support for a legal complaint against the oil company Pluspetrol in relation to a 500-barrel oil spill that had occurred the previous year. Much of the speech addressed the unsustainability of oil operations in the region, especially in relation to the "constant oil spills," which had degraded the productivity of local crops, diminished the quality and quantity of fish (the communities' primary food staple), and harmed human health. Given these impacts, Lopez argued that, for the region's indigenous groups, "oil operations have not signified development" but rather, produced "impoverishment, sickness, contamination, and death."

Lopez's larger target in this speech was Peru's policy to "sell the Amazon," which was driven by a vision of development which equated company profits with local development. According to Lopez, the common thread in a range of projects, whether for oil operations, biofuel expansion, land privatization, or a host of other policies, was the aim to change land ownership and to "disappear" indigenous communities, so as to facilitate the entry of large companies to deforest, plant monocultures, or otherwise procure more income from the forest. Government policies, in this view, were driven by the "neoliberal economic order" that "brings people to destroy the earth."

In the face of these threats, Lopez called for communities to unite to defend their lives and the lives of future generations. He emphasized that indigenous people are inseparable from their territory and that "water is life," and therefore defense of life included the defense of their territory and the environment. Finally, Lopez noted that they were not alone in their fight—that many people in the world were seeking a "different model that doesn't destroy the forests . . . That is why they say that only indigenous [peoples] can save the planet."

For indigenous leaders like Lopez, environmentally unsustainable projects are not seen as aberrant, but rather as part and parcel of an unsustainable economic development model, and critiques of projects play an important role in critiquing dominant development models. The fact that this is a speech given by an indigenous leader to people in his own communities also suggests the value and function of the discourse in fortifying internal unity in resistance movements. Finally, references to unsustainability prompt considerations about alternative visions of development that have more to do with quality of life, access to clean water, and leaving a natural inheritance to future generations, than with securing target levels of cash or cement.

Case study B: Mainland Japanese framings of an Okinawan coral festival

Similar contestations over whose practices are unsustainable yield different results on the other side of the world, in western Okinawa, Japan. Yabiji reef, located 10 kilometers north of Miyako Island, is often described as a "phantom continent" because of its impressive breadth. The reef comes into view only at low tide. While reefs seldom appear as features on maps (even contemporary ones), Tokugawa cartographers noted Yabiji in their renderings as early as 1645. The reef has long been important to islanders.

Starting in the early 1980s, the local government has promoted the reef as a prime place to celebrate the third day of the third lunar month, when Okinawan women traditionally cleanse their bodies and souls with ocean water. For two days, car ferries that usually shuttle between other nearby islands are commandeered by festival organizers and filled with tourists eager to view the coral reef. As the car ferry plunks its steel ramp onto the protruding coral, thousands of guests disembark on the reef to discover the treasures cradled by the phantom continent.

Environmentalists in Miyako, most of whom are originally from mainland Japan, have long argued that this event destroys the fragile coral reef (Kajiwara and Matsumoto 2004). They protest about the way the festival unfolds. They are concerned by how participants are encouraged to walk on the reef, touch organisms they come across, and collect shellfish they may find. To the mainlander environmentalists, this illustrates how the local organizers lack awareness of the consequences of their actions. In these narratives, the festival becomes evidence of yet another unsustainable Okinawan practice. Referencing the festival to illustrate the lack of Okinawan environmental awareness is intriguing because the overwhelming majority—in 2012, an estimated 95 percent—of attendees come from mainland Japan. Okinawans themselves celebrate the festival closer to home. Mainland environmentalists ignore the broader political economy of the event when they use the festival to prove their point about unsustainable Okinawan practices.

Environmental awareness for mainland conservationists means the ability to anticipate and predict how the reef will look in the future. Okinawans, however, argue that the festival highlights a fundamental lack of mainlander awareness of the present-day environment. The reef teems with life as the tide recedes, but the mainlanders are not able to see it. Okinawans tell stories about collecting and then releasing shellfish on the coral reef just before the mainlanders disembark to increase their chances of "finding" sea life. Without the help of the Okinawans, they wouldn't know how to see the nature that surrounds them. Calling certain events like the festival unsustainable masks the larger political economy of these kinds of practices in Okinawa, which in this case is driven by mainlanders themselves.

For mainland environmentalists, this festival illustrates the necessity of their interventions. Viewed in the context of historically fraught Japanese–Okinawan relations, this is unsurprising

(Hook and Siddle 2003). Not only is the festival called "unsustainable," this label becomes projected onto Okinawans themselves, enforcing and extending narratives of Okinawans as "backwards." This reproduces existing narratives of what it means to be "modern" and what it means to be "primitive" in Japan, validating the perspective that mainlanders are the best stewards of the nation's nature.

Section II: Unstable temporalities of unsustainability

Case study A: The critique of swidden agriculture

Swidden agriculture is a quintessential example of the importance of temporality in a discourse of sustainable versus unsustainable environmental relations. For at least a century, the orthodox narrative of tropical swidden agriculture has been that it is a destructive system of resource use or, if not destructive in the present tense, it has inherent dynamics that will lead to resource destruction in the future. The primary driver of this future destruction has almost always been assumed to be the linearly extrapolated pressures of assumed population growth and static technology on a fixed resource base. Anthropologists have long critiqued the premises of this calculus (e.g. Carneiro 2008 [1960]), but not the wider issue of how temporality is being strategically deployed here.

Central to the orthodox view of swidden agriculture among government officials and scientists, therefore, has been not simply a critique of present practices, but a critique of a predicted future state. An enduring concern with the future—a concern not just with what is but what will be—has consumed the mainstream discourse on swidden agriculture. The role of the imagination has thus been central to this discourse, as an imagined future has been invoked, ubiquitously, to critique the present. Power has been exercised through "owning" not simply a representation of the present, therefore, but a representation of the future—which in consequence has made the future into a contested dimension.

A half-century of study led to an anthropological critique of this disparagement of swidden agriculture, suggesting that the real basis for the animosity toward swidden was its relative imperviousness to state control and extraction (Scott 2009; Dove 2011, 2015). The orthodox, "declensionist" view of swidden agriculture also has been shown to represent a curious forgetting of the not-so-distant European and American histories of swidden agriculture, which rarely ended in the sort of Malthusian collapse predicted (Sigaut 1979; Otto and Anderson 1982). Finally, the declensionist view of collapse ignores the emic view of swidden agriculturalists themselves, many of whom anticipate a very different future, one that incorporates more trading, cash cropping, and even the exit of their children from agriculture altogether through education (Cramb 2007). In short, the emic view is often focused more on the sustainability of a socio-cultural system as opposed to the sustainability of an agricultural system, and in some cases this explains the persistence of swidden (van Vliet *et al.* 2013; cf. Bebbington 1993). Widespread inattention to these emic perspectives illustrates how little agency is accorded to swidden cultivators themselves in the orthodox critique.

Emic views aside, the long-held etic view that any swidden agricultural system would inevitably end in Malthusian collapse is almost never borne out by actual cases. In some instances, swidden cultivators have been documented practicing their system of agriculture for decades, even centuries, with no noticeable degradation of the environment (Lawrence and Schlesinger 2001). Even shortening fallows do not necessarily entail the imminent demise of swidden systems (Schmidt-Vogt *et al.* 2009). There are many documented cases where swidden cultivators have intensified their system of agriculture in the absence of critical population/land pressures, in some cases due to state conservation policies, but in other cases without any such external coercion. Access to markets and their demand for cash crops often drives a move away from swiddens, but some scholars have suggested that continued swiddening may even complement the cultivation of high-yielding rubber and oil palm (Mertz *et al.* 2013; cf. Dove 2011). In addition, diversification of both on-farm and off-farm sources of income may actually decrease pressure on swidden cultivation and thus offer space for its continued practice (van Vliet *et al.* 2013). Finally, swidden cultivation is sometimes retained simply as a safety net in regions where other sources of income are present but not always dependable (van Vliet *et al.* 2012). Actual cases of severe environmental degradation are often due to appropriation of land by political-economic elites, confining swidden cultivators to ever-smaller territories and thus ever-increasing population/land ratios.

There has been a spate of recent articles concerning the current status of swidden agriculture in Southeast Asia (Mertz *et al.* 2009; Padoch *et al.* 2010). The orthodox declensionist discourse does such a poor job of explaining modern swidden history that some of these articles actually ask: what has happened to swidden agriculture? The swidden futures that have actually come to pass do not reflect the temporality of the century-old critique of swidden agriculture. This demonstrates the remarkable degree to which this critique of swidden was in fact an imagined trajectory of unsustainability.

Case study B: Renewable energy in Germany

Distributed renewable energy production has been described as "of the future" but "not ready for the mainstream" in many contexts. When renewables are defined as technologies of the future, they are simultaneously defined as unsustainable in the present. The market price of renewables vis-à-vis fossil fuels is often given as the necessary criterion for their sustainability. However, whether renewables are used or not is not solely an issue of economics (Schumacher 1973; Lovins 1977). Their adoption also depends on political struggles for social power and control of the future.

Germany—the state with the greatest renewable energy capacity of any in Europe or North America—offers an example of how claims of economic unsustainability and technological futurity can depend on many factors, particularly the claimant's stake in existing economic and infrastructural arrangements. With the passage of the Electricity Feed-in Act in 1991, the German state incentivized distributed renewables for actors outside centralized utilities. Following the Act's introduction, the country went from producing less than 3 percent of its electricity from solar and wind sources to producing more than 23 percent year-round by 2012 (Lovins 2013, 2014), with daytime peaks of 60 percent (Wesoff 2013). The vast majority of the funding for these projects came from sources outside the traditional energy utilities. Ninety percent of this investment came from individual citizens and citizens organized into co-operatives (Scheer 2012: 41). By 2012, 65 percent of Germany's renewable energy capacity was owned by such individuals and groups (Hedges 2012).

Most Germans express approval for the ongoing expansion of this distributed renewable energy generation capacity. Many industry experts and representatives, however, have consistently criticized these energy sources. "The widespread [90 percent] popularity of renewable energy has developed despite decades of extensive denunciation by the traditional power industry and the majority of energy experts," noted Hermann Scheer (2012: 2), one of Germany's pioneering proponents of the *energiewende* (energy transition). The industry's justification of its opposition to *energiewende* has changed over time. At first the arguments were ontological: distributed renewable technologies were inherently unable to displace the centralized model. In 1991, for instance, industry advocates contended that: " 'exotic' energies simply don't offer more than a 5 percent potential" (Scheer 2012: 24). When the actual expansion of renewables contradicted those estimates by growing rapidly, traditional utilities and their supporters began to criticize the unsustainable *pace* of the expansion of renewable generation, arguing that a too-rapid transition would necessarily harm the German economy (Scheer 2012; Lovins 2013). After an intense lobbying and advertising effort, in 2014, the traditional industries were able to get the German government to "stage" the pace of expansion of dispersed renewable generation, slowing the *energiewende* by setting temporal limits on the overall share of renewables in the energy mix. The Germany economy's rate of expansion under *energiewende* suggests that these experts were, in all likelihood, expressing concern for a particular sector of the economy: the traditional, centralized energy utilities and their long-standing business models.

German struggles over the timelinessness of decentralized renewable energy not only suggest that cost-evaluation and perceptions of unsustainability involve social power, but that controlling people by way of concepts of time is also involved (Berry 1977). Energy transitions, however, are not simply about swapping one source or system for another, but rather involve far-reaching social and economic changes with often unpredictable ramifications (Melosi 2006). This recognition of energy transitions as struggles over the future should caution against the idea of any inherent energy market teleology—that is, that fossil fuels will inexorably phase out while renewables lose their unsustainability and inevitably phase in. Energy infrastructures are always produced and maintained through ongoing social negotiation.

Case study C: Self-perpetuating but unsustainable? Examining chronic malnutrition in Bolivia

In biomedical terms, "stunting" refers to the condition of low height for age, caused by chronic malnutrition. Stunting is the result of multiple dietary and environmental factors, but in contrast to wasting (low weight for height), stunting can occur even when a child consumes enough calories if the *quality* of the diet, in terms of key vitamins and minerals, is inadequate (e.g. WHO Multicentre Growth Reference Study Group 2006). Stunting represents undesirable but self-perpetuating conditions, which entrench socio–economic and health inequalities. Although stunting is seldom described in terms of "sustainability/unsustainability," examining the goodness-of-fit of these terms to the problem sheds light on the way the future is imagined—and for whom—in broader sustainability debates.

Stunting should be understood as an indicator of a larger set of adverse conditions experienced by the child and his or her care group. Low growth for age is correlated with poor physical and intellectual development, such that "damage suffered in early life leads to permanent impairment" (Victora *et al.* 2008: 340). Childhood malnutrition has later-life repercussions, potentially making it more difficult for that child to perform in school, or on the job, than his or her peers (Hoddinott *et al.* 2008). The feedback loops surrounding child nutrition are effectively a mechanism for the intergenerational transmission of poverty (Victora *et al.* 2008).

Observations from Bolivia demonstrate how this transmission may be not only biophysical, but also socio-cultural. Bolivia has the highest levels of malnutrition in South America. In 2008, approximately 27 percent of Bolivian children under the age of five had low height-for-age (Coa and Ochoa 2009). Although children are often born with height and weight within the norm for infants, children's comparison to World Health Organization (WHO) growth references tends to drop off as they are weaned from breastfeeding and solid foods are introduced (Cruz Agudo *et al.* 2010).

In Bolivian households, both rural and urban, starchy carbohydrates, such as potatoes, rice, and pasta, are a central component of any given meal. For most Bolivians, the "ideal-type" meal would also include meat, but many poor households eat relatively little meat on a daily basis. Vegetables are consumed frequently, but in limited variety and small quantities. Integrating more such legumes and vegetables into children's diets might represent a lower-cost way to improve nutrient intake. However, discussions with food preparers during qualitative, participatory research suggested that few consider this an attractive option, given the strong cultural preference for a "meat-and-potatoes" meal.

Policies to address the high levels of stunting in Bolivia have been implemented, but the coverage of such programs is patchy. These rely largely on the provision of free or low-cost nutritional supplements to mothers and children under the age of five. In rural areas, mothers of small children may live far from health centers, limiting their ability to attend the regular check-ups, which would allow health-care providers to identify children with stalled growth. In urban areas, daytime hospital hours may not suit working mothers' schedules. Even if enrolled in malnutrition-combatting programs, poor or indigenous parents may be hesitant to return to health centers after receiving disrespectful or indifferent treatment by formal health-care practitioners. And sometimes, even when parents are eager for assistance, the medicines themselves may simply be out of stock, or otherwise unavailable.

Few would disagree that Bolivia's high levels of malnutrition are undesirable, but, notably, the term "unsustainable" is nearly absent from policy discussions surrounding stunting. Indeed, the application of this term would represent something of a logical fallacy, given that in biophysical, biocultural, and socio-economic terms, chronic malnutrition has all the grounds to be self-perpetuating, or self-"sustaining" in a literal sense. To change this confluence of cultural food preferences, received culinary knowledge, and discriminatory health-care systems would require significant investment. However, such investment would imply a transfer of wealth from some richer segment of society—a politically volatile proposition, and one which richer populations might themselves consider "unsustainable."

This examination of chronic malnutrition in Bolivia demonstrates a broader issue in the framework of "un/sustainability." Although conflicts over what is environmentally "sustainable" are often also conflicts over competing sets of values, combatting child malnutrition is a relatively indisputable "social good." However, the barriers to achieving more socially beneficial outcomes are closely entangled with the context of Bolivia's entrenched socio-economic inequality. As this example suggests, asking what changes would be necessary to imagine an alternative future implicitly raises a question about the theory of change embedded in sustainability debates: who will bear the costs, and who will reap the benefits? Or, in other words: sustainability, but for whom?

Conclusion

The most strident critiques of sustainable development suggest that it is a relatively unitary notion, a big discursive tent where many can gather, an inoffensive position from which to launch mild, non-threatening demands for environmental and economic change. These arguments tend to trace a neat line from Brundtland to the present, suggesting that all who think with the concept accept the clean sense of synergy between neoliberal capitalism and environmental protection. At the most basic level, our ethnographic investigations of unsustainability-in-action complicate this argument, laying bare the myriad economic and ecological arrangements that sustainability's other is used to invoke. In the hands of Alfonso Lopez, sustainability and capitalist development are cast as directly oppositional projects. Meanwhile, energy experts in Germany argue that distributed renewable production's potential to disrupt a well-oiled economy make it an "unsustainable" option for the country. In practice, we contend, "unsustainable" is a label that gets put to many uses on the ground, some that advance searing critiques of capitalist economic relations.

For all the diversity of the cases we examine, however, a common thread seems to unite the discussions of unsustainability. A subject's positionality will fundamentally shape what she or he perceives or labels as unsustainable. This is not to argue that "sustainability" is an empty signifier or its history irrelevant, but rather to demand careful attention to the conditions of the concept's deployment. What, exactly, is the system, practice, or community that the speaker is labeling as unsustainable? What are the benefits (or harms) that the current arrangements are providing this person? Teasing out these elements in a particular case is crucial to understanding the power relations that structure conversations about sustainability.

As our examinations of unsustainability's temporality suggest, to label something unsustainable is to make a particular kind of claim about its future, tracing a specific type of speculative fiction—which, as the swidden and German energy cases show, does not necessarily coincide with the eventual lived reality. Labeling a system like swidden as "of the past" or one of distributed renewables as "of the future" makes an important claim about what is possible in the present, one that can severely circumscribe potential courses of environmental or economic action. Just as we do well to acknowledge the uneven impacts of contemporary environmental and economic processes, analysis of these suggested "futures" must always grapple with the question of what groups or systems they're imagined to be sustaining (or not). Our Bolivian case—examining the long-standing, self-sustaining cycle of chronic poverty and bodily stunting that is rarely labeled as "sustainable"—illustrates this point effectively. Contemporary talk of sustainability quietly elides steady reproducibility with widespread desirability. For many, however, certain self-sustaining systems promise a future of continued harm. With all this in mind, we argue that debates over unsustainability serve as rich sites to explore the anthropology of the future, key moments where messy questions of "what can be" and "what should be" are worked through.

Notes

1 Co-author Lauren Baker accompanied Lopez, the federation president, to 38 of these community visits, where he gave variations of the roughly 45-minute stump speech.

References

Agyeman, Julian, Robert Bullard and Bob Evans (eds) 2003. *Just Sustainabilities: Development in an Unequal World*. Cambridge, MA: The MIT Press.

Arce, Moiseìs. 2014. *Resource Extraction and Protest in Peru*. Pittsburgh, PA: University of Pittsburgh Press.

Bebbington, Anthony. 1993. "Modernization from Below: An Alternative Indigenous Development?" *Economic Geography* 69(3): 274–292.

Bebbington, Anthony. 2009. "The New Extraction: Rewriting the Political Ecology of the Andes?" *NACLA Report on the Americas* 42(5): 12–20.

Bebbington, Anthony, Nicholas Cuba and John Rogan. 2014. "The Overlapping Geographies of Resource Extraction." *ReVista: Harvard Review of Latin America* XIII(2): 20–23.

Berry, Wendell. 1977. *The Unsettling of America: Culture & Agriculture*. San Francisco, CA: Friends of the Earth Press.

Carneiro, Robert. 2008 [1960]. "Slash-and-Burn Agriculture: A Closer Look at its Implications for Settlement Patterns." In Michael R. Dove and Carol Carpenter (eds) *Environmental Anthropology: A Historical Reader*. Malden, MA: Blackwell, pp. 249–253.

Coa, R. and Ochoa, L. H. 2009. Encuesta Nacional de Demografía y Salud (ENDSA) 2008. Measure DHS Program/Ministerio de Salud y Deportes. www.dhsprogram.com/pubs/pdf/FR228/FR228 [08Feb2010].pdf (accessed 21 January 2015).

Cramb, Rob. 2007. *Land and Longhouse: Agrarian Transformation in the Uplands of Sarawak*. Copenhagen: NIAS.

Cronon, William. 1992. "A Place for Stories: Nature, History and Narrative." *Journal of American History* 78(4): 1347–1376.

Cruz Agudo, Yesmina, Andrew Jones, Peter Berti and Sergio Larrea Macías. 2010. "Lactancia materna, alimentación complementaria y malnutrición infantil en los Andes de Bolivia." *Archivos Latinoamericanos de Nutricion* 60(1): 7–13.

de la Flor, Pablo. 2014. "Mining and Economic Development in Peru: A Time of Resurgence. *ReVista: Harvard Review of Latin America* XIII(2): 24–27.

Derrida, Jacques. 1994. *Specters of Marx: The State of the Debt, the Work of Mourning, and the New International* (transl. P. Kamuf). London: Routledge.

Dove, Michael R. 2011. *The Banana Tree at the Gate: The History of Marginal Peoples and Global Markets in Borneo*. New Haven, CT: Yale University Press.

Dove, Michael R. 2015. "Linnaeus' Study of Swedish Swidden Cultivation: Pioneering Ethnographic Work on the 'Economy of Nature'." *Ambio* 44(3): 239–248.

Escobar, Arturo. 1995. *Encountering Development: The Making and Unmaking of the Third World*. Princeton, NJ: Princeton University Press.

Fabian, Johannes. 1983. *Time and the Other: How Anthropology Makes its Object*. New York: Columbia University Press.

Fairhead, James and Melissa Leach. 1996. *Misreading the African Landscape: Society and Ecology in a Forest–Savanna Mosaic*. Cambridge, UK: Cambridge University Press.

García Pérez, Alan. 2007. "El Síndrome del Perro del Hortelano." *El Comercio Perú*, 28 October .

Greenberg, Miriam. 2013. "What on Earth is Sustainable? Towards a Critical Sustainability Studies." *Boom: A Journal of California* 3(4): 54–66.

Hajer, Martin. 1995. *The Politics of Environmental Discourse: Ecological Modernization and the Policy Process*. Oxford: Oxford University Press.

Harvey, David. 1996. *Justice, Nature, and the Geography of Difference*. Oxford: Blackwell.

Hedges, Thomas. 2012. "How Germany Is Getting to 100 Percent Renewable Energy." *TruthDig*, posted 15 November. www.truthdig.com/report/item/how_germany_is_getting_to_100_percent_renewable_energy_20121115 (accessed 15 October 2015).

Hoddinott, John, John Maluccio, Jere Behrman, Rafael Flores and Reynaldo Martorell. 2008. "Effect of a Nutrition Intervention during Early Childhood on Economic Productivity in Guatemalan Adults." *The Lancet* 371(9610): 411–416.

Hook, Glenn and Richard Siddle. 2003. *Japan and Okinawa: Structure and Subjectivity*. London and New York: Routledge.

Kajiwara, Kenji and Hisashi Matsumoto. 2004. "Kankou (Tourism)." In Ministry of Environment and Japan Coral Reef Society (eds) *Nihon No Sango Sho (Japan's Coral Reefs)*. Tokyo: Ministry of Environment, pp. 122–129.

Keil, Roger. 2007. "Sustaining Modernity, Modernizing Nature: The Environmental Crisis and the Survival of Capitalism." In Rob Krueger and David Gibbs (eds) *The Sustainable Development Paradox: Urban Political Economy in Europe and the United States*. New York: Guilford, pp. 41–65.

Kopnina, Helen and Eleanor Shoreman-Ouimet (eds) 2015. *Sustainability: Key Issues*. New York: Routledge/Earthscan.

Krueger, Rob and David Gibbs. 2007. *The Sustainable Development Paradox: Urban Political Economy in Europe and the United States*. New York: Guilford.

Lawrence, Deborah and William Schlesinger. 2001. "Changes in Soil Phosphorus during 200 Years of Shifting Cultivation in Indonesia." *Ecology* 82(10): 2769–2780.

Lovins, Amory. 1977. *Soft Energy Paths: Toward a Durable Peace*. San Francisco, CA: Friends of the Earth Press.

Lovins, Amory. 2013. "Separating Fact from Fiction in Accounts of Germany's Renewables Revolution." *RMI*, 15 August. http://blog.rmi.org/separating_fact_from_fiction_in_accounts_of_germanys_renewables_revolution (accessed 15 October 2015).

Lovins, Amory. 2014. "Amory's Angle: Ramping up Renewable Energy." *Solutions* 7(1). www.rmi.org/winter_2014_esj_ramping_up_renewable_electricity (accessed 15 October 2015).

Masco, Joe. 2010. "Bad Weather: On Planetary Crisis." *Social Studies of Science* 40(1): 7–40.

Melosi, Martin. 2006. "Energy Transitions in Historical Perspective." In Brendan Dooley (ed.) *Energy and Culture: Perspectives on the Power to Work*. Aldershot, UK: Ashgate, pp. 3–18.

Mertz, Ole, Christine Padoch, Jefferson Fox, R. A. Cramb, Stephen J. Leisz, Nguyen Thanh Lam and Tran Duc Vien. 2009. "Swidden Change in Southeast Asia: Understanding Causes and Consequences." *Human Ecology* 37(3): 259–264.

Mertz, Ole, Kelvin Egay, Thilde Bech Bruun and Tina Svan Colding. 2013. "The Last Swiddens of Sarawak, Malaysia." *Human Ecology* 41(1): 109–118.

Mol, Arthur and David Sonnenfeld (eds) 2000. *Ecological Modernisation around the World: Perspectives and Critical Debates*. London and New York: Routledge.

Otto, J. S. and N. E. Anderson. 1982. "Slash-and-Burn Cultivation in the Highlands South: A Problem in Comparative Agricultural History." *Comparative Study of Society and History* 24: 131–147.

Padoch, Christine, Kevin Coffey, Ole Mertz, Stephen J. Leisz, Jefferson Fox and Reed L. Wadley. 2010. "The Demise of Swidden in Southeast Asia? Local Realities and Regional Ambiguities." *Geografisk Tidsskrift–Danish Journal of Geography* 107(1): 29–41.

Sayre, Nathan. 2012. "The Politics of the Anthropogenic." *Annual Review of Anthropology* 41: 57–70.

Scheer, Hermann. 2012. *The Energy Imperative: 100 Percent Renewable Now*. New York: Earthscan.

Schmidt-Vogt, Dietrich, Stephen Leisz, Ole Mertz, Andreas Heinimann, Thiha Thiha, Peter Messerli, Michael Epprecht, Pham Van Cu, Vu Kim Chi, Martin Hardiono and Truong Dao. 2009. "An Assessment of Trends in the Extent of Swidden in Southeast Asia." *Human Ecology* 37(3): 269–280.

Schumacher, Ernst. 1973. *Small Is Beautiful: Economics as if People Mattered*. London: Blond & Briggs Ltd.

Scott, James. 2009. *The Art of Not Being Governed*. New Haven, CT: Yale University Press.

Sigaut, François. 1979. "Swidden Cultivation in Europe: A Question for Tropical Anthropologists." *Social Science Information* 18(4/5): 679–694.

Stetson, George. 2012. "Oil Politics and Indigenous Resistance in the Peruvian Amazon: The Rhetoric of Modernity against the Reality of Coloniality." *Journal of Environment & Development* 21(1): 76–97.

Stewart, Kathleen and Susan Harding. 1999. "Bad Endings: American Apocalypsis." *Annual Review of Anthropology* 28: 285–310.

Swyngedouw, Erik. 2007. "Impossible 'Sustainability' and the Postpolitical Condition." In Rob Krueger and David Gibbs (eds) *The Sustainable Development Paradox: Urban Political Economy in the United States and Europe*. New York: Guilford, pp. 13–40.

Swyngedouw, Erik. 2010. "Apocalypse Forever? Post-Political Populism and the Spectre of Climate Change." *Theory, Culture & Society* 27(2–3): 213–232.

van Vliet, Nathalie, Ole Mertz, Andreas Heinimann, Tobias Langanke, Unai Pascual, Birgit Schmook, Cristina Adams, Dietrich Schmidt-Vogt, Peter Messerli, Stephen Leisz, Jean-Christophe Castella, Lars Jørgensen, Torben Birch-Thomsen, Cornelia Hett, Thilde Bech Bruun, Amy Ickowitz, Kim Chi Vu, Kono Yasuyuki, Jefferson Fox, Christine Padoch, Wolfram Dressler and Alan D. Ziegler. 2012. "Trends, Drivers and Impacts of Changes in Swidden Cultivation in Tropical Forest-Agriculture Frontiers: A Global Assessment." *Global Environmental Change* 22(2): 418–429.

van Vliet, Nathalie, Ole Mertz, Torben Birch-Thomsen and Birgit Schmook. 2013. "Is there a Continuing Rationale for Swidden Cultivation in the 21st Century?" *Human Ecology* 41(1): 1–5.

Victora, Cesar, Linda Adair, Caroline Fall, Pedro Hallal, Reynaldo Martorell, Linda Richter and Harshpal Sachdev. 2008. "Maternal and Child Undernutrition: Consequences for Adult Health and Human Capital." *The Lancet* 371(9609): 340–357.

Wesoff, Eric. 2013. "Germany Hits 59% Renewable Peak, Grid Does Not Explode." *Green Tech Media*, posted 30 October. www.greentechmedia.com/articles/read/Germany-Hits-59-Renewable-Peak-Grid-Does-Not-Explode (accessed 15 October 2015).

WHO Multicentre Growth Reference Study Group. 2006. *WHO Child Growth Standards: Length/Height-for-Age, Weight-for-Age, Weight-for-Length, Weight-for-Height and Body Mass Index-for-Age: Methods and Development*. Geneva: World Health Organization. www.who.int/childgrowth/standards/Technical_report.pdf?ua=1 (accessed 21 February 2015).

World Commission on Environment and Development. 1987. *Our Common Future*. Oxford: Oxford University Press.

15
ANTHROPOLOGICAL APPROACHES TO ENERGY

Peter Wynn Kirby

Introduction

Energy—its production, its consumption, its very conception and articulation—circulates at the core of human endeavor, and yet as a topic of anthropological scrutiny it has been relatively overlooked until recently. This scholarly neglect is both puzzling and regrettable, as the value of an anthropological approach to energy is its rigorous focus on the sociocultural conditions of energy, as well as attention to the dizzying range of phenomena that might constitute 'energy' variously defined. (These include carbs, kilowatt-hours, kerosene, chi, chakra, chili peppers, tonics, ginseng, fat, feng shui, fuel rods, aphrodisiacs, animism, and Keynes's 'animal spirits of capitalism,' to name but a few.) The fluid and wide-ranging methodology of ethnographic fieldwork generally does a very good job of sketching out the complex sociopolitical situation of energy beyond its narrow material or technical/thermodynamic specifications. For this reason, anthropologists attend to both the 'material substance' and the 'environmental and social context' of forms of energy (Strauss *et al.* 2013: 20) in order to understand the complex of factors that drive energy matters. Hydrocarbons like coal and oil, for instance, have been so lucrative and sought-after since the nineteenth century that they have had the potential to transform whole regions—witness the grave socioeconomic and ecological distortions caused by coal mining in 1860s Colorado or by extraction in the Alberta Tar Sands of Canada and the Niger Delta of West Africa in this century.

Not all energy sources find their way into automobile gas tanks, smartphone batteries, and nuclear reactor cores, of course. Expanding our definitions of energy to include the full range of relevant phenomena—from fat cells to fuel cells, from Sellafield to self-help literature—furnishes valuable insight into links between diverse social domains. Anthropologists in particular have analyzed folk understandings of life-force, virility, fertility, power, and health, which all exude associations with energy in subtle and important ways—yet these have frequently been examined under numerous different rubrics and with varied terminology, to the extent that these phenomena have rarely been considered aspects of 'energy' at all. Indeed, much of the ambiguity and confusion surrounding the term is, on the one hand, the literal reference to energy as a thermodynamic quantity or material; and, on the other, metaphorical invocations of the term to refer to everything from social behavior to the supernatural. Throughout this discussion, 'energy' as studied by anthropologists manifests as:

1   a thermodynamic quantity;
2   materialities (with oil or coal, for example, serving as metonyms for energy itself);
3   systems of metaphor and other tropes; and
4   pervasive cultural and political contexts dominated by energy extraction, production, and/or consumption.

In crafting a concise and cogent account of approaches to energy in anthropology, these pages eschew an exhaustive listing of all work, instead selecting important and evocative scholarly material in order to bring out the above four dimensions of 'energy' in a relatively engaging manner.

Figurative invocations

Early usage of 'energy' in sociocultural anthropology leant heavily on the metaphorical. In his *Elementary Forms of the Religious Life*, the great social theorist Émile Durkheim (2008 [1912]: 210) spoke of the 'moments of effervescence' that could animate social gatherings like rituals. Durkheim also observed the 'special energy' that circulated amongst celebrants and within mobs as well, for instance, leading people to take actions when 'carried away' in crowds that they would never have taken if alone (Durkheim 1982 [1895]: 56). This sort of approach to 'energy' in human societies soon diverged even further into woolly territory in early anthropological writings. One of the earliest preoccupations of *fin-de-siècle* anthropologists was with *mana*, a phenomenon said to represent 'energy' or 'life-force' in a range of Polynesian societies. At the time, some writers—notably Marcel Mauss (1909 [1904]; Mauss and Hubert 1904)—took these 'primitive' societies to be windows into the spiritual and social development of all societies, including those of now-industrialized parts of the world. The very breadth and cultural salience of *mana* that caught the imagination of early ethnographers might at first glance seem incomprehensible to contemporary readers—as Lévi-Strauss (1987 [1950]: 64) puts it, the seductive symbolic logic of *mana* represented 'force and action; quality and state; [noun], adjective and verb all at once; abstract and concrete; omnipresent and localised.' Yet it is worth pointing out that *mana* bears a strong similarity to concepts of energy and life-force in traditional Chinese medicine (and by extension linked notions elsewhere in East Asia and South Asia), as explained in these pages.

Joseph Alter's work on Indian *Pahalwani* wrestlers offers an evocative example of how more contemporary anthropologists explore such 'energy' concepts in complex cultural settings, demonstrating both the salience and the encompassing breadth of such embodied practices, and thus the importance of their careful analysis. Indian wrestlers, as well as other martial artists in India and in other cultures, scrupulously stay celibate to retain semen as part of their training in order to conserve energy and build power and endurance. Going far beyond the typical period of enforced celibacy during 'training camp' for mainstream professional pugilists for days, weeks, or perhaps months before big bouts—for a discussion of the seminal strategies of American boxers, see Wacquant 1995—Indian wrestlers, under the careful tutelage of their guru, conserve semen ideally on a continuing basis, steadily cultivating energy over time (Alter 1994a, 1995). With strong cultural–nationalist associations with landscapes and native purity, the very earthen ground of the outdoor gymnasium is, furthermore, believed by practitioners to become infused with the energy of (unejaculated) 'semen,' imbuing the precincts of the training compound with the combined power of these men, sometimes accumulated over many decades and generations (Alter 1992, 1994b). In this valenced milieu, 'semen' not only constitutes a powerful rationale for training and a Spartan lifestyle, but a pervasive cultural logic that becomes entwined with the perceived primordialist Hindu-nationalist foundations of India itself (Alter 1994a). In turn, this preoccupation with control of sexual fluid fits within a larger Hindu ideology of restraint, renunciation, and moral citizenship—most famously embodied by the celibate and politically/ morally iconic Mahatma Gandhi—and coheres with health practices in India such as yoga and Ayurveda, including cultivation and circulation of *prana* (life-force). Through breathing coordination, restrained diet, and training, practitioners and Hindu nationalists alike believe that celibate martial training can transmute 'semen' into edifying energy, purity, and 'biomoral' development (Alter 1994a: 62).

While this notion of 'semen' in India might be explained away as just a distinctive North Indian analogue for 'virility' or 'strength,' it hardly occurs in isolation. The anthropological literature brims with vast folk-belief systems linking corporeal 'energies' with landscape and environmental forces. Animist traditions like Japanese Shinto map Japan's uneven spiritual topography, identifying powerful features of the landscape that give off positive or negative energy, as well as leveraging a complex set of protocols for managing risk and maintaining purity (e.g. Namihira 1985; Nelson 1996). The notion of *chi/qi* (energy, life-force) in traditional Chinese medicine and the Taoist worldview governs not only health and illness, but longevity, fertility/virility, skill, mental and artistic acuity, harmony and balance in society and in environment (e.g. Chen 2003). How this plays out in complex industrialized settings powerfully influenced by biomedicine and technoscience (to name a few) is subtle and important, not only in China but also in nations like Japan, Korea, and elsewhere. (For example, people might frequently use traditional Chinese medicine to *stay* 'healthy'—or for particular sorts of symptoms—and then visit a modern-style biomedical hospital when they require operations or other interventions. Much of 'modernity' in a range of societies is a rich conjoining of such interpenetrating, hybridized cultural traditions and practices.) An intriguing anthropological approach scrutinizes overlaps between different hybrid 'relational knowledge systems' incorporating human, animal, and material landscapes and considers how 'energy' is understood in Alaska (Chapman 2013: 96–97), juxtaposing customary Native American notions of 'energy' and power with nearby energy extraction initiatives in Alaska. Chapman shows that such contested sites are not only multinational, but also

> *multinatural* in the ways that they exist in many natures, diverse cosmologies of resources, society, and environment. . . . A relational ontology of energy is, here, one in which energy exists not in the form of neutral, fungible "natural resources" but in circulating social obligations among people and other nonhuman beings.
>
> *(Chapman 2013: 96–97; emphasis added)*

Along the extraction-scarred terrain of Alaska's petro-industrial landscape,

> many people in Native communities would disagree with being labeled poor when they feel themselves to be rich, if not in cash or carbon fuels [then] in healthy spirit, food, and land, interwoven qualities that together produce vital individual and social energy.
>
> *(Chapman 2013: 102–103)*

In this way, such diverse notions of 'energy' can impact how conventional energy extraction—like that of oil—is conceived of, promoted, mobilized, and contested.

Cultural thermodynamics

While anthropology as a discipline tends to immerse itself in ethnographic fieldwork in particular contexts and (sub-)cultures more than other social science fields, some past anthropologists have taken a more macro-scale view and embraced energy as a vehicle for analysis and indeed comparison between different social milieux. Most notoriously, the neo-evolutionist Leslie White (1943) constructed an elaborate system of comparative analysis looking at how different societies through time and space have succeeded at producing energy, rehashing flawed nineteenth-century theories of cultural/racial evolution in the process. White elevates the exploitation of resources from the environment in an abstract and unsubtle manner, while placing much less attention on cultural practices and subtleties of context. (For example, the following typical excerpt from his writing demonstrates his style of turning cultures into sets of variables that could literally be phrased in terms of mathematical equations [see below]: 'Other things being equal, the degree of cultural development varies directly as the efficiency of the technological means with which the harnessed energy is put to work' [White 1943: 338].) White identifies technological and organizational advances that create forms of thermodynamic and nutritional abundance in societies, which he believes determine these societies' developmental 'progress' in material culture, artistic production, defense, political structure, demographics, and so on. To be sure, humans require shelter, warmth, and sustenance. It is doubtless true that a human wielding an axe has finite ability to chop wood. An iron axe is more efficient at cutting logs than a stone axe, and so on. All axes are surpassed, unsurprisingly, by the modern chainsaw, and the huge machines that contemporary loggers use to fell mature trees in a matter of seconds constitute a technological advance on the fuel-gathering abilities of hunter-foragers almost inconceivable in its scale. White should be recognized for his pioneering realization of the salience of energy in societies, but in his zeal to chart evolutionary trajectories for societies and their technology, and to fashion equations that purport to measure and quantify their 'progress'—such as '$E \times T = P$, in which E represents the amount of energy expended per capita per unit of time, T the technological means of its expenditure, and P the magnitude of the product per unit of time' (White 1943: 336)—he reduces energy production to a shallow variable that does little to communicate the vast importance of understanding energy as conceived and enacted in varied communities.

Over the ensuing decades, anthropologists shied away, for the most part, from such macro-scale analyses in general and from analyzing energy in particular—with some important exceptions. For example, regarding the latter point, Marvin Harris's analysis (1966) of the counterintuitive efficiency of India's 'sacred cattle,' long viewed as a wasteful Hindu extravagance by appalled Western economists, is less an attempt to construct an approach to energy than a contrarian, hard-nosed interpretation of the data, including the labor that animals provide, the dung used for fuel, the animals' conversion of waste sources of nutrition, and so on. It has only been in recent years, against the backdrop of vitriolic controversy over pollutant fossil fuels, costly nuclear accidents, the planetary-scale risk of climate change, and related contemporary issues that anthropologists have begun to study energy with the rigor and attention that it deserves. (For some of the multidisciplinary backdrop to this shift, see Nader 2010.)

One major issue of importance to environmental anthropology involves the structural resource imbalance and rapaciousness of capitalism and industrialization as they impact peripheries. Alf Hornborg (2001) launches a comprehensive analytical assault on skewed capitalist forces that propel headlong consumption of material and labor resources from far-flung marginal regions to generate products and to create profits for industrialized consumer economies in more metropolitan nodes. His close analysis of entropy and how the second law of thermodynamics shapes modern institutions shows how industrialized societies are dissipative structures whose processes of accumulation lead, apparently inexorably, to entropy (i.e. disorder: pollution and degradation). (This stands as a more comprehensive and sophisticated updating of the early musings of Richard Adams [1975], regarding technology-led human development and its thermodynamic and ecological ramifications.) Such unequal global modes of exchange serve as backdrop to the numerous eco-focused anthropological studies of environmental defilement and injustice in varied cultural contexts that pepper this handbook.

Materialities and contexts

To the extent that exploited energy resources are transportable, their trade and use have been a richly trans-border endeavor. The rapacious pursuit of whales during the eighteenth and nineteenth centuries was mostly (though not exclusively) driven by demand for whale oil as a clean-burning indoor light source, an often overlooked point. Throughout the nineteenth century, primarily North American and European whaling ships scoured the seas from the Arctic Circle to the South Pacific and Antarctica in search of this sought-after lamp oil, in the process bringing many cetacean species to the brink of extinction. The price of a gallon of whale lamp oil skyrocketed as the century went on and remained high even after Abraham Gesner patented kerosene in 1854 as a more easily exploited fuel alternative, derived from the newly discovered energy source of coal. Through both the 'coal transition' and the 'petroleum transition' (Melosi 2010), hydrocarbon-abundant regions attracted migrant workforces from around the world, creating a booming energy trade that sent these potent and sought-after commodities sometimes considerable distances. Naturally, this highly trans-border and asymmetrical enterprise continues into the twenty-first century, frequently involving large corporations listed in the wealthiest industrialized nations that voraciously prospect for oil and other hydrocarbons in subterranean or deep-water deposits around the planet. Anthropologists continue to dig analytically into contemporary multinational-led exploitation of fossil-fuel resources in a range of fascinating and contested social contexts. (See e.g. Nuttal 2010; Strauss *et al.* 2013; Dove 2014.)

The quest for wealth and power through discovery, exploitation, and commoditization of fossil-fuel resources like petroleum and coal is a drama worthy of Hollywood. (Those interested might, indeed, refer to the acclaimed film *There Will Be Blood* [2007, dir. Paul Thomas Anderson], which depicts the turbulent, cut-throat early years of the oil business in the American West. See also Upton Sinclair's novel *Oil!* [1927].) The scale of riches posed by coal seams, oil fields, and so on was so vast that resource extraction exerted a powerful influence, with the potential to warp entire communities and regions (Andrews 2008; Yergin 2008 [1992]; see also the abundant literature on the so-called 'resource curse' vis-à-vis systemic problems of governance in petro-states).

Yet viewed another way, energy enacts community. The distribution lines, insulated cables, and conduits that connect electricity provision for households and neighborhoods, the pipelines, tanks, and tubing that allow hydrocarbons to circulate, the utilities that read meters and process fees, are constitutive of social relationships and demarcate a form of thermodynamic citizenship. (In countries like France, this link becomes even more explicit—a person's original electricity bill or gas bill becomes an essential document certifying residency in bureaucratic spheres.) This is also apparent, of course, in alternative communities that opt to live together entirely 'off the grid,' remaining fiercely independent from state or corporate control and the pollutant, immoral lifestyles that they represent. 'Smart grids' and 'super grids' not only allow more efficient transfer, scheduling, and husbanding of energy in a region, but can facilitate a form of democratic energy revolution; roof-mounted solar panels, wind turbines, and other green household contrivances often generate surplus energy that can be sold to utilities, reversing the power vector and potentially ushering in a more egalitarian, grass-roots subversion of erstwhile centralized power provision that will probably shape energy use and social/political action in coming decades (e.g. Scheer 2004; Yergin 2012). If we normally notice grids through their absence—i.e. blackouts and other failures (Howe forthcoming, autumn 2016)—developments in coming years will probably bring social and material transformations that will prove a good deal more conspicuous. Regardless, people's everyday understandings of energy remain hazy and contradictory. Relatively recent work (e.g. Rupp 2013) has taken the intriguing line of identifying folk-like, vernacular understandings of energy in contemporary industrialized contexts like New York City, for example, which draws important links between technical/material/thermodynamic properties of energy and the sometimes flawed, imperfect associations with energy that dominate everyday engagement with energy *as lived*.

Much of the carbon-fueled energy production apparatus is highly pollutant—not just reckless coal combustion, but familiar oil-furnaces, factories, and automobile exhausts create air pollution, for example, that cause many hundreds of thousands of premature deaths each year. (According to the World Health Organization [2014; see also WHO 2013], outdoor air pollution alone causes an estimated 3.7 million premature deaths globally each year, with most of this thanks to fossil fuels. Then there are the grave health complications that afflict many more among the living, such as serious respiratory disorders and additional stress on those suffering heart disease.) Pollution from multinational energy development projects also builds up in groundwater and streams, following multiple environmental pathways into the bodies of humans and other organisms. One example: in *Flammable*, an important study of controversies over toxic pollution in a particularly fraught cultural context, ethnographers Javier Auyero and Débora Swistun (2009: 6) delve into the 'toxic uncertainty' and 'symbolic violence' suffered by inhabitants of a shanty-town exposed to pollutant emissions from a Shell oil refinery in Argentina, as well as the intriguing responses and coping strategies of shantytown residents. Or take the unprecedented 2010 Deepwater Horizon oil spill, which released many millions of barrels of crude into the Gulf of Mexico from a gusher on the ocean floor, about 1,600 meters below sea level. For three chaotic months during which authorities and scientists struggled even to grasp the scale and indeed the very nature of the unfolding disaster, over a million gallons of chemical dispersants helped to break the oil down to the extent that the debacle unfolded at the abstruse level of deep-sea microbes measurable only with retrofitted scientific instruments. The unruly processes of administrative, political, scientific, and social destructuring (and restructuring) furnished a vantage not only on a remote marine ecosystem that was previously little understood, but also on a dynamic epistemic and ideological battleground on which networks, institutions, corporations, and governments leveraged competing notions of 'environment' toward divergent ends (see e.g. Bond 2013). This material demonstrates how even close scrutiny of the prospecting for and processing of hydrocarbons—tightly linked to commonly conceived mainstream notions of 'energy' as conventional fuel sources—can quickly spill into diverse domains including toxic pollution, environmental health, citizen science, community protest, political economy, and frictions between divergent knowledge practices.

Nevertheless, the uncanny, pernicious threat of meltdown and radiation exposure make nuclear power provision a particular target of concerns over environmental risk. After the 1979 partial meltdown at Three-Mile Island in the USA and, in particular, after the 1986 catastrophic meltdown and widespread radiation from the Soviet-era Chernobyl debacle in Ukraine, anthropologists (e.g. Petryna 2002, 2004) and others not only studied the tragic aftermath, but began to ask whether such nuclear power station failures could be called 'accidents' at all. (Indeed, Charles Perrow's 1999 [1984] timely analysis of the defects of such tightly coupled, highly complex technological systems concluded that these should be reconceived as 'normal accidents' that would continue in the future and, in the case of nuclear reactors, would present an intolerable environmental health risk.) The calamitous 2011 triple meltdowns at Fukushima Daiichi in Japan only confirmed this view, highlighting the devastating impact of widespread radiation and evacuations and exposing the complacency and ineptitude of the nuclear establishment, whose poor emergency planning and shoddy plant design and siting oversight helped to create the nuclear debacle. In time, the publications of anthropologists working on the irradiated aftermath of the Japan disaster, and attitudes to energy in Japan generally, will enter the scholarly literature, but a solid interim ethnographic treatment of the disasters appears in the collection *Japan Copes with Calamity* (Gill *et al.* 2013). Work in the pro-nuclear French context offers intriguing insight into nuclear cultures more broadly. For example, anthropologist Françoise Zonabend (1993) provides a vivid and insightful ethnography of life next to a nuclear facility on Normandy's notorious 'nuclear peninsula'—this is complemented by Gabrielle Hecht's compelling postwar history of the tangled nationalist political terrain of France's zealously promoted nuclear sector, entitled *The Radiance of France* (Hecht 2009 [1998]). Strong and motivated pro- and anti-nuclear factions in a range of industrialized nations will doubtless provide a continuing ethnographic panoply of material on nuclear issues for anthropologists to study as new Generation IV reactor projects, old irradiated reactor decommissioning, ongoing disaster remediation, and continuing radiation exposure create controversy in fraught sociocultural contexts.

Energy is, thus, central to how societies conceive of and engage with environments, technologies, knowledge practices, health, citizenship, and even identity itself. Anthropologists are uniquely qualified to scrutinize such captivating material linking cultural thermodynamics in all its diverse manifestations. Whether it is called 'energy,' 'life-force,' 'power,' 'energo-power,' or 'energopolitics' (e.g. Boyer 2014), energy animates human interaction, galvanizes political disputes, and lies at the core of the cultural and semantic labor that drives human social action. Like the wondrous fossils of swampland flora that coal miners discover in dank, tenebrous subterranean shafts, imprinted in pitch-black coal seams from the accumulated sun-energy of untold quantities of 'ancient vegetal matter' over tens of millions of years (Andrews 2008: 145), sociocultural 'finds' related to energy will doubtless continue to stimu-late curious spelunking anthropologists, their analytical picks and headlamps at the ready, keeping them engaged with this rich complex of material well into the future.

References

Adams, Richard N. (1975). *Energy and Structure: A Theory of Social Power.* Austin: University of Texas Press.

Alter, Joseph (1992). *The Wrestler's Body: Identity and Ideology in North India.* Berkeley and Los Angeles: University of California Press.

Alter, Joseph (1994a). Celibacy, Sexuality, and the Transformation of Gender into Nationalism in North India. *Journal of Asian Studies* 53(1): 45–66.

Alter, Joseph (1994b). Somatic Nationalism: Indian Wrestling and Militant Hinduism. *Modern Asian Studies* 28(3): 557–588.

Alter, Joseph (1995). The Celibate Wrestler: Sexual Chaos, Embodied Balance and Competitive Politics in North India. *Contributions to Indian Sociology* (new series) 29(1–2): 109–131.

Andrews, Thomas G. (2008). *Killing for Coal: America's Deadliest Labor War.* Cambridge, MA: Harvard University Press.

Auyero, Javier and Débora A. Swistun (2009). *Flammable: Environmental Suffering in an Argentine Shantytown.* Oxford and New York: Oxford University Press.

Bond, David (2013). Governing Disaster: The Political Life of the Environment during the BP Oil Spill. *Cultural Anthropology* 28(4): 694–715. doi:10.1111/cuan.12033

Boyer, Dominic (2014). Energopower: An Introduction. *Anthropological Quarterly* 87(2): 309–333.

Chapman, Chelsea (2013). Multinatural Resources: Ontologies of Energy and the Politics of Inevitability in Alaska. In Sarah Strauss, Stephanie Rupp and Thomas Love (eds) *Cultures of Energy: Power, Practices, Technologies.* Walnut Creek, CA: Left Coast Press, pp. 96–109.

Chen, Nancy (2003). *Breathing Spaces: Qigong, Psychiatry, and Healing in China.* New York: Columbia University Press.

Dove, Michael (2014). *The Anthropology of Climate Change: An Historical Reader.* Malden, MA and Oxford: Wiley–Blackwell.

Durkheim, Émile (1982 [1895]). *The Rules of Sociological Method.* (*Les règles de la méthode sociologique*). New York: The Free Press.

Durkheim, Émile (2008 [1912]). *The Elementary Forms of the Religious Life.* New York: Dover.

Gill, Tom, Brigitte Steger and David H. Slater (eds) (2013). *Japan Copes with Calamity: Ethnographies of the Earthquake, Tsunami and Nuclear Disasters of March 2011.* Oxford and Bern: Peter Lang.

Harris, Marvin (1966). The Cultural Ecology of India's Sacred Cattle. *American Anthropologist* 7(1): 51–59.

Hecht, Gabrielle (2009 [1998]). *The Radiance of France: Nuclear Power and National Identity after World War II.* Cambridge, MA and London: The MIT Press.

Hornborg, Alf (2001). *The Power of the Machine: Global Inequalities of Economy, Technology, and Environment.* Walnut Creek, CA: AltaMira Press.

Howe, Cymene (forthcoming, autumn 2016). Grids. In Jennifer Wenzel, Imre Szeman and Patricia Yaeger (eds) *Fueling Cultures: 100 Words for Energy and Environment.* New York: Fordham University Press.

Lévi-Strauss, Claude (1987 [1950]). *Introduction to the Work of Marcel Mauss.* London: Routledge and Kegan Paul.

Mauss, Marcel (1909 [1904]). L'origines des pouvoirs magiques dans les sociétés Australiennes. Republished in Marcel Mauss and Henri Hubert, *Mélanges d'histoires des religions.* Paris: Félix Alcan, pp. 131–187.

Mauss, Marcel and Henri Hubert (1904). Esquisse d'une théorie générale de la magie. *L'Année Sociologique* 7: 1–146.

Melosi, Marvin (2010). Energy Transitions in Historical Perspective. In Laura Nader (ed.) *The Energy Reader.* Malden, MA and Oxford: Blackwell, pp. 45–60.

Nader, Laura (ed.) (2010). *The Energy Reader.* Malden, MA and Oxford: Blackwell.

Namihira, Emiko 1985. *Kegare (Ritual Pollution).* Tokyo: Tōkyōdō.

Nelson, John K. 1996. *A Year in the Life of a Shinto Shrine.* Seattle: University of Washington Press.

Nuttal, Mark (2010). *Pipeline Dreams: People, Environment, and the Arctic Energy Frontier.* Copenhagen: IWGIA.

Perrow, Charles (1999 [1984]) *Normal Accidents: Living with High-Risk Technologies.* 2nd edn. Princeton, NJ: Princeton University Press.

Petryna, Adriana (2002). *Life Exposed: Biological Citizens after Chernobyl.* Princeton, NJ: Princeton University Press.

Petryna, A. (2004). Biological Citizenship: The Science and Politics of Chernobyl-Exposed Populations. *Osiris* (2nd series) 19: 250–265.

Rupp, Stephanie (2013). Considering Energy: E = MC² = (Magic.Culture)². In Sarah Strauss, Stephanie Rupp and Thomas Love (eds) *Cultures of Energy: Power, Practices, Technologies.* Walnut Creek, CA: Left Coast Press, pp. 79–95.

Scheer, Hermann (2004). *The Solar Economy: Renewable Energy for a Sustainable Global Future.* London: Earthscan.

Sinclair, Upton (1927). *Oil!* New York: Albert & Charles Boni.

Strauss, Sarah, Stephanie Rupp and Thomas Love (2013). Powerlines: Cultures of Energy in the Twenty-First Century. In Sarah Strauss, Stephanie Rupp and Thomas Love (eds) *Cultures of Energy: Power, Practices, Technologies*. Walnut Creek, CA: Left Coast Press, pp. 10–40.

Wacquant, Loïc (1995). Pugs at Work. Bodily Capital and Bodily Labor among Professional Boxers. *Body & Society* 1(1): 65–93.

White, Leslie (1943). Energy and the Evolution of Culture. *American Anthropologist* 45(3–1): 335–356.

WHO (2013). *Review of Evidence on Health Aspects of Air Pollution – REVIHAPP Project (Technical Report)*. Bonn, Germany: World Health Organization. www.euro.who.int/__data/assets/pdf_file/0004/193108/REVIHAAP-Final-technical-report-final-version.pdf?ua=1 (accessed March 2015).

WHO (2014). Ambient (Outdoor) Air Quality and Health: Factsheet No. 313. World Health Organization. www.who.int/mediacentre/factsheets/fs313/en/ (accessed March 2015).

Yergin, Daniel (2008 [1992]). *The Prize: The Epic Quest for Money, Oil and Power*. New York: Free Press.

Yergin, Daniel (2012). *The Quest: Energy, Security, and the Remaking of the Modern World*. Revised edn. New York: Penguin.

Zonabend, Françoise (1993). *The Nuclear Peninsula*. Cambridge, UK: Cambridge University Press.

PART IV

Climate change, resilience, and vulnerability

16

DISASTERS AND THEIR IMPACT

A fundamental feature of environment

Susanna M. Hoffman

Introduction

Not every environment is serene.

Almost all have embedded within them one or more sorts of upheaval: earthquakes or harrowing fault-line movements; volcanic eruptions with concomitant lava flows, ash shrouds, and devastating shockwaves; gyrating or bombardment-like wind storms that emanate over land or sea and annihilate everything in their path; ravaging floods, routine and unforeseen, stemming from snow melts and torrential rain storms; pernicious droughts that deepen and spread like afflictions; deleterious wildfires that char turf, forest, and edifice; cascading slides and avalanches that tumble down coulees and shear off hillsides; extremes of heat and cold onerous to the point that air becomes unbreathable while ground ices over or near-to-simmers. Yet, most environmentally focused socio-cultural studies, as well as socio-cultural studies in general, have passed over the existence of these upheavals. Instead, the vast majority treat environmental settings, along with the cultures and societies seated upon them, as if they maintain a perpetual steady state.

Now and again in the early archives of social studies the idea appears that geographical disturbances bore major impact upon human communities and their locales. In anthropology, Anthony F. C. Wallace initiated the topic as the primary concern in a 1956 story of the Worcester Tornado of 1953. He was followed by Belshaw in 1951, Schneider (1957), Firth (1959), and Schwimmer (1969), although these researchers, as opposed to Wallace, happened to be examining unrelated issues in places that then unexpectedly endured disasters. In recent years, however, the topic of disaster began to arise in earnest within a number of social science fields including cultural geography, sociology, history, and economics, along with anthropology. At first those taking up the topic had again undergone unanticipated calamities in their study sites. Others joined in because the problems ensuing from disasters were becoming so prevalent. Among the anthropologists were Anthony Oliver-Smith (Chapter 17 in this volume), Gregory Button (2010), myself, and a few others, an incipient group now joined by a growing wave of scholars. A number have come from environmental anthropology, others from political ecology, medical anthropology, ethnography, archaeology, and still more crisscrossing interests. Nonetheless, even among the many whose primary emphases are ecology and environment, calamities remain treated as departures from the norm, and communities and landscapes are addressed as if the fabric of the site had never been rent by some catastrophe and does not bear the patchwork that results from such events (Hoffman 2005).

The truth is, disasters, when they occur, are all-encompassing events. Both where calamitous episodes constitute a chronic norm and where they occur only intermittently, they sweep across every aspect of human life: the environmental, the biological, and the socio-cultural (Oliver-Smith and Hoffman 1999). Moreover, the occurrence of disasters and their deleterious effects are expanding. Over the last few decades a tremendous increase in catastrophes of all descriptions has transpired around the world. The upsurge is coupled with the fact that more and more people are living in hazardous zones, almost every region of the world is undergoing urbanization, the worldwide population shift to coast lines, Westernization, immigration, and the junctures and the demands of global networks are mounting. Layered on top of all these dire factors are the initial effects of global warming. Altogether, these collective agencies are placing more and more people in tenuous situations, a circumstance that will only increase. The accompanying effects and costs on human communities, already enormous, are exploding. Meanwhile, the effects of globalism and climate change are coming to mean that a disaster in one place brings about grievous effects upon others far distant.

To delve further into the issue of disaster and the environment, a number of factors must be addressed: first, that humans do not dwell upon a sole environmental underpinning but rather upon an amalgamated one; second, that exactly what constitutes a disaster once again uncoils not from a single event or happening, but from a coalescence of agents and even understandings; and finally, that many core elements involved derive not from the bedrock of earth beneath people, but the grounding of their culture.

Not one, but four environments

At the virtual bottom line of every human habitation lies the ground it sits on. At least that is the general assumption. Humans, however, do in fact not dwell in just one environment, but in four. Each and every one contributes to, and in many cases initiates, the disasters that people undergo.

The first environment is the basal terrain in which a people dwell. This is what is usually referred to by the term "environment," although it might be better termed the "physical plane." The second is a people's "modified" environment. Humans rarely live in a place without altering it. Rather, they sculpt their surroundings. They terrace hillsides, channel streams, lob off mountain tops, purloin sea beds, tunnel into ore loads, pile up bulwarks, contour flats, move rocks, fashion inlets, take down timber, and revise vegetation. In all these maneuvers, they potentially make their domain less stable and allow for, or create, fresh hazards. In addition, wherever humans reside, there abides a third environment: the built one. Upon their basic orbit, humans erect houses, barns, barracks, skyscrapers, temples, memorials, castles, walkways, docks, and marinas. They employ mud, straw, brick, wood, concrete, steel, glass, and stucco. They implant pylons and metal rods, pave roadways, string bridges, erect power plants, and assemble industrial complexes. They encourage communities to spread up and out all the while superimposing a contrived milieu in which the inhabitants live, eat, sleep, and work.

All three of the environments, physical, modified, and built, can give rise to disturbances in quotidian lives. Moreover, it could further be said that there is yet a fourth environment in which people reside: their culture. It is a people's culture that in the first place dictates how an environment is utilized. Culture prescribes how the physical plane is modified and what is built upon it. At a more abstract level, a people's culture then formulates another encompassing habitat: one of thinking and doing. Human engagement with a place is never completely a biological nor a direct response to physical or material conditions, prevailing or constructed. A people's culture involves a complex grid of knowledges and meanings, beliefs and laws, customs and habits, traditions and innovations, shared more or less by all, although at times differentiated by individuals, families, and groupings. It encompasses a set of social, political, economic, and ideological institutions and practices. In the contemporary world, it further includes the impingements of regional, national, and international and other non-local constructs (Hoffman and Oliver-Smith 2002).

What then is a disaster?

Exactly how to define what constitutes a disaster has been the topic of much discussion (Westgate and O'Keefe 1976; Kroll-Smith and Couch 1991; Qurantelli 1998). Multiple factors and certainly opinions come into play. However, after much examination and development in the field, all agree on one basic premise: disasters do not spring up like sudden riddles from some incognito sphere. All disasters are caused by humans in one way or another. It matters not if they spring forth from the fundamental terrain, from the modifications that have taken place, or from the contrivances of human manufacture; all have a "people" part to their creation and unfolding.

It follows, therefore, that there is no such thing as a "natural" disaster. To attribute a disaster to the mere ecological happening is like assigning a noise to "one hand clapping" or asking "If a tree falls in an empty forest, does it make a sound?" Without the presence of humans, earth's disruptions are merely events of environmental process, not calamities (Blaikie *et al.* 1994; Oliver-Smith and Hoffman 1999; Hartman and Squires 2006). To constitute a disaster, people are present. They have planted themselves in a certain place. They have done or made things. Disasters only take place through the conjuncture of two essential factors: a human population and a potentially destructive agent. Both are part of a total ecological system, including all natural, modified, and constructed features. Both are embedded in natural and social systems that unfold as processes over time. As such, they render disasters also as processual phenomena, rather than events that are isolated and temporally demarcated in exact time frames (Oliver-Smith and Hoffman 2002: 3–5).

If there is any hidden factor to disasters, it is the third one. The conjunction of simply a human population and a potentially destructive circumstance, such as a volatile fault line or a leaky factory, does not inevitably produce a disaster. Rather, a disaster only manifests itself in the context of a historically produced pattern of "vulnerability" evidenced in the location, infrastructure, socio-political organization, production and distribution systems, and ideology of a society. Indeed, a society's pattern of vulnerability is a core element of a disaster. It conditions the behavior of individuals and organizations throughout the full unfolding of a disaster far more profoundly than will the physical force of the destructive agent (Oliver-Smith and Hoffman 2002: 3–5).

Accordingly, disasters not only have people and place, they have story and chronology. They are assembled over years, decades, sometimes centuries within human domains and systems (Oliver-Smith 1999) and there is a tale to their making. That tale often includes miscalculations, misperception, lack of foresight, deficient discernment, lack of care, greed, and more. The eucalyptus trees that burned so fiercely in the Oakland–Berkeley firestorm of 1991 were imported by Spanish land grantees centuries earlier (Hoffman 1994, 1998). The Tennessee Valley ash spill (2008) resulted from the gross actions of a flagrant industry (Button 2010: 135–159). The severity of the Kobe earthquake in Japan (1995) stemmed from cheap dense housing reconstructed after World War II to serve the rebirth of an industrial hub. Those most injured by Hurricane Katrina (2005) had been pushed into the low-lying Ninth Ward by nefarious economics, politics, and racial machinations long compiled (Hartman and Squires 2006; Browne 2015).

These same examples demonstrate another factor lying within the connection between people and disasters. Not all members of a locale are equally imperiled. Disasters, and the vulnerability to them, exhibit what many call "unequal shares of safety." Most commonly, those unduly affected belong to sectors of the population less culturally valued—as determined generally by gender, class, and ethnicity—and are made more vulnerable by a conscripted place in environment, economics, politics, social structure, ethos, and prejudices (Harvey 1996). Sometimes, vulnerability is reversed and the more privileged segments turn into the more imperiled, especially when those segments elect to inhabit precarious places. Note that the elements leading to vulnerability and disaster may further be openly acknowledged by a community or be hidden.

A disaster thus takes place then only through a pattern of events and processes within the evolved and tooled context of a community, overt and covert. I venture a definition lifted from a work by Anthony Oliver-Smith and myself.

A disaster is:

> A process/event combining a potentially destructive agent/force from the natural, modified, or built environment and a population in a socially and economically produced condition of vulnerability, resulting in a perceived disruption of the customary relative satisfaction of individual and social needs for physical survival, social order, and meaning.
>
> *(Oliver-Smith and Hoffman 2002: 4)*

Since the definition of disaster can therefore not be entirely separated from the concomitant matter of hazard, I also venture a definition of hazard. To do so, it is essential first to note that not all disasters are environmentally triggered or derived from the modified environment. Many, especially nowadays, spring from the "third" environment, the "built" one. They, and the vulnerability to them, arise from structures fabricated by human hand or detrimental practices of human enterprise, acknowledging that there is often an underlying aspect of the physical plane to the location of the structures and actions, such as a convenient river, an oil-rich stratum. Such disasters are generally called "technological" disasters. They include the ground water contamination in Hinkley, California (1952 onward); the deadly chemical leak in Bhopal, India (1984); the nuclear meltdowns of Chernobyl, Ukraine (1986) and Fukushima, Japan (2011); the Exxon (1989) and the Deepwater Horizon (2010) oil spills in the United States. Lethal epidemics also fall into the domain of disasters. They, too, frequently have human action at their genesis, some sort of animal-or-insect-to-human contact that fans out through human interaction. The Spanish influenza pandemic of 1918–1919 probably arose from pig farms in Kansas. Africa's recent outbreak of Ebola (2014) apparently issued from the consumption of bat meat. Technological and epidemic disasters generally differ from other kinds in that they most often cause little structural damage but great injury. Exceptions exist. The infamous Johnstown flood (1889), which sprang from a man-made dirt dam and recreational lake, caused massive structural damage as well as death

(Erikson 1976). Technological disasters can also deliver extensive environmental harm, destroying a people's relations to their patch of ground for decades to come.

A hazard can, therefore, be defined as:

> The forces, conditions, or technologies that carry a potential for social, infra-structural, or environmental damage. A hazard can be a hurricane, earthquake, or avalanche, but it can also be a nuclear facility or a socio-economic practice, such as using pesticides. The issue of hazard further incorporates the way a society perceives the danger or dangers, either environmental and/or technological, they face and allows the danger to enter their calculation of risk.
>
> *(Oliver-Smith and Hoffman 2002: 4)*

Disasters arrive in two ways: by rapid onset, as with an earthquake or meltdown; or by slow onset, as with a drought or toxic pollution. As well as having developmental histories, when disasters occur, they immediately ensnare the present and engulf the future. People act and react to them in diverse ways. Their eventuation and reverberation often take years during which the needs and interests of many rise up, necessitate articulation, and require negotiation. No matter how large or small, at first all disasters are furthermore experienced at a local level. Even when the area impacted is enormous and the numbers touched are legion, every disaster comes down to the particular consequences and reactions of the local communities affected. Because of that, one disaster may have any number of manifestations as each different spot experiences it. Each undergoes a catastrophe in the first place in the context of its own profile of vulnerability. Each may feel the experience in differing degrees. The same disaster agent will show great fluctuation in both patterns of destruction as well as interpretation of cause, effect, and responsibility, thus confounding any singular or overarching understanding, approach, or response (Oliver-Smith and Hoffman 2002: 1–22).

Cultural factors

Since all disasters derive from human causation, the crux of each comes down to one element: the "fourth" environment, the people's culture. From origin to development, reaction to recovery, culture is the driver that facilitates, frames, and guides disaster.

Numerous aspects are involved. Some have a direct association with a people's physical circumstance. Others are more indirect. They include: choice of location, pattern of settlement, utilization of locale, economics, material goods, architecture, tools, social arrangements, politics, beliefs, laws, art, literature, and more. A particular few stand out in pertinence.

Adaptation

Adaptation has been a central concept in anthropology since the field's inception. The term refers to the patterns of behavior that enable a people to cope with their environmental surroundings and to subsist upon it. As humans have clearly flourished in a wide variety of ecologies since the beginning of the species, various scholars posit that adaptation operates as the juncture between human biology and human existence and is possibly the origin of culture (Goodman and Leatherman 1998; Hruschka *et al.* 2005).

As, at its foremost level, adaptation involves how a people acquire food and the goods and actions necessary for basic survival, it is deemed largely ecological and economic in operation.

Yet, humans address their environments differently from most biological forms. They interact with nature and gain subsistence not in a purely straightforward fashion, but rather through a set of behaviors, which are socially constituted and meaningful (Patterson 1994). Hunting, gathering, farming, herding, fishing, extracting materials, trading, building houses, laying pipelines, arguing in court, performing surgery, all these ways of thriving, whether environmentally entwined or not, are accomplished through social co-ordinations and presume a cultural system. They also contain history and are directed at perpetuity; that is, they have been constituted over time and intend persistence (Crumley 1994; Redmond 1999).

To repeat, however, most of the environments in which humans live are not serene: thus, adaptation for most human groups both environmentally and socially has included some degree of familiarity and accommodation to the hazards and disasters that are systemic to their terrain. Studies show that before colonization, globalization, and other interferences, most societies in their native practices expressed knowledge of their physical surroundings and had strategies to deal with it, to the point that, for many, the various physical events they experienced did not constitute in their view a "disaster," but were simply part of their existence and experience (Schneider 1957). Archaeologist Payson Sheets (1999) similarly argues that most simpler societies understood hazards and evolved ways of dealing with disruptive events. Numerous people, for example, recognized volcanic eruptions and moved away from ash spills only to move back 20 years later. The more complex the society, the less reconciled it is to disturbance. Sahelian nomads adapted to periodic droughts through linkages with sedentary farmers and altering migration routes (Lovejoy and Baier 1976). McCabe (2002) notes that the Turkana of Africa simply moved to better grasslands when drought struck, until the concepts of nation state and borders interfered. They also had a well-developed sequence to the slaughter of their animals that enabled survival. Archaeologist Michael Moseley states that even more complex societies, such as the Inca, took into account the hazards in their environment and could endure chronic upheavals, as long as the upheavals were singular. It is only when two or more calamities occurred in close succession there, or by implication anywhere—that is, compound disruptions—that societies cannot accommodate them (Moseley 1999, 2002).

When hazards become activated, the degree to which they bring about a disaster is an index of a culture's adaptation or maladaptation to its location. Even today, certain people construct movable houses that they can carry away from flooding rivers only to set them back down again when the river recedes later. Numerous contemporary urban communities have mandated adjustments to threatening environments, although usually only to one extant peril and rarely an all-hazard composite. The problem today is that all too often native strategies have been disrupted by governmental policies, economic development, population increase, or nation-state boundaries to the degree that maladaptation has mushroomed. In consequence, the magnitude of death and destruction resulting from today's interplay of culture, society, environment, and calamity has burgeoned equally. Successful adaptation is undeniably intertwined with the highly specific circumstances of locale, not the outer world, which is why many involved in the disaster field clamor for the use of "local" knowledge rather than top-down programs when dealing with either preparation for or recovery from a calamity.

Perception

People not only adapt to their environments to one degree or another, they also engineer how they perceive it. In every society, people let some features of their locale enter their awareness while they dismiss or recast others. As Cosgrove and Daniels (1988: 1) say, "A landscape is a cultural image, a pictoral way of representing or symbolising surrounding."

As always in perceptual matters, a number of components are involved. People of different cultures do not see color the same way. All people "see" the entire color spectrum, but from one culture to another, people merge colors into different sets they adjudge similar (Berlin and Kay 1969). Different people see space differently as well. Some grow up accommodating to objects at a distance, animals in a field or clouds on the horizon, while others calibrate their vision to the near requirements of machines. The same sort of tailoring pertains to sound, touch, and smell. Nor do all people share a distinction of what is the natural world versus what is human, or cultural, habitat. To some, the physical plane and living quarters are intermingled without boundary or differentiation; while other people, particularly in Western societies, think of nature, from which many risks stem, as separate and untamed (Lévi-Strauss 1966; Horigan 1988). As Gibson (1979) states, the environment in which people are active should not be confused with the actual physical world of "nature."

Whether nature is considered a separate realm or not bears consequence in terms of disaster, especially in efforts to reduce risk and calamity. Those who consider nature as apart from human contrivance often attempt to control it, generally by physical means. They erect levees, raise fire walls, and re-direct rivers. But since nature does not actually exist separate from ourselves, harnessing it to achieve safety, as many in the disaster field recognize, is rarely the answer. Risk reduction is a socio-cultural and perceptual problem, not a physical one.

How a people arrange the space they inhabit also affects vulnerability (Feld and Basso 1996; Low and Lawrence-Zuniga 2003). Some people consider any and all of the space around them as available for occupation and expand into it whether deemed safe or not. Other groups, according to sacred parameters or legal codes, strictly define what can be lived on and what must be left unoccupied. Cultures also narrate the density of human habitat upon their environments. Some cultures demonstrate a preference for clustered habitations, thus potentially making denizens more vulnerable to mudslides, firestorms, and earthquakes. Others mandate that people live spread out with yards and distances between them, potentially making people less vulnerable, or not. It depends on the surrounding hazards.

Far more crucial are a culture's concepts of what constitutes a peril. Danger and risk are, after all, not the same thing. Danger is an extant hazard that exists manifestly in the surroundings: a floodplane, an earthquake fault, a leaky factory. Risk is a calculation. Risk sits between people and danger much like a water faucet (Ingold 1992; Ruck 1993; Paine 2002). The faucet can be completely open so that a people comprehend all the dangers around them—flood, fire, oil rig. The faucet can be only partly open so that people acknowledge only some of the surrounding hazards, but are blind to others. Californians, for example, perceive that earthquakes are a threat and prepare for them, yet they are in almost total denial over firestorms, floods, and avalanches, which are more common and destructive on a yearly basis than earthquakes. Or a culture's perceptual faucet can be turned off completely so that a people recognize no danger at all. An illuminating instance comes from the Greeks who live on the island of Santorini. Santorini is an active volcano seven times larger than Krakatoa. Despite the fact that the volcano erupted twice in the twentieth century, caused a tremendous earthquake in 1956 and three small ones recently, the people voice no alarm. After I told a young woman there what I did, she declared, "Thank goodness we don't have problems like that here" (Hoffman 2014). Occasionally, people see the risk of exploiting a particular environment as too high and move, as have some on the Mississippi River flood bank. Others have discerned a serious peril in the built environment, as the people of Bhopal, India, actually did to no avail (Rajan 1999, 2002). Overall, however, it is when disasters are embedded in an environment, but are intermittent as opposed to chronic in their happening, like earthquakes or the recent destructive flash floods in Epirus, Greece, and Albania, that leads to most denial (Nellas and Semini 2015).

Part of a people's perception of both environment and risk also lies in their expressive culture, something few environmental or even disaster researchers consider. In every culture, the character of the landscape and the disasters within it have been the subject of mythology, legend, art, and literature for millennia. Hanging up on a wall, told around a campfire, or read in books, the portrayals carry profound impact. They set forth an illustration of potential risks and foretell what a disaster will be like. They function as an oracle and speak of consequence. Most of the portrayals are greatly repeated in a culture's lore; thus their continued depiction compounds their fixedness and seeps into the culture's capital like an echo of Jung's collective unconscious. Such stories range from Sodom and Gomorrah, Noah, the Eddas, Emperor Yao, Manu, Atlantis, Pompeii, but also encompass current fantasies and tales, such as stories of apocalypses, monumental eruptions, and gigantic tidal waves. Likewise, artistic depictions and, in contemporary times, factual and fictional movie and television portrayals inculcate images of disaster in people's impressions. People's prior experiences of disaster also create a pervasive idea of what peril exists or what a disaster will entail. Tales of former disasters led people to deny weather predictions and remain in their houses during both Hurricanes Sandy and Katrina (Hoffman 2002, 2005).

Anthropologist George Lakoff (Lakoff and Johnson 1980) and Nobel Prize-winning psychologist Daniel Kahneman (2011) both tell us that pre-formed concepts tend to become the formats by which people filter happenings and determine action, whether those formats take into account actuality or not. A culture's perceptions and images of both peril and the environment do just that. They tender a template by which people recognize, disregard, or readjust factualness. Moreover, when a compelling impression clashes with fact, it is the impression, not the fact, that usually prevails. Kahneman calls it the "illusion of validity." Memory, he says, automatically provides the narrative about what is going on, true or not, and suppresses alternatives. A people's environmental and disaster concepts thus affirm two old adages: the power of a tale "told a thousand times" and "a picture is worth a thousand words."

To put it another way, a people that experience or anticipate disaster in their environments stand on a pivot differentiating what their culture provides as a model "of" their environs and/or a calamity, and what becomes a model "for" their physical plane and/or a calamity. A model "of" is the symbolic presentation of the existing relationship between them and their physical, social, or spiritual environment. A model "for" presents an image of a post-ulated reality, complete with meanings, which could be realized with any happening to come. That is, whatever the culture has told them about the risk contained in their ecological, modified, or constructed surroundings is what they will perpetuate.

A people's treatment of time, like space, is also cardinal to how they envision their environment and disasters, as is the style in which they think. Some people think about the components of their surroundings and calculate the passage of time in a linear fashion. They see the physical plane as evolving and life unfolding in a progression, occasionally punctuated by notable episodes. Others, such as the Hindu, Tibetan, and ancient Mayans think of events and assess time in a cyclical fashion, meaning that all manner of things, including disasters, transpire on a re-occurring calendar no matter what intervenes. The implication for both locale and catastrophic events is that linear thought and time imply hope of change. Mitigation can potentially alter what might transpire. With cyclical thinking, mitigation is often dis-missed as useless since all situations and happenings are preordained (Friedel *et al.* 1993;

Hoffman 2002). Still, styles of thinking are not always as simple as they appear on a surface level. Occasionally, a people such as those in Western societies who seemingly think and calculate in a lineal fashion indulge the covert view that environmental processes, like climate change and disasters, are in fact cyclical. Some, even scientists, claim a calamity to be "the one hundred year flood" or "the fifty year eruption." Doing so instills the notion that a similar calamity will not occur again for a specified amount of time, though in truth, the same sort of incident can happen on any calendar (Hoffman 2002).

Place attachment

The most mysterious factor in people's relation to the environment, and subsequently in their vulnerability to disaster, is place attachment. The "why" of why people cling to a particular place remains enigmatic. In consequence of it, however, people hunker down and often refuse to leave a particular place despite the threat or arrival of a calamitous incident. They also return to the place after the calamity as rapidly as possible, undeterred by embedded peril or looming threat.

Some researchers have suggested that place attachment may be left over from early human evolution, only now instead of a hunting and gathering sphere, people prey on their local tavern and ravage the familiar grocery. Others link the phenomenon to familiarity of sights, smells, and sounds, citing that these generate comfort and security, however false (Altman and Low 1992). Whatever place attachment comes from, it is strong and it is global. Virtually everywhere, people adhere to their home notwithstanding cataclysm.

To describe place attachment, I have come to borrow a term from epicurean vocabulary, *terroir*. *Terroir* describes the loam of the earth, the texture of climate, and waft of air that engenders a special nature to what grows there, like wines. The marrow of a people's life also seems a product of the ground they occupy, the atmosphere they breathe, and the way they live. Denizens of a place feel it, smell it, taste it, as much as they maneuver it and manipulate it, and in some sense they themselves—their accents, dress, gestures—are a product of *terroir*. Despite the risks, they prefer to remain where they are. Along the Gulf Coast of Mississippi after Hurricanes Katrina, Rita, Ike, and Gustav, where new codes prohibit rebuilding, inhabitants have turned their old house foundations into picnic platforms on which they congregate every weekend. Various survivors of the Oakland–Berkeley firestorm rebuilt not only on the same house lot, but exactly the same house. Place attachment also seems to call out to people whose whole community has voluntarily moved to ensure safety. Slowly, but surely, many "drift back" to the former location.

The mystery of place attachment calls into question whether culture is embedded in a specific physical location and/or whether those retaining a particular culture are seeking to re-root it in its fermenting soil. Place attachment also bears critical implications toward the looming matter of climate change, storms, exigencies, and population resettlement. Place attachment could well stem from yet another matrix of reasons, including the visual landscape and the activities inherent in a distinct location. As Tim Ingold says,

> A place owes its character to the experiences it affords to those who spend time there – to the sights, sounds and indeed smells that constitute its specific ambience. And these, in turn, depend on the kinds of activities in which its inhabitants engage. It is from this relational context of people's engagement with the world, in the business of dwelling, that each place draws its unique significance.
>
> *(Ingold 2011: 192)*

Meanings also are not just attached to a certain landscape, they are "gathered from it" (Ingold 2011: 192). Separation from a specific place, therefore, bears implication not only for people's engagement, but for deeper significance and spirituality, which can seem irreplaceable. In Japan, the idea of *furusato*, meaning "home" or "ancestral" town, has great symbolic identity even for those who were not born there and may never have seen it (Gill 2013).

Land use, ownership, and inheritance systems also intermesh with place attachment. Fields, grazing pastures, or house lots are often so tenaciously held that holders or legatees squat upon them rather than seek aid or safety. After earthquakes, floods, or fires, Greeks will not leave their house plots to seek a disaster center. Instead, they camp in cars and tents on their demolished properties. After the 2004 tsunami in Sumatra, villagers placed flags directly into heaps of debris to mark the location of their individual gardens.

Other cultural elements

Without question, many other aspects of culture are intertwined with both the environments in which people live and the disruptions those environments chronically or intermittently undergo. I name but a few.

A people's social structure at times often corresponds to how the physical environment is owned and used, and also how disaster survival is accomplished (Altman and Low 1992). Bilateral kinship, where people consider blood relations to extend through both parents, for example, has been hypothesized as giving hunting and gathering people more flexibility to separate and unite in relation to available foodstuffs, but it also offers people in situations of chronic calamity greater availability for aid and shelter. Contrarily, unilineal kinship, where people calculate their kin through only one parent, provides collective resources of groupings such as clans, enabling the losses of some to be readily absorbed by the many. Whatever the kinship system, without a doubt, family in every society, including those far dispersed in contemporary society, plays a key role in disaster response (Hoffman 1994, 1998, 1999a). Kinsfolk descend upon disaster victims everywhere. Indeed, among certain groups, response to a calamity does not take place by isolated individuals or small nuclear families, but rather by extended family confederacies acting as a single entity (Browne 2015). Class, race, ethnicity, gender, and age also have great bearing on disaster vulnerability and survival worldwide (Enarson and Morrow 1998; Hoffman 2004).

That a people's religion and cosmology mirror their surroundings and their means of subsistence has deep grounding in anthropology. Animism has long been correlated with natural resource communities; calendars and weather deities are postulated as going hand in hand with agriculture. Rarely, though, has it been noted that certain religious ideologies correspond with embedded calamities. Numerous places where environmental upheavals are a chronic occurrence feature double-sided deities that are at times beneficent and at other times violent. Damballah and Kali figure among them. In other cases, certain deities are directly representative of catastrophic elements. Pele, for example, is specifically a goddess of volcanoes. Very often, communities that undergo calamities conceive of nature itself as two-sided. It is both mother and monster (Hoffman 2002). Particular religious mandates—for instance, belief in god's will—also influence disaster preparation and recovery, as do concepts of material property, whether a culture considers objects like furniture, weavings, pottery, photographs to be permanent or transitory. Also influential is a culture's innate flexibility. Some groups seem to recognize the need to adjust and do so with ease; others entomb the past and rigidly resist alteration.

Conclusion

One of the truly interesting things about disasters everywhere is that they are "revealers" (Garcia-Acosta 2002). They expose what has covertly taken place, in not just one, but all four environments—the physical, modified, built, and cultural—as well as in adaptation, perception, attachment, alliances, stratification, gender, symbolism, material culture, and more. Hurricane Katrina uncovered aspects of the Mississippi Delta's physical reality, along with severe defects within the modified environment, faulty construction of the levees that had been built, and also deeply persistent cultural biases, classism, racism, sexism, economic and political forces, family structure, housing archetypes, community function and dysfunction, ideals, religion, food preferences, dress styles, and on and on. Students of disaster have used such terms to describe them and their effects upon people and communities as "sweeping," "total," and "comprehensive," and that they are.

One final note: hand in hand with adaptation, the role of hazards and disasters in mobilizing forces of cultural change remains vastly understudied. Cultures are not static, and disasters almost inevitably compel societies to undertake immediate revisions in surroundings, habitats, and life ways. Along with short-term, emergency adjustments, they can also set in motion long-term adaptations (Sjoberg 1962; Hoffman 1999b), a facet of their occurrence that bears heed in times of changing use of environment, changing climate, and the need for risk reduction.

References

Altman, Irwin and S. Low (eds). 1992. *Place Attachment*. Human Behavior and the Environment series, Volume 12. Thousand Oaks, CA: Sage Publications.

Belshaw, Cyril. 1951. "Social Consequence of the Mount Lamington Eruption." *Oceania* 21(4): 241–251.

Berlin, Brent and P. D. Kay. 1969. *Basic Color Terms*. Berkeley: University of California Press.

Blaikie, Piers, T. Cannon, I. Davis and B. Wisner. 1994. *At Risk: Natural Hazards, People's Vulnerability and Disasters*. London: Routledge.

Browne, Katherine. 2015. *Standing in the Need: Culture, Comfort, and Coming Home after Katrina*. Austin: University of Texas Press.

Button, Gregory. 2010. *Disaster Culture*. Walnut Creek, CA: Left Coast Press.

Cosgrove, Denis and S. Daniels. 1988. "Introduction: Iconography and Landscape." In D. Cosgrove and S. Daniels (eds) *The Iconography of Landscape*. Cambridge, UK: Cambridge University Press, pp. 1–10.

Crumley, Carole (ed.). 1994. *Historical Ecology*. Santa Fe, NM: School of American Research Press.

Enarson, Elaine and B. Morrow (eds). 1998. *The Gendered Terrain of Disasters: Through Women's Eyes*. Westport, CT: Greenwood Publishing Group.

Erikson, Kai. 1976. *Everything in its Path: Destruction of Community in the Buffalo Creek Flood*. New York: Simon and Schuster.

Feld, Steven and K. Basso (eds). 1996. *Senses of Place*. Santa Fe, NM: School of American Research Press.

Firth, Raymond. 1959. *Social Change in Tikopia*. London: Allen & Unwin.

Friedel, David, L. Schele and J. Parker. (1993). *Maya Cosmos*. New York: Morrow.

Garcia-Acosta, Virginia. 2002. "Historical Disaster Research." In S. M. Hoffman and A. Oliver-Smith (eds) *Catastrophe and Culture: The Anthropology of Disaster*. Santa Fe, NM: School of American Research Press, pp. 49–68.

Gibson, James J. 1979. *The Ecological Approach to Visual Perception*. Boston, MA: Houghton Mifflin.

Gill, Thomas. 2013. "This Spoiled Place: People, Place and Community in an Irradiated Village in Fukushima Prefecture." In T. Gill, B. Steger and D. Slater (eds) *Japan Copes with Calamity*. Bern: Peter Lang Publishers, pp. 201–234.

Goodman, Alan and T. Leatherman (eds). 1998. *Building a New Biocultural Synthesis*. Ann Arbor: University of Michigan Press.

Hartman, Chester and G. Squires (eds). 2006. *There is No Such Thing as a Natural Disaster: Race, Class and Hurricane Katrina*. New York: Routledge.

Harvey, David. 1996. *Justice, Nature, and the Geography of Difference*. Cambridge, MA: Blackwell.

Hoffman, Susanna M. 1994. "Up from the Embers: A Disaster Survivor's Story." *Clinical Quarterly, National Center for Post-Traumatic Stress* 4(2): 15–16.

—— 1998. "Eve and Adam among the Embers: Gender Patterns after the Oakland Berkeley Firestorm." In E. Enarson and B. H. Morrow (eds) *The Gendered Terrain of Disasters: Through Women's Eyes*. Westport, CT: Greenwood Publishing Group, pp. 55–61.

—— 1999a. "The Regenesis of Traditional Gender Patterns in the Wake of Disaster." In A. Oliver-Smith and S. M. Hoffman (eds) *The Angry Earth: Disasters in Anthropological Perspective*. New York: Routledge, pp. 173–191.

—— 1999b. "After Atlas Shrugs: Cultural Change or Persistence after a Disaster." In A. Oliver-Smith and S. M. Hoffman (eds) *The Angry Earth: Disasters in Anthropological Perspective*. New York: Routledge, pp. 302–326.

—— 2002. "The Monster and the Mother: The Symbolism of Disaster." In S. M. Hoffman and A. Oliver-Smith (eds) *Catastrophe and Culture: The Anthropology of Disaster*. Santa Fe, NM: School of American Research Press, pp. 113–142.

—— 2004. "Hidden Victims of Disaster." *Environmental Hazards* 5(2): 67–70.

—— 2005. "Katrina and Rita: A Disaster Anthropologist's Thoughts." *Anthropology News* 46(8): 19.

—— 2014. "Culture: The Crucial Factor in Hazard, Risk and Disaster Recovery: The Anthropological Perspective." In A. Collins (ed.) *Hazards, Risks, and Disasters in Society*. London: Elsevier.

Hoffman, Susanna M. and A. Oliver-Smith. 2002. *Catastrophe and Culture*. Santa Fe, NM: School of American Research Press.

Horigan, Stephen. 1988. *Nature and Culture in Western Discourses*. London: Routledge.

Hruschka, Daniel, D. Lende and C. Worthman. 2005. "Biocultural Dialogues: Biology and Culture in Psychological Anthropology." *Ethos* 33(1): 1–19.

Ingold, Tim. 1992. "Culture and the Perception of the Environment." In E. Cross and D. Parkin (eds) *Bush, Base: Forest Farm*. London: Routledge, pp. 39–55.

—— 2011. *The Perception of the Environment*. New York: Routledge.

Kahneman, Daniel. 2011. *Thinking Fast and Slow*. New York: Farrar, Strauss and Giroux.

Kroll-Smith, J. Stephen and S. R. Couch. 1991. "What Is a Disaster: An Ecological Symbolic Approach to Resolving the Debate." *International Journal of Mass Emergencies and Disaster* 9(3): 355–366.

Lakoff, George and M. Johnson. 1980. *Metaphors We Live By*. Chicago, IL: University of Chicago Press.

Lévi-Strauss, Claude. 1966. *The Savage Mind*. Chicago, IL: University of Chicago Press.

Lovejoy, Paul and S. Baier. 1976. "The Desert-Side Economy of the Central Sudan." In Michael Glantz (ed.) *The Politics of Natural Disaster*. New York: Praeger, pp. 145–175.

Low, Setha and D. Lawrence-Zuniga. 2003. *The Anthropology of Space and Place: Locating Culture*. Oxford: Blackwell.

McCabe, J. Terrence. 2002. "Impact of and Response to Drought, among Turkana Pastoralists: Implications for Anthropological Theory and Hazard Research." In S. M. Hoffman and A. Oliver-Smith (eds) *Catastrophe and Culture: The Anthropology of Disaster*. Santa Fe, NM: School of American Research Press, pp. 213–236.

Moseley, Michael. 1999. "Convergent Catastrophe: Past Patterns and Future Implications of Collateral Natural Disasters in the Andes." In A. Oliver-Smith and S. M. Hoffman (eds), *The Angry Earth: Disaster in Anthropological Perspective*. New York: Routledge, pp. 59–72.

—— 2002. "Modeling Protracted Drought, Collateral Natural Disaster, and Human Responses in the Andes." In S. M. Hoffman and A. Oliver-Smith (eds) *Catastrophe and Culture: The Anthropology of Disaster*. Santa Fe, NM: School of American Research Press, pp. 187–212.

Nellas, Demetris and L. Semini. 2015. "Flash Floods Hit Greece, Albania, Force Evacuations." *Associated Press*, 1 February 2015.

Oliver-Smith, Anthony. 1999. "Peru's Five-Hundred Year Earthquake." In A. Oliver-Smith and S. M. Hoffman (eds) *The Angry Earth: Disaster in Anthropological Perspective*. New York: Routledge, pp. 74–88.

Oliver-Smith, Anthony and S. M. Hoffman (eds). 1999. *The Angry Earth: Disaster in Anthropological Perspective*. New York: Routledge.

—— 2002. "Introduction." In S. M. Hoffman and A. Oliver-Smith (eds) *Catastrophe and Culture: The Anthropology of Disaster*. Santa Fe, NM: School of American Research Press, pp. 3–4.

Paine, Robert. 2002. "Danger and the No-Risk Thesis." In S. M. Hoffman and A. Oliver-Smith (eds) *Catastrophe and Culture: The Anthropology of Disaster*. Santa Fe, NM: School of American Research Press, pp. 67–90.

Patterson, Thomas. 1994. "Toward a Properly Historical Ecology." In C. Crumley (ed.) *Historical Ecology: Cultural Knowledge and Changing Landscapes*. Santa Fe, NM: School of American Research Press, pp. 223–238.

Quarantelli, Enrico (ed.). 1998. *What Is a Disaster? Perspectives on the Question*. New York: Routledge.

Rajan, S. Ravi. 1999. "Bhopal: Vulnerability, Routinization, and Chronic Disaster." In A. Oliver-Smith and S. M. Hoffman (eds) *The Angry Earth: Disaster in Anthropological Perspective*. New York: Routledge, pp. 257–277.

—— 2002. "Missing Expertise, Categorical Politics, and Chronic Disasters: The Case of Bhopal." In S. M. Hoffman and A. Oliver-Smith (eds) *Catastrophe and Culture: The Anthropology of Disaster*. Santa Fe, NM: School of American Research Press, pp. 237–260.

Redmond, Charles. 1999. *Human Impact on Ancient Environments*. Tucson: University of Arizona Press.

Ruck, Bayerische (ed.). 1993. *Risk Is a Construct: Perceptions of Risk Perception*. Munich: Knesebeck.

Schneider, David. 1957. "Typhoons on Yap." *Human Organization* 16(2): 10–15.

Schwimmer, Eric. 1969. *Cultural Consequences of a Volcanic Eruption Experienced by the Mt. Lamington Orokaiva*. Salem: University of Oregon Press.

Sheets, Payson. 1999. "The Effects of Explosive Volcanism on Ancient Egalitarian, Ranked, and Stratified Societies in Middle America." In A. Oliver-Smith and S. M. Hoffman (eds) *The Angry Earth: Disaster in Anthropological Perspective*. New York: Routledge, pp. 36–58.

Sjoberg, Gideon. 1962. "Disasters and Social Change." In G. Baker and D. Chapman (eds) *Man and Society in Disaster*. New York: Basic Books, pp. 356–384.

Wallace, Anthony F. C. 1956. *Human Behavior in Extreme Situations*. Washington, DC: National Academy of Sciences–National Research Council.

Westgate, Kenneth N. and P. O'Keefe. 1976. Some Definitions of Disaster. Occasional Paper No. 4. Bradford, UK: University of Bradford Disaster Research Unit.

17

ADAPTATION, VULNERABILITY, AND RESILIENCE

Contested concepts in the anthropology of climate change

Anthony Oliver-Smith

Introduction

Understanding the effects that climate change has on human communities depends on developing appropriate conceptual tools that can adequately frame the socio-cultural construction of risks and effects and the impacts of those effects. Adaptation, vulnerability, and resilience are concepts that have been deployed to understand the effects of climate change and to inform the development of strategies and practices to reduce both the risks and impacts of climate change (Fiske *et al.* 2014). Originally developed in biology, adaptation plays a central role in natural selection and evolution. In cultural anthropology, adaptation has been used to understand how cultures use their natural resources for social reproduction and long-term survival in their total environment. Vulnerability and resilience, emerging from disaster research and ecology respectively, are framed as conditions that in some sense serve as indices of the success or failure of adaptive strategies. Employing the three concepts engages multiple socio-cultural variables in articulation with the uncertainties in evolving climate change scenarios. Moreover, as social processes, adaptation, vulnerability, and resilience evolve in the relational and emergent nature of socio-ecological systems (Murphy *et al.* 2016). In that sense, the frequent deployment of these concepts as apolitical and technocratic tools for neutral interventions for the protection of society may actually undermine local efforts to adjust to climate change effects (Smucker *et al.* 2015).

The social impacts of climate change involve a specific articulation between local social and cultural organization and increasingly complex and uncertain climate and weather phenomena (Crate and Nuttall 2009). Human adaptation to the natural environment is neither a biological nor a technical response of an undifferentiated population to physical or material conditions. It is always internally complex, involving the diverse interests, knowledge, and meanings of a differentiated population, interacting within both the material processes of a complex and dynamic physical setting and a set of social, political, economic, and ideological institutions and practices. Today this interaction is made more complex by local engagement with international, national, regional, and other non-local institutions and the constraints and options they involve for decision-making, often making adaptation an even more political process. Moreover, these interacting variables occur on multiple spatial and temporal scales for a wide variety of adaptive agents (individuals, families, communities, etc.), each with differing values, priorities, and goals, which are all inflected by ethical considerations (Johnson 2013).

These ethical concerns partially mobilize international and national policies for mitigating and adapting to climate change effects. The United Nations Framework Convention on Climate Change (UNFCCC 1992: online) defines climate change as "a change of climate which is attributed directly or indirectly to human activity that alters the composition of the global atmosphere and which is in addition natural climate variability observed over comparable time periods." Climate is generally characterized by averages and human adaptation is normally directed and conditioned by these norms. Extreme events are fundamentally weather events, although extremes become factored into climate variability (Lavell 2011). Both climate and weather and their effects are influenced locally by such factors as topography, ground cover, and human action.

It is within these parameters of variability, between averages and extremes, that the notions of adaptation (and mitigation), vulnerability, and resilience in human individuals, communities, and societies must be understood. Under specific conditions of vulnerability, even relatively minor events in terms of the physical energy released can create extreme disasters. Since many of the harshest effects of climate change will manifest as natural hazards (storms, floods, droughts, etc.), the fields of disaster research and disaster risk reduction will be highly relevant. Indeed, even a small increase in averages can push people living at the margins from chronic risk into acute risk. Here efforts to assist local adaptation are more appropriately focused on extreme vulnerability than extreme events. It will be largely a response to changes in climate averages that will guide new forms of production, energy uses, and resource (water) storage capacities and technologies. However, to the extent possible, extremes must be integrated into the overall adaptation framework, although it is generally impossible to mitigate irregular or unpredictable events completely (Lavell 2011).

Adaptation, vulnerability, and resilience are seen today as essential in framing and developing responses to climate change, despite debates over their overall value. These concepts pose complex problems for both analysis and application, in part because they suffer from a lack of precision in the way they have been used. Their adoption by multiple disciplines has resulted in considerable inconsistency and a lack of clarity, particularly with regard to issues of temporal and spatial scales, cross-scale interactions, and the fundamental units of analysis and application. Some of the definitions derive from different conceptual starting points and assumptions, posing different questions about adaptation, vulnerability, and resilience, some focusing mainly on human security issues and others adopting a more holistic perspective (O'Brien *et al.* 2007). In their presentation as neutral, technocratic instruments, the political dimensions of their application are obscured (Smucker *et al.* 2015). This variation has the potential to either reveal or obscure important questions. Nevertheless, this lack of coherence and consistency has not impeded their deployment as policy instruments for purposes of multiple agendas across a wide range of social and political interests. However, anthropological perspectives on adaptation, vulnerability, and resilience, grounded in a tradition of holistic research on local lifeways, often vary significantly from those used in the climate change literature and policy frameworks.

This chapter has started with a consideration of the use of the concepts of adaptation, vulnerability, and resilience in the framing of the challenges of climate change. The second section deals with the way adaptation has been used in anthropological research in general, followed by an analysis of its use in the study of climate change effects. The chapter then considers the transformation of the concept of adaptation into a policy instrument in climate change governance and practice. The next three sections examine the subsidiary concepts of vulnerability and resilience in terms of their salience in understanding climate change impacts and their practical and policy implications for adaptation projects. Since it has recently been concluded that climate change will produce effects for which no adaptation is deemed possible, the question of the limits of adaptation is considered for its conceptual, practical, and ethical problems as a final topic.

Adaptation: the anthropological perspective

Originating in biological ecology, adaptation, defined as the process of developing or enhancing structural, physiological, and/or genetically coded behavioral characteristics that improve an organism's chances for survival and reproduction, is inherent in natural selection. However, when a concept traverses the terrain between the natural and social sciences, it may undergo an alteration in its definition. It is useful to distinguish between adaptation and adaptability as the capacity to adjust to changing circumstances (Hetherington 2012). From a cultural anthropological perspective, adaptation now refers to learned behavior in response to environmental change and is the fundamental conceptual nexus of a socio-ecological system. In anthropology, adaptation generally refers to changes in belief and/or behavior in response to altered circumstances to improve the conditions of existence, including a culturally meaningful life. In the process of adaptation, human and natural systems co-construct socio-ecological systems (Collins *et al.* 2013).

The socio-cultural system is the primary means by which humans adjust to the resources and hazards of their total environment. Human adaptation has a wider number of attendant features for adaptive capacity including complex human cognition, social organization, values and meanings. Thus, human beings do not just adapt unconsciously as reactive organisms. Through cultural means humans perceive changes, consider their implications and possible responses through a grid of individually interpreted cultural knowledge and meaning, and make decisions and elaborate responses, including the deployment of technology, that may reflect a variety of value positions. This enables them to reconfigure themselves without losing functionality (Folke *et al.* 2002a). Further, the complexity of human societies virtually ensures that outcomes will be equally complex, often with unequal and/ or unanticipated results.

Two dimensions are crucial to the process of adaptation. The first involves the interplay between individual and group or between differently constituted groups. What may be adaptive for the individual may be maladaptive for the group, and vice versa. How choices are made is not purely an issue of biological adaptation, but is cultural, or specifically, political in nature, reflecting social values and power relations. The second dimension involves the issue of choices and action in a proximate time frame that may bear unanticipated longer-term adaptive implications.

To survive, to ensure maintenance, demographic replacement, and social reproduction, including culturally meaningful lives, humans interact with nature, both shaping and being shaped, through a set of material practices that are socially constituted and culturally meaningful (Patterson 1994: 223). Socially constructed meanings create frameworks through which alternative material and social practices are analyzed, evaluated, and prioritized (Crane 2010). All are accomplished through social arrangements; all modify the natural and social world in ways that enable to some degree the persistence of the society, which also entails the sustainability of the environment, through time. The goals of survival, maintenance, demographic replacement, social reproduction, and meaning are culturally extremely variable, which complicates interpretation and application in specific circumstances.

Humans also must adapt to a set of socially constructed institutional circumstances (Bennett 1996). That is, they do not just adapt to natural features, land, or water, for example; but also to human institutions such as labor, economics, markets, schools, governments, and churches and the resources and constraints they present. In that sense, our institutions are at once part of our adaptation, but must be adapted to as well through "second order adaptations" (Birkmann 2011). Moreover, human adaptation is not simply a function of technical adjustment, but also involves the need to frame responses that accord with social and cultural parameters (Crate 2008).

Therefore, an adaptation is part of a lifeway, in effect, an "evolved practice or perspective," the way things are done, that is both culturally sanctioned and socially enacted. This differs from coping, often conflated with adaptation, which refers to decision-making in novel situations when there is no ready culturally integrated institutionalized response. Coping behavior involves immediate problem-solving and decision-making, including improvisation and creativity. Adaptations, on the other hand, are part of the fund of general knowledge and practice in a culture, in effect, part of the overall "toolkit" for survival in a particular environment. Coping strategies that effectively address challenges without longer-term negative outcomes may be adopted as established practices and come to constitute culturally sanctioned and socially enacted adaptations or adaptive strategies (Bennett 1996).

In effect, adaptation implies social and cultural change, which is rarely purely reactive and usually complex, involving the articulation of a change in belief or behavior with many, if not all, other dimensions of life. For example, the relatively integrated nature of culture suggests that a change in livelihood strategies may reverberate in other aspects of local life (Bennett 1996). Although rarely happening rapidly, sometimes the occurrence of a severe disaster will stimulate rapid alterations in the way of doing things, but the tendency—some might say, the resilience—of pre-disaster systems to reassert themselves in the aftermath is evidence that such rapid change is not inevitable.

Adaptation as climate change policy instrument

The adaptation concept is now central in climate policy domains. It is now considered to be a policy option since it was recognized that mitigation policies directed toward reducing greenhouse gas emissions had, in large part, failed. In effect, the use of the term adaptation has shifted from referring to a basic and omnipresent process of change in life to being a policy-driven set of formal strategies and projects (Nelson *et al.* 2007).

In 2001, the Intergovernmental Panel on Climate Change (IPCC: 89–90) defined adaptation as an "Adjustment in natural or human systems to a new or changing environment." Various types of adaptation were noted, including anticipatory (otherwise known as mitigation) and reactive adaptation, private and public adaptation, and autonomous and planned adaptation. In the domain of climate policy, the concept of mitigation refers primarily to the reduction of greenhouse gases, while adaptation refers to adjusting to or managing changing conditions (Smit and Wandel 2006).

Adaptation projects address a wide variety of issues related to climate change, such as drought and desertification, water management, disease vector expansions (malaria, dengue, cholera), agricultural diversification, river basin management, seasonal forecasting, flooding, sea-level rise, and conservation, to mention only a few. In many instances, such projects, sponsored by governments, international organizations, and civil society, are similar to externally generated sustainable development projects, something to promote perhaps, but not automatically adaptations. Such projects may become adaptations when they themselves are adapted to and integrated into cultural knowledge and practice, in effect becoming part of the "toolkit."

There is concern about the way adaptation has become a key element in climate change policy, despite failing to capture the full impacts of climate change. Nor, as it is used, does it accurately represent local perceptions or priorities of affected people or the options available to them. Critics complain about the excessive focus on specific biophysical stressors and the tendency to ignore broader social and cultural ramifications of interventions (Orlove 2009; Lavell 2011; Oliver-Smith 2013). These questions in turn are complicated by issues of scale both in analysis and application. The time frames in which natural and social processes unfold are different. Generally, responses to current problems are short-term and often produce unintended consequences. Short-term responses are largely coping strategies that tend to make societies more vulnerable in the long run. Long-term responses, however, are usually not appreciated, when the problem is immediate and people want to see quick results (Giddens 2009). Spatially, adaptations that may be effective in one context may prove to have negative effects either up or down spatial and organizational scales, underscoring the importance of local institutions in the way adaptation programs and practices are developed and applied (Agrawal 2008).

The question then is whether adaptation projects are truly adaptive, or are they basically coping strategies for specific biophysical stressors, which fail to address fundamental problems of risk and vulnerability. Although the research literature engages with this issue (Pelling 2011), the question of systemically imposed vulnerability does not usually get factored into adaptation projects. In effect, people may be adapting more to systemic vulnerability imposed by society, and thus, actually reinforcing it, than to climate change itself. The question, then, is whether adaptation as it is being currently framed, is at least in part, adjusting so that the status quo can persist? The problems of the poor and vulnerable did not start with climate change. They may have become worse with the effects of climate change, but focusing on limiting specific effects of climate change fails to address systemically imposed social vulnerability.

The social construction of vulnerability

The concept of vulnerability emerged in the 1970s from the field of disaster research. Geographers and anthropologists researching hazards and disasters in the developing world found mainstream disaster literature to be lacking explanations for why disasters were so much worse in the global South and proposed that it was necessary to take "the naturalness out of natural disasters" (O'Keefe *et al.* 1976: 566). Their focus shifted toward the multiple social causes at various scales in the normal order of things that imposed risk on specific populations and increased disaster impact (Hewitt 1983). Vulnerability, therefore, encompasses many complex and interconnected social, economic, demographic, environmental, and political processes and parameters, making it difficult to define exactly because many of the social forces that drive it are harder to conceptualize succinctly and to quantify (Thywissen 2006).

Although the term vulnerability is now used in many fields, for disaster researchers and practitioners, it describes the extent to which a community, family, or individual is either susceptible or resilient to the impact of the natural hazards of its particular socio-ecological system. The condition of vulnerability is the result of various factors, including awareness of hazards, settlement and infrastructural patterns, public policy and administration, the level of societal development, socio-economic structure, and institutional capacities in disaster and risk management (Wisner *et al.* 2004).

There are many approaches and models for vulnerability, some focusing on broadening and deepening spatial and temporal scales to identify causal linkages between root causes, dynamic pressures, and unsafe conditions which, when combined with a natural hazard, produce a disaster (Wisner *et al.* 2004; Integrated Research on Disaster Risk 2011). Others, for example Turner *et al.* (2003), reduce the temporal dimension and focus on detailing exposure, susceptibility, coping, impact response, capacity, adaptive capacity, and interactions with perturbations and stressors as elements of vulnerability. However, at the most basic level, there is general agreement that vulnerability is a necessary precondition for a disaster to take place and refers to the social characteristics and conditions of a group that place people at risk in terms of their abilities to anticipate, respond to, and recover from a disaster impact (Wisner *et al.* 2004). Since vulnerability is socially produced, risk in society is therefore unevenly distributed, indicating that not everyone in specific environments will be equally vulnerable to climate change effects. Vulnerability thus explicitly ties environmental issues, such as hazards, in with the structure and organization of society, and the rights accorded to membership in that society. Since total environmental security is not possible, every social context is characterized by some level of vulnerability. In that sense vulnerability is an intrinsic, but dynamic, multi-dimensional aspect of every society that is independent of the magnitude of any particular hazard (Oliver-Smith 2002).

However, some researchers claim that the widespread acceptance of the vulnerability concept results in underestimating the importance of exposure to specific hazards (Birkmann 2011). Others caution that the frequent conflation of vulnerability with poverty overlooks many communities, though extremely poor, that have high levels of social organizational adaptive capacity (otherwise known as resilience) and have developed effective strategies for dealing with environmental threats (Laska and Peterson 2013). Still others see vulnerability as a potentially disempowering concept for local populations (Cannon 2008; Cameron 2012). Defining a community as vulnerable may mask important forms of social organizational agency, representing it as helpless in the face of environmental forces. Vulnerability began as a critical concept, but is now frequently used simply as a term to describe a set of conditions. In that sense, it has been de-historicized and has lost some of its critical edge.

Social vulnerability and climate change effects and impacts

The climate change literature generally takes a different approach to social vulnerability from that taken by disaster research. The IPCC (2007) definition is concerned with

> the degree to which a system is susceptible to and unable to cope with adverse effects of climate change, including climate variability and extremes. Vulnerability is a function of the character, magnitude, and rate of climate change and variation to which a system is exposed, its sensitivity, and its adaptive capacity.
>
> *(IPCC 2007: 6)*

This approach can be seen as a return to an emphasis on exposure to physical processes rather than the social construction of risk (Kelman and Gaillard 2010). Designing a policy-relevant research agenda on vulnerability and the social impacts of climate change is challenging because it requires combining global projections, their local and regional manifestations, and local patterns of vulnerability that are constructed by local, regional, and global processes. Although more extreme events in the future are very likely, most of the effects of climate change will probably be gradual, affecting communities already dealing with high levels of social vulnerability. These processes potentially turn creeping, chronic risk or disaster into rapid-onset disaster (Lavell 2011). Therefore, climate change will tend to increase the frequencies and exacerbate impacts of existing hazards, the effects of which are largely the outcome of existing local social vulnerabilities. Moreover, by undermining local resilience, climate change effects may increase the vulnerability of people to earthquakes and other hazards not linked to climate change. Even when the hazard driven by climate change is novel, its impacts will still be expressed, coped with, and/or adapted to in the context of local patterns of social vulnerability. Effective interventions, therefore, should begin with a sustainable development orientation aimed at reducing vulnerability and enhancing resilience in changing environmental conditions. Efforts should be focused on the social vulnerabilities, including deficits in wealth and power, which render people susceptible to hazards, as well as on the challenges in adapting to biophysical changes in those hazards.

Since many climate change effects will accentuate existing hazards, adaptation projects should draw on measures developed in disaster risk reduction to focus on the processes that increase exposure and vulnerability and strain the capacity of communities to cope with events made more extreme by climate change processes (Birkmann and von Teichman 2010). Climate change adaptation and disaster risk reduction should be complementary, designed to address those social and economic features that render people vulnerable to environmental hazards in general, which are fundamentally development-related phenomena (Kelman and Gaillard 2010). This approach to vulnerability and resilience is consistent with development that directly addresses problems of poverty, malnutrition, health, education, and access to resources, as well as ecological integrity that can at the same time increase local resilience (Cannon and Müller-Mahn 2010).

Resilience and adaptive capacity

When the concept of vulnerability emerged in the 1970s, ecological science, drawing on physics and engineering, began to refer to an ecosystem's capacity to respond to disturbance by resisting damage and recovering quickly as resilience (Holling 1973). Resilience in ecology was seen as an outcome of an adaptive cycle (exploitation, conservation, release, and reorganization), developed to understand the character and dynamics of change in socio-ecological systems at various stages (Gunderson and Holling 2002; Folke *et al.* 2002b, 2004). By building system-wide resilience through "analysis, adaptive resource management, and adaptive governance" (Walker *et al.* 2004: 5), ecologists hope to reverse the decline in biodiversity.

Resilience now figures importantly in both climate change research and policy, but largely without the adaptive cycle framework. Resilience refers to the ability to prepare and plan for, absorb, recover from, or more successfully adapt to actual or potential adverse events (National Research Council 2012). In this view, resilience in a community is portrayed as a function of internal coherence, social solidarity, and the capacity to organize and work on its own behalf in dealing with climate change effects. When resilience is framed this way, it begins to resemble adaptation rather closely.

There are considerable reservations about the utility of the resilience concept, but many social scientists and policy makers still apply the concept to society, defining resilience as the ability of social groups or individuals to bear or absorb sudden or slow changes and variation without collapsing (Holling and Meffe 1996). Community resilience is rooted in the historical, social, and cultural constructions that govern social interaction, local management institutions, and material development. To understand how communities can reduce risk and losses from climate change, attention should be paid to feedbacks in adaptive governance for preparedness and disaster mitigation activities, through social learning that eventually may enhance adaptive capacity over longer periods of time (Cutter *et al.* 2008).

Adaptive governance is a recurrent theme in resilience research. Approaches to resilience building in communities range from centralized, top-down projects, focusing on specific biophysical climate change effects to efforts that also draw on science, but stress engagement with community building and multi-level politics (Brunner and Lynch 2010; Cote and Nightingale 2012). Politically feasible and equitable resilience projects must engage diverse stakeholders and their implementation must adapt when conditions change.

However, resilience theory lacks the archaeological and/or historical attention to time and space scales that can capture not only rapid variables, but also the slower-changing processes at work in what appear to be stable systems (Crumley 2013). In the context of climate change, longer time frames are useful to see that landscapes are not stable: impacts on land use, culture, politics, and environments do matter, at time scales both short and long. From the perspective of longer time frames, the resilience concept does prove useful in conceptualizing socio-ecological processes of change and stability.

However, resilience is still problematical in that it is both an analytic scientific lens and a normative cultural concept. Analysis of socio-ecological resilience based on empirical research must engage with normative culturally-framed value propositions (Crane 2010). Local patterns of resilience are culturally defined and socially enacted. In resilience-building projects, social constructions of meaning (culture) must be integrated with materialist analysis of adaptive socio-ecological processes. Adaptive strategies may impart resilience to the ecological material components of a socio-ecological system, but such changes for local people may impact deeply held traditional values and beliefs, enacting significant and unanticipated transformation of the culture (Crane 2010).

The cultural side of resilience requires that livelihoods which fulfill both material and moral needs be supported to maintain a sense of continuity of meaning and coherence in contexts of major change (Marris 1975; Crane 2010). Research on rapid or radical change suggests that disruption driven by climate change will have severe cultural impacts on physical and mental health, including an increased incidence of mental health problems (Willcox *et al.* 2013). These findings are consistent with research in disaster studies and development-forced displacement and resettlement (Turton 2006). Moreover, top-down adaptation projects imposed with or without a resilience framework carry a similar disruptive potential with concomitant second-order adaptations necessary (Birkmann 2011).

Questions have also been raised about the implications of resilience for stability or change. Adaptation from a resilience standpoint, rather than replicating the present, is seen by some to promote the capacity to deal with future change (Nelson *et al.* 2007). Resilience is thus oriented toward maintaining flexibility and adaptive capacity to handle future stressors. However, resilience defined as the ability to absorb disturbance, be reorganized, and retain the same basic structure and ways of functioning, contains an emphasis on stability and continuity, which may include patterns of vulnerability, inequality, and exploitation. In effect, resilience, which has garnered considerable policy salience, tends to shift the burden of responsibility and action toward communities and away from addressing the systemically imposed vulnerabilities.

Like adaptation and vulnerability, resilience as a broad concept must be specified to be of use in research, policy, and practice. For example, resilience can be applied to a wide range of units of analysis, such as an individual or household, to socially defined groups such as the elderly, the private sector, or even infrastructure (such as levees) (Nelson *et al.* 2009). From a spatial perspective, resilience may be seen as a property of communities, cities, or ecosystems (Cutter *et al.* 2008). An issue with far-reaching policy implications pertains to what the unit of analysis is resilient to. Is a community resilient to the ongoing stressors of a social system that distributes risks and losses unequally? Or to a set of biophysical changes set in motion by climate change effects, implying a return to a pre-1970s model of natural hazards as drivers of risk and disasters (Kelman and Galliard 2010)?

Limits of adaptation to climate change

The first major policy response to climate change developed under the Kyoto Protocol, adopted in 1997 and entered into force in 2005, promoted mitigation to reduce the amount of greenhouse gas emissions. However, it soon became clear that it was too late to fully mitigate climate change. Subsequently, the Cancun Adaptation Framework (2010) was developed to help affected communities and regions to adapt to current and future changes. Now it is increasingly recognized that adaptation processes are complex and may face limitations in their applications and effectiveness. The recent climate talks in Doha (2012) and Warsaw (2013) have focused on policy responses to the limits of adaptation. Such limitations have been discussed in terms of absolute thresholds in biological, economic, or technological parameters (Adger *et al.* 2009). For human systems, discussions of supposedly absolute economic or technological adaptation limits do not generally recognize them as culturally defined and socially enacted; in effect, a matter of choice and decision-making (Oliver-Smith 2013). Some limits on adaptation may actually be purposeful strategies to protect a status quo that favors the interests of some groups over others, thus reflecting a conservative dimension in resilience. Therefore, adaptation limits for human systems involve more than biophysical risks, raising questions about adaptation goals, acceptable and unacceptable risks, and the malleability of culture and society.

If adaptive capacity is seen as open-ended, indefinitely elastic, responsibility shifts away from mitigating greenhouse gases toward strategies and resources for adaptation (Dow *et al.* 2013). Since human adaptation is basically socio-cultural, and therefore at least somewhat flexible, then it is difficult to actually define absolute limits, beyond those endangering physical existence. However, defining limits as cultural suggests that they can then be overridden, thus rendering the community open to top-down adaptation interventions that serve non-local agendas and possible violations of human rights. In that sense—defining an adaptation limit ultimately as a function of local culture—establishing absolute adaptation limits thus presents significant conceptual, practical, and ethical problems. By the same token, conceptualizing adaptation limits as essentially flexible suggests that communities will be adaptable to risks that might actually be overwhelming and thus creates a similar set of problems.

Furthermore, adaptive capacity is not uniform throughout a community, but inflected by social, economic, and political factors. Each case will involve a complex interaction between local factors, such as knowledge, resources, power, adaptive capacity, and cultural values, and the intensity of an environmental threat. The capacity of people to adapt will be limited not only by the intensity of environmental risk or impact, but also by the vulnerability or resilience of their circumstances. Since the circumstances of vulnerability and resilience manifest in multiple ways and through differential access to resources, many "limits" may actually be externally imposed. The array of responses, adaptive and otherwise, will involve a range of strategies in belief and/or behavior that may engage social, cultural, and technological change that nonetheless, if they are to be successful, must be integrated into the fabric of local understandings, attitudes, and values.

Conclusion

Adaptation, vulnerability, and resilience, despite the inconsistencies in definitions and applications, have become central to academic research and policy frameworks on climate change. Each concept is articulated with and involved in the formulation and application of the others. Indeed, changes in conditions of vulnerability and/or resilience are currently leading to situations that are exceeding any capacities to adapt, bringing about irrevocable losses.

Adaptation requires change, but the direction and purpose of that change must be defined. In one context, adaptation as currently deployed may foster approaches that more deeply embed current environmental relations, power and wealth differences, and exploitation (Felli and Castree 2012). Interventions that do not challenge current systemic practices may promote or exacerbate vulnerability. Vulnerability analysis therefore becomes a virtual requirement prior to any adaptation intervention if it is to have any transformational potential (Ribot 2011). Is transformational adaptation, in the sense of "a change in the fundamental attributes of a system based on altered paradigms, goal or values" possible (IPCC 2013: 27)? As currently practiced, much climate change adaptation today does not address the real adaptive challenge which requires questioning the beliefs, values, commitments, loyalties, and interest that have created and perpetuated the structures, systems, and behaviors that drive climate change (O'Brien 2012). Indeed, current definitions of climate change adaptation are positioned far more to accommodate change rather than to challenge the causes and drivers, leaving current development approaches essentially unchallenged (Pelling 2011).

All three concepts have proved important in our understanding of climate change effects, but as yet have produced only uneven results in reducing risk, losses, or damages from climate change (Dupuis and Knoepfel 2013). In effect, climate change is a "wicked" problem, requiring "clumsy solutions" involving the articulation of diverse world views, forms of social organization, interests, knowledge systems and meanings of populations within their dynamic physical settings and socio-cultural circumstances, including the interactions of local to global decision-making processes (Verweij and Thompson 2006). Such "clumsy solutions" must generate policies that creatively articulate multiple perspectives on the causes, effects, adaptations, resiliences, and vulnerabilities associated with climate change that are embedded in global, national, and local priorities and practices of societal organization and development. In the final analysis, climate change presents some daunting challenges to exposed and vulnerable peoples around the globe, variously increasing their exposure and vulnerability, testing their resilience and their adaptive capacity in both the material and cultural dimensions.

References

Adger, W. N., S. Dessai, M. Goulden, M. Hulme, I. Lorenzoni, D. R. Nelson, L. O. Naess, J. Wolf and A. Wreford 2009. "Are there Social Limits to Adaptation to Climate Change?" *Climatic Change* 93(3): 335–354.

Agrawal, A. 2008. The Role of Local Institutions in Adaptation to Climate Change. Paper prepared for the Social Dimensions of Climate Change, Social Development Department, The World Bank, Washington, DC (5–6 March).

Bennett, J. 1996. *Human Ecology as Human Behavior*. New Brunswick, NJ: Transaction Publishers.

Birkmann, J. 2011. "First and Second Order Adaptation to Natural Hazards and Extreme Events in the Context of Climate Change." *Natural Hazards* 58(2): 811–840.

Birkmann, J. and K. von Teichman 2010. "Integrating Disaster Risk Reduction and Climate Change Adaptation: Key Challenges—Scales, Knowledge, and Norms." *Sustainability Science*. doi: 10.1007/s11625-010-0108-y

Brunner, R. D. and A. H. Lynch 2010. *Adaptive Governance and Climate Change*. Boston, MA: American Meteorological Society.

Cameron, E. S. 2012. "Securing Indigenous Politics: A Critique of the Vulnerability and Adaptation Approach to the Human Dimensions of Climate Change in the Canadian Arctic." *Global Environmental Change* 22: 103–114.

Cannon, T. 2008. Reducing People's Vulnerability to Natural Hazards: Communities and Resilience. UNU–WIDER Working Paper No. 2008/34. Bonn, Germany: United Nations University.

Cannon, T. and D. Müller-Mahn 2010. "Vulnerability, Resilience and Development Discourses in Context of Climate Change." *Natural Hazards* 55(3): 621–635. doi 10.1007/s11069-010-9499-4

Collins, S. L., S. R. Carpenter, S. M. Swinton, D. E. Orenstein, D. L. Childers, T. L. Gragson, N. B. Grimm, J. M. Grove, S. L. Harlan, J. P. Kaye, A. K. Knapp, G. P. Kofinas, J. J. Magnuson, W. H. McDowell, J. M. Melack, L. A. Ogden, G. P. Robertson, M. D. Smith and A. C. Whitmer 2013. "An Integrated Framework for Long-term Social-ecological Research. *Frontiers in Ecology and Environment* 9(6): 351–357. doi: 10.1890/100068

Cote, M. and A. J. Nightingale 2012. "Resilience Thinking Meets Social Theory: Situating Social Change in Socio-ecological Systems (SES) Research." *Progress in Human Geography* 36(4): 475–489.

Crane, T. A. 2010. "Of Models and Meanings: Cultural Resilience in Socio-ecological Systems." *Ecology and Society* 15(4): 19.

Crate, S. A. 2008. "Gone the Bull of Winter: Grappling with the Cultural Implications of and Anthropology's Role(s) in Global Climate Change." *Current Anthropology* 49(4): 569–595.

Crate, S. A. and M. Nuttall 2009. *Anthropology and Climate Change: From Encounters to Actions*. Walnut Creek, CA: Left Coast Press.

Crumley, C. L. 2013. "New Paths into the Anthropocene." In C. Isendahl and D. Stump (eds) *Oxford Handbook of Historical Ecology and Applied Archaeology*. Oxford: Oxford University Press.

Cutter, S. L., L. Barnes, M. Berry, C. Burton, E. Evans, E. Tate and J. Webb 2008. "A Place-based Model for Understanding Community Resilience to Natural Disasters." *Global Environmental Change* 18(4): 598–606.

Dow, K., F. Berkhout, B. L. Preston, R. J. T. Klein, G. Midgley and M. R. Shaw 2013. "Limits to Adaptation." *Nature Climate Change* 3: 305–307.

Dupuis, J. and P. Knoepfel 2013. "The Adaptation Policy Paradox: The Implementation Deficit of Policies Framed as Climate Change Adaptation." *Ecology and Society* 18(4): 31. doi.org/10.5751/ES-05965-180431

Felli, R. and N. Castree 2012. "Commentary." *Environment and Planning* 44(1): 1–4.

Fiske, S. J., S. A. Crate, C. L. Crumley, K. Galvin, H. Lazrus, L. Lucero, A. Oliver-Smith, B. Orlove, S. Strauss and R. Wilk 2014. *Changing the Atmosphere. Anthropology and Climate Change*. Final Report of the AAA Global Climate Change Task Force. Arlington, VA: American Anthropological Association. http://s3.amazonaws.com/rdcms-aaa/files/production/public/FileDownloads/pdfs/cmtes/commissions/upload/GCCTF-Changing-the-Atmosphere.pdf (accessed 5 March 2016).

Folke, C., S. Carpenter, T. Elmqvist, L. Gunderson, C. S. Holling and B. Walker 2002a. "Resilience and Sustainable Development: Building Adaptive Capacity in a World of Transformations." *Ambio* 31(5): 437–440.

Folke, C., J. Colding and F. Berkes 2002b. "Building Resilience for Adaptive Capacity in Social-ecological Systems." In F. Berkes, J. Colding and C. Folke (eds) *Navigating Social-ecological Systems: Building Resilience for Complexity and Change*. Cambridge, UK: Cambridge University Press, pp 352–387.

Folke, C., S. Carpenter, B. Walker, M. Scheffer, T. Elmqvist, L. Gunderson and C. S. Holling 2004. "Regime Shifts, Resilience, and Biodiversity in Ecosystem Management." *Annual Review of Ecology, Evolution, and Systematics* 35: 557–581.

Giddens, A. 2009. *Global Politics and Climate Change*. Cambridge, UK: Polity Press.

Gunderson, L. and C. S. Holling 2002. *Panarchy: Understanding Transformations in Human and Natural Systems*. Washington, DC: Island Press.

Hetherington, R. 2012. *Living in a Dangerous Climate: Climate Change and Human Evolution*. Cambridge, UK: Cambridge University Press.

Hewitt, K. 1983. *Interpretations of Calamity*. Boston, MA: Allen & Unwin.

Holling, C. S. 1973. "Resilience and Stability of Ecological Systems." *Annual Review of Ecology and Systematics* 4: 1–23.

Holling, C. S. and G. K. Meffe 1996. "Command and Control and the Pathology of Natural Resource Management." *Conservation Biology* 10(2): 328–337.

Intergovernmental Panel on Climate Change (IPCC) 2001. *Climate Change 2001: The Scientific Basis. Contribution of Working Group I to the Third Assessment Report of the Intergovernmental Panel on Climate Change* (edited by J. T. Houghton, Y. Ding, D. J. Griggs, M. Noguer, P. J. van der Linden, X. Dai, K. Maskell and C. A. Johnson). New York: Cambridge University Press.

Intergovernmental Panel on Climate Change (IPCC) 2007. "Summary for Policymakers." In *Climate Change 2007: The Physical Science Basis. Contribution of Working Group I to the Fourth Assessment Report of the Intergovernmental Panel on Climate Change* (edited by S. Soomon, C. Qin, M. Manning, Z. Cher, M. Marquis, K. B. Avery, M. Tignor and H. L. Miller). Cambridge, UK and New York: Cambridge University Press, pp. 23–73.

Intergovernmental Panel on Climate Change (IPCC) 2013. "Summary for Policymakers." In *Climate Change 2013: The Physical Science Basis. Contribution of Working Group I to the Fifth Assessment Report of the Intergovernmental Panel on Climate Change* (edited by T. F. Stocker, D. Qin, G. K. Plattner, M. Tignor, S. K. Allen, J. Boschung, A. Nauels, Y. Xia, V. Bex and P. M. Midgley). Cambridge, UK and New York: Cambridge University Press, pp. 1–30. doi:10.1017/CBO9781107415324.004

Integrated Research on Disaster Risk (IRDR) 2011. *The FORIN Project*. Paris: ICSU.

Johnson, C. A. 2013. "Governing Climate Displacement: The Ethics and Politics of Human Resettlement." *Environmental Politics* 21(2): 308–328.

Kelman, I. and J. C. Gaillard 2010. "Embedding Climate Change Adaptation within Disaster Risk Reduction." In R. Shaw, J. M. Pulhin and J. J. Pereira (eds) *Climate Change Adaptation and Disaster Risk Reduction: Issues and Challenges*. Bingley, UK: Emerald Group Publishing Limited, pp. 23–46.

Laska, S. and K. Peterson 2013. "'Between Now and Then': Tackling the Conundrum of Climate Change." *Canadian Risk and Hazards Newsletter* 5(1): 5–8. http://207.23.111.231/sites/default/files/library/HazNet_2013-10_v5n1.pdf

Lavell, A. 2011. Unpacking Climate Change Adaptation and Disaster Risk Management: Searching for the Links and the Differences: A Conceptual and Epistemological Critique and Proposal. Unpublished paper for the IUCN–FLACSO (Facultad Latinoamericana de Ciencias Sociales) Project on Climate Change Adaptation and Disaster Risk Reduction, San José, Costa Rica.

Marris, P. 1975. *Loss and Change*. Garden City, NY: Anchor Books.

Murphy, D., C. Wyborn, L. Yung and D. Williams 2016. "Engaging Future Climate Change Vulnerability and Adaptation Using Landscape-scale Iterative Scenario-building." *Human Organization* 75(1): 33–46.

National Research Council 2012. *Disaster Resilience: A National Imperative*. Washington, DC: National Academies Press.

Nelson, D. R., W. N. Adger and K. Brown 2007. "Adaptation to Environmental Change: Contributions of a Resilience Framework." *Annual Review of Environment and Resources* 32: 395–419. doi:10.1146/annurev.energy.32.051807 (accessed 7 August 2013).

Nelson, D. R, C. T. West and T. J. Finan 2009. Introduction to "In Focus: Global Change and Adaptation in Local Places." *American Anthropologist* 11(3): 271–274.

O'Brien, K. 2012. "Global Environmental Change II: From Adaptation to Deliberate Transformation." *Progress in Human Geography* 36(5): 667–676.

O'Brien, K., S. Eriksen, L. P. Nygaard and A. Schjolden 2007. "Why Different Interpretations of Vulnerability Matter in Climate Change Discourses." *Climate Policy* 7(1): 73–88.

O'Keefe, P., K. Westgate and B. Wisner 1976. "Taking the Naturalness out of Natural Disasters." *Nature* 260(5552): 566–567.

Oliver-Smith, A. 2002. "Theorizing Disasters: Nature, Culture, Power." In S. M. Hoffman and A. Oliver-Smith (eds) *Culture and Catastrophe: The Anthropology of Disaster*. Santa Fe, NM: School of American Research Press.

Oliver-Smith, A. 2013. "A Matter of Choice." *International Journal of Disaster Risk Reduction* 3: 1–3.

Orlove, B. 2009. "The Past, the Present and Some Possible Futures of Adaptation." In W. N. Adger, I. Lorenzoni and K. O'Brien (eds) *Adapting to Climate Change: Thresholds, Values, Governance.* Cambridge, UK: Cambridge University Press, pp. 131–163.

Patterson, T. 1994. "Toward a Properly Historical Ecology." In C. L. Crumley (ed.) *Historical Ecology: Cultural Knowledge and Changing Landscapes.* Santa Fe, NM: School of American Research Press, pp. 223–237.

Pelling, M. 2011. *Adaptation to Climate Change: From Resilience to Transformation.* London and New York: Routledge.

Ribot, J. 2011. "Vulnerability Before Adaptation: Toward Transformative Climate Action." *Global Environmental Change* 21: 1160–1162.

Smit, B. and J. Wandel 2006. "Adaptation, Adaptive Capacity and Vulnerability." *Global Environmental Change* 16: 282–292.

Smucker, T. A., B. Wisner, A. Mascarenhas, P. Munishi, E. E. Wangui, G. Sinha, D. Weiner, C. Bwenge and E. Lovell 2015. "Differentiated Livelihoods, Local Institutions, and the Adaptation Imperative: Assessing Climate Change Adaptation Policy in Tanzania." *Geoforum* 59: 39–50.

Thywissen, K. 2006. "Core Terminology of Disaster Reduction: A Comparative Glossary." In J. Birkmann (ed.) *Measuring Vulnerability to Natural Hazards: Towards Disaster Resilient Societies.* Tokyo: United Nations University Press, pp. 448–496.

Turner, B. L., R. E. Kasperson, P. A. Matson, J. J. McCarthy, R. W. Corell, L. Christenson, N. Eckley, J. X. Kasperson, A. Luers, M. L. Martello, C. Polsky, A. Pulsipher and A. Schiller 2003. "A Framework for Vulnerability Analysis in Sustainability Science." *Proceedings of the National Academy of Sciences of the United States of America* 100(14): 8074–8079.

Turton, D. 2006. "Who Is a Forced Migrant?" In Chris de Wet (ed.) *Development-induced Displacement: Problems, Policies, and People.* Oxford: Berghahn Books.

United Nations Framework Convention on Climate Change (UNFCCC) 1992. Definitions. http://unfccc.int/files/essential_background/background_publications_htmlpdf/application/pdf/conveng.pdf (accessed 23 February 2016).

Verweij, M. and M. Thompson (eds) 2006. *Clumsy Solutions for a Complex World: Governance, Politics and Plural Perception.* Basingstoke, UK: Palgrave/Macmillan.

Walker, B., C. S. Holling, S. R. Carpenter and A. Kinzig 2004. "Resilience, Adaptability and Transformability in Social-ecological Systems." *Ecology and Society* 9(2): 5.

Willcox, A. C., S. L. Harper, J. D. Ford, V. L. Edge, K. Landman, K. Houle, S. Blake and C. Wolfrey 2013. "Climate Change and Mental Health: An Exploratory Case Study from Rigolet, Nunatsiavut, Canada." *Climatic Change* 121(2): 255–270.

Wisner, B., P. Blaikie, T. Cannon and I. Davis 2004. *At Risk: Natural Hazards, People's Vulnerability, and Disasters.* 2nd edn. London: Routledge.

18

CLIMATE, ENVIRONMENT, AND SOCIETY IN NORTHWEST GREENLAND

Mark Nuttall

Introduction

According to the most recent reports from the Intergovernmental Panel on Climate Change (IPCC), the average temperature on the Earth's surface increased by 0.85° C between 1880 and 2012 (IPCC 2013, 2014). Climate scientists no longer appear hesitant to say that the warming observed in the past 50 years or more is attributed to human activities, particularly those activities related to the burning of fossil fuels. The Anthropocene does indeed seem an apt term to describe human influence on the planet and how we are implicated as agents of geophysical reconfiguration and climate change in our current environmental predicament.

Some of the consequences of Earth's warming trend are most immediately observable in the Arctic. For many northern residents, particularly indigenous hunters in northern Alaska, Canada, and Greenland who now have to travel on thinning sea ice in the winter or on increasingly stormy waters during summer, Fennoscandian and Siberian reindeer herders who struggle to find good pasture for their animals, or communities facing the dangers of thawing permafrost or coastal erosion, climate change is a lived experience (e.g. Henshaw 2009; Marino 2015). One critical task for anthropology is to understand how people not only respond to, manage, and live with such change, but how they reflect upon past changes to negotiate present circumstances and anticipate future conditions. Yet, while residents of northern places observe and experience significant shifts in Arctic marine and terrestrial environments, it does not necessarily follow that they will think about climate change as the most pressing issue affecting their lives. This is not to say they dismiss climate change, are skeptical of it, or do not feel the effects. Rather, they face a number of contemporary challenges that also act to limit them in how they are able to respond to climate change, most notably by reducing their options for adaptation and narrowing their anticipatory gaze as they imagine themselves and their livelihoods into the future.

In this chapter I illustrate this point by drawing on long-term and recurring research in hunting and fishing communities in the Upernavik region of northwest Greenland, an area in which I have worked since the late 1980s. By doing so, I argue for understanding the consequences of climate change in a broader context – rapid social, economic, and demographic change, wildlife management, oil exploration, quota systems for marine mammals and fish, environmentalist campaigns, and trade barriers have significant implications for everyday life in the Arctic and, in many cases, what climate change does is magnify existing societal, political, economic, legal, institutional, and other challenges that affect northern peoples (Nuttall *et al.* 2005). While the effects of climate change are stark in the Arctic, people are navigating northern waters that are not just being transformed by shifting sea ice or warmer currents, but are being threatened by oil exploration and by neoliberal views of northern ocean environments and how the animals and fish in them should be managed, caught, and marketed. As one long-time friend, a hunter, put it to me, travelling on, across, and around thin and dangerous sea ice is not so difficult, but getting around a quota system that privileges the knowledge of scientists and the interests of those concerned with the management of marine mammals and fish over local hunters and fishers is seemingly impossible.

Greenland and the Arctic: at the epicentre of global change

There is a regional texture to climate change and so, as in other parts of the world, there are regional variations throughout the Arctic due to atmospheric winds and ocean currents, with some areas showing more warming than others and a few areas even showing a slight cool-ing; but for the Arctic as a whole, the scientific evidence suggests a clear warming trend; temperatures are expected to increase several times that of the global mean (IPCC 2013), leading to sea ice retreat, melting of glaciers, and thawing of permafrost (ACIA 2005; AMAP 2012). The melting of parts of the Greenland inland ice is increasing (Box and Decker 2011), and summer sea ice is decreasing at a rate faster than foreseen in any model and may fully disappear before 2050 (Wang and Overland 2009). The changing climate has been cited as having a substantial negative impact on northern community resource-use activities as thinning ice conditions, shifting animal migration routes, and generally changing weather patterns place significant limitations on hunters and fishers (Huntington and Fox 2005; Nuttall *et al.* 2005). In addition, environmental pollutants and the contamination of the Arctic food chain have raised concerns relating to the consumption of traditional foods among health-care professionals and indigenous peoples' organizations alike.

The changing climate and reduced sea-ice cover, however, inspire a narrative about opportunities for development of the Arctic, which is often expressed in talk of a rush to claim rights over access to northern resources such as hydrocarbons, minerals, and fish (Dodds and Nuttall 2016). Changes currently underway in sea ice, and market demands for new resources, have resulted in a significant global interest in the prospects for resource development. Oil and gas companies are securing exploration and development licences – according to some sources, Baffin Bay and the Greenland Sea potentially hold some of the largest undiscovered oil and gas resources in the Arctic (AMAP 2007; Circum-Arctic Resource Appraisal 2008), and mining companies are surveying rich mineral deposits, including diamonds, gold, iron, zinc, copper, uranium, and rare earth elements, in what are seen as high-latitude resource frontiers (Dodds and Nuttall 2016).

Greenland, a self-governing territory of the Kingdom of Denmark, achieved Home Rule in 1979, and greater autonomy in the form of self-government in June 2009. Politicians and business elites have aspirations to develop a still more self-reliant economy and the exploitation of both renewable and non-renewable resources is a cornerstone of economic development policy. Following the introduction of self-government in June 2009, the Greenland Parliament (*Inatsisartut*) and the Government of Greenland (*Naalakkersuisut*) have confirmed a strong interest in the potential of industrialized resource development with a focus on extractive industries for the overall economic development of Greenlandic society. Greenland is being positioned as a resource frontier and source of raw materials and hydrocarbons for the global economy within the contexts of a changing climate and a political quest for greater autonomy (Nuttall 2012). Yet there are concerns that strong environmental and social-impact assessment processes, regulatory regimes, and decision-making processes are not yet in place to ensure that extractive industries proceed in accordance with environmental protection and social and economic sustainability in mind (Nuttall 2013). In other work, I have explored emergent forms, imaginings, and narratives at the intersection of politics and corporate transnationalism, and have considered the political discourse surrounding resource development, public responses to it, and the nature of extractive industries (Nuttall 2012, 2015). Looking at social impact assessment, environmental impact assessment, and public participation, I have shown how public disquiet over lack of appropriate consultation (and criticism over the absence of information about planned megaprojects) is leading to a situation where demands for legitimate public engagement in democratic and transparent discussion and debate over extractive industries are increasing, and how this challenges both the representations and governance of resource development.

Hunting and fishing communities of northwest Greenland

In Greenland today, some 47,000 people (out of a total population of around 57,000) live in urban spaces; over 80 per cent of Greenland's population live in towns of 1,000 people or more, with 60 per cent concentrated in six towns on the west coast (Nuuk, the capital, has the largest population with around 15,500 people living there). There are 18 towns in Greenland and 110 smaller settlements, including hunting villages around the coast and the often remote sheep farms of the southern part of the country. Although the Greenlandic population is growing, the country's total population has remained steady since the 1980s, mainly as a result of the decline in the number of Danes and other non-Greenlanders living and working there, but also as a result of Greenlanders moving to Denmark for education, work, family reasons, or retirement.

For many who live in the smaller villages and settlements along the southern, northern, and east coasts, the resources of both land and sea continue to provide the basis for local economies and people's livelihoods. The Upernavik area of northwest Greenland is an archipelago of scattered islands, headlands, and peninsulas – the town of Upernavik, the district's administrative centre, has around 1,100 inhabitants and about 1,700 people live in nine villages along a coast which stretches some 450 kilometres. Since the first movements of Inuit cultures along the northwest coast some 4,500 years ago, following their migrations from northern Canada, people in this area have depended on hunting marine mammals and on fishing – today, marine mammals (such as seals, walrus, narwhals, beluga, fin, and minke whales) and polar bears are hunted; and fishing for fjord cod, Greenland halibut, salmon, and Arctic char is an important seasonal activity. Terrestrial animals such as reindeer and Arctic foxes have also been of some importance, as have musk-oxen in some areas. Animals continue to sustain these hunting and fishing communities in an economic and nutritional way, but are also vital for social identity and everyday life, and this is recognized, reflected, and celebrated in community hunting regulations, in hunting practices and in patterns of sharing and gift-giving which are informed by ideas of close social relatedness (Dahl 2000; Nuttall 2000).

In Upernavik's small communities, the ability to hunt and fish is not only made possible by or is dependent on a person's skills and knowledge and the availability and seasonal presence of animals, but on the amount of money that comes into and circulates around the hunting household and that can be allocated for supporting hunting and fishing activities. The technologies and equipment used in modern hunting and fishing activities – boats, snowmobiles, engines, rifles, fishing gear, to name just a few items – are extremely expensive to obtain and maintain. And for those hunters and fishers who keep sled dogs, the preferred foods to feed a hungry team are fish and seal or walrus meat, but procuring a ready supply involves considerable time and effort in going hunting and fishing in the first place; as an indication of changing attitudes or changing resource-use patterns, sacks of imported prepared sled dog food are now piled in the store in Upernavik and in the store in some of the settlements – buying it is an easier option for feeding one's dogs, though one that is still expensive.

The hunting and fishing communities of the Upernavik area are characterized by a combination of informal and formal economic activities; on the one hand, there are those activities that may be called traditional subsistence ways of making a living – catching marine mammals and fish, and sharing the meat within and between households and community networks, and utilizing sealskins or reindeer and musk-ox pelts for clothing; while on the other hand, there are those activities that are recognized as more commercial fisheries, with the aim of selling everything one catches, as well as employment (although jobs are rather more limited in the smaller communities than in the town of Upernavik). Hunting and fishing activities satisfy important social, cultural, and nutritional needs of families, house-holds, and communities, as well as economic ones. Foods purchased from the local store supplement people's diets, which are comprised mainly of meat and fish caught locally. Individuals and households lacking the means or ability to hunt find that it is often essential to be able to obtain traditional foods through local distribution channels and sharing networks. In some cases, the money earned from the sale of meat or fish, and from employ-ment, makes it possible to continue hunting and fishing, rather than contributing to its decline, as cash buys items like boats, rifles, and snowmobiles. Cash also meets demands for a rising standard of living: to purchase oil to heat homes, buy consumer goods, or travel beyond one's community. While food procured from hunting and fishing continues to provide Arctic peoples throughout the northern circumpolar world, not just in northern Greenland, with important nutritional, socio-economic, and cultural benefits, finding ways to earn money is a major concern in many small communities. The seasonal and often irregular nature of wage-generating activities (such as those derived from a small number of tourists to the Upernavik area, mainly in summer) means that families and households often face major problems in ensuring a regular cash-flow.

Until recently, it was still possible for many hunting households to earn money through the sale of sealskins (indeed, this had been for some their main source of income). However, international campaigns directed by animal rights groups towards seal hunting in northern regions from the 1970s and 1980s onwards have had a lasting legacy – most significantly in international trade bans such as the European Union's restrictions on imports of sealskins – and northern households in Greenland, Canada, and Alaska have encountered considerable difficulties in selling the products of the hunt (Wenzel 1991). Even though the EU has recently moved to ease these restrictions, the public perception of hunting and wearing items of sealskin clothing as morally questionable has had a deep impact on markets, making it almost impossible for hunting households to find an outlet for the skins they prepare for sale. Indeed, in the town of Upernavik, the small sealskin house at the harbour to which skins would usually be sold is now rarely open. Preparing a sealskin is a time-consuming business and it is women's work. Skins need to be scraped, all the fat and blubber removed, then washed and dried. Increasingly, women feel it is hardly worth the time and effort. Yet, sealskins are still needed for winter clothing (as are the furs from other marine mammals such as polar bears) and not all are sold, but the skills needed to prepare them and turn them into effective protection against the winter are disappearing.

When I began my first period of fieldwork in the Upernavik area in spring 1987, the effects of the European trade ban were beginning to bite hard and hunters were turning to small-scale fishing for Greenland halibut as a way of earning some money (Nuttall 1992). Today, the inshore fishery, comprised mainly of small boats – dinghies of less than six metres in length and fitted with outboard engines – has developed considerably and it remains the most significant way of earning an income for many in the town and for the majority of village households, as well as making an important contribution to the wider Greenlandic economy. At the time of the first experimental fisheries in the mid- to late 1980s, encouraged by the municipal authorities and the Home Rule government, people felt optimistic that there might be a future for small community life. This was not dulled by any notion of what was, in fact, the first sign that the neoliberalism of the oceans and the commodification of fish stocks happening in other parts of the world (Høst 2015) was about to make its presence felt in northwest Greenland. From the perspective of the household, fishing at the time was (and still is today) often seen as one of a range of many activities that make up the seasonal round, and of these, perhaps the only one for many people that provides the money necessary to allow for the continuation of a hunting way of life. For the managers of fish stocks, the owners of the Greenlandic fishing industry, and for the government of Greenland, fish such as Greenland halibut have become important resources that can bring in revenue for the development of the national economy.

In the early 1990s, the Upernavik area underwent a major transition from hunting to fishing. Not all hunters abandoned seal hunting, but the opportunities apparent by turning more or less full time to fishing for Greenland halibut were difficult to resist. Soon many people were giving up their sled dogs in favour of snowmobiles and were moving away from standing for hours on end at a seal's breathing hole to fishing camps on the sea ice in the winter; they were also establishing new summer camping places near good fishing prospects deep in iceberg-filled glacial bays. Several communities, such as Innaarsuit, Aappilattoq, Kangersuatsiaq, Tasisusaq, and Nutaarmiut, became known as fishing villages, whereas once they had reputations as exclusively hunting settlements, drawing people there either as seasonal residents or through permanent relocation. Later on, Upernavik Seafood, a locally-based company established to purchase and process the products of the fishery, provided loans to fishers to allow them to obtain snowmobiles and new boats. The fishery grew, as did the size of the boats some of the fishers used. At the same time, large boats from places south of the Upernavik district, such as Uummannaq, Ilulissat, and Nuuk, also began to venture to these lucrative fishing grounds and compete with those who fish from dinghies. The Greenland halibut fishery has been subject to an individual transferrable quota (ITQ) system for some years now (Jacobsen and Delaney 2014), itself part of recent reforms in Greenlandic fisheries more generally to propel coastal fisheries towards greater economic profitability (Jacobsen and Raakjær 2014), and contested ideas of property rights vested in fish stocks have come to the fore in discussions of the economic development of the district. These reveal an ongoing conflict between those advancing the interests of the small settlements and the interests of the national government and those who oversee and run the fishing industry (Jacobsen and Delaney 2014).

Exploratory activity related to extractive industries has also brought different kinds of pressures and anxieties, as well as hopes for economic benefits in the Upernavik area. Mining companies are engaged in prospecting and developing plans for a number of projects in

223

northwest Greenland, but Baffin Bay and Melville Bay have also been the focus of recent international interest in the prospects for the discovery of oil (Nuttall 2012, 2013). In 2012 and 2013 several oil companies carried out a series of seismic site surveys, some of which overlapped with the protection zone for narwhals in Melville Bay. Narwhals are highly sensitive to anthropogenic activities, especially noise, so there is concern that the high-energy airgun pulses used in marine seismic surveys could cause the animals to abandon important summer grounds in Melville Bay and change their migration patterns, increasing the possibility of ice entrapment (Heide-Jørgensen *et al.* 2013). Indeed, after these surveys had finished, hunters from Melville Bay communities reported that narwhal behaviour was different and that the hunt had been influenced negatively due to the seismic activities in the area. Canadian Inuit narwhal hunters believe that narwhal migrations have changed since seismic surveys have been carried out in Baffin Bay (as was emphasized in a press release by the Inuit Circumpolar Council in September 2013). Marine biologists and hunters in Greenland have also begun to express their worries over the possible effects of intense seismic survey activities and increased shipping on marine mammals and the future of hunting communities, and are calling for long-term monitoring programmes to be put in place (see e.g. Heide-Jørgensen *et al.* 2013; Nuttall 2016). It is likely that exploratory activities will increase in the coming years and there could be a range of likely impacts on narwhals and other marine mammals, with consequences for hunting communities. Hunters have also expressed concern that they are not too well informed about the activities of seismic vessels. Improved communication and dialogue seem particularly important in this regard.

Shifting worlds

Extreme weather events have become increasingly common for the residents of the Upernavik district. During the conversations I have had during my field visits in recent years, hunters have said they now experience far more difficult and uncertain ice conditions in winter and spring than they did several years ago, and they have remarked on the shifting currents, more powerful waves, stronger winds, and fiercer storms that are becoming a part of daily life during summer and autumn. In northern Greenland, sea ice (*siku*) is central to people's lives for several months of the year. Its formation and stability open up all kinds of possibilities for hunting, fishing, and travelling, and connect communities in a significantly different way from the open water. Yet considerable changes to the sea ice are being observed and experienced. It now tends to form later and break up earlier than many people have known it to do during their lifetimes, making connections between communities increasingly tenuous and precarious. By way of example, the period of travel by dogsled on good, solid sea ice is around three months during winter and spring, compared with five or six months some 10 to 15 years ago. Around the villages of Nuussuaq and Kullorsuaq in the northern part of the Upernavik district, hunters have remarked that the ice is now best, in terms of its thickness and texture to travel on, in March and April, which reduces significantly the amount of time hunters are able to hunt and fish (although there is still ice in January and February, its consistency and thickness are often not considered to be good). At the same time, around Kullorsuaq, hunters have, in recent years, been hunting by boat during some periods when there is open water during winter and spring.

Hunters report that the sea ice is also of a different texture and consistency. Its instability is beginning to make ice-edge hunting more difficult and dangerous. For example, some hunters in communities north of Upernavik town have remarked that travelling to the edge of the ice makes them anxious in a way it has never done – they say the ice is "more slippery" than they have known it, and that they feel more secure travelling by dogsled on the solid ice that is attached to the shore (although this is a considerably rougher ice environment on which to move along and across), thus placing limits on how far from land they can travel on ice (Nuttall 2009). Changes in snow cover on both the sea ice and land are also causing difficulty in accessing hunting and fishing areas by dogsled or snowmobile, making local adjustments in winter travel, and in hunting and fishing strategies necessary. Hunters and fishers are utilizing new adaptive strategies that include travelling to new fishing grounds, seeking alternative sources of income, preparing for the unexpected and increased reliance on boat transportation during the winter and when there are increasingly ice-free waters.

An increasingly large body of published scientific work focuses on the changing Greenland inland ice and its outlet glaciers, and chronicles an alarming annual deficit of the ice sheet's mass as well as a decline in its reflectivity (e.g. Box and Decker 2011). Such writings warn that the inland ice is approaching a tipping point (see e.g. Wassmann and Lenton 2012, for a broader discussion of Arctic tipping points). When I talk with people in northwest Greenland about the changes occurring in their surroundings that are so obvious and immediate, I am struck by the way they do not consider the shifting sea ice or areas where glaciers have receded as indigenous accounts of what scientists could be looking for in terms of local evidence of tipping points or changes in thresholds; in such places where the ice has moved back several kilometres in recent years, there is now open water which means that new areas in the locality have emerged in which to fish or hunt, and to travel; and the melting ice has revealed islands or parts of the mainland where people can establish new campsites or hunting lookouts and explore the possibilities an extended vista has to offer. In summer 2014, a hunter from the village of Aappilattoq, just to the northeast of Upernavik town, showed me just how far back a nearby tidal glacier had receded since my last visit a few years previously. The glacier, the Upernavik Isstrøm, has long been an object of scientific interest – up until around 1950 it had one terminus, but is today characterized by a number of separate termini and their retreat has seen the development of new islands. Between 2000 and 2010, the ice loss for the combined termini of the glacier was 7.9 square kilometres per year (Box and Decker 2011).

My friend did not talk about this change in the locality as something that was worrying or indicative of environmental catastrophe as many of my colleagues in the physical sciences have considered such glacial retreat to be. Rather, he talked about the new places he and his family now enjoyed visiting as part of their seasonal round, and of the possibilities for fishing. The area, he remarked, is now full of redfish – few had usually been seen or caught this far north before the glacier receded – and he and his fellow villagers felt there were opportunities to develop a new fishery. However, Royal Greenland, the fish processing company that operates throughout Greenland and which took over control of Upernavik Seafood in 2015, only buys Greenland halibut from fishers and refuses to take any other species that are landed. While scientists may consider redfish to be an indicator species of climate change, local hunters and fishers are welcoming of such new fish coming into their area. The problem for them is the market and the reliance on a single type of fish as the basis for the local economy; this fish, the Greenland halibut, however, has become the object of larger fishing vessels from further south which fish the quota before the fisher in his dinghy can get out into the fjords.

With this in mind, a challenge for decision-making related to climate threats is to understand and evaluate such change in this context of local perceptions and experiences. It is also important to understand the regional texture to climate change effects – for example, while hunters in northern Greenland are navigating their way around melting sea ice and are noticing changes in the migration of marine mammals and fish, sheep farmers in south Greenland are expanding their grazing ranges and cultivating land for vegetable production. And while Inuit leaders and activists in northern Canada frame climate change as an issue of human rights and worry about the disappearance of Inuit culture along with the ice (Watt-Cloutier 2015), politicians and business leaders in Greenland do not always consider climate change to bring environmental disaster, but see it as something that will allow the implementation of empowering political and economic decisions (Nuttall 2009). Melting glacial ice, for instance, means the possibility for hydropower development, oil exploration, and access to mineral resources. And while the Upernavik fjords may be filled with the debris of collapsing glaciers, people living within these surroundings see them as filled with fish and the prospects for making a living.

The future of community life

Over the next two or three decades, the gradual depopulation and possible abandonment of many settlements in the Upernavik area and the continued decline of livelihoods based on small-scale hunting and fishing may well be likely. Certainly, in the years I have worked in northwest Greenland there have been significant demographic shifts and profound socio-economic changes in the places I have come to know. But to say this is because of changes in climate and environment is perhaps to overstate the effects and to ignore how people have lived with, responded to, and anticipated considerable seasonal changes in the past. Movement away from the hunting and fishing villages of the far north is the reality of a continuing trend of social and economic change, but it is also going to be an effect of government attitude and policy towards non-urban centres with small populations. Many settlements are indeed experiencing a population drain, mainly of young women. Migration from small communities to the urban centres of Greenland – and on to Denmark – continues in response to employment opportunities, education, and changes in lifestyle. Today in Greenland I have often heard it said by young women who come from small settlements that, "Just because I am the daughter of a seal hunter doesn't mean I am going to stay here in this place and be a seal hunter's wife." In many of the small settlements in which I have worked and researched, old people and young single men are now in the majority. In Kangersuatsiaq, once a place renowned throughout northern Greenland for its young, aspiring population, around a third of the houses are now empty as young people have moved to Upernavik or to other communities. One reason for this is that the fish processing plant closed down because of the difficulties of providing it with a supply of fresh water – this has nothing to do with climate change; the village is on a small island with no source of fresh water other than from the icebergs that surround it. Fishing has declined in importance and people have returned to being full-time hunters. The settlements have only one shop with relatively few goods and offer few opportunities for paid employment. Conversely, many of the larger towns offer a better choice in terms of schools and education, which in turn gives access to a larger number and variety of jobs.

One argument put forward when accounting for the changes being experienced in small communities is that climate change will lead to people migrating from small Arctic communities. I have often heard Greenlandic politicians remark how hunters can no longer hunt because of the impacts of climate change on sea-ice conditions and that few choices are left to people if they cannot continue to practise traditional ways of living off the land and sea (e.g. Nuttall 2009). I see it differently: people are already leaving their home communities for other places in Greenland (and even beyond, to Denmark) for reasons that have little to do with climate change and a lot to do with a lack of economic opportunities, as well as lifestyle choices, ambition, education, and the desire for an urban, cosmopolitan future. This is true of many other parts of the Arctic, not just Greenland. Migration away from small communities has been ongoing for decades and it may well be that climate change just becomes another push factor rather than a primary reason.

Although the economic significance of the traditional way of life is steadily decreasing, hunting is still a crucial part of Greenlandic identity and this is reflected in the fact that more people hunt for leisure than those for whom it is their sole occupation. Yet the divide between town and village life has come to stand for and perhaps define the whole idea of political and economic development in Greenland. Today, there are many politicians in Greenland who would like to see the country's population concentrated in a few main towns. Although few politicians would publicly admit that it would be better to close some hunting communities and relocate their inhabitants to larger villages or towns, the reality is that hunting, while informing Greenlandic cultural identity, contributes little to the economy of this nation in formation (Nuttall 1992).

When Home Rule was given to Greenland in 1979, the new indigenous government inherited a Danish colonial policy of subsidies for trade in hunting and fishing products and a system of fixed prices on basic consumer goods, water, electricity, and fuel throughout Greenland. The Royal Greenland Trade Company, which had operated in Greenland since the late eighteenth century until the mid-1980s, had introduced this system to make it possible for hunters and their families to continue to live in remote places and play their part as producers of the hunting and fishing products that formed the backbone of the Danish trade monopoly. A litre of milk, or the cost of providing lighting for homes, has until recently cost the same wherever people may live, whether in Nuuk or the most northerly settlements. While keeping small communities populated, the system has also been criticized as a way of forestalling the introduction of development policies for them by Greenland's government.

The recent abolition of this system, beginning in 2005, ostensibly to reflect the true value of providing and importing goods and services, has been disputed and debated in the parliament in Nuuk. In reality, it was costly for Greenland's government to maintain this system of subsidies, as well as hindering the effective implementation of economic development plans. A new system of differentiated prices has been introduced throughout Greenland. This may lead to some villages diversifying their economic base and emerging in a stronger position – an outcome the government intends. Yet some government critics see it as a way of encouraging the depopulation of some communities and long-term policies of demographic shift and investment in a few major centres. This is often countered by the argument that by subsidizing hunting settlements to continue to hunt seals and not allowing them to develop other economies would be paramount to creating reserves in which hunters and their families are expected to practise lifestyles that belong to the past. It would appear that statements from politicians such as "hunters are not able to hunt anymore because of thinning sea ice or changing climatic conditions" are simplistic (Nuttall 2009). At the same time, the introduction of management regulations for the conservation and sustainable use of living resources often inhibits the abilities of hunters and fishers to continue customary practices. For example, recent research in East Greenland has shown that the introduction of quotas on narwhal hunting has had a negative cultural impact (Nielsen *et al.* 2013). Such management policies have been criticized because they are implemented by government authorities and are based on scientific research without local consultation.

Conclusion

As in many places around Greenland's coasts, people who live in small hunting and fishing communities of the northwest are observing and experiencing considerable shifts in the environment as a result of climate change. Climate change, however, has to be understood in a wider context of other drivers of social and economic change, as well as political life and governance – for instance, everyday life is circumscribed by the institutions of wider Greenlandic society and the regulations and quotas that are implemented by management systems for living marine resources. These combine with environmental and climate change to often restrain the abilities of local people to travel and move around the locality and to hunt and fish certain species (Nuttall *et al.* 2005). Furthermore, the presence of exploratory activity related to extractive industries has brought different kinds of pressures and anxieties, as well as hopes for the future. So while climate change is noticeable in northwest Greenland, and is certainly having some impacts, the changing nature of hunting practices and hunting households and the declining fortunes of some villages are a consequence of many other factors, including Greenland's nation-building and state-formation processes and its push towards greater self-governance and eventual independence (Nuttall 2015). Hulme's (2011) warning that the future should not be reduced to climate change is apt in the north Greenlandic context. The viability of the livelihoods of people living in Greenlandic villages must be understood within this context of multiple stress factors, including institutional, political, social, and economic changes that reduce flexibility and adaptive capacity, leaving people with little room to move about in a world that is undergoing constant change, meeting its challenges and seizing its opportunities.

Acknowledgements

This chapter draws on research in northwest Greenland carried out over a number of years. More recent fieldwork has been conducted under the auspices of the Climate and Society Research Programme at the Greenland Climate Research Centre, and funded by the Danish Agency of Science, Technology and Innovation, as well as work done as part of the EU project Ice, Climate, Economics–Arctic Research on Change (ICE–ARC) funded by the Seventh Framework Programme. My thanks also go to Eleanor Shoreman-Ouimet and Helen Kopnina for their critical reading and editorial suggestions.

References

ACIA 2005. *Arctic Climate Impact Assessment.* ACIA Scientific Report. Cambridge, UK: Cambridge University Press.

AMAP 2007. *Arctic Oil and Gas 2007.* Oslo: Arctic Monitoring and Assessment Programme.

AMAP 2012. *Arctic Climate Issues 2011: Changes in Arctic Snow, Water, Ice and Permafrost.* Oslo: Arctic Monitoring and Assessment Programme.

Box, Jason E. and David T. Decker 2011. "Greenland marine-terminating glacier area changes: 2000–2010." *Annals of Glaciology* 52(59): 91–98.

Circum-Arctic Resource Appraisal 2008. *Estimates of Undiscovered Oil and Gas North of the Arctic Circle.* Washington, DC: U.S. Geological Survey. http://pubs.usgs.gov/fs/2008/3049/ (accessed 6 March 2016).

Dahl, Jens 2000. *Saqqaq: An Inuit Hunting Community in the Modern World.* Toronto, ON: University of Toronto Press.

Dodds, Klaus and Mark Nuttall 2016. *The Scramble for the Poles: The Geopolitics of the Arctic and Antarctic.* Cambridge, UK: Polity Press.

Heide-Jørgensen, Mads P., Rikke G. Hansen, Kristin Westdal, Randall Reeves and Anders Mosbech 2013. "Narwhals and seismic exploration: Is seismic noise increasing the risk of ice entrapments?" *Biological Conservation* 158: 50–54.

Henshaw, Anne 2009. "Sea ice: The sociocultural dimensions of a melting environment in the Arctic." In Susan A. Crate and Mark Nuttall (eds) *Anthropology and Climate Change: From Encounters to Actions*. Walnut Creek, CA: Left Coast Press, pp. 153–165.

Høst, Jeppe 2015. *Market-Based Fisheries Management: Private Fish and the Captains of Finance*. Dordrecht, the Netherlands: Springer.

Hulme, Mike 2011. "Reducing the future to climate change: A study of climate determinism and reductionism." *Osiris* 26(1): 245–266.

Huntington, Henry P. and Shari Fox 2005. "The changing Arctic: Indigenous perspectives." In *Arctic Climate Impact Assessment. ACIA Scientific Report*. Cambridge, UK: Cambridge University Press, pp. 61–98.

IPCC 2013. *Climate Change 2013: The Physical Science Basis. Contribution of Working Group I to the Fifth Assessment Report of the Intergovernmental Panel on Climate Change*. Cambridge, UK: Cambridge University Press.

IPCC 2014. *Fifth Assessment Report. Working Group I: The Physical Science Basis and Working Group II: Impacts, Adaptations and Vulnerability*. Cambridge, UK: Cambridge University Press.

Jacobsen, Rikke and Alyne Delaney 2014. "When social sustainability becomes politics: Perspectives from Greenlandic fisheries governance." *Maritime Studies* 13(6). doi: 10.11186/2212-9790-13-6

Jacobsen, Rikke and Jesper Raakjær 2014. "Who defines the need for fishery reform? Participants, discourses and networks in the reform of the Greenland fishery." *Polar Record* 50(4): 391–402.

Marino, Elizabeth 2015. *Fierce Climate, Sacred Ground: An Ethnograpy of Climate Change in Shishmaref, Alaska*. Fairbanks: University of Alaska Press.

Nielsen, Martin R. and Henrik Meilby 2013. "Quotas on narwhal (*Monodon monoceros*) hunting in East Greenland: Trends in narwhal killed per hunter and potential impacts of regulations on Inuit communities." *Human Ecology* 41(2): 187–203.

Nuttall, Mark 1992. *Arctic Homeland: Kinship, Community and Development in Northwest Greenland*. Toronto, ON: University of Toronto Press.

Nuttall, Mark 2000. "Choosing kin: Sharing and subsistence in a Greenlandic hunting community." In Peter Schweitzer (ed.) *The Dividends of Kinship: Meanings and Uses of Social Relatedness*. London: Routledge, pp. 33–60.

Nuttall, Mark 2009. "Living in a world of movement: Human resilience to environmental instability in Greenland." In Susan A. Crate and Mark Nuttall (eds) *Anthropology and Climate Change: From Encounters to Actions*. Walnut Creek, CA: Left Coast Press, pp. 292–310.

Nuttall, Mark 2012. "Imagining and governing the Greenlandic resource frontier." *The Polar Journal* 2(1): 113–124.

Nuttall, Mark 2013. "Zero-tolerance, uranium and Greenland's mining future." *The Polar Journal* 3(2): 368–383.

Nuttall, Mark 2015. "Subsurface politics: Greenlandic discourses on extractive industries." In Leif C. Jensen and Geir Hønneland (eds) *Handbook of the Politics of the Arctic*. Cheltenham, UK: Edward Elgar, pp. 105–127.

Nuttall, Mark 2016. "Narwhal hunters, seismic surveys and the Middle Ice: Monitoring environmental change in Greenland's Melville Bay." In Susan A. Crate and Mark Nuttall (eds) *Anthropology and Climate Change: From Actions to Transformations*. London: Routledge, pp. 354–372.

Nuttall, Mark, Fikret Berkes, Bruce Forbes, Gary Kofinas, Tatiana Vlassova and George W. Wenzel 2005. "Hunting, herding, fishing and gathering: Indigenous peoples and renewable resource use in the Arctic." In *Arctic Climate Impact Assessment. ACIA Scientific Report*. Cambridge, UK: Cambridge University Press, pp. 649–690.

Wang, Muyin and James E. Overland 2009. "A sea ice free summer Arctic within 30 years?" *Geophysical Research Letters* 36(7): L07502. doi:10.1029/2009GL037820

Wassmann, Paul and Timothy Lenton 2012. "Arctic tipping points in an Earth system perspective." *Ambio* 41(1): 1–9.

Watt-Cloutier, Sheila 2015. *The Right to Be Cold*. Toronto, ON: Penguin Canada.

Wenzel, George 1991. *Animal Rights, Human Rights: Economy, Ecology and Ideology in the Canadian Arctic*. Toronto, ON: University of Toronto Press.

19

TAKING RESPONSIBILITY FOR CLIMATE CHANGE

On human adaptation, sustainable consumption, and environmental governance[1]

Cindy Isenhour

Introduction: history and the current consumption–climate anomaly

Anthropology, with its deep historical and cross-cultural lens, reminds us that humans have adapted to a remarkable variety of conditions, both environmental and social. At the same time, a historical perspective also highlights the exceptional nature of the current moment, raising questions about adaptive capacity. The last several centuries are an anomaly, an outlier, which combine significant increases in population growth and environmental impact with intense social and economic interconnection at the global scale. While it is increasingly clear that global consumption and emissions patterns must be adapted in order to avoid resource depletion and dangerous climate change, the interdependent nature of the global economic system makes most governments hesitant to act unilaterally for fear of losing competitive advantage. A deeply popular alternative has emerged in the absence of adequate international and state-level governance – the idea that concerned individuals take responsibility for climate change. This chapter traces the development of the contemporary emphasis on consumer responsibility and explores its transformative potential relative to the urgency of adaptation in the age of climate change and high consumption.

The chapter begins with an historical review of the emergence of sustainable consumption as a dominant theme in international sustainable development, in environmental movements, and more recently, governmental climate mitigation policies. The second section discusses the promise of encouraging more consumer responsibility and briefly reviews empirical studies to illustrate some positive outcomes. The third section addresses critiques of consumer-based environmental governance. In the final section, the chapter links various perspectives to their policy implications and proposes strategies that might help to reconcile both the promise and perils of efforts to achieve more sustainable consumption patterns and reduce associated emissions.

A history of sustainable consumption

The contemporary emphasis on sustainable consumption is fairly recent, with roots reaching back only a few decades. I suggest here it emerged from the convergence of three parallel movements:

1   an increased emphasis on global equity in international governance organizations
2   a growing concern with personal engagement in the environmental movement
3   the dominance of free-market policies since the 1980s.

Global institutions and sustainability discourse

The earliest discussions about "sustainability" were focused on population growth and environmental degradation in the "third world" (Adams 2001). Inspired by Paul and Anne Ehrlich's *The Population Bomb* (1968) and Meadows and colleagues' *The Limits of Growth* (1972), neo-Malthusian ideas were popular during the 1972 United Nations Conference on the Human Environment, resulting in the development of environment-centric conservation agendas, often referred to as "coercive conservation" (Conca 2005). Developing nations, however, argued that in laying so much blame on localized resource use and population growth, global connections had been mystified and the need for basic human development and poverty alleviation ignored.

These concerns were acknowledged in the Brundtland Report (UN World Commission on Environment and Development 1987) which placed greater emphasis on issues of justice. Yet as Cohen (2005) observed, the resource-intensive lifestyles of the global North continued to escape critical scrutiny thanks to "a broad coalition of affluent countries, led by the US (which) was loath to include any substantive treatment of the environmental implications of consumption" (2005: 23–24). With the approach of the 1992 Earth Summit in Rio de Janeiro, however, a vocal coalition of developing countries "insisted on broadening the list of actors that contributed to ecological deterioration beyond the obligatory reference to population growth" (Cohen 2005: 23–24). This shift can be seen in the World Conservation Union's 1991 document *Caring for the Earth* which argued that a "concerted effort is needed to reduce energy and resource consumption by upper income countries" (1991: 44). One year later in Rio, the UN Conference on the Environment and Development directed increased attention toward sustainable consumption. Consider, for example, the following passage from chapter 4 of the Rio Declaration: "While poverty results in certain kinds of environmental stress, the major cause of the continued deterioration of the global environment is the unsustainable pattern of consumption and production, particularly in industrialized countries" (UNCED 1992: 4.3).

The Rio Declaration encouraged voluntary efforts to eliminate unsustainable production and consumption patterns. This call was taken up in earnest by some governments (Fuchs and Lorek 2005; Isenhour 2010a) but sustainable consumption continued to be conceptually imagined as a subset of sustainable production (Cohen 2005), resulting in ecological modernization policies based on the conviction that ecological crises could be overcome by supply chain and infrastructural innovation, but this failed to engage consumers (Feichtinger and Pregernig 2005).

By the 2002 World Summit on Sustainable Development (WSSD) in Johannesburg, consumption had emerged as a dominant theme in sustainability discourse (Cohen 2005). Voluntary "Marrakech Process" frameworks were launched in 2003, with the intent of mobilizing "multi-stakeholder groups" to "accelerate the shift toward sustainable consumption" (UNEP 2015: online). The adoption of a new 10-year framework at the Rio+20 meetings in 2013 continues this work to encourage voluntary sustainable consumption and production patterns. These developments certainly helped to give rise to the current emphasis on sustainable consumerism, but not in isolation. During the same time period there was also a strong push within the environmental movement to broaden support by encouraging personal responsibility.

Individual environmental practice and new social movements

Over the last several decades we've seen the rapid expansion of markets for green, eco-labeled, fair trade, and organic goods. Meanwhile systems for local and alternative provisioning have grown more robust with the development of community-supported agriculture, farmers' markets, and urban gardening initiatives. Others are going further to reduce total consumption through second-hand purchases or participating in voluntary simplicity, freeganism (also known colloquially as dumpster diving), or compacter movements. We can tie these movements to several decades of environmental and social education programs driven by non-governmental organizations (NGOs). The World Wide Fund for Nature (WWF), Greenpeace, and Friends of the Earth have long focused on increasing awareness and encouraging individuals to take responsibility for their personal choices.

This engagement with individuals is reflective of "new social movements" which emerged in the 1960s and 1970s. They are characterized by a novel relationship between the citizen, state, and market – one which focuses on self-determination, individual identity, and "quality of life" issues (Habermas 1984 [1981]). Niklas Rose has argued that this new arrangement, which places more emphasis on individual responsibility, is characteristic of "advanced liberalism" in which governance is no longer achieved by regulating society, but rather through the "regulated choices of individual citizens, now construed as subjects of choices and aspirations to self-actualization and fulfillment" (Rose 1996: 41).

The market logic and policies of advanced liberalism

Finally, the focus on sustainable consumption can also be linked to growing disappointment in the ability or willingness of the state to solve environmental and social problems in many international contexts (Guthman 2008; Allen 2010). The alternative "power in numbers" approach was intended to signal collective environmental values and thus build legitimacy for more progressive policies. Ironically, however, the movement's acceptance of consumer responsibility enabled states to devolve responsibility for environmental welfare and move further away from environmental regulation (Princen *et al.* 2002). Thus the push toward individual responsibility was both a response to and an affirmation of the free-market logics which have grown increasingly dominant since the 1980s. Based on the assumption that free consumers will make rational choices, ultimately resulting in the public good (Carrier and Miller 2000; Lyon 2006), market logic favors the removal of state regulation in favor of voluntary market-based mechanisms. These ideas were captured by Milton and Rose Friedman (1980: 65–66) who wrote at the dawn of neoliberal ideologies in 1980, "When you vote daily in the supermarket, you get precisely what you voted for, and so does everyone else. The ballot box produces conformity without unanimity; the marketplace, unanimity without conformity."

On the promise of sustainable consumption: pragmatism, democracy, and incrementalism

Leveraging the market

There is evidence to suggest that consumers want more environmentally, socially, and economically efficient market alternatives and that many industries are responding. A comparative study in the EU suggests that between a quarter and a third of consumers report boycotting or intentionally buying (buycotting) a product in order to support a cause (Kjærnes *et al.* 2007). In the United States, a survey conducted in 2012 found that more than half of the respondents (54 percent) reported having bought a product with social or environmental benefit in the past year, and 42 percent self-reported boycotting a product, brand, or company after learning about irresponsible behavior (Cone Communications 2013). Corporations have strong incentives to respond to consumer interests and demands, given that they benefit from exploiting rapidly expanding markets, like those associated with green product lines. Corporations are also heavily invested in protecting the value of their brands from environmental and social criticisms. Corporations must, at a minimum, demonstrate movement toward environmental and social responsibility in order to avoid regulation (Marsden *et al.* 2000), and ensure adequate employee motivation and morale (Jacobsen and Dulsrud 2007).

Well-publicized consumer boycotts can achieve significant results – bringing about modified investment, sourcing, and production priorities and policies (Conroy 2001; Clouder and Harrison 2006; Munro and Schurman 2008). In 2010, for example, Greenpeace launched a social media campaign and boycott targeting Nestlé's Kit Kat brand to highlight tropical deforestation associated with palm oil production. After more than 1.5 million people viewed the campaign's spoof ad and 200,000 emails were sent to Nestlé headquarters, the company agreed to a plan for sustainable palm oil sourcing. Conroy (2001: 18) argues that in the context of a global trading system and increasing privatization and deregulation, efforts to place market pressure on firms constitute "powerful alternatives to simple invocations of corporate altruism and civic responsibility" and "may be the only alternative to the competitive downgrading of social and environmental practices by firms worldwide."

Political participation and democratic movement

Proponents of the focus on sustainable consumption also claim that these movements provide a new, expanded, and promising means for democratic political participation (Micheletti 2003). Ulrich Beck has argued (as paraphrased by Sassatelli 2006: 223) that "if modernity was a democracy oriented to producers, late modernity is a democracy oriented to consumers: a pragmatic and cosmopolitan democracy where the sleepy giant of the 'sovereign citizen-consumer' is becoming a counterweight to big transnational corporations." Here, in what Trentman (2004) calls the new orthodoxy of the active consumer, individuals are seen as active and rational agents who, in aggregate, have the power to challenge dominant economic and political structures and contribute to a new "globalized democracy" (Dolan 2002).

Cognitive consistency, moral subjectivity, and relations of care

Sustainable consumption can also help to elucidate global commodity chains (Goss 2004), making more apparent the ecological and social conditions of production, helping to increase "knowledge of chains of consequences" (Barnett *et al.* 2005: 24). Many respond to increased knowledge of the social and environmental consequences of production through the expression of solidarity and moral obligation, enacted through alternative consumer behaviors (Connolly and Prothero 2008). These actions, regardless of their objective efficacy, allow consumers to realign their consumption behaviors in ways consistent with their personal values and in opposition to impersonal market logics which reduce us to self-interested actors concerned primarily with personal financial costs and benefits (Wright and Middendorf 2008: 278; Carrier and Leuchford 2012).

Barnett and his colleagues (2005) describe this process of resistance and alternative identity formation as "moral selving". There is evidence to suggest that participation in "nourishing networks" (Whatmore and Thorne 1997), "moral economies" (Luetchford 2008), or "ethics of care" (Bauman 2008; Featherstone 2011) have helped consumers to feel a sense of internal consistency (Jaffee *et al.* 2004: 184; Lyon 2006; Shreck 2008). By participating in such networks, sustainable consumers can create more ethical and internally consistent identities (Lyon 2006; Bauman 2008; Binkley 2008). Soper and colleagues (2009) suggested that alternative consumerism can thus be about a re-imagination of the good life, one in which consumers achieve satisfaction by realigning their behaviors and values. There is also some evidence to suggest that the act of creating an alternative consumer identity, and the efforts required to maintain it, can facilitate entry into more significant participation (Barnett *et al.* 2005; Guthman 2008).

Inspiration, hope, and pragmatic change

Uncountable individuals have responded to their concerns for sustainability through modifications of their consumption behavior. Their rationales for doing so are surely varied and complex, but studies suggest a shared desire to make a difference and lead by example. The movement has to start somewhere and many concerned about sustainability hope their early adoption might help to inspire fellow citizens and policy makers to do their "fair share." While consumers' actions are highly individual, there is a sense that their values are shared with others and that "individualized collective action" can add up (Micheletti 2003).

On the challenges of sustainable consumption: power, structure, and scale

Despite several decades of consumer education, the growing availability of alternatives on the market, significant optimism, and the efforts of uncountable consumers and citizens – sustainable consumption patterns have clearly failed to emerge. Hobson writes, "Although reducing levels and impacts from production and consumption has been a pivotal socio-environmental goal for decades, resource use continues to grow rapidly" (2013a: 1082). This section traces several prominent critiques of the contemporary focus on consumer responsibility in an attempt to explore why efforts to encourage more sustainable consumption have not been more successful.

Information is not sufficient

The most common explanations for increased resource use and degradation are linked to the assumption that people are not adequately aware of or interested in environmental problems. The implication is that more information is necessary to inform consumers who will then, voluntarily, make the right choice (Halkier 2001). These ideas make perfect sense in the context of advanced liberal capitalist societies which are hesitant to regulate choice or impinge on market freedoms for fear of damaging the economy and collective well-being – but empirical research has long questioned their validity.

Public opinion polling suggests that large majorities in the world's most consumptive societies are aware of and concerned about environmental problems (European Commission 2014; Gallup 2014). In the United States, home to one of the most consumptive economies in the world, citizens have consistently prioritized environmental protection over economic growth during times of economic stability (Gallup 2014).

Decision scientists have long observed significant "gaps" between environmental know-ledge, attitudes, and behaviors (Ölander and Thøgersen 1995). Even those most concerned about the environment frequently make choices contrary to their environmental values and concerns (Isenhour 2010a). Indeed, consumers are often ambivalent and inconsistent as they balance multiple consumption priorities like convenience, price, quality, and prestige (Halkier 2001). In fact, consumers frequently report much higher levels of pro-environmental con-sumption than analyses of their behavior suggest. What is more disturbing is that consumers who report engaging in behaviors designed to reduce their environmental impact frequently have ecological and climate footprints similar to – and in some circumstances, larger than – consumers without an interest in environmental issues (Csutoria 2013). This is often due to rebound effects, when decisions to conserve energy or resources result in the transfer of savings into other spending categories with more significant environmental impact. This phenomenon, variously referred to as "take back", "the rebound effect," or "Jevon's Paradox" has been demonstrated in a variety of contexts (Greening *et al.* 2000; Andrews 2013).

These research findings are not presented to argue that consumer education is unnecessary; certainly it is an important part of the solution (Kopnina 2011). But these data raise questions about whether our long-standing emphasis on providing consumers with more education and then trusting them to make green choices is adequate (Wilk 2004). If even the most aware and committed consumers find it difficult to objectively reduce their environmental impact, there are clearly other factors at play.

Lack of opportunity and structural barriers

Ölander and Thøgersen (1995) propose that "opportunity" is an important variable mediating the relationship between environmental awareness and attitudes and behaviors. They write (1995: 360), "consistency between attitudes and behavior can be expected only if that behavior depends solely on the actor's free choice, that is, if the actor commands the necessary and sufficient will-power, abilities, resources and technical means to perform the behavior"; they go on to acknowledge that "many, maybe most, environmentally relevant behaviors are not completely volitional in this strict sense."

Barriers linked to sociality and normativity are particularly salient. Consumption decisions are shaped by cultural imaginaries and a whole array of socially derived behavioral norms. Celebrated anthropologist Mary Douglas once wrote:

> Instead of starting from the individual confronting his own basic needs, cultural theory starts from a system in which a consumer knows that s/he is expected to play some part or s/he will not get any income. Everything that s/he chooses to do or to buy is part of a project to choose other people . . . the forms of consumption which s/he prefers are those that maintain the kind of collectivity s/he likes to be in.
>
> *(Douglas 2004: 145)*

Understanding the social nature of consumption allows us to move beyond individualist explanations for sustainable consumption's failures – such as a lack of information, non-virtuous behavior, or problems associated with a lack of willpower (Jacobsen and Dulsrud 2007). Further, it helps us to recognize the productive functions of consumption including the expression of care (Miller 2001a), identity construction, and symbolic communication (Shove 2004). Given the social and symbolic functions of consumption, Baudrillard has argued that asking consumers to voluntarily restrict consumption is nothing more than "naïve and absurd moralism" (1970: 68).

Without collective movement and social validity, it is no wonder that many sustainable consumers have reported that their environmental values threaten to isolate them. Without seeing other people engaging in similar pro-environmental behaviors, they feel as though they are shouldering an unfair burden (Isenhour 2010b) and are reluctant to act more progressively in the face of the seeming inactivity of others (Hobson 2013b).

The individualization of risk and responsibility

I've argued elsewhere (Isenhour 2010a, 2010b) that sustainable consumption's contemporary focus on voluntary, individual choice is implicated in its failure. The devolution of responsibility for environmental welfare away from states and toward individual actors constricts the state's primary role to that of an information provider. If consumers or producers do not respond to social marketing campaigns, the state isn't implicated. Rather, it succeeds in having promoted both environmental welfare and the interests of the market. Yet this strategy puts a lot of pressure on caring individuals when many contemporary environmental problems have roots that grow far beyond the consumer's sphere of influence and control.

As Dolan writes:

> [C]onsumer practices are cultural and social practices that have historically developed and are manifestations of both local and global linkages of social interdependencies. To continually look at the consumer as the cause of the ecological problem effectively decontextualizes consumption acts from such interdependencies.
>
> *(Dolan 2002: 171)*

While we blame consumers for their inability to engage it is certainly true that consumers have very little influence over corporate marketing practices, product design, or larger structural issues associated with global finance and the dismantling of environmental regulations. This of course raises the question about how wise it is to rely on voluntary niches to operate on the scale necessary to address contemporary environmental and social problems (Hobson 2013b).

Further, if our actions become overly intimate and limited to the private realm, they become "silent routines" (Halkier 1999). Wright and Middendorf write that:

> altering your habits of milk consumption, or of any consumable good for that matter . . . is localized change . . . it is unlikely to bring about wider transformative change unless diffused to a broader audience that has the power to effect change . . . collective action stands a better chance of realizing systemic change.
>
> *(Wright and Middendorf 2008: 15)*

Indeed, many researchers have observed that individuals are more powerful when acting in the civic realm (Gabriel and Lang 2005; Johnston 2008) and warn that if responsibility for environmental welfare becomes overly individualized, "there is little room to ponder institutions, the nature and exercise of political power, or ways of collectively changing . . . society" (Maniates 2002: 45).

A second, related critique of the focus on individual choice is related to the channeling of participation and activism through the market – where signaled preferences and values are intercepted by trend spotters and marketers rather than public leaders with the power to enact more significant structural changes. There is certainly an irony in the commodification and marketing of consumer dissent, as Naomi Klein has persuasively argued (1999; see also Gladwell 2000).

Finally, many argue that the emphasis on individual choice may be dangerously misleading. Sustainable consumption is framed in the realm of choice, but the reality is that many people do not have access to choice. We can certainly all "vote with our wallets," but the richer the consumer in this system, the more powerful and "ethical," "sustainable," or "moral" he or she becomes (Dolan 2002). One wallet does not equal one vote in this inherently non-democratic conceptualization of culture change. It is little wonder then that the movement toward sustainable consumption is viewed with skepticism by those who see it as an elite practice in which relatively wealthy consumers often buy exclusive products without thinking reflexively about consumption as a practice. Consumption has increasingly come to be seen as an individual right in wealthy post-industrial societies (Fuchs and Lorek 2005). But many see this evocation of rights as a means for the world's most privileged to defend their ability to choose products that are extremely harmful, particularly for the world's most vulnerable communities and ecosytems. Vulnerable locales often do not have the ability to choose whether their waters are used for the production of goods destined for foreign markets or their rainforests should be felled to make room for oil palm plantations. The emphasis on consumer choice rather than restriction in contemporary manifestations of sustainable consumption is thus seen by critics as a defense of power and privilege rather than an earnest attempt to limit, through collective means, irresponsible and damaging consumption and production practices. Guthman (2003: 151) writes, "making risk management a matter of consumer choice rather than public choice is troubling . . . as if it is sufficient to make a personal decision as to whether a particular material or practice constitutes harm."

Reproduction of an existing system

Critics of the movement toward consumer responsibility also argue that these movements have played right into the hands of the problem, helping to reproduce the same ideologies they portend to resist. Indeed there is an irony associated with practices that seek to solve problems of unregulated markets and overconsumption – with less regulated markets and more consumption (Lyon and Moberg 2010). Johnston writes that this "conservation through consumption" approach "maximizes commodity choice, while minimizing the citizen's ecological responsibilities to restrain consumption" (2008: 259). Further, the very focus on consumption as a solution solidifies the centrality and significance of consumption practice (Dolan 2002).

Conclusion: reconciling movement potential and the urgency of adaptation

The goal to encourage more sustainable consumption patterns and reduce associated emissions is certainly important, but more substantial movement will require policies that can move the majority, not just the committed fringe, toward less environmentally destructive practices (Miller 2001b). As Allen reminds us, "no social advances have ever been made without a combination of social movements and legislation" (2010: 306).

Further, sustainable consumption practices are more likely to be adopted if they are regulated by collective means (Ölander and Thøgersen 1995), overcoming problems associated with free riding or accusations of unequal access. Consumption decisions are significantly influenced by reference groups and social comparison (Welsch and Kühling 2009), making it much more likely that people will modify behaviors if their social and reference groups have acted similarly under a uniform policy.

The world economy, resource use, and global greenhouse gas concentrations continue to grow quickly and most analysts suggest that the global middle class will triple by 2030, creating even greater strain on natural resources and earth systems. While humans have proven resourceful and adaptive in a wide variety of contexts, the challenges we face are unique and increasingly urgent. It is certainly imperative that production and consumption systems adapt to reflect growing understanding of ecological limits and dangerous climate change, but the contemporary focus on consumer responsibility is an insufficient strategy. As Dauvergne (2010: 5) has remarked, "changing the environmental choices of enough consumers fast enough to make a global difference is very hard and getting harder."

Notes

1 A longer and modified version of this chapter was previously published under the title "Sustainable Consumption and its Discontents" in *Sustainability: Key Issues*, edited by Helen Kopnina and Eleanor Shoreman-Ouimet, Routledge, 2015. Reproduced material is reprinted here with permission from and thanks to Routledge.

References

Adams, W. (2001) *Green Development. Environment and Sustainability in the Third World*. New York: Routledge.

Allen, P. (2010) Realizing Justice in Local Food Systems. *Cambridge Journal of Regions, Economy and Society* 3(2): 295–308.

Andrews, C. (2013) Empowering Sustainable Consumption. *IEEE Technology and Society Magazine* Fall: 8–9.

Barnett, C., P. Cloke, N. Clarke and A. Malpass (2005) Consuming Ethics: Articulating the Subjects and Spaces of Ethical Consumption. *Antipode* 37(1): 23–45.

Baudrillard, J. (1970) *The Consumer Society: Myths and Structures*. London: Sage.

Bauman, Z. (2008) *Does Ethics Have a Chance in a World of Consumers?* Cambridge, MA: Harvard University Press.

Binkley, S. (2008) Liquid Consumption: Anti-Consumerism and the Fetishized De-Fetishization of Commodities. *Cultural Studies* 22(5): 599–623.

Carrier, J. and D. Miller (2000) From Private Virtue to Public Vice. In H. L. Moore (ed.) *Anthropological Theory Today*. Malden, MA: Blackwell, pp. 24–47.

Carrier, J. and P. Leuchford (2012) *Ethical Consumption: Social Value and Economic Practice*. New York: Berghahn Books.

Clouder, S. and R. Harrison (2006) The Effectiveness of Ethical Consumer Behavior. In R. Harrison, T. Newholm and D. Shaw (eds) *The Ethical Consumer*. London: Sage, pp. 89–102.

Cohen, M. J. (2005) Sustainable Consumption in National Context: An Introduction to the Special Issue. *Sustainability: Science, Practice and Policy* 1(1): 22–28.

Conca, K. (2005) Environmental Governance after Johannesburg: From Stalled Legalization to Environmental Human Rights? *Journal of International Law and International Relations* 1(1–2): 121–138.

Cone Communications (2013) Cone Communications Social Impact Study: The Next Cause Evolution. www.conecomm.com/2013-social-impact (accessed 20 November 2015).

Connolly, J. and A. Prothero (2008) Green Consumption: Life-Politics, Risk and Contradictions. *Journal of Consumer Culture* 8(1): 117–154.

Conroy, M. E. (2001) Can Advocacy-Led Certification Systems Transform Global Corporate Practices? Evidence and Some Theory. Political Economy Research Institute Working Paper Series, No. 21.

Csutoria, M. (2013) One More Awareness Gap: The Behavior–Impact Gap Problem. *Journal of Consumer Policy* 35(1): 145–163.

Dauvergne, P. (2010) The Problem of Consumption. *Global Environmental Politics* 10(2): 1–10.

Dolan, P. (2002) The Sustainability of "Sustainable Consumption." *Journal of Macromarketing* 22(2): 170–181.

Douglas, M. (2004) Consumers Revolt. In D. B. Clarke, M. A. Doel and K. M. L. Housiaux (eds) *The Consumption Reader*. New York: Routledge, 144–149.

Ehrlich, P. (1968) *The Population Bomb*. New York: Ballantine Books.

European Commission (2014) Special Eurobarometer 416: Attitudes of European Citizens towards the Environment. http://ec.europa.eu/public_opinion/archives/ebs/ebs_416_en.pdf (accessed 11 November 2014).

Featherstone, M. (2011) Foreword. In T. Lewis and E. Potter (eds) *Ethical Consumption: A Critical Introduction*. New York: Routledge, pp. xvii–xxviii.

Feichtinger, J. and M. Pregernig (2005) Imagined Citizens and Participation: Local Agenda 21 in Two Communities in Sweden and Australia. *Local Environment* 10(3): 229–242.

Friedman, M. and R. Friedman (1980) *Free to Choose: A Personal Statement*. New York: Harcourt Brace Jovanovich.

Fuchs D. A. and S. Lorek (2005) Sustainable Consumption Governance: A History of Promises and Failures. *Journal of Consumer Policy* 28(3): 261–288.

Gabriel, Y. and T. Lang (2005) A Brief History of Consumer Activism. In R. Harrison, T. Newholm and D. Shaw (eds) *The Ethical Consumer*. Thousand Oaks, CA: Sage, pp. 39–53.

Gallup (2014) Americans Again Pick Environment over Economic Growth. www.gallup.com/poll/168017/americans-again-pick-environment-economic-growth.aspx (accessed 15 November 2014).

Gladwell, M. (2000) The Coolhunt. In E. Schor and D. Holt (eds) *The Consumer Society Reader*. New York: New York Press, pp. 360–374.

Goss, J. (2004) Geography of Consumption. *Progress in Human Geography* 28(3): 369–380.

Greening, L A., D. L. Greene and C. Difiglio (2000) Energy Efficiency and Consumption: The Rebound Effect—A Survey. *Energy Policy* 28(6–7): 389–401.

Guthman, J. (2003) Eating Risk: The Politics of Labeling Genetically Engineered Foods. In R. Schurman and D. D. Kelso (eds) *Engineering Trouble: Biotechnology and its Discontents*. Los Angeles: University of California Press, pp. 130–151.

—— (2008) Neoliberalism and the Making of Food Politics in California. *Geoforum* 39(3): 1171–1183.

Habermas, J. (1984 [1981]) *Reason and the Rationalization of Society*. Volume 1 of *The Theory of Communicative Action* (English transl. by T. McCarthy). Boston, MA: Beacon Press.

Halkier, B. (1999) Consequences of the Politicization of Consumption: The Example of Environmentally Friendly Consumption Practices. *Journal of Environmental Policy and Planning* 1(1): 25–41.

Halkier, B. (2001) Consuming Ambivalences: Consumer Handling of Environmentally Related Risks in Food. *Journal of Consumer Culture* 1(2): 205–224.

Hobson, K. (2013a) "Weak" or "Strong" Sustainable Consumption? Efficiency, Degrowth and the 10 Year Framework of Programmes. *Environment and Planning C: Government and Policy* 31(6): 1082–1098.

Hobson, K. (2013b) On the Making of the Environmental Citizen. *Environmental Politics* 22(1): 56–72.

Isenhour, C. (2010a) Building Sustainable Societies: A Swedish Case Study on the Limits of Reflexive Modernization. *American Ethnologist* 37(3): 511–525.

—— (2010b) On Conflicted Swedish Consumers, the Effort to "Stop Shopping" and Neoliberal Environmental Governance. *Journal of Consumer Behavior* 9(6) (Special Issue on Anti-Consumption and Sustainability): 454–469.

Jacobsen, E. and A. Dulsrud (2007) Will Consumers Save the World? The Framing of Political Consumerism. *Journal of Agricultural and Environmental Ethics* 20(5): 469–482.

Jaffee, D., J. R. Kloppenburg and M. B. Monroy (2004) Bringing the "Moral Charge" Home: Fair Trade within the North and within the South. *Rural Sociology* 69(2): 169–196.

Johnston, J. (2008) The Citizen–Consumer Hybrid: Ideological Tensions and the Case of Whole Foods Market. *Theory and Society* 37(3): 229–270.

Kjærnes, U., M. Harvey and A. Warde (2007) *Trust in Food. A Comparative and Institutional Analysis.* London: Palgrave Macmillan.

Klein, N. (1999) *No Logo.* Toronto, ON: Knopf Canada.

Kopnina, H. (2011) What about that Wrapper? Using Consumption Diaries in Green Education. In H. Kopnina and E. Shoreman-Ouimet (eds) *Environmental Anthropology Today.* New York and Oxford: Routledge, pp. 118–139.

Luetchford, P. (2008) *Fair Trade and a Global Commodity: Coffee in Costa Rica.* London: Pluto Press.

Lyon, S. (2006) Migratory Imaginations: The Commodification and Contradictions of Shade Grown Coffee. *Social Anthropology* 14(3): 377–390.

Lyon, S. and M. Moberg (2010) *Fair Trade and Social Justice: Global Ethnographies.* New York: New York University Press.

Maniates, M. (2002) Individualization: Plant a Tree, Buy a Bike, Save the World? In T. Princen, M. Maniates and K. Conca (eds) *Confronting Consumption.* Cambridge, MA: The MIT Press, pp. 43–66.

Marsden, T., A. Flynn and M. Harrison (2000) *Consuming Interests: The Social Provision of Foods.* London: UCL Press.

Meadows, Donella, Dennis Meadows, J. Randers and W. Behrens (1972) *The Limits to Growth.* New York: Universe Books.

Micheletti, M. (2003) *Political Virtue and Shopping: Individuals, Consumerism, and Collective Action.* New York: Palgrave Macmillan.

Miller, D. (2001a) *The Dialectics of Shopping.* Chicago, IL: University of Chicago Press.

—— (2001b) The Poverty of Morality. *Journal of Consumer Culture* 1(2): 225–244.

Munro, W. A. and R. Schurman (2008) Sustaining Outrage: Motivating Sensibilities in the U.S. Anti-GE Movement. In W. Wright and G. Middendorf (eds) *The Fight over Food: Producers, Consumers, and Activists Challenge the Global Food System.* University Park: Pennsylvania State University Press, pp. 145–176.

Ölander, F. and J. Thøgersen (1995) Understanding of Consumer Behaviour as a Prerequisite for Environmental Protection. *Journal of Consumer Policy* 18: 317–357.

Princen, T., M. Maniates and K. Conca (2002) *Confronting Consumption.* Cambridge, MA: The MIT Press.

Rose, N. (1996) Governing "Advanced" Liberal Democracies. In A. Barry, T. Osborne and N. Rose (eds) *Foucault and Political Reason: Liberalism, Neo-Liberalism and Rationalities of Government.* Chicago, IL: University of Chicago Press, pp. 37–64.

Sassatelli, R. (2006) Virtue, Responsibility and Consumer Choice: Framing Critical Consumerism. In J. Brewer and F. Trentmann (eds) *Consuming Cultures, Global Perspectives: Historical Trajectories, Transnational Exchanges* Oxford: Berg Publishers, pp. 219–250.

Shove, E. (2004) *Comfort, Cleanliness and Convenience: The Social Organization of Normality.* London: Berg.

Shreck, A. (2008) Resistance, Redistribution, and Power in the Fair Trade Banana Initiative. In W. Wright and G. Middendorfl (eds) *The Fight over Food: Producers, Consumers, and Activists Challenge the Global Food System.* University Park: Pennsylvania State University Press, pp. 121–144.

Soper, K., M. Ryle and L. Thomas (2009) *The Politics and Pleasures of Consuming Differently.* London: Palgrave Macmillan.

Trentmann, F. (2004) Beyond Consumerism: New Historical Perspectives on Consumption. *Journal of Contemporary History* 39(3): 373–401.

UNCED (1992) Rio Declaration on Environment and Development. Rio de Janeiro, Brazil: United Nations Conference on Environment and Development.

UNEP (2015) Marrakech Process. UN Environment Programme Division of Technology, Industry and Economics: Sustainable Consumption and Production Branch. www.unep.fr/scp/marrakech/ (accessed 23 March 2015).

UN World Commission on Environment and Development (1987) *Our Common Future.* Oxford and New York: Oxford University Press.

Welsch, H. and J. Kühling (2009) Determinants of Pro-Environmental Consumption: The Role of Reference Groups and Routine Behavior. *Ecological Economics* 69(1): 166–176.

Whatmore, S. J. and L. B. Thorne (1997) Nourishing Networks: Alternative Geographies of Food. In D. Goodman and M. Watts (eds) *Globalizing Food: Agrarian Questions and Global Restructuring*. London and New York: Routledge, pp. 287–304.

Wilk, R. (2004) Questionable Assumptions about Sustainable Consumption. In L. Reisch and I. Røpke (eds) *The Ecological Economics of Consumption*. Current Issues in Ecological Economics series. Cheltenham, UK: Edward Elgar, pp. 17–22.

World Conservation Union (1991). *Caring for the Earth: A Strategy for Sustainable Living*. Gland, Switzerland: WCU.

Wright, W. and G. Middendorf (2008) Introduction: Fighting over Food – Change in the Agrifood System. In W. Wright and G. Middendorf (eds) *The Fight over Food: Producers, Consumers, and Activists Challenge the Global Food System*. University Park: Pennsylvania State University Press, pp. 1–28.

20

CLIMATE CHANGE ADAPTATION AND DEVELOPMENT PLANNING

From resilience to transformation?

Bob Pokrant

Introduction

Adaptation is a central concept in climate change research and policy-making and is increasingly being integrated into development planning under rubrics such as mainstreaming, climate-resilient development, and climate-compatible development. This chapter examines the relationship between climate change adaptation (CCA) and development, drawing on anthropological and related disciplines to examine how selected national governments, non-governmental organisations (NGOs), business, and local communities engage with the coupling of CCA to development planning. It shows that current mainstreaming policies seek to accommodate adaptation initiatives within established development paradigms and projects using a resilience-based framework. These policies have been criticised as insufficient to bring about long-term sustainability. Critics argue that a shift towards more transformative initiatives and a rethinking of current development paradigms are required.

Anthropologists are engaged in climate change (CC) and development studies in a variety of ways (Baer and Singer 2014; Barnes and Dove 2015; Barnes *et al.* 2013; Crate 2011; Crate and Nuttall 2009; Dove 2014; Inderberg *et al.* 2015; Krauss 2015; Rudiak-Gould 2009, 2014; Strauss 2012). A key focus of anthropological and related disciplinary research is how local communities in developing countries are affected by and respond to human-induced and natural hazards, including those related to climate change and variability; how their responses are affected by cultural values and political relations, and the ways in which climate change issues are embedded in wider social, historical, and development contexts (Barnes *et al.* 2013). Of particular cross-disciplinary importance is how CCA initiatives and development processes and projects intersect nationally and locally.

The chapter summarises the background to development and climate change studies; looks critically at the nexus between CCA and development planning and practice in selected developing countries; and discusses current debates on climate-resilient and climate-compatible development pathways.

Part 1: Climate change, adaptation, and development

Anthropological research on CC and development brings together the multi-disciplinary fields of development studies and climate change. The anthropology of development originates in the Cold War in the 1950s with antecedents in the evolutionary anthropology of the nineteenth century, archaeology, and the twentieth-century shift to fieldwork-based studies of yet-to-become developing societies. Anthropological studies of contemporary anthropogenic climate change date from the 1990s (Crate 2011), although weather and climate variability have been topics of anthropological inquiry since the discipline's founding (Dove 2014). This renewed interest has found official expression in the 2014 American Anthropological Association final report entitled *Changing the Atmosphere: Anthropology and Climate Change* (Fiske *et al.* 2014), which provides a summary of anthropology's engagement with climate change and recommendations for future research and policy direction.

Most climate scientists agree that contemporary climate change, manifested in rising global average temperatures, sea-level rise, changing weather patterns and ecological systems, is largely human-induced and the product of the last two centuries' fossil fuels and energy- and material-intensive economic growth in today's developed countries – with more recent increases in greenhouse gas emissions (GGEs) from China, India, Brazil, and South Africa (IPCC 2014). The main agents of this historical process have been the political and economic elites of those countries located at particular times and places (Malm and Hornborg 2014). Contemporary climate change is one manifestation of a wider domestication and subordination of the non-human world to serve human needs since the beginning of human inhabitation of the planet. This domestication and subordination took a global turn from the sixteenth century when a world economy centred in Europe began to emerge out of the unequal incorporation of diverse peoples into networks of trade, conquest, plunder of natural resources, and new systems of production and extraction based on new forms of property ownership and labour exploitation (Mannion 2014; Radkau 2008; Richards 2005; Wolf 1982). This transformation intensified after 1945 with the rise to global pre-eminence of the USA and the Soviet Union and the race for what became known as development, an ideologically charged attempt to control the economic and political direction of the majority of the world's human populations variously characterised as underdeveloped, developing, emerging, and transitional.

Today, 'development' has several referents (Crewe and Axelby 2012). It refers to processes of industrial change since the eighteenth century (Cowen and Shenton 1996), which in its initial stages saw the growing mechanisation of production and natural resource extraction linked to the ideology of capitalism organised around the private ownership and control of the productive process, and the emergence of a non-property owning and legally free wage-labour force supported by the dominant political elites of the day. These technological and legal changes were buttressed by discourses or sets of ideas about how to think about development in order to shape and legitimate its meaning and direction (Escobar 1995; Ziai 2013). These historic material and discursive processes have underpinned the post-1945 development project defined as 'the purposeful pursuit of economic, social and political goals through planned intervention' (Crewe and Axelby 2013: 3). Such planned intervention is aimed officially at improving people's material and other conditions. This aim has shifted since the 1980s from a national and largely state-directed project (the development project) to more market-directed change operating across national boundaries (the globalisation project) (McMichael 2011).

Dryzek (2005: 52) describes this period as guided by a Promethean view of the relationship between society, economy, and the rest of nature in which humans were considered to possess an unlimited technological and organisational capacity to deal with any problem. This view and its material outcomes have transformed the world to such a degree that a new and controversial term, the Anthropocene, has been used to describe the growing role of humans in shaping earth systems, calling into question traditional dichotomies between culture and nature and the capacity of humans to provide effective planetary stewardship (Ehlers 2006; Hamilton *et al.* 2015; Lövbrand *et al.* 2015).

From 1945 to the 1980s, development planning in developing countries put wealth creation, rapid economic growth, and the raising of material living standards above environmental protection. From the 1970s, accumulating evidence on development-induced environmental damage (Millennium Ecosystem Assessment 2005) and growing pressure from civil society led to a reassessment of the way humans related to the non-human world and to each other, which culminated in the establishment of Sustainable Development (SD) as the grand, if contested, official narrative of the age. The SD narrative seeks to legitimate particular economic growth-based and environmentally sensitive development pathways that satisfy particular sets of global, national, and regional interest coalitions (Du Pisani 2006; Mitcham 1995; Mosse 2005). Its derivatives include ecological modernisation (Hajer 1995; Mol and Spaargaren 2000), green growth (Jacobs 2013; UNEP 2011), the new climate economy (GCEC 2014), and eco-modernism (Shellenberger and Nordhaus 2011). This reassessment has intensified with concerns over climate change, and was reiterated by governments at the 2012 Rio+20 United Nations Summit. They committed themselves to develop sustainable development goals (SDGs) to be incorporated into the Millennium Development Goals (MDGs) by 2015 (Kumi *et al.* 2014; UNDESA 2015). Two goals proposed are that climate change should be integrated into all national development plans through 'sustained, inclusive and sustainable economic growth, full and productive employment and decent work for all' (UNDESA 2015: SDG 8). One means of integration is through linking of CCA strategies to development planning at the local and national levels, referred to variously as mainstreaming, climate-proofing (C-P), climate-resilient development (CRD), and climate-compatible development (CCD).[1] Of these, CCD seeks to incorporate both adaptation and mitigation strategies[2] and provide what is referred to as 'triple-wins' in adaptation, mitigation, and development (Boyle *et al.* 2013).

Developing countries, for historical reasons, have regarded mitigation as the responsibility of high-income countries (Hurrell and Sengupta 2012). Such responsibility is being extended to several developing countries (Brazil, China, India, South Africa) with rapidly increasing total and per capita GGEs, and there are pressures on other developing countries with lower per capita and total emissions to act on mitigation to avoid future environmental deterioration and as a means to obtain increased global financing (Urban 2014).

Part 2: Mainstreaming practices in local communities

Mainstreaming of CCA is the generic and officially sanctioned term within the United Nations Development Programme (UNDP) and the United Nations Environment Programme (UNEP) Poverty–Environment Initiative (PEI), used to describe the integration of environment and CCA into development planning (Benson *et al.* 2014).[3] It is defined as:

> the iterative process of integrating considerations of climate change adaptation into policy-making, budgeting, implementation and monitoring processes at national,

sector and subnational levels. It is a multi-year, multi-stakeholder effort grounded in the contribution of climate change adaptation to human well-being, pro-poor economic growth, and achievement of the MDGs. It entails working with a range of government and non-governmental actors, and other actors in the development field.

(UNDP–UNEP PEI 2011: 3)

Many countries have CCA and mainstreaming policy frameworks (Massey *et al.* 2014; Rauken *et al.* 2015). The focus here is on the 'developing world',[4] particularly the Least Developed Countries,[5] where mainstreaming (Benson *et al.* 2014) has become a central policy direction among governments and donor agencies. Climate change is considered an obstacle to development as it raises the social, economic, and environmental costs of doing business and improving people's lives and livelihoods (Warner *et al.* 2012). Stand-alone climate change policies, such as National Adaptation Programmes of Action (NAPAs), which seek to ameliorate CC impacts do not address fully the social vulnerabilities that make people more susceptible to CC risk (Ayers and Dodman 2010; Ayers *et al.* 2014; Schipper and Pelling 2006). These vulnerabilities are the product of proximate and more deep-seated causes, including previous national development initiatives and historical patterns of development. Mainstreaming is thought to provide policy, institutional, and financial efficiencies through linking it to development policy (Lebel *et al.* 2012).

There are at least three overlapping variants of mainstreaming. Climate-proofing (C-P) refers to modifying existing development projects 'to ensure that they are no longer at risk from climate change or no longer contribute to the vulnerability of its recipients' (Klein *et al.* 2007: 26). Climate-proofing focuses on ensuring that climate change impacts are understood so investments can be adapted to them to minimise them and protect existing development pathways (Ayers *et al.* 2014; Brooks and Grist, 2008); for example, encouraging farmers to use salt-tolerant crops to combat water and soil salinization. Climate-resilient development (CRD) involves making development initiatives robust enough to 'bounce back' from climate impacts through a focus on the underlying drivers of vulnerability, variously referred to as context vulnerability, starting-point vulnerability, adaptation as development or mainstreaming plus (Ayers and Dodman 2010; Ayers *et al.* 2014; O'Brien *et al.* 2007) in order to create improved adaptive capacity. This approach contrasts with end-point vulnerability policies that focus on reducing a population's exposure and sensitivity to biophysical hazards. Climate-compatible development (CCD) extends CRD to include mitigation or low-carbon policies (Ellis *et al.* 2013) to achieve 'triple wins' in national planning (Mitchell and Maxwell 2010). For example, shifting to renewable energy resources can have adaptation and development benefits as well as mitigating GGEs. Mitchell and Maxwell (2010: 1) define CCD as 'development that minimises the harm caused by climate impacts, while maximising the many human development opportunities presented by a low emissions, more resilient, future'.

Over 40 developing country governments, including Bangladesh, Nepal, Cambodia, the Dominican Republic, Laos, Kenya, Tanzania, The Gambia, Rwanda, Zanzibar, Mozambique, Ethiopia, Uganda, and Morocco, have begun to incorporate CC mainstreaming[6] into their development planning.[7] Research into mainstreaming consists of (a) country studies of its integration and implementation at regional and community levels; and (b) a broader critical examination of mainstreaming as a resilience-building strategy.

Several country studies show a disjuncture between policy and practice in that governments and other agencies often focus on meeting immediate development needs when longer-term CC planning is required (Ludi *et al.* 2014: 44). For example, the Future Climate for Africa

(FCFA)[8] programme reports that in Malawi, Rwanda, Zambia, Ghana, and Mozambique there has been little integration of climate adaptation into development planning, resulting from the immediacy of conventional development issues requiring rapid and short-term attention; nesting of climate change policy in weak and under-resourced ministries; scarcity of donor funding; a lack of suitability of longer-term climate information to local circumstances; and a lack of mediating organisations to link policy-makers, scientists, and local people (Jones *et al.* 2015). Newell *et al.* (2014) report that the Kenyan government supports investment in both renewable energy (solar and geo-thermal) and non-renewable sources (coal and LPG) to increase electricity supply and has plans for offshore oil development. In other words, the purported 'triple wins' of such policies actually involve trade-offs between adaptation, mitigation, and development, which can mean less attention to the most vulnerable. 'The drivers of policy have not, on the whole, been concerns for pro-poor energy access, but rather concerns around energy security and the competitiveness of industry in Kenya' (Newell *et al.* 2014: 32).

Quan *et al.* (2014) in their study of carbon forestry and REDD+[9] in Mozambique demonstrate the difficulties of linking mitigation objectives through tree planting, conservation, and carbon trading with the promotion of sustainable livelihoods and climate adaptation. They point to differing agendas of interest coalitions ranging from large-scale private control of forests linked to external carbon markets to national NGOs who reject REDD+ as a means to alleviate poverty and assist local communities to adapt to climate change impacts. Tompkins *et al.* (2013) show that in Sub-Saharan Africa, Latin America, and Southeast Asia, achieving triple wins is possible, but that trade-offs are sometimes preferable or likely, depending on local circumstances. They argue that certain hard infrastructure and land-use change projects generate more costs (have higher regrets). Thus, coastal defences provide greater physical security to some populations and protect agricultural land from seawater inundation, but they can also increase emissions and reduce economic security for other populations through use of carbon-intense concrete, destruction of wetlands and biodiversity, and reduction in fishing grounds.

Saywack (2013) reports on Guyana's efforts to protect and restore coastal mangroves in order to provide triple wins in shoreline protection, carbon sequestration, and financial benefits and improved ecosystem services and livelihoods. Government and business continue to remove mangroves for agricultural and other uses, while at the same time the government supports mangrove restoration. He criticises mangrove restoration to counter sea-level rise as there are no landward buffer zones (zones of retreat) due to population density and infrastructural impediments; no integrated official institutions to imple-ment policy; and few alternative livelihoods attractive to local people. Trade-offs can also serve the interests of the more powerful, which can mean poorer adaptation outcomes for the poor and greater social injustice. Such criticisms mirror the wider critique of adaptation as a response to biophysical impacts, rather than challenging wider institutional and social structures that create the vulnerabilities in the first place (Bassett and Fogelman 2013; O'Brien *et al.* 2007).

Some critics argue that the disjuncture between mainstreaming policy and practice is the product of the top-down and culturally insensitive approach of the political and technocratic classes of developing countries whose aim is greater global market integration (De Boer *et al.* 2010; Huq and Reid 2004; Huq *et al.* 2003; Rigg and Oven 2015). Local communities are seen as beneficiaries rather than active agents engaged deliberatively in decision-making to use and expand local capacities and practices to set priorities and shape daily activities (O'Brien *et al.* 2007; Schipper *et al.* 2014). For example, Ethiopia's Climate-Resilient Green

Economy strategies are considered world leaders in CCD. However, Eriksen and Marin (2015) show how Ethiopian pastoralists have been marginalised by drought and other weather-related conditions and also by government policies that removed land for grazing, diverted water resources for other uses, and allowed tree cutting for charcoal and other purposes. They report little evidence of systematic deliberative negotiations with local people and show that government policies to expand irrigated agriculture and demand for biofuels can result in a conflict between the two goals of adaptation and mitigation. Milman and Arsano (2014), working in another region of Ethiopia, argue that local development policies conflict with reducing vulnerability to climate change and reflect the state's desire to sedentarise the populations, shift them into export-oriented commercial agriculture, and allow greater state control of local ethnic communities.

The claim of a top-down and culturally insensitive approach to development planning has been a long-standing debate within anthropology and development studies (Cooke and Kothari 2001; Dodman and Mitlin 2013; Mansuri and Rao 2004; Mosse 2005) and has re-surfaced in the climate change adaptation literature with calls for Community-based Adaptation to Climate Change (CBA) and Ecosystem-based Adaptation (EbA). Community-based Adaptation seeks to empower local communities to identify problems that are due to climate change rather than climate variability alone, and to use their local knowledge and experience to set their own priorities for climate-friendly development. Ecosystem-based Adaptation complements CBA and wider sustainable development goals through drawing on ecosystems as sources of human well-being and enhanced biodiversity (Ford *et al.* 2014; Forsyth 2013; Ojea 2015; Reid and Schipper 2014). These approaches are said to allow alternative or counter-narratives to the dominant CC discourse to emerge, to locate vulnerability within particular social contexts that vary across communities, to enhance the possibility for greater distributive and procedural justice for the poor and their descendants, and to strengthen the resilience of social-ecological systems, particularly where populations are highly dependent on resource extraction.

There is a growing body of CBA and EbA research, much of it focused on sectoral areas such as agriculture and disaster and risk management rather than the most vulnerable groups (Ford *et al.* 2014). As noted earlier, it shows that local communities often prioritise more immediate concerns such as sanitation, food security, job opportunities, and the like, which can conflict with government climate policies and partly account for government compromises in CCD policies. For example, in Ghana, artisanal fishers opposed Ghanaian government decarbonisation measures to reduce fossil-fuel subsidies to small-scale fishers, which led to the policy being shelved (Tanner *et al.* 2014). Fishers were more concerned with immediate benefits from government policy rather than longer-term adaptation benefits arising from a shift away from fossil-fuel use. Losing the subsidy meant increased poverty for many fishers, especially as no economic alternatives were provided. The fishers also saw the policy as unjust, as pressures on the Ghanaian government to remove subsidies came from the EU, which continued massive fuel subsidies to its fishing fleets.

A study of coastal adaptation to climate change in two coastal villages in southwest Bangladesh (Rahman and Pokrant 2015) showed that members of different occupational groups regarded climate change as an abstract and remote concept and of little relevance to their current concerns. They had observed recent changes in local weather as intensifying pressures on existing livelihood strategies and drew on traditional adaptation practices to meet their own livelihood priorities. For example, rice farmers complained of salinisation caused by shrimp farming and cyclones; fishers referred to banditry, official corruption, declining fish yields resulting from bad governance, over-fishing and changing weather patterns, and increased local tiger attacks from declining tiger prey caused by cyclonic disruption to forested areas. Despite the Bangladesh government's policy commitment to both CRD and CDD, local government authorities did little to inform local people of the need for longer-term CC planning and focused on traditional development objectives such as improved roads.

In India, Adam (2015) examined how a public works programme, the Mahatma Gandhi National Rural Employment Guarantee Act (MGNREGA), became linked to India's climate change policy. This wage employment programme provides poor families with work on public projects, which include 'eco-restoration' services such as water conservation and afforestation. Adam (2015) points out that any adaptation and mitigation benefits were not part of the original design, remained poorly evaluated and monitored, and could be used by the Indian government, whose national development strategy is highly carbon-intensive, to show it is doing something for the planet and the poor at the same time. More generally, such programmes can lock the poor into longer-term maladaptive development pathways.

Part 3: From resilience to transformation?

A central feature of CC mainstreaming is building resilience. An early version of resilience defines it as: 'the ability to absorb disturbances, to be changed and then to re-organise and still have the same identity (retain the same basic structure and ways of functioning)' (Resilience Alliance 2014: online). It derives from ecology and engineering and serves a system-maintaining or enhancing function described as a 'buffer for conserving what you have and recovering to what you were' (Folke *et al.* 2010: 6). What is being bounced back to is taken as a normal or baseline.

The focus is on 'resistance' or a system's capacity to withstand stress without change. A later version includes notions of adaptive learning and reflexivity as people affected learn from experience and can change their practices to meet new circumstances, which may involve seeking to return to a previous societal state using known adaptation strategies (Kates *et al.* 2012; Matyas and Pelling 2015).

The capacity to accommodate to change through resilience-building is central to human and non-human survival (Hastrup 2009). For example, when there is a flood, cyclone, drought, or other climate-related hazard, taking infrastructural and other initiatives can be positive social assets in that they assist local communities to 'resist' or re-establish themselves. Similarly, efforts to preserve biodiversity through refugia or wildlife corridors contribute to ensuring ecological integrity (Poiani *et al.* 2011). This view of resilience as the capacity to absorb and/or adapt to hazards is said to focus on incremental change (Kates *et al.* 2012), adaptation-as-resilience (Pelling 2011), practical adaptation (O'Brien *et al.* 2015), or adjustment adaptation (Bassett and Fogelman 2013). Such strategies involve building local and national adaptive capacity, defined as the ability to mobilise various resources to respond to actual and potential physical and social stressors in order to assist communities to recover from the impact of a hazard (Joakim *et al.* 2015; Lemos *et al.* 2013; Walker *et al.* 2004). However, such initiatives can be maladaptive from both a developmental and climate change perspective if they (a) fail to address the diverse bases of social vulnerability (class, gender, age, ethnicity) that existed prior to the hazard event or process; and (b) do not prepare for the longer-term effects of slow-acting climate change (Joakim *et al.* 2015).

Such criticism has led to calls for socially transformational adaptation, understood as the recognition that a change in the system under consideration may be desirable and/or inevitable in order to achieve positive climate change and development outcomes (Kates *et al.* 2012; O'Brien 2012; Pelling 2011). There is considerable variation among researchers as to what is meant by transformation (Feola 2014). All share a view of transformation as a qualitative change of a system, but vary in regard to the system considered; the change undergone; the main drivers, agents, and desirability of the change; the means by which transformation is to be achieved; and the effectiveness of transformational strategies in the longer term. Two broad approaches can be identified. The first operates within an ecological modernisation or green economy paradigm. Examples include moving from fossil-fuel dependence to greater reliance on renewable energy sources (Dangerman and Schellnhuber 2013); replacing traditional crop strains with salt- or drought-tolerant varieties to adapt to changing weather patterns and growing freshwater salinization (Kates *et al.* 2012; SeinnSeinn *et al.* 2015); increasing mechanisation of agriculture and focus on economic benefits rather than wider community needs (Feola 2014); moving affected populations to new locations (Kates *et al.* 2012); seeking new lands to cultivate as temperatures change (Park *et al.* 2012); and building new barrage locations rather than improving existing defences against sea-level rise (Smith *et al.* 2011). Such transformations take place within sub-systems nested within economic and political systems, which are not the object of transformation although some institutional changes may be required or eventuated. Versions of this kind of transformational adaptation are increasingly accepted by the major global environmental governance institutions such as the IPCC (Noble *et al.* 2014).

A second body of research engages more directly with the relationship between development, climate change, and social justice. It draws on world-systems theory, dependency theory, neo-Marxism, radical geography, political ecology, and other critical approaches to development and modern capitalism (Baer and Singer 2014; Taylor 2014). According to this body of research, incremental adaptation or traditional resilience studies have neglected the unequal distribution of national and global economic, social, and political power, which is both a driver of, and barrier to, realising greater social, economic, and climate justice. Rudiak-Gould (2014) refers to this as the 'industrial blame' viewpoint in which industrialisation, rich nation consumer culture, and capitalism are held responsible for the vulnerability of the poor in both developed and developing countries. Researchers are encouraged to explore transformative approaches to a fairer and more environmentally sustainable future by 'reform in over-arching political-economy regimes and associated cultural discourses on development, security and risk' (Pelling 2011: 50). This involves working cooperatively and reflexively with local communities, particularly the most marginalised, to challenge existing paradigms, policies, and practices of development (Bahadur and Tanner 2014; Feola 2014; Inderberg *et al.* 2015).

Such 'deliberate transformation' (O'Brien 2012) means that researchers, co-workers, and local people should ask what is transformation for, whose interests does it serve, can it be engineered or does it come about inadvertently, and will it have positive societal consequences? Ribot (2014) argues for a more sophisticated causal-chain analysis that goes beyond enhancing adaptive capacity as a locally situated practice to a wider critique and action by the vulnerable and their supporters (including activist researchers) of the political economic structures and agents that shape their lives. By linking responsibility to causal-chain analysis, a more complete explanation of the socially and ecologically unequal distribution of vulnerability can be found and provide a basis for politically informed action by local communities.

Final comments

Anthropology and related disciplines increasingly recognise that CC is a development issue in that historic development trajectories have caused CC, and responding to it requires changes to current development policy and practice. There have been two main academic and policy responses. At the policy level, CCA is being mainstreamed into development planning, focusing on reducing social vulnerabilities through adaptation policies that build societal resilience. Research shows that mainstreaming is driven by global and national agencies and is at an early stage of implementation. It has been criticised for its top-down approach, and uneven and slow implementation, and has met with opposition from some intended beneficiaries on economic and social justice grounds. The second response is a critique of adaptation-as-resilience and calls for more transformational strategies to meet the uncertain and longer-term impacts of climate change. Such strategies range from application of innovative technologies and reform of land-use practices to changes to the 'business-as-usual' development pathways that dominate the climate change and development discourse.

Notes

1 Also referred to as low carbon-resilient development (Fisher 2013).
2 The concept of adaptation is long established in anthropology (Fiske *et al.* 2014; Simonet 2010). In the climate change field, it refers to processes of accommodation to the expected impacts of existing climate change, while mitigation refers to the reduction of greenhouse gas emissions (GGEs) at source and the shift to low carbon development pathways. A third potential strategy is geo-engineering or the deliberate manipulation of the climate system. Such a strategy is not presently a policy priority but may become so in the future.
3 It received official endorsement at the 2012 Rio+20 Summit as part of the Sustainable Development agenda that included poverty eradication, sustainable consumption and production, improved natural resource management, inclusive and equitable growth, gender empowerment, and democracy (UNDESA 2014).
4 The concept of developing countries continues to be used as a descriptive and normative term to refer to countries that are materially poorer than so-called developed countries and that seek to attain higher material living standards comparable to those of the developed countries. There is great diversity in levels of living standard across the so-called developing world and also considerable debate about what constitutes development.
5 The LDCs consist of a group of countries classified by the UN as having profound poverty, weak economic, institutional, and human resources, and which are often exposed to major geophysical hazards. As of 2014, 48 countries fell into this category (www.un.org/en/development/desa/policy/cdp/ldc/ldc_list.pdf).
6 Mainstreaming has a wider reference in development studies and has been applied to gender, environmental degradation, and HIV/AIDS (Oates *et al.* 2011).
7 Several developed country governments such as Norway and the Netherlands have adopted mainstreaming of CCA as part of national policy (GLOBE International 2013; Rauken *et al.* 2015; Veraart *et al.* 2014).
8 Future Climate for Africa (FCFA) is a five-year international research programme funded by the UK's Department for International Development (DFID) and the Natural Environment Research Council (NERC).
9 REDD+ stands for Reducing Emissions from Deforestation and Forest Degradation. It is a UN-backed programme which seeks

> to create a financial value for the carbon stored in forests, offering incentives for developing countries to reduce emissions from forested lands and invest in low-carbon paths to sustainable development. 'REDD+' goes beyond deforestation and forest degradation, and includes the role of conservation, sustainable management of forests and enhancement of forest carbon stocks.

> (*www.un-redd.org/Home/tabid/565/Default.aspx*)

References

Adam, H. N. (2015). Mainstreaming adaptation in India: The Mahatma Gandhi National Rural Employment Guarantee Act and climate change. *Climate and Development* 7(2): 142–152. doi: 10.1080/17565529.2014.934772

Ayers, J. and Dodman, D. (2010). Climate change adaptation and development: The state of the debate. *Progress in Development Studies* 10(2): 161–168.

Ayers, J. M., Huq, S., Faisal, A. M. and Hussain, S. T. (2014). Mainstreaming climate change adaptation into development: A case study of Bangladesh. *Wiley Interdisciplinary Reviews: Climate Change* 5(1): 37–51.

Baer, H. and Singer, M. (2014). *The Anthropology of Climate Change: An Integrated Critical Perspective.* New York: Routledge.

Bahadur, A. and Tanner, T. (2014). Transformational resilience thinking: Putting people, power and politics at the heart of urban climate resilience. *Environment and Urbanization* 26(1): 200–214.

Barnes, J. and Dove, M. R. (eds) (2015). *Climate Cultures: Anthropological Perspectives on Climate Change.* New Haven, CT: Yale University Press.

Barnes, J., Dove, M. R., Lahsen, M., Mathews, A., McElwee, P., McIntosh, R., Moore, F., O'Reilly, J., Orlove, B., Puri, R., Weiss, H. and Yager, K. (2013). Contributions of anthropology to the study of climate change. *Nature Climate Change* 3: 541–544. doi:10.1038/ncli

Bassett, T. J. and Fogelman, C. (2013). Déjà vu or something new? The adaptation concept in the climate change literature. *Geoforum* 48: 42–53.

Benson, E., Forbes, A., Korkeakoski, M., Latif, R. and Lham, D. (2014). Environment and climate mainstreaming: Challenges and successes. *Development in Practice* 24(4): 605–614. doi: 10.1080/09614524.2014.911819

Boyle, J., Harris, M., Bizikova, L., Parry, J. E., Hammill, A. and Dion, J. (2013). *Exploring Trends in Low-Carbon, Climate-Resilient Development.* London: IIED.

Brooks, N. and Grist, N. (2008). Development Futures in the Light of Climate Change: Creating New Insights into the Past, the Present and Global Futures. Background Paper. Policy Forum: International Development in the Face of Climate Change: Beyond Mainstreaming.

Cooke, B. and Kothari, U. (eds) (2001). *Participation: The New Tyranny?* London: Zed Books.

Cowen, M. and Shenton, R. W. (1996). *Doctrines of Development.* London: Taylor & Francis.

Crate, S. A. (2011). Climate and culture: Anthropology in the era of contemporary climate change. *Annual Review of Anthropology* 40: 175–194.

Crate, S. A. and Nuttall, M. (2009). *Anthropology and Climate Change: From Encounters to Actions.* Walnut Creek, CA: Left Coast Press.

Crewe, E. and Axelby, R. (2012). *Anthropology and Development: Culture, Morality and Politics in a Globalised World.* New York: Cambridge University Press.

Dangerman, T. C. J. and Schellnhuber, H. J. (2013). Energy systems transformation. *Proceedings of the National Academy of Sciences of the United States of America* 110(7): E549–E558.

De Boer, J., Waerdekker, J. A. and van der Sluijs, J. P. (2010). Frame-based guide to situated decision-making on climate change. *Global Environmental Change* 20(3): 502–510.

Dodman, D. and Mitlin, D. (2013). Challenges for community-based adaptation: Discovering the potential for transformation. *Journal of International Development* 25(5): 640–659.

Dove, M. (ed.) (2014). *The Anthropology of Climate Change. An Historical Reader.* Malden, MA: Wiley–Blackwell.

Dryzek, J. S. (2005). *The Politics of the Earth: Environmental Discourses.* Oxford: Oxford University Press.

Du Pisani, J. A. (2006) Sustainable development: Historical roots of the concept. *Environmental Sciences* 3(2): 83–96. doi: 10.1080/15693430600688831

Ehlers, E. (2006). *Earth System Science in the Anthropocene.* Berlin and Heidelberg: Springer.

Ellis, K., Cambray, A. and Lemma, A. (2013). Drivers and Challenges for Climate Compatible Development. Working Paper, Climate and Development Knowledge Network, London.

Eriksen, S. and Marin, S. (2015). Sustainable adaptation under adverse development? In T. H. Inderberg, S. Eriksen, K. O'Brien and L. Sygna (eds) *Climate Change Adaptation and Development: Transforming Paradigms and Practices.* London and New York: Routledge, pp. 178–199.

Escobar, A. (1995). *Encountering Development: The Making and Unmaking of the Third World.* Princeton, NJ: Princeton University Press.

Feola, G. (2014). Societal transformation in response to global environmental change: A review of emerging concepts. *Ambio* 44(5): 376–390.

Fisher, S. (2013). Low Carbon Resilient Development in the Least Developed Countries. IIED Issue Paper. International Institute for Environment and Development, London.

Fiske, S. J., Crate, S. A., Crumley, C. L., Galvin, K., Lazrus, H., Lucero, L., OliverSmith, A., Orlove, B., Strauss, S. and Wilk, R. 2014. *Changing the Atmosphere. Anthropology and Climate Change*. Final report of the AAA Global Climate Change Task Force (137 pages). Arlington, VA: American Anthropological Association.

Folke, C., Carpenter, R. S., Walker, B., Scheffer, M., Chapin, T. and Rockstrom, J. (2010). Resilience thinking: Integrating resilience, adaptability and transformability. *Ecology and Society* 15(4): article 20. www.fs.fed.us/pnw/pubs/journals/pnw_2010_folke.pdf (accessed June 2015).

Ford, J. D., Berrang-Ford, L., Bunce, A., McKay, C., Irwin, M. and Pearce, T. (2014). The status of climate change adaptation in Africa and Asia. *Regional Environmental Change* 15(5): 801–814.

Forsyth, T. (2013). Community-based adaptation: A review of past and future challenges. *Wiley Interdisciplinary Reviews: Climate Change* 4(5): 439–446.

GCEC (2014). *Better Growth Better Climate: The New Climate Economy Report. The Synthesis Report* (edited by F. Calderon and N. Stern) Washington, DC: The Global Commission on the Economy and Climate.

GLOBE International (2013). *The GLOBE Climate Legislation Study*. London: GLOBE International and CDKN.

Hajer, M. A. (1995). *The Politics of Environmental Discourse: Ecological Modernisation and the Policy Process*. Oxford: Oxford University Press.

Hamilton, C., Gemenne, F. and Bonneuil, C. (eds) (2015). *The Anthropocene and the Global Environmental Crisis: Rethinking Modernity in a New Epoch*. London and New York: Routledge.

Hastrup, K. (2009). Waterworlds: Framing the question of resilience. In K. Hastrup (ed.) *The Question of Resilience. Social Responses to Climate Change*. Copenhagen: The Royal Danish Academy of Science and Letters, pp. 11–30.

Huq, S. and Reid, H. (2004). Mainstreaming adaptation in development. *Institute for Environment and Development Bulletin* 35(3): 15–24.

Huq, S., Rahman, A., Konate, M., Sokona, Y. and Reid, H. (2003). *Mainstreaming Adaptation to Climate Change in Least Developed countries (LDCS)*. London: International Institute for Environment and Development.

Hurrell, A. and Sengupta, S. (2012). Emerging powers, North–South relations and global climate politics. *International Affairs* 88(3): 463–484.

Inderberg, T. H., Eriksen, S., O'Brien, K. and Sygna, L. (eds) (2015). *Climate Change Adaptation and Development: Transforming Paradigms and Practices*. London: Routledge.

IPCC (2014). *Climate Change 2014: Synthesis Report. Contribution of Working Groups I, II and III to the Fifth Assessment Report of the Intergovernmental Panel on Climate Change* [Core Writing Team, R. K. Pachauri and L. A. Meyer (eds); 151 pages]. Geneva, Switzerland: Intergovernmental Panel on Climate Change.

Jacobs, M. 2013. Green growth. In R. Falkner (ed.) *The Handbook of Global Climate and Environment Policy*. Chichester, UK: John Wiley & Sons, pp. 197–214.

Joakim, E. P., Mortsch, L. and Oulahen, G. (2015). Using vulnerability and resilience concepts to advance climate change adaptation. *Environmental Hazards* 14(2): 137–155. doi: 10.1080/17477891. 2014.1003777

Jones, L., Carabine, E., Roux, J-P. and Tanner, T. (2015). *Promoting the Use of Climate Information to Achieve Long-Term Development Objectives in Sub-Saharan Africa: Results from the Future Climate for Africa Scoping Phase*. London: CDKN.

Kates, R. W., Travis, W. R. and Wilbanks, T. J. (2012). Transformational adaptation when incremental adaptations to climate change are insufficient. *Proceedings of the National Academy of Sciences of the United States of America* 109(19): 7156–7161.

Klein, R. J., Eriksen, S. E., Næss, L. O., Hammill, A., Tanner, T. M., Robledo, C. and O'Brien, K. L. (2007). Portfolio screening to support the mainstreaming of adaptation to climate change into development assistance. *Climatic Change* 84(1): 23–44.

Krauss, W. (2015). Anthropology in the anthropocene: Sustainable development, climate change and interdisciplinary research. In H. M. Greschke and J. Tischler (eds) *Grounding Global Climate Change*. Dordrecht: Springer Netherlands, pp. 59–76.

Kumi, E., Arhin, A. A. and Yeboah, T. (2014). Can post-2015 sustainable development goals survive neoliberalism? A critical examination of the sustainable development–neoliberalism nexus in developing countries. *Environment, Development and Sustainability* 16(3): 539–554. doi 10.1007/s10668-013-9492-7

Lebel, L., Li, L., Krittasudthacheewa, C., Juntopas, M., Vijitpan, T., Uchiyama, T. and Krawanchid, D. (2012). *Mainstreaming Climate Change Adaptation into Development Planning*. Bangkok: Adaptation Knowledge Platform and Stockholm Environment Institute.

Lemos, M. C., Agrawal, A., Eakin, H., Nelson, D. R., Engle, N. L. and Johns, O. (2013). Building adaptive capacity to climate change in less developed countries. In A. Ghassem and J. W. Hurrell (eds) *Climate Science for Serving Society*. Dordrecht: Springer Netherlands, pp. 437–457.

Lövbrand, E., Beck, S., Chilvers, J., Forsyth, T., Hedrén, J., Hulme, M., Lidskog, R. and Vasileiadou, E. (2015). Who speaks for the future of Earth? How critical social science can extend the conversation on the Anthropocene. *Global Environmental Change* 32: 211–218.

Ludi, E., Wiggins, S., Jones, L., Lofthouse, J. and Levine, S. (2014). Adapting development: How wider development interventions can support adaptive capacity at the community level. In E. L. F. Schipper, J. Ayers, H. Reid, S. Huq and A. Rahman (eds) (2014). *Community-Based Adaptation to Climate Change: Scaling it Up*. London and New York: Routledge, pp. 36–52.

McMichael, P. (2011). *Development and Social Change: A Global Perspective*. 5th edn. Los Angeles/London/New Delhi/Singapore/Washington, DC: Sage Publications.

Malm, A. and Hornborg, A. (2014). The geology of mankind? A critique of the Anthropocene narrative. *The Anthropocene Review* 1(1): pp. 62–69.

Mannion, D. A. (2014). *Global Environmental Change: A Natural and Cultural Environmental History*. London and New York: Routledge.

Mansuri, G. and Rao, V. (2004). Community-based and -driven development: A critical review. *The World Bank Research Observer* 19(1): 1–39.

Massey, E. Biesbroek, R., Huitema, D. and Jordan, A. (2014). Climate policy innovation: The adoption and diffusion of adaptation policies across Europe. *Global Environmental Change*. http://dx.doi.org/10.1016/j.gloenvcha.2014.09.002

Matyas, D. and Pelling, M. (2015). Positioning resilience for 2015: The role of resistance, incremental adjustment and transformation in disaster risk management policy. *Disasters* 39(s1): s1–s18. doi: 10.1111/disa.12107

Millennium Ecosystem Assessment (2005). *Ecosystems and Human Well-Being: Synthesis*. Washington, DC: Island Press.

Milman, A. and Arsano, Y. (2014). Climate adaptation and development: Contradictions for human security in Gambella, Ethiopia. *Global Environmental Change* 29: 349–359.

Mitcham, C. (1995). The concept of sustainable development: Its origins and ambivalence. *Technology in Society* 17(3): 311–326.

Mitchell, T. and Maxwell, S. (2010). Defining Climate-Compatible Development. CDKN Policy Brief. London: Climate and Development Knowledge Network.

Mol, A. P. and Spaargaren, G. (2000). Ecological modernisation theory in debate: A review. *Environmental Politics* 9(1): 17–49.

Mosse, D. (2005). *Cultivating Development: An Ethnography of Aid Policy and Practice*. Anthropology, Culture and Society series. London: Pluto Press.

Newell, P., Phillips, J. and Pueyo, A. with Kirumba, E., Ozor, N. and Urama, K. (2014). The Political Economy of Low Carbon Energy in Kenya. IDS Working Paper 445. Institute of Development Studies, University of Sussex, Brighton, UK.

Noble, I. R., S. Huq, Y. A. Anokhin, J. Carmin, D. Goudou, F. P. Lansigan, B. Osman-Elasha and A. Villamizar (2014). Adaptation needs and options. In IPCC (edited by C. B. Field *et al.*) *Climate Change 2014: Impacts, Adaptation, and Vulnerability. Part A: Global and Sectoral Aspects. Contribution of Working Group II to the Fifth Assessment Report of the Intergovernmental Panel on Climate Change*. Cambridge, UK and New York, pp. 833–868.

Oates, N., Conway, D. and Calow, R. (2011). The 'Mainstreaming' Approach to Climate Change Adaptation: Insights from Ethiopia's Water Sector. Background Note, Overseas Development Institute, London.

O'Brien, K. (2012). Global environmental change II: From adaptation to deliberate transformation. *Progress in Human Geography* 36(5): 667–676.

O'Brien, K., Eriksen, S., Nygaard, L. P. and Schjolden, A. (2007). Why different interpretations of vulnerability matter in climate change discourses. *Climate Policy* 7(1): 73–88.

O'Brien, K., Eriksen, S., Inderberg, T. H. and Sygna, L. (2015). Climate change and development: Adaptation through transformation. In T. H. Inderberg, S. Eriksen, K. O'Brien and L. Sygna (eds) *Climate Change Adaptation and Development: Transforming Paradigms and Practices*. London: Routledge, pp. 273–289.

Ojea, E. (2015). Challenges for mainstreaming Ecosystem-based Adaptation into the international climate agenda. *Current Opinion in Environmental Sustainability* 14: 41–48.

Park, S. E., Marshall, N. A., Jakku, E., Dowd, A. M., Howden, S. M., Mendham, E. and Fleming, A. (2012). Informing adaptation responses to climate change through theories of transformation. *Global Environmental Change* 22(1): 115–126.

Pelling, M. (2011). *Adaptation to Climate Change: From Resilience to Transformation*. New York: Routledge.

Poiani, K. A., Goldman, R. L., Hobson, J., Hoekstra, J. M. and Nelson, K. S. (2011). Redesigning biodiversity conservation projects for climate change: Examples from the field. *Biodiversity and Conservation* 20(1): 185–201.

Quan, J., Otto Naess, L., Newsham, A., Sitoe, A. and Corral Fernandez, M. (2014). Carbon Forestry and Climate Compatible Development in Mozambique: A Political Economy Analysis. IDS Working Paper 448. Institute of Development Studies, University of Sussex, Brighton, UK.

Radkau, J. (2008). *Nature and Power. A Global History of the Environment*. Cambridge, UK: Cambridge University Press.

Rahman, M. and Pokrant, B. (2015). Changing local weather and adaptation in two coastal villages in Bangladesh. *Journal of the Indian Ocean Region* 11(1): 74–97. doi:10.1080/19480881.2015.1019995

Rauken, T., Mydske, P. K. and Winsvold, M. (2015). Mainstreaming climate change adaptation at the local level. *Local Environment: The International Journal of Justice and Sustainability* 20(4): 408–423. doi: 10.1080/13549839.2014.880412

Reid, H. and Schipper, E. L. F. (2014). Upscaling community-based adaptation. An introduction to the edited volume. In E. L. F. Schipper, J. Ayers, H. Reid, S. Huq and A. Rahman (eds) *Community-Based Adaptation to Climate Change: Scaling it Up*. London and New York: Routledge, pp. 3–21.

Resilience Alliance (2014). Key concepts. www.resalliance.org/index.php/key_concepts (accessed 9 May 2014).

Ribot, J. (2014). Cause and response: Vulnerability and climate in the Anthropocene. *Journal of Peasant Studies* 41(5): 667–705.

Richards, J. (2005). *The Unending Frontier: An Environmental History of the Early Modern World*. Berkeley, London, and Los Angeles: University of California Press.

Rigg, J. and Oven, K. (2015). Building liberal resilience? A critical review from developing rural Asia. *Global Environmental Change* 32(5): 175–186.

Rudiak-Gould, P. (2009). *The Fallen Palm: Climate Change and Culture Change in the Marshall Islands*. Saarbrücken, Germany: VDM Verlag.

Rudiak-Gould, P. (2014). Climate Change and Accusation. *Current Anthropology* 55(4): 365–386.

Saywack, M. (2013). Mangrove Management in Guyana: A Case of Climate Compatible Development? Unpublished dissertation, Master of Science in Climate Change and Development, University of Sussex, Brighton, UK.

Schipper, L. and Pelling, M. (2006). Disaster risk, climate change and international development: Scope for, and challenges to, integration. *Disasters* 30(1) 19–38.

Schipper, E. L. F., Ayers, J., Reid, H., Huq, S. and Rahman, A. (eds) (2014). *Community-Based Adaptation to Climate Change: Scaling it Up*. London and New York: Routledge.

SeinnSeinn, M. U., Ahmad, M. M., Thapa, G. B. and Shrestha, R. P. (2015). Farmers' adaptation to rainfall variability and salinity through agronomic practices in lower Ayeyarwady Delta, Myanmar. *Journal of Earth Science & Climatic Change* 6(2): 258. doi: 10.4172/2157-7617.1000258

Shellenberger, M. and Nordhaus, T. (2011). Evolve: The case for modernization as the road to salvation. In M. Shellenberger and T. Nordhaus (eds) *Love Your Monsters: Postenvironmentalism and Anthropocene*. Oakland, CA: The Breakthrough Institute, pp. 8–16.

Simonet, G. (2010). The concept of adaptation: Interdisciplinary scope and involvement in climate change. *S.A.P.I.EN.S* [open-access journal] 3(1).

Smith, M. S., Horrocks, L., Harvey, A. and Hamilton, C. (2011). Rethinking adaptation for a 4 C world. *Philosophical Transactions of the Royal Society of London A: Mathematical, Physical and Engineering Sciences* 369(1934): 196–216.

Strauss, S. (2012). Are cultures endangered by climate change? Yes, but . . . . *Wiley Interdisciplinary Reviews: Climate Change* 3(4): 371–377.

Tanner, T., Mensah, A., Lawson, E. T., Gordon, C., Godfrey-Wood, R. and Cannon, T. (2014). Political Economy of Climate Compatible Development: Artisanal Fisheries and Climate Change in Ghana. IDS Working Paper 446. Institute of Development Studies, University of Sussex, Brighton, UK.

Taylor, M. (2014). *The Political Ecology of Climate Change Adaptation: Livelihoods, Agrarian Change and the Conflicts of Development.* London: Routledge.

Tompkins, E. L., Mensah, A., King, L., Long, T. K., Lawson, E. T., Hutton, C. W., Hoang, V. A., Gordon, C., Fish, M., Dyer, J. and Bood, N. (2013). An Investigation of the Evidence of Benefits from Climate Compatible Development. Sustainability Research Institute Paper No. 44; Centre for Climate Change Economics and Policy, Working Paper No. 124, University of Leeds, UK.

UNDESA (2015). Open Working Group Proposal for Sustainable Development Goals. UN Department of Economic and Social Affairs. https://sustainabledevelopment.un.org/focussdgs.html (accessed 2 January 2015).

UNDP–UNEP PEI (2011). *Mainstreaming Climate Change Adaptation into Development Planning: A Guide for Practitioners.* New York: United Nations Development Programme–United Nations Environment Programme Poverty–Environment Initiative.

UNEP (2011). *Towards a Green Economy: Pathways to Sustainable Development and Poverty Eradication.* Nairobi: United Nations Environment Programme.

Urban, F. (2014). *Low Carbon Transitions for Developing Countries.* London: Routledge.

Veraart, J. A., van Nieuwaal, K., Driessen, P. P. and Kabat, P. (2014). From climate research to climate compatible development: Experiences and progress in the Netherlands. *Regional Environmental Change* 14(3): 851–863.

Walker, B., Holling, C. S., Carpenter, S. R. and Kinzig, A. (2004). Resilience, adaptability and transformability in social-ecological systems. *Ecology and Society* 9(2): article 5. www.ecologyandsociety.org/vol9/iss2/art5 (accessed June 2015).

Warner, K., van der Geest, K., and Kreft, S., Huq, S., Harmeling, S., Kusters, K. and de Sherbinin, A. (2012). *Evidence from the Frontlines of Climate Change: Loss and Damage to Communities despite Coping and Adaptation.* Loss and Damage in Vulnerable Countries Initiative. Policy Report. Report No. 9. Bonn, Germany: United Nations University Institute for Environment and Human Security (UNU-EHS).

Wolf, E. (1982). *Europe and the People without History.* Berkeley and Los Angeles: University of California Press.

Ziai, A. (2013). The discourse of 'development' and why the concept should be abandoned. *Development in Practice* 23(1): 123–136. doi: 10.1080/09614524.2013.752792

PART V

Justice, ethics, and governance

21

JUSTICE FOR ALL

Inconvenient truths and reconciliation in human–non-human relations

Veronica Strang

Introduction

Anthropologists have long assisted disadvantaged human communities in their endeavours to achieve social justice, and they are now paying increasing attention to the need to extend notions of justice to non-human species. The emergence of more fluid and relational social theories, along with some useful experiments with interspecies ethnography, have served to promote bioethical approaches suggesting that justice for people should not – and indeed cannot – come before ecological justice. Animal rights debates have continued to raise moral questions about the provision of justice to those who cannot speak for themselves. Environmental concerns have foregrounded the interdependence of humans and other species and the potential for the disruption of these relationships to have major impacts on whole ecosystems. And, with extinction rates rocketing, it is clear that a dualistic vision of Culture and Nature that produces separate 'social' and 'environmental' categories is both theoretically and practically inadequate. This chapter therefore seeks to articulate a theoretical approach that reconciles the human and non-human, and underlines the reality that sustainable relationships between them can only be achieved by the provision of justice for all.

Justice and equity

Why should anthropology, a discipline focused on understanding human beings, consider those that are non-human? Is that not the role of zoologists and biologists, or our closer cousins, the primatologists? And why should we extend notions of justice to non-human kinds when, in some instances, this may only be achieved by sacrificing the immediate interests of the disadvantaged human groups for whom we have traditionally acted as advocates?

This chapter suggests that a concern for the non-human should be encompassed by anthropologists for reasons that are ethical, practical, and intellectual. First, the notion of justice is fundamentally concerned with equalising relations between those who have power and those who do not. This raises a moral question about the provision of justice to those who can speak for themselves, in preference to those who cannot. Second, humans, other species, and the material world are bound together in communal processes of production and

259

Figure 21.1 Orangutan, Singapore Zoo.

Source: Photo by Veronica Strang.

reproduction that are interdependent, such that disruption for any of the participants has potentially major impacts on the others. A short-term focus on immediate human interests has longer-term detrimental effects on humans and non-humans alike. Third, the dualistic vision of Culture and Nature, which underpins the putatively separate categories of 'social' and 'environmental', is theoretically inadequate, and theory is manifested in practice. A theoretical frame in which human needs and interests are separated and prioritised inevitably gives insufficient weight to the needs of the non-human.

A more theoretically robust approach would recognise the artificiality of such dualism, reintegrate the human and non-human, and thus enable reconciliation between the critical perspectives on these issues. In sum: giving humankind priority in the provision of justice leads down a path that is morally questionable, carries high risks, and is intellectually problematic. What is needed, instead, is the simultaneous provision of justice for all human and non-human beings. Thus, in defining a theory of ecological justice, Baxter argues that non-human species have a moral right to distributive justice, which entails 'recognizing their claim to a fair share of the environmental resources which all life-forms need to survive and to flourish' (2005: 4).

The concept of justice is fundamentally ideological. It was first used in English in the mediaeval period to express the idea that the 'right order' of things involved some degree of equity (Hunt 2009). It therefore implies collaborative rather than competitive relationships. A later usage, from the seventeenth century, 'to do justice to', contained the slightly broader meaning: that justice means 'to render fully and fairly, showing due appreciation' (Harper 2014: 1). Justice is therefore underpinned by an idea that maintaining a proper order in the world involves 'appreciating': recognising and upholding the value of others. With the

Figure 21.2 Mustering cattle in Cape York.

Source: Photo by Veronica Strang.

emphasis on 'others', it seems both categorically and ethically questionable to confine notions of justice, equity, and value to relationships between humans.

Prioritising justice as a means of ensuring equity leads directly to issues of power and agency. In the last few centuries, large industrialised societies have embarked upon hegemonic colonial enterprises, creating wildly unequal power relations between and within human societies. In many cases, relatively egalitarian indigenous forms of social organisation have been subsumed by hierarchical and patriarchal forms of governance in which indigenous communities, minorities, and women have been relegated to second- and sometimes third-class citizenship, assuming they even achieve the latter. For example: in European nations, women generally only achieved full suffrage after 1900 and in some cases not until the second half of the century.[1] Aboriginal Australians were not given Australian citizenship until 1967 (Attwood and Markus 1999; Howard 2003).

Anthropological interests in justice have therefore tended to focus on the social and economic rights of disadvantaged human groups. As well as articulating ideas about citizenship and enfranchisement, these interests are often entangled with promoting 'development' and more equitable access to resources. Much work has been done on the ownership of property and resources, highlighting the inequities generated by globalisation and the neo-colonial economic expansion of transnational corporations (Anderson and Berglund 2003; Paavola and Lowe 2005; Strang 2009a; Strang and Busse 2011).

Sometimes obscured in these debates is the reality that both the early colonial and the recent hegemonies of the global 'market' have exported to all corners of the globe highly unsustainable economic practices (Franklin 2006; Griffiths and Robin 1997). Their defining characteristic is ever-greater instrumentalism in human engagements with the material world and its non-human inhabitants. Though acknowledging its deep historical roots, Horkheimer and Adorno (2002 [1944]) suggest that this instrumentalism became firmly established in the post-Enlightenment period, when through 'rational sovereignty', human-kind achieved the 'mastery' of Nature, manifested in the all-consuming engine of an ever-expanding capitalist economy. Illich (1999) is similarly critical of obsessions with growth and the 'Promethean transgression' represented by the abandonment of sustainable 'balance and limits' in favour of development's constant expectation of 'more' (1999: 14). Moran (2006) notes that 'addictive' patterns of consumption became particularly aspirational in the post-war era. In this period, technological advances enabled particularly rapid intensifications in the use of land and water resources, and commensurately detrimental impacts on non-human species and ecosystems. Thus economic growth has been achieved – and continues to be achieved – via the externalisation of multiple costs to less powerful human *and* non-human communities (Johnston *et al.* 2012; Moran 2006; Plumwood 2002).

With the most powerful societies living in unsustainable affluence, it is difficult to suggest that other people should be prevented from enjoying the material benefits that industrialised economic practices allow. Discourses on justice often imply that the most disadvantaged human groups should have special rights to redress long-term imbalances, and clearly there is a case to be made. However, if the result is only a short-term gain at the long-term expense of the non-human (and thus humans too), this is not a sustainable way to achieve either social or ecological equity. Special rights to resources, like other forms of positive discrim-ination, tend to reify disparities in power as much as they address them. And there remains a thorny moral question as to whether anyone, advantaged or disadvantaged, has the right to prioritise their own interests to the extent that those of the non-human are deemed expendable.

An ethnographic example from my own fieldwork illustrates this dilemma. Should Aboriginal communities in Australia have the 'right' to adapt their traditional practices to shoot rather than spear wallabies, to the point that the population of wallabies in Cape York has sometimes dipped dramatically? The complexities of the issue surfaced at a meeting between Aboriginal elders and representatives of the Queensland National Parks service, while legislation was being tabled to prevent hunting in Australia's national parks. One of the elders, Colin Lawrence, referred to the history of settlement in the area. In the early 1900s, a European grazier had shot a number of Aboriginal people until being speared by one of their leaders, now regarded as a local hero. The grazier had shot Aboriginal people 'like dogs', said Lawrence pointedly, 'and now you want to tell us we can't even shoot a wallaby!' (Strang: field notes 1991).

Yet the number of wallabies has become more variable, not just because the possession of cars and rifles has enabled new forms of hunting, but also because of the competition for food within a fragile habitat created by ever-intensifying cattle farming. At some point, the population may drop to less viable levels. Should this be an Aboriginal choice? Should it be anyone's choice? This opens up a question about justice and cultural relativity, and whether anthropologists should promote cultural relativity to the degree that no universal human – or other – rights carry any weight. In anthropological debates about ethics (Caplan 2003), some of us have argued that extreme cultural relativity, in which it is possible to ignore major abuses of human rights (such as domestic violence), is an abdication of moral responsibility. If we extend this to non-human rights, then one might say precisely the same thing.

This implies that we all share a moral responsibility to prevent abuse of the non-human as well as the human. Though there is wide cultural and sub-cultural diversity in what people

Figure 21.3 Wallabies are an important traditional bush food for Aboriginal communities in Australia.

Source: Photo by Veronica Strang.

consider to be abuse (for example, the range between promoting the humane slaughter and eating of animals and extreme veganism), many indigenous communities would probably agree. Aboriginal Australian and Maori ideologies certainly valorise respect for and collaboration with the non-human, and I will come back to this point. Many anthropologists are – in my view quite rightly – concerned with disempowered human groups and advocates for their rights. But perhaps, in engaging in these issues, it is important not to separate people from the non-human and from the larger world that we all inhabit.

Casualties

Abstract concepts of environmental and ecological justice tend to subsume the reality that 'the environment' and its ecosystems are composed of thousands of individual species, ranging from the smallest microbial organisms (vital to healthy soil and to aquatic balance) to the largest creatures such as whales and elephants, which tend to get most of the public press about animal rights. But human destruction is undiscriminating: according to the International Union for the Conservation of Nature (IUCN) and the UN Environmental Programme (UNEP), the effects of the Anthropocene – that is, the period of human history since the Holocene – have been increasingly disastrous for most of the non-human inhabitants of the planet.

Figures 21.4a and 21.4b Bull catching in Cape York.

Source: Photos by Veronica Strang.

The list of causal factors is long, but includes extensive deforestation; the burning of fossil fuels and the production of carbon dioxide (CO_2) (leading to the melting of glaciers and arctic ice, and thus the loss of freshwater resources, and rising sea levels); the overuse of fertilisers, herbicides, and pesticides; pollution from multiple forms of mining and manufacturing. Overall, there have been massive diversions of freshwater and other resources into human processes of production and consumption, and competition for these resources has produced millions of (human) refugees. 'The exponential increase in all of these measurable phenomena is tied most fundamentally to two factors: the increase in the human population and our consumption habits. Indeed one must think of these two factors in tandem' (Moran 2006: 2–3).

What I want to underline here, though, is that this competition is not just between humans: all of these activities have entailed the loss of habitats and resources for non-human beings and, with depressing frequency, their demise. Throughout the Anthropocene, and in particular over the last 500 years, there has been an exponential acceleration in the rate of species extinction, even taking into account previous peaks caused by major environmental events, such as volcanic eruptions. The IUCN (2014) calculates that humankind has now anthropogenically increased 'normal' rates of extinction by about 10,000 per cent. Within the next 40–50 years, the coral reefs, on which about a quarter of the oceans' species depend, will have disappeared. About 25 per cent of the mammals on this planet will be extinct, as will about 41 per cent of its amphibians. Thousands of species, large and small, will have been sacrificed to human societies' endeavours to achieve the continual 'growth' and 'development' that require constant intensification in the use of 'our' resources. In all senses of the term, how can this be justified?

Figure 21.5 Seal pup, Kangaroo Island, South Australia.

Source: Photo by Veronica Strang.

Even if a justification could be made, this is a critically short-term mode of environmental engagement, echoing on a planetary scale the dynamics that have already caused more localised forms of societal collapse (Caldararo 2004; Diamond 2005). As Dobson points out (1998), the self-interested argument that the non-human should be protected because it is essential to human societies (as encapsulated in the Brundtland Report [UN World Commission on Environment and Development 1987]) is not sufficient in itself. But there is no doubt that it has become more pressing. The physical interdependences between humankind and other species are fundamental and complex. As much interdisciplinary work has shown, complex adaptive systems can be sensitive to relatively minor social and/or ecological events (Holland 2001; Lansing 2003). Ecosystemic integrity or resilience – what Moran calls 'the web of life' – relies on biodiversity and, it has been argued, cultural diversity too (Moran 2006; Orlove and Brush 1996; Posey and Plenderleith 2004). Little ecological expertise is required to see that removing multiple participants in such a complex array of interdependent relationships is not a viable long-term option. Approximately 500 million people depend on the aquatic resources supported by the coral reefs currently being destroyed by the impacts of unsustainable energy use. About three-quarters of the crops planted by humans are pollinated by bees, and these crops comprise about a third of the world's food. In the UK, recent controversies have drawn attention to the use of neonicotinoids to control crop pests, and their potential to endanger bee populations, and yet their use continues. Prioritising the rights of manu-facturers or farmers to make short-term profits at the expense of the non-human is likely to become very expensive for humans themselves. The growing number of environmental refugees around the world, and the human populations suffering in conflicts over resources, are only the first tranche of casualties in a combative engagement with 'the other' that, if it were aimed directly towards human groups, we would have no difficulty in recognising as a war.

Reconciling the other

It is of course the non-humanity, the 'otherness' of non-human species that gives licence to their destruction, just as it does when fellow humans are 'de-humanised'. Categorised firmly as 'other', non-human beings can be domesticated and enslaved; actively destroyed if troublesome; or merely extinguished by a disregard for their interests. They can be consumed as food, killed for sport, or used to provide resources such as leather, fertiliser, and oil. Such usage only becomes problematic when they acquire anthropomorphic person-hood as pets and companions: a categorical repositioning which may gain them much pampering and affection – at least until they become elderly and commit the capital crime of incontinence.

There is, of course, a rich anthropological literature on the complex and diverse relations between humans and animals, addressing long-term issues of domestication (Clutton-Brock 1988; Crosby 1994; Ellen and Fukui 1996) and examining categorical distinctions (Atran 1990; Bulmer 1967; Douglas 1973; Durkheim and Mauss 1963; Willis 1989). There is also close interest in the various ways in which animals become persons, as totemic ancestors (Durkheim 1961); as the mediaeval perpetrators of crimes (Phillips 2013);[2] as pets (Manning and Serpell 1994; Serpell 1996); and as what conservation organisations describe as 'iconic' species (Milton 1993, 2003). All depend on some acknowledgement of animals as persons (Carrithers et al. 2011; Fuentes and Wolfe 2002; Knight 2005; Noske 1989, 1997; Ritvo 1987).

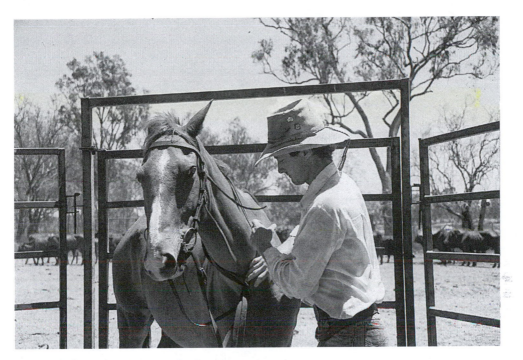

Figure 21.6 Horsebreaking in North Queensland.

Source: Photo by Veronica Strang.

This literature illustrates the myriad entanglements of human and non-human lives, and the often symbiotic interdependencies that these create. However, although it highlights the contingency of ideas about personhood, and its potential to be extended beyond human boundaries, it tends generally to retain a vision of personhood as human. Animals acquire personhood by becoming anthropomorphised; by being perceived as having human characteristics, emotions, or behaviours; or by being encompassed by individual or collective constructions of human identity. In large-scale industrialised societies at least, this does not imply an alternate, non-human form of personhood, or challenge more fundamental distinctions between human and other.

It is useful to relocate this categorical separation in its historical context. Moran suggests that:

> The nature-culture dichotomy has been central to Western thinking since time immemorial. . . . Dichotomous thinking led us to think of people as apart from nature, and charged with controlling nature for human purposes – and crucially, as distinct from the inherent dynamics of the Earth system itself.
>
> *(Moran 2006: 7–8)*

One might question the 'since time immemorial', but Nature–Culture dualism has certainly been a dominant model for a long time. Following Durkheim (1961), it may be said to have followed a (putatively) progressive trajectory away from 'nature religions' valorising non-human deities; towards religions worshipping humanised gods; into increasingly patriarchal and hierarchical monotheisms and scientific deconstructions of the world (Harrison

1999; Hocart 1970 [1952]; Strang 2014a). A dualistic vision of (supposedly rational, male) Culture and (primal, feminised) Nature introduced not only a critical separation between them, but also encouraged widening inequities in their perceived power and status – inequities that continue to be reflected in their differential access to justice (Adams 1993; Ortner 1976; Plumwood 1993, 2002).

Nature–Culture dualism has been so normalised over time that it has become seemingly fundamental in everyday discourses and in many areas of 'natural' science. However, theorists such as Strathern (1992), Verdery and Humphrey (2004), Escobar (1999, 2015), and Descola and Pálsson (1996) have questioned its intellectual validity. In this area, as in others, anthropological theories have gained from engagement with diverse cultural ways of understanding the world.[3] A sharply dualistic vision of Nature and Culture, or for that matter human and non-human, does not pertain in all societies' worldviews, and is notably absent in many indigenous cosmologies (Greenough and Lowenhaupt Tsing 2003). This has real implications for the environmental values that they promote, and for the relationships with the non-human that they compose, encouraging more egalitarian and reciprocal approaches that are – demonstrably – more sustainable in the longer term (Moran 2006; Strang 1997).

Such statements tend to attract the ire of conservative writers, anxious about the romanticisation of indigenous peoples' relationships with their environments. But it is necessary to put aside the historical imagery about Noble Savages, as well as the popular representations of indigenous 'harmony with nature' utilised by conservation organisations and sometimes (with astute political aims) by indigenous groups themselves (Ellen 1986; Hames 2007). There are real differences to consider in the ways that some indigenous groups conceptualise human and other beings. For example, Aboriginal Australian understandings about what it means to be human, and how human and other beings interconnect, are unencumbered by dualistic siloes. These differences are revealed in their ideas about the fluid movement of the human spirit over space and time, into and out of material being, via various human and non-human forms. The human spirit's generation from ancestral forces held in the land; its corporate manifestation as a human person; and its eventual reunification with, or dissolution into, an invisible totemic (non-human) ancestral being, highlight a cultural understanding in which human-ness is seen as 'contingent matter' (Strang 2002, 2009b, 2014b).

On the matter of being

While issues of materiality may seem tangential to the attainment of ecological justice, the emergent literature in this area emphasises the fact that matter matters. Humans are bio-cultural beings, sharing huge amounts of genetic material with other organic species, and subject to the same evolutionary and biological processes (Ingold and Pálsson 2013). We depend absolutely upon complex interrelationships, not only between ourselves and non-human beings, but also with ecological processes and the range of organic and inorganic materials that constitute these. For instance, every cell in the human body is irrigated by water; the human body is about 67 per cent water; even our thoughts depend upon the electric charges enabled by water molecules. We may sit at the top of the food chain (until arriving eventually at the bottom of it), but we are still dynamically composed – and decomposed – of the material of the world.

Foregrounding materiality enables us to reconsider ecological justice in several ways. First, it conceptually relocates humankind firmly within the material interdependencies that compose ecology. A useful impetus to these ideas has been provided by network theories and socio-technical systems (STS) approaches, which question and perceptually dissolve the boundaries of relationality in human and non-human interactions (Latour 2005; Mol and Law 1994; Mol 2002). Materialist thinking has been taken further by writers such as Bennett (2009), Tsing (2004), and Ingold (2012) who have elucidated the dynamism of the 'vibrant matter', 'friction', and 'flux' through which the 'matter of being' emerges in spatio-temporal processes of 'becoming' (Deleuze and Guattari 1993 [1980]). Coole and Frost argue that these 'vitalist' approaches require a new materialist ontology which is post- rather than anti-Cartesian, and which 'avoids dualism or dialectical reconciliation by espousing a monological account of emergent, generative material being' (2010: 8). Examining human–non-human relationships from this perspective therefore presents a direct challenge to a dualistic vision of Nature and Culture, and opens up new opportunities to rethink its positionalities.

Such reconsideration has generated humbler, more bioethical – i.e. biocentric – approaches in which humans no longer automatically hold the centre stage (Chen *et al.* 2013; Haraway 2008; Tsing 2004).[4] Related forays into 'multispecies ethnography' (e.g. Kirksey and Helmreich 2010; Tsing 2015) have provided insights into how human–non-human interactions affect a diverse range of 'others', including plants (Head and Atchison 2009), microbes (Helmreich 2009), viruses (Lowe 2010), and corals (Hayward 2010), as well as those, such as primates, that are more easily seen in – literal – relation to humankind (Fuentes 2010). The 'thought experiment' of considering their emic perspectives provides fresh ideas about personhood, and thus issues of ecological justice, establishing a vision of multiple forms of participants and persons in human–environmental relations.

Figure 21.7 Stockman with pet dingo pup.

Source: Photo by Veronica Strang.

A quite different approach is provided by specialists in material culture, and this too seems unrelated to issues of ecological justice until we consider its capacity to highlight the agency of things. There is no space here to engage with lengthy debates about material agency (e.g. Ingold 2007; Knappett and Malafouris 2008; Strang 2015), but I want to highlight the value of starting with a question about 'what things do'. Like studies of human–animal relations, those concerned with material things have benefited from exchanges of knowledge about indigenous lifeworlds containing sentient landscapes and objects, providing – again – highly fluid ideas about personhood, agency, and identity. While it is obviously critical to separate contemporary theories of materiality from traditional beliefs in animism, the capacity of the latter to imagine an active material world has proved fruitful. Research on how things and persons act upon each other (Gell 1998; Tilley *et al.* 2006) is now extending usefully into a consideration of how, via their particular properties and behaviours, aspects of the material environment – including its 'resources' – play an agentive, recursive role in human–non-human engagements (Bakker and Bridge 2006; Boivin 2008; Strang 2014b).

Rather than being constituted anthropocentrically, as merely the passive subject of human action, this provides a more dynamically reciprocal view of the non-human material environment. As with non-human species, this repositioning reframes it as an active participant in a mutually constitutive relational process, thus enabling an 'appreciation of the other' and highlighting the need to consider its interests. In this sense, it adds to the case for the extension of justice to encompass the non-human.

Figure 21.8 Author with favourite work horse.

Source: Photo by Clare Blackman.

Justice for all

The issue of value or 'appreciation' underpins each part of a rationale for the extension of notions of justice beyond humankind. Destructive modes of human–non-human engagement are enabled by a dualistic understanding of Culture and Nature which permits the devaluation of non-human beings, casting them as exploitable and expendable economic subjects. The alienation of 'the other' at a fundamental level also encourages human societies to make dangerously short-term choices while determinedly refusing to consider the 'inconvenient truths' of their likely consequences (Guggenheim 2006).

As noted previously, there is a rational case to be made, on self-interest alone, for humankind to deal more reciprocally with other species and the material environment. The UN World Commission on Environment and Development, the IUCN, Greenpeace, and other environmental organisations have made just such a case, as have the alarming scenarios presented by climate change scientists. Another approach purportedly aimed at conservation, and self-defined as 'rational', is an all-pervasive push to commoditise 'ecosystem services' or 'environmental services' by attaching monetary value to all of the elements and processes of ecosystems according to the extent that they serve humankind.

Jonathan Porritt argues that such marketisation has been genuinely effective in persuading governments and industry to adjust their activities to conserve non-human species and the material environment. He suggests that framing human–environmental relationships in this way is the only realistic way to achieve these changes (personal communication). He may well be right – his extraordinary track record means that he is better qualified to say this than just about anyone. But, as he also acknowledges, there remains a major question as to whether an approach that evaluates the non-human in reductive monetary terms (which inevitably excludes many unmeasurable factors), and which positions the environment and its non-human inhabitants as a 'service' to humankind, can ever deliver the level of reciprocity required to ensure that non-human interests are protected in the longer term.[5] My own view – because theoretical models inevitably manifest themselves in practice – is that an approach that places humankind in such a position of primacy, and which further entrenches the conceptual alienation between human and non-human, contains an inherent contradiction in terms of reciprocal relations, and will inevitably give priority to human interests 'when push comes to shove'.

And the problem is that push comes to shove all the time. Protecting 'ecosystem services' may work when there is the luxury of flexibility, but it is readily subsumed by more immediate pressures. It is plain that rationality rarely outweighs people's capacities for denial. This is amply illustrated by most societies' unaltered commitment to growth-based economic modes and their collective ineptitude in reducing CO_2 emissions. And there is an additional ethical question, which returns us to the issue of justice, as to whether, in any case, humankind has the right to impose on non-human species its own evaluation of their fiscal worth in terms of 'service'.

Deep ecologists have argued that real changes in practice are more likely to come, not from purportedly rational arguments about cause and effect, but from fundamental changes in values. For some writers, this is a spiritual matter: Sponsel suggests that 'spiritual ecology' is needed to 'tear many of our societies away from the forces of materialism which distort our values' (2000: 95). Atran and Norenzayan (2004) argue that religion needs to challenge science and secularism if humankind is to break away from self-interest and re-establish 'organic solidarity'.

Given the Durkheimian contradictions to this vision of equality contained in most major religions, and their historic contribution to dualistic and unequal relationships with the non-human, I am dubious about the utility of looking to religion in this endeavour. But, whether religious or secular, a shift in values is key: any sustainable way forward requires a 'rendering of justice to' and 'due appreciation' of the non-human. Clearly a large-scale return to the kinds of pre-Christian 'nature religions' that valorised and appreciated the non-human is unlikely, but there is some potential to learn from those that pertain in indigenous communities. As noted above, indigenous worldviews in Australia and elsewhere generally construct relationships with other species and things that are more egalitarian and reciprocal, and more based on notions of partnership, thus ensuring 'due appreciation' for the non-human.

However, appreciation, co-identification, and affective ties are not enough; deep ecology – or as Milton puts it, 'loving nature' (2002) – is not enough. What is most important about alternate worldviews is that they offer a genuinely different constellation of relations: a closely integrated model of human and non-human beings interacting within a single conceptual community. My concluding point, then, is that this provides exemplars about what is needed *theoretically* for long-term sustainability: a radical re-conceptualisation of human–non-human relationships and the notion of 'community' itself.

This suggests that there is a need to incorporate into social anthropology the theorisations of writers interested in the bioethics of non-human and material worlds. These enable the repositioning of humankind and the inclusion of all species and materials as collaborative partners within a shared 'monological' process of becoming (Coole and Frost 2010). In these more inclusive visions, the idea of community can be 're-imagined' to encompass the non-human (Strang in press). In these terms, 'justice for all' is neither 'social' nor 'ecological', but is both conceptually and practically reconciled into a single vision of equity and order.

Notes

1 Greece 1952, Switzerland 1971, Liechtenstein 1984.
2 It is clear that animals were regarded as having sufficient 'personhood' in mediaeval Europe to be subjected to human forms of justice and punishment in the famous animal trials of that period (Phillips 2013).
3 As I have noted elsewhere, anthropological theories have been co-constituted by ethnographic involvement and knowledge exchanges with multiple cultural perspectives (Strang 2006).
4 These resonate with longer-running debates about biocentric versus anthropocentric human–environmental relationships, or 'deep' and 'shallow' ecology (Moran 2006).
5 Porritt notes the example provided by the Yasuni National Park in Ecuador, where efforts have been made to persuade the international community to pay to prevent the exploitation of rich oil reserves in a region critical for biodiversity. A tentative agreement has been reached, but the story is far from over. The list of less positive examples, where conservation has been overridden by short-term efforts to extract resources or generate energe, is vastly longer, including for example, the tar sand oil extractions in Canada, the Three Gorges dams in China, and myriad other instances where pressing economic needs or desires have subsumed all non-human interests.

References

Adams C 1993. *Ecofeminism and the sacred*. New York: The Continuum Publishing Company.
Anderson D and Berglund E (eds) 2003. *Ethnographies of conservation: Environmentalism and the distribution of privilege*. New York and Oxford: Berghahn Books.
Atran S 1990. *Cognitive foundations of natural history*. Cambridge and New York: Cambridge University Press.
Atran S and Norenzayan A 2004. Religion's evolutionary landscape: Counterintuition, commitment, compassion, communion. *Behavioral and Brain Sciences* 27: 713–770.

Attwood B and Markus A 1999. *The struggle for Aboriginal rights: A documentary history*. Cambridge and New York: Allen & Unwin.

Bakker K and Bridge G 2006. Material worlds? Resource geographies and the 'matter of nature'. *Progress in Human Geography* 30(1): 5–27.

Baxter B 2005. *A theory of ecological justice*. London and New York: Routledge.

Bennett J 2009. *Vibrant matter: A political ecology of things*. Durham, NC: Duke University Press.

Boivin N 2008. *Material cultures, material minds: The impact of things on human thought, society, and evolution*. Cambridge and New York: Cambridge University Press.

Bulmer R 1967. Why is a cassowary not a bird? A problem of zoological taxonomy among the Karam of the New Guinea Highlands. *Man* (new series) 2(1): 5–25.

Caldararo N 2004. *Sustainability, human ecology, and the collapse of complex societies: Economic anthropology and a 21st century adaptation*. New York and London: Edwin Mellen Press.

Caplan P (ed.) 2003. *The ethics of anthropology: Debates and dilemmas*. New York: Routledge.

Carrithers M, Bracken L and Emery S 2011. Can a species be a person? A trope and its entanglements in the Anthropocene era. *Current Anthropology* 52(5): 661–685.

Chen C, Macleod J and Neimanis A (eds) 2013. *Thinking with water*. Montreal, QC: McGill–Queens University Press.

Clutton-Brock J (ed.) 1988. *The walking larder: Patterns of domestication, pastoralism, and predation*. London and Boston, MA: Unwin Hyman.

Coole D and Frost S 2010. *New materialisms: Ontology, agency and politics*. Durham, NC and London: Duke University Press.

Crosby A 1994. *Germs, seeds and animals: Studies in ecological history*. Armonk, NY: M.E. Sharpe.

Deleuze G and Guattari F 1993 [1980]. *A thousand plateaus: Capitalism and schizophrenia* (transl. B Massumi). Minneapolis: University of Minnesota Press.

Descola P and Pálsson G (eds) 1996. *Nature and society: Anthropological perspectives*. London and New York: Routledge.

Diamond J 2005. *Collapse: How societies choose to fail or succeed*. New York: Penguin.

Dobson A 1998. *Justice and the environment: Conceptions of environmental sustainability and theories of distributive justice*. Oxford: Oxford University Press.

Douglas M (ed.) 1973. *Rules and meanings: The anthropology of everyday knowledge*. Harmondsworth, UK: Penguin Education.

Durkheim É 1961. *The elementary forms of the religious life*. New York: Collier Books.

Durkheim É and Mauss M 1963. *Primitive classification* (transl. and edited by R Needham). London: Cohen & West.

Ellen R 1986. What Black Elk left unsaid: On the illusory images of Green primitivism. *Anthropology Today* 2(6): 8–13.

Ellen R and Fukui K (eds) 1996. *Redefining nature: Ecology, culture and domestication*. Oxford and Washington, DC: Berg.

Escobar A 1999. After nature: Steps to an anti-essentialist political ecology. *Current Anthropology* 40(1): 1–16.

—— 2015. Sustaining the pluriverse: The political ontology of territorial struggles. Paper presented at the Centre for the Anthropology of Sustainability Inaugural Conference on 'Anthropological visions of sustainable futures', University College London, 12–14 February 2015.

Franklin A 2006. *Animal nation: The true story of animals and Australia*. Sydney: UNSW Press.

Fuentes A 2010. Naturalcultural encounters in Bali: Monkeys, temples, tourists and ethnoprimatology. *Cultural Anthropology* 25(4): 600–624.

Fuentes A and Wolfe L (eds) 2002. *Primates face to face: Conservation implications of human and nonhuman primate interconnections*.Cambridge and New York: Cambridge University Press.

Gell A 1998. *Art and agency: An anthropological theory*. Oxford and New York: Berg.

Greenough P and Lowenhaupt Tsing A (eds) 2003. *Nature in the global south: Environmental projects in south and southeast Asia*. Durham, NC and London: Duke University Press.

Griffiths T and Robin L (eds) 1997. *Ecology and empire: Environmental history of settler societies*. Keele, Staffordshire, UK: Keele University Press.

Guggenheim D (dir.) 2006. *An inconvenient truth*. Los Angeles, CA: Film Paramount Classics.

Hames R 2007. The ecologically Noble Savage debate. *Annual Review of Anthropology* 36(1): 177–190.

Haraway D 2008. *When species meet*. Minneapolis: University of Minnesota Press.

Harper D 2014. *Online etymology dictionary* (multiple sources). www.etymonline.com/index.php?term= justice (accessed 26 April 2014).

Harrison P 1999. Subduing the Earth: Genesis 1, early modern science, and the exploitation of nature. *The Journal of Religion* 79(1): 86–109.

Hayward E 2010. Fingereyes: Impressions of cup corals. *Cultural Anthropology* 25(4): 577–599.

Head L and Atchison J 2009. Cultural ecology: Emerging human-plant geographies. *Progress in Human Geography* 33(2): 236–245.

Helmreich S 2009. *Alien ocean: Anthropological voyages in microbial seas.* Berkeley: University of California Press.

Hocart A 1970 [1952]. *The life-giving myth and other essays.* London: Methuen.

Holland J 2001. Understanding the complexity of economic, ecological and social systems. In E Stein (ed.) *Lectures in the sciences of complexity.* Reading, MA: Addison-Wesley, pp. 619–712.

Horkheimer M and Adorno T 2002 [1944]. *Dialectic of enlightenment* (transl. J Cumming). New York: Continuum.

Howard B 2003. *Indigenous peoples and the state: The struggle for native rights.* DeKalb: Northern Illinois University Press.

Hunt J 2009 *Medieval justice: Cases and laws in France, England and Germany, 500–1500.* Jefferson, NC: McFarland and Company.

Illich I 1999. The shadow our future throws. *New Perspectives Quarterly* 16(2): 14–18. www.digitalnpq.org/archive/2009_fall_2010_winter/12_illich.html (accessed 25 April 2014).

Ingold T 2007. Materials against materiality. *Archaeological Dialogues* 14(1): 1–16.

—— 2012. Toward an ecology of materials. *Annual Review of Anthropology* 41(1): 427–442.

Ingold T and Pálsson G (eds) 2013. *Biosocial becomings: Integrating social and biological anthropology.* Cambridge and New York: Cambridge University Press.

International Union for Conservation of Nature (IUCN) 2014. Red list of threatened species. www.iucnredlist.org/ (accessed 23 April 2014).

Johnston B, Hiwasaki L, Klaver I, Ramos-Castillo A and Strang V (eds) 2012. *Water, cultural diversity and global environmental change: Emerging trends, sustainable futures?* Paris: UNESCO.

Kirksey S and Helmreich S 2010. The emergence of multispecies ethnography. *Cultural Anthropology* 25(4): 545–576.

Knappett C and Malafouris L (eds) 2008. *Material agency: Towards a non-anthropocentric approach.* New York: Springer.

Knight J (ed.) 2005. *Animals in person: Cultural perspectives on human–animal interaction.* Oxford and New York: Berg.

Lansing S 2003. Complex adaptive systems. *Annual Review of Anthropology* 32: 183–204.

Latour B 2005. *Reassembling the social: An introduction to Actor-Network-Theory.* Oxford: Oxford University Press.

Lowe C 2010. Viral clouds: Becoming H5N1 in Indonesia. *Cultural Anthropology* 25(4): 625–649.

Manning A and Serpell J (eds) 1994. *Animals and human society: Changing perspectives.* London and New York: Routledge.

Milton K (ed.) 1993. *Environmentalism: The view from anthropology.* London and New York: Routledge.

—— 2002. *Loving nature: Towards an ecology of emotion.* London and New York: Routledge.

—— 2003. Comment on human–animal relations. *Anthropology Today* 19(1): 19–20.

Mol A 2002. *The body multiple: Ontology in medical practice.* Durham, NC and London: Duke University Press.

Mol A and Law J 1994. Regions, networks and fluids: Anaemia and social topology. *Social Studies of Science* 24(4): 641–671.

Moran E 2006. *People and nature: An introduction to Human Ecological Relations.* Malden, MA and Oxford: Blackwell Publishers.

Noske B 1989. *Humans and other animals.* London: Pluto Press.

—— 1997. *Beyond boundaries: Humans and animals.* Montreal, QC and London: Black Rose.

Orlove B and Brush S 1996. Anthropology and the conservation of biodiversity. *Annual Review of Anthropology* 25: 329–352.

Ortner S 1976. Is female to nature as male is to culture? In M Rosaldo and L Lamphere (eds) *Women, culture and society.* Stanford, CA: Stanford University Press, pp. 67–87.

Paavola J and Lowe I (eds) 2005. *Environmental values in a globalising world: Nature, justice, and governance.* London and New York: Routledge.

Phillips P 2013. *Medieval animal trials: Justice for all*. Lewiston, NY: Edwin Mellen Press.

Plumwood V 1993. *Feminism and the mastery of nature*. London and New York: Routledge.

—— 2002. *Environmental culture: The ecological crisis of reason*. London and New York: Routledge.

Posey D and Plenderleith K 2004. *Indigenous knowledge and ethics: A Darrell Posey reader*. London and New York: Routledge.

Ritvo H 1987. *The animal estate: The English and other creatures in the Victorian age*. Cambridge, MA: Harvard University Press.

Serpell J 1996. *In the company of animals: A study of human–animal relationships*. Cambridge and New York: Cambridge University Press.

Sponsel L (ed.) 2000. *Endangered peoples of Southeast and East Asia: Struggles to survive and thrive*. Westport, CT: Greenwood Press.

Strang V 1997. *Uncommon ground: Cultural landscapes and environmental values*. Oxford and New York: Berg.

—— 2002. Life down under: Water and identity in an Aboriginal cultural landscape. *Goldsmiths College Anthropology Research Papers*. No. 7. London: Goldsmiths College.

—— 2006. A happy coincidence? Symbiosis and synthesis in anthropological and indigenous knowledges. *Current Anthropology* 47(6): 981–1008.

—— 2009a. *Gardening the world: Agency, identity, and the ownership of water*. Oxford and New York: Berghahn Books.

—— 2009b. Water and indigenous religion: Aboriginal Australia. In T Tvedt and T Oestigaard (eds) *The idea of water*. London: I.B. Tauris, pp. 343–377.

—— 2014a. Lording it over the goddess: Water, gender and human-environmental relations. *Journal of Feminist Studies in Religion* 30(1): 83–107.

—— 2014b. Fluid consistencies: Meaning and materiality in human engagements with water. *Archaeological Dialogues* 21(2): 133–150.

—— 2015. On the matter of time. *Interdisciplinary Science Reviews* 40(2): 101–123.

—— in press. Re-imagined communities: A bioethical approach to water policy. In K Conca and E Weinthal (eds) *The Oxford handbook on water politics and policy*. Oxford and New York: Oxford University Press.

Strang V and Busse M 2011. *Ownership and appropriation*. Oxford and New York: Berg.

Strathern M 1992. *After nature: English kinship in the late twentieth century*. Cambridge and New York: Cambridge University Press.

Tilley C, Keane W, Küchler S, Rowlands M and Spyer P (eds) 2006. *Handbook of material culture*. London, Thousand Oaks, CA and New Delhi: Sage.

Tsing A 2004. *Friction: An ethnography of global connections*. Princeton, NJ: Princeton University Press.

—— 2015. Life in past and coming ruins. Conference paper presented at the Centre for the Anthropology of Sustainability Inaugural Conference on 'Anthropological Visions of Sustainable Futures', University College London, 12–14 February 2015.

UN World Commission on Environment and Development 1987. *Our common future*. Oxford and New York: Oxford University Press.

Verdery K and Humphrey C (eds) 2004. *Property in question: Value transformation in the global economy*. Oxford and New York: Berg.

Willis R (ed.) 1989. *Signifying animals: Human meaning in the natural world*. London and Boston, MA: Unwin Hyman.

22

ENVIRONMENTAL ETHICS AND ENVIRONMENTAL ANTHROPOLOGY

Holmes Rolston III

Introduction

Anthropology, including environmental anthropology, is a science, as also is ecology. Philosophy, including environmental ethics, analyzes issues often to make value judgments about right and wrong. Science deals with the facts of the matter; ethics needs such facts, but moves from *is* to *ought*. Science and philosophy are both theoretical and applied, however; and applied anthropology, like ecology, must cross over into applied ethics, willy-nilly. How activist will environmental anthropologists be? Will they be allies of those they study? Whose needs, what needs are served? Environmental ethics will inevitably hope to shape, focus, and inspire action. Here theory without application is wasted time—unless perhaps the theorist is facilitating policies or practices set or done by others. Almost half of the people in the world still live in close encounter with their surrounding landscapes. Urban as well as rural people depend on supporting landscapes, near or far. So situated, what ought they, what ought we to do?

So, right at the start, we face a challenge: clarifying the intermingling of science and conscience, which has never been more demanding than in this first of the 45 million centuries of life on Earth in which one species with its escalating populations, powers, and appetites, can jeopardize the planet's future. The *logos* of *anthropos* is the problem. *Homo sapiens* needs wisdom desperately, along with its knowledge, *sapientia* with its *scientia*. Environmental ethics is theory and practice about values in, or carried by, and duties to, or concerning, the natural world. Environmental ethics needs to address concerns about humans living well in their natural environments, about equitable resource use, about domestic and wild animals, plants and living organisms, endangered species and biodiversity, ecosystems and communities of life, and about the global Earth.

We will move through these levels, wondering what special contributions environmental anthropologists might bring to bear. We here invite dialogue between environmental ethicists and anthropologists. As a philosopher, I am more interested in your forming your own answers than in delivering answers to you. But such crosstalk will result in better answers if the questions are well formed. Expect some probing. I found thinking through these ideas and cases probing myself. If you need to know where I am coming from, what answers I have reached, Christopher Preston has written my intellectual biography (Preston 2009).

Aboriginal humans on their landscapes

What is all over most landscapes is not wild nature, but nature linked with people who inhabit these landscapes. So we need an "anthropology which puts more than usual emphasis on the interface between cultural and ecological factors" (Thin 1996: 186; Townsend 2009). In their dialogue with philosophical ethicists, environmental anthropologists may insist that environmental ethics too is as social as it is natural. Most of life for most people takes place on anthropogenic biomes that are a hybrid tapestry of nature and culture. More than 80 percent of all people live in densely populated rural, village, and urban landscapes (Ellis and Ramankutty 2008). Natural systems are inextricably entwined with cultural systems, which introduce new levels of complexity (Liu *et al.* 2007). So far as they can, these peoples purposefully transform nature, sometimes more, sometimes less, into a desirable humanized form. Often also, accepting trade-offs or degrading landscapes unintentionally results. Human values and natural values are synthetic, or symbiotic. If nature means pristine nature, totally unaffected by human activities, past or present, there is relatively little remaining on Earth. If culture means totally re-constructed, civilized, de-natured lands with no dependence on natural systems, there is none of that on Earth either.

So environmental ethics is a synthesis of humans and nature, with humans hoping to live well on their Earth. Still, by many accounts, humans are the focus: "Human beings are at the centre of concerns . . ." So the *Rio Declaration* begins, formulated at the United Nations Conference on Environment and Development, and signed by almost every nation on Earth (UNCED 1992a: online). This was once to be called the *Earth Charter*, but the developing nations were more interested in asserting their rights to develop, and only secondarily in saving the Earth. The Rio claim is, in many respects, quite true. The human species is causing all the concern. Environmental problems are people problems, not gorilla or tiger problems. The problem is to get people into "a healthy and productive life in harmony with nature" (UNCED 1992a: online).

Environmental ethics, continuing this account, is sometimes founded on what we can call a human right to nature. The UN World Commission on Environment and Development claims: "All human beings have the fundamental right to an environment adequate for their health and well-being" (1987: 9). This includes the basic natural givens—air, soil, water, functioning ecosystems, hydrologic cycles, and so on. These could previously be taken for granted. But now the right must be made explicit and defended. This is not any claim against or for nature itself; rather it is a claim made against other humans who might deprive some humans of such nature. But note that this might still support the argument that humans need to sustain nature on these landscapes they inhabit, at least insofar as it sustains their well-being.

So caution: in the lives of local peoples, natural process and forces are still very much on the landscape they inhabit; the natural is as important as the social, even more so. Much more than those in developed societies, local peoples depend on ecosystems services. Also, while the anthropologists are focused on their social needs, these peoples themselves typically have their own traditional worldviews in which nature may feature as much as culture: they may believe in spirits good and bad, in gods and goddesses abroad on the landscape. They often take animals as totems for their tribes.

In 1996, I was at Uluru or Ayer's Rock in Australia, a spectacular huge red sandstone mountain dome isolated on its landscape, one of the most recognizable landmarks in the nation, and a favorite climb, especially to be on top at daybreak. This is now on designated Aboriginal land. A tribe named the Anangu are the traditional owners. Signs at the base welcome visitors, and give them permission to climb, but request that they not do so. By their tradition, only Mala warriors (men who take the name of the Mala, or hare wallaby) are permitted to climb. Tourists are invited to see sites at the base where Anangu women, who were not permitted to climb either, prepared food for the warriors. Outsiders, and women, they say, will pollute the tracks of their ancient warriors.

You are invited to view, from a distance, Mala Puta, a cave (eroded pocket) in the sandstone wall, said to be the pouch of the female hare wallaby, where the Anangu believe they were created by or from the hare wallaby, though you are sternly forbidden to photograph the cave, lest you desecrate it. I climbed Uluru, torn between respect for their culture, disbelief in their creation story, doubts about their macho men insisting that their women not climb, but serve them, doubts about whether a small local tribe should impose their wishes on half a million others each year wishing to visit a World Heritage geological site. Since my visit, there has been ongoing debate whether the right thing to do is to forbid the climb to outsiders (and native women?) (Uluru–Kata Tjuta National Park 2012). Now I am wondering whether environmental anthropologists have any insight in such conflicts. They might set forth the Anangu worldview, empathetically enabling ethicists better to evaluate aboriginal rights traded off against more global rights to a natural heritage.

In 2004, in Taiwan, I was invited to an aboriginal site of the Paiwan tribe. Entering the reservation, my host, the chief, and I had to stop at a shrine to placate the local spirits. In the mountains there lives, or once lived, the Taiwan clouded leopard, now perhaps extinct. Some research scientists had set cameras to see if they could photograph any leopards. Some researchers "disappeared," as they put it.

The locals claimed they had angered the spirits. In the ceremony, the chief, now acting as priest, was pouring rice wine into a foot-long bamboo stick. He was to drink out of one end and I out of the other, to show that we were friends and the local goddess would welcome me. In the midst of pouring the wine, his cell phone rang. The goddess was put on hold, and the ceremony resumed later. I found this a curious mix of reverence, superstition, and high technology.

The reason I was there is that the tribe hoped to open up a part of their reservation to eco-tourism. They wanted my impression of the possibilities. We hiked a trail a mile or so to two interesting waterfalls. At the second I heard that the most spectacular falls were still further off, and suggested that we could hike there too. "Oh, no," I was told. "An ornery spirit lives there, and it would be dangerous for you to go." I began to doubt whether eco-tourism was feasible, not because of the landscape, but because of their beliefs about spirits inhabiting their lands.

Indigenous peoples may live in an enchanted world, one of spirits, good and bad, witches, demons, fairies to which they may ascribe their fortunes and misfortunes, their good luck, or disease, seeking to please or placate these spirits with rituals and taboos. Neither ethicists nor anthropologists themselves personally live in any such enspirited world, nor can they take seriously—at least not literally—these local animisms, though they may have their ways of pretending to "go native," or of de-mythologizing these beliefs, perhaps still holding to some convictions about the sacred depths of nature.

Environmental justice

Environmental justice demands an equitable distribution of burdens and benefits to racial minorities, the poor, and those in developing nations (Attfield and Wilkins 1992). The ethical issues here typically involve who gets the benefits and who bears the costs—equity and consent issues. The rich may argue that some people and nations have achieved more than others; they earned their wealth by hard work and Yankee ingenuity. If one compares, say, Sweden with Uganda, the Swedes have an earned prosperity that the Ugandans lack, unfortunately. But Idi Amin Dada and his supporters did make a series of mistakes that left the country in a shambles (Kaufman 2003). Fairness nowhere commands rewarding all parties equally; justice is giving each his or her due.

True, but this is not the whole truth. The rich in developed nations—also within the developing nations—have power to exploit the poor, and capitalists will soon exploit them. The vast inequities in wealth are impossible to justify on the basis of merit. All who benefit from capitalism are complicit in the injustice. The victims downwater or downwind never gave any free, informed consent and usually have no means of proving their damages or asserting their rights. The wealthy (some of whom are producing the toxic substances, all are enjoying benefits) can afford to protect themselves. Environmental justice seeks protection from such injustice, empowering local peoples against outside threats and using moral, as well as social and political, convictions to do this. On this environmental ethicists and environmental anthropologists will entirely agree, and environmental anthropologists may be in a better position to estimate the local damages.

Some prefer here to use the term "ecojustice," arguing that we ought to blend justice in the social order and integrity in the natural order (see Veronica Strang, Chapter 21 in this volume). Ecojustice may claim to be a more inclusive ethic than environmental justice, which is mostly about people. Caring for humanity requires caring for the Earth; these are complements—not opposites as so often argued. One does not need to sacrifice nature to benefit people; rather, people benefit from a nature that is protected and conserved. Environmental anthropologists hope to put human and biotic communities together comprehensively. They seek sustaining communities in which people are fulfilled; beyond that, they hope to sustain the entire community of life. Although this caring-for-people-justice which complements the caring-for-nature-justice sounds vaguely reasonable so long as it is kept reasonably vague, on closer analysis one wonders whether the fulfillment of the human community is historically possible with the simultaneous fulfillment of the whole biotic community (Wenz 1988). Ethicists may also wonder whether the concept of "justice" is appropriate to trees or butterflies, preferring such terms as respecting their life, their "intrinsic value," or a "good of their own."

One place where concern for both human and biotic communities does coincide is in environmental health. Health is not only skin-in; it is skin-out. It is hard to be healthy in a sick environment. In "conservation medicine," physicians and veterinarians now realize that "health effects ripple throughout the web of life. Health connects all species" (Tabor 2002: 9). Developed countries, which may have thought themselves protected with their advanced medical systems, discover they are still linked with health, human and animal, to the developing world, even to wild nature, and vulnerable to disruptions there, to which they may also be contributing. Before jumping to humans, HIV/AIDS existed in primate populations in Africa, with which it had co-evolved. It might never have emerged as a pandemic if it were not for the social disruptions in post-colonial and sub-Saharan Africa: with the bush-meat trade; the movement of rural populations to large and crowded cities, caught in poverty there; with disrupted family structures promoting promiscuity and prostitution—all of which facilitate HIV transmission (Morens *et al.* 2004). The ill-health effects of pollution often show up first in women, especially pregnant women, and in children.

A further complication is that aboriginal peoples are likely to have diseases or malnutrition that we know how to cure or treat (polio vaccine, smallpox, AIDS, vitamins). But does our desire for their welfare require introducing them to such medicine, if this will destroy their cultural folklore? Environmental anthropologists are in a good position to adapt the flexibility in aboriginal worldviews to find ways to combine modern medicine and traditional healing.

Environmentalists concerned with the health of local peoples will have to set this in a more comprehensive context. They will have to consider the environmental policies of the World Bank, the North American Free Trade Agreement (NAFTA), the World Trade Organization (WTO), and the International Monetary Fund (IMF). These will affect, sometimes dramatically, the living conditions of the poor, their wages, their taxes, and their health. They may be poor because they are living on degraded landscapes, owing to their long habitation there, such degradation intensified by colonial empires, continued by global capitalists, who now protect themselves with NAFTA and WTO. Such peoples are likely to remain poor, even if developers arrive, because they will be too poorly paid to break out of their poverty. In terms of social as well as natural surroundings, their health, again, is not just skin-in, but skin-out; it must be seen in terms of their larger welfare, which often depends as much on global forces as on locally available resources and medical care.

Joseph Stiglitz, Nobel laureate, became increasingly ethically concerned:

> While I was at the World Bank, I saw firsthand the devastating effect that globalization can have on developing countries, and especially the poor within those countries . . . Especially at the International Monetary Fund . . . decisions were made on the basis of what seemed a curious blend of ideology and bad economics, dogmas that sometimes seemed to be thinly veiling special interests . . . The IMF's policies, in part based on the outworn presumption that markets, by themselves, lead to efficient outcomes, failed to allow for desirable government interventions in the market, measures which can guide economic growth and make *everyone* better off.
>
> (Stiglitz 2002: ix, xiii, xii)

Nor are governments, pushed by such financial interests, always willing so to guide growth. Stiglitz wrote in April 2000: "I was chief economist at the World Bank from 1996 until last November, during the gravest global economic crisis in a half-century. I saw how the IMF, in tandem with the U.S. Treasury Department, responded. And I was appalled" (Stiglitz 2000: 56). "While there may be underlying economic forces at play, politics have shaped the market, and shaped it in ways that advantage the top at the expense of the rest" (Stiglitz 2012: xix–xx).

One ought first to seek fair trade, after that free trade. Environmental anthropologists can join environmental ethicists in this conviction, and both may add "environmentally sustainable trade."

> Global inequalities in income increased in the 20th century by orders of magnitude out of proportion to anything experienced before. The distance between the incomes of the richest and poorest country was about 3 to 1 in 1820, 35 to 1 in 1950, 44 to 1 in 1973, and 72 to 1 in 1992.
>
> (UNDP 2000: 6)

That inequity has since become even more extreme. "Economic inequality is rapidly increasing in the majority of countries. The wealth of the world is divided in two: almost half going to the richest one percent, the other half to the remaining 99 percent" (Oxfam 2014: 1). Free trade moves capital and goods across national boundaries, but the labor also required for production is confined within nations, which means that capital can relocate production, exploiting the cheapest labor.

Environmental ethicists may now also be faulted for overlooking the poor (often of a different race, class, or sex) in their concern to save wildlife. The poor are kept poor because their development is not only constrained by the wealthy rich, but by the setting aside of biodiversity reserves, forest reserves, hunting and catching limits. The livelihood of such poor people may be adversely affected by protected elephants, who trash their crops (Tidsell 2014). There may be concern, as we next see, about the rights of indigenous peoples in nature reserves, which they may claim as their native lands.

Wild animals

Several indigenous groups in the United States, especially Alaska, maintain their right to cultural whaling. The Makah tribe in Washington State has reinstated their right to whaling, going back the Treaty of Neah Bay (1855) in which they ceded to the United States over half of their ancestral land to ensure their right to continue hunting whales. They may be traditional people, but they know how to enlist excellent lawyers (Miller 2000/2001). From the 1920s until the 1980s, the tribe ceased hunting, concerned about whale survival. After the gray whale was removed from the Endangered Species list in 1994, they decided to hunt again, revitalizing their ancient tradition. They harpoon the whale from a cedar canoe manned by eight men, trained for the hunt both physically and spiritually. They claim great respect for the whales they kill. They now shoot the whale with a rifle after it is harpooned, so that it dies with less pain. A number of Makah tribal members opposed resuming the hunt.

In 1999, the United States Government allowed the Makah to take five whales a year for their ancestral hunt. They killed their first whale on 17 May 1999, with TV cameras in helicopters overhead, and with threat of harassment by protestors' boats. Environmentalists are concerned about viable whale populations, especially if other native peoples make similar claims. There is a quota of 124 whales for native groups in the Northwest. Many also hold that eating whales, like eating chimpanzees, is immoral. Several hundred environmentalist and animal rights groups from over two dozen countries opposed the hunt, though Greenpeace and the Sierra Club did not.

Their permission to hunt was reversed in 2001. The issue has remained contorted by differing decisions, often involving environmental impact. Some of the 1999 Makah hunters, though now unauthorized, killed a whale in September 2007; the whale was immediately seized by the US Coast Guard, and sank unharvested (this is the word used by the Makah). The question posed for environmental anthropologists is what insights they can offer for enriching, or resolving, this issue, especially those relative to the ethical issues: the rights of the Makah, the "rights" of the whales, and their conservation.

Members of the Hopi tribe in northeastern Arizona engage in a ceremony that requires ritual suffocation of golden eagles, sending their spirits to fly to the world of their ancestors, informing them of what Hopis need in today's world. However, they were refused admission to capture eagles in Wupatki National Monument, outside Flagstaff, Arizona, which they claim as ancestral land (Shaffer 1999; Stevens and Velushi 1999). Elsewhere, US Forest Service officials have deferred to their preferences, but environmental ethicists will wonder: is it right to sacrifice eagles, a threatened species, to satisfy these traditional tribal beliefs? Most environmental ethicists, even if they compromise to tolerate such beliefs, would not find this an appropriate way to treat eagles; many would endorse prohibiting such behavior where this involves taking eagles by trapping on public lands. Anthropologists often make the point that these aboriginal worldviews are not static, but dynamic, and partially at least, adaptable to new situations (Grossman and Parker 2012). Can they find ways of resolving this dispute?

Plants—Botanical life

Local peoples are often gatherers, who must eat from their landscapes, and also gather firewood, and materials for shelter. In this respect they can be expected to know their landscapes better than outsiders, such as Westerners who visit, including botanists. Anthropologists can illuminate this ethnobotany and ethnoecology. Some of this knowledge might lead to effective conservation, of which an environmental ethicist will approve. But from the fact that they know what a plant is good for, it may or may not follow that they have means for ensuring a sustainable harvest, or that they even know when they are over-harvesting, especially if their population is increasing. This is likely to differ with different tribes.

Ginseng (*Panax quinquefolius*) is a native plant in Appalachian forests, with rather precise habitat requirements. The plant adds diversity, interest, and richness to the woods. The Orientals had already eradicated a prized Asian ginseng when a Jesuit priest in Canada in the early 1700s found the American plant. Many tons were shipped to Asia, and ginseng became known as "Appalachian gold." Chinese herbal medicine claims that drinking tea made from the roots enhances virility and sexual prowess, especially in the elderly. The Chinese still cultivate some domesticated plants. Conservation biologists will deplore the present trade in roots as nothing more than catering to mistaken superstition. Chinese folk beliefs that lead to exploiting ginseng are not supported by contemporary medicine, and those who hold them would be better off if they knew better. Can environmental anthropologists help? They might consider cases where folk medicine did lead to discoveries of useful medicines, such as metformin for diabetes, made from a Chinese plant. This could lead to discussions of mistakes the folk healers have recognized and corrected (snake oil?), and then to reconsidering ginseng.

Horticulturists in 1962 took a wild tomato (*Lycopersicon chmielewski*) and bred it into and enhanced the commercial tomato for the United States industry, resulting in $8 million a year profits: no one in Peru, where it was found, was paid anything for this. Vandana Shiva has lambasted this as unjust, claiming that "this wild material is owned . . . by local people" there (1991: 260–261). The UN *Convention on Biological Diversity* insists that "States have sovereign rights over their own biological resources" (UNCED 1992b: Preamble, Article 15). But the tiny tomato, more like a yellow ball nettle, was not cultivated or even known by these local people. The horticulturalists claim that germplasm is not subject to local or national ownership, although individual plants and cultivars may be. No one owns the basic genetic information in tomatoes, apples, pineapples, or bananas (even if they may patent specific horticultural varieties), much less in wild plants, which may happen to be on lands where they live. The commercial value from its use resulted from the high-tech skills of geneticists, not from any knowledge or activities of the local peoples in Peru (Rolston 1994: 54–58).

Again, might environmental anthropologists have insights here? The local peoples are themselves likely to hold that some things found in nature are not subject to ownership, perhaps that wild plants have intrinsic value, or a good of their own to be respected, in contrast to what they can own, such as plants they cultivate and garden. Even these high-tech geneticists, under Western law, do not own the genetic information (what is *discovered*), though they can patent and own what they may have *invented* using such information. Cross-cultural discussions of ownership could lead to dialogue between anthropologists, local peoples, and ethicists.

Biodiversity, ecosystems, and communities of life

Half of the remaining tigers in the world are in India. A recent estimate is 1,410 in more than 43 reserves. India launched a flagship program, Project Tiger, in the 1970s, with powerful support from then prime minister Indira Gandhi. That has been praised as a success, although recent studies find that management effectiveness ranges from very good to poor. India has over four times the population of the United States in a land area one-third the size. The world's most densely inhabited democracy—over a billion people—is today challenged to save the world's largest population of tigers. The main threats are loss of habitat and poaching for body parts, largely sold in China and Tibet. To preserve habitat, some local peoples have been given nearby lands outside the reserves and moved.

In 2006, the Indian Parliament passed The Scheduled Tribes and Other Traditional Forest Dwellers (Recognition of Forest Rights) Act. Those who once lived in the forest are given rights to collect, use, and dispose of forest products; this includes grazing, though not hunting and trapping. Each family that has been living in an area is entitled to four hectares of land in the forest. This greatly fragments the reserve (with over 2.5 million such claims) and often makes it impossible to keep sufficient areas free of human presence for tiger conservation. Such people are likely both to kill tigers that threaten their safety, and to sell poached body parts. The Act has been much abused, with corruption in local politics, and with urban people staking windfall claims on the basis of their ancestry (Tilson and Nyhus 2010: 306–314). Implementing the Act—with concern for ecojustice, concern for saving the tiger, as well as concern for forest ecosystems—is complex and dynamic. This would seem to be an ideal situation for the insights of environmental anthropology to enlighten environmental ethics, speaking both to the local peoples, who both live on the land and have had the tiger deeply embedded in their mythology for millennia, and to wildlife conservationists, determined to save the world's most charismatic cat.

Local peoples typically depend heavily on ecosystem services, which figure into the environmental justice as we have noted. Thirty percent of the Millennium Ecosystem Assessment Development Goals depend on access to clean water. A third of the people on the planet lack readily available safe drinking water. The principal authors conclude:

> We lack a robust theoretical basis for linking ecological diversity to ecosystem dynamics and, in turn, to ecosystem services underlying human well-being. . . . Relations between ecosystem services and human well-being are poorly understood. One gap relates to the consequences of changes in ecosystem services for poverty reduction. The poor are most dependent on ecosystem services and vulnerable to their degradation.
>
> *(Carpenter et al. 2006: 257)*

The concern becomes how to combine these uncertainties in scientific knowledge with the protection of such local peoples, and how to get these peoples also to protect their ecosystems (Orlove and Brush 1996). The Yamuna River is a major watercourse that flows from sources in the Himalayas through Delhi, and into the Ganges and Bay of Bengal. Pristine in its origins and dangerously polluted downstream, the river has (or is) a mother goddess. When I was at that river recently, some conservationists claimed that accentuating local beliefs that the pollutants were making the mother goddess sick, raising fears of her anger, was a more effective strategy than teaching local people any science. Keep their myths! But is there a better way to combine these forces for ecosystem conservation, conserving the communities of life?

Living on Earth/on earth—at home on a planet

Anthropology typically features local communities at home on their earth, but were it not for their contact with the West, they would not even know they lived on Earth. Even in the West, for millennia, we did not know that we lived on a planet. Encountering this global sphere, such communities meet destructive forces that threaten their lifestyle. Local peoples in the past underwent changing climates, which changed their fortunes. But they did not know anthropogenic climate change on global scales (Dove 2014). They also meet radical worldviews, far removed from their traditional ones, that can overwhelm them cognitively as well as environmentally.

For example, global leaders may now urge that we manage the planet. We have entered the Anthropocene epoch, the latest global claim. Anthropologists will need to look twice at this, once to see what they make of it themselves, and second to see how local peoples can possibly fit into this contemporary picture. These peoples know their local landscapes; but they have never thought about managing a planet. Anthropocene, a novel word, is reminiscent of anthropology, established among the sciences. But this immediately becomes high-profile discourse, taken to showcase the expanding human empire on the planet. We are now "the God species." "Nature no longer runs the Earth. We do" (Lynas 2011: 8). Richard Alley (2011) provides us with: *Earth: The Operator's Manual*. This God species, with its operator's manual, makes human enterprise now a fully coupled, interacting component of the Earth system itself.

Here environmental anthropologists might seem to be left far behind. Traditional cultures did not come within light years of such possibilities. They were subsistence peoples, who lived at the mercy of storms, droughts, diseases. They managed to find enough food to survive, make it through winter, barely raise enough children to keep their tribes alive, often with noble resolution and courage, using what beliefs they had to muddle through, sustaining themselves for centuries. Maybe sympathetic anthropologists might hope that such peoples can learn from the West to improve their lot; maybe Western capitalists can be brought to treat them more justly. But these Anthropocene proposals will simply make all such antiquarian views irrelevant.

But there is another possibility, more topsy turvy. Our encounter with these worldviews that we take to be naïve, pre-modern, prescientific systems may expose the metaphysics that drives our science. Our global high-tech cultures may be infected by hubris, by desire for power and domination. Traditional views may render perceptible something authentic in nature to which science blinds us. No one is the worse for having his or her receptive faculties increased, whether by science, religion, art, philosophy, myth, or whatever.

Science has discovered the community of life on Earth in ways not known to traditional cultures—through microscopes, explorations around the globe, fossil evidence, and the labors of taxonomists with their phylogenetic insights. But the same science licenses our uses of this Earth. The axiology with which we interpret natural history interlocks with the axiology that drives our cultural development. What we must push for, according to the Royal Society of London, the world's oldest scientific society, is "sustainable intensification" of reaping the benefits of exploiting the Earth (Royal Society 2009). Biological knowledge has fueled technology, agricultural development, the control of disease organisms, declines in infant mortality, lengthening spans of life, the elimination of predators, and the exploitation of genetic resources. The logic at the bottom of this is that a valueless nature can be put to any cultural use we please; humans are constrained only by prudence and regard for our fellow humans.

These local peoples have by now seen the marvelous photographs of Earth taken from space, so they too know that they live on Earth. They know more immediately that they live on Earth with their feet on the ground and the sky over their heads, and they have attitudes about belonging on earth. Compare these with the Anthropocene zealots, celebrating themselves as the first species ever to be able to re-engineer the planet, who are at the same time the first species ever to imperil its future. Even the most enlightened exploiters are not residents of a community of life, only consumers of materials. They reduce their environment to a place to gather food or deposit waste, to resource and sink. The environment must be this much, of course, but it can be much more.

Though traditional cultures do not have ecology as a science, they often have what ecology means etymologically: a logic of a home. They may have worldviews in which they are meaningful residents in a meaningful world—as did the ancient Hebrews in their promised land. It can hardly be said that science has yet given us a worldview in which we readily find ourselves at home. The West with its growth ethic has tended to replace ecology, the logic of a home, with economics, a logic of efficient resource use. Such an ethic of dominance in the only moral creature becomes one of arrogance, an Earth-eating mentality that has become consumptive and no longer resides in any place in peace.

Compared with the traditionalists who believe that the myriad natural kinds all have a place under the sun, that creation is to be reverenced, that a spiritual integrity places claims on human conduct, we moderns are the ones who seem axiologically naïve. Yes, humans are standouts, on Earth. But perhaps we are on a wild yang trip. We see more comprehensively than the old-timers biologically, but sometimes they see more comprehensively than we do axiologically. They have a more inclusive ethic than we have yet attained. Not always, of course, for teachings about reverence for life mingle with contradictory abuses. Meanwhile, those of us who embrace the modern scientific and technological worldview have little to brag about in our Anthropocene enthusiasm.

The worldview that has triggered the great losses of biological diversity in recent centuries did not arise from traditional cultural values, either classical or primitive. These losses began when science-based models were exported to traditional societies. The environmental damage done within primitive and classical cultures (which was sometimes considerable) pales beside damages done in our own centuries when these cultures are "opened up" for development, when they get entangled in world markets, when they aspire to Western standards of living, and when they are secularized. Our escalating consumer mentality may need to reform its values as much as do the unfortunately foolish folk who desire ginseng to keep their sexual prowess or who sacrifice eagles to get help from ancestors in their poverty. In a worldview without value except by human preference assignments, science-based values are not part of the solution; they are the root of the problem.

We in the dominant West cannot return to superstitious folklore, to an enchanted world. It is unlikely that we can lift intact from traditional cultures any pre-scientific, mythological way of valuing nature. But partly as a result of our dialogue with these cultures, we might accept non-human life on Earth as neighbors, with a good of their own, of value for what they are in themselves, not simply as our global stock. Perhaps we can begin to see ourselves not so much as maximizers of human development, but as fellow residents in a global community of life. Using traditional values as a catalyst, we might draw our model of Earth from ecology, rather than from physics, chemistry, computing, or mechanics. No model of development can be "right" in terms of inter-human justice unless it is "right" in terms of adapted fit to the land. So, somewhat to our surprise, we might well reach the conclusion that both our science-based, secular, ever more exploitative cultures and traditional cultures alike need a revised environmental ethic.

References

Alley R 2011. *Earth: The Operator's Manual*. New York: W. W. Norton & Company.

Attfield R and B Wilkins (eds) 1992. *International Justice and the Third World: Essays in the Philosophy of Development*. London: Routledge.

Carpenter S R, R DeFries, T Dietz, H A Mooney, S Polasky, W V Reid and R J Scholes 2006. Millennium Ecosystem Assessment: Research Needs. *Science* 314(5797): 257–258.

Dove M R (ed.) 2014. *The Anthropology of Climate Change*. Chichester, UK: John Wiley & Sons Ltd.

Ellis E C and N Ramankutty 2008. Putting People in the Map: Anthropogenic Biomes of the World. *Frontiers in Ecology and the Environment* 6(8): 439–447.

Grossman Z and A Parker (eds) 2012. *Asserting Native Resilience: Pacific Rim Indigenous Nations Face the Climate Crisis*. Corvalis: Oregon State University Press.

Kaufman M 2003. Idi Amin, Murderous and Erratic Ruler of Uganda in the 70's, Dies in Exile. *The New York Times*, 17 August, p. 32.

Liu, J, T Dietz, S R Carpenter, M Alberti, C Folke, E Moran, A N Pell, P Deadman, T Kratz, J Lubchenco, E Ostrom, Z Ouyang, W Provencher, C L Redman, S H Schneider and W W Taylor 2007. Complexity of Human and Natural Systems. *Science* 317(5844): 1513–1516.

Lynas M 2011. *The God Species: Saving the Planet in the Age of Humans*. Washington, DC: National Geographic.

Miller R J 2000/2001. Exercising Cultural Self-Determination: The Makah Indian Tribe Goes Whaling. *American Indian Law Review* 25(2): 165–273.

Morens D M, G K Folkers and A S Fauci 2004. The Challenge of Emerging and Re-emerging Infectious Diseases. *Nature* 430(6996): 242–249.

Orlove B S and S B Brush 1996. Anthropology and the Conservation of Biodiversity. *Annual Review of Anthropology* 25: 329–352.

Oxfam 2014. *Working for the Few: Political Capture and Economic Inequality*. Oxford: Oxfam International.

Preston C J 2009. *Saving Creation: Nature and Faith in the Life of Holmes Rolston, III*. San Antonio, TX: Trinity University Press,

Rolston III H 1994. *Conserving Natural Value*. New York: Columbia University Press.

Royal Society 2009. *Reaping the Benefits: Science and the Sustainable Intensification of Global Agriculture*. London: Royal Society.

Shaffer M 1999. Wupatki Won't Let Hopis Gather Golden Eagles. *Arizona Republic* (Phoenix), 31 July, p. A1.

Shiva V 1991. *The Violence of the Green Revolution*. London: Zed Books.

Stevens J and L Velushi 1999. Hopi Eaglet Ceremonies Thwarted. *Arizona Daily Sun* (Flagstaff), 29 July, pp. 1, 11.

Stiglitz J E 2000. The Insider: What I Learned at the World Economic Crisis. *The New Republic* 222(16/17), pp. 56–60.

—— 2002. *Globalization and its Discontents*. New York: W. W. Norton & Company.

—— 2012. *The Price of Inequality*. New York: W. W. Norton & Company.

Tabor G M 2002. Defining Conservation Medicine. In A Aguire, R S Ostfeld, G M Tabor, C House and M C Pearl (eds) *Conservation Medicine: Ecological Health in Practice*. Oxford: Oxford University Press, pp. 8–16.

Thin N 1996. Environment. In A Barnard and J Spencer (eds) *Encyclopedia of Social and Cultural Anthropology*. London: Routledge, pp. 185–188.

Tidsell C 2014. *Human Values and Biodiversity Conservation: The Survival of Wild Species*. Cheltenham, UK: Edward Elgar.

Tilson R and P J Nyhus (eds) 2010. *Tigers of the World: The Science, Politics, and Conservation of* Panthera tigris. 2nd edn. Boston, MA: Elsevier/Academic Press.

Townsend P K 2009. *Environmental Anthropology*. 2nd edn. Long Grove, IL: Waveland Press.

Uluru–Kata Tjuta National Park 2012. *Knowledge Handbook for Tour Guides*. Published by the Anangu people under the auspices of the Australian Government, National Parks. www.environment.gov.au/resource/knowledge-handbook-tour-guides-uluru-kata-tjuta-national-park (accessed 22 February 2016).

United Nations Conference on Environment and Development (UNCED) 1992a. *The Rio Declaration on Environment and Development*. UNCED Document A/CONF.151/5/Rev. 1, 13 June. www.unep.org/documents.multilingual/default.asp?documentid=78&articleid=1163 (accessed 22 February 2016).

United Nations Conference on Environment and Development (UNCED) 1992b. *Convention on Biological Diversity*. www.cbd.int/convention/text (accessed 22 February 2016).

United Nations Development Programme (UNDP) 2000. *Human Development Report 2000*. Oxford: Oxford University Press.

United Nations World Commission on Environment and Development (UNWCED) 1987. *Our Common Future*. New York: Oxford University Press.

Wenz P 1988. *Environmental Justice*. Albany: State University of New York Press.

23

BATTLE OF THE ECOLOGIES: DEEP VERSUS POLITICAL

An investigation into anthropocentrism in the social sciences

Bernard Daley Zaleha

Introduction

Animals and birds are dying because of the wickedness of our people, people who say, "God doesn't see what we are doing."

(*Jeremiah 12: 4, Today's English Version Bible*)

The above epigraph from the Hebrew Bible is attributed to Jeremiah, a prophet of Ancient Israel active around the beginning of the sixth century BC (Coogan 2006: 366–376). The passage posits that morally dubious actions by humans cause significant mortality and destruction to non-human nature, demonstrating that concern for non-human life is not only a nineteenth and twentieth century phenomenon. Jumping ahead two and a half millennia to the cultural currents following the first Earth Day, the movie *Silent Running* (Trumbull 1972; screenwritten by Michael Cimino, Steven Bochco, and Deric Washburn; see also Kermode 2014: 14–15) voices a similar concern. It envisions a future earth where all non-human life (both plants and animals) has been eliminated, people survive completely on synthetic nutrition, and the only remaining non-human life is maintained in geodesic domes in deep space on space ships for possible reintroduction to earth in some undetermined time in the future. All people in this imagined future do not miss having non-human life around (having never known any) because "there is hardly any more disease, there's no more poverty, and nobody's out of a job." The film's protagonist, Freeman Lowell, is the lone dissenter from glad acceptance of this state of affairs, and is the sole objector when the order comes to destroy the life-sustaining domes so that the ships can be returned to "commercial services" (Trumbull 1972: 13 min., 18 min.).

While the Book of Jeremiah and *Silent Running* may have articulated a concern for the fate of non-human life, such a concern is by no means universal. Representative of a widespread and contrary position is that expressed by plant biologist Erle Ellis who exhorts "nature is gone. . . . If this bothers you, get over it" (Ellis 2009: para. 2). Echoing Julian Simon's view "that human ingenuity . . . is limitlessly bountiful" (Simon 1981: 41), Ellis argues:

[T]here really is no such thing as a human carrying capacity ... We transform ecosystems to sustain ourselves. This is what we do and have always done. Our planet's human-carrying capacity emerges from the capabilities of our social systems and our technologies more than from any environmental limits.

(Ellis 2013: paras. 6, 9)

Notable in both of Ellis's statements is his indifference to what human expansion—in numbers, in affluence, in technology, and/or in resource extraction—has meant for humans and non-human life. He is thus a harbinger of an implicit (and sometimes explicit) religion of extreme anthropocentrism, the presence of which in the contemporary academy is explored and documented in this chapter.

The Western philosophical tradition is traditionally broken down into three inquiries: What is reality? (*metaphysics*); How do we know what we know about that reality? (*epistemology*); and, Given what we know, how should we behave? (What is good? What is bad? What is right? What is wrong?) (*ethics*) (Silverman 2008). Postmodern/poststructural thought as developed since the 1970s directs much of its energy at questioning epistemology, often questioning previous claims to knowledge developed in the course of the modernist/ Enlightenment era. But these theorists go even further. Challenging whether a reliable grasp of reality (metaphysics) is even possible, poststructuralism is described as "a theoretical approach to knowledge and society that embraces the ultimate undecidability of meaning" (Gibson-Graham 2000: 95). Within this poststructuralist regime, individual humans may have opinions about "what it all means," but there are no universally agreed-upon standards to adjudicate such "meaning" in any given situation. The third project of the Western philosophical tradition, ethics, is thus reduced to an enumeration and cataloguing of conflicting opinions incapable of adjudication.

Notwithstanding poststructuralism's asserted denial of "decidable meaning," human activities—including those within research projects across the academy—contain and reflect embedded ethical values. But what values, ethics, and/or morals are at play is often not expressly discussed. In the different sections of this chapter, I will do the following. I will briefly lay out the social psychological research explaining the theoretical foundation for evaluating the real-world effects of environmental values. I will describe the historical development of environmental sociology as a sub-discipline of sociology; and then the development of the interdisciplinary field of political ecology. I will consider the indications of where on the egoistic/humanistic/biospheric scale the two fields fall, and whether there are clear divides within the fields as to these environmental values. Finally, I will reflect on the ramifications, if any, of these value systems for both environmental sociology and political ecology.

The social psychology of environmental values

I use a broad definition of religion, the theoretical foundation for which I have laid out in detail elsewhere (Zaleha 2013). In short, relying on Max Weber and Clifford Geertz, anthropologist Carolyn Rouse argues that because "any strongly held belief and [cultural] orientation to the world" is religion, "atheism, secular humanism, Marxism, and of course Judaism, Christianity, and Islam" are all manifestations of religion and "all individuals are [therefore] religious" (Rouse 2004: 139). Supplemental to this, the social psychologists Batson, Schoenrade, and Ventis define religion as "whatever we as individuals do to come to grips personally" with the existential questions arising from our unavoidable mortality

(Batson *et al.* 1993: 8). In capsule form then, religion is *strong beliefs* (which need not include supernatural claims) *embraced to answer existential questions*. As such, it is not confined to religious institutions as conventionally understood.

Environmental sociology and political ecology, my focus here, are communities of academic practice made up of individual humans. These communities inevitably express, at least in part, the personal meaning systems (the religions) of these academic practitioners. And because each field involves the environment, the positions articulated by these practitioners are also an expression of their environmental values and ethics.

Dietz *et al.* (2005), reviewing the sociological and social psychological literature on environmental values, divide environmental values into three types: (1) self-interest (or ego-istic) values; (2) humanistic altruism; and (3) biospheric (sometimes labeled as ecocentric or biocentric) altruism. Egoistic environmental concern prioritizes one's own well-being and, usually, the well-being of family and friends. Humanistic altruism values the environment out of concern for humanity's well-being. Biospheric altruism extends the circle of moral concern beyond humanity to include other species and/or the state of ecosystems themselves. Humanity remains important, but the non-human world is brought within the circle of moral concern, cohering with Aldo Leopold's famed land ethic (Leopold 1949: 201). Biospheric altruism views non-human nature as intrinsically valuable, whereas self-interest and humanistic altruism do not (Dietz *et al.* 2005: 344).

Another useful model for assessing various advocates and theorists is Johnston's biocentrism/humanistic–anthropocentrism scale. Johnston (2013: 32) visualizes environmental constituencies as a series of "concentric circles, moving from a dark green center, to light green, to light brown, to dark brown on the outside." Dark green represents those who resonate with nature-as-sacred religion or otherwise accept nature as intrinsically valuable. Light green participants recognize "some correlation between social justice and ecological degradation," but do not necessarily accept that nature is intrinsically valuable or sacred, but are instead "weakly anthropocentric." Light brown sustainability advocates "frame their activism in purely human-centered terms" and reject "any human obligations to non-humans. Those with no environmental or sustainability concerns occupy the dark brown circle . . . [and] do not support the central aims of sustainability." People within the "light brown" and "dark brown" circles see biophysical reality only as a storehouse of resources for humanity with no intrinsic value itself, and see any suggestion to the contrary as mere romantic naïveté. The following sections will explore the explicit and implicit values within environmental sociology and political ecology, understanding that these values often amount to a form of implicit, though usually unstated, religion for these practitioners.

Environmental sociology

Environmental sociology arose out of the spike in public concern triggered by events in the United States such as an ignitable Cuyahoga River (1969) and the Santa Barbara oil spill of the same year, by the pesticide DDT and other pollution issues brought to light by the 1962 publication of *Silent Spring* (Carson 2002), by increasingly severe air and water pollution, and by the plight of certain high-profile endangered species such as the bald eagle in the late 1960s and 1970s. In light of these developments and the massive public event that became the first Earth Day in 1970, some sociologists began to research the connection between human culture and the natural environment. Investigating whether this upsurge in environ-mental concern represented a significant shift in worldview, public attitudes, and/or behavior became interesting to a small cadre of sociologists.

The late William Catton and Riley Dunlap were two sociologists who took an early interest in this new research direction. In 1978, they proposed a new, less anthropocentric, sociological frame of interpretation, which they labeled the "New Environmental Paradigm" or "NEP," and contrasted it with the then dominant "Human Exemptionalism Paradigm" or "HEP" within sociology (Catton and Dunlap 1978: 41–42). In embracing the NEP, "the study of the interaction between the environment and society" would become "the core of environmental sociology" (Catton and Dunlap 1978: 44).

In the *Annual Review of Sociology*, Dunlap and Catton (1979: 244) explained that by embracing the NEP, the sub-field of environmental sociology would stimulate a renewed recognition that "physical environments can influence (and in turn be influenced by) human societies and behavior," contrary to "the traditional sociological insistence that social facts can be explained only by other social facts." Sociology's tendency to disregard "the salience of physical environments" (1979: 245) led to its "Human Exemptionalism Paradigm" (1979: 250). Humans were deemed somehow exempt from ecological influences. By rejecting this, sociology would again investigate a "diverse range of societal-environmental interactions" (1979: 244).

Catton also articulated a theory of impending catastrophe. He argued that through the use of ever more sophisticated technologies and fossil fuels, *Homo sapiens* has become *Homo colossus*, and that humans were now destructive of their own future. Borrowing a term from population dynamics in wildlife biology, he also declared that humanity was already in a state of "overshoot," a condition where a given species has already overshot its ecological carrying capacity, but still continues to grow exponentially, leading eventually to rapid die-off (Catton 1980: 106, 173).

Catton and Dunlap also accepted the IPAT model developed by Holdren (who later served as President Obama's science advisor) and Ehrlich which posited that environmental impacts (I) resulted from the interplay of three variables: human population (P), the level of affluence of particular human sub-groups (A), and the varying types of technologies (T) utilized to attain varying types of affluence (Ehrlich and Holdren 1972).

What has come to be known as the environmental justice movement became a major concern beginning in the late 1980s, and continues as a substantial focus into the present (Taylor 2000). Eventually, both the social movements and the researchers delving into this subject matter shifted their focus from concerns about a given "contaminated community," particular landfills, or particular bad actors in the chemical industry, to a more systemic critique of "a whole system of technology and chemical production, driven by profit," which was not effectively regulated by a government that primarily "serves private wealth rather than [the] public interest" (Szasz 1994: 80–81). During the 1990s and 2000s, some environmental sociologists would join in the poststructuralist turn underway in political ecology. I will return to this development below, after discussing political ecology.

Political ecology

No annual review of political ecology has been done, but the book *Political Ecology: A Critical Introduction* by the influential political ecologist Paul Robbins (2012) serves as an effective summary of the field. Robbins (2012) dates the beginnings of political ecology to Blaikie and Brookfield's *Land Degradation and Society* (1987). According to Robbins (2012: 15), that work defined political ecology as combining "the concerns of ecology and a broadly defined political economy," which together encompass "the constantly shifting dialectic between society and land-based resources" occurring between competing "classes and groups."

Robbins sees contemporary political ecology as an interdisciplinary field joining a wide variety of academic disciplines such as anthropology, geography, environmental history, and sociology, and in "a series of 'disciplinary transgressions'" creating a "community of practice" that addresses the "condition and change of social/environmental systems, with explicit consideration of relations of power. This project assumes "that there are better, less coercive, less exploitive, and more sustainable ways of doing things" (Robbins 2012: 20). Thus, political ecology is activist in its orientation, not merely descriptive, and seeks to advocate for new, more progressive norms. While Marxian tradition has always theorized about "relations of power," Robbins explains that political ecology also relies on "poststructural" theories of "power/knowledge" developed by Michel Foucault, quoting his famous passage: "Each society has its regime of truth, its general politics of truth: that is, the types of discourse that it accepts and makes function as true." For Robbins, Foucault established "that truth is an effect of power, one that is formed through language and enforces social order by seeming intuitive or taken for granted." Foucault is supplemented by political ecologists with Derrida's techniques of "deconstruction" whereby "rigorous analysis of text and its interpretations" allows an "ongoing habit of aggressively evaluating taken-for-granted dominant stories" (Robbins 2012: 70). This aggressive deconstruction, according to Robbins (2012: 127–128), leads to a "radical constructivism" among some political ecologists where "science" is only one method of investigation that "cannot be used for adjudicating disputes between different claims about what is real." Instead, environmental conflicts are merely

> struggles over ideas about nature, in which one group will prevail not because they hold a better or more accurate account of a process—soil erosion, global warming, ozone depletion—but because they access and mobilize social power to create consensus on the truth.
>
> *(Robbins 2012: 128)*

In this approach, humanity's "symbolic systems" are "sovereign over all other reality . . . disabling empirical investigation" by natural science, and opening space to valorize "alternative constructions of the environment held by other social communities, like forest dwellers, nomadic herders, and religious philosophers." Robbins sees this radical constructivism as a minority position, and argues that most political ecologists accept that "the objective world is real and independent of our categorization," even if our understanding of the world is "filtered through subjective conceptual systems and scientific methods that are socially conditioned." This "soft constructivism" assumes that humanity's "concepts of reality" reflect "incomplete, incorrect, biased, and false understandings of an empirical reality" (Robbins 2012: 127–128). An example of this softer constructivism is Escobar's statement that "nature is always constructed by our meaning-giving and discursive processes," even as he acknowledges "biophysical reality" (Escobar 1999: 1–2). Thus, even in its softer form, epistemology and metaphysics are held in a state of radical doubt.

"Marginalized" and "disenfranchised" human communities are identified as political ecology's "explicit concern" (Robbins 2012: 28), and finding the "causes" that lead to "general and pernicious" exploitation "for limited gain at collective cost" is one of its goals (Robbins 2012: 20). Whether it is "peasants," "nomadic herders," "slash-and-burn agriculturalists" in former colonial countries, or "disempowered communities" of color subjected to disproportionately large toxic exposures in developed nations, underdog human communities are the primary targets of political ecology's moral concern (Robbins 2012: 63, 74, 117).

Robbins hints at the outset of his book that "non-humans" might "perhaps" also have "interests" of their own (Robbins 2012: 4), and further declares that political ecology is not in "opposition to the defense of ambient ecological systems, biodiversity, non-human flora and fauna, or areas of relatively low human impact" (his trope for "wilderness") (Robbins 2012: 181). Robbins suggests that political ecology, therefore, is not *per se* opposed to wildlife and wildlands preservation, and notes (2012: 88) that "injustice can be extended to the environment itself, insofar as ecosystems or species may lose or suffer for the benefit of" human elites. Political ecology, he asserts, provides better analysis than "straightforward animal and environmental rights accounts," because political ecology seeks to reveal "the deep structural economic drivers of unjust outcomes" inflicted on the non-human while attending "to the simultaneous marginalization of disempowered people" inflicted by "the same systems and processes." Political ecology also views resource use by marginal human communities as "relatively benign," "environmentally innocuous" (Robbins 2012: 21–22), or positively beneficial. He attacks the "wilderness" that capitalist elites from Europe and the United States seek to preserve because it has been "created" by human presence, and a land without people has "actually *never existed before*" (Robbins 2012: 177–178; Robbins' emphasis). Robbins thus denies the archeological record that humans are relative newcomers to the Americas, arriving no earlier than about 25,000 years ago (Gugliotta 2013).

Robbins notes the strong influence on political ecology of William Cronon's still influential and still controversial essay of 1995, "The trouble with wilderness; or, getting back to the wrong nature" (Robbins 2012: 130). Sackman (2006) notes that Cronon's essay utilized Judith Butler's (1999 [1990]) analysis "that there is nothing natural about sex, about 'men' or 'women' as such," (2006: 210) and used Butler's method to show "how wilderness discourse created the object it claimed to simply represent" (2006: 210). In his first paragraph, Cronon (1995: 70) declares that "wilderness is not quite what it seems. Far from being the one place on earth that stands apart from humanity, it is quite profoundly a human creation" and "is not a pristine sanctuary where the last remnant of an untouched, endangered, but still transcendent nature" exists; instead, it is a mere "product of that civilization, and could hardly be contaminated by the very stuff of which it is made." Wilderness, in this view, is just "the reflection of our own unexamined longings and desires." In his next paragraph, Cronon tried to walk some of this back, saying, "let me hasten to add that the nonhuman world we encounter in wilderness is far from being merely our own invention. I celebrate with others who love wilderness the beauty and power of the things it contains" (Cronon 1995: 70). It was too late. The preceding paragraph stands as the main "take away" for the essay.

In the ensuing controversy (see Soulé and Lease 1995; Worster 1997; Brower 2014), Cronon declared that "the religion I was critiquing is my own," that he too was among "those who worship at the altar of wilderness," even if he was also attempting to demonstrate to his co-religionists that "their God (like all deities) has a complicated and problematic past" (Cronon 1996: 54). His efforts to qualify or limit his initial "jeremiad" (Cronon 1996: 55), however, have been mostly ignored or missed altogether. Cronon now gets cited for the proposition that wilderness has "never existed" (Robbins 2012: 177–178) or is a merely "elite concern" (Rudy and Konefal 2007: 496). And environmental historian Anya Zilberstein (in-person conversation, 12 August 2012) argues that Cronon's essay demonstrates why national parks and designated wilderness areas were a policy mistake and should now be dismantled and de-established. While Cronon says he "would feel deep regret" if his words were "used toward such an end" (Cronon 1996: 47), Zilberstein's comments show that his creation is now beyond his control. Calls to "roll back" the protection of natural areas are coming not just from the quarters of neoliberal capitalism sponsored by fossil fuel and mining interests, but from the academic left, including his fellow environmental historians, and from political ecologists such as the anthropologist Robert Fletcher (2010), who has reinvigorated the "trouble with wilderness" thesis, but without any of Cronon's limiting caveats. Fletcher instead argues that the "concept of wild" is simply one of the "lies" humans "tell about ourselves," and that so long as humans think they "need wilderness," humanity "will never be free." Once the romantic attachment to both the idea of "the wild" and "wilderness" is abandoned, a move to "a 'post-conservation' perspective more concerned with social and environmental justice than biodiversity preservation" can be accomplished (Fletcher 2010: 177–178).

Unlike Robbins, Fletcher's political ecology expressly rejects the idea that non-human reality can make any moral claims upon humanity. The historian Clarence Glacken noted that from Genesis 1 to Psalms 8 and 115, the theme that humans, "sinful" though they are, occupy "a position on earth comparable to that of God in the universe . . . has been one of the key ideas in the religious and philosophical thought of Western civilization regarding [humanity's] place in nature" (Glacken 1967: 155). Fletcher, as an exemplar of a particular strand of political ecological thought, supports Robert H. Nelson's argument that new "secular religions" which "den[y] any connection with Christianity" nevertheless retain "an essentially Christian worldview." Contrary to theorists of secularism who see Christianity's influence in Europe and North America to be waning, Nelson argues that "Christian ideas" have "a greater influence and more powerful impact" because they have camouflaged themselves and become invisible by moving "outside" their traditional Christian institutional setting and shedding their express Christian terminology (Nelson 2010: 347). Fletcher shows that the radical anthropocentrism and extreme humanism that Lynn White (1967) associated with Christianity lives on in secular garb.

Some strands of contemporary environmental sociology have aligned and included themselves with the above-described political ecology. Rudy and Konefal, for example, see "early environmental sociology . . . as a mix of progressive conservationism and neo-Malthusian apocalypticism" that continued the historical "elite concerns with wildlife and wilderness conservation" and eventually extended to "middle-class concerns about (sub)urban aesthetics, personal public health, and outdoor activities and athleticism." Rudy and Konefal pejoratively describe environmental sociology as furthering the interests of "patrician hunters of charismatic megafauna, suburban mothers pursuing clean air and water, neo-Malthusian ecologists focused on overpopulation, technophilic recycling engineers or innovators in appropriate technology" through "top-down, scientific, and technological policy determination and implementation" (Rudy and Konefal 2007: 496, 500). For them, all this retrograde thinking is solved by aligning environmental sociology with political ecology.

In summary, the defining traits of political ecology (and its sympathetic partners in environmental sociology) are the following:

1   Marxian or neo-Marxist anti-capitalism;
2   concern for marginalized communities, whether in the developed or developing world;
3   an anarchistic skepticism of government actors; and
4   a prevailing anti-wilderness and anti-biodiversity preservation ideology.

As to the last item, political ecology sees "those dearly held wildernesses that sell so many Sierra Club calendars" (Robbins 2012: 4) as a fetish for developed-nation elites that obstructs progress on behalf of political ecology's intended communities of concern. Many, probably most, political ecologists would join in with post-colonial theorist Edward Said's 1994 dismissal of wilderness advocacy as "the indulgence of spoiled tree huggers who lack a proper cause" (cited by Nixon 2011: 332). This anti-wilderness ideology among political ecologists is seldom explicitly stated but is frequently implied. Some, like Zilberstein and Fletcher, state their anti-nature agenda outright.

Environmental values in environmental sociology and political ecology

Biospheric value/deep ecological precursors in Marx

In analyzing the environmental values in environmental sociology and political ecology, I assess to what extent they are humanistic or biospheric within Dietz *et al.*'s (2005) framework. What I have laid out in the foregoing demonstrates that neither discourse forms around egoistic or individualistic value orientations, something that would be expected from what I term *neoliberal ecology* (which sees the generation of capitalist monetary wealth as the ultimate value, and sees most people and all of non-human nature as merely instrumental to this goal). So the focus of my primary exploration is the extent to which the value orientations of environmental sociology and political ecology are primarily humanistic or biospheric. In recognizing the intrinsic value of non-human reality, the biospheric value orientations are very similar to or identical with the environmental philosophy first articulated in 1972 by Arne Naess and known as deep ecology, though it has much deeper roots before the coining of this particular label (Zaleha 2010).

While deep ecology is most often associated with various movements of radical environ-mentalism (Taylor 2010: 71–102), critical geographer David Harvey (1996: 157) noted that Marx himself came "very close to endorsing the view that money has destroyed earlier and perhaps recoverable intrinsic natural values," citing Marx's famed (at least among eco-Marxists) and most biospherecentric passage:

> Money is the jealous God . . . beside which no other god may exist. Money abases all the gods of [humanity] and changes them into commodities. Money is the universal and self-sufficient value of all things. It has, therefore, deprived the whole world, both the human world and nature, of their own proper value . . . he worships it [as Money . . .] become[s] the god of this world . . . The mode of perceiving nature, under the rule of private property and of money, is a real contempt for, and a practical degradation of, nature . . . It is . . . intolerable "that every creature should be transformed into property—the fishes in the water, the birds of the air, the plants of the earth: the creature too should become free" [citing Protestant theologian Thomas Münzer]. Christianity . . . alienat[es] . . . man from himself, and from Nature . . . turn[ing] alienated man and alienated Nature into alienable, saleable objects . . . and attributing to them the significance of an alien entity, namely money.
>
> *(Marx 1978 [1843]: 50–52)*

Harvey noted that Marx had prefigured Leopold's famed land ethic of a century later (Harvey [1996: 157], quoting Leopold [1949: 223–225]).

The overall tenor of much of Harvey's work is to put distance between the progressive socialist project and the deep ecological thought systems that see intrinsic value in the non-human world. Harvey acknowledges here, however, the attraction of such an approach by

295

citing Aldo Leopold, the figure that many commentators and environmental historians regard as giving rise to the field of environmental ethics and philosophy (Callicott 2005: 1166), and notes the affinity to Leopold's land ethic that is shown in Marx's thought. While Leopold may be little known among most environmental sociologists or political ecologists, both Marx and Harvey are major influences, hinting that the gap between political and deep ecology may not be unbridgeable.

Environmental values in environmental sociology

Applying Dietz *et al.*'s (2005) model to environmental sociology, it is apparent that both biospheric and humanistic value systems are present. Early environmental sociology and those practitioners who carry its concerns into the contemporary era have not embraced the postmodern concerns embodied in most political ecology. While most, if not all, environmental sociologists would acknowledge the role of capitalism in environmental degradation, many nevertheless leave space for market-sympathetic scholars who might seek to reform rather than replace capitalism. In like manner, environmental sociology has included theorists who value the non-human biophysical world as having more than merely instrumental value to humans. Catton was probably a deep ecologist and he is highly regarded among the radical environmentalist community (Devall and Sessions 1985: 46). In like manner, the late Humboldt State University sociologist Bill Devall provides another example of a biospheric/deep ecological environmental sociologist who was also active in the radical environmental movement, and indeed was one of its primary academics in the United States (Devall and Sessions 1985; Taylor 2010: 113). However, there is little to indicate that a biospheric orientation is anything more than a small current in an otherwise predominantly humanistic orientation within contemporary environmental sociology. This is especially the case for the more postmodern/poststructural forms of environmental sociology exemplified by Rudy and Konefal.

Environmental values in political ecology

One way that political ecology is different from some parts of environmental sociology is that its practitioners seem to be exclusively humanistic, even radically anthropocentric, in their value orientations, seeing the non-human biophysical world as important primarily, or only, for human use. Robbins admits that the "non-human elements of conservation ecology are sometimes lost" because "political ecology . . . proceeds from an anthropocentric perspective, which . . . underplays the role of animals, plants, and soil in delimiting and directing conservation histories" (Robbins 2012: 192). Robbins himself, however, told me that environmental theorists "need to let go of Leopold" and his land ethic (in-person conversation, 4 November 2013). He is squarely on record with a thoroughgoing anthropocentrism, even if he occasionally leaves a small space for biospheric values.

As David Harvey notes, "Marxism has shared with much of bourgeois social science a general abhorrence of the idea that 'nature' can control, determine, or even limit any kind of human endeavor" (1996: 193), and both "liberal and Marxian theory" appear to have "at least this [in] common," namely, they accept human "domination of nature . . . as fundamental to their emancipatory projects" (Harvey 1996: 127). Notwithstanding Marx's possible intrinsic valuation of non-human nature, in the Marxist tradition as it evolved post-Marx, moral consideration for nature has generally been ruled out of bounds from the start. It was this very tendency that led Russell Means, one of the co-founders of the American

Indian Movement, to reject the idea that AIM or indigenous peoples anywhere should ally themselves with Marxist movements (Means 1980).

Conclusion

Criticizing and questioning the illegitimate over-optimism of modernism's grand utopian project and casting light on oppressive imperialistic abuses has been a valuable contribution of some of the academic discourses that travel under the postmodernist/poststructuralist banner. These critiques, however, are ultimately applying Enlightenment rationality in an effort, to some extent successful, to correct misguided and/or unfounded claims, and are primarily making positivist arguments that earlier modernist assertions simply lacked an actual evidentiary foundation. To this extent, then, in David Harvey's words, postmodernism/poststructuralism is merely a "revolt within modernism" (Harvey 1990: 42) that ultimately carries the modernist project forward.

At its relativistic worst, the postmodern turn does indeed seem to be something new. It is not really that "nothing" can be said to be "true." The idea is, instead, that only human thought is true and worthwhile. Charlene Spretnak argues that when

> deconstructive postmodernists conclude that there is nothing to life but arbitrary social construction and utter groundlessness, they continue and intensify the diminished conceptualization of the human that was begun by Renaissance humanism, the scientific revolution, and the Enlightenment. These foundational movements of modernity cumulatively framed the human story apart from the larger unfolding story of the earth community. Deconstructive postmodernists shrink the human story even further, insisting that it is entirely a matter of power plays and language games.
>
> *(Spretnak 1997: 433)*

Deconstructive postmodernism, ironically, with its focus on linguistic creation, can be understood as a Judeo-Christian heresy.

> The vision of a human subject constituting itself through language . . . recalls biblical understandings of human special creation. For poststructuralists, as in the Genesis creation account and Saint John's vision of cosmic beginnings (when "The word was with God, and the Word was God" [John 1: 1]), naming wields constitutive power. While the mechanism differs—divine fiat versus the play of signifiers—the conclusion is strikingly similar: humans are alone among animals insofar as the clue to their origins lies not in the physical world and the body but in the realm of ideas or spirits.
>
> *(Peterson 2001: 60–61)*

Humans are "still the only animal[s] that really matter" (Peterson 2001: 61). In its above-described manifestations, poststructuralist/postmodernist thought is just the latest, and an especially strident, assertion of the "human exemptionalism" first noted by Dunlap and Catton during the period of early environmental sociology. In this model, humanity is the ultimate creator, now unconstrained by any external limits imposed by an external transcendent supernatural being or beings or even by the biophysical cosmos itself, à la Julian Simon or Erle Ellis.

This approach undergirds the way Cronon's 1995 essay has been taken up and is being carried forward, notwithstanding Cronon's own contrary desires. Another famed environmental historian, equal in stature to Cronon and one of environmental history's founders, is Donald Worster. In 1997, Worster gave a short, blunt, even blistering, assessment of both Cronon's original piece and the lines of argument that his fellow environmental historians were making in reliance upon it. He laid out three errors: "Error #1— North America (we are told) was never a 'wilderness'—not any part of it"; "Error #2— The wilderness is nothing real but is only a cultural construct dreamed up by rich white romantics"; and "Error #3: The preservation of wilderness has been a distraction from addressing other, more important environmental problems" (Worster 1997: 10–12). He elaborated that if

> you assume that standard account [that] . . . the love of wilderness was . . . simply the "discovery" or "invention" of a few rich men with Harvard or Yale degrees . . . then it becomes very easy to turn the entire story into a polemic against elitist snobs who seek the sanctuary of wilderness at the expense of peasants, workers, Indians, or the poor of the world. Of course there were and are people like that. If the story didn't have a kernel of truth in it, the revisionists would not get any kind of hearing at all. But it is a small kernel, not the whole complicated truth of what wilderness has meant to people through the ages or what draws them to protect wilderness today. Contrary to the established story, the love of Nature (i.e., wilderness) was not merely a "cultural construct" of the Romantic period in Europe. It has much older cultural roots, and it may even have roots in the very structure of human feelings and consciousness going far back into the evolutionary past, transcending any cultural patterns. Historians of late have been far too quick to dismiss as "essentialist" any deep residuum of humanity and to reduce all thought and feeling to shifting tides of "culture." Nineteenth-century Romanticism, with its glorification of the sublime, was indeed a cultural expression, but it also may be understood as an effort to recover and express those deeper feelings which in all sorts of cultures have linked the beauty of the natural world to a sense of wholeness and spirituality. The enthusiasm for wilderness in America was undeniably a cultural fashion, but it also drew on that other-than-cultural hunger for the natural world that persists across time and space [and] was felt by poor folks as well as rich.
>
> *(Worster 1997: 11)*

That last sentence is particularly instructive. As an activist for both social justice and wildlands preservation for over three decades, I know it to be true. Love of wilderness is not the sole or even primary province of wealthy white Americans or Europeans, contrary to assertions of it being only an "elitist" concern. Some radical environmentalists of my acquaintance live in a state of homelessness and dumpster dive for food in order to pursue and engage in activities to defend the wilderness and biodiversity.

Along with Worster, sociologist and science and technology theorist Eileen Crist (2004: 8) suggests that one way to rebut Cronon's trouble-with-wilderness and other social constructivist models is, instead of inquiring "how people assign meaning to the world," ask instead "how people receive meaning from the world." People,

> as well as other animals, are able to tune into, tap, decipher, or directly receive those meanings. Wilderness advocates, deep ecologists, naturalists, poets, farmers who live with the land, scientists, and phenomenologists, in differing ways, have expressed opposition to the world view of a passive natural world.
>
> *(Crist 2004: 9)*

Put another way, meaning "*derived from* the world within which the human species evolved," is not "rendered meaningful by the human *cogito*" (Crist 2004: 8–9; emphasis in original). In seeking to de-legitimize the affective bond that non-elites feel for wild spaces, these postmodern theorists of the academic left become the parties guilty of an imperialist imposition of their elitist value norms stemming from their own extreme humanism. Worster, Crist, and others set forth strong aguments why this imposition should be rejected.

I will assume the goodwill of these postmodern theorists. The fact that they are attempting such an imposition is strong evidence that they themselves have a humanistic environmental orientation, and genuinely lack the affective biophilia posited by Wilson, Kellert, and others (Kellert and Wilson 1993) that manifests itself in biospheric value orientations. If that is their affective orientation, Fletcher, Konefal, Robbins, Rudy, and their like-minded colleagues can indeed imagine they are maintaining a challenge against elites and in favor of marginal human communities. Undoubtedly, there are instances where they are doing exactly that. But love of the non-human biophysical world is not the exclusive domain of neoliberal elites who are the traditional target of postmodernist critique.

From whence comes a biospheric value orientation? Some research has shown that early positive childhood experiences in natural environments are important (Chawla 1998). Earth First! co-founder Dave Foreman posits the existence of a "wilderness gene" (Foreman 1991: 55–58), an idea elaborated by Kellert and Wilson (Wilson 1984; Kellert and Wilson 1993). Wherever it comes from, what Dietz *et al.*'s research (2005) shows is that people who have the orientation are more likely than those who exhibit only humanistic value orientations to undertake pro-environmental behavior. If one takes the present alarming environmental projections seriously, the presence within humanity of people possessing biospheric value orientations should be welcome, even if one possesses only instrumentalist, humanistic attitudes toward the non-human. In the final analysis, the postmodernists and extreme humanists are working against their own asserted interests.

References

Batson, C D, Schoenrade, P and Ventis, W L (1993). *Religion and the individual: A social-psychological perspective*. New York: Oxford University Press.

Blaikie, P M and Brookfield, H C (1987). *Land degradation and society*. London: Methuen.

Brower, K (2014). Leave wilderness alone. *Outside* [online], 13 October 2014.www.outsideonline.com/1926421/leave-wilderness-alone (accessed 5 March 2016).

Butler, J (1999 [1990]) *Gender trouble: Feminism and the subversion of identity*. New York: Routledge.

Callicott, J B (2005). Natural history as natural religion. In B Taylor (ed.) *Encyclopedia of religion and nature*. London and New York: Continuum International.

Carson, R (2002). *Silent spring*. Boston, MA: Houghton Mifflin.

Catton, Jr, W R (1980). *Overshoot, the ecological basis of revolutionary change*. Urbana: University of Illinois Press.

Catton, Jr, W R and Dunlap, R E (1978). Environmental sociology: A new paradigm. *American Sociologist* 13: 41–49.

Chawla, L (1998). Significant life experiences revisited: A review of research on sources of environmental sensitivity. *Environmental Education Research* 4(4): 369–382.

Coogan, M D (2006). *The Old Testament: A historical and literary introduction to the Hebrew scriptures*. New York: Oxford University Press.

Crist, E (2004). Against the social construction of nature and wilderness. *Environmental Ethics* 26(1): 5–24.

Cronon, W (1995). The trouble with wilderness; or, getting back to the wrong nature. In W Cronon (ed.) *Uncommon ground: Toward reinventing nature*. 1st edn. New York: W. W. Norton & Company, pp. 69–90.

Cronon, W (1996). The trouble with wilderness: A response. *Environmental History* 1(1): 47–55.

Devall, B and Sessions, G (1985). *Deep ecology*. Salt Lake City, UT: G. M. Smith.

Dietz, T, Fitzgerald, A and Shwom, R (2005). Environmental values. *Annual Review of Environment and Resources* 30(1): 335–372.

Dunlap, R E and Catton, Jr, W R (1979). Environmental sociology. *Annual Review of Sociology* 5: 243–273.

Ehrlich, P R and Holdren, J (1972). A bulletin dialogue on the "Closing Circle": Critique: One dimensional ecology. *Bulletin of the Atomic Scientists* 28(5): 16–27.

Ellis, E C (2009). Op-ed: Stop trying to save the planet. *Wired* [online]. Available: www.wired.com/wiredscience/2009/05/ftf-ellis-1/ (accessed 5 March 2016).

Ellis, E C (2013). Overpopulation is not the problem. *The New York Times* [online], 13 September 2013. Available: www.nytimes.com/2013/09/14/opinion/overpopulation-is-not-the-problem.html (accessed 5 March 2016).

Escobar, A (1999). After nature: Steps to an antiessentialist political ecology. *Current Anthropology* 40(1): 1–30.

Fletcher, R (2010). Neoliberal environmentality: Towards a poststructuralist political ecology of the conservation debate. *Conservation and Society* 8(3): 171–181.

Foreman, D (1991). *Confessions of an eco-warrior*. New York: Harmony Books.

Gibson-Graham, J K (2000). Poststructural interventions. In E S Sheppard and T J Barnes (eds) *A companion to economic geography*. Oxford: Blackwell.

Glacken, C J (1967). *Traces on the Rhodian shore: Nature and culture in Western thought from ancient times to the end of the eighteenth century*. Berkeley: University of California Press.

Gugliotta, G (2013). When did humans come to the Americas? *Smithsonian Magazine* [online]. Available: www.smithsonianmag.com/science-nature/when-did-humans-come-to-the-americas-4209273 (accessed 5 March 2016).

Harvey, D (1990). *The condition of postmodernity: An enquiry into the origins of cultural change*. Oxford, UK and Cambridge, MA: Blackwell.

Harvey, D (1996). *Justice, nature, and the geography of difference*. Cambridge, MA: Blackwell.

Johnston, L F (2013). *Religion and sustainability: Social movements and the politics of the environment*. Sheffield, UK and Bristol, CT: Equinox.

Kellert, S R and Wilson, E O (1993). *The biophilia hypothesis*. Washington, DC: Island Press.

Kermode, M (2014). *Silent running*. London: Palgrave Macmillan.

Leopold, A (1949). *A Sand County almanac, and sketches here and there*. New York: Oxford University Press.

Marx, K (1978 [1843]). On the Jewish question. In R C Tucker (ed.) *The Marx-Engels reader*. New York: W. W. Norton & Company.

Means, R (1980). Fighting words on the future of the earth. *Mother Jones*, December, pp. 22–38.

Nelson, R H (2010). *The new holy wars: Economic religion vs. environmental religion in contemporary America*. University Park, PA/Oakland, CA: Pennsylvania State University Press/Independent Institute.

Nixon, R (2011). *Slow violence and the environmentalism of the poor*. Cambridge, MA: Harvard University Press.

Peterson, A L (2001). *Being human: Ethics, environment, and our place in the world*. Berkeley: University of California Press.

Robbins, P (2012). *Political ecology: A critical introduction*. Malden, MA: John Wiley & Sons Inc.

Rouse, C M (2004). *Engaged surrender: African American women and Islam*. Berkeley: University of California Press.

Rudy, A P and Konefal, J (2007). Nature, sociology, and social justice: Environmental sociology, pedagogy, and the curriculum. *American Behavioral Scientist* 51(4): 495–515.

Sackman, D C (2006). The gender trouble with wilderness. *Reviews in American History* 34(2): 208–213.

Silverman, A (2008). Plato's middle period metaphysics and epistemology. *Stanford Encyclopedia of Philosophy* [online]. Available: http://plato.stanford.edu/archives/win2008/entries/plato-metaphysics/ (accessed 5 March 2016).

Simon, J L (1981). The scarcity of raw materials. *The Atlantic Monthly* 247(6): 33–41.

Soulé, M E and Lease, G (1995). *Reinventing nature? Responses to postmodern deconstruction*. Washington, DC: Island Press.

Spretnak, C (1997). Radical nonduality in ecofeminist philosophy. In K Warren and N Erkal (eds) *Ecofeminism: Women, culture, nature*. Bloomington: Indiana University Press, pp. 425–435.

Szasz, A (1994). *Ecopopulism: Toxic waste and the movement for environmental justice*. Minneapolis: University of Minnesota Press.

Taylor, B (2010). *Dark green religion: Nature spirituality and the planetary future.* Berkeley: University of California Press.

Taylor, D (2000). Rise of the environmental justice paradigm: Injustice framing and the social construction of environmental discourses. *American Behavioral Scientist* 43(4): 508–580.

Trumbull, D (dir.) (1972). *Silent running.* Universal City, CA: Universal Studios.

White, L (1967). The historical roots of our ecologic crisis. *Science* 155(3767): 1203–1207.

Wilson, E O (1984). *Biophilia.* Cambridge, MA: Harvard University Press.

Worster, D (1997). The wilderness of history. *Wild Earth* Fall: 9–13.

Zaleha, B D (2010). Nature and nature religions. In P W Williams (ed.) *Encyclopedia of religion in America.* Newbury Park, CA: Sage Publications.

Zaleha, B D (2013). "Our only heaven": Nature veneration, quest religion, and pro-environment behavior. *Journal for the Study of Religion, Nature and Culture* 7(2): 131–153.

24

GOOD GOVERNANCE, CORRUPTION, AND FOREST PROTECTION

Critical insights from environmental anthropology

Pauline von Hellermann

Introduction

Since the 1990s, the idea of 'good governance' has become one of the leading paradigms in tropical forest conservation, as in international development as a whole. 'Bad' governance – weak institutions, inefficiency, corruption, and illegal activities – is now widely regarded as a major cause of deforestation; 'good' governance – institutional reform, the combat of corruption and crime and the promotion of efficiency, rule of law, transparency, accountability, and participation – as the route towards forest protection. These principles have informed recent policy initiatives in tropical forest conservation in various ways. Advocated and supported by the World Bank, the United Nations (UN), and other donors, there has been a widespread shift towards decentralised and participatory forms of forest management, as greater participation is believed to reduce opportunities for mismanagement and corruption. In addition, a series of Forest Law Enforcement and Governance (FLEG) initiatives, including the European Commission's Action Plan on Forest Law Enforcement, Governance and Trade (FLEGT) have been established since 2001, with the aim to combat illegal logging and corruption in the forest sector through various measures, including licensing schemes (Brown *et al.* 2008). Greenpeace, too, responsible for one of the first investigations into illegal logging in the 1990s, campaigns for the setting up and improvement of verification schemes. The promotion of good governance is also a core component of the United Nations Collaborative Programme on Reducing Emissions from Deforestation and Forest Degradation (UN-REDD and REDD+), which aims to prevent deforestation by creating a financial value for the carbon stored in old-growth high forest. The activities and funding of REDD+, as well as those of the related Forest Carbon Partnership Facility, have so far focused on helping producer governments to demonstrate their 'readiness' to participate, through democratic governance, anti-corruption initiatives, and improving transparency.

However, despite its popularity and ubiquity, the good governance agenda has only partially, if at all, achieved its goals. Numerous studies have shown that community forest projects can be marred as much by elite capture, corruption, and mismanagement as can centralised forms of forest management, and do not necessarily improve forest protection (Charnley and Poe 2007; German *et al.* 2010). Timber verification schemes, too, are difficult to implement and have only had limited success so far (Brown *et al.* 2008). In international development in general, anti-corruption measures and governance restructuring undertaken under the banner of good governance have, at best, had mixed results; in several African countries, corruption has been on the increase since good governance reforms were introduced (Szeftel 1998; Blundo and Olivier de Sardan 2006; Anders 2010), and there is little evidence so far that good governance actually fosters economic development (see Gray and Khan 2010; Grindle 2010).

In conjunction with empirical observations of its shortcomings, a number of powerful critiques of the good governance agenda in international development have emerged. Drawing on this larger critical literature, this chapter provides an overview of the ways in which environmental anthropology and related fields offer critical perspectives on good governance initiatives in forest conservation. Three main approaches, overlapping yet distinct, can be identified here. The first focuses on decentralised and participatory resource management projects and on their theoretical underpinnings, namely common–pool resources (CPR) theory. A second line of critique focuses more specifically on corruption and the way its role in deforestation is conceptualised. The third is provided by recent insights in ecology and historical ecology, which problematise key ecological assumptions informing the good governance agenda in forestry. Before discussing each of these three approaches in detail, however, I begin with a brief account of the rise of the good governance agenda in international development generally and forest conservation specifically.

The emergence of the good governance agenda

Several factors combined in bringing about the focus on governance in forest con-servation. The overall interest in governance in recent decades is linked to the emergence of neoliberalism and its advocacy of privatisation, deregulation, and scaling down of state government. In fact, while the term governance can be used quite broadly to describe 'a method of government or regulation' irrespective of historical context, as the *New Webster's International Dictionary*, for example, does (Weiss 2000: 795), it is also used specifically to describe only recent, neoliberal forms of governance that rely on a combination of public and private actors (Pierre and Peters 2000). The *good* governance agenda is rooted in this neoliberal understanding of governance, promoting as it does participation of civil society and the private sector in government. But it also presents a renewed recognition of the importance of institutions, emerging in response to the widespread failure of neoliberal structural adjustment programmes in the Global South as well as the havoc caused by the unchecked eruption of capitalist market forces in the former Soviet bloc. 'Bringing the state back in', the good governance agenda is strongly informed by new institutional economics (Gray and Khan 2010; Grindle 2010).

In the promotion of good governance, the fight against corruption soon took centre stage. This was epitomised by then World Bank President James Wolfensohn's famous 'Cancer of Corruption' speech at the World Bank's Annual Meeting in 1996, during which he identified corruption as a major hindrance to economic development. The 1990s also saw the establishment of the NGO Transparency International by Graf Lambsdorff (a former World Bank employee), which publishes the influential annual Corruption Perceptions Index. Initiatives such as these have helped to expose and draw attention to corruption to an unprecedented degree: anti–corruption initiatives are now not only a prerequisite for the receipt of development aid and loans; they have also in many countries become an integral part of domestic politics (Werbner *et al.* 2014).

These trends have coincided with a shift in the understanding of the causes of deforestation. Traditionally more focused on the destruction caused by small-scale farmers, the deforestation literature has begun to highlight the 'underlying' causes of deforestation (Contreras-Hermosila 2000; Geist and Lambin 2002), and to draw attention to deforestation caused by larger-scale agricultural projects and industrial logging and the political processes behind these (Hecht and Cockburn 1990; Dauvergne 1993; Dove 1993; Rudel 2007). Much of this work is rooted in political ecology, the inter-disciplinary field concerned with the interaction between political economy and the environment (Peet and Watts 2004). Meanwhile environmental anthropologists have also long challenged the orthodoxy that small-scale farmers are the main agents of deforestation, by showing that many indigenous populations have sophisticated environmental knowledge and often manage their environments well, at times even contributing to forest increase and biodiversity (e.g. Conklin 1957; Fairhead and Leach 1996; Guyer and Richards 1996).

There is thus a powerful (and remarkable) convergence between a diverse range of actors and voices supporting the principles of good governance in conservation: World Bank economists, anthropologists, environmental and human rights activists all largely agree that it is the underlying causes of deforestation that need to be tackled and that local people should have more control over their own resources. However, this new-found common language of participation, accountability, transparency, and sustainability has not translated into unmitigated success for forest conservation initiatives inspired by good governance, and by now an important critical scholarship on the good governance agenda as a whole and its specific manifestations in forest conservation has emerged. The rest of this chapter examines in detail three key critiques, deriving both from the broader literature on the good governance agenda and corruption, and from the concerns and insights of environmental anthropology.

Environmental governance beyond common-pool resources theory

The first line of critique focuses on the theoretical underpinnings of the recent drive for decentralisation and participation in natural resource management, namely common-pool resources (CPR) theory. Rooted in new institutional economics, CPR theory is most associated with the work of Elinor Ostrom (1990), who showed that common-pool resources could be successfully managed by locally developed common property regimes. Ostrom acknowledged that variability in human–ecosystem interaction meant there was no single institutional 'panacea', but identified eight 'design principles' that would ensure stable local common-pool resource management. These principles include clearly defined boundaries, locally adapted rules, and the recognition of the community by higher-level authorities (Ostrom 1990).

Common-pool resources theory has played a crucial role in challenging the 'tragedy of the commons' hypothesis (Hardin 1968) and its policy implications – namely, that common-pool resources require either state or private property regimes – and has given much impetus to the global drive towards decentralisation and participation in natural resource management, including tropical forest conservation. In Latin America and India, community forestry had already emerged in the 1970s and 1980s, linked to indigenous rights and environmental movements as well as frustration with the shortcomings of centralised forest administration (Rival 2003; Charnley and Poe 2007). But World Bank and other donor support for such programmes under the banner of good governance, informed by CPR theory, has taken decentralisation much further in recent decades. In many parts of Africa, for example, forest decentralisation and the promotion of community participation are directly linked to donor conditionalities (Charnley and Poe 2007; German *et al.* 2010).

However, in view of the limited tangible success of many recent participatory initiatives, a growing body of work has begun in turn to critique the simplistic application of CPR theory, focusing in particular on the rigidity with which it distinguishes between formal and informal institutions, its ahistorical, apolitical, and decontextualised understanding of institutions, and its valorisation of 'the community' (Mehta *et al.* 2001; Arts and Visseren-Hamakers 2012).

Informed by historical, sociological, anthropological, and political ecology approaches, a number of authors have put forward alternative, more nuanced understandings of how environmental governance actually works in practice, focusing on the 'messy middle' (Mehta *et al.* 2001) between formal and informal arrangements. Thus, Cleaver suggests that 'real governance' (Cleaver *et al.* 2013) is best understood as 'institutional bricolage', the uneven patching together of old practices and accepted norms with new arrangements (Cleaver 2001). Steins (2001) draws on Actor–Network Theory (ANT) to explore how individuals interact with human and non-human 'actors' in natural resource management, while Li (2007) uses the analytic of 'assemblages' (Deleuze and Guattari 1987) to capture the complex dynamics of practices involved in community forestry. Others employ Bourdieu (1990) to analyse contemporary practices in natural resource management (e.g. Zimmer and Sakdapolrak 2012; Caine 2013).

As well as conceptualising environmental governance in processual, practice-based terms, such critical works also draw attention to power relations. Power is often remarkably absent in official good governance programmes and policy statements, including forest-related ones; in fact, Li (2007) identifies 'anti-politics' (Ferguson 1990) as a key practice in contemporary community forestry. In general, interventions under the banner of good governance are presented as technical, bureaucratic measures, thereby providing something of a 'figleaf' (Grindle 2010) for what are often heavily political interferences (Brown and Cloke 2004). Cloaked in the language of participation, devolution, and civil society involvement, good governance actually presents ever more pervasive forms of power (Orlandini 2003). This line of analysis draws theoretically on Foucault's concepts of governmentality and biopower, the idea that government is about letting subjects govern themselves, 'the conduct of conduct' (Foucault 2000; Arts and Visseren-Hamakers 2012). Foucauldian approaches have also been important in critical analyses of decentralisation in natural resource management. Thus Agrawal (2005a, 2005b) uses the term 'environmentality' to describe how villagers develop environmental consciousness through their involvement in community forest councils, and how through this consciousness they become willing agents of government forest conservation policies; how 'technologies of self and power are involved in the creation of new subjects concerned about the environment' (Agrawal 2005b: 166).

The anti-politics of the good governance agenda not only disguise global forms of power with technocratic language; they are also manifest in a lack of appreciation by policy-makers of local politics and power relations. Leftwich argues that good governance proponents are politically naïve to believe that a few measures can address governance problems, since 'good governance is not simply available on order, but requires a particular kind of politics both to institute and sustain it' (Leftwich 1993: 607; cited in Corbridge 2005: 186), a politics that is, almost by definition, absent in the places where good governance programmes are being implemented (see also Szeftel 1998). The same critique applies to the idealised conceptualisation of 'the community' that informs the promotion of participatory projects and mainstream CPR theory itself (Sharpe 1998; Agrawal and Gibson 1999; Charnley and Poe 2007). In forest areas, like anywhere else, local communities are difficult to define, heterogeneous, conflict-ridden, and shaped by uneven power relations. Working with 'the community' in forest conservation in practice often means working with the powerful – mostly men – thus effectively reinforcing existing inequalities. New work on environmental governance therefore seeks to provide ways of taking account of local politics and power relations (e.g. Mehta *et al.* 2001; Agrawal 2003; Zimmer and Sakdapolrak 2012).

There is also a growing recognition of the need for a more historically contextualised understanding of current forest reform than CPR-inspired mainstream resource management analyses provide (Mehta *et al.* 2001; Agrawal 2003; Batterbury and Fernando 2006). In fact, the existing historical and political ecology literature on scientific forestry and its adoption in colonial Asia and Africa can provide pertinent insights into contemporary reform efforts. For one, it shows that scientific forestry was an integral part of the rise of the modern state; a key arena of new forms of governmentality emerging in seventeenth- and eighteenth-century Europe. For this reason, James Scott begins *Seeing Like a State*, his seminal study of large (and failed) state-led projects of rural and urban transformation, with a chapter on scientific forestry, using it as 'something of a model' for the processes he is concerned with (Scott 1998: 11). In a similar vein, colonial forestry, built on French and German principles of scientific forestry, has been examined as a form of colonial 'statemaking' (Sivaramakrishnan 1999) and as a perfect example of Weberian 'formal rationalisation' (Bryant 1998).

These reminders of the roots of forestry in modern state practice are important because despite the recent shift towards more participatory approaches, several of its key principles actually remain unchanged. For example, even if by now many former government-run forest reserves have been put under community control, the principle of reservation itself, that an area of forest is demarcated and rights of access are heavily curtailed, largely remains integral to forest protection, both in biodiversity conservation and timber-production-oriented forest management. In this context, it is important to remember that government reserves were first and foremost necessary for the practice of scientific forestry, which required complete control over forest tracts. As will be discussed in more detail below, the actual ecological benefits of reservation, both in terms of ensuring a regular timber supply and of preserving biodiversity, cannot always be taken for granted.

Historical studies also show that, despite forestry's centrist origins and orientation, decentralisation is in fact not new: in parts of West Africa, local authorities were put in charge of forest administration from the 1920s onwards (Wardell and Lund 2006; von Hellermann and Usuanlele 2009). It would, however, be misleading to assume that these early decentralisation initiatives presented actual community engagement. In the Benin Division in southern Nigeria, the native authority put in charge of forestry was the *Oba* (king) of Benin, whose urban-based administration did not include local communities living in or near forests (von Hellermann and Usuanlele 2009). It is nevertheless illuminating to study these early decentralisation policies. The limits of actual power devolved, the struggles over revenue and labour, and the motivation and tactics of colonial administration as well as native authorities in many ways anticipate contemporary dynamics and problems with decentralisation efforts. Bose *et al.* (2012) explore a different aspect of the historical roots of contemporary decentralisation efforts, by showing how these employ wider social categories created in the colonial period, namely those of 'scheduled tribes' in India.

Finally, the wider political, economic, and ecological context, too, shapes the trajectory and outcomes of institutional reforms, a wider context that is often missed in the narrow focus on 'design principles' in mainstream CPR approaches. Thus Mehta *et al.* (2001) stress that the contemporary world is characterised by fundamental ecological, economic, and political uncertainty; and that this uncertainty needs to be taken into account in natural resource management analyses. Li (2001), for example, discusses how agrarian change in the context of the global cocoa boom of the 1990s had a far more profound effect on rural livelihoods and land management practices than institutional reform in the forest sector. Environmental changes, too, can shape policy outcome far more than institutional design itself (Agrawal 2007; Charnley and Poe 2007). I will discuss in the last section how new insights in ecology and historical ecology can further help to understand current governance reforms in their wider ecological context.

Anthropological perspectives on corruption in the forest sector

With the fight against corruption high on the agenda in policy circles and the media, there has been a marked increase in academic interest in corruption since the 1990s. Anthropologists, too, traditionally shying away from the subject (Haller and Shore 2005: 7), have begun to discuss corruption, and there is now a distinct anthropology of corruption (for overviews, see Pardo 2004; Haller and Shore 2005; Blundo and Olivier de Sardan 2006). Methodologically and theoretically, anthropology can make a valuable contribution not only to our understanding of corruption as a whole, but also to critical assessments of the current focus on the combat of corruption in forest conservation.

Thus, a prominent theme in the anthropology of corruption is the analysis of corruption discourses and their political uses (Haller and Shore 2005). Here, an important body of work analyses global corruption discourses; in particular, the good governance agenda and recent anti-corruption campaigns. As Elizabeth Harrison (2007: 676) points out, the focus on corruption 'provides a neat explanation for the ills of both countries and continents that leaves moral culpability entirely with the supposedly corrupt'. Similarly, the current focus on 'bad' governance as a key cause of deforestation puts most blame on locals, no longer poor farmers, but corrupt forest officials and politicians. Just as powerful environmental crisis narratives served to justify colonial and post-colonial conservation intervention (Leach and Mearns 1996), so, arguably, the identification of corruption as a key cause of deforestation presents the combination of both environmental and political crisis narratives, again used to justify political and environmental intervention (von Hellermann 2007; see also Fortmann 2005).

Second, anthropologists have explored the links between social norms, moral economy, and corruption. Overall, anthropologists have been at pains to disassociate themselves from the idea that corruption in Africa, for example, is rooted in a 'culture of corruption', and only a few have tackled this topic directly (Smith 2007). Instead of evoking a 'culture of corruption', Olivier de Sardan (1999) argues that African moral economy – in parti-cular the logics of gift giving, brokerage, solidarity networks, predatory authority, and redistributive accumulation – serves to banalise and generalise corruption. Generally anthropologists have helped to point out that corruption, and indeed good governance, are not understood by all people in the same way, that such ideas are socially embedded (Poluha and Rosendahl 2002; Orlandini 2003; Haller and Shore 2005; Siegel 2011). Such approaches are also relevant for understanding 'corrupt' practices in forestry. My research in southern Nigeria showed how social relations between forest staff, loggers, and farmers are deeply embedded in local social and political practices, such as the sealing of farm land allocations with kola nut and 'hot' (local gin), or the flow of 'gifts' from loggers to forest staff (von Hellermann 2013). Legal pluralism in access to land, such as exists in many parts of Africa, can also facilitate licensing ambiguity and therefore illegal logging practices (Siebert and Elwert 2004).

Third, as well as bringing out how 'corrupt' practices may be socially embedded, ethnographic work helps to achieve a more nuanced, differentiated, and sector-specific understanding of corruption, showing that even in one locality, there is never just one moral economy shaping everyone's behaviour (Anders 2004). Nigerian forest officers do not all have the same attitudes and do not participate in corrupt practices in the same way: some are far more committed to forest conservation and correct procedures than others. There is also considerable condemnation of corrupt and illegal practices amongst villagers, which sometimes results in active obstruction and resistance to illegal loggers (von Hellermann 2013: 120–121). Moreover, ethnographic work helps to distinguish between grand and petty forms of corruption, a distinction that is often curiously absent from good governance discourses (Walton 2013). Yet it is important to make distinctions: a farmer providing the visiting forest officer with kola nut, 'hot' and a 'dash' in order to obtain two hectares instead of the one hectare of reserve land he is officially allowed under the Taungya scheme in Nigeria's Edo State, is not the same, in nature and scale, as state ministers awarding many square miles of reserve land to political cronies (von Hellermann 2013). Finally, sector-specific ethnographic research helps to show how particular practices are rooted as much in sector-specific policies and institutions as in local moral economy, if not more. Timber logging, for example, is regulated by a system of on-the-ground 'stamping' by forest officers to mark legally felled trees, a system which has been subject to abuse throughout its history, in eighteenth-century France (Rochel 2005) as much as in contemporary Nigeria. Equally, the widely used concession system, whereby loggers gain a licence for logging a particular piece of forest for a particular piece of time, is intrinsically prone to patronage as well as informal, additional uses (see also Hardin 2011).

In this respect, a fourth point raised by the anthropology of corruption is particularly pertinent, namely the need to understand contemporary practices in their historical context. There is a general tendency to associate corrupt practices with recent, post-independence governments in Africa; but in fact, colonial administrations, generally run on a shoestring, were often governed in a slapdash, arbitrary manner and saw widespread corruption and illegal activities (Chabal and Daloz 1999; Blundo and Olivier de Sardan 2006). Moreover, as I have just discussed above, logging regulations have been abused throughout their existence. An appreciation of the long-term history of corruption in forestry in fact adds new perspectives on a well-entrenched but limiting debate about the roots of corruption in post-colonial countries – whether it is 'the modern state [that] is corrupted by traditional culture or traditional culture [that] is corrupted by the advent of the modern state' (Blundo and Olivier de Sardan 2006: 29). As an examination of forestry shows, it may be neither, because contemporary practices have even deeper, sector-specific roots.

Finally, my research in southern Nigeria also highlighted the need for understanding 'corrupt' practices in their wider economic and political context. Since the 1980s and 1990s, economic decline and widespread 'retrenchment' and financial shortages in the public sector have brought with them a drastic drop in employment opportunities and pensions, forcing many people to return to farming 'for survival', creating a huge demand for farmland. Local demand for timber, too – for years fostered by the colonial forest department – is now huge, and Edo State's economy is heavily dependent on the timber industry, with over 200 saw mills and countless carpenters and furniture makers operating in Benin City. Yet while southern Nigeria has seen significant economic and demographic shifts over the last few decades – with Nigeria's population more than tripling between 1963 and 2013 – official policies and procedures in forestry have largely remained unchanged, a phenomenon also observed by Anders (2004) in his study of the civil service in Malawi. Moreover, there are generally few democratic channels available for ordinary citizens to influence or change policy. In this context, the only way in which citizens can effectively change policy is through informal, 'corrupt' alterations of official policy on the ground. This point was already made much earlier by James Scott (1969), who suggested that where interest structures and institutionalised forms through which demands can be made are weak or non-existent, a sizeable number of demands reach the political system after laws are passed, at the enforcement stage.

Thus, since the 1980s, in Nigeria's Edo State, the agroforestry Taungya Scheme has not been practised as originally designed by colonial foresters: while it continues to flourish as a system of land allocation, no trees are planted, more land is allocated to farmers than officially allowed, and farms are re-allocated every three years. Its transformation is often described as one of forestry's biggest failures in Edo State. However, this new form of Taungya has played a significant role in meeting the large rise in demand for subsistence farmland, in a remarkably peaceful way (von Hellermann 2007). Similarly, the cocoa and plantain farms that have sprung up in forest reserves in recent decades are indeed illegal, but they provide a vital source of livelihood for the small-scale farmers and traders involved. Some of these important functions of informal 'corrupt' and 'illegal' practices that have emerged on the ground have been belatedly recognised in policy: a 1994 edict allowed Taungya farmers to return to the same piece of land; and in 2006, the Edo State forest department started granting licences to cocoa farmers (von Hellermann 2013). These developments are reminiscent of Mosse's (2004) analysis that development policy changes are in practice often made from below, rather than top-down.

Such a pragmatic interpretation of corruption is somewhat unfashionable at the moment. In contrast to the 1960s, when there was a debate between 'functionalist' and 'moralistic' analyses of corruption (Farrales 2005), there is a nearly universal consensus now that the effects of corruption are detrimental. Yet ethnographic work in the forest sector shows that this is not always the case; some 'corrupt' practices can be viewed in a different light. In addition to the social and economic effects just discussed, an in-depth examination of the ecological outcomes of corruption further challenges received wisdom on the effects of corruption.

New ecologies and forest governance

The overall aim of the good governance agenda in forestry is, of course, to improve forest protection. Mismanagement and corruption result in deforestation, so combating corruption and establishing the rule of law, it is reasoned, will protect forests. True, there is no doubt that uncontrolled logging and especially the large-scale conversion of forests to agricultural uses do significantly contribute to deforestation. Nevertheless, the connections between 'bad' governance and deforestation, and 'good' governance and forest protection, are not always as self-evident as they seem. On-the-ground observations by foresters and anthropologists as well as conceptual shifts in ecology as a whole unsettle some of the key assumptions informing the good governance agenda, and suggest that, from an ecological point of view, too, a more differentiated understanding of what constitutes 'good' and 'bad' forest governance is required.

Modern forestry is based on the assumption that forests are stable environments, which through the application of scientific methods can be managed in such a way so as to ensure long-term sustainable yields. A key condition for this is that forests are protected from all human disturbances other than expert treatment methods and carefully regulated logging. For much of the twentieth century, the idea that forests are stable 'climax' ecosystems was also core to the discipline of ecology, rooted as it was in a fundamental belief in the balance of nature. Since the 1970s, however, something of a paradigm shift has occurred amongst ecologists; now disequilibrium and instability are increasingly seen as the defining characteristics of 'nature' (Botkin 1990; Sprugel 1991). At the same time, the sub-field of historical ecology emerged, like political ecology, as a critical response to cultural ecology, but also as a critique of ecology's traditional focus on environments undisturbed by humans. Thinking about ecology historically and bringing together environmental anthropologists, ecologists, and archaeologists, historical ecology research has powerfully shown just how fundamentally all environments, including all forests, are shaped by humans and how the impact of humans on forest growth and biodiversity can be positive as well as negative (Balée 2006).

Informed by these insights, localised historical and ethnographic studies can further unsettle established ideas of what constitutes good and bad forest management. In Nigeria's Edo State, forests were seemingly managed well in the colonial period: over 64 per cent of land was under reservation by the 1930s, and from the 1940s onwards, carefully drawn-up working plans regulated logging activities and prescribed timber regeneration methods. In recent decades, however, reserves have officially shrunk to less than 20 per cent, and there is widespread illegal farming and logging in what remains. It is not surprising, therefore, that the *Conservation Atlas of Tropical Forests* states that Nigeria's 'natural forests were carefully managed in the early part of the century, [but] they have since been severely over-exploited' (Lowe *et al.* 1992: 230; see also Oates 1999). This view is widely shared by conservationists, foresters, and local people alike, who all participate in this particular version of the much-repeated Nigerian 'things fall apart' narrative: that forests were managed well in the colonial period and that political decline in recent decades has caused environmental destruction. But this is not, in fact, correct.

The colonial forest department not only experienced financial and staff shortages, delays, internal conflict, illegal logging, and corruption: my archival research showed that even in its most successful periods, colonial forest management did not actually result in sustainable timber production. This is because it was widespread shifting cultivation in the pre-colonial period that had created the conditions for the abundance of timber species, many of which are light-demanding in their early stages and grow best in opened areas. In this context, forest reservation effectively curtailed the conditions that had facilitated the regeneration of timber species. Inside reserves, now no longer farmed, timber species could not regenerate well under the closed forest canopy, while outside reserves, farming necessarily intensified, shortening fallow periods and reducing opportunities for timber species to fully regenerate here too. The separation of forests and farmland that forest reservation created thus protected forest tracts, but not the overall number of trees, least of all timber trees.

Working plans, too, did not constitute successful environmental stewardship: the extensive application of arborial treatment did not improve regeneration inside reserves (see also Plumptre 1996). Moreover, the cooperation of logging companies in these restrictive plans was only gained by the introduction, in the 1950s, of 'salvage felling', completely unregulated felling outside reserves. Upon close inspection, therefore, colonial forest management, well organised and orderly as it might have been, did not represent sustainable management.

The environmentally destructive effects of mismanagement and corruption in more recent decades are not a given, either. Thus, illegal cocoa and plantain farmers in western Edo

State, frequently condemned as a major source of forest destruction, compare rather well to the officially sanctioned oil palm and rubber monocultures established on large-scale plantations, in that both cocoa and plantain farmers leave a substantial amount of original trees and plants and are much more biodiverse (von Hellermann 2013; see also Schroth and Harvey 2007). Meanwhile, Taungya farming as it is practised today does result in forest clearance inside reserves, but also allows farmers to prolong fallow periods on community land, facilitating quite substantial forest regeneration outside reserves. Informal Taungya arrangements on the ground therefore provide opportunities for community-based conservation practices that would otherwise not exist.

Of course, not all instances of corruption can be reinterpreted in this way: when a political crony of a state minister is given a large area of reserved forest land, clears and then abandons it, or if trees of smaller and smaller girth sizes are felled for timber, there are few environmental, or indeed, social benefits. Nevertheless, my research showed that the links between corruption and environmental destruction are not inevitable. Indeed, there is a growing recognition of the need for more empirical research into the actual outcomes of corruption in natural resource management (Robbins 2000; Corbridge and Kumar 2002; Robbins *et al.* 2006).

Conclusion

The three critical perspectives presented here do not challenge the overall validity of the good governance agenda in forest management: accountability, participation, transparency, rule of law, and sustainability all remain worth striving for. Rather, they highlight shortcomings in the ways in which these goals are currently conceptualised and approached by policy-makers. The critical scholarship on CPR theory shows how disappointing outcomes of its practical applications are linked to a preoccupation with institutional design, without a sufficient appreciation of historical, politico-economic, and indeed, ecological context. Anthropological approaches to corruption challenge us to think more carefully about the different ways in which forest policies and laws are subverted, again highlighting the need for a historically contextualised understanding of contemporary 'corrupt' practices. Historical ecology research and new approaches in ecology, finally, raise questions about the ecological assumptions underlying the good governance agenda.

Each of these three approaches is distinct in its intellectual roots, concerns, and affiliations, and each offers different insights. Yet all three are firmly situated within environmental anthropology; indeed they are a testament to the field's breadth and versatility. It is through its ability to draw on such different approaches – from within anthropology, but also from other social and natural sciences – that environmental anthropology is perhaps particularly well equipped to provide us with a critical, holistic understanding of the shortcomings of the good governance agenda in tropical forest conservation. At the same time, the good govern-ance agenda presents a fruitful focus for thinking through different strands of environmental anthropology and exploring their effective combination.

References

Agrawal, A 2003. "Sustainable Governance of Common-Pool Resources: Context, Methods, and Politics." *Annual Review of Anthropology* 32: 243–262.
—— 2005a. *Environmentality: Technologies of Government and the Making of Subjects.* Durham, NC: Duke University Press.

——— 2005b. "Environmentality. Community, Intimate Government, and the Making of Environmental Subjects in Kumoan, India." *Current Anthropology* 46(2): 161–190.

——— 2007. "Forests, Governance, and Sustainability: Common Property Theory and its Contributions." *International Journal of the Commons* 1(1): 111–136.

Agrawal, A and C C Gibson 1999. "Enchantment and Disenchantment: The Role of Community in Natural Resource Conservation." *World Development* 27(4): 629–649.

Anders, G 2004. "Like Chameleons. Civil Servants and Corruption in Malawi." *Le bulletin de l'APAD* 23–24: 43–67.

——— 2010. *In the Shadow of Good Governance: An Ethnography of Civil Service Reform in Africa.* Leiden, the Netherlands: Brill.

Arts, B and I J Visseren-Hamakers 2012. "Forest Governance: Mainstream and Critical Views." *ETFRN News* 53 (April): 3–8.

Balée, W 2006. "The Research Program of Historical Ecology." *Annual Review of Anthropology* 35(1): 75–98.

Batterbury, S P J and J L Fernando 2006. "Rescaling Governance and the Impacts of Political and Environmental Decentralization: An Introduction." *World Development* 34(11): 1851–1863.

Blundo, G and J-P Olivier de Sardan 2006. *Everyday Corruption and the State: Citizens and Public Officials in Africa.* London: Zed Books.

Bose, P, B Arts and H van Dijk 2012. "'Forest Governmentality': A Genealogy of Subject-Making of Forest-Dependent 'Scheduled Tribes' in India." *Land Use Policy* 29(3): 664–673.

Botkin, D B 1990. *Discordant Harmonies. A New Ecology for the Twenty-First Century.* Oxford: Oxford University Press.

Bourdieu, P 1990. *The Logic of Practice.* Cambridge, UK: Polity Press.

Brown, D, K Schreckenberg, N Bird, P Cerutti, F Del Gatto, C Diaw, T Fomété, C Luttrell, G Navarro, R Oberndorf, H Thiel and A Wells 2008. *Legal Timber. Verification and Governance in the Forestry Sector.* London: Overseas Development Institute.

Brown, E and J Cloke 2004. "Neoliberal Reform, Governance and Corruption in the South: Assessing the International Anti-Corruption Crusade." *Antipode* 36(2): 272–294.

Bryant, R L 1998. "Rationalising Forest Use in British Burma 1856–1942." In R H Grove, V Damodaran and S Sangwan (eds) *Nature and the Orient.* New Delhi: Oxford University Press.

Caine, K J 2013. "Bourdieu in the North: Practical Understanding in Natural Resource Governance." *Canadian Journal of Sociology / Cahiers canadiens de sociologie* 38(3): 333.

Chabal, P and J-P Daloz 1999. *Africa Works. Disorder as Political Instrument.* Oxford: James Currey.

Charnley, S and M R Poe 2007. "Community Forestry in Theory and Practice: Where Are we Now?" *Annual Review of Anthropology* 36(1): 301–336.

Cleaver, F 2001. "Institutional Bricolage, Conflict and Cooperation in Usangu, Tanzania." *IDS Bulletin* 32(4): 26–35.

Cleaver, F, T Franks, F Maganga and K Hall 2013. "Beyond Negotiation? Real Governance, Hybrid Institutions and Pastoralism in the Usangu Plains, Tanzania." *Environment, Politics and Development Working Paper Series*, Department of Geography, King's College London.

Conklin, H 1957. *Hanunoo Agriculture. A Report on an Integral System of Shifting Cultivation in the Philippines.* Rome: FAO.

Contreras-Hermosila, A 2000. "The Underlying Causes of Forest Decline." Bogor, Indonesia: Centre for International Forestry Research.

Corbridge, S 2005. *Seeing the State: Governance and Governmentality in India.* Cambridge, UK: Cambridge University Press.

Corbridge, S and S Kumar 2002. "Community, Corruption, Landscape: Tales from the Tree Trade." *Political Geography* 21(6): 765–788.

Dauvergne, P 1993. "The Politics of Deforestation in Indonesia." *Pacific Affairs* 66(4): 497–518.

Deleuze, G and F Guattari 1987. *A Thousand Plateaus: Capitalism and Schizophrenia.* Minneapolis: University of Minnesota Press.

Dove, M R 1993. "A Revisionist View of Tropical Deforestation and Development." *Environmental Conservation* 20(1): 17–24.

Fairhead, J and M Leach 1996. *Misreading the African Landscape. Society and Ecology in a Forest–Savanna Mosaic.* Cambridge, UK: Cambridge University Press.

Farrales, M J 2005. "A History of Corruption Studies and the Great Definitions Debate." Available at http://Ssrn.Com/Abstract=1739962 (accessed 18 February 2015).

Ferguson, J 1990. *The Anti-Politics Machine: "Development", Depoliticization, and Bureaucratic Power in Lesotho*. Cambridge, UK: Cambridge University Press.

Fortmann, L 2005. "What we Need Is a Community Bambi: The Perils and Possibilities of Powerful Symbols." In P J Brosius, A Lowenhaupt Tsing and C Zerner (eds) *Communities and Conservation: Histories and Politics of Community-Based Natural Resource Management*. Walnut Creek, CA: Altamira Press, pp. 195–205.

Foucault, M 2000. *Power: The Essential Works of Michel Foucault 1954–1984, Volume 3*. London: Penguin Books.

Geist, H J and E F Lambin 2002. "Proximate Causes and Underlying Driving Forces of Tropical Deforestation." *Bioscience* 52(2): 143–150.

German, L, A Karsenty and A-M Tiani (eds) 2010. *Governing Africa's Forests in a Globalized World*. London: Earthscan.

Gray, H S and M H Khan 2010. "Good Governance and Growth in Africa: What Can we Learn from Tanzania?" In V Padayachee (ed.) *The Political Economy of Africa*. London: Routledge, pp 339–356.

Grindle, M 2010. "Good Governance: The Inflation of an Idea." *Harvard Kennedy School Faculty Research Working Paper Series*. Boston, MA: Harvard Kennedy School.

Guyer, J and P Richards 1996. "The Invention of Biodiversity: Social Perspectives on the Management of Biological Variety in Africa." *Africa* 66(1): 1–13.

Haller, D and C Shore (eds) 2005. *Corruption. Anthropological Perspectives*. London: Pluto Press.

Hardin, G 1968. "The Tragedy of the Commons." *Science* 162(3859): 1243–1248.

Hardin, R 2011. "Concessionary Politics. Property, Patronage, and Political Rivalry in Central African Forest Management." *Current Anthropology* 52(S3): S113–S125.

Harrison, E 2007. "Corruption." *Development in Practice* 17(4/5): 672–678.

Hecht, S and A Cockburn 1990. *The Fate of the Forest*. London: Penguin.

Leach, M and R Mearns (eds) 1996. *The Lie of the Land. Challenging Received Wisdom on the African Environment*. Oxford: James Currey.

Leftwich, A 1993. "Governance, Democracy and Development in the Third World." *Third World Quarterly* 14(3): 605–624.

Li, T M 2001. "Agrarian Differentiation and the Limits of Natural Resource Management in Upland Southeast Asia." *IDS Bulletin* 32(4): 88–94.

—— 2007. "Practices of Assemblage and Community Forest Management." *Economy and Society* 36(2): 263–293.

Lowe, R G, J Caldecott, R Barnwell and R W J Keay 1992. "Nigeria." In J Sayer, C S Harcourt and N M Collins (eds) *Conservation Atlas of Tropical Forests: Africa*. London: Macmillan, pp. 230–239.

Mehta, L, M Leach and I Scoones 2001. "Editorial: Environmental Governance in an Uncertain World." *IDS Bulletin* 32(4): 1–9.

Mosse, D 2004. *Cultivating Development: An Ethnography of Aid Policy and Practice*. London: Pluto.

Oates, J F 1999. *Myth and Reality in the Rain Forest. How Conservation Strategies Are Failing in West Africa*. Oakland, CA: University of California Press.

Olivier de Sardan, J-P 1999. "A Moral Economy of Corruption in Africa?" *The Journal of Modern African Studies* 37(1): 25–52.

Orlandini, B 2003. "Consuming 'Good Governance' in Thailand." *The European Journal of Development Research* 15(2): 16–43.

Ostrom, E 1990. *Governing the Commons: The Evolution of Institutions for Collective Action*. Cambridge, UK: Cambridge University Press.

Pardo, I 2004. *Between Morality and the Law: Corruption, Anthropology and Comparative Society*. Aldershot, UK: Ashgate.

Peet, R and M Watts 2004. *Liberation Ecologies. Environment, Development, Social Movements*. London: Routledge.

Pierre, J and G Peters 2000. *Governance, Politics and the State*. London: Macmillan.

Plumptre, A J 1996. "Changes Following 60 Years of Selective Timber Harvesting in the Budongo Forest Reserve, Uganda." *Forest Ecology and Management* 89(1–3): 101–113.

Poluha, E and M Rosendahl 2002. *Contesting 'Good' Governance: Crosscultural Perspectives on Representation, Accountability and Public Space*. London: RoutledgeCurzon.

Rival, L 2003. "The Meanings of Forest Governance in Esmeraldas, Ecuador." *Oxford Development Studies* 31(4): 479–501.

Robbins, P 2000. "The Rotten Institution: Corruption in Natural Resource Management." *Political Geography* 19(4): 423–443.

Robbins, P, K McSweeney, T Waite and J Rice 2006. "Even Conservation Rules Are Made to Be Broken: Implications for Biodiversity." *Environmental Management* 37(2): 162–169.

Rochel, X 2005. "The 18th Century Paintings of Raon L'etape: A Geo-Historical Interpretation." Paper presented at the 3rd International Conference of the European Society for Environmental History, Florence, February.

Rudel, T K 2007. "Changing Agents of Deforestation: From State-Initiated to Enterprise Driven Processes, 1970–2000." *Land Use Policy* 24(1): 35–41.

Schroth, G and C A Harvey 2007. "Biodiversity Conservation in Cocoa Production Landscapes: An Overview." *Biodiversity and Conservation* 16(8): 2237–2244.

Scott, J C 1969. "The Analysis of Corruption in Developing Nations." *Comparative Studies in Society and History* 11(3): 315–341.

—— 1998. *Seeing Like a State. How Certain Schemes to Improve the Human Condition Have Failed.* New Haven, CT: Yale University Press.

Sharpe, B 1998. "'First the Forest': Conservation, 'Community' and 'Participation' in South-West Cameroon." *Africa* 68(1): 25–45.

Siebert, U and G Elwert 2004. "Combating Corruption and Illegal Logging in Benin, West Africa." *Journal of Sustainable Forestry* 19(1–3): 239–261.

Siegel, D 2011. "Corruption and the Global Diamond Trade." In A Graycar and R G Smith (eds) *Handbook of Global Research and Practice in Corruption.* Cheltenham, UK: Edward Elgar Publishing, pp. 224–240.

Sivaramakrishnan, K 1999. *Modern Forests. Statemaking and Environmental Change in Colonial Eastern India.* Stanford, CA: Stanford University Press.

Smith, D J 2007. *A Culture of Corruption: Everyday Deception and Popular Discontent in Nigeria.* Princeton, NJ: Princeton University Press.

Sprugel, D G 1991. "Disturbance, Equilibrium, and Environmental Variability: What Is 'Natural' Vegetation in a Changing Environment?" *Biological Conservation* 58: 1–18.

Steins, N A 2001. "New Directions in Natural Resource Management: The Offer of Actor–Network Theory." *IDS Bulletin* 32(4): 18–25.

Szeftel, M 1998. "Misunderstanding African Politics: Corruption and the Governance Agenda." *Review of African Political Economy* 25(76): 221–240.

von Hellermann, P 2007. "Things Fall Apart? Management, Environment and Taungya Farming in Edo State, Southern Nigeria." *Africa* 77(3): 371–392.

—— 2013. *Things Fall Apart? The Political Ecology of Forest Governance in Southern Nigeria.* New York: Berghahn Books.

von Hellermann, P and U Usuanlele 2009. "The Owner of the Land: The Benin Obas and Colonial Forest Reservation in the Benin Division, Southern Nigeria." *Journal of African History* 50(2): 223–246.

Walton, G W 2013. "Is All Corruption Dysfunctional? Perceptions of Corruption and its Consequences in Papua New Guinea." *Public Administration and Development* 33(3): 175–190.

Wardell, A and C Lund 2006. "Governing Access to Forests in Northern Ghana: Micro-Politics and the Rents of Non-Enforcement." *World Development* 34(11): 1887–1906.

Weiss, T G 2000. "Governance, Good Governance and Global Governance: Conceptual and Actual Challenges." *Third World Quarterly* 21(5): 795–814.

Werbner, P, M Webb and K Spellman-Poots (eds) 2014. *The Political Aesthetics of GlobalProtest. The Arab Spring and Beyond.* Edinburgh, Scotland: Edinburgh University Press.

Zimmer, A and P Sakdapolrak 2012. "The Social Practices of Governing. Analysing WasteWater Governance in a Delhi Slum." *Environment and Urbanization in Asia* 3(2): 325–341.

25

CULTURAL ECOTOURISM AS AN INDIGENOUS MODERNITY

Namibian Bushmen and two contradictions of capitalism

Stasja Koot

Introduction

So-called indigenous[1] people, such as the Bushmen of Namibia, are often seen as 'traditional conservationists'. Based on their indigenous knowledge of nature, they are frequently imagined and positioned as primordial people who belong to nature and therefore protect it better than anyone else. This kind of representation also creates the impression that they are still in need of development, as if they are 'not yet modern'. Today, such images flourish in what I call 'cultural ecotourism' and its marketing strategies. Such cultural ecotourism also generates an expansion of neoliberal capitalism to the world of indigenous people, which creates two contradictions. First, through ecotourism, 'authentic' indigenous people earn money and adapt to an 'inauthentic' modern life in a capitalist world. To do so, it is necessary that they remember or reinvent their 'traditions' and thereby continue to act as 'authentic' people of nature. Second, ecotourism is supposed to 'develop' indigenous people, but the values of this 'development' are based on neoliberal capitalism, the system that creates many environmental problems today. Therefore, 'developing' people based on capitalist values might add to global environmental pressure. At first glance, these contradictions might create the impression that indigenous people are victims of a more dominant political economy, due to their limited economic possibilities. Yet, in cultural ecotourism, they can also take up a more active part in modernisation, creating 'indigenous modernities' in which indigenous people bend aspects of modernisation to their own benefit and strengthen their indigenous image.

'Nature' is often the main attraction of so-called 'ecotourism'. Some authors, such as Crist (2004) or Kidner (2000), argue against a social construction of nature, while others believe that there is no 'single nature', but many different constructions of what nature is or should be (see e.g. Cater 2006: 25). Using an interpretative approach in this chapter, I explore the indigenous 'people of nature' – in particular the Bushmen of Namibia – who play a crucial role in cultural ecotourism. Although ecotourism has been given many definitions, in general it can be seen as a type of alternative tourism or nature-based tourism, in which serious attention is paid to environmental and local concerns, as opposed to conventional mass tourism (Cater 1994: 3–4; Fennell 2003: 18). The term is often used in conservation literature and misapplied to nature-based tourism, but ecotourism encompasses a much wider set of environmental concerns on accommodation and local ownership, while nature-based tourism is a form of conventional tourism (Brockington *et al.* 2008: 134–135). Therefore, the term can lead to confusion and is used and abused in the tourism and travel industry (Cater 1994: 3–4).

My aim here is to show how ecotourism has become a concept that is dominated by neoliberal capitalist ideologies, actions (e.g. consumption), values, and institutions originating in the West (see e.g. Cater 2006: 25; West and Carrier 2004), which has a big influence on the way in which local societies are changing, and how these indigenous people respond to these processes. I suggest that indigenous groups have not only become victims of more powerful forces that are shaping their environment, such as colonialism, capitalism, and modern technology; they are also agents who are actively engaging in the contemporary modern environment. To be able to do so, they sometimes embrace their indigenous status as 'authentic' and/or marginalised people. This means that indigenous societies are neither traditional, in the sense of 'authentic', nor modern, in the sense of 'inauthentic', but hybrid.

My findings are based on ongoing visits to the Bushmen of southern Africa since 1999. The first time I stayed with them as an anthropology student doing ethnographic fieldwork for six months in 1999; and later, from 2002 to 2007, I lived among the Hai//om in Tsintsabis, northern Namibia. I was then working on a community-based ecotourism project called Treesleeper Camp (see Hüncke and Koot 2012; Koot 2012, 2015, submitted). Later, based on six months of fieldwork in 2010, I studied three Namibian Bushmen groups (and one South African group) for a PhD dissertation (Koot 2013).

Cultural ecotourism and neoliberal capitalism

What makes ecotourism particularly interesting is that there is a general tendency to regard it as a 'good' phenomenon, in which nature is conserved, cultures are preserved, and simultaneously the people of these cultures are developed (see e.g. Cater 2006; West and Carrier 2004). Concerning the conservation of nature, recent evidence shows that the global conservation of wildlife species can be supported by ecotourism activities (see e.g. De Vasconcellos Pegas *et al.* 2015), although animals can also be disadvantaged, for example, because ever more 'ecotourists' join boat tours which affect the stress levels of whales and dolphins, and can even kill them (Cressey 2014).

In this chapter, however, I focus on ecotourism's conflation with 'ethnic tourism', 'indigenous tourism' or 'cultural tourism', because I look specifically at the role of indigenous people, who tend to be seen as part of nature – something I have previously dubbed 'cultural ecotourism' (Koot 2013: 49–52). Therefore, the use of 'ecotourism' in this chapter is focused on indigenous peoples' engagement in tourism, in association with nature activities.

For example, when I worked at Treesleeper Camp, we used solar energy, focused on the contemporary and traditional culture of the local !Xun and Hai//om Bushman groups and built a campsite in a beautiful natural setting (see also Koot 2012). Although the project was initially aimed at the economic development of the local community (with serious consideration for the natural environment), various companies in the Namibian tourism industry were eager to promote it as an ecotourism destination. In a way this made sense, because all important elements of ecotourism were there up to a degree; it was only our initial focus that was on the 'community-based' aspect. The vicinity of 'pure nature' – in this case, the Etosha National Park which is also an important part of the original Hai//om habitat – might have added to the 'ecotouristic image' of Treesleeper Camp. Moreover, the image of the indigenous Bushmen as people of nature should not be underestimated (see also Koot 2015).

Tourism in general is an exponent of contemporary neoliberal capitalism and helps to spread its values (Duffy 2013). This also applies to cultural ecotourism, which creates various problems that are associated with capitalist development, such as the creation of 'inauthenticity' and poverty. These problems are then often addressed using capitalist mechanisms (Fletcher and Neves 2012).

Instead of earlier state-led types of capitalism that were focused on welfare, today's neoliberal capitalism concentrates power more than ever in the capitalist class, which creates structural impoverishment for most people outside this class (Kotz 2003). Nevertheless, the rise of neoliberal capitalism is often presented as "a gospel of salvation . . . to transform the universe of the marginalized and disempowered" (Comaroff and Comaroff 2001: 2), neglecting the increasing global imbalances in incomes. This can happen because many people assume that marginalisation can be eradicated through the 'trickling down' of finances in a free market. Private enterprises and entrepreneurial initiatives are believed to be crucial to create wealth through an increase in production (Harvey 2005), which means that consumption, industrialisation, and extraction need to be increased as well.

From this point of view, development based on neoliberal capitalist ideas, values, and assumptions throws a very different light on the 'eco' in ecotourism. The two contradictions that I describe in this chapter, one about authenticity and the other one about development, often stay hidden behind the positive messages of ingenious marketing rhetoric about the advantages that ecotourism brings to develop these marginalised communities and keep them authentic. Today, ecotourism, with its strong focus on wildlife, has become an important element in the rhetoric of nature conservation, in which a business approach dominates (Spenceley 2008: 180).

Indigenous modernities

Today, indigenous peoples have also become dependent on modern means of production, communication, and transportation, such as rifles, radios, and motorised vehicles (Robins 2003; Sahlins 1999). They can acquire such products with money from payments, wage labour, and so on. This integration of industrial technologies and systems into indigenous cosmologies is what Marshall Sahlins has referred to as "indigenous modernities" (1999: vi–vii):

> Many of the peoples who were left for dead or dying by dependency theory we now find adapting their dependencies to cultural theories of their own. Confronted by cultural processes and forms undreamed of in an earlier anthropology, such as the integration of industrial technologies in indigenous sociologies and cosmologies, we are not leaving the twentieth century with the same ideas that got us there.
>
> *(Sahlins 1999: vi)*

For the Bushmen, because of the remoteness of the areas where many live, cars and cell phones are among the most valuable modern items that they embrace today which enable them to continue some 'authentic' indigenous practices, albeit altered. Cars, for example, are being used to distribute elephant meat to nearby settlements, thereby being a helpful tool for the social element of hunting. This means that Bushmen do not necessarily create a first response to the encroachment of the capitalist world and its ideas in which they try to imitate 'us'; they can also use consumer products and capitalist ideas as indigenous modernities to strengthen their identity as themselves, to become *more* 'authentic'. For this, 'our' commodities can be helpful, but people are selective and can transform usage of these commodities for themselves. Western goods can be used to develop their own ideas, so that the indigenisation of Western objects takes place. In this way, many non-industrial people have not entered the capitalist world economy as passive objects of exploitation, but as active agents (Sahlins 1992).

In what follows, I provide in-depth descriptions of two contradictions of capitalism in cultural ecotourism. First I explain a contradiction about the search for authenticity; and second, I describe a contradiction about the idea of development. In these sections I also analyse my own fieldwork findings from cultural ecotourism among Namibian Bushmen. I then wrap up by relating both contradictions to Sahlins' concept of indigenous modernities.

The two contradictions

In 2010, I held an interview with a development fieldworker from a non-governmental organisation (NGO) about (eco)tourism among the southern African Bushmen (or San). Having worked with Bushmen for decades, she explained to me that

> For us with a Western background and coming from a capitalist mindset, you see so clearly the potential of something that can be done but you don't see the community networks that exist around it. And those community networks is their [the Bushmen's] economy. We don't see that economy, we just see "Oh, but you can get much more money" but you don't see how that economy imposed on their economy is going to destroy the fibre of the other one . . . Tourism has in its core the force of destruction [of] what it is that we want to sell. So you want to sell this product, the beauty of it, while the capitalist world and culture and means that we bring in that they also want, that has the potential of destroying what we try to sell. How do you toss that game? . . . It has positive elements of self-esteem and cultural knowledge, preservation and also income-generation, but it has in its core . . . the people fear that it keeps them back, it keeps them who they were and they want to move on.
>
> *(Koot 2010: fieldwork interview)*

In the above quote, two contradictions of neoliberal capitalism are revealed that come about through the implementation of cultural ecotourism among the so-called indigenous peoples.

The first contradiction: authenticity

The search for authenticity is an important characteristic of tourist modernity and is based on the belief that authenticity was lost somehow and only exists in the past or in other, faraway places. Modernity, with its Western tourists and dominant capitalist values, is associated with inauthenticity (Goffman 1959; MacCannell 1976), which implies that the search for authenticity can serve as a remedy against modernity's maladies: this often leads to the commodification of indigenous cultures; they are reduced to a good or product with a financial exchange value (Cohen 1988).

Today, the Bushmen are often still considered an icon of nature, while in reality they have gone through a brutal history and live under harsh and marginalised conditions. The perpetuation of their image as people of nature is also called the Bushman myth (Gordon and Douglas 2000), which creates the first contradiction that I discuss here. It refers to the role that many indigenous people (have to) play when engaging in cultural ecotourism. The ecotourists' search for 'authenticity' not only involves 'authentic nature', but also the 'authentic people of nature'. This means that the local people are supposed to live closer to nature, while in reality they are an important tourist attraction. In fact, by acting authentic, the local people have taken up a position in a capitalist system in which they have become (a part of) an ecotourism product. In the above quote, the NGO worker refers to this, for example, by mentioning the "destruction" of what "we want to sell" (the product) and that "it keeps them who they were and they want to move on". However, this does not necessarily mean that without tourism, Bushmen would be left 'untouched'; it is only one such influence, and therefore should be seen as a phenomenon of the wider political economy.

In cultural ecotourism, indigenous people are often characterised as the ethically superior, wise protectors of the land who can function as an example for non-indigenous people, something that David Fennell (2008) calls the "myth of indigenous stewardship". For example, a former client of Treesleeper Camp, Nomad Africa Adventure Tours, would explain that the Bushmen "have much to offer our modern way of living in terms of a sustainable existence with nature" (Nomad Africa Adventure Tours 2015). However, if the ecological impact within traditional societies was often low, this is not necessarily because of conservation-mindedness, but it should also be attributed to local conditions, such as low population density, the absence of a market, and poor technology (Fennell 2008; see also Ingold 2000: 68), conditions that have now undergone profound changes and continue to do so.

So in the marketing of cultural ecotourism, local people are often 'naturalised' for tourist consumption and are shown in photographs, for example, in traditional dress with the local flora and fauna (Brockington *et al.* 2008; Igoe 2010; Koot 2015). Their mythical images are being sold and used in advertising, not least in ecotourism. Often, that which is sold does not have anything to do with the actors, but with the encouragement of consumption for profit. Ironically, the people used for this advertising may well be unable to afford the products themselves (Tomaselli 2005: 136). Western idea(l)s about nature and the people living in nature are enacted through the free market, creating products based on the tourists' consumptive needs. In this way, tourists spread 'inauthentic' capitalist ideas, values, and the market system instead of supporting 'authentic' indigenous practices (West and Carrier 2004), or the 'preservation' of these cultures.

Such marketing leads to encounters between hosts and guests, in which there are various ideas about what is authentic (Van Beek 2007: 88). These encounters have often resulted in the villagers' adoption of the tourists' expectations, based on the tourists' pre-existing image of the villages, leading to performances with little resemblance to local traits, original rituals, or normal conduct (Tomaselli 1996: 102). Therefore, tourists get to see a 'staged authenticity' ('front regions' or frontstage), as opposed to 'back regions' (backstage) where the hosts' lives take place (MacCannell 1976). This staged authenticity is constructed by the hosts who represent the 'other' they are searching for. It seems as if the attraction the Bushmen hold for tourists is the focus on their (ascribed) identity as the primitive others of a pristine fantasy, semi-officially marked and marketed as being a scarce resource, off the beaten track, almost extinct, and so on (Garland and Gordon 1999: 271; Guenther 2002: 51–52).

For example, when I met a Dutch tourist in the Nyae Nyae Conservancy, Namibia, he explained that he was looking for authenticity and spirituality among the Bushmen. After watching three movies about Bushmen including the influential *The Great Dance* (Foster and Foster 2000), he had become inspired by the Bushmen's "spiritual experience of nature". To find this, he contacted the director of *The Great Dance,* who recommended him to "go to [the Ju/'hoansi of] Tsumkwe, because there it is accessible and according to his feeling it would be *more authentic*" (my italics). This quote shows how some people tend to consider some Bushmen to be 'more authentic' than others, based on their preconceptions of what is authentic and what is not. In general, the Ju/'hoansi of the Nyae Nyae Conservancy in Namibia and the Dobe Area in Botswana are often regarded as the 'pure' or 'real' Bushmen, based on historical and anthropological accounts (Koot 2013: 60). In this line, a tour guide at Treesleeper Camp explained that during the activity of a village tour, they show the tourists !Xun[2] houses. She explained that "[t]he village tour is just a show . . . One of the !Xun houses is not exactly built in the style as these people used to build houses . . . They also do not always speak !Xun, but I as a guide just say that they do" (cited in Hüncke and Koot 2012: 683). As Garland and Gordon (1999: 280) stated, what counts as authentic has no fixed content and even though cultural characteristics, such as ethnic originality and historical stasis are conflated with authenticity, these are not the same thing. Indeed, the same Dutch tourist explained that he was "more interested in their [the Bushmen's] own roots instead of what they have taken over from the West". It is this search for authenticity that can explain why tourists often do not want to be tourists; it is because they *are* the West, the modern, the 'inauthentic'.

Altogether, this led the Hai//om manager of Treesleeper Camp to wonder rhetorically: "What do tourists want to see? Do they want to see how Bushmen [are]? Should we change because of tourists or should tourists accept how we are?" (cited in Hüncke and Koot 2012: 682). In many cases, ecotourism activities lead indigenous groups to (re)invent their traditions, to create commodities for the tourist market, often because the tourist market becomes a way of facilitating the 'preservation' of the cultural traditions that would otherwise perish (Cohen 1988: 382). For Bushmen, cultural ecotourism is a potential strategy for generating income and regaining control over the production, reproduction, and packaging of their own image (Suzman 2001: 135). A clear example of a commodified aspect of Bushmen culture is the trance or healing dance. Today, Bushmen engage in dancing work and expect to be paid for it, except when healing their own family members. As dance has gained monetary value, it has become a product and a service to be paid for by their own (ill) community members and by 'outsiders', mostly tourists. The latter types of dance have changed a lot compared to the original and are mostly devoid of any curing (Guenther 2005). This shows how Bushmen's relations, with fellow Bushmen too, are evolving under the influence of tourism as an exponent of capitalism.

So simply by their attendance, cultural ecotourists impose neoliberal capitalism on the local cultures that are thereby commodified. Within capitalism, this is covered under a "psychological fix" (Fletcher and Neves 2012: 66); marketing isolates the mysterious indigenous cultures in the tourists' minds. This happens as if the indigenous people are excluded from the problems of the 'modern' world. Instead of accepting a situation in which local cultures are turned into products because of the tourists' presence, the creation of an image that is mysterious, harmless, and authentic protects the tourists from potential feelings of guilt (Fletcher and Neves 2012: 65–66).

In this process, ethnic commodities become contradictory in the sense that, seen from the conventional assumptions about value and price, the appeal of such commodities lies in the idea that they resist the rationality of ordinary economics based on neoliberal capitalism. However, this does not mean that those who commodify their identities will always remain dupes of the market, although it might seem to be this way at first. There are numerous examples in which they enter into their own small businesses based on the commodification of their culture, in which there is a good level of tactical and critical consciousness (Comaroff and Comaroff 2009: 20–27). When Hobsbawm (1983) wrote about invented traditions, he stated that those inventions may initially be seen as a simplification of traditional cultures, but that they are important cultural responses to the forces of modernity. Today, ever more Bushmen are taking an active part in the process of imaging (Tomaselli 1999: 131–132). To distinguish themselves, some indigenous people compromise with the dominant groups and their ideas. In many cases, they have no problem claiming to be the best ecologists in the world (Fennell 2008; Sahlins 1993), because this image has become a commodity.

The second contradiction: development

The second contradiction refers to the development of the local, indigenous people, described in the quote from the NGO worker at the beginning of this section as achieved by "self-esteem and cultural knowledge, preservation and also income-generation". Indeed, in ecotourism, a type of development is promoted that is essentially based on values and assumptions from capitalism. Ecotourism is a mainly Western-centric approach (e.g. Cater 2006: 25), resulting in values from the capitalist world, such as cash and commodities, which cross a permeable barrier and are converted into values of 'traditional economies' that are often based on sharing (Lee 2005: 24–25). Contemporary neoliberal capitalism has been responsible for most of the recent global environmental decline through its support of consumerism and related resource extraction and industrialisation. Therefore, the contemporary global domination and spread of neoliberal capitalism should be critically analysed, especially in relation to ecological 'solutions' such as ecotourism.

Development in ecotourism takes place based on a rhetoric of socio-economic values that are inherent in neoliberal capitalist individualism (West and Carrier 2004: 485), while the extraction and industrialism that it supports have often proven to be disastrous for the environment. By attaching financial value to nature and culture, development of indigenous people through ecotourism supports the promotion of an unsustainable livelihood that is based on an increase of consumption (see e.g. Cater 2006: 34–35). This shows the penetration of market forces into their small-scale, subsistence, and exchange-based economies (Lee 2005: 16). In development discourse, Western economic terms are used as being necessary for concepts such as "efficiency" and "economic growth", that are rarely justified but are automatically assumed to be based on "economic correctness" (Ferguson 2006: 77–79). The focus of institutions such as the World Bank and the International Monetary Fund (IMF) is on competitive advantages in Africa, which are there to be utilised efficiently so that economic growth and, as is assumed, development, can take place (Ferguson 2006: 77–79).

Under this influence, the current identity of the Bushmen in ecotourism has gained a double nature, in which they are both the primitive (authentic) cultural objects as well as modernising producers of tourism, thereby creating hybridity. This hybridity has led to a sometimes inconvenient "double vision" among NGOs (Robins 2001): on the one hand, they promote Western values and ideas, such as democracy and income-generating activities, to help indigenous peoples socialise into becoming 'modern citizens'. On the other hand, however, they promote the preservation of an 'authentic' culture based on traditional leadership, cultural survival, and the promotion of Bushmen languages. In Western development thinking by the state, donors, and NGOs alike, there is a tendency to continue the artificial divide between modernity and tradition, instead of recognising this hybridity (Robins 2001: 843–844; Robins 2003: 279–280; Sahlins 1999: vi–vii). Ecotourism, with its strong focus on authenticity and development, strongly resembles this double vision of NGOs and donors, which is no surprise when realising that ecotourism is often supported and instigated by these actors. This is partly also due to the dependency of NGOs on Western donors who, in some cases, promote the image of homogeneous and communal authentic people, while at the same time advocating capitalist and democratic values to them (Robins 2001: 845–851), such as individualism, to imitate the Western lifestyle and to 'become like us'. However, this does not necessarily mean that Bushmen are only passively 'accepting' their development, acquiescing in the imposition of modernist values and ideas. Quite the contrary: as 'indigenous' people, they grapple with modernity based on a history and culture that is classified as poor and marginalised. Bushmen, as indigenous people, are not only "objects for tourist consumption; as modernizing subjects, they must also be seen as producers, agents in the production and marketing of tourist artifacts and experiences" (Garland and Gordon 1999: 275). As modern producers of tourism, indigenous peoples have become a new genre in tourism that emphasises not only their cultural difference from Westerners, but also the ways in which they are similar, behaving as willing producers and consumers in capitalism. The first label of authentic Bushmen 'others' locates them almost automatically outside modern time and space, and often in nature. The second, modernist label posits them as active agents and participants in the tourism industry from which they choose to benefit by commodifying themselves through commercial and legal transactions. Interestingly, in cultural ecotourism, both discourses co-exist comfortably and sometimes their status as 'others' is the very thing that makes their modern role possible at all; it is the 'authentic other' that they ultimately have to sell (Garland and Gordon 1999: 275–279).

Some advantages of modernity and development are embraced by the local poor (Robins 2003: 280–284), whereas others are utterly rejected. According to some researchers, the commodification of culture could be a panacea for development, whereas others worry that it will exacerbate or even reinvent long-standing behaviours and relations of extraction and inequality (Comaroff and Comaroff 2009: 140–143). For example, the Treesleeper Camp manager explained that when the NGO NACOBTA (Namibia Community-Based Tourism Assistance Trust) supported the project with marketing, they misrepresented the project by using a picture which he felt did not do any good for the project. Nevertheless, he was later able to set up additional marketing activities through donor funding, because he followed a course on marketing, benefiting from capitalism to represent their indigenous project in their own way (Koot 2013: 238). In another example from the 1990s, the Intu Afrika lodge advertised Bushmen at their lodge as the last of their kind and few in number, while the stories told to the tourists about them were fanciful (Garland and Gordon 1999: 276–277). However, they lived in a village about two kilometres from the tourists and only dressed up in traditional outfits for tourist performances (Guenther 2002: 49). The hybrid, non-local, and in-migrated community was advertised as having traditional skills, but lacked the basic training they required to turn their skills into income generation. Intu Afrika and the tourists served as benevolent do-gooders, taking the Bushmen out of their primitive, disempowered, and traditional state (Garland and Gordon 1999: 277). Nevertheless, for the Bushmen at Intu Afrika, working there was not a choice as they felt pressured into it by their poverty and unemployment. They complained of social tensions, unfulfilled promises of land acquisition, and a tourist levy by the owners. Moreover, the labour conditions led some workers to explain that they were just a duplication of those found on commercial farms (Sylvain 2002: 1080–1081; cf. Koot 2016).

In my fieldwork I also experienced that it is very common to emphasise the economic importance of tourism for Bushmen, so that tourists will be encouraged to consider themselves as helpful agents in the Bushmen's process of development. This happens in guidebooks and brochures and at guest farms, lodges, NGOs, and among tour operators. For example, I have myself written marketing texts about Treesleeper Camp in which I explained that this tourism project "will stimulate the small scale economy" (Treesleeper Camp 2015); and the Nomad tour operator mentioned above explains that tourism provides "much needed funding for the conservation of the area and their way of life" (Nomad Africa Adventure Tours 2015). Interestingly, at Nomad it is even assumed that funding is now a necessity for Bushmen to continue "their way of life", instead of an outside influence that will, for good or bad, change the local dynamics.

However, there are tourists who seek an authentic experience in which they are willing to accept that the tourist product itself does not necessarily have to be authentic. Tourism then becomes a quest for authenticity, in which the tourists are looking for an ideology that enables them to see their modern selves as authentic, even if the Bushmen are clearly not (Garland and Gordon 1999). Tourists might easily regard Bushmen who are engaged in tourism as primitive and modern at the same time, halfway through an imagined development process. This ideology of the tourist is the one of Western socio-economic development, which encompasses Bushmen as both being and becoming (developed). In this way, tourists can consider themselves patrons of the Bushmen instead of exploitative consumers. This authentic quest then denies the historic circumstances that have contributed to the current marginalised status of Bushmen, while positioning them below the fully modern status of the developed tourist (Garland and Gordon 1999: 281–283).

In this process, what is a benefit to one is a loss for another, and individuals may change and experience new circumstances. In many cases, the costs are regarded in terms of natural resources; and the benefits in terms of development (projects), training, and opportunities to join the market economy (Brockington *et al.* 2008: 73–74). In this discourse, cultural ecotourism is often regarded a kind of 'fair trade tourism', based on a so-called "social fix" (Fletcher and Neves 2012: 65), which suggests that local communities, who were often unjustly treated in the past, are now developed into equal world-citizens who receive proper wages and good treatment. Through marketing, rhetoric, and certification systems, tourism mediators become the power holders, negotiating between the indigenous people and the outside world. For these mediators, it is important to show that they 'do good', thereby increasing the value of their business by using rhetoric about fair trade and assumed economic trickle-down effects (see also Cater 2006: 26). Furthermore, by being an ecotourist, instead of just an 'ordinary' tourist, tourists themselves show that they act in a socially responsible way through the support they generate for the development of marginalised indigenous peoples.

Conclusion

A dual nature exists in cultural ecotourism, in which indigenous people, such as the Bushmen of Namibia, are positioned as authentic and modern at the same time. As an exponent of neoliberal capitalism, this type of tourism creates contradictions, and environmental anthropologists doing research on ecotourism should be aware of those and the dynamics they create. The first contradiction is the tourists' search for authenticity, while the tourists' presence is itself an imposition of values and ideas from the modern capitalist world; it makes the authentic people inauthentic. The second contradiction is the development of the indigenous people, which is an essential element of ecotourism. Because development tends to be focused on Western, capitalist, modern ways of life, it creates consumers when successful. This creates an increase of consumption and therefore supports polluting and unsustainable phenomena such as extraction and industrialism. Thus, cultural ecotourists can either look for the authentic Bushmen or, in case they follow an ideology that is focused on development, for the marginalised Bushmen. In the latter case, development is mostly based on the Western ideology of economic growth that is supposed to 'trickle down' to the local people. This makes sure that tourists can now feel good about themselves as supporting consumers of helpless indigenous people.

However, indigenous people are not only victims of outside pressures from the contemporary dominating neoliberal capitalist system; through indigenous modernities, they can also use the values and ideas created in this system for their own benefit, even to increase their indigenous identity. They can use them to construct an indigenisation of modernity, in which they acquire their own cultural space in the dominant political economy. Today, there are Bushmen who think in a more business-like manner when it suits them or who want to apply national (formal) law instead of traditional law, or who want to open a bank account for their monthly salary because it means they do not have to share it with family members. Such examples show a continuously changing life-world, which does not automatically mean that the modern takes over the traditional, but simply that values of modernisation are integrated into indigenous Bushmen communities, just as rifles, cars, cement houses, and cell phones have been. Therefore, 'indigenous modernities' are material *and* immaterial. Today, values such as democracy, human rights, national law, profit maximisation, marketing, and entrepreneurialism have become influences and ideas in the daily life of the Bushmen of Namibia and they exercise agency in their complex negotiations with external agents and forces.

In cultural ecotourism, Bushmen are still portrayed as the authentic people who know nature best, but who are not yet modern and therefore still in need of development. This image can be heavily criticised, and up to a degree it should be and it is, but it is also an immaterial indigenous modernity that is claimed by the Bushmen themselves when it suits them. From an indigenous perspective, it makes sense to claim it because it will increase one's possibilities in neoliberal capitalism. Whether it is true or not that (s)he really *is* 'the best ecologist' does not matter; it is *the idea* that (s)he is the best ecologist that matters and that can now be regarded as a commodity that the Bushmen can use to their advantage.

Notes

1 I am aware of the contentious character of the term 'indigenous' (see, for example, Béteille 1998; Kuper 2003), but that discussion goes beyond the scope of this chapter.
2 The Ju/'hoansi in the previous example are in fact a sub-group of the !Xun (see e.g. Barnard 1992: 39–40), so also here the !Xun are regarded as the 'real', 'pure', or more 'authentic' Bushmen.

References

Barnard A 1992. *Hunters and Herders of Southern Africa: A Comparative Ethnography of the Khoisan Peoples.* New York: Cambridge University Press.

Béteille A 1998. The Idea of Indigenous People. *Current Anthropology* 39(2): 187–192.

Brockington D, Duffy R and Igoe J 2008. *Nature Unbound: Conservation, Capitalism and the Future of Protected Areas*. London: Earthscan.

Cater E 1994. Introduction. In E Cater and G Lowman (eds) *Ecotourism: A Sustainable Option?* New York: John Wiley & Sons Inc., pp. 3–17.

Cater E 2006. Ecotourism as a Western Construct. *Journal of Ecotourism* 5(1–2): 23–39.

Cohen E 1988. Authenticity and Commoditization in Tourism. *Annals of Tourism Research* 15(3): 371–386.

Comaroff J and Comaroff J L 2001. Millennial Capitalism: First Thoughts on a Second Coming. In J Comaroff and J L Comaroff (eds) *Millennial Capitalism and the Culture of Neoliberalism*. London: Duke University Press, pp. 1–56.

Comaroff J L and Comaroff J 2009. *Ethnicity, Inc.* Chicago, IL: University of Chicago Press.

Cressey D 2014. Ecotourism Rise Hits Whales. *Nature* 512(7512): 358.

Crist E 2004. Against the Social Construction of Nature and Wilderness. *Environmental Ethics* 26(1): 5–24.

De Vasconcellos Pegas, F, Grignon J and Morrison C 2015. Interdependencies among Traditional Resource Use Practices, Sustainable Tourism, and Biodiversity Conservation: A Global Assessment. *Human Dimensions of Wildlife* 20(5): 454–461.

Duffy R 2013. The International Political Economy of Tourism and the Neoliberalisation of Nature: Challenges Posed by Selling Close Interactions with Animals. *Review of International Political Economy* 20(3): 605–626.

Fennell D A 2003. *Ecotourism*. 2nd edn. New York: Routledge.

Fennell D A 2008. Ecotourism and the Myth of Indigenous Stewardship. *Journal of Sustainable Tourism* 16(2): 129–149.

Ferguson J 2006. *Global Shadows: Africa in the Neoliberal World Order*. London: Duke University Press.

Fletcher R and Neves K 2012. Contradictions in Tourism: The Promise and Pitfalls of Ecotourism as a Manifold Capitalist Fix. *Environment and Society: Advances in Research* 3(1): 60–77.

Foster C and Foster D (dirs.) 2000. *The Great Dance*. Cape Town: Sense Africa: Foster Brother Film Productions.

Garland E and Gordon R J 1999. The Authentic (In)Authentic: Bushman Anthro-Tourism. *Visual Anthropology* 12(2–3): 267–287.

Goffman E 1959. *The Presentation of Self in Everyday Life*. London: Penguin.

Gordon R J and Douglas S S 2000. *The Bushman Myth: The Making of a Namibian Underclass*. 2nd edn. Boulder, CO: Westview Press.

Guenther M 2002. Ethno-Tourism and the Bushmen. *Senri Ethnological Studies* 60: 47–64.

Guenther M 2005. The Professionalisation and Commoditisation of the Contemporary Bushman Trance Dancer and Trance Dance, and the Decline of Sharing. In T Widlok and W G Tadesse (eds) *Property and Equality, Volume 2: Encapsulation, Commercialization, Discrimination*. New York: Berghahn Books, pp. 208–230.

Harvey D 2005. *A Brief History of Neoliberalism*. Oxford: Oxford University Press.

Hobsbawm E 1983. Introduction: Inventing Traditions. In E Hobsbawm and T Ranger (eds) *The Invention of Tradition*. Cambridge, UK: Cambridge University Press, pp. 1–14.

Hüncke A and Koot S 2012. The Presentation of Bushmen in Cultural Tourism: Tourists' Images of Bushmen and the Tourism Provider's Presentation of (Hai//om) Bushmen at Treesleeper Camp, Namibia. *Critical Arts* 26(5): 671–689.

Igoe J 2010. The Spectacle of Nature in the Global Economy of Appearances: Anthropological Engagements with the Spectacular Mediations of Transnational Conservation. *Critique of Anthropology* 30(4): 375–397.

Ingold T 2000. *The Perception of the Environment: Essays on Livelihood, Dwelling and Skill*. London: Routledge.

Kidner D W 2000. Fabricating Nature: A Critique of the Social Construction of Nature. *Environmental Ethics* 22(4): 339–357.

Koot S 2012. Treesleeper Camp: A Case Study of a Community Tourism Project in Tsintsabis, Namibia. In W E A Van Beek and A Schmidt (eds) *African Hosts & their Guests: Cultural Dynamics of Tourism*. Woodbridge, UK: James Currey, pp. 153–175.

Koot S 2013. Dwelling in Tourism: Power and Myth amongst Bushmen in Southern Africa. PhD thesis, African Studies Centre, Leiden, the Netherlands.

Koot S 2015. White Namibians in Tourism and the Politics of Belonging through Bushmen. *Anthropology Southern Africa* 38(1&2): 4–15.

Koot S 2016. Contradictions of Capitalism in the South African Kalahari: Indigenous Bushmen, their Brand and *Baasskap* in Tourism. *Journal of Sustainable Tourism*. doi:10.1080/09669582.2016.1158825

Koot S submitted. Perpetuating Power through Autoethnography: My Unawareness of Research and Memories of Paternalism among the Indigenous Hai//om in Namibia. *Critical Arts* 30(6).

Kotz D M 2003. Socialism and Global Neoliberal Capitalism. Paper presented at the international conference on The Works of Karl Marx and Challenges for the XXI Century, Havana, Cuba, 5–8 May.

Kuper A 2003. The Return of the Native. *Current Anthropology* 44(3): 389–402.

Lee R B 2005. Power and Property in Twenty-First Century Foragers: A Critical Examination. In T Widlok and W G Tadesse (eds) *Property and Equality Volume 2: Encapsulation, Commmercialization, Discrimination.* New York: Berghahn Books, pp. 16–31.

MacCannell D 1976. *The Tourist: A New Theory of the Leisure Class.* Los Angeles: University of California Press.

Nomad Africa Adventure Tours 2015. Bushmen – San People. http://nomadtours.co.za/discover/highlights/bushman-san-people/ (accessed 6 August 2015).

Robins S 2001. NGOs, 'Bushmen' and Double Vision: The ≠Khomani San Land Claim and the Cultural Politics of 'Community' and 'Development' in the Kalahari. *Journal of Southern African Studies* 27(4): 833–853.

Robins S 2003. Whose Modernity? Indigenous Modernities and Land Claims after Apartheid. *Development and Change* 34(2): 265–286.

Sahlins M 1992. The Economics of Develop-Man in the Pacific. *RES: Anthropology and Aesthetics* 21: 12–25.

Sahlins M 1993. Goodbye to Tristes Tropes: Ethnography in the Context of Modern World History. *The Journal of Modern History* 65(1): 1–25.

Sahlins M 1999. What Is Anthropological Enlightenment? Some Lessons of the Twentieth Century. *Annual Review of Anthropology* 28(1): i–xxiii.

Spenceley A 2008. Impacts of Wildlife Tourism on Rural Livelihoods in Southern Africa. In A Spenceley (ed.) *Responsible Tourism: Critical Issues for Conservation and Development.* New York: Earthscan, pp. 159–186.

Suzman J 2001. *An Assessment of the Status of the San in Namibia.* Windhoek, Namibia: Legal Assistance Centre.

Sylvain R 2002. 'Land, Water and Truth': San Identity and Global Indigenism. *American Anthropologist* 104(4): 1074–1085.

Tomaselli K G 1996. *Appropriating Images: The Semiotics of Visual Representation.* Højbjerg, Denmark: Intervention Press.

Tomaselli K G 1999. Encounters in the Kalahari: Some Points of Departure. *Visual Anthropology* 12(2): 131–136.

Tomaselli K G 2005. *Where Global Contradictions Are Sharpest: Research Stories from the Kalahari.* Amsterdam: Rozenberg Publishers.

Treesleeper Camp 2015. Background. www.treesleeper.org/backgrounds.html (accessed 9 August 2015).

Van Beek W E A 2007. African Tourist Encounters: Effects of Tourism on Two West African Societies. *African Analyst* 2(2): 87–101.

West P and Carrier J G 2004. Ecotourism and Authenticity: Getting Away from it All? *Current Anthropology* 45(4): 483–498.

PART VI

Health, population, and environment

26

LOCAL AND ORGANIC FOOD MOVEMENTS

Ryan T. Adams

Introduction

Brooklyn, New York is an area of New York City recently known as a hotspot for "hipsters" with their long beards, nerd glasses, throwback fashions, and hyper-specific food preferences. Beyond the hipster scene are signs of a fascination with local food among the emblematic food trucks, anti-fashion restaurant scene, amid dinner party conversations, and at public events. The fascination with local food is drawn from a constellation of critiques of capitalism, food production practices, nutrition, and globalization along with a sense of nostalgia for lost "authentic" foodways.[1] In Julie Guthman's (2004) study of organic farming in California, she found that thirty-five percent of the organic farms sold their crops at farmers' markets, indicating that there is a connection between the organic food movement (OFM) and the local food movement (LFM), even if local food is not always organic, and organic food is sometimes shipped long distances. While the LFM and OFM are present across the globe, my focus in this chapter will be on the way these movements have taken place in the United States and how anthropologists have studied the American versions of these food movements.

These particular social movements centered on food are relatively new, but the fact that people organize themselves around a food issue as a means of political and social transformation is not new (Wilk 2006a). Around the world, there is a wide universe of alternative food system practices, such as the cooperative movement, indigenous food rights, heritage gardening, the anti-GMO (genetically modified organisms) movement, and various diet-related movements such as veganism or the paleo diet. If these represent a collective reaction to a constellation of concerns about an impersonal industrial food system polluting the earth with pesticides, harming rural communities with farm consolidation, and moving food through supply chains dominated by corporate agribusiness, while providing consumers with unhealthy mass-produced, highly-processed food, then the complexity and breadth of these concerns explain why the solutions vary considerably. Specifically, "organic" or "local" as designations for good food address these concerns differently.

Chad Lavin (2012) addressed the distinctions between the OFM and the LFM, arguing that organic agriculture is driven by a concern about alienation in the broad relationship between people and the earth, while "locavorism" is a retreat from politics into a postmodern protest centered in an alienation from place. Beyond the distinct qualities of the OFM and

LFM, I work here to understand the cultural practices associated with each, and the similarities and differences in the ways the associated practices and narratives shift through time. In separating these food movements conceptually, and focusing my analysis on their differences in practice, I will illustrate the different motives and concerns of food reformers associated with each, and then document how these movements change similarly over time in relation to the mainstream food system. I start by outlining the history of anthropological engagement with food and farming as a research topic, demonstrating how anthropologists study the OFM and the LFM, and then examine its manifestation in Brooklyn, based on my ethnographic fieldwork there.

The research for this chapter was conducted over more than a dozen visits to Brooklyn. In addition to these visits, I lived in Brooklyn during the summer of 2015, visiting the stores, markets, and restaurants that I report on, generally participating in as much of the local food scene as I could, and conducting interviews with people involved in local food politics.[2] The approach was ethnographic, intended to understand the prevailing ideas and ways of thinking, so the sampling technique was purposeful and too small to produce direct claims from empirical evidence about the behavior and practices of a city borough with a population of more than 2.5 million people.

Anthropological studies of food and farming

While food consumption has been studied throughout the history of anthropology, comparing early food research in anthropology to the current fascination indicates a growth in interest (Nestle 2002; Counihan and Van Esterik 2013). Sidney Mintz and Christine Du Bois (2002) reviewed early analyses of food consumption, noting that they were concerned with meals as rituals, the effects of food exchange, with the meaning of particular food items, and with social changes that were mirrored in changes in diet. During World War II, Margaret Mead (1943) called attention to the potential problems of the increased use of pesticides, herbicides, and changes in diet, recommending a broad and systematic research agenda related to diet, nutrition, and foodways. Audrey Richards (1961) studied the way that food exchange was related to social cohesion in Zambia (then Northern Rhodesia), and Claude Lévi-Strauss (1983 [1964]) and Mary Douglas (1966) squarely addressed food consumption as a research problem, using food consumption to reveal cultural categories that advanced their theoretical concerns in relation to Structuralism. The quantity of research examining food consumption, however, paled in comparison to the attention being given to food production.

Julian Steward's concept of Cultural Ecology illustrates the way earlier generations of anthropologists looked at food production as a factor that drove features more central to the discipline of anthropology, such as how food scarcity or abundance produced particular social arrangements among the Shoshoni (Steward 1937). Later anthropological studies of farming systems were based on analyses of energy inputs, resource efficiencies and allocations, and efforts to develop holistic, systematic models of the farming system using the ecosystem concept.

> In a wild food economy, a person, under given environmental conditions, expends a certain amount of energy (we will assume it is an average person so that the question of skill may be ignored) and in return he will secure, on the average, so much meat, fish, or plant food.
>
> *(White 1943: 341)*

Systematic studies that conceived of food as an energetic and nutritional input for humans who carried out activities and organized their societies toward productive ends (see Carneiro 1961; Gross 1975) had the advantage of an empirical method and a bounded frame of reference, but also had the disadvantage of ignoring or overly simplifying the meaning of food, and the cultural context of its production.

Anthropological studies of food production with specific attention to the role of economic inequality and trade policy are associated with the increased concern with political economy in anthropological studies of human–environment interactions following the emergence of Political Ecology. Sidney Mintz (1986) and Eric Wolf (1982), in particular, were concerned with trading and labor arrangements related to food and drink as a central element in their development of a historically and geographically broad analytical approach to understanding the types of social patterns still found in Latin America and the Caribbean. Anthropologists began to trace global trade networks, exploitative landholding systems, and commodification of land and forests near the communities they studied (Escobar 1999). These studies generally took place in rural communities outside the United States and Europe, however, as studies of industrial farming followed another trajectory.

An early study of American farmers by Alexander Goldenweiser and Leon Truesdell (1924) was ahead of its time, in terms of the scope of anthropological interest in food and farming; but works by John Bennett (1969) and Peggy Barlett (1980) marked a growth in interest in North American farming by anthropology where previously the topic had primarily been the purview of Rural Sociology. In the mid-twentieth century, the scope of anthropology expanded to include middle-class America, generally, and ethnographies of North American middle-class farmers, in particular, in addition to the more traditional studies of pastoral, foraging, and horticultural societies. Chibnik (1987) pointed out the division of labor between anthropologists who had worked with tribal and peasant people, and the rural sociologists, geographers, and economists who studied modern industrial agriculture. In organizing the edited volume *Farm Work and Fieldwork*, he announced:

> My primary goal in compiling the volume is to demonstrate how anthropological methods can be used to study agriculture in an industrial society; an important secondary goal is to show how technological and economic changes have affected rural American communities.
>
> *(Chibnik 1987: 12)*

Generally speaking, the anthropological studies were more critical of "development" than the preceding sociological studies had been (Lewis and Mosse 2006).

By the late twentieth century, anthropological interest in food had grown, and around the same time a number of single food studies were published, tracing a particular food diachronically, as it traverses various political, social, and cultural units (Ohnuki-Tierney 1993; Kurlansky 1997; Rosenblum 1996). As the social organizations of production and consumption vary through time, the singular focus on a particular food item brings the other contrasting elements of its "social life" into bright contrast (following Appadurai 1986 and Marcus 1995). At the same time, the earlier focus on the meaning of food consumption has been revived in studies that examine what eating locally means to consumers and activists (Wilk 2006b; DeLind 2011; Isenhour 2012; Nonini 2013; Cronin *et al.* 2014). The historical and social contexts of global commodity chains can thus illustrate the meaning and impact of our global food system, while studies of food consumers reveal their reactions to these changes in our food system.

By the time anthropologists had finally turned their attention to farming in the United States, global food trading networks, farm consolidation, chemical inputs, and large-scale Fordist food-processing techniques had resulted in a food system dominated by only a few companies sourcing foods from all over the world for consumers who were disconnected from the origins and production conditions of that food. There were many ways in which consumers (and consumers as citizens) reacted to this situation, as the OFM and LFM in Brooklyn demonstrate.

Environmentalism and the organic food movement

In studying environmentalism, anthropologists developed methods and theories suited to the study of activism that are also relevant to the study of food movements (Guthman 1998). Environmentalism was examined as an emergent trend driven by a combination of factors related to generational differences, disenchantment with "progress," and practical concerns about the growing impact of pollution on the daily lives of Americans (Milton 1996; McMichael 2000; Morgan and Murdoch 2000). In Northern California at least, some of the same people were involved in generating a wave of environmentalism in the 1960s and in beginning to push for organic foods soon after (Belasco 2007). At that time crop and agrochemical research was focused almost exclusively on increasing the scale of production, with farm consolidation, increasing reliance on chemical applications to crops, and the increased use of confined animal feeding operations (CAFOs), which concentrated animals in unhealthy conditions in order to increase the economic efficiency of meat production (Lobao and Stofferahn 2008). Pesticide use, in particular, served as a marker for the constellation of concerns by critics of this type of high-modernist agriculture related to both food safety and worker safety, leading to the emergence of organic agriculture as a logical alternative to address these various concerns (Tompkins 2009). At that moment, organic agriculture represented a full and radical break from the trajectory of the American food industry.

Organic agriculture eventually was absorbed into the mainstream food system through a process of institutionalizing the goals of the movement. The non-governmental organizations (NGOs) which were working to popularize organics turned to regulatory standards as a way to insure basic compliance with the practices of organic agriculture (Guthman 2014). Through this process, organic became embedded in the mainstream food system, allowing for its expansion, but removing the early elements related to social transformation, following a trajectory that anthropologists have noted in regard to environmentalism generally (Milton 2003). During the anti-environmental backlash of the 1980s in America, upper-middle-class consumers who were not associated with the 1970s counterculture movement looked to organic products as a way to provide "clean," "healthy," and "safe" foods for their children (Guthman 2014). Accelerating from the modest gains in the 1960s and 1970s, the organic food industry expanded rapidly in the 1980s due to demand growth (Guthman 2014). During the 1990s, "super-naturals" (big-box grocery chains specializing in organic foods) opened across the United States, and these businesses encouraged intermediaries to develop a range of organic products beyond produce, such as organic processed foods, with these stores in mind (Marsden and Arce 1995).

As it was absorbed into the mainstream food system, the organic label became a recognizable signal for more expensive, but "cleaner" and "healthier" food divorced from concerns about animal welfare and class politics related to farm worker conditions and land distribution issues, for instance (Guthman 2013). By limiting the critique to the application of synthetic agrochemicals, many of the original anti-mainstream food values were excised from the OFM, and global food corporations took a seat at the table (Allen and Kovach 2000). The agribusiness giant Tyson Foods, for instance, was among the strong advocates for strict organic standards for chicken (Weinraub 2003). For vegetarians, placing an organic label on meat became a further irony, demonstrating the cooption of the original critique of an impersonal mainstream food system by a food industry unconcerned about systematically turning animals into food (Adams 2010). The contemporary, coopted OFM has gentrified the space where a radical critique of American foodways had once been.

The local food movement emerges from Slow Food

The central critique of the local food movement is that exchange has become impersonal and unsustainably energy-intensive. The critique of LFM extends to emotional, social, cultural, and moral aspects of our relationship with food producers and the supply chains that bring the food to us (Goodman and Goodman 2007). In *Food Justice*, Gottlieb and Joshi (2010) trace the origins of the local food movement to Carlo Petrini and the International Slow Food Movement, which is a reaction against an impersonal and modernized food system—"fast food," in other words (Leitch 2013).

> Slow Food, on the other hand, means giving the act of nourishing oneself the impor-tance it deserves, learning to take pleasure in the diversity of recipes and flavors, recognizing the variety of places where food is produced and the people who produce it, and respecting the rhythm of the seasons and of human gatherings.
>
> *(Petrini 2003: xvii)*

Savoring good flavors, eating communally, learning about food history, and maintaining a diverse source of foods are all aspects of Slow Food, but the element that was most directly related to the LFM was its call for consumers to purchase, learn about, and celebrate fresh, regional food items. As the LFM grew, three aspects of consumers' views on food came together: a political concern with industrial production systems; an ethical concern with preserving the culture of regional foodways; and a gastronomic concern with improving the flavor of food by shielding it from the deleterious effects of mass production, processing, and shipping (Gottlieb and Joshi 2010).

In the United States, Gary Nabhan's (2002) book *Coming Home to Eat* was influential for many people who joined the LFM. In this book he describes his efforts to eat only food grown within 250 miles of his home in Arizona for a year. Barbara Kingsolver's (2007) attempt to eat locally has also garnered widespread attention, along with film and television coverage of this type of diet challenge, such as the film *Eating Alabama* (Grace 2012). I would run across this same idea applied to Brooklyn in 2012, in a foraging class I took in Prospect Park with Leda Meredith, whose fascinating journey into the LFM is chronicled in her book *Botany, Ballet, and Dinner from Scratch* (2008).

Community activists still see locally produced food as a way to build stronger community ties (Alaimo *et al.* 2010; Meadow 2013), and to empower people who are economically disadvantaged by the industrial food system (Cobb 2011; Gottlieb and Joshi 2010). Lisa Markowitz notes that, in Louisville, Kentucky, "the creation of farmers' markets in low-income neighborhoods has been central in efforts to create a more equitable local food economy" (Markowitz 2012: 532). However, as Guthman (2011), and McIlvaine-Newsad and Porter (2013) note, community gardens are often located in impoverished minority neighborhoods with middle–class and affluent whites being the main participants, which is clearly not a fully realized social justice vision. The make–up of local food activists might, therefore, be indicative of a coming repetition of the gentrification process that organic food demonstrated. Mirroring the way in which organic food became a marker of class, Kenji Tierney and Emiko Ohnuki-Tierney assert that locavorism "marks not so much a democratization of taste as new vehicles for asserting distinction" (2012: 126).

Brooklyn

Brooklyn was transformed by a recent wave of young, highly educated, new residents who moved to the borough seeking a cool neighborhood, and unable to afford the high rents of Manhattan during the 1990s and 2000s. To quote Eisenberg (2010: xiv), "Throughout the gentrified neighborhoods, where twenty- and thirty-somethings create a new Brooklyn, they've developed a cottage industry of artisan restaurants, food boutiques, and other businesses devoted to the ingestible." The food scene that Eisenberg describes grew out of some common ideas the new residents had in combination with local Brooklyn values, but importantly, also grew out of a desire to embrace "authenticity" in contrast with the vacant, image-conscious avant-garde food scene in 1990s Manhattan (Parasecoli 2009).

The current Brooklyn scene has many components, including restaurants that source locally, urban farms, abundant farmers' markets, food-stall fairs, and the iconic food trucks often purveying local, "made from scratch" dishes. The food trucks grew out of a long tradition of lunch trucks for working-class New Yorkers selling sandwiches and coffee.

> Beginning in the 1990s, food trucks began to proliferate in the city. Some of the pioneers of this resurgence sold coffee, desserts, or both, but they were soon joined by young entrepreneurs offering an array of ethnic specialties: Chinese dumplings, Belgian waffles, wienerschnitzel, fish tacos, and Margherita pizza.
>
> *(Smith 2013: 79)*

Food-truck meals were appealing in Brooklyn because of their association with authentic working-class New York City, but if they also sold gourmet food, then that was the best of both worlds.

The growth in farmers' markets, called "greenmarkets" in Brooklyn, urban gardens, and composting initiatives can be traced to a transition in the agency responsible for running the farmers' markets from a bureaucratic Council on the Environment of New York City to a more dynamic and food-centered GrowNYC in 2007 (Smith 2013). Other emblematic Brooklyn food initiatives are more radical in their vision for environmental and fiscal sustainability, like the Brooklyn Grange, "the leading rooftop farming and intensive green roofing business in the US" according to their website (http://brooklyngrangefarm.com). This rooftop farm produces acres of produce that they sell to restaurants, in farmers' markets, and direct to the consumer, but they also host school groups, tours, and even weddings at their picturesque location in the Brooklyn Navy Yard overlooking the Manhattan skyline.

The older organic food movement on the other hand predates the arrival of hipsters and the new gentrifying Brooklynites, and by the time I arrived, seems to have been almost entirely absorbed by the mainstream food system in Brooklyn, when I found widespread organic offerings in grocery stores and chain restaurants. The organic label is so common that independent restaurants rarely use it to distinguish themselves and their food, although some indicate that they try to source organic food when possible.

Organic food in Brooklyn

Many consumers in Brooklyn are concerned about the health effects of the foods they eat and turn to organic as a way to keep their families healthy. The literature has demonstrated a number of traits for organic consumers, including their perceptions of organic food as being healthier, more nutritious, and better tasting (Hughner *et al.* 2007), and their demographic status as young adults or older middle-aged consumers (Lohr 2001). Among the Brooklynites I spoke with, there is a widespread belief that organic agriculture is better for the environment. A young man shopping at the Fort Greene Park Greenmarket explained, "I always choose organic over conventional, because of the environment. It causes pollution." A customer at the Grand Army Plaza Greenmarket explained, "I came here with my wife first. I'm not uptight about food, but after kids we just want to eat better. You know? Eat more organic produce. Biodiversity is a real concern." The correlation between organic food and parenting corresponds to research in England. According to Kneafsey *et al.* (2008: 117), "Indeed, a common catalyst for buying 'organic' and joining schemes was the desire to feed young children a healthy and less adulterated diet." In Park Slope, a neighborhood in northwest Brooklyn, there are a number of health food stores that had previously emphasized the fact that they sold organic food, when that was a mark of distinction. A manager at one of these stores explains the reduced focus on organic labels: "Appearance remains a continuing concern with how the produce looks. It really isn't about organic or local but about trust. Our customers trust us and we work to put out good food, even if the practices aren't certified." These stores now mix signs related to organic, local, and a range of other food types, including gluten-free, GMO-free, and vegan, for instance. At some larger grocery stores (Union Market, Park Slope Coop), organic food is no longer confined to specific sections, but scattered throughout the store, indicative of organic food's mainstream status.

In 2012, the organic label was found on menus in both chain restaurants and independent restaurants, although for upscale independent restaurants, their menus used terms like "local," "seasonal," or "artisanal" as often as organic. According to employees at some of these independent restaurants, the use of organic as a label for particular menu items was more common in the 1990s and early 2000s, and while they recognize that their Brooklyn customers have a range of standards for finding good food, the shift away from an organic label was motivated by their changing "concept" rather than consumer demand. By 2015, many restaurants had adopted a technique of a menu statement describing their approach to sourcing, usually indicating that organic foods were preferred when possible (Figure 26.1). This is not to say that "organic" was not visible as a label, because there were still examples of restaurants featuring "organic" in their signage and displays, but these were mixed in with a number of other qualities that those foods possessed.

At the farmers' markets, vendors and market staff both indicated a certain degree of frustration with the lack of understanding by some customers in regard to organic food and how it may or may not be related to the safety and health of the food being sold. A Brooklyn greenmarket stand manager explained, "The customers arrive with clear ideas and buzzwords, but this is New England and there are going to be pests, fungus, and mold so these are conditions that make organic very difficult." The farmers were glad to explain their growing techniques and decision-making process when they were not buried in a long line of customers, and in fact, some relished the chance to educate consumers about the relative risks and advantages of the choices they had made even if they felt like they were swimming against the tide. As one farmer put it, "You want to tell them, but they don't always want

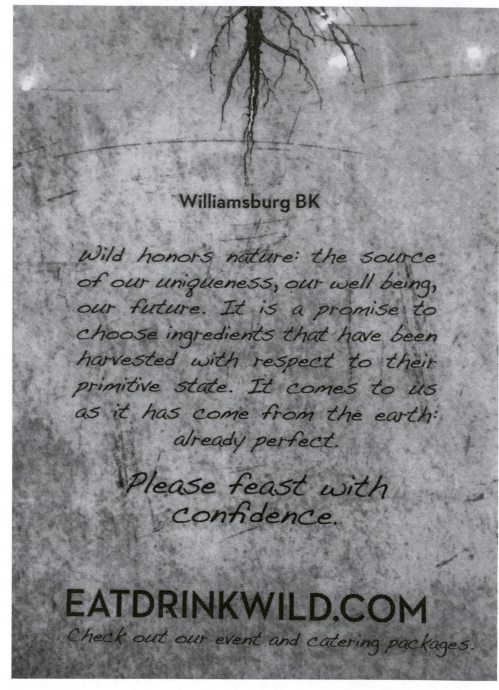

Figure 26.1 A passage on the menu for Wild in Williamsburg, a neighborhood in Brooklyn, indicating the care they take to source their food without an explicitly "organic" label.

Source: Photo by Ryan T. Adams.

to hear. They think they know a lot about farming because of something they read." The personal connection and ability to help consumers understand the challenges of farming is a real advantage he saw to selling their crops locally.

Local food in Brooklyn

Brooklyn is caricatured as a community of hipsters with hyper-specific fussy tastes, and one of the most emblematic consumer items associated with this hipster lifestyle is local food. The foods which are seen to be authentic, locally produced, and otherwise suitable choices for an extremely well-informed food consumer are among the foods that are loved; while processed foods which are associated with thoughtless mainstream American food consumers motivated by advertisements and gimmicks are among the foods that these same Brooklynites reject. One Brooklyn chef noted the shift in how people moved away from the mainstream food system:

> People were disenchanted and frustrated. They over-read and got jargony and fussy. The baseline is about taste, aroma, flavor. Of course you try to buy organic and local, but in the end it is about freshness and quality. We produce good food that is intentionally archaic and time-honored.
>
> *(Adams: personal interview, June 2015)*

This way of thinking about authenticity in relation to local food mirrors the results of Rebecca Sims' (2012) study of tourists seeking "authentic" local food in England, where the consumers were more concerned about avoiding "fake" foods associated with the mainstream food system than with finding locally grown food. Ideally, the local foods that Brooklynites love would also be considered unlikely to be prized by the mainstream food consumers, in order to generate a clean matrix of food aversions and preferences, allowing them to be differentiated from the mainstream food consumer (Wilk 1997). An example might be found in the novel food combinations with detailed food sourcing stories (Indian tacos, locally sourced Scotch eggs, burgers with ramen noodle buns, etc.) at the food stalls in Smorgasburg, the weekly food vendor marketplace (Figure 26.2).

Buying locally in Brooklyn represents an attempt to build cultural capital and stage authenticity (Lindholm 2008). There are a number of restaurants in Brooklyn that have made their reputation due to their local sourcing, with "farm to table" replacing other, earlier ways of distinguishing their food and giving their clientele a chance to exercise their cultural capital. In Brooklyn, the key to this cultural capital is an awareness of the evils of the modern food system and an appreciation of the local foods for their authenticity, "realness," and connection to community. At L'Albero dei Gelati in Park Slope, the owners see these three elements as vitally intertwined. They view the connection they establish with customers as the basis of their belonging in the community, and are determined to be completely honest and sincere when they indicate that the food they sell is worthwhile, fresh, healthy, and delicious. This usually means that they must have the same kind of holistic, honest relationship with their vendors. They indicated to me that because "good food" has so many layers, in terms of taste, sustainability, community, seasonality, etc., they choose to take an approach wherein the producers and consumers are both seen as essential members of their personal community. The value of these relationships helps them discern between thoughtlessly produced food that may have an organic certification and a fresh, local supplier who is very careful and dedicated to producing delicious, healthy food, but does not have the government

Figure 26.2 Smorgasburg on the waterfront in Williamsburg, a neighborhood in Brooklyn.

Source: Photo by Ryan T. Adams.

certification. One of the few certified organic producers at another greenmarket sympathized with that position while still advocating for organic food, saying "The USDA [U.S. Department of Agriculture] has diluted and corrupted what organic used to mean, but we have no choice if we want to raise the bar."

Most market workers and farmers were aware of how consumers conflated fresh, healthy, local, and organic, and were glad to have customers who trusted them. One market-stand worker explained:

> They want organic because of fear, but they don't understand that farmers need to make money and sometimes have pest problems. The food here is remarkable. They think it is an 'organic market' even though it isn't, but it is really good food.
>
> *(Adams: personal interview, May 2015)*

The personal connections lead to trust, and that trust presents an alternative means of allaying fears, apart from an organic certification.

In part, the appeal of "real food," sourced locally, and prepared by people you know well is easily understood as a reaction against the impersonal character of life in one of the largest cities in the United States. Drawing on David Graeber (2001), Jeffrey Pratt (2007) sees a drive for authenticity through symbolic food purchases as a protest against the harms of our industrial food system, positioning this transaction as central to the motives of the LFM. The advantage seen by LFM advocates whom I interviewed in Brooklyn is that local food can address so many of the concerns Brooklynites are experiencing, from urban social disconnection, to health problems related to a poor diet, to supply chains that stock the shelves with flavorless mass-produced food, to a sense of helplessness at the negative environmental impact of life in a big city. Finding meaningful personal connection as an essential element of the local food economy has been noted in the literature.

> For some there was an intense desire for closeness (to production and producer, to process and outcomes), and recognition of the need to preserve the connectedness of networks established by what were sometimes implied to be brave or challenging schemes, so that future generations could benefit from them and not be beholden to one type of food source.
>
> *(Kneafsey et al. 2008: 116)*

Many local food buyers in Brooklyn indicated that shopping at a farmers' market was just fun and allowed them to make an event out of stocking their kitchen, so I should not overstate the sense of anxiety provoking a trip to the market or the meaningful connections that the markets sometimes provide.

The producers who sell their crops through the LFM also appreciate the connections with market customers who may not understand farming, but who can afford to pay enough to let the farmers make a decent living. A farmer described his financial position to me:

> It's family land. There is no way I could have bought it and farmed it, but that is exactly what I am doing now. I am growing all kinds of things that I could never sell at these prices. I have almost 25,000 heirloom tomato plants! Where would I sell that, if it wasn't for the interest people in Brooklyn have for kale and stuff like that?
>
> *(Adams: personal interview, June 2015)*

Another farmer explained how he was able to take over his father's farm and expand it: "The markets are a way to prosper, unlike wholesale. There are a lot of hipsters now. Farming is cool, I guess, and that's different than when I grew up." A vendor at the Greenmarket in front of Washington Park has a photo album out alongside the organic kale and lettuce he is selling, and describes the way his farm and the market experience are intertwined for customers. In observing his interactions with customers, I came to understand how the customers get to experience a vicarious thrill of an Arcadian fantasy while bonding with the farmer over the traffic he is about to experience as he makes his way back through Manhattan once the last of his produce is sold.

Conclusion

The OFM and LFM have distinct origins, motives, and influences on the mainstream food system, but their trajectory demonstrates that the food system in the United States is flexible and prone to periodic reconfigurations in relation to the social and cultural context of food in consumers' lives. Activists have used these tendencies to reconfigure as a way to shape the environmental impact that food production has, in the case of organic food. While the organic food movement has been absorbed by the mainstream food system in Brooklyn, the impact on the environment by reducing the application of synthetic agrochemicals might be worth the trade-off of dropping the broader critique of our food system.

The LFM has not been coopted through a simplification and regularization of the meaning of local (to a simple mileage standard, for instance). Activists have advocated for local food to reconstitute some aspects of a more personal connection to food following the conversion of the food system in the United States into an industrial economy, and the diversity of meanings give the movement a real vitality and political currency. Local food in Brooklyn is about sharing an experience of producing food, about connecting to members of your community through honest descriptions of food, about demonstrating your ability to discern "authenticity" in an advertisement-saturated environment, and more. The various parts of the movement do not always share the same motives, definitions, or enemies, but that is what gives the LFM strength and leverage to serve as a narrative space to transform the food system.

Acknowledgements

Thank you to the Brooklynites who shared their stories with me. Research was made possible through a Faculty Research Grant from Lycoming College. Thank you to Richard Wilk, Eleanor Shoreman-Ouimet, Helen Kopnina, Sarah Quick, and Trisha Stubblefield for your comments on earlier drafts of the manuscript. All errors and omissions are my own responsibility.

Notes

1 The foods, food traditions, and culinary culture associated with a group of people.
2 I conducted interviews with several farmers or market-stand managers (n = 22), restaurant owners, chefs, and managers (n = 45), restaurant and farmers' market customers (n = 23), and others such as farmers' market managers and rooftop farmers (n = 7).

References

Adams, Carol. 2010. *The Sexual Politics of Meat: A Feminist-Vegetarian Critical Theory*. New York: A & C Black.
Alaimo, Katherine, Thomas M. Reischl and Julie Ober Allen. 2010. "Community Gardening, Neighborhood Meetings, and Social Capital." *Journal of Community Psychology* 38(4): pp. 497–514.
Allen, Patricia and Martin Kovach. 2000. "The Capitalist Composition of Organic: The Potential of Markets in Fulfilling the Promise of Organic Agriculture." *Agriculture and Human Values* 17(3): 221–232.
Appadurai, Arjun. 1986. *The Social Life of Things: Commodities in Cultural Perspective*. Cambridge, UK: Cambridge University Press.
Barlett, Peggy F. 1980. *Agricultural Decision Making: Anthropological Contributions to Rural Development*. New York: Academic Press.
Belasco, Warren J. 2007. *Appetite for Change: How the Counterculture Took on the Food Industry*. Ithaca, NY: Cornell University Press.
Bennett, John W. 1969. *Northern Plainsmen: Adaptive Strategy and Agrarian Life*. Chicago, IL: Aldine Publishing Co.
Carneiro, Robert. 1961. "Slash-and-burn Cultivation among the Kuikuru and its Implications for Cultural Development in the Amazon Basin." In J. Wilbert (ed.) *The Evolution of Horticultural Systems in Native South America*. Caracas, Venezuela: Sociedad de Ciencias Naturales La Salle.

Chibnik, Michael. 1987. *Farm Work and Fieldwork: American Agriculture in Anthropological Perspective*. Ithaca, NY: Cornell University Press.

Cobb, Tanya D. 2011. *Reclaiming our Food: How the Grassroots Food Movement Is Changing the Way we Eat*. North Adams, MA: Storey Publishing.

Counihan, Carole and Penny Van Esterik. 2013. *Food and Culture: A Reader*. New York: Routledge.

Cronin, James M., Mary B. McCarthy and Alan M. Collins. 2014. "Covert Distinction: How Hipsters Practice Food-based Strategies in the Production of Identity. *Consumption Markets and Culture* 17(1): 2–28.

DeLind, Laura. 2011. "Are Local Food and the Local Food Movement Taking us Where we Want to Go? Or Are we Hitching our Wagons to the Wrong Stars?" *Agriculture and Human Values* 28(2): 273–283.

Douglas, Mary. 1966. *Purity and Danger: An Analysis of Concepts of Pollution and Taboo*. New York: Praeger.

Eisenberg, Sherri. 2010. *Food Lovers' Guide to Brooklyn: Best Local Specialties, Markets, Recipes, Restaurants, and Events*. Guilford, CT: Globe Pequot Press.

Escobar, Arturo. 1999. "After Nature: Steps to an Antiessentialist Political Ecology." *Current Anthropology* 40(1): 1–30

Goldenweiser, Alexander and Leon E. Truesdell. 1924. *Farm Tenancy in the United States: An Analysis of the Results of the 1920 Census Relative to Farms Classified by Tenure Supplemented by Pertinent Data from Other Sources*. Issue 4. Washington, DC: U.S. Government Publishing Office.

Goodman, David and Michael Goodman. 2007. "Localism, Livelihoods and the 'Post-organic': Changing Perspectives on Alternative Food Networks in the United States." In Damian Maye, Lewis Holloway and Moya Kneafsey (eds) *Alternative Food Geographies: Representation and Practice*. Oxford: Elsevier Science, pp. 23–28.

Gottlieb, Robert and Anupama Joshi. 2010. *Food Justice*. Cambridge, MA: The MIT Press.

Grace, Andrew B. 2012. *Eating Alabama: A Story about Why Food Matters*. Moon Winx Films in association with the Independent Television Service and Alabama Public Television.

Graeber, David. 2001. *Toward an Anthropological Theory of Value: The False Coin of our Own Dreams*. New York: Palgrave.

Gross, Daniel. 1975. "Protein Capture and Cultural Development in the Amazon Basin." *American Anthropologist* 77(3), 526–549.

Guthman, Julie. 1998. "Regulating Meaning, Appropriating Nature: The Codification of California Organic Agriculture." *Antipode* 30(2): 135–154.

—— 2004. *Agrarian Dreams: The Paradox of Organic Farming in California*. 1st edn. Oakland, CA: University of California Press.

—— 2011. *Weighing In: Obesity, Food Justice, and the Limits of Capitalism*. Berkeley: University of California Press.

—— 2013. "Fast Food/Organic Food: Reflexive Tastes and the Making of 'Yuppie Chow'." In Carole Counihan and Penny Van Esterik (eds) *Food and Culture: a Reader*. New York: Routledge, pp. 496–509.

—— 2014. *Agrarian Dreams: The Paradox of Organic Farming in California*. 2nd edn. Oakland, CA: University of California Press.

Hughner, Renée Shaw, Pierre McDonagh, Andrea Prothero, Clifford J. Shultz and Julie Stanton. 2007. "Who Are Organic Food Consumers? A Compilation and Review of Why People Purchase Organic Food." *Journal of Consumer Behaviour* 6(2–3): 94–110.

Isenhour, Cindy. 2012. "On the Challenges of Signalling Ethics without the Stuff: Tales of Conspicuous Green Anti-consumption." In James G. Carrier and Peter G. Luetchford (eds) *Ethical Consumption: Social Value and Economic Practice*. New York: Berghahn Books.

Kingsolver, Barbara. 2007. *Animal, Vegetable, Miracle*. New York City: HarperCollins.

Kneafsey, Moya, Rosie Cox, Lewis Holloway, Elizabeth Dowler, Laura Venn and Helena Tuomainen. 2008. *Reconnecting Consumers, Producers, and Food: Exploring Alternatives*. Oxford: Berg Publishers.

Kurlansky, Mark. 1997. *Cod: A Biography of the Fish that Changed the World*. New York: Walker and Co.

Lavin, Chad. 2012. "The Year of Eating Politically." In Psyche Williams-Forson and Carole Counihan (eds) *Taking Food Public: Redefining Foodways in a Changing World*. New York: Routledge, pp. 576–591.

Leitch, Alison. 2013. "Slow Food and the Politics of 'Virtuous Globalization'." In Carole Counihan and Penny Van Esterik (eds) *Food and Culture: A Reader*. 3rd edn. New York: Routledge, pp. 409–425.

Lévi-Strauss, Claude. 1983 [1964]. *The Raw and the Cooked: Mythologiques, Volume 1* (reprint edn. from *Le Cru et le cuit*). Chicago, IL: University of Chicago Press.

Lewis, David and David Mosse. 2006. *Development Brokers and Translators: The Ethnography of Aid and Agencies*. Boulder, CO: Kumarian Press.

Lindholm, Charles. 2008. *Culture and Authenticity*. Hoboken, NJ: Wiley–Blackwell,

Lobao, Linda and Curtis Stofferahn. 2008. "The Community Effects of Industrialized Farming: Social Science Research and Challenges to Corporate Farming Laws." *Agriculture and Human Values* 25(2): 219–240.

Lohr, Luanne. 2001. "Factors Affecting International Demand and Trade in Organic Food Products." In Anita Regmi (ed). *Changing Structure of Global Food Consumption and Trade*. WRS-01-1. Washington, DC: United States Department of Agriculture, Economic Research Service, pp. 67–79.

McIlvaine-Newsad, Heather and Rob Porter. 2013. "How Does your Garden Grow? Environmental Justice Aspects of Community Gardens." *Journal of Ecological Anthropology* 16(1): 69–75.

McMichael, Philip. 2000. "The Power of Food." *Agriculture and Human Values* 17(1): 21–33.

Marcus, George. 1995. "Ethnography in/of the World System: The Emergence of Multi-sited Ethnography." *Annual Review of Anthropology* 24: 95–117.

Markowitz, Lisa. 2012. "Expanding Access and Alternatives." In Psyche Williams-Forson and Carole Counihan (eds) *Taking Food Public: Redefining Foodways in a Changing World*. New York: Routledge, pp. 531–541.

Marsden, Terry and Alvaro Arce. 1995. "Constructing Quality: Emerging Food Networks in the Rural Transition." *Environment and Planning A* 27(8): 1261–1279.

Mead, Margaret. 1943. "The Problem of Changing Food Habits." *Bulletin of the National Research Council* 108(325): 20–31.

Meadow, Alison. 2013. "Alternative Food Systems at Ground Level: The Fairbanks Community Garden." *Journal of Ecological Anthropology* 16(1): 76–84.

Meredith, Leda. 2008. *Botany, Ballet, and Dinner from Scratch: A Memoir with Recipes*. New York: Heliotrope Books.

Milton, Kay. 1996. *Environmentalism and Cultural Theory: Exploring the Role of Anthropology in Environmental Discourse*. London and New York: Routledge.

—— 2003. *Environmentalism: The View from Anthropology*. ASA Monographs 32. New York: Routledge.

Mintz, Sidney W. 1986. *Sweetness and Power: The Place of Sugar in Modern History*. New York: Penguin Books.

Mintz, Sidney W. and Christine Du Bois. 2002. "The Anthropology of Food and Eating." *Annual Review of Anthropology* 31: 99–119.

Morgan, Kevin and Jonathan Murdoch. 2000. "Organic vs. Conventional Agriculture: Knowledge, Power and Innovation in the Food Chain." *Geoforum* 31(2): 159–173.

Nabhan, Gary P. 2002. *Coming Home to Eat: The Pleasures and Politics of Local Foods*. New York: W. W. Norton & Company.

Nestle, Marion. 2002. *Food Politics: How the Food Industry Influences Nutrition and Health*. Berkeley: University of California Press.

Nonini, Donald. 2013. "The Local-food Movement and the Anthropology of Global Systems". *American Ethnologist* 40(2): 267–275.

Ohnuki-Tierney, Emiko. 1993. *Rice as Self: Japanese Identities through Time*. Princeton, NJ: Princeton University Press.

Parasecoli, Fabio. 2009. "The Chefs, the Entrepreneurs, and their Patrons: The Avant-garde Food Scene in New York City." In Annie Hauck-Lawson and Jonathan Deutsch (eds) *Gastropolis: Food and New York City*. New York: Columbia University Press, pp. 116–131.

Petrini, Carlo. 2003. *Slow Food: The Case for Taste*. New York: Columbia University Press.

Pratt, Jeffrey. 2007. "Food Values: The Local and the Authentic." *Critique of Anthropology* 27(3): 285–300.

Richards, Audrey. 1961. *Land, Labour and Diet in Northern Rhodesia; An Economic Study of the Bemba Tribe*. Published for the International African Institute. London: Oxford University Press.

Rosenblum, Mort. 1996. *Olives: The Life and Lore of a Noble Fruit*. New York: North Point Press.

Sims, Rebecca. 2012. "Food, Place and Authenticity: Local Food and the Sustainable Tourism Experience." In Psyche Williams-Forson and Carole Counihan (eds) *Taking Food Public: Redefining Foodways in a Changing World*. New York: Routledge, pp. 475–490.

Smith, Andrew. 2013. *New York City: A Food Biography*. New York: Rowman & Littlefield.

Steward, Julian. 1937. "Linguistic Distributions and Political Groups of the Great Basin Shoshoneans." *American Anthropologist* 39(4): 625–634.

Tierney, R. Kenji and Emiko Ohnuki-Tierney. 2012. "Anthropology of Food." In Jeffrey Pilcher (ed.) *The Oxford Handbook of Food History*. New York: Oxford University Press, pp. 117–134.

Tompkins, Adam. 2009. "Cancer Valley, California: Pesticides, Politics, and Childhood Disease in the Central Valley." In Michael Egan and Jeff Crane (eds) *Natural Protest: Essays on the History of American Environmentalism*. New York: Routledge.

Weinraub, Judith. 2003. "Chicken Feed Politics." *The Washington Post* [online], posted 19 March. www.washingtonpost.com/archive/lifestyle/food/2003/03/19/chicken-feed-politics/ff40080d-618d-4659-a741-35d42b4b7c42/ (accessed 13 October 2015).

White, Leslie. 1943. "Energy and the Evolution of Culture." *American Anthropologist* 45(3): 335–356.

Wilk, Richard. 1997. "A Critique of Desire: Distaste and Dislike in Consumer Behavior." *Consumption Markets & Culture* 1(2): 175–196.

—— (ed.) 2006a. "From Wild Weeds to Artisanal Cheese." In Richard Wilk (ed.) *Fast Food/Slow Food: The Cultural Economy of the Global Food System*. Lanham, MD: AltaMira Press.

—— 2006b. *Fast Food/Slow Food: The Cultural Economy of the Global Food System*. Lanham, MD: AltaMira Press.

Wolf, Eric R. 1982. *Europe and the People without History*. Berkeley: University of California Press.

27

ANTHROPOCENTRISM AND THE MAKING OF ENVIRONMENTAL HEALTH

Merrill Singer

Introduction

There is embedded in English common law the dictum that "an Englishman's home is his castle." This legal principle, dating to the seventeenth century and the writings of the celebrated jurist Sir Edward Coke (Sheppard 2005), but echoing ideas from at least as far back as the Roman Empire, proposes that a man (and gender here is no accident) can do as he pleases within the confines of his own house. The linguist and progressive political analyst Noam Chomsky has raised some highly pertinent questions about ownership and behavior on an even grander scale by enquiring "who owns [castle] Earth [and who] owns the global atmosphere being polluted by the heat-trapping gases" (Chomsky 2013: para. 22). His query was informed by recognition that growing social inequalities have resulted in those most responsible for environmental disruption suffering the least consequences, and those least responsible enduring the gravest penalties. Social elites, those with the greatest wealth and the most power, Chomsky argues, act as if they are the titleholders of our planet and hence free to do as they please as if the whole planet was their rightful estate. As a result, history has witnessed a process of environmental takeover that "has proceeded acre by acre, island by island, region by region, and continent by continent, reaching its current global apogee with the final loss of wild places and the corollary sixth mass extinction underway" (Crist 2012: 149). Without diminishing the fundamental importance of Chomsky's concern about environmentally mediated expression of social inequity, but with a focus on the broader issue of anthropocentrism in human life, this chapter addresses the question: do humans own the Earth and its global atmosphere? Our actions in the world, as scrutinized here, suggest that we think we are the proprietors of the planet and therefore are entitled to do what is in our immediate self-interest without too much regard for non-human Earthlings, less powerful human sectors, and the planet's ecosystems. Yet whether we deny it, feel overwhelmed by the complexity of understanding it, or experience a sense of powerlessness to do something about it, as historian Tony Judt (2010: 1) bluntly states, the truth remains that there "is something profoundly wrong with the way we are living today." Our current environmental problems are not really new, but reflect a long march—at an ever faster pace—toward grave environmental uncertainties and consequences. Of specific focus in this chapter, from the perspective of a critical environmentally-informed medical anthropology, is the issue of environmental health in both senses of the term: the health of the environment and human health as shaped by the environment (Kopnina and Keune 2013); and, especially, the interrelationship of these two core arenas of the anthropological project. This type of analysis requires a multidisciplinary approach that views health as the complex product of inter-acting social structures and activities and human and natural ecologies. Examination of these issues suggests a pathway for framing future work in the anthropological study of environmental health.

The complexities of environmental health

The statement above by Judt hints at the powerful relationship that exists between the health of the environment and the health of people. In part this is because, as Wendell Berry points out:

> While we live our bodies are moving particles of the earth, joined inextricably both to the soil and to the bodies of other living creatures. It is hardly surprising then that there should be some profound resemblances between our treatment of our bodies and our treatment of the earth.
>
> *(Berry 1977: 93)*

Consequently one gauge of how extensively human activity has adversely changed Earth is what might be called "the rebound effect,"[1] which I use here to refer to changes in the burden of human health problems caused by anthropogenic environmental changes, such as the everyday discharge of harmful toxins by agriculture, industry, construction, mining, and mechanized transportation, as well as the health impacts of accidental releases like oil spills.

One consequence of the complexity of ecological systems is that their disruption can have far-reaching and unexpected reverberations in human health. The explosion in Lyme disease in the United States in recent decades illustrates the multiple ways in which human disordering of the environment has produced rebound effects on our own well-being. This vector-borne disease, named after the town of Lyme, Connecticut, is spread by ticks. Ticks are known to transmit a wide array of pathogens, and new disease-causing tick-borne microorganisms are being discovered regularly (Paddock and Telford 2011). Lyme disease, the best-known tick-borne disease, is now the most prevalent vector-borne disease in North America and "both the annual incidence and geographic range are increasing" (Levia *et al.* 2012).

Although the significant jump in Lyme disease cases is relatively recent, ticks are not new to the area where the disease was first identified and named in the United States (although it had been previously recognized in Europe). The presence of ticks in the Northeast was established in the mid-eighteenth century by the Swedish botanist Pehr Kalm (1773). Kalm reported that the forests he visited in New York "abound" with ticks. But much of the forest that once covered the Northeast was removed as migrants from Europe began cutting trees and developing farms during the eighteenth and nineteenth centuries. In Concord, Massachusetts, the location of Walden Pond, made famous by Henry David Thoreau, for example, arriving European settlers found a landscape in which: "Oaks and chestnuts abound on hillsides. Dry sites are covered with sprouting oaks and somewhat-scrubby pitch pines" (Concord Historical Commission 2001: online). As the settlement expanded, however, wandering livestock grazed down the limited forage of the forest. Firewood demands for inefficient home-fireplaces cleaned out the forest understory. Trees were logged to build homes, typically framed with huge oak timbers following a cultural tradition used in English domestic construction. As the forest was penetrated and pushed back, pitch pines and sprouting oaks declined. Cultivation, pastures, and wandering livestock caused erosion and sedimentation of waterways. By the beginning of the American Revolution in 1775, only about 30 percent of the area surrounding Concord was forested, dropping to 25 percent by the end of the eighteenth century. The unrelenting deforestation process continued into the nineteenth century, resulting in a removal of 90 percent of local forests by 1850. With their natural habitat under assault, there was a significant drop in the numbers of white-tailed deer as well as forest-dwelling white-footed mice, and presumably of the ticks that feed upon these mammalian species.

With the rise of the Industrial Revolution, however, small New England farms were abandoned in large numbers, with younger generations migrating to the cities and their growing demands for labor. The resulting slow-down in tree cutting allowed forests to grow back over abandoned farmed land. By the end of the nineteenth century, forests once again covered 40 percent of Concord's environs. With the new trees, the deer and mice returned—and so too the black-legged tick, the immediate Lyme disease vector. Not just to Concord, but more broadly in New England where the emergence of suburbia thrust people into growing contact with Lyme disease vectors.

"If an acorn falls in the forest, will you contract Lyme disease?" This curious question appeared in an account reporting the findings of a study by Richard Ostfeld of the Cary Institute of Ecosystem Studies showing a statistical relationship between the bountifulness of forest acorn production in autumn and rates of nearby human Lyme disease (2011). As part of their evolutionary adaptation to species that gobble up their fallen seeds, oak trees drop few or even no acorns in most years. This strategy makes acorns an unreliable food source and dissuades mice and chipmunk populations from concentrating around oaks and consuming all of the acorns that might otherwise sprout new trees. In some years, however, oaks produce a bumper crop of acorns. These are called mast years, from the old English word for the nuts of forest trees accumulated on the ground. This tactic is called *predator satiation*, or safety in numbers (Molles 2002). Mice especially favor acorns because they are so large that they provide abundant proteins, carbohydrates, and fats, as well as minerals and vitamins. Acorns, in turn, are so big because of an adaptation to forested areas with thick layers of leaf litter collected over the years on top of the soil. Big acorns provide the energy needed for a seedling whose tap root must penetrate this barrier of decaying leaf litter to reach the mineral-rich soil below.

The study by Ostfeld found that autumns in which forests produced an abundance of acorns are followed the next summer by a significant jump in mice populations. High numbers of mice provide multiple hosts for ticks, including Lyme-infected ticks. Ostfeld's research showed that 90 percent of ticks that feed on mice in some areas are infected with Lyme. Ticks are dormant for almost a year after feeding on mice and then resume feeding on new hosts, including, if they are present in the environment, humans. As a result, there is more Lyme disease among nearby humans two years after a high acorn year. Notably, the size of deer populations in the area was not found to be predictive of more Lyme disease. The answer to Ostfeld's query, it appears, is yes: if acorns falls in the forest, especially in great numbers, the likelihood of contracting Lyme disease goes up for people living near or visiting infested areas.

But this story is even more complex, as it must include the role of Japanese Barberry. This hardy semi-deciduous shrub (specifically *Berberis thunbergii*), native to Japan and East

Asia, was brought to the United States in the late nineteenth century as landscape ornamentation, because it was seen as particularly attractive due to its red almost football-shaped berries, its requirement of minimum care, and its resistance to grazing deer predation. The original seeds in North America were sent from St. Petersburg, Russia to the Arnold Arboretum in Boston in 1875, and were the source of seeds planted in the New York Botanical Garden the following year (Silander and Klepis 1999). Decorative planting was promoted in various areas in New England, leading to the discovery that Barberry grew well in abandoned farm areas that were reverting to forest. It often was planted as a hedge to cordon off properties, as its thorny branches create an effective natural fence. The plant is hearty and is a prolific seed-producer with a high germination rate. Animals spread its seeds when they consume its berries, as do hikers in the treads of their boots. Because of its rapid spread and tendency to form dense stands in woodlands, wetlands, and meadows that displace native plant species, by the last decades of the twentieth century it had come to be redefined as an invasive species in at least 20 states.

Barberry is part of the story of Lyme disease, however, because its dense foliage creates a perfect, humid micro-environment on the ground that fosters the growth of mice and tick populations. According to Jeffrey Ward from the Department of Forestry and Horticulture at the Connecticut Agricultural Experiment Station in New Haven:

> When we measure the presence of ticks carrying the Lyme spirochete (*Borrelia burgdorferi*) we find 120 infected ticks where Japanese barberry is not contained [i.e. not under control], 40 ticks per acre where Barberry is contained, and only 10 infected ticks where there is no Barberry.
>
> *(Foran 2012: para. 8)*

Ward and colleagues studied several features of the triangular relationship between deer, ticks, and Barberry at 28 study sites in Connecticut. They found that in open grassy areas, ticks are only able to be active and feeding for 15–16 hours per day, but if they are protected by Japanese Barberry, the period of activity increases to 23 or 24 hours. This increases the likelihood of contracting Lyme disease for people passing through an area populated by Barberry plants. The intentional introduction by humans of what eventually came to be seen as an invasive—if decorative—landscaping plant, they found, contributed to the growing prevalence of Lyme disease.

Forest fragmentation is another human impact that promotes Lyme disease. This occurs when large, continuous forests are broken into smaller patches by the construction of roads, clearing for agriculture, suburbanization, or other human development projects. White-footed mice are more abundant in forest fragments in some parts of the countryside, probably because fewer of their common predators, like coyotes and foxes, and competitors, like rabbits, remain in fragmented patches. The mice, by contrast, tend to be particularly abundant in forested land segments smaller than five acres. Further, research by Ostfeld and co-workers found that forest patches smaller than three acres have an average of three times as many ticks as do larger fragments, and seven times more infected ticks (Allan *et al.* 2003). In the smallest patches, these researchers discovered that as many as 80 percent of the ticks are infected, the highest rate they have seen in their tick studies.

Additionally, there is the issue of tick-borne infection and anthropogenic climate change (Singer and Bulled 2014). Vector-borne diseases have been identified as one of the biggest health threats produced by climate change (Randolph 2009). Research by Jore (2013) in Norway, for example, found that the *Ixodes ricinus* (castor bean) tick has spread over an ever wider geographic range and at higher altitudes in mountainous areas because of factors like climate change. In her research, Jore explored the relationship between the distribution of infected ticks and microclimatic conditions at seven data collection points along the southern coast of Norway. She and her colleagues report that the degree of humidity has a substantial impact on the ability of the tick-borne encephalitis virus to survive and reproduce in the *Ixodes ricinus* tick and then be transmitted to humans in areas where these ticks previously were absent (Andreassen *et al.* 2012). Supporting Jore's work, Munderloh and Kurtti (2011: A148) note that "areas that are likely to experience increased or prolonged seasonal tick activity are . . . those located at the current extremes of the current range of distribution, areas where climate change will be felt most acutely." Especially important, then, is climate warming along the cold edges of species distribution, such as the changes promoting the movement of Lyme disease into Canada and tick-borne encephalitis to higher altitudes in Slovakia (Kilpatrick and Randolph 2012).

In an interesting twist that further reveals the unforeseen consequences of adverse human effects on the environment, it has been proposed that the extinction of passenger pigeons at the beginning of the Industrial Revolution may have facilitated the expansion of tick populations in reforested areas. Since these birds were exterminated, mice have been free of a major competitor for the windfall of acorns during mast years. Nomadic wanderers that specialized on a diet of mast acorns, the enormous flocks of passenger pigeons would have consumed huge quantities of their favored food source. The birds were so efficient at denuding the woods of acorns and other nuts that observers noted that both local wildlife and feral hogs struggled to find sufficient food after a passenger pigeon flock passed through an area. As a result of this fierce competition, mast years may not, in the past, have led to explosions in mice populations and the disease-bearing parasites that feed on them. As David Blockstein (1998: 1831), who has studied the history of passenger pigeons, writes: "Could the outbreaks of Lyme disease in the late 20th century have been a delayed consequence of the extinction of the passenger pigeon a century earlier?"

More broadly, this example raises the question of how many other diseases that now produce considerable human suffering and death are the hidden or not well-understood products of very complex environmental restructurings and disruptions caused by human activities. A partial answer to this question is found in the New York University Medical Center guide *Staying Healthy in a Risky Environment* which lists a vast number of health conditions that are adversely impacted by anthropogenic environmental factors (Upton and Graber 1993). Written by environmental health experts at New York University's Norton Nelson Institute of Environmental Medicine, this book examines the negative effects of environmental contaminants like pesticides and industrial water pollution on dermatological, neurological, respiratory, immunological, musculoskeletal, cardiological, and reproductive systems of the body.

Of critical importance in this regard is the vast array of chemicals that humans produce and use in enormous quantities. Over 140,000 different manufactured chemicals, as well as an equally immense number of unintentional chemicals produced by mining, burning fossil fuels, and waste disposal, are routinely dispersed around the planet (McDonough and Braungart 2002). Each year, 1,000 new industrial chemicals, most of which are untested for human and environmental health and safety, are added to this list. This figure reflects the continuous growth in the global production, trade, and use of chemicals and the expanding chemical intensification of both economies around the world and environments across the globe. In North America alone in 2006, the United Nations Environmental Programme (UNEP) (2012) estimates that 5.6 million tons of manufactured chemicals entered the environment; 1.8 million tons of this massive reconfiguring of the composition of the environment were substances classified as persistent, bioaccumulative in the bodies of living organisms, and poisonous to humans and other species. Among the chemicals annually released into the environment, 857,000 metric tons are compounds considered to be reproductive or developmental toxicants; that is, they are detrimental to fetuses in the womb and young children growing up in a chemicalized world (United Nations Environmental Programme 2012).

The abundant chemicals that originate in industrial activities are being released into the environments of both developed and developing countries. The developed world, with its comparatively longer industrial history, is the source of many examples of toxin rebound effects.

A telling case is that of lead, one of the best-known environmental threats to human health, and seen as "the mother of all industrial poisons [. . . .] [and] the paradigmatic toxin [linking] industrial and environmental disease" (Markowitz and Rosner 2002: 137). Lead has been used in human communities for over 5,000 years, but environmental levels in inhabited areas began to rise dramatically with the Industrial Revolution. Lead poisoning is linked to a wide range of health problems, including nervous system damage, decreased IQ, stunted growth, sterility, hyperactivity, impaired hearing, seizures, and death. Historically, in developed nations, lead was an ingredient in paint, gasoline, and a myriad consumer products. By the 1980s, people living in the United States were being exposed to ten times the levels that had occurred in the lead-using European civilizations of antiquity. In the period between 1978 and 1993, after the use of lead in gasoline in the United States was banned, people's blood-lead levels in the country declined by 78 percent (Kitman 2000). But significant damage had already been done. It is estimated that the average American lost about 6 IQ points from exposure to leaded gasoline and paint (Moench 2013). It took some time for the general public to realize how gravely the environment had been infused with industrial lead because the big producers, the Ethyl Corporation, General Motors, Standard Oil, Du Pont, and the American Petroleum Institute concealed information in their possession and aggressively fought efforts to regulate or curtail the use of lead (Shy 1990). The continued (and ongoing) use of lead long after its health and environmental consequences were well documented, reflects a far broader and worsening pattern of environmental health "mistakes" that characterizes human history. And that history continues. Although no level of lead has been found to be safe for human ingestion, lead continues to be used in personal products like lipstick and chapstick (Liu *et al.* 2013).

Who is in harm's way?

In developing nations, generally those with the fewest pollution controls and weakest health-care systems, which are places where chemical release into the environment is growing most rapidly, major contaminants include: pesticides from agricultural run-off; heavy metals from the production of cement; dioxins released during the recycling of electronic appliances; mercury and other heavy metals from mining and coal combustion; butyltins, heavy metals, and asbestos released during ship breaking and materials recycling activities; heavy metals used by tanneries; mutagenic dyes and heavy metals employed in the production of textiles; and toxic metals, solvents, polymers, and flame retardants used during the manufacture of electronic goods. Often the chemicalization of environments in developing countries is a consequence of their role in global production and consumption chains, such as the manufacture of leather goods in Bangladesh for large American clothing corporations, or the vigorous promotional efforts of sales representatives of multinational pesticide companies among small farmers in India (Hansen and Wethal 2015).

In Bangladesh, the tanning industry is centered in Hazaribagh, a commercial and industrial neighborhood of the capital city of Dhaka. In the period from June 2011 to July 2012, Bangladesh's increasingly lucrative leather industry exported over $650 million worth of leather products, including shoes, purses, suitcases, and belts. These goods are purchased by consumers in stores like Gap, Walmart, and Target. The tanneries in Hazaribagh operate in an enforcement-free zone that protects them from most government oversight and environmental regulations. Common chemicals in use in tanneries include sulfuric acid and sodium sulfide, both of which burn human skin, eye membranes, and the respiratory tract. Other chemicals harmful to humans which are used to tan hides include formaldehyde (used as a re-tanning agent and a preservative), azo colorants (used in the dyeing process), and pentachlorophenol (a preservative), all three of which are confirmed or potential human carcinogens which produce delayed health effects that only appear years after exposure. Leather dust, which fills the tanneries, is also carcinogenic in humans. Studies of tannery workers show that they display a notable array of health problems: premature aging, acid-burned and rash-covered skin, corroded fingers, body aches, dizziness and nausea, and disfigured or amputated limbs. People who live near tanneries, through which chemical releases pass in open gutters on their way to being dumped in the highly polluted rivers of Dhaka also report a high rate of health conditions, such as diarrhea, respiratory problems, and skin, stomach, and eye problems (Human Rights Watch 2012).

With the regular use of powerful chemicals comes the potential for calamitous accidents and these are not rare events. The U.S. National Response Center and Environment Canada (Parran 2009) reports that on average there are more than 40,000 reported chemical spill events annually in North America. Exemplary is a spill event that occurred in Charleston, West Virginia on 9 January 2014 when 10,000 gallons of the unregulated chemical known as 4-methylcyclohexane methanol (MCHM) leaked from an above-ground storage tank down to the waters of the Elk River. The flow of MCHM overwhelmed the carbon filtration system based in the West Virginia American Water treatment plant just downstream from the spill. Within a few days, over 400 people who consumed or were exposed to the contaminated water had to be treated for various symptoms including rashes, nausea, and vomiting. In response, Congress began hearings to establish why the leakage had occurred and how the crisis was handled. In the midst of the hearings, in February 2014, 82,000 tons of coal ash spilled into the Dan River in the border area between North Carolina and Virginia. Given the toxic character of the ash, state health officials quickly warned people to avoid swimming in or eating fish caught in the Dan River. A byproduct of burning coal, coal ash, which contains arsenic, mercury, lead, thallium, and other dangerous contaminants, is a significant threat to water quality. Across the country in California, scientists at the University of California at Davis reported in 2012 that over 250,000 people in the Tulare Lake Basin and Salinas Valley are at significant risk for nitrate contamination in their drinking water because of leaching into groundwater from heavily fertilized farm areas (Friend 2014). Examples like these could fill this Handbook. Together they affirm that the environmental balance sheet produced by our behaviors on the planet is rapidly being tilted toward disaster as the ecosystems and habitat sites of the world are converted into toxic hotspots contaminated by one or more deadly or damaging pollutants.

Recent assessment by the Pure Earth/Blacksmith Institute, an international non-profit organization focused on identifying and ameliorating areas with high toxin concentrations, concluded that air, water, and chemical pollution is now one of the major threats to health in the developing world, where it is responsible for over 10 million deaths per year, more than any of the world's major infectious diseases. The human casualties of pollution now number three times the combined total of the big three infectious killers: malaria, HIV/AIDS, and tuberculosis (Blacksmith Institute 2013). But, like other consequences of a global system structured by extensive social inequalities, the lion's share of pollution-related deaths occur among the poor in low- and middle-income countries, people who have the least resources to respond to a life threat they were not primarily responsible for creating. In essence, the poor of the world have become "the poisoned poor" (Global Alliance on Health and Pollution 2014). And in the words of Richard Fuller, president of the Pure Earth/Blacksmith Institute, for them, "the consequences are dire" (Leahy 2014: para. 3).

The work of organizations like the Blacksmith Institute is vital because calculating the full impact of environmental pollution is a challenging task. It is difficult to track the relationship between health and pollution for a number of reasons. First, the kinds of health statistics that are collected by public health offices and programs around the world measure diseases (which is a specific consequence), rather than pollution (which is diverse and the cause of various diseases). By contrast, in the case of infectious diseases, usually the cause (if not always the precise pathogen) is comparatively easy to establish. Second, debates over the science of environmental health are considerable and often intense. Complications include the fact that the scientific knowledge is never complete. For any given exposure, data may not be available about specific health effects, about health effects of exposures at specific dose levels, about responses among specific sub-groups of the population (e.g. by age or gender differences), or about effects of concomitant exposures to multiple substances (Johnson 2005: 976). Commonly, levels of exposure to environmental risks are uncertain or unknown because of limitations in the availability of detailed monitoring of pollutant release, and inevitable variations across local settings and among different population groups, such as different social classes. Toxic exposures can involve diverse pathways and complex processes. Third, although individual pollutants may be implicated in a range of health outcomes, few diseases are easily or directly attributable to single environmental pollutants. Frequently, there is an "evidence gap" between the experiences of sufferers from toxic exposures and the narrow parameters used in official records or that have been set by existing law. Finally, as Briggs (2003: 1) points out, prolonged "latency times, the effects of cumulative exposures, and multiple exposures to different pollutants which might act synergistically" are all factors that create additional difficulties in unraveling the connection linking environmental pollution and health outcomes.

Despite these challenges, in his book, *Poisoned Planet: How Constant Exposure to Man-made Chemicals is Putting your Life at Risk*, science writer Julian Cribb (2014) reviews a growing body of scientific evidence linking exposure to contaminants in food, water, air, and consumer products to a startling array of diseases, including various cancers, heart disease, diabetes, obesity, joint disorders, attention deficit hyperactivity disorder (ADHD), autism, Alzheimer's disease, and depression. In Cribb's assessment, Earth is now a poisoned planet that is infused with the substances deliberately or inadvertently formed in the process of extracting, making, using, burning or discarding the commodities of industrial production. Chemicals, some known to be harmful and others of unknown effect are in most of the possessions in our homes, the clothes we wear, the farms that produce the food we consume, the medicines and cosmetics we purchase, the roads we traverse, and the places where we work. The thousands of anthropogenic chemicals that are the life blood of modern industrial living have "infiltrated each and every one of our own bodies, the bodies of our growing children, our newborn infants, and even our unborn" (Schwartz-Nobel 2007: xvii) and remain as a body burden "in our blood, our brains, our flesh, and the deepest marrows of our bones" (2007: xviii)

Exposure occurs through multiple pathways, including inhalation of contaminated air and dust, ingestion of contaminated water and food, skin contact with chemical or contaminated products, and through both the placental barrier during pregnancy and from the consumption of contaminated breast milk (Prüss-Ustün *et al.* 2011).

Occupational exposures to various dusts, gases, fumes, and chemicals are contributing to chronic obstructive pulmonary disease, asthma, acute lower respiratory infections, and diseases like asbestosis, bronchitis, and silicosis. Maternal exposure to pesticides and chemicals in consumer products is tied to low-birth-weight newborns and pre-term infants. Very tiny particles of heavy metals like lead, cadmium, and mercury, as well as solvents, pollutant gases, and pesticides, are linked to heart disease and cerebrovascular disease. Crystalline silica dust, produced by abrasive blasting, stonecutting, rock drilling, quarrying, and tunneling, can be inhaled and causes the lungs to form scar tissue, reducing the ability to take in oxygen and making sufferers more susceptible to lung infections. Hearing loss, as well as mood changes, lethargy, and chest pains, are associated with workplace exposure to carbon disulfide during the manufacture of rayon, cellophane, synthetic rubber, and pesticides. Various skin diseases stem from exposures to antiseptics, aromatic amines in textiles, dyes, cement, glues, and preservatives in food.

The human immune system appears to be particularly sensitive to environmental pollutants like lead and cadium (Dietert and Piepenbrink 2006). Effects include impaired regulation of immune cell functioning. This disruption is especially found in children exposed to these pollutants. Another pollutant, gallium arsenide, which is used in the production of integrated circuits, LED lights, solar cells, and optical windows, inhibits the immune system from mounting appropriate responses to specific pathogens (Lewis 1996). Contaminant exposures are beginning to be seen as a disruptive force in vaccine-induced protection against infection and in the development of autoimmune diseases (Forrest 2008).

We now live in a world in which we are surrounded and permeated by human-produced chemicals. The vast array of toxins poured into the environment has triggered a silent, deadly, and disabling epidemic among humans and among the other species on the planet as well. It is part of the steep price we are paying for the ways that we live and the considerable profits that chemicals and chemical-releasing commodities bring to their producers.

Conclusion: anthropology and the risks of the anthropocene

Health has entered a new historic epoch in which environmental factors, under adverse human influence, are becoming a primary driver. This recognition prompted the leading British medical journal, *The Lancet*, to launch the Planetary Health initiative. The program, which is motivated by acceptance of the fundamental need to collectively achieve a world "that nourishes and sustains the diversity of life with which we coexist and on which we depend" (Horton 2014: 847), has significant implications for the anthropology of health and the environment.

The shift toward a planetary health perspective in population health thinking was triggered by the awareness that not only are human communities worldwide now multiply linked together by flows of commodities, ideas, people, and health-related influences from vectors to medicines, but the health and well-being of human communities also are multiply linked to the environment and to the other species on Earth. Internally, we are not fully human, in that our bodies are home to massive numbers of microorganisms, some of which are vital to our health; and externally, our survival, from the air we breathe to the food we consume, depends on numerous plant, animal, and other species. But these relationships are at grave risk today. As accurately stated in the Planetary Health manifesto: "Our patterns of overconsumption are unsustainable and will ultimately cause the collapse of our civilisation. The harms we continue to inflict on our planetary systems are a threat to our very existence as a species" (Horton *et al.* 2014: 847). A planetary health perspective, in short, reveals the fundamental ways in which human beings are not just agents of environmental change, but are also vulnerable objects of that change.

Humans have acquired through their ability to harness ever more powerful levels of energy, produce prodigious quantities of toxic waste, and rapidly increase their population size, the dangerous ability to overtax planetary boundaries and initiate significant and potentially irreversible environmental changes that may be catastrophic. From the standpoint of living systems, human and otherwise, we stand on the precipice of conditions that "can be called, without hyperbole, threatened apocalypse" (Foster *et al.* 2010: 109).

Moreover, central to the incipient planetary health movement, as it must be to any meaningful response to the dangers of climate change, is a commitment to equity in a world of unjust societies and unequal relations among societies. As articulated in the Planetary Health manifesto, there is a critical need for a vision of life on Earth that values social justice and fairness for all. Planetary health, in short, presents a model for guiding examination and action in the anthropology of health and the environment.

Notes

1 This definition differs considerably from the conventional one found in the field of energy economics, where the term labels systemic responses that take place with the introduction of new technologies that increase the efficiency of use of a particular resource.

References

Allan B, Keesing F and Ostfeld R 2003. Effect of forest fragmentation on Lyme disease risk. *Conservation Biology* 17(1): 267–272.

Andreassen A, Jore S, Cuber P, Dudman S, Tengs T, Isaksen K, Hygen H O, Viljugrei H, Anestad G, Ottesen P and Vainio K 2012. Prevalence of tick borne encephalitis virus in tick nymphs in relation to climatic factors on the southern coast of Norway. *Parasites & Vectors* 5: 177.

Berry W 1977. *The unsettling of America: Culture & agriculture.* San Francisco, CA: Sierra Club Books.

Blacksmith Institute 2013. *The top ten toxic threats: Cleanup, progress, and ongoing challenges.* New York: Blacksmith Institute.

Blockstein D 1998. Lyme disease and the passenger pigeon? *Science* 279(5358): 1831–1833.

Briggs D 2003. Environmental pollution and the global burden of disease. *British Medical Bulletin* 68(1): 1–24.

Chomsky N 2013. Who owns the Earth? *TruthOut*, Op-Ed, posted 5 July. www.truth-out. org/opinion/item/17402-who-owns-the-earth (accessed 1 April 2014).

Concord Historical Commission 2001. A brief visual history of Concord. In *Historic Resources Masterplan of Concord, Massachusetts.* www.concordlibrary.org/scollect/bhc/bhc.html (accessed 1 June 2014).

Cribb J 2014. *Poisoned planet: How constant exposure to man-made chemicals is putting your life at risk.* Crows Nest, NSW: Allen & Unwin.

Crist E 2012. Abundant Earth and the population question. In P Cafaro and E Crist (eds) *Life on the brink: Environmentalists confront overpopulation.* Athens: University of Georgia Press, pp. 141–153.

Dietert R and Piepenbrink M 2006. Lead and immune function. *Clinical Reviews in Toxicology* 36: 359–385.

Foran S 2012. Controlling Japanese Barberry helps stop spread of tick-borne diseases. *Uconn Today*, posted 22 February. http://today.uconn.edu/blog/2012/02/controlling-japanese-barberry-helps-stop-spread-of-tick-borne-diseases/ (accessed 5 June 2014).

Forrest B 2008. Correlation of cellular immune responses with protection against culture-confirmed influenza virus in young children. *Clinical and Vaccine Immunology* 15(7): 1042–1053.

Foster J B, Clark B and York R 2010. *The ecological rift: Capitalism's war on the Earth*. New York: Monthly Review Press.

Friend T 2014. Water in America: Is it safe to drink? *National Geographic*, posted 17 February. http://news.nationalgeographic.com/news/2014/02/140217-drinking-water-safety-west-virginia-chemical-spill-science/# (accessed 7 February 2015).

Global Alliance on Health and Pollution 2014. The poisoned poor: Toxic chemical exposures in low- and middle-income countries. www.gahp.net/new/wp-content/uploads/2013/09/GAHPPoisonedPoor_Report-Sept-2013.pdf (accessed 8 July 2014).

Hansen A and Wethal U 2015. *Emerging economies and challenges to sustainability theories, strategies, local realities*. Abingdon, UK: Routledge.

Horton R 2014. Reimagining the meaning of health. *The Lancet* 384(9939): 218.

Horton R, Beaglehole R, Bonita R, Raeburn J, McKee M and Wall S 2014. From public to planetary health: A manifesto. *The Lancet* 383(9920): 847.

Human Rights Watch 2012. *Toxic tanneries: The health repercussions of Bangladesh's Hazaribagh leather*. Amsterdam: Human Rights Watch.

Johnson B 2005. Environmental health policy. In H Frumkin (ed.) *Environmental Health from Global to Local*. San Francisco, CA: Jossey-Bass, pp. 961–987.

Judt T 2010. *Ill fares the land*. New York: Penguin Press.

Kalm P 1773. *Travels into North America, Volume 1. American journeys: eye witnessed accounts of early American explorations and settlement*. www.americanjourneys.org/aj-117a/summary/index.asp (accessed 3 August 2014).

Kilpatrick M and Randolph S 2012. Drivers, dynamics, and control of emerging vector-borne zoonotic diseases. *Lancet* 380(9857): 1946–1955.

Kitman J 2000. 8,500 years of lead, 79 years of leaded gasoline. *The Nation*, 20 March. www.thenation.com/article/timeline (accessed 14 November 2014).

Kopnina H and Keune H (eds) 2013. *Health and environment: Social science perspectives*. New York: Nova Science Publishers.

Leahy S 2014. In developing world, pollution kills more than disease. Inter Press Service. www.ipsnews.net/2014/06/in-developing-world-pollution-kills-more-than-disease/ (accessed 6 October 2015).

Levia T, Kilpatrick M, Mangel M and Wilmers C 2012. Deer, predators, and the emergence of Lyme disease. *Proceedings of the National Academy of Sciences of the United States of America* 109(20): 10942–10947.

Lewis T 1996. Gallium arsenide selectively suppresses antigen processing by splenic macrophages for CD4+ T cell activation. *The Journal of Pharmacology and Experimental Therapeutics* 278(3): 1244–1251.

Liu S, Hammond K and Rojas-Cheatam A 2013. Concentrations and potential health risks of metals in lip products. *Environmental Health Perspectives* 121(6): 705–710.

McDonough W and Braungart M 2002. *Cradle to cradle: Remaking the way we live*. New York: North Point Press.

Markowitz G and Rosner D 2002. *Deceit and denial: The deadly politics of industrial pollution*. Berkeley: University of California Press.

Moench B 2013. Mankind: Death by corporation. *Truthout*, Op-Ed, posted 26 June. http://truth-out.org/opinion/item/17178-mankind-death-by-corporation (accessed 23 June 2014).

Molles M 2002. *Ecology: Concepts and applications*. New York: McGraw-Hill.

Munderloh U and Kurtti T 2011. Emerging and re-emerging tick-borne diseases: New challenges at the interface of human and animal health. In Committee on Lyme Disease and Other Tick-Borne Diseases *et al. Critical needs and gaps in understanding: Prevention, amelioration, and resolution of Lyme and other tick-borne diseases: The short-term and long-term outcomes. Workshop report*. Washington, DC: National Academies Press, pp. A142–A166.

Ostfeld R 2011. *Lyme disease: The ecology of a complex system*. Oxford: Oxford University Press.

Paddock, C and Telford S 2011. Through a glass darkly: The global incidence of tick-borne diseases. In Committee on Lyme Disease and Other Tick-Borne Diseases *et al. Critical needs and gaps in* understanding: Prevention, amelioration, and resolution of Lyme and other tick-borne diseases: The short-term and long-term outcomes. Workshop report.* Washington, DC: National Academies Press, pp. 221–266.

Parran S 2009 Preparing for chemical spill containment in the 21st century. *Environmental Science & Engineering Magazine* 22(3), pp. 40–41.

Prüss-Ustün A, Vickers C, Haefliger P and Bertollini R 2011. Knowns and unknowns on burden of disease due to chemicals: A systematic review. *Environmental Health* 10: 9.

Randolph S 2009. Tick-borne disease systems emerge from the shadows: The beauty lies in molecular detail, the message in epidemiology. *Parasitology* 136(12): 1403–1413.

Schwartz-Nobel L 2007. *Poisoned nation: Pollution, greed, and the rise of deadly epidemics.* New York: St Martin's Press.

Sheppard S (ed.) 2005. *The selected writings of Sir Edward Coke.* Indianapolis, IN: Liberty Fund.

Shy C 1990. Lead in petrol: The mistake of the XXth century. *World Health Statistics Quarterly* 43(3): 168–176.

Silander J and Klepis D 1999. The invasion ecology of Japanese Barberry (*Berberis thunbergii*) in the New England landscape. *Biological Invasions* 1: 189–201.

Singer, M and Bulled N 2014. Ectoparasitic syndemics: Polymicrobial tick-borne disease interactions in a changing anthropogenic landscape. *Medical Anthropology Quarterly.* doi: 10.1111/maq.12163

Soveig J 2013. The impact of climatic factors upon Zoonotic diseases: An epidemiological investigation. Doctoral dissertation, Norwegian School of Veterinary Sciences, Oslo.

United Nations Environmental Programme 2012. *Towards sound management of chemicals: Health and environmental effects.* McClean, VA: GPS Publishing.

Upton A and Graber E (eds) 1993. *Staying healthy in a risky environment.* New York: Simon and Schuster.

28

MULTI-SPECIES ENTANGLEMENTS, ANTHROPOLOGY, AND ENVIRONMENTAL HEALTH JUSTICE

Melanie Rock

Introduction

In medical anthropology, environments tend to be treated as background or context. Further, medical anthropologists often imply that environments consist of inert spaces occupied by humans, rather than as lively places that are also inhabited by non-human species. It is no wonder, then, that anthropologists who care deeply about environments or multi-species interactions have tended to work in subfields other than medical anthropology. This state of affairs, however, is changing as medical anthropologists and allied researchers concern themselves with multi-species interactions, hierarchies, and ecologies during fieldwork and in their writings (Green 2012; Hinchliffe 2015; Rock *et al.* 2007; Rock *et al.* 2009; Singer 2009; Singer *et al.* 2011). The growing popularity of the term 'entanglement' relates to these trends (Nading 2013).

In anthropology and beyond, references to 'entanglement' signal attention to how human bodies entwine and intermingle with one another, as well as with non-human bodies, technologies, other materials, and physical environments. Conceptually, ethically, and methodologically, the notion of entanglement lends itself to ethnographic engagements with "how humans – even in the context of disease – strive to live well together with animals" (Nading 2013: 67). Indeed, multi-species interactions may encompass emotional bonds, affective registers, and institutionalized protections (Nading 2013; Rock and Degeling in press). Yet multi-species entanglements do not all bring about advantages, or at least not for all humans or other animals (Blue and Rock 2011; Haraway 2008; Rock and Degeling 2015).

Accordingly, the concept of 'environmental health justice' must be expanded beyond its anthropocentric foundations. Initially, advocates and allied scholars rallied around the concept of environment health justice to address inequity in the socio-spatial distribution of risk, including pollution (Masuda *et al.* 2010). More recently, scholars have framed inequity in people's access to and capacity to derive benefits from environmental features, such as attractive parks and beachfronts, as a political matter (Frohlich and Abel 2014; Masuda *et al.* 2010). A third wave in the conceptualization of environmental health justice is now underway, which emphasizes multi-species entanglements (Rock and Degeling 2015).

This chapter considers the growing interest in multi-species entanglements as an opportunity to bring medical anthropology and environmental anthropology into deeper dialogue, through discussions of social justice that acknowledge the presence and absence of non-human animals in shared environments. At the same time, consideration for multi-species entanglements could connect medical anthropology and environmental anthropology with related discussions in other disciplines and fields, including geography and public health. The chapter begins with an overview of medical anthropology, particularly as regards theories of disease, illness, sickness, and suffering. This overview highlights the fact that non-human species have not featured prominently in medical anthropology and that anthropologists interested in non-human animals have had little to say about disease or health. Next, I review parallel developments in geography. This review suggests that, by comparison with anthropology, conversations regarding non-human species are more advanced in that discipline. Finally, to demonstrate the importance of multi-species interactions and ecologies for medical anthropology, I discuss three recent monographs that pivot on somewhat different conceptualizations of 'entanglement' (Lock 2013; Nading 2014; van Dooren 2014). These monographs and related sources imply that scholars are referencing interdependence among humans, non-human species, and environments through six overlapping uses of the term 'entanglement':

1 descriptive, sometimes explicitly evoking evolutionary theory;
2 rhizomatic, in the sense of being intrinsically connected and diffusely grounded;
3 phenomenological, in the sense of subjective embodiment;
4 physical or material, sometimes despite temporal and spatial distance;
5 manifold, to the extent that coherence requires coordination over time and space;
6 synergistic, to the extent that deleterious effects compound one another, while flourish-ing entails multiple bodies, species, and spaces.

Medical anthropology: an overview

In a landmark paper, titled "The Anthropologies of Illness and Sickness," Young (1982) made a substantial contribution to the establishment and development of medical anthropology as a distinctive field of study. Disease, according to what Young (1982: 270) wrote at the time, consisted of "organic pathologies and abnormalities." As such, he considered diseases to be the proper preserve of scientists and physicians and to be off-limits to anthropologists as a suitable object of inquiry.

Young recognized that anthropologists might study illness, which he defined (following Kleinman *et al.* 1978) as "a person's perceptions or experiences of certain socially devalued states including, but not limited to, disease" (Young 1982: 265). But he argued that anthropologists ought to pay more attention to sickness, which he defined as

the process through which worrisome behavioral and biological signs, particularly ones originating in disease, are given socially recognizable meanings i.e., they are made into symptoms and socially significant outcomes . . . *Sickness is, then a process for socializing disease and illness.*

(*Young 1982: 270; emphasis in original*)

In a crucial move, Young (1982) reinterpreted the anthropology of magic and religion as consonant with the anthropology of illness and sickness. He regarded *Witchcraft, Oracles and Magic among the Azande* (Evans-Pritchard 1976 [1937]) as an exemplar. Evans-Pritchard was writing about multi-species interactions because the infectious disease known as trypano-somiasis was central to his research project (Singer *et al.* 2011). Trypanosomiasis circulates via tsetse flies and continues to have devastating impacts in Africa (Palmer *et al.* 2014). Neither Young (1982) nor, apparently, Evans-Pritchard (1976 [1937]) asked how non-human species and ecological conditions fit into local cosmology and corresponding practices of relevance to sickness and health.

Meanwhile, anthropologists regard Evans-Pritchard's (1960 [1940]) *The Nuer* as a milestone in both environmental anthropology and in multi-species ethnography (Mullin 1999; Shanklin 1985). Even as Evans-Pritchard emphasized that environmental conditions and cattle were crucial to Nuer well-being and their ideas about living well, *The Nuer* is not generally regarded as highly relevant to medical anthropology. Current thinking about environmental health justice renders Evans-Pritchard's work among the Nuer, as well as his research with the Azande, as highly relevant to connecting environmental anthropology with medical anthropology.

A little more than a decade later after the publication of Young's review, Lock (1993a) pointed to wide-ranging analyses of embodiment in anthropology and beyond, and she distinguished between studies of individuated bodies, collective bodies, and political bodies (see also Lock 1993b; Scheper-Hughes and Lock 1987). In reviewing the anthropology of embodiment, Lock (1993a) emphasized what she called "local biologies" to account for variation, at multiple scales, in people's ways of defining disease, responding to societal pressures, and conceptualizing health. In her rendering of local biologies, environments were given prominence, yet in ways that pointed to complexity in the nexus among epistemology, ontology, and embodiment (see also Lock 1993b). This concept has proven influential in medical anthropologists' engagements with the imprint of social hierarchies, geographies, lifestyles, and symbolism on disease, illness, and sickness (Brotherton and Nguyen 2013). Recently, Lock's conceptualization of local biologies anchored ethnographic research focused on multi-species entanglements in health and disease (Nading 2014), as will be discussed in more detail below.

In keeping with developments beyond anthropology, and especially in the philosophy and sociology of science, biomedicine has increasingly become framed as suitable for ethno-graphic study (Franklin 1995). In doing so, the historical, political, economic, and geographic conditions that account for the presence of certain diseases have tended to be treated as "context" (Lock *et al.* 2000). Diseases, by consequence, no longer appeared off-limits for ethnographic study by anthropologists or other ethnographers (see also Young 1980). The coordination of bodies and disease, temporally and geographically, has become a key analytic concern in medical anthropology and related fields (Kearns and Moon 2002; Mol 2002; Mykhalovskiy and Weir 2004).

But why do some sicknesses manifest or materialize to a greater extent than others in a given place or time? Nguyen and Peschard (2004) addressed this question through a synthesis of research from medical anthropology and the field of public health known as social epidemiology (i.e. the study of the extent to which hierarchy impacts on the distribution of diseases in human populations). To take into account what might be termed broadly as social or political environments, their discussion emphasized human suffering (Kleinman *et al.* 1997). Nevertheless, Nguyen and Peschard (2004) did not emphasize that people share environments with non-human life forms. For example, they describe HIV/AIDS as a purely human phenomenon, whereas non-human primates were probably HIV's original source (Rock *et al.* 2009). Furthermore, the very forces that create and exacerbate impoverishment in human populations also put pressure on non-human primates to adapt; for instance, in situations of armed conflict and habitat loss (Fuentes 2012). Environmental health justice ought to encompass humanity's closest biological relatives still alive today; that is, non-human primates such as chimpanzees, gorillas, and orangutans.

Similar to the review of medical anthropology and social epidemiology undertaken by Nguyen and Peschard (2004), recent *Annual Review of Anthropology* articles on global health (Janes and Corbett 2009) and on resiliency (Panter-Brick 2014), respectively, do not make much of non-human life in problematizing inequity. A closer look, however, reveals that non-human animals are deeply implicated in the globalization of sickness and health, as well as in localized embodiments of resiliency. Trypanosomiasis is a prime example (Palmer *et al.* 2014; Singer *et al.* 2011), and so is dengue (Nading 2014). More broadly, non-human animals are key sources of food for human populations, and nutrition remains crucial to resisting and surviving infections (Rock *et al.* 2009).

In addition, discussions about globalized and localized inequities in relation to pharmaceuticals and biomedicine have begun to extend to non-human animals, for non-human animals routinely serve as surrogates for human beings in biomedical research. This state of affairs complicates discussions of social suffering, public policy, empathy, biomedical science, and multi-species entanglements (Davies 2012; Dennis 2013; Rock *et al.* 2007; Schlich *et al.* 2009; Schlünder and Schlich 2009). For example, dogs served as experimental models in the research that led to insulin therapy, and then slaughtered cattle and pigs provided the insulin used to treat diabetes in people (Bliss 2000 [1982]). Today, most insulin to treat diabetes is based on recombinant DNA technology, but now the systematic slaughter of cattle and pigs converts into a reliable source of insulin to extend the lives of people's diabetic cats and dogs, and pet-food besides (Blue and Rock 2011; Rock and Babinec 2008). Dogs and cats, overall, tend to receive more sympathy and better treatment than do farm animals (Blue and Rock 2011; Haraway 2008; Keck and Ticktin 2015). Thus environmental health injustice manifests not only in relationships among humans, but also in people's hierarchal distinctions among non-human animals.

Whereas medical anthropologists have not paid much attention to non-human animals, anthropological reviews of human interactions with non-human animals have not emphasized disease, sickness, suffering, or health (Mullin 1999; Shanklin 1985). In his recent article on humans' interactions with non-human primates, however, Fuentes (2012) stresses that hierarchy and conflict among humans has resulted in suffering among non-human primates. In particular, agricultural expansion has eroded the habitats of chimpanzees and gorillas, while countless female orangutans have been slaughtered so that their babies can be taken away to sell as pets. Earlier, Sapolsky (2004) argued that health outcomes are unevenly spread along hierarchical lines in primate populations, including human populations. With regard to social epidemiology, Sapolsky's (2004) synthesis overlaps with that of Nguyen and Peschard (2004). Yet unlike Fuentes (2012), neither Sapolsky (2004) nor Nguyen and Peschard (2004) concerned themselves with non-human primates and the environmental conditions that these animals require to survive – never mind thrive – as matters of social justice.

Ingold (2012) includes some discussion of primatology and ethology, but even when arguing that more attention ought to be paid to life forms, he does not pose questions about disease, sickness, suffering, or health. Nevertheless, Ingold's (2011) examination of "being alive" provides insights for conceptualizing health and well-being as multi-species flourishing

(Rock and Degeling 2015; Rock *et al.* 2014). Meanwhile, recent review articles by anthropologists on climate change have pointed to ecological changes as drivers of disease incidence in non-human animals (Cassidy 2012; Crate 2011). These articles do not, however, emphasize the extent to which multi-species interactions and environmental conditions matter for both human and non-human lives (except for Fuentes 2012).

Indeed, to bring together questions about human health, environmental integrity, and animal welfare, as is being done under the auspices of "One Health" (Craddock and Hinchliffe 2015; Green 2012; Rock *et al.* 2009), is to posit associations and equivalencies that run counter to foundational thinking in Western "common sense" (Povinelli 2001). That is because Western philosophy, science, and law all presume a sharp distinction and hierarchal distinction between human and non-human lives (Descola 2013 [2005]). Accordingly, it can seem sensible, even ethical, to imagine that humans should be masters of all other animals and ought to shape environmental conditions to serve human interests (Rock and Degeling 2015). Rather than confirming psychological divergence, however, biomedical research ultimately demonstrates that many non-human animals resemble human beings, not only physically, but also socially and emotionally (Dennis 2013; Johnson and Degeling 2011; Schlich *et al.* 2009). Overall, selectivity in people's commitments to one another cannot be adequately understood without consideration of selectivity in people's commitments to non-human beings (Rock and Degeling 2015). When heterogeneity in people's commitments to non-human beings are taken into account, then questions about the environmental dimensions of inequality, sickness, suffering, and health become more complicated but also, perhaps, more tractable in anthropological terms. Anthropologists concerned with environmental conditions have much to offer studies and reflections about the relevance of multi-species entanglements for health equity.

Medical, health, and animal geographies: an overview

Geographers increasingly differentiate 'medical' from 'health' research, whereas anthropologists may not. Research in 'medical geography' regards biomedical definitions of disease as foundational, interfaces with social epidemiology, and often involves spatial analyses to optimize the delivery of professional services (Kearns and Moon 2002; Parr 2004). By contrast, research in 'health geography' tends to question biomedical definitions of disease, attend to embodied experience in diverse environments, and distill subjective meanings (Kearns and Moon 2002; Parr 2004). Spatial arrangements for healthcare have been prioritized in medical geography, while concerns such as self-help, family dynamics, and community engagement have received more attention in health geography (Parr 2003).

Differences in orientation between medical and health geography resonate with the distinctions between disease, illness, and sickness in medical anthropology (Young 1982). Also, a preoccupation with spatialized hierarchy in both medical and health geography (Parr 2004) overlaps with medical anthropology (Kleinman *et al.* 1997; Lock 1993a; Nguyen and Peschard 2004; Young 1982). This preoccupation is also central to explorations of environmental health justice in public health (Frohlich and Abel 2014; Masuda *et al.* 2010). Indeed, key contributors to the contemporary conceptualization of environmental health justice in public health are, in fact, geographers by training (Masuda *et al.* 2010). Overall, geographers have tended to place greater emphasis on human–environment interfaces in sickness and with more emphasis overall on what is meant by health than have medical anthropologists.

Geographers have recently turned their attention toward human interactions with non-human animals, toward interactions among non-human animals, and toward non-human species such as plants, bacteria, and parasites that circulate among and between human bodies. The concept of dwelling, as developed by the anthropologist Ingold (2000, 2008) to express a phenomenological orientation that acknowledges non-human animals and ecological dynamics in theorizing embodiment, has been taken up enthusiastically in the emerging subfield of animal geography (Buller 2014; Johnston 2008). In fact, a growing number of geographers are uncomfortable with the very notion of "human geography" because social relations are never solely or purely human in nature (Buller 2014). More-than-human geography draws attention to non-human entities such as land and water, but also to non-human animals and to the dynamic interplay between non-human and human life, at scales ranging from the microscopic to the macroscopic.

Animal geography, furthermore, increasingly straddles medical and health geographies. Crises and controversies that implicate non-human animals have captivated the attention of geographers (Buller 2014). Even when these studies focus on the spatial distribution of diseases, as compared with human suffering, they still expand the domain of medical geography simply by calling attention to non-human life. And when geographers do broach subjective experiences of illness, suffering, and well-being by way of animal-involved diseases or injuries, their analyses differ from mainstream medical geography in that humanist suppositions are challenged. Such questioning implies an expansion and recasting of geographers' research techniques along with broader philosophical and ethical commitments (Buller 2015a). For example, geographers have studied biomedical laboratories as networked places where select humans interact with select non-human animals (Davies 2012), whereas cities everywhere teem with human and non-human life (Hinchliffe and Whatmore 2006).

Entanglements in sickness and in health

In a compelling review article, Nading (2013) explores the implications of multi-species entanglements for social studies of disease, sickness, suffering, and health. Starting off with the supposition (2013: 60) that "health" comprises "the combination of practice and epistemology by which people confront *disease*, the manifestation of symptoms associated with biophysical disorder, and *illness*, the socially and culturally mediated experience of suffering," Nading goes on to say that health ultimately entails "the production of life itself" (2013: 61). Yet as observed by Nading (2013: 61), sicknesses may prompt local people, health professionals, and social researchers to ask penetrating questions about how and to what extent "humans are materially, economically and even symbolically connected to animals."

In historical works, insect-borne infectious diseases, such as malaria and yellow fever, have been prominent. These works concern themselves with disease ecology, but Nading (2013) argues that the disease ecology tradition has tended to reify species categories. More specifically, rather than highlighting fluidity among individual bodies and variation within species, which are essential to biological mutations and evolutionary theory, Nading contends that the disease ecologists have tended to regard non-human species as homogenous things that behave like discrete variables. Interest is resurging in linkages between humans and non-human species in contemporary disease ecology; yet, instead of concentrating on historical origins, disease ecologists today pride themselves on being future-oriented and proactive. In these respects, studies in disease ecology reflect the current concern with preparedness (Lakoff 2008). Studies of disease ecology in the vein of 'conservation medicine' (e.g. preservation of non-human primates' habitats) pay close attention to anthropogenic changes and social inequality among humans and between humans and non-human animals (e.g. Saj *et al.* 2006).

Nevertheless, "the political side of disease ecology remains largely unexamined" (Nading 2013: 65). Whereas future-oriented and proactive applications have become prominent in disease ecology, they are absolutely central to discussions of non-human populations in relation to economic growth and international security (Nading 2013). The extent to which multi-species realities are implicated in politics is only now being theorized (Hinchliffe *et al.* 2013). In doing so, multi-species entanglements are receiving emphasis (Nading 2013: 67).

Yet multi-species entanglements can involve emotional affinity with non-human animals in roles such as family pets and service animals for people with disabilities, as well as a sense of attachment to wildlife or farm animals (Blue and Rock 2011; Buller 2015b; Nading 2013; Rock and Degeling 2015; Solomon 2010). In other words, not all ways of life seek to separate humans from non-human species, even though differentiation to the extent of outright segregation on the basis of biological species has often been idealized in biomedicine and public health (Hardy 2003). To deepen appreciation for the growing interest in human–animal studies among anthropologists and geographers, in particular, I turn now to three recent ethnographies by Lock (2013), Nading (2014), and van Dooren (2014) that differ by topic, yet have in common a core concern with entanglements.

Mosquito Trails: Ecology, Health, and the Politics of Entanglement

Nading's (2014) *Mosquito Trails: Ecology, Health and the Politics of Entanglement* presents a sensitive portrait of multi-species relations and political ecology in urbanized Nicaragua. Through a focus on dengue fever, Nading shows that whereas donors and senior government officials may orient toward biosecurity and disease eradication, householders and front-line community health workers positively emphasize entanglement with non-human species, notably – but by no means exclusively – with mosquitos. There are aesthetic and affective dimensions to local people's entanglements with mosquitos and other non-human life forms. For example, the participants in Nading's fieldwork manifested keen interest in insect ecology as a way to think deeply about the place where they lived (see also McNaughton 2012; Patterson 2015). Yet public health directives may overlook, dismiss, or even preclude local priorities and preferences.

In *Mosquito Trails*, Nading (2014: 11) defines entanglement as "the unfolding, often incidental attachments and affinities, antagonisms and animosities that bring people, non-human animals and things into each other's worlds." Accordingly, entanglement "is at once a material, temporal and spatial condition" (Nading 2014: 11).

Nading turns to quantum physics to buttress his conceptualization of entanglement in material terms. In this scientific field, entanglement refers to the realization that particles may be linked, to the extent that a change in one is accompanied by a change in another, even when far apart. A historical treatment describes the concept of entanglement in quantum physics as follows:

> Any time two entities interact, they entangle. It doesn't matter if they are photons (bits of light), atoms (bits of matter), or bigger things made of atoms like dust motes, microscopes, cats or people. The entanglement persists no matter how far these entities separate, as long as they don't subsequently interact with anything

else – an almost impossibly tall order for a cat or a person, which is why we don't notice the effect.

(Gilder 2009: 3)

Quantum physics thus disrupts classical models of reality, embodiment, and causality in ways that are only beginning to be taken up in anthropology and other social sciences (Barad 2007). Inspired by the meaning of entanglement in quantum physics, Nading (2014: 11) says, "In dengue, human and mosquito bodies, like mosquito and viral bodies, are both two and one at the same time." His approach builds on Haraway's (2008) analytic focus on *relationships*, rather than on seemingly discrete objects, things, or bodies. Nading also follows Mol's (2002) concern with bodily multiplicity in biomedicine, which has since been extended to non-human species, veterinary medicine, and environmental health justice (Law and Mol 2008, 2011; Rock and Babinec 2008; Rock and Degeling 2015).

Entanglements have temporal dimensions, which Nading (2014: 11) regards as "results of contemporary material attachments," but also as the basis for narratives. Relevant narratives for dengue fever in Nading's fieldwork included the post-colonial history of Nicaragua (e.g. the Sandinista movement's emphasis on community participation in public policy), along with epidemiological and biomedical accounts of global risk. Specifically, once people have been exposed to one of a handful of serotypes of dengue, then they are known to be much more likely to become severely ill following exposure to another of dengue's serotypes. This epidemiological truth helps to shape, but never wholly determines, the actions of community health workers charged with the prevention and control of dengue. Community health workers evinced sophistication as regards environmental health injustice; for example, to appreciate why some of their neighbors stockpiled garbage to sell on the international market for recyclables, even as backyard stockpiles breed mosquitos and thus increase the likelihood of dengue infection.

Spatially, entanglements may vary in scale and in geographic characteristics. Regarding dengue in Nicaragua, Nading (2014: 11) notes that the disease is spatially "rhizomatic," for "clear beginnings, middles, and ends" are lacking (see Colman 2010 for elaboration). Moreover, dengue in the place where Nading (2014: 11) was based "is both a story of a community's struggle with a 'global' pandemic and that of a highly local set of problems, from earthquakes and floods to gang violence and municipal politics." In other words, environmental health injustice was a central concern in the field setting, even if not phrased in precisely these terms.

In tracing how dengue viruses, mosquitos, and human bodies combine over time in a particular place, Nading (2014) expands Lock's (1993b) conceptualization of local biologies to consider how material and social conditions are reproduced *not only within and via human bodies, but also within and via non-human bodies*. Environments, from this perspective, do not cause health problems except insofar as "humans and non-humans incorporate each other's actions" (Nading 2014: 11). Such "incorporations" sometimes occur through direct interactions; at other times, they take place over long distances and extended periods of time. Nading's ethnography thus suggests that environmental health justice entails careful consideration of local conditions and observable interactions, but of how multi-species networks with global reach (Blue and Rock 2011).

The Alzheimer Conundrum: Entanglements of Dementia and Aging

Lock's latest monograph (2013), titled *The Alzheimer Conundrum: Entanglements of Dementia and Aging*, builds on her earlier work on biomedical and broader societal responses to aging

(Lock 1993b). This time, however, she has focused her energies on brain science and medical treatments for types of dementia, especially Alzheimer's disease (AD). In orienting toward the persistence of uncertainty, despite and even as a result of brain scientists' efforts to prevent and treat different types of dementia, Lock contrasts a 'localization theory' with an 'entanglement theory' of AD. The localization thesis predominates in brain science and biomedicine, and emphasizes neuropathology within individual bodies. By contrast, the entanglement thesis emphasizes that human experience, including dementia, is inextricable from surrounding environments. Alzheimer's disease scientists who emphasize entanglements are in the minority, and "their research is driven less by a search for a cure and more by an effort to find out who among us are at increased risk for AD on the basis, largely, of social, political, and environmental factors" (Lock 2013: 20).

Lock's rendering of bodily entanglements with environments does not emphasize multi-species dimensions. Nevertheless, Lock's examination of AD underlines that genetically speaking, people exhibit diversity, but also share a great deal with non-human animals – to the extent of underpinning laboratory research with non-human animals such as mice. Yet as one AD researcher stressed in an interview, "The mouse is a good model but we have to keep in mind that a mouse is just a mouse – they are not human" (Lock 2013: 151).

As Lock (2013) repeatedly emphasizes, disparities persist in people's capacity to live in accordance with recommendations on healthy lifestyles. In combination with ongoing discussions in public health (Frohlich and Abel 2014; Masuda *et al.* 2010), Lock's (2013) mediations on AD point in the direction of environmental health justice. Furthermore, environmental health justice as regards AD implicates multi-species entanglements. In particular, the potential for nutrition to have a positive impact on AD outcomes certainly carries implications for plant and animal life. Meanwhile, regular walking can help in preventing AD and in curbing its progression. Plants and non-human animals are connected to outdoor walking, to an extent that is gaining notice in professional fields such as urban planning and public health. For example, regular dog-walking could help in averting AD, as well as in controlling Type 2 diabetes or warding off depression (Peel *et al.* 2010; Toohey *et al.* 2013). Yet discussions of policies or programs to encourage dog-walking, or bird-watching for that matter, do not fit readily into medical anthropology at the present time (Pinder 2007; Rock *et al.* 2007). With more attention paid to environmental health justice in anthropology, the importance of multi-species entanglements for preventing disease and promoting well-being could become more visible.

Flight Ways: Life and Loss at the Edge of Extinction

Whereas multi-species entanglements remain implicit to Lock's (2013) discussion of environmental dimensions in healthy aging and social justice, non-human beings are central to Thom van Dooren's (2014) *Flight Ways: Life and Loss at the Edge of Extinction*. More specifically, van Dooren's monograph centers on "avian entanglements" (van Dooren 2014: 4). By this phrasing, van Dooren means to say that birds and their relationships with one another and with other species, including humans, were pivotal to how his study was conceived and conducted. Methodologically, his approach could meaningfully be described as a synthesis of ethnology with ethology (Lestel 2006). Indeed, van Dooren's writing evinces immersion and empathy in the tradition of ethnography (Stewart 1998), even as he takes pains to stop short of anthropomorphizing.

Thom van Dooren's engagement with ethnological and ecological research is fundamentally sympathetic as regards the scientists and the birds themselves, allowing him to elaborate on scientific sources with feeling. He calls into question people's selective affinities with non-human beings; for example, the extent to which people's dogs are permitted to disrupt the lives of penguins in Sydney, Australia. Furthermore, as illustrated by his investigation of the lives and deaths of vultures along with those of people in India, poverty implicates both human and non-human beings. Poor farmers use veterinary drugs to prolong the lives of cattle as agricultural labor; yet vultures feed on the carcasses of cattle, and these drugs are painfully toxic to vultures; the resulting decimation of vulture populations means that vultures can no longer reliably dispose of human remains; increasingly, feral dogs feed on cattle carcasses, and one additional consequence is to increase poor people's rabies risk.

Ethical questions about the kinds of lives that are possible and desirable, for people and for fellow creatures, underpin *Flight Ways*. Thom van Dooren reserves his most critical stance for research and applications that privilege the species body over quality of life for individual birds, most notably when discussing efforts to revitalize whooping-crane populations in North America. Mainly due to hunting and habitat loss (i.e. environmental health injustice as regards not only these birds, but also in the displacement and decimation of Indigenous peoples), only 20 or so whooping cranes remained by the early twentieth century (van Dooren 2014: 89–90). Yet as van Dooren takes pains to document, efforts to preserve whooping cranes as a species entail inflicting harm on individual birds of other species, as conscripts to care for whooping-crane eggs. And some whooping cranes live in captivity, so that their offspring might experience the freedoms typical of wildlife.

To conceptualize "avian entanglements" as a matter of social justice in the burgeoning field of environmental humanities, Haraway (2008) was a key source of inspiration (van Dooren 2014: 4). In turn, Haraway's concern with the element of selection that is inherent to any instantiation of multi-species flourishing might recall the closing chapter of *On the Origin of Species*, wherein Darwin (1870) invites readers

> to contemplate an entangled bank, clothed with plants of many kinds, with birds singing on the bushes, with various insects flitting about, and with worms crawling through the damp earth, and to reflect that these elaborately constructed forms, so different from one another, and dependent on each other in so complex a manner, have all been produced by laws acting around us.
>
> (Darwin 1870: 425)

Extinctions are the focus for van Dooren in *Flight Ways*, but urbanization also displaces some humans and non-human animals, even as cities make possible hitherto unimaginable ways of life (Hinchliffe and Whatmore 2006; van Dooren and Rose 2012). The farming of animals, whether fish or fowl or mammalian, is another vivid example of how multi-species entanglements selectively foster and eliminate ways of life – and actual lives (Blue and Rock 2011; Buller 2013).

Following on from Haraway (2008), van Dooren (2014: 8) elaborates on a distinction that has been made between "life forms" and "forms of life." Whereas "life forms" refer to organisms within ecosystems, "forms of life" have been defined as "those cultural, social, symbolic, and pragmatic ways of thinking and acting that organize *human* communities" (Helmreich 2008: 6; emphasis added). Yet as demonstrated by van Dooren (2014), non-human animals have – and may lose – their ways of living. And many "collectives," to use the terminology preferred by Descola (2013 [2005]), have both human and non-human members. Thus, environmental health justice is a more-than-human affair. At a minimum, solidarity with other people often entails respect for their views on and interdependence with non–human animals (Rock and Degeling 2015).

Keeping in mind that van Dooren draws inspiration from Haraway (2008), who in turn builds on Barad's (2007) engagements with quantum physics, multi-species entanglements clearly extend beyond classic cause–effect mechanisms (see also Nading 2014). Multi-species entanglements in environmental health justice could be both deeper and more diffuse than imagined in either conventional physics or biomedicine. In his work, van Dooren exemplifies this point in his attention to "becoming with" the birds that anchor his inquiries into the losses and non–human suffering imposed by human-mediated extinctions. This stance is not just a matter of research ethics or methodology. Environmental changes abetted by social inequality have worsened the quality of life and increased disease risks among many members of our own species, along with countless members of non–human species.

Concluding remarks

This chapter highlights the fact that greater attention to non–human animals in socio-ecological systems is long overdue in medical anthropology. At the same time, environmental anthropologists have much to offer discussions about health and well-being. Our discipline's hallmark anthropocentrism need not become a barrier to recognizing how non–human lives figure in the social organization of experience (Hurn 2010), including that of sickness, suffering, and health. Moreover, anthropologists might fruitfully investigate the imprint of human hierarchies, activities, and ideas on ecological dynamics and the lives of non–human animals, as van Dooren (2014) has done by focusing his attention on birds; and Nading (2014) has shown by accounting for dengue through the entanglement of poor people's lives with mosquitos in a Nicaraguan city.

Anthropologists could play crucial roles in envisioning and realizing environmental health justice for fellow humans and fellow creatures. This chapter has treated the current interest in multi-species entanglements as an occasion for encouraging environmental anthropologists and medical anthropologists to engage in discussions regarding environmental health justice. Over the past 30 years, medical anthropologists have examined the profound imprint of social inequality on human suffering, and biomedical knowledge has been subjected to ethnographic scrutiny. The extent to which human health hinges on environments and non–human species will, I hope, receive more attention from anthropologists in the years to come.

Acknowledgements

I am grateful to the editors for the invitation to submit a chapter for this volume. The writing process was advanced by a Visiting Scholar Award funded by the Canadian Institutes of Health Research, Institute of Population and Public Health (CIHR–IPPH, ICT-138054) and hosted by Steve Hinchliffe in the Natures, Materialities and Biopolitics Research Group at the University of Exeter in November 2014. This CIHR–IPPH award allowed me to attend the British Animal Studies Network conference coordinated by Henry Buller at the University of Exeter, where some of the ideas expressed here were developed. I also wish to thank Gwendolyn Blue and Lydia Vaz for commenting on an earlier version of the manuscript.

References

Barad, K 2007. *Meeting the Universe Halfway: Quantum Physics and the Entanglement of Matter and Meaning*. Raleigh, NC: Duke University Press.

Bliss, M 2000 [1982]. *The Discovery of Insulin*. Toronto, ON: University of Toronto Press.

Blue, G and M J Rock 2011. Trans-Biopolitics: Complexity in Interspecies Relations. *Health: An Interdisciplinary Journal for the Social Study of Health, Illness and Medicine* 15(4): 353–368.

Brotherton, P S and V-K Nguyen 2013. Revisiting Local Biology in the Era of Global Health. *Medical Anthropology* 32(4): 287–290.

Buller, H 2013. Individuation, the Mass and Farm Animals. *Theory, Culture & Society* 30(7–8): 155–175.

Buller, H 2014. Animal Geographies I. *Progress in Human Geography* 38(2): 308–318.

Buller, H 2015a. Animal Geographies II: Methods. *Progress in Human Geography* 39(3): 374–384.

Buller, H 2015b. Animal Geographies III: Ethics. *Progress in Human Geography*: doi: 10.1177/0309132 515580489

Cassidy, R 2012. Lives with Others: Climate Change and Human–Animal Relations. *Annual Review of Anthropology* 41(1): 21–36.

Colman, F 2010. Rhizome. In A Parr (ed.) *The Deleuze Dictionary*. Edinburgh, Scotland: Edinburgh University Press, pp. 232–235.

Craddock, S and S Hinchliffe 2015. One World, One Health? Social Science Engagements with the One Health Agenda. *Social Science & Medicine* 129: 1–4.

Crate, S A 2011. Climate and Culture: Anthropology in the Era of Contemporary Climate Change. *Annual Review of Anthropology* 40: 175–194.

Darwin, C 1870. *On the Origin of Species by Means of Natural Selection: Or the Preservation of Favoured Races in the Struggle for Life* (original edn.). New York: D. Appleton & Company.

Davies, G 2012. Caring for the Multiple and the Multitude: Assembling Animal Welfare and Enabling Ethical Critique. *Environment and Planning D: Society and Space* 30(4): 623–638.

Dennis, S 2013. Ambiguous Mice, Speaking Rats: Crossing and Affirming the Great Divides in Scientific Practice. *Anthrozoos: A Multidisciplinary Journal of the Interactions of People and Animals* 26(4): 505–517.

Descola, P 2013 [2005]. *Beyond Nature and Culture*. Chicago, IL: Chicago University Press.

Evans-Pritchard, E E 1960 [1940]. *The Nuer: A Description of the Modes of Livelihood and Political Institutions of a Nilotic People*. Oxford: Clarendon Press.

Evans-Pritchard, E E 1976 [1937]. *Witchcraft, Oracles and Magic among the Azande* (abridged with an introduction by E Gillies). Oxford: Clarendon Press.

Franklin, S 1995. Science as Culture, Cultures of Science. *Annual Review of Anthropology* 24: 163–184.

Frohlich, K L and T Abel 2014. Environmental Justice and Health Practices: Understanding how Health Inequities Arise at the Local Level. *Sociology of Health & Illness* 36(2): 199–212.

Fuentes, A 2012. Ethnoprimatology and the Anthropology of the Human–Primate Interface. *Annual Review of Anthropology* 41(1): 101–117.

Gilder, L 2009. *The Age of Entanglement: When Quantum Physics Was Reborn*. New York: Vintage.

Green, J 2012. One Health, One Medicine, and Critical Public Health. *Critical Public Health* 22(4): 377–381.

Haraway, D 2008. *When Species Meet*. Minneapolis, MN and London: University of Minnesota Press.

Hardy, A 2003. Animals, Disease, and Man: Making Connections. *Perspectives in Biology and Medicine* 46(2): 200–215.

Helmreich, S 2008. *Alien Ocean: Anthropological Voyages in Microbial Seas*. Berkeley: University of California Press.

Hinchliffe, S 2015. More than One World, More than One Health: Re-Configuring Interspecies Health. *Social Science & Medicine* 129: 28–35.

Hinchliffe, S and S Whatmore 2006. Living Cities: Towards a Politics of Conviviality. *Science as Culture* 15(3): 123–138.

Hinchliffe, S, J Allen, S Lavau, N Bingham and S Carter 2013. Biosecurity and the Topologies of Infected Life: From Borderlines to Borderlands. *Transactions of the Institute of British Geographers* 38(4): 531–543.

Hurn, S 2010. What's in a Name? Anthrozoology, Human–Animal Studies, Animal Studies or . . .? *Anthropology Today* 26(3): 27–28.

Ingold, T 2000. *The Perception of the Environment: Essays on Livelihood, Dwelling and Skill*. London and New York: Psychology Press.

Ingold, T 2008. Bindings against Boundaries: Entanglements of Life in an Open World. *Environment and Planning A* 40(8): 1796–1810.

Ingold, T 2011. *Being Alive: Essays on Movement, Knowledge and Description*. London: Routledge.

Ingold, T 2012. Toward an Ecology of Materials. *Annual Review of Anthropology* 41: 427–442.

Janes, C R and K K Corbett 2009. Anthropology and Global Health. *Annual Review of Anthropology* 38: 167–183.

Johnson, J and C Degeling 2011. Animals-as-Patients: Improving the Practice of Animal Experimentation. *Between the Species* 15(1): 43–57.

Johnston, C 2008. Beyond the Clearing: Towards a Dwelt Animal Geography. *Progress in Human Geography* 32(5): 633–649.

Kearns, R and G Moon 2002. From Medical to Health Geography: Novelty, Place and Theory after a Decade of Change. *Progress in Human Geography* 26(5): 605–625.

Keck, F and M Ticktin 2015. La souffrance animale à distance: Des vétérinaires dans l'action humanitaire. *Anthropologie et Sociétés* 39(1–2): 145–163.

Kleinman, A, L Eisenberg and B Good 1978. Culture, Illness, and Care: Clinical Lessons from Anthropologic and Cross-Cultural Research. *Annals of Internal Medicine* 88(2): 251–258.

Kleinman, A, V Das and M Lock 1997. *Social Suffering*. Berkeley: University of California Press.

Lakoff, A 2008. The Generic Biothreat, or, How we Became Unprepared. *Cultural Anthropology* 23(3): 399–428.

Law, J and A Mol 2008. The Actor-Enacted: Cumbrian Sheep in 2001. In L Malafouris and C Knappett (eds) *Material Agency towards a Non-Anthropocentric Approach*. New York: Springer, pp. 57–78.

Law, J and A Mol 2011. Veterinary Realities: What Is Foot and Mouth Disease? *Sociologia Ruralis* 51(1): 1–16.

Lestel, D 2006. Ethology and Ethnology: The Coming Synthesis. *Social Science Information* 45(2): 147–153.

Lock, M 1993a. Cultivating the Body: Anthropologies and Epistemologies of Bodily Practice and Knowledge. *Annual Review of Anthropology* 22: 133–155.

Lock, M 1993b. *Encounters with Aging: Myths of Menopause in Japan and North America*. Berkeley and Los Angeles: University of California Press.

Lock, M 2013. *The Alzheimer Conundrum: Entanglements of Dementia and Aging*. Princeton, NJ: Princeton University Press.

Lock, M, A Young and A Cambrosio 2000. *Living and Working with the New Biomedical Technologies: Intersections of Inquiry*. Cambridge, UK: Cambridge University Press.

McNaughton, D 2012. The Importance of Long-Term Social Research in Enabling Participation and Developing Engagement Strategies for New Dengue Control Technologies. *PLoS: Neglected Tropical Diseases* 6(8): e1785.

Masuda, J R, B Poland and J Baxter 2010. Reaching for Environmental Health Justice: Canadian Experiences for a Comprehensive Research, Policy and Advocacy Agenda in Health Promotion. *Health Promotion International* 25(4): 453–463.

Mol, A 2002. *The Body Multiple: Ontology in Medical Practice*. Durham, NC: Duke University Press.

Mullin, M 1999. Mirrors and Windows: Sociocultural Studies of Animal–Human Relationships. *Annual Review of Anthropology* 28: 201–224.

Mykhalovskiy, E and L Weir 2004. The Problem of Evidence-Based Medicine: Directions for Social Science. *Social Science & Medicine* 59(5): 1059–1069.

Nading, A M 2013. Humans, Animals, and Health: From Ecology to Entanglement. *Environment and Society: Advances in Research* 4(1): 60–78.

Nading, A M 2014. *Mosquito Trails: Ecology, Health, and the Politics of Entanglement*. Berkeley: University of California Press.

Nguyen, V-K and K Peschard 2004. Anthropology, Inequality, and Disease: A Review. *Annual Review of Anthropology* 32: 447–474.

Palmer, J J, A H Kelly, E I Surur, F Checchi and C Jones 2014. Changing Landscapes, Changing Practice: Negotiating Access to Sleeping Sickness Services in a Post-Conflict Society. *Social Science & Medicine* 120: 396–404.

Panter-Brick, C 2014. Health, Risk, and Resilience: Interdisciplinary Concepts and Applications. *Annual Review of Anthropology* 43(1): 431–448.

Parr, H 2003. Medical Geography: Care and Caring. *Progress in Human Geography* 27(2): 212–221.

Parr, H 2004. Medical Geography: Critical Medical and Health Geography? *Progress in Human Geography* 28(2): 246–257.

Patterson, P B 2015. Bug Wood: Climate Change, Mountain Pine Beetles and Risk in the Southeastern British Columbia Logging Industry. *Research in Economic Anthropology* 35, 47–64.

Peel, E, M Douglas, O Parry and J Lawton 2010. Type 2 Diabetes and Dog Walking: Patients' Longitudinal Perspectives about Implementing and Sustaining Physical Activity. *The British Journal of General Practice* 60(577): 570–577.

Pinder, R 2007. On Movement and Stillness. *Ethnography* 8(1): 99–116.

Povinelli, E A 2001. Radical Worlds: The Anthropology of Incommensurability and Inconceivability. *Annual Review of Anthropology* 30: 319–334.

Rock, M and P Babinec 2008. Diabetes in People, Cats and Dogs: Biomedicine and Manifold Ontologies. *Medical Anthropology: Cross-Cultural Studies in Health and Illness* 27(4): 324–252.

Rock, M and C Degeling 2016. Toward One Health Promotion. In M Singer (ed.) *A Companion to Environmental Health: Anthropological Perspectives*. West Sussex, UK: Wiley–Blackwell, pp. 68–82.

Rock, M J and C Degeling 2015. Public Health Ethics and More-than-Human Solidarity. *Social Science & Medicine* 129: 61–67.

Rock, M J, E Mykhalovskiy and T Schlich 2007. People, Other Animals and Health Knowledges: Towards a Research Agenda. *Social Science & Medicine* 64: 1970–1976.

Rock, M J, B Buntain, J Hatfield and B Hallgrímsson 2009. Animal–Human Connections, 'One Health,' and the Syndemic Approach to Prevention. *Social Science & Medicine* 68: 991–995.

Rock, M J, C Degeling and G Blue 2014. Toward Stronger Theory in Critical Public Health: Insights from Debates Surrounding Posthumanism. *Critical Public Health* 24(3): 337–348.

Saj, T L, C Mather and P Sicotte 2006. Traditional Taboos in Biological Conservation: The Case of Colobus Vellerosus at the Boabeng-Fiema Monkey Sanctuary, Central Ghana. *Social Science Information* 45(2): 285–310.

Sapolosky, R M 2004. Social Status and Health in Humans and Other Animals. *Annual Review of Anthropology* 33: 393–418.

Scheper-Hughes, N and M Lock 1987. The Mindful Body: A Prolegomenon to Future Work in Medical Anthropology. *Medical Anthropological Quarterly* 1(1): 6–39.

Schlich, T, E Mykhalovskiy and M Rock 2009. Animals in Surgery—Surgery in Animals: Nature and Culture in Animal–Human Relationships and Modern Surgery. *History and Philosophy of the Life Sciences* 31(3–4): 321–354.

Schlünder, M and T Schlich 2009. The Emergence of "Implant-Pets" and "Bone-Sheep": Animals as New Biomedical Objects in Orthopaedic Surgery. *History and Philosophy of the Life Sciences* 31(3–4): 429–460.

Shanklin, E 1985. Sustenance and Symbol: Anthropological Studies of Domesticated Animals. *Annual Review of Anthropology* 14: 375–403.

Singer, M C 2009. Doorways in Nature: Syndemics, Zoonotics, and Public Health. *Social Science & Medicine* 68: 996–999.

Singer, M C, A Herring, J Livingston and M Rock 2011. Syndemics in Global Health. In M Singer and P I Erickson (eds) *Companion to Medical Anthropology*. Chichester, UK: Blackwell Publishing, pp. 159–180.

Solomon, O 2010. What a Dog Can Do: Children with Autism and Therapy Dogs in Social Interaction. *Ethos* 38(1): 143–166.

Stewart, A 1998. *The Ethnographer's Method*. Thousand Oaks, CA: Sage.

Toohey, A M, G R McCormack, P K Doyle-Baker, C L Adams and M J Rock 2013. Dog-Walking and Sense of Community in Neighborhoods: Implications for Promoting Regular Physical Activity in Adults 50 Years and Older. *Health & Place* 22: 75–81.

van Dooren, T 2014. *Flight Ways: Life and Loss at the Edge of Extinction*. New York: Columbia University Press.

van Dooren, T and D B Rose 2012. Storied-Places in a Multispecies City. *Humanimalia* 3(2): 1–27.

Young, A 1980. The Discourse on Stress and the Reproduction of Conventional Knowledge. *Social Science & Medicine* 14B(3): 133–146.

Young, A 1982. The Anthropologies of Illness and Sickness. *Annual Review of Anthropology* 11: 257–285.

29

CHALLENGING THE CONVENTIONAL WISDOM

Breast cancer and environmental health

Mary K. Anglin

Introduction

Why might a disease such as breast cancer be linked to exposure to synthetic chemicals and other environmental contaminants, including ionizing radiation? What are the arguments for and against this proposition, and whose voices have come to matter most in public debates over the prevention of breast cancer? Further, what might that set of disagreements indicate about the health of the public or the status of "the environment" in capitalist and increasingly post-industrial settings, or about activist practices in the Global North? The present chapter draws upon ethnographic literature in anthropology and related social sciences, as well as research in public health articulating an eco-social perspective, to examine the social contexts of an ongoing discussion about environmental and political factors in health. Likewise, this chapter provides an opportunity to examine anthropological insights about breast cancer, as a social phenomenon, in conjunction with the foundational assumption of eco-social perspectives on health: that humans incorporate biologically, or come to "embody," the social and material worlds in which we live.

Educational campaigns offered by federal agencies and major foundations in the United States, especially during the month of October, broadcast the message that breast cancer is a major health concern warranting public awareness. And, indeed, a multitude of statistics support that claim. Within the United States, as the nation with the highest incidence rates in the world, 2.9 million women were living with breast cancer during 2013, while an additional 39,620 women died from this disease (American Cancer Society 2013; Surveillance Epidemiology and End Results [SEER] 2014). Despite the declaration of a "war on cancer" in 1971 by then President Nixon, breast cancer incidence rose by more than 30 percent during the late twentieth century in the United States, and the population-based probability of a breast cancer diagnosis, over the course of a lifetime, is currently one in eight (Howe and Clapp 2012; Howlader *et al.* 2013). Moreover, while first-generation immigrants have lower probabilities of developing breast cancer, congruent with their countries of origin, successive generations experience rates of incidence that are consistent with the U.S. population at large. On a global level, one measure of breast cancer's significance pertains to the costs of premature death and disability, which are estimated to be $88 billion annually (Rudel *et al.* 2014: 881; see also American Cancer Society 2010; IBCERCC 2013). Clearly, efforts to treat and contain this disease have so far met with limited success, and the suffering of countless numbers of women continues.

A central point of concern and debate pertains to whether, and through what means, breast cancer might be prevented. Mainstream approaches, such as those communicated through health campaigns in the United States, emphasize the element of personal responsibility in cancer prevention—namely, through women's regular participation in mammography screening and modification of behaviors to minimize their individual risks for the disease. However, screening technologies at best offer the prospect of early detection, with its twin aims of less invasive and more effective treatment, rather than the avoidance of disease. Then, too, the conditions of living, reproductive decisions, and cultural practices regarded as "lifestyle choices" and "established risk factors" by much of American biomedicine are associated with just 25–30 percent of the diagnosed cases, leaving three-quarters of breast cancer diagnoses unexplained (Kelsey and Gammon 1990).[1] Genetic factors, including the much-heralded BRCA 1 and BRCA 2, account for 5–10 percent of breast cancer diagnoses (King *et al.* 1993; Newman *et al.* 1997). Thus, the matter of breast cancer etiology remains largely unresolved, and routes of effective prevention are far from apparent.

Responding to this fundamental uncertainty, cancer activists, environmental justice advocates, "community scientists," public health researchers, and even members of the President's Cancer Panel (2008–2009) have identified a potential environmental connection; namely, the correlation between ever-greater production and use of chemical compounds over the late twentieth and early twenty-first centuries and a notable increase in the incidence of breast cancer. Their argument proceeds along two axes: 1) the plausibility of this association, with its (limited) evidentiary basis; and 2) the further implications for health and regulatory policies in the United States. Focusing on the harmful effects of exposure to synthetic chemicals—as well as their persistence within the environment—enables us to think about the ways that diseases like cancer are socially produced and not simply the byproduct of poor decisions or unlucky genetic inheritance. That perspective also provides insight about ways to alter, if not fully eliminate, a significant source of health risks: pollution.

Making the link

> In my fantasy, the millions of us who have become society's cancer victims will simultaneously come out of our houses and offices and factories, and we will surge into the streets. "Enough," our voices will shout. "Enough of your poisons, enough of your death!" There are so many of us that industry and commerce stop. And we, the people with cancer, will not let it start up again until we know it can start up clean, free of the pollutants which are still creating cancers in more and more of our bodies.
>
> *(Judy Brady 1991a: 33)*

Over the past 20 years or more, cancer has become the subject matter of ethnographic research, as well as a locus for the application of clinically and socially driven anthropological insights. As with the anthropology of HIV/AIDS, many of the anthropological analyses of cancer address health inequities, including economic and social barriers to timely diagnosis and treatment; tendencies within the health-care arena to oversimplify, if not stereotype, cultural difference; the limitations and authoritative status of biomedical approaches to disease; marked variance in rates of morbidity and mortality, along the lines of race, ethnicity, and class; and other salient questions (Anglin 2006; Balshem 1993; Chavez *et al.*

1995; Kagawa-Singer 2001; Lannin *et al.* 1998; McMullin and Weiner 2008; Mathews *et al.* 2015).

A primary goal of this ethnographic work, as with anthropological analyses of HIV/AIDS, has been to elucidate the viewpoints of those most closely affected, thereby augmenting our knowledge base about cancer and advancing the cause of social justice. Nowhere is the relationship between co-producers of knowledge more readily apparent than in the study of environmental factors in breast cancer, where social science and public health researchers have worked closely with—and learned from—women living with breast cancer and environmental justice advocates.

The origins of American public and scientific concern over the role of synthetic chemicals as pollutants and environmentally based carcinogens can be traced to the path-breaking work of Rachel Carson (1962), a marine biologist and science writer who did not disclose her own breast cancer diagnosis lest that be taken as evidence of personal bias. Carson looked to World War II as a defining moment in the production of organic compounds as insecticides and for other wartime applications, and their subsequent adaptation for usage in domestic and agricultural settings. What most concerned Carson about the new reliance on "the chemical death rain" was not simply the proliferation of synthetic compounds, but their build-up in the earth, air, and waterways, and cumulative impact on a wide array of life forms (1962: 12). The potency of synthetic compounds, she wrote, resides in the fact that

> they destroy the very enzymes whose function is to protect the body from harm, they block the oxidation processes from which the body receives its energy, and they may initiate in certain cells the slow and irreversible change that leads to malignancy.
>
> *(Carson 1962: 16–17)*

These arguments became influential due to the quality of Carson's scientific analysis, in conjunction with her status as an independent researcher (albeit a former and well-regarded staff scientist with the U.S. Bureau of Fisheries). Rachel Carson's testimony before Congress and the President's Science Advisory Committee, moreover, had proven an important factor in the eventual banning of use of the pesticide DDT within the United States and continues as a model for environmental policy-making.

Thus, in the 1990s, when women with cancer began to name breast cancer an "epidemic" in the United States and examine potential reasons for the well-documented secular trend, they turned to Rachel Carson and others influenced by her work (Arditti and Schreiber 1993; Batt 1994; Brady 1991b; Epstein 1998 [1978]; Steingraber 1997; Stocker 1993; Tempest Williams 1991). As Sandra Steingraber wrote in her "letter to Rachel":

> This is what I can tell you: that groups like this are forming in many American cities, that women with cancer are reframing the debate on environmental protection, that our knowledge compels us.
>
> These are the sea changes that I feel.
>
> *(Steingraber 1993: 198)*

It was the organization, 1 in 9: The Long Island Breast Cancer Action Coalition, to which Steingraber referred. Residents of Long Island learned in the 1980s, through a report by the

New York State Department of Health, that breast cancer incidence rates were higher for Nassau and Suffolk Counties than elsewhere in the state; the increased incidence could be measured as a transition from the 1 in 10 lifetime probability of developing breast cancer, common to the United States as a whole, to that of 1 in 9.[2] They acted on this information by forming the grassroots coalition in 1990; initiating a community-based mapping project to determine which women had been diagnosed with breast cancer and where they lived; staging protests at the Nassau County Courthouse in order that women's voices be heard directly and to hold state officials accountable for providing further information; and petitioning Congress for federally funded research to investigate the causes of a burgeoning epidemic (Baralt and McCormick 2010; McQuiston 1992; Osuch *et al.* 2012; Winn 2005).

Similar efforts were initiated in other parts of the United States. In 1991, women in Massachusetts created the Massachusetts Breast Cancer Coalition (MBCC) with the objectives of having the state legislature publicly acknowledge breast cancer as an epidemic and of acquiring state funding to address this public health crisis. Whereas the organizing activities of 1 in 9 resulted in the inclusion of a proviso within Public Law 103-43 (U.S. Congress 1993), authorizing a sequence of studies to be funded and administered through the National Cancer Institute, MBCC acquired state funding to establish "'a laboratory of their own' and named it Silent Spring Institute in tribute to Rachel Carson" (Silent Spring Institute 2014; see also McQuiston 1992; Massachusetts Breast Cancer Coalition 2014a, 2014b; Winn 2005). Twenty years later, and now privately funded, Silent Spring Institute continues its research on environmental factors in breast cancer, along with other studies of environmental exposures (Brody *et al.* 2007, Brody *et al.* 2009, Brown *et al.* 2006).

In California, grassroots organizations worked under the rubric of a statewide advocacy network—California Breast Cancer Organizations (CABCO)—to encourage the passage of 1993 legislation establishing the California Breast Cancer Research Program (CBCRP) and funding the program, at least in part, via a $.02 increase to the state tobacco tax. From its inception, CBCRP listed as one of its priorities, "the identification and elimination of environmental causes of breast cancer," and that continues to the present (California Breast Cancer Research Program 2014a, 2014b; see also Milliken 2004). Equally notable was the founding of the Toxic Links Coalition (TLC), bringing together cancer organizations and environmental justice organizations in the San Francisco Bay Area. During its ten-year history, 1994–2004, TLC engaged in annual tours identifying sites of the "Cancer Industry," along with other ways of calling attention to practices of environmental contamination and the immiseration of local communities (Klawiter 2008; Ley 2009).[3]

While other grassroots coalitions and areas of the United States participated in the development of an "environmental breast cancer movement," as it is often called, the aforementioned are the examples most frequently cited. In each instance, a factor prompting the consideration of environmental determinants was the discovery of locally relevant cancer "hot spots" or regions with discernably higher rates of breast cancer incidence: Nassau and Suffolk Counties on Long Island, Cape Cod in Massachusetts, and the nine-county San Francisco Bay Area of California. The specificity of the cancer clusters, moreover, undermined the reasoning that "successes" of mammography screening might account for increased incidence or that the cancer rates were attributable to demographic patterns alone. Cancer activists drew upon this well-documented geography of breast cancer to argue for the examination of other causes, rooted in political, economic, and environmental practices, as Anglin (1998) and Klawiter (2008) have noted.[4] Through such challenges to the "dominant paradigm for addressing the breast cancer problem," Ley observes (2009: 3), activists articulated "a new vision for public health, biomedicine, science, and environmental policy" with far-reaching implications (see also Baralt 2010; Clorfene-Casten 1993).

Forging an eco-social paradigm of cancer

The problem is not one of the environment per se. The problem derives from capital's presumption that the natural environment—land, trees, oil, minerals, water—is exploitable and renewable. Bodily health is not viewed as integral to its environs. The hypothesis of a porous genetic body that absorbs environmental processes over time requires a humanized standpoint that recognizes the racialized and class aspects of those processes.

(Zillah Eisenstein 2001: 95)

The environmental turn in breast cancer activism in the United States has been characterized as an embodied health movement wherein notions of "the biological body," informed by accounts of those living with illness, inspire a politicized and collective identity (Brown et al. 2004: 50, 60–61; see also Klawiter 2008 and Ley 2009). In addition, narratives of environmental *exposure*—as, for example, Tempest Williams's (1991: 282–287) depiction of the above-ground atomic tests that spewed radioactive fallout throughout the deserts of Utah and Nevada—played a crucial role in linking personal (and familial) experience to critiques of societal arrangements and structural forces (see also Diaz 1991; Eisenberg 1991; Epperson 1991; Steingraber 1997). Having "watched the women in my family die common, heroic deaths" from breast and ovarian cancer, Tempest Williams (1991: 285, 286) reached the conclusion that "the price of obedience has become too high" and engaged in public protest.

The American environmental justice (EJ) movement proved influential through its legacy of social change, as well as via specific instances of collaboration with cancer activists.[5] As Checker (2012) argued in another context, EJ readings of the body politic have characteristically included skepticism about the place of science in measuring exposure to environmental toxins and/or investigating the nature of their effects on human health (see also Jain 2013; Klawiter 2008). If risk-assessment techniques and other scientific analyses of environmental contaminants more frequently produced doubt instead of conclusive results, local advocates found other ways to register findings from practical, community-derived knowledge (see Checker 2007; Michaels 2008; Ottinger and Cohen 2011; Russell et al. 1992). Thus, conferences, hearings, and events such as those sponsored by the Toxic Links Coalition replaced the notion of "behavioral risks" for cancer with an understanding derived from the histories of EJ struggles and health activism (Brulle and Pellow 2006; Lorde 1980, 1988; Morgen 2002). These were public opportunities for calling attention to "the hidden maze of linkages and networks connecting the bodies of state agencies, politicians, charities, and profit-driven corporations to the unhealthy bodies of people involuntarily exposed to toxins and living in contaminated communities" (Klawiter 2008: 210).

From the outset, breast cancer activists worked to establish what some have characterized as "different science" or "citizen science": an independent approach much in the spirit of Rachel Carson's work, explicitly in the public interest, and constituting new forms of alliance between scientists and representatives of affected communities in the United States (Anglin 1998: 196; McCormick et al. 2003: 547; see also Brown et al. 2006). As Cohen and Ottinger noted of environmental justice studies, broadly configured, research partnerships of this sort have led to methodological innovations as well as the general "transform[ation of] scientific and technological practices" (2011: 8, 15; see also Morello-Frosch *et al.* 2011). Thus, for example, the Long Island Breast Cancer Study Project (1992–2002) offered invaluable lessons as to how the peer-review process itself sharply limited the involvement of advocates in scientific research, as well as the need for more explicitly defined procedures of collaboration (Ley 2009; Osuch *et al.* 2012).[6] Cancer activists pressed for an active role as reviewers evaluating proposals at the national level—for example, through the National Breast Cancer Coalition's Project Lead (Platner *et al.* 2002)—and a voice in establishing relevant questions for research, as with the community-driven, participatory approach of Silent Spring Institute and "A Woman's Cancer Agenda" formulated by the Women's Community Cancer Project (1993). To quote Ellen Parker, a participant in the founding and early directing of Silent Spring, "It was a new experience for the scientists to work so closely with activists and the people affected by the illness they were studying" (Silent Spring 2014; see also Brody *et al.* 2005). As another measure of "clear science" with relevance for a broader audience, the advocacy organization known as the Breast Cancer Fund has, since 2002, provided a review of "the scientific evidence linking exposures to environmental chemicals and radiation to breast cancer" (Gray 2010: 3); the sixth edition addresses critical feedback from scientists and other readers on a prior version of the review, published in the *International Journal of Occupational and Environmental Health* (Gray 2010; Gray *et al.* 2009; see also Breast Cancer Fund 2015; Kopelson 2013).

The portrait that emerges from these analyses is not one of simple causality, tying specific chemical exposures to increased risk of breast cancer, as had been the objective of the Long Island Breast Cancer Study Project and other early studies (Gammon *et al.* 2002; Hunter *et al.* 1997, Krieger *et al.* 1994; Winn 2005; Wolff *et al.* 1993). Instead, and congruent with eco-social perspectives, research on environmental factors in breast cancer now investigates a class of chemicals known as endocrine disruptors, given their impact on hormonally mediated biological functioning. One dimension of this research considers the various forces influencing the availability of multiple chemicals (and routes of exposure) in particular environmental contexts. Equally important are the societal, historical, and biological processes affecting bodies at the individual and population levels (Colborn *et al.* 1996; Davis *et al.* 1993; Krieger 2013; Krieger *et al.* 2011; Sherman 2000; Steingraber 1997). The uncertainties and processual character of this framework may be partly understood to reflect the dearth of toxicity data on synthetic chemicals, as noted by the Breast Cancer Fund's review, along with other methodological problems in the study of environmental carcinogens (Gray 2010: 14; Rudel and Perovich 2012; Rudel *et al.* 2007). However, in the words of Birnbaum (2013: 322), it is equally a matter of moving beyond the "classical dichotomy of toxic versus non-toxic" to examine "time- and life stage-specific" effects of exposure to the synthetic chemicals that have become ubiquitous within human-altered environments:

> The human body is not a closed system—medicines are delivered orally, intranasally, and transdermally, and environmental chemicals are delivered similarly, in the water we drink, the food we eat, and the air we breathe. . . . In the same way as physicians endeavor to understand and monitor the effect of medicines on endocrine pathways, we ought to achieve the same understanding and control of the effects of environmental chemicals.
>
> *(Birnbaum 2013: 322)*

These were the points underlined by environmental justice and cancer activists, following the lead of Rachel Carson, and more recently also Theo Colborn, through toxic tours, narratives of exposure, community-based research, along with presentations at conferences and hearings (Carson 1962; Colborn *et al.* 1993; Ley 2009). As Eisenstein (2001: 91, 92) has argued, Carson's approach to the environment "requires an episteme that sees the unseeable, thinks in multiplicity, and over long periods of time."

Thus, in a presentation for the Joint Informational Hearing on Breast Cancer and the Environment before the California Senate Health and Human Services Committee and the Assembly Health Committee, Karen Holly (2002) narrated the trans-generational occupational exposures of her family, her own reproductive strategies and the breast cancer diagnosis she received at the age of 34, and the preventive health measures still undertaken routinely as the resident of a working-class neighborhood "not too far from the chemical plants." As Holly explained, poverty might also be considered a "carcinogen," since economic factors constrained the choices and living conditions for communities of color such as her own. Holly's testimony aptly illustrates the

> ecosocial premise . . . that clues to current and changing population patterns in health, including social disparities in health, are to be found in the dynamic social, material, and ecological contexts into which we are born, develop, interact, and endeavour to live meaningful lives.
>
> *(Krieger 2005: 350)*

Yet her aim was to communicate more than just the state of scientific inquiry. Representing this as "one story among many," Karen Holly asked the Committees: "I meet more and more African American women under the age of 40 being diagnosed with breast cancer. How do I save my sisters, our families, and our communities?"

As with many cancer activists and organizations such as 1 in 9 or the Breast Cancer Fund, Holly used her testimony to advocate for the precautionary principle, which emphasizes preventive health measures and the value of public safety over activities that could do harm to the environment (Brody *et al.* 2005; Grandjean 2004; Klawiter 2008; Ley 2009). The precautionary principle takes seriously "the potential for catastrophic effects on global eco-logical systems" through inadequate regulation of synthetic chemicals and other commercial practices, and the need to redirect environmental policy in the United States as well as other nations of the Global North (Kriebel *et al.* 2001: 871). It is an approach that recalls Brady's (1991a: 33) image of demonstrators shouting, "Enough of your poisons, enough of your death," and finally forcing industry "to start up clean."

While the United States has yet to fully endorse the precautionary principle, as the European Union and other international entities have done (Bergman *et al.* 2013; Kopnina 2010; United Nations Conference on Environment and Development 1992), there are hopeful signs of change. Among them are the passage of the Breast Cancer and Environmental Research Act of 2008 (U.S. Congress 2008), federal legislation that had been debated and defeated over nine years, as well as promotion of the precautionary principle through the report issued by the 2008–2009 President's Cancer Panel and the "action agenda" resulting from a "national conversation on public health and chemical exposures" (Brown 2011: a484; IBCERCC 2013; Leadership Council 2011; Leffall *et al.* 2010). Each of these achievements reflects the influence of decades of grassroots cancer advocacy and what Brody *et al.* (2005: 921) refer to as "activist-governed research," with its commitments to radical democracy and improving the health of the public (see also McCormick *et al.* 2003).

The challenge posed by breast cancer as Eisenstein (2001), Steingraber (1997), and Krieger (2013) have argued, is to gain a better comprehension of the porousness of human bodies in relation to the social worlds and physical landscapes we occupy over time. In the spirit of Rachel Carson's work, it is equally to appreciate the dynamism of physical environments as an outgrowth of political decision-making and global economic circuits, along with material processes that at the very least reflect the impact of local/regional climates, biochemistries, and inhabitants. Disease and disability, from this vantage point, can be viewed as the embodiment of specific histories of interaction between ecological settings, social forces, and individual/population-level biologies.

In tracing the contours of a debate over the causes of and potential routes of prevention for breast cancer, this chapter has endeavored to show the impact of cancer and environmental justice activism on scholarly views about health and the environment, as well as scientific methodologies and practices of collaboration. As organizations like the Massachusetts Breast Cancer Coalition and the Breast Cancer Fund make clear, however, their aim is not simply to understand the environmental foundation of diseases like breast cancer, but to "end the epidemic." Accordingly, one further direction for scholarly work will be to follow the impact of health activist discourses on emerging environmental policy in the United States and other settings within the Global North.

Notes

1 Traditional risk factors include a woman's chronological age, family history of breast cancer, benign breast disease, age at menarche, maternal age at birth of first child, nulliparity or childlessness, age at menopause, genetic influence, ethnicity, race, and socioeconomic status. The list of "possible," or likely, risks for breast cancer includes obesity (as measured by body mass index), diet and physical exercise, consumption of alcohol, use of oral contraceptives and, more recently, also hormone replacement therapy (Clarke *et al.* 2006; Glass *et al.* 2007; Kelsey and Berkowitz 1988; Kelsey and Gammon 1991; Newman *et al.* 1997, Ravdin *et al.* 2007, Stewart *et al.* 2007).

2 Judy Brady (1991b: 9) notes in the Introduction to *1 in 3: Women with Cancer Confront an Epidemic*, "My own case was diagnosed in 1980; at that time the statistics indicated that one in fourteen women in the United States would be diagnosed with breast cancer. Five years later, the figures were one in ten. Six years after that—now, in 1991—the figures are one in nine."

3 Another endeavor, closely aligned, was the making of a documentary film in the late 1990s, *Rachel's Daughters: Searching for the Causes of Breast Cancer* (Light and Saraf 1997). The distributor, Women Make Movies, describes the film in the following way:

> [T]his fascinating documentary follows a group of women—all breast cancer activists who are fighting or have survived the disease—who are on a personal mission to unearth the causes of breast cancer. The result is *Rachel's Daughters*, an engaging detective story and detailed analysis of the science and politics of this epidemic.
>
> *(www.wmm.com/filmcatalog/pages/c401.shtml*
> *[accessed 22 September 2015])*

4 Thus, a 1995 public hearing was convened in San Francisco on Women, Health and the Environment. The hearing featured the testimony of 19 activists/organizations—primarily those related to women living with breast cancer—before a panel of representatives from the Environmental Protection Agency (EPA), the Food and Drug Administration (FDA), the federal cancer registry (Surveillance, Epidemiology and End Results [SEER]), the American Cancer Society, the California State Legislature, city/county Departments of Health, the Indigenous Peoples' Network, and the Human Rights Commission. Several presenters specifically addressed the 1994 edition of the *Greater Bay Area Cancer Registry Report*, which stated that white women in the San Francisco Bay Area had the highest rates of breast cancer incidence globally, and African American women in the San Francisco Bay Area had the fourth highest incidence globally (Northern California Cancer Center [1994], cited in Klawiter [2008: 211; see also 356, note 9]; see also Anglin 1998: 187–188).

The San Francisco hearing served as the inaugural event for a series of conferences across the United States—organized under the sponsorship of Greenpeace and the Women's Environment & Development Organization (WEDO)—which brought cancer activists and environmental activists together to "make the link" between environmental pollution and cancer (see also Ley 2009). Moreover, in the San Francisco Bay Area, at least two more grassroots organizations were formed in response to the *Greater Bay Area Cancer Registry Report* and the issues presented at the hearing: the Breast Cancer Fund and Marin Breast Cancer Watch, which is now Zero Breast Cancer.

5 These collaborations were not without tensions over inclusivity, or the lack thereof, insofar as cancer activists focused on cancer as the major health issue and concerns about the environment were framed from the vantage point of a white, middle-class constituency (Anglin 1998; Klawiter 2008; Ley 2009; see also Kaufert 1998; Lorde 1980, 1988; Morgen 2002; Viviansayles 1993).

6 Social scientists have been present as observers and, at times, also participants in debates over the various roles of community representatives in conducting scientific research. For example, through their analysis of the Breast Cancer and Environment Research Centers (BCERC) projects funded by the National Institute of Environmental Health Sciences and the National Cancer Institute, Baralt and McCormick (2010) inspired public discussion as to how "advocate-scientist" research partnerships should be evaluated; and whether or not participants' expressions of "frustration" reflected "an ongoing, interactive, collaborative, critical process of science and advocacy" (Wolff and Barlow 2011: A201; Baralt and McCormick 2011). In other instances, social scientists have joined teams of investigators engaged in community-based participatory research (CBPR) on environmental exposures (see e.g. Brown *et al.* 2012).

References

American Cancer Society 2013. *Breast Cancer Facts and Figures, 2013–2014*. Atlanta, GA: American Cancer Society, Inc.

Anglin, Mary K 1998. "Dismantling the Master's House: Cancer Activists, Discourses of Prevention, and Environmental Justice." *Identities: Global Studies in Culture and Power* 5(2): 183–218.

—— 2006. "Whose Health? Whose Justice? Examining Quality of Care and Breast Cancer Activism through the Intersections of Gender, Race, Ethnicity, and Class." In Amy Schulz and Leith Mullings (eds) *Health at the Intersections of Gender, Race, and Class*. New York: Jossey-Bass/Pfeiffer, pp. 313–341.

Arditti, Rita and Tatiana Schreiber. 1993. "Killing us Quietly: Cancer, the Environment, and Women." In Midge Stocker (ed.) *Confronting Cancer, Constructing Change: New Perspectives on Women and Cancer*. Chicago, IL: Third Side Press, pp. 231–259.

Balshem, Martha 1993. *Cancer in the Community: Class and Medical Authority*. Washington, DC: Smithsonian Press.

Baralt, Lori 2010. "Biomedical and Environmental Health Perspectives: The Example of Confronting Breast Cancer." In Helen Kopnina and Hans Keune (eds) *Health and Environment: Social Science Perspectives.*, Hauppauge, NY: Nova Science Publishers, pp. 139–155.

Baralt, Lori B and Sabrina McCormick 2010. "A Review of Advocate-Scientist Collaboration in Federally Funded Environmental Breast Cancer Research Centers." *Environmental Health Perspectives* 118(12): 1668–1675.

—— 2011. "Breast Cancer Environment Centers and Advocacy: Baralt and McCormick Respond." *Environmental Health Perspectives* 119(5): A 201–A202.

Batt, Sharon 1994. *Patient No More: The Politics of Breast Cancer*. Charlottetown, PE, Canada: Gynergy Books.

Bergman, Ake, Jerrold J Heindel, Susan Jobling, Karen A Kidd and R Thomas Zoeller (eds) 2013. *The State of the Science of Endocrine Disrupting Chemicals*. Geneva, Switzerland: World Health Organization and United Nations Environmental Programme. http://apps.who.int/iris/bitstream/10665/78102/1/WHO_HSE_PHE_IHE_2013.1_eng.pdf?ua=1

Birnbaum, Linda S 2013. "When Environmental Chemicals Act Like Uncontrolled Medicine." *Trends in Endocrinology and Metabolism* 24(7): 321–323.

Brady, Judy 1991a. "The Goose and the Golden Egg." In Judy Brady (ed.) *One in Three: Women with Cancer Confront an Epidemic*. Pittsburgh, PA: Cleis Press, pp. 13–35.

—— (ed.) 1991b. *One in Three: Women with Cancer Confront an Epidemic*. Pittsburgh, PA: Cleis Press.

Breast Cancer Fund 2015. "Clear Science." www.breastcancerfund.org/clear-science/ (accessed 12 October 2015).

Brody, Julia Green, Joel Tickner and Ruthann A Rudel 2005. "Community-Initiated Breast Cancer and Environmental Studies and the Precautionary Principle." *Environmental Health Perspectives* 113(8): 920–925.

Brody, Julia Green, Kirsten B Moysich, Olivier Humblet, Kathleen R Attfield, Gregory Beehler and Ruthann A Rudel 2007. "Environmental Pollutants and Breast Cancer." *Environmental Factors in Breast Cancer*. Supplement to *Cancer* 109(S12): 2667–2711.

Brody, Julia Green, Rachel Morello-Frosch, Ami Zota, Phil Brown, Carla Perez and Ruthann A Rudel 2009. "Linking Exposure Assessment Science with Policy Objectives for Environmental Justice and Breast Cancer Advocacy: The Northern California Household Exposure Study." *American Journal of Public Health* 99 (Supplement 3): S600–S609.

Brown, Phil, Stephen Zavestoski, Sabrina McCormick, Brian Mayer, Rachel Morello-Frosch and Rebecca Gasior Altman 2004. "Embodied Health Movements: New Approaches to Social Movements in Health." *Sociology of Health and Illness* 26(1): 50–80.

Brown, Phil, Sabrina McCormick, Brian Mayer, Stephen Zavestoski, Rachel Morello-Frosch, Rebecca Gasior Altman and Laura Senier 2006. "'A Lab of our Own': Environmental Causation of Breast Cancer and Challenges to the Dominant Epidemiological Paradigm." *Science, Technology, and Human Values* 31(5): 499–536.

Brown, Phil, Julia Green Brody, Rachel Morello-Frosch, Jessica Tovar, Ami R Zota and Ruthann A Rudel 2012. "Measuring the Success of Community Science: The Northern California Household Exposure Study." *Environmental Health Perspectives* 120 (3): 326–331.

Brown, Valerie 2011. "Are we on the Same Page? Action Agenda of the National Conversation on Public Health and Chemical Exposures." *Environmental Health Perspectives* 119(11): a484–a487.

Brulle, Robert J and David N Pellow 2006. "Environmental Justice: Human Health and Environmental Inequalities." *Annual Review of Public Health* 27: 103–124.

California Breast Cancer Research Program 2014a. "About us." http://cbcrp.org/about/index.html (accessed 20 October 2014).

—— 2014b. "Special Research Initiatives." http://cbcrp.org/priorities/sri/index.html (accessed 20 October 2014).

Carson, Rachel 1962. *Silent Spring*. Boston, MA: Houghton Mifflin.

Chavez, Leo, F Allen Hubbell, Juliet M McMullin, Rebecca G Martinez and Shiraz I Mishra 1995. "Structure and Meaning in Models of Breast and Cervical Cancer Risk Factors: A Comparison of Perceptions among Latinas, Anglo Women, and Physicians." *Medical Anthropology Quarterly* 9(10): 40–74.

Checker, Melissa 2007. "'But I Know it's True': Environmental Risk Assessment, Justice, and Anthropology." *Human Organization* 66(2): 112–124.

—— 2012. "'Make us Whole': Environmental Justice and the Politics of Skepticism." *Capitalism Nature Socialism* 23(3): 35–51.

Clarke, C A, S L Glaser, C S Uratsu, J V Selby, L H Kushi and L J Herrinton 2006. "Recent Declines in Hormone Therapy Utilization and Breast Cancer Incidence: Clinical and Population-Based Evidence, Letter to the Editor. *Journal of Clinical Oncology* 24: e49–e50.

Clorfene-Casten, Liane 1993. "The Environmental Link to Breast Cancer." *Ms.* (magazine) 3(6), pp. 52–56.

Cohen, Benjamin R and Gwen Ottinger 2011. "Introduction: Environmental Justice and the Transformation of Science and Engineering." In Gwen Ottinger and Benjamin R Cohen (eds) *Technoscience and Environmental Justice: Expert Cultures in a Grassroots Movement*. Cambridge, MA: The MIT Press, pp. 1–18.

Colborn, Theo, Frederick S vom Saal and Ana M Soto 1993. "Developmental Effects of Endocrine-Disrupting Chemicals in Wildlife and Humans." *Environmental Health Perspectives* 101(5): 378–384.

Colborn, Theo, Dianne Dumanoski and John Peterson Myers 1996. *Our Stolen Future: Are we Threatening our Fertility, Intelligence, and Survival? A Scientific Detective Story*. New York: Dutton.

Davis, Devra L, H Leon Bradlow, Mary Wolff, Tracey Woodruff, David G Hoel and Hoda Anton-Culver 1993. "Medical Hypothesis: Xenoestrogens as Preventable Causes of Cancer." *Environmental Health Perspectives* 101(5): 372–377.

Diaz, Reina 1991. "The Harvest of Poison." In Judy Brady (ed.) *One in Three: Women with Cancer Confront an Epidemic*. Pittsburgh, PA: Cleis Press, pp. 71–78.

Eisenberg, Susan 1991. "Exposure." In Judy Brady (ed.) *One in Three: Women with Cancer Confront an Epidemic*. Pittsburgh, PA: Cleis Press, p. 88.

Eisenstein, Zillah 2001. *Manmade Breast Cancers*. Ithaca, NY: Cornell University Press.

Epperson, Zinna 1991. "The Story of a Downwinder." In Judy Brady (ed.) *One in Three: Women with Cancer Confront an Epidemic*. Pittsburgh, PA: Cleis Press, pp. 89–96.

Epstein, Samuel S 1998 [1978]. *The Politics of Cancer Revisited*. Fremont Center, NY: East Ridge Press.

Gammon, Marilie, Alfred I Neugut, Regina M Santarella, Susan L Teitlebaum *et al*. 2002. "The Long Island Breast Cancer Study Project: Description of a Multi-Institutional Collaboration to Identify Environmental Risk Factors for Breast Cancer." *Breast Cancer Research and Treatment* 74: 235–254.

Glass, Andrew G, James V Lacey Jr, J Daniel Carreon and Robert N Hoover 2007. "Breast Cancer Incidence, 1980–2006: Combined Roles of Menopausal Hormone Therapy, Screening Mammography, and Estrogen Receptor Status." *Journal of the National Cancer Institute* 99(15): 1152–1161.

Grandjean, Philippe 2004. "Implications of the Precautionary Principle for Primary Prevention and Research." *Annual Review of Public Health* 25(1): 199–223.

Gray, Janet 2010. *State of the Evidence: The Connection between Breast Cancer and the Environment*. 6th edn. San Francisco, CA: Breast Cancer Fund.

Gray, Janet, Nancy Evans, Brynn Taylor, Jeanne Rizzo and Marissa Walker 2009. "State of the Evidence: The Connection between Breast Cancer and the Environment." *International Journal of Occupational and Environmental Health* 15(1): 43–78.

Holly, Karen 2002. "Personal Testimony Regarding Breast Cancer and the Environment." Testimony to the Senate and Senate Health and Human Services Committee and Assembly Health Committee, Joint Informational Hearing on Breast Cancer and the Environment, San Francisco, CA: San Francisco City Hall, 23 October 2002.

Howe, Genevieve K and Richard W Clapp 2012. "Are we Winning or Losing the War on Cancer? Deciphering the Propaganda of the NCI's 33-Year War." In Richard W Clapp (ed.) *From Critical Science to Solutions: The Best of Scientific Solutions*. Amity, NY: Baywood Publishing, pp. 131–146.

Howlader, N, A M Noone, M Krapcho, J Garshell, N Neyman, S F Altekruse, C L Kosary, M Yu, J Ruhl, Z Tatalovich, H Cho, A Mariotto, D R Lewis, H S Chen, E J Feuer and K A Cronin (eds) 2013. "4. Breast." In *SEER Cancer Statistics Review, 1975–2010*. Bethesda, MD: National Cancer Institute. http://seer.cancer.gov/csr/1975_2010/ (based on November 2012 SEER data submission, posted to the SEER web site, April 2013; accessed 20 April 2014).

Hunter, David J, Susan E Hankinson, Francine Laden, Graham A Colditz, JoAnn E Manson, Walter C Willett, Frank E Speizer and Mary S Wolff 1997. "Plasma Organochlorine Levels and the Risk of Breast Cancer." *New England Journal of Medicine* 337: 1253–1258.

IBCERCC (Interagency Breast Cancer and Environmental Research Coordinating Committee) 2013. *Breast Cancer and the Environment: Prioritizing Prevention*. Research Triangle Park, NC: National Institute of Environmental Health Sciences.

Jain, S Lochlann 2013. *Malignant: How Cancer Becomes Us*. Berkeley: University of California Press.

Kagawa-Singer, Marjorie 2001. "From Genes to Social Science: Impact of the Simplistic Interpretation of Race, Ethnicity, and Culture on Cancer Outcome." *Cancer* 91 (Issue Supplement 1): 226–232.

Kaufert, Patricia A 1998. "Women, Resistance, and the Breast Cancer Movement." In Margaret Lock and Patricia A Kaufert (eds) *Pragmatic Women and Body Politics*. Cambridge, UK: Cambridge University Press, pp. 287–309.

Kelsey, Janet L and Gertrud S Berkowitz 1988. "Breast Cancer Epidemiology." *Cancer Research* 48(20): 5615–5623.

Kelsey, Janet L and Marilie D Gammon 1990. "Epidemiology of Breast Cancer." *Epidemiologic Reviews* 12(1): 228–240.

Klawiter, Maren 2008. *The Biopolitics of Breast Cancer: Changing Cultures of Disease and Activism*. Minneapolis: University of Minnesota Press.

King, Mary-Claire, Sarah Rowell and Susan Love 1993. "Inherited Breast and Ovarian Cancer: What are the Risks? What are the Choices?" *Journal of the American Medical Association* 269(15): 1975–1980.

Kopelson, Karen 2013. "Risky Appeals: Recruiting to the Environmental Breast Cancer Movement in an Age of 'Pink Fatigue'." *Rhetoric Society Quarterly* 43(2): 107–133.

Kopnina, Helen 2010. "Health and Environment Policies in the European Union." In Helen Kopnina and Hans Keune (eds) *Health and Environment: Social Science Perspectives*. Hauppauge, NY: Nova Science Publishers, pp. 229–245.

Kriebel, David, Joel Tickner, Paul Epstein, John Lemons, Richard Levins, Edward Loechler, Margaret Quinn, Ruthann Rudel, Ted Schettler and Michael Stoto 2001. "The Precautionary Principle in Environmental Science." *Environmental Health Perspectives* 109(9): 871–876.

Krieger, Nancy 2005. "Embodiment: A Conceptual Glossary for Epidemiology." *Journal of Epidemiology and Community Health* 59: 350–355.

—— 2013. "History, Biology, and Health Inequities: Emergent Embodied Phenotypes and the Illustrative Case of the Breast Cancer Estrogen Receptor." *American Journal of Public Health* 103(1): 22–27.

Krieger, Nancy, Mary S Wolff, Robert A Hiatt, Marilyn Rivera, Joseph Vogelman and Norman Orentreich 1994. "Breast Cancer and Serum Organochlorines: A Prospective Study among White, Black, and Asian Women." *Journal of the National Cancer Institute* 86(8): 589–599.

Krieger, Nancy, Jarvis T Chen and Pamela D Waterman 2011. "Temporal Trends in the Black/White Breast Cancer Case Ratio for Estrogen Receptor Status: Disparities are Historically Contingent, not Innate." *Cancer Causes and Control* 22(3): 511–514.

Lannin, Donald R, Holly F Mathews, Jim Mitchell, Melvin S Swanson, Frances H Swanson and Maxine S Edwards 1998. "Influence of Socioeconomic and Cultural Factors on Racial Differences in Late-Stage Presentation of Breast Cancer." *Journal of the American Medical Association* 279(22): 1801–1807.

Leadership Council 2011. *Addressing Public Health and Chemical Exposures: An Action Agenda.* www.nationalconversation.us/wp-content/uploads/2014/05/national-conversation-action-agenda.pdf (accessed 27 January 2014).

Leffall Jr, LaSalle D and Margaret D Kripke 2010. "Preface." In Suzanne H Reuben (ed.) *Reducing Environmental Cancer Risk: What we Can Do Now*, 2008–2009 Annual Report of the President's Cancer Panel. Washington, DC: U.S. Department of Health and Human Services, National Institutes of Health, National Cancer Institute.

Ley, Barbara L 2009. *From Pink to Green: Disease Prevention and the Environmental Breast Cancer Movement.* New Brunswick, NJ: Rutgers University Press.

Light, Allie and Irving Saraf 1997. *Rachel's Daughters: Searching for the Causes of Breast Cancer.* San Francisco, CA: Light-Saraf Films. www.lightsaraffilms.com/Rachels.html (accessed 22 September 2015).

Lorde, Audre 1980. *The Cancer Journals.* Argyle, NY: Spinsters, Ink.

—— 1988. *A Burst of Light.* Ithaca, NY: Firebrand Books.

McCormick, Sabrina, Phil Brown and Stephen Zavestocki 2003. "The Personal is Scientific, the Scientific is Political: The Public Paradigm of the Environmental Breast Cancer Movement." *Sociological Forum* 18(4): 545–576.

McCormick, Sabrina, Julia Brody, Phil Brown and R Polk 2004. "Public Involvement in Breast Cancer Research: An Analysis and Model for Future Research." *International Journal of Health Services* 34(4): 625–646.

McMullin, Juliet and Diane Weiner (eds) 2008. *Confronting Cancer: Metaphors, Advocacy, and Anthropology.* Santa Fe, NM: School for Advanced Research Press.

McQuiston, John T 1992. "Citing Breast Cancer Rates in Nassau and Suffolk, Group Asks for Research." *The New York Times*, 12 May. www.nytimes.com/1992/05/12/nyregion/citing-breast-cancer-rates-in-nassau-and-suffolk-group-asks-for-research.html (accessed 19 October 2014).

Massachusetts Breast Cancer Coalition 2014a. http://mbcc.org/breast-cancer-prevention/ (accessed 1 February 2014).

—— 2014b. "Breast Cancer and the Environment." http://mbcc.org/breast-cancer-prevention/be-informed/breast-cancer-and-the-environment/ (accessed 1 February 2014).

Mathews, Holly F, Nancy Burke and Eirini Kampriani (eds) 2015. *Anthropologies of Cancer in Transnational Worlds.* New York: Routledge.

Michaels, David 2008. *Doubt is their Product: How Industry's Assault on Science Threatens your Health.* New York: Oxford University Press.

Milliken, Robert C 2004. "Maximizing the Impact of the California Breast Cancer Research Program: Studying Environmental Influences and Breast Cancer." White Paper. Oakland, CA: California Breast Cancer Research Program.

Morello-Frosch, Rachel, Phil Brown, Julia G Brody, Rebecca G Altman, Ruthann A Rudel, Ami Zota and Carla Perez 2011. "Experts, Ethics, and Environmental Justice: Communicating and Contesting Results from Personal Exposure Science." In Gwen Ottinger and Benjamin R Cohen (eds) *Technoscience and Environmental Justice: Expert Cultures in a Grassroots Movement.* Cambridge, MA: The MIT Press, pp. 93–118.

Morgen, Sandra 2002. *Into our Own Hands: The Women's Health Movement in the United States, 1969–1990.* New Brunswick, NJ: Rutgers University Press.

Newman, Beth, Robert C Millikan and Mary-Claire King 1997. "Genetic Epidemiology of Breast and Ovarian Cancers." *Epidemiologic Reviews* 19(1): 69–79.

Northern California Cancer Center 1994. "Breast Cancer in the Greater Bay Area: Highest Incidence Rates in the World." *Greater Bay Area Cancer Registry Report 5.* Fremont, CA: NCCC.

Osuch, Janet, Kami Silk, Carole Price, Janice Barlow, Karen Miller, Ann Hernick and Ann Fonfa 2012. "A Historical Perspective on Breast Cancer Activism in the United States: From Education and Support to Partnership in Scientific Research." *Journal of Women's Health* 21(3): 355–362.

Ottinger, Gwen and Benjamin R Cohen (eds) 2011. *Technoscience and Environmental Justice: Expert Cultures in a Grassroots Movement.* Cambridge, MA: The MIT Press.

Platner, Janice H, L Michelle Bennett, Robert Millikan and Mary D G Barker 2002. "The Partnership between Breast Cancer Advocates and Scientists." *Environmental and Molecular Mutagenesis* 39: 102–107.

Ravdin, Peter M, Kathleen A Cronin, Nadia Howlader, Christine D Berg, Rowan T Chlebowski, Eric J Feuer, Brenda K Edwards and Donald A Berry 2007. "The Decrease in Breast-Cancer Incidence in 2003 in the United States." *New England Journal of Medicine* 356(16): 1670–1674. doi: 10.1056/NEJMsr070105

Rudel, Ruthann and Laura Perovich 2012. "Accurate Risk-Based Chemical Screening Relies on Robust Exposure Estimates." Letter to the Editor. *Toxicological Sciences* 128(1): 295–296.

Rudel, Ruthann A, Kathleen R Attfield, Jessica N Schifano and Julia Green Brody 2007. "Chemicals Causing Mammary Gland Tumors in Animals Signal New Directions for Epidemiology, Chemicals Testing, and Risk Assessment for Breast Cancer Prevention." *Environmental Factors in Breast Cancer* Supplement to *Cancer* 109(S12): 2635–2666.

Rudel, Ruthann A, Janet M Ackerman, Kathleen R Attfield and Julia Green Brody 2014. "New Exposure Biomarkers as Tools for Breast Cancer Epidemiology, Biomonitoring, and Prevention: A Systematic Approach Based on Animal Evidence." *Environmental Health Perspectives* 122(9): 881–895.

Russell, Dick, Sanford Lewis and Russell Keating 1992. *Inconclusive by Design: Waste, Fraud, and Abuse in Federal Environmental Health Research, an Investigative Study by the Environmental Health Network and the National Toxics Campaign Fund.* https://archive.org/details/InconclusiveByDesignWasteFraudAndAbuseInFederalEnvironmentalHealth (accessed 1 February 2014).

Surveillance, Epidemiology, and End Results (SEER) 2014. "Stat Fact Sheets: Breast Cancer." Bethesda, MD: National Cancer Institute. http://seer.cancer.gov/statfacts/html/breast.html (accessed 1 February 2014).

Sherman, Janette 2000. *Life's Delicate Balance: Causes and Prevention of Breast Cancer.* New York: Taylor & Francis.

Silent Spring 2014. "History of Silent Spring Institute." http://silentspring.org/history-silent-spring-institute (accessed 20 October 2014).

Steingraber, Sandra 1991. "We All Live Downwind." In Judy Brady (ed.) *One in Three: Women with Cancer Confront an Epidemic.* Pittsburgh, PA: Cleis Press, pp. 36–48.

—— 1993. "'If I Live to Be 90 Still Wanting to Say Something': My Search for Rachel Carson." In Midge Stocker (ed.) *Confronting Cancer, Constructing Change: New Perspectives on Women and Cancer.* Chicago, IL: Third Side Press, pp. 181–199.

—— 1997. *Living Downstream: An Ecologist Looks at Cancer and the Environment.* Reading, MA: Addison-Wesley Publishing Co.

Stewart, S L, S A Sabatino, S L Foster and L C Richardson 2007. "Decline in Breast Cancer Incidence 1999–2003." *Morbidity and Mortality Weekly Report* 56 (8 June 2007): 549–553.

Stocker, Midge (ed.) 1993. *Confronting Cancer, Constructing Change: New Perspectives on Women and Cancer.* Chicago, IL: Third Side Press.

Tempest Williams, Terry 1991. *Refuge: An Unnatural History of Family and Place.* New York: Vintage Books.

United Nations Conference on Environment and Development 1992. "Rio Declaration on Environment and Development." www.unep.org/Documents.multilingual/Default.asp?DocumentID=78&ArticleID=1163 (accessed 9 September 2015).

U.S. Congress 1993. U.S. Congress, National Institutes of Health Revitalization Act of 1993, Study of Elevated Breast Cancer Rates in Long Island, Public Law 103–43, June 10, 1993, Section 1911. Potential Environmental and Other Risks Contributing to Incidence of Breast Cancer. Washington,

DC: U. S. Government Publishing Office. http://epi.grants.cancer.gov/past-initiatives/LIBCSP/PublicLaw.html (accessed 7 March 2016).

U.S. Congress 2008. U.S. Congress, Breast Cancer and Environmental Research Act of 2008, Public Law 110–354, October 8, 2008. Washington, DC: U.S. Government Publishing Office. www.gpo.gov/fdsys/pkg/PLAW-110publ354/pdf/PLAW-110publ354.pdf (accessed 7 March 2016).

Viviansayles, P J 1993. "The Politics of Breast Cancer." Commentary, *Ms.* (magazine) 3(6), pp. 54–55.

Winn, D M 2005. "Science and Society: The Long Island Breast Cancer Study Project." *Nature Reviews Cancer* 5(12): 986–994.

Wolff, Mary S and Janice Barlow 2011. "Breast Cancer Environment Centers and Advocacy." *Environmental Health Perspectives* 119(5): A200–A201.

Wolff, Mary S, Paolo Toniolo, Eric W Lee, Marilyn Rivera and Neil Dubin 1993. "Blood Levels of Organochlorine Residues and Risk of Breast Cancer." *Journal of the National Cancer Institute* 85: 648–652.

Women's Community Cancer Project 1993. "A Women's Cancer Agenda." In Midge Stocker (ed.) *Confronting Cancer, Constructing Change: New Perspectives on Women and Cancer.* Chicago, IL: Third Side Press, pp. 261–263.

30

EXCESSIVE HUMAN NUMBERS IN A WORLD OF FINITE LIMITS

Confronting the threshold of collapse

J. Kenneth Smail

Stretch a bow to the very full and you will wish you had stopped in time.

Lao-Tse

Introduction

In this chapter I call attention to the growing disconnection between reasonably accurate demographic projections of future global population growth (to more than 9 billion by the mid-twenty-first century) versus prudent scientific estimates of the Earth's likely long-term sustainable human carrying capacity (perhaps no more than 2 billion at a modest first-world standard of living). In addition to identifying the recent emergence of several other critical global challenges, I speculate about the nature of the profound evolutionary, ecological, and sociocultural consequences that could well appear during the twenty-first century. In essence, I argue that an important emergent phenomenon has become increasingly likely; namely, the growing potential for a global "synchronous failure," a cascading political, economic, social, environmental, and demographic breakdown (or generalized collapse) stimulated by the mutually-reinforcing convergence of multiple "inconvenient truths." This poses a fundamental existential question. Unless significant mitigating steps are soon undertaken, could the future of modern agricultural/industrial/technological civilization, as well as the lives of several billion human beings, be at considerable risk?

It has become increasingly apparent over the past half-century that there is a growing tension between two seemingly irreconcilable trends. On the one hand, moderate to conservative demographic projections indicate that global human numbers—currently around 7.4 billion—will almost certainly reach between 8.5 and 9 billion by the mid-twenty-first century, less than two generations from the present. On the other hand, prudent and increasingly reliable scientific estimates suggest that the Earth's long-term sustainable human carrying capacity, at what might be defined as a "minimally adequate" to "moderately comfortable" developed-world standard of living, may not be much greater than 2 billion. It may in fact be considerably less, perhaps in the range of 1 billion, particularly if the normative lifestyle (level of consumption) aspired to is anywhere close to that currently characterizing North America.

Consider the following thought experiments. Take any late twentieth/early twenty-first-century problem, whether environmental, economic, political, social, or moral, and ask whether its solution would be made easier—or more difficult—by a steadily growing population. Or conversely, imagine trying to resolve, or at least accommodate, these same problems in a context where population size—whether global or local—has either stabilized or slowly begun to decline. Or consider the following challenge posed by Bartlett (1998): can you think of any problem, on any scale, from microscopic to global, whose long-term solution is in any demonstrable way aided, assisted, or advanced by having larger populations at the local level, the state level, the national level, or globally? Or finally, might it be legitimate to ask whether the Earth suffers not so much from a "shortage" of resources as it does from a "longage" (or surfeit) of people (Hardin 1999)?

In what follows, I take the position that increasingly rapid population growth during the past century has played a central role in causing, or at least in further exacerbating, the numerous systemic problems—ecological, economic, political, social, and moral—that currently face our species. Although recognition of this fundamental fact has been slow in coming, there is now a growing realization that "demographic fatigue" can not only overwhelm the efforts of many less-developed nations, particularly those whose populations and corresponding infrastructural needs double (or more) every generation, but can also sap the strength of even the most robust and stable political and economic systems (Brown *et al.* 1999).

In fact, the magnitude and rapidity of this rampant and seemingly unregulated demographic expansion, particularly since the mid-twentieth century, have led some researchers to see certain fundamental similarities between the spread of the human species and the growth of a malignant melanoma (or other cancer). Consider the following criteria for identifying a cancerous malignancy (Gregg 1955; Hern 1993, 1999):

1   rapid, uncontrolled tissue growth;
2   invasion and destruction of adjacent normal tissue;
3   de-differentiation: loss of functional (adaptive) distinctiveness of individual tissue components;
4   metastasis: dissemination to and/or invasion of distant tissue sites; and
5   production of toxic metabolites.

Notwithstanding a difference in scale of several orders of magnitude, humanity:

1   has also grown explosively;
2   has invaded, destabilized, and simplified numerous adjacent ecosystems;
3   has become increasingly amalgamated into a single, undifferentiated global phenomenon (agro/techno/urban civilization);
4   has now metastasized into a monocultural "juggernaut" (Grant 1996) in the process of spreading to (colonizing) all corners of the Earth; typically accompanied by
5   an excessive production of ecologically dangerous waste and pollution.

In short, one could argue that the human species has now become a growing cancer—a malignant ecotumor—on the planet, and further that this cancerous process has increasingly been reinforced by what has become a runaway (positive feedback) relationship between continued population growth and ongoing cultural/technological elaboration (Hern 1993). In the simplest terms, this human cancer has the potential to, significantly and perhaps permanently, destabilize the planetary ecosystem.

Global population reduction

I thus begin with the following general propositions:

1   that there are indeed finite limits to global human numbers;
2   that these limits have not only been reached, but already exceeded; and
3   that population stabilization and subsequent significant decline are not only desirable, but almost certainly inevitable.

However, as is usually the case, the devil is in the details, and there is obviously considerable disagreement about appropriate means to this end. While many have tended to focus on rapid population growth as the primary causal mechanism underlying many (if not most) of our current global difficulties, others have preferred to explain these critical challenges (including population growth) as the consequence, or outcome, of the operation of various other factors. As with so many problems of this nature, particularly those dealing with complex and non-linear adaptive systems, the reality, of course, is probably somewhere in between, the synergistic result of numerous feedback mechanisms, both positive and negative, operating in a complex causal network.

At any rate, as a consequence of this modern-day "Malthusian dilemma," it seems reasonable to suggest that it is now time—indeed, past time—to think boldly about the mid-range future, and to consider alternatives that go beyond merely slowing the growth, or even achieving the stabilization, of global human numbers. In this partly hortatory chapter, I take the position that it has now become necessary for the human species to develop and implement, as quickly as possible, a well-conceived, clearly articulated, flexibly designed, broadly equitable, and internationally coordinated program focused on bringing about a *very significant reduction in global human numbers* over the next two or more centuries.

In simple quantitative terms, given the above-mentioned "irreconcilable numbers," this will probably require a global population "shrinkage" of at least 75–80 percent, from a probable mid-to-late twenty-first-century "peak" in the range of 9 to 11 billion to a future (twenty-second century and beyond) "population optimum" of not more than 2 billion, or perhaps even fewer. While these tentative target figures may at first glance seem draconian, it is surely worth remembering that global human numbers only passed the 1 billion mark in the early nineteenth century, barely two centuries ago, and only reached the 2 billion mark in the late 1920s, a time still within living memory.

Obviously, a demographic change of this magnitude, whether brought about by conscious human design or ultimately by forces beyond human control, will require a major reorientation of human thought, values, expectations, and lifestyle(s). Unfortunately, there is no guarantee that such a program will be successful. Moreover, if humanity fails in this effort, it seems likely that nature's even harsher realities will almost certainly be imposed. Speaking as a professional physical anthropologist/human evolutionary biologist, it is entirely possible that this rapidly metastasizing—yet still partly hidden—demographic and environmental crisis could emerge as the greatest evolutionary/ecological "bottleneck" that our species has yet encountered.

To the best of my knowledge, any claim to originality on my part stems primarily from my willingness, in several published essays and papers over the past two decades, to speak more openly and candidly than most about *the next logical step beyond global population stabilization* (Smail 1995, 1997a, 1997b, 1997c, 2002a, 2002b, 2003a, 2003b, 2004, 2008). Specifically, I refer here to my central argument: *first*, that a significant *decrease* in global human numbers is now a necessary—and probably inevitable—consequence of a century-long period of "explosive" population growth that now shows numerous signs of having already exceeded the Earth's long-term optimal human carrying capacity; and *second*, that the unsustainable "tensions" resulting from this complex dynamic could potentially lead to the fragmentation and eventual collapse of modern agricultural/industrial/technological civilization, perhaps *within* the lifetimes of those now living.

Validating the hypothesis

It is important to recognize that this admittedly controversial proposition—that there must be a very significant reduction in global human numbers over the next one or two centuries—is presented here in the form of a testable scientific hypothesis, one that is amenable not only to continued empirical confirmation, but also to potential falsification. In other words, this hypothesis may be quickly and easily *rejected* (i.e. empirically falsified), if it can clearly be demonstrated that ongoing estimates for global population size over the next few hundred years *will not exceed* what will presumably be increasingly accurate projections of both current and future optimal human carrying capacities. For the purposes of this chapter, an "optimal" carrying capacity may be defined as a population size, typically *less than* the sustainable maximum, that is most likely to produce a good and sustainable (i.e. broadly acceptable) quality of life for its members, without adversely affecting the quality of life of people who live elsewhere or of people who will live in future times.

However, this hypothesis is *confirmed* if future global population size *continues to exceed* (by a significant margin) these same carrying capacity estimates. Moreover, such confirmation would be true regardless of whether human numbers continue to grow at current rates, grow more slowly, stabilize, or even begin to decline. For example, even if future research shows that the 2 billion (or smaller) optimal carrying capacity utilized in this chapter has been significantly underestimated (i.e. is "off-target" by a factor of two or more), the argument put forth here loses little, if any, of its persuasive power; nor is the above hypothesis in any way invalidated. The reason for this is simple. Even a global population optimum of 4 to 5 billion, more than double the figure recommended here, would still necessitate a very substantial reduction (of some 50 percent or more) from the 9 to 10 billion projected for the mid-to-late twenty-first century.

Notwithstanding the numerous difficulties in addressing a problem of such complexity, it is nonetheless surprising how little scientific and public attention has been directed toward establishing empirically quantifiable, scientifically testable, and socioculturally agreed-upon parameters for what the Earth's long-term human carrying capacity—or flexibly defined "optimal population range"—might actually be. Unfortunately, with only a few notable exceptions, many otherwise well-qualified scientific investigators and public policy analysts have been rather hesitant to take a clear and forthright position on this profoundly important matter, certainly destined to become the overarching issue of the current century.

It is difficult to say whether this unfortunate reticence is due to ingrained investigatory caution, concerns about professional reputation and advancement (particularly among younger investigators), the increasingly specialized structure of both the scientific and political enterprises, personal qualms about reaching conclusions that have potentially unpalatable social and political ramifications, or other unspecified (and perhaps deeply-rooted) ideological, moral, or religious reservations (Beck and Kolankiewicz 2000). Or perhaps, given its global nature and seemingly endless ramifications, the chief difficulty in dealing with the complex population/environment conundrum represents little more than a manifestation of "scale paralysis," that enervating sense of individual and collective powerlessness when confronted by problems that seem overwhelming in their magnitude.

Certainly, the rough approximations of global human carrying capacity put forth during the past century show considerable variation, ranging from fewer than 1 billion to well beyond 20 billion, an order of magnitude or more (Cohen 1995). It is, however, important to note that since the 1990s, a growing number of investigators (and organizations) have articulated reasonably well-thought-out positions on future global population optimums. Interestingly enough, most of these estimates have clustered in the 1 to 3 billion range. This is an important development, since it is patently obvious that it will be difficult to engender any sort of effective public response to the above-mentioned global crisis if future population goals (i.e. desired demographic optimums) continue to be imperfectly understood and poorly articulated.

Multiple challenges

Quite frankly, I hope the above hypothesis is wrong and that various demographic optimists are correct in their claims that, thanks to a number of significant recent developments—from effective and inexpensive contraceptive techniques to advances in women's education and empowerment—human numbers will begin to show a "natural" stabilization and subsequent decline somewhat sooner than expected. Presumably, when this welcome demographic trend is coupled with enhanced efficiencies in energy production, resource utilization, and materials conservation, and is further reinforced by efforts toward significantly reduced per capita consumption levels (particularly in the more developed world), it might allow for somewhat larger carrying capacities, or optimal population sizes, than we currently imagine.

But this sort of optimism is warranted only by corroborative data; that is, only if the above-mentioned "irreconcilable numbers" show unmistakable evidence of coming into much closer congruence. For it is now increasingly apparent that any such optimism should be tempered by an honest and full consideration of the problems surrounding a broad range of rapidly emerging (and converging) "inconvenient truths"—global phenomena whose powerful downstream effects will undoubtedly become manifest within the next few decades, if they have not done so already. In addition to the overpopulation/carrying capacity conundrum, the two "truths" that have thus far generated the most public interest and controversy, both scientific and political, are of course:

1   *Unpredictable climatic trends:* or the broad-scale ecological, economic, political, and cultural consequences of ongoing "climate change," or increasing "climatic instability" (or more popularly, anthropogenic "global warming"). Based on the evidence now provided by extensive scientific research and analysis since the 1980s, these wide-ranging climatic phenomena and longer-term trends are empirically quite well documented, certainly resting on a strong "preponderance of evidence" as they come ever closer to the level of "beyond reasonable doubt."

2   *Post-peak fossil energy supplies:* or the unpredictable consequences—including the potential for wide-scale political, economic, and social destabilization—of passing the global "production peak" of oil, coal, and natural gas. For it seems increasingly likely that the "post-carbon" world will soon be engaged in a massive struggle to adapt to a long-term and significant decline in the availability of cheap and abundant energy from fossil fuels, the aptly named "ancient sunlight" that for the past two centuries has fueled

the exuberant growth of modern agricultural/industrial/technological civilization (Hartmann 2004; Heinberg 2005; Greer 2008; Klare 2012).

More specifically, the evidence from recent "peak energy" research and analysis increasingly suggests that by the middle of the twenty-first century, humanity will be faced with a global population of some 9 billion, struggling to maintain—or in many instances still trying to acquire—some semblance of modern first-world civilization on but a third to a half of the oil and gas the world *currently* produces, exacerbated still further by a notable deficit of "proven" or "environmentally benign" energy substitutes (renewable or otherwise) on anywhere near the scale that would be necessary.

This of course is in addition to dealing with the growing constraints and pressures due to a broad range of other important "limiting factors," most of which have been the subject of considerable scientific study, public concern, and increased political attention over the past generation and more. Chief among these multiple and complexly interconnected "critical challenges" are:

1 continuing rapid population growth, particularly in the less-developed world;
2 the diminishing availability of fresh water, particularly for agricultural use;
3 the ongoing degradation of topsoil, both in terms of fertility decline and erosional losses;
4 maintaining an adequate food supply (plant, animal, and fish protein) for growing populations;
5 growing shortages of, and geopolitical competition for, essential minerals and materials;
6 the steady constriction of wilderness areas and reduced global biodiversity;
7 the warming and increasing acidification of the oceans (around 70 percent of the Earth's surface);
8 growing stresses on public health due to breakdowns in the epidemiological environment;
9 the increasingly sclerotic malfunctioning of basic political, economic, and social institutions;
10 a pervasive economic mindset based on the fallacy of unlimited growth in a finite world;
11 the growing potential for a major collapse of the world's debt-based financial system;
12 the growing power and influence of "non-state" actors (criminal gangs, terrorist groups, etc.);
13 ongoing and uncontrolled mass migration, not only cross-border, but also within-border;
14 the ever-present danger posed by weapons of mass destruction (nuclear, chemical, biological);
15 and surely others that the reader might identify . . .

Acknowledging our dilemma

Given the above, it is obvious that assertions that the Earth might be able to support a population of 10 to 15 billion people for an indefinite period of time at a standard of living similar to or superior to the present are not only cruelly misleading, but almost certainly false. Notwithstanding our current addiction to continued and uninterrupted economic growth, surely the dominant political mantra of the twentieth and early twenty-first centuries (what some have aptly termed "growthmania"), it is essential for humanity to recognize that there are, in fact, *finite physical, biological, and ecological limits to the Earth's long-term sustainable carrying capacity* (i.e. the "natural capital" that supports us). And to recognize further that we are now drawing down on the principal, as well as the interest, of these precious "capital assets," as many of these finite limits have already been reached (and in a number of instances surpassed).

Consequently, because at some point in the not-too-distant future, the negative ramifications and ecological damage stemming from the mutually reinforcing effects of excessive human reproduction and over-consumption of resources could well become irreversible, and since there is only one Earth with which to experiment, it would undoubtedly be better for our species to err on the side of prudence, exercising wherever possible a cautious and careful stewardship.

Surely it is time to suggest that the burden of proof on these matters, so long shouldered by so-called "neo-Malthusian pessimists," be increasingly shifted to the "cornucopian optimists." In other words, for those who might be inclined to ignore (or summarily reject) the hypothesis put forth here, the *scientific* "burden of proof" should be quite clear: *what is the evidence that the Earth can withstand—without irreparable damage—another two or more centuries during which global human numbers and per capita consumption greatly exceed the Earth's optimal (sustainable) carrying capacity?*

In any event, having established in this chapter an empirically "quantifiable" and "falsifiable" frame of reference, it seems obvious that it is now time to go one step further, and at the very least begin to make the case that current rhetoric about "slowing the growth," or even achieving the "stabilization," of global human numbers *is clearly insufficient to the task that lies before us*. Quite simply, both the empirical data and inexorable logic suggest with increasing clarity that what will be required for the foreseeable future—the "default position" for the next two or three centuries—is a *very significant reduction* in global human numbers.

Admittedly, this presents a vexing "temporal disconnection" that may be difficult (perhaps even impossible) to resolve, particularly in a manner that will be perceived as equitable, voluntary, and humane. It seems all too likely that the period of time—*at least two centuries*— that will be minimally necessary for initial population stabilization and subsequent reduction, eventually to a desired global optimum in the 1 to 2 billion range, is clearly inconsistent with the much more "restricted" time frame suggested by the rapidly swelling chorus of those who project significant fossil-energy production declines, and steadily growing problems associated with global climatic change and accompanying food shortages, appearing within the next generation or two.

I refer here to the distinct possibility of an environmental "critical threshold," or quasi-evolutionary "bottleneck," or cascading political, economic, and social "breakdown," or global "synchronous failure," all emerging over the *next several decades* (by the mid-twenty-first century or before), while demographic momentum remains an active force and global human numbers continue to increase.

I am therefore only cautiously optimistic that the human species will be able successfully to confront the complex and interrelated problems we have managed to create for ourselves— what some have begun to characterize as an ecological, demographic, economic, political, sociocultural, and moral "perfect storm." In fact, when I see how little traction various mitigating (or ameliorative) efforts have gained over the past 30 to 40 years, I have become increasingly pessimistic that humanity—potentially some 9-plus billion of us within our children's and grandchildren's lifetimes—will be successful in staving off some very difficult times over the next several generations.

Collapse scenarios

Given this, it is certainly time—indeed, past time—to give serious consideration to steps that might avert, or at least to some extent mitigate, the growing possibility of a partial-to-full collapse of what we have come to know as modern agricultural/industrial/technological civilization. A number of reasonably well-articulated "collapse scenarios" have been recently put forth, ranging from gradual to rapid. Though hardly an exhaustive overview, the following examples are representative:

1   *A slow and inexorable decline* (i.e. gradual destabilization, fragmentation, and break-down) over a considerable period of time; what some have termed a "long emergency," eventually resulting in much smaller—as well as more "localized" and "resilient"—political, economic, and social units; a more-or-less "soft landing" collapse, extending over multiple generations and several centuries.

2   *A gradual but "step-wise" collapse,* characterized by repeated periods of decline that alternate with temporary—but ultimately unsuccessful—attempts at reintegration and stability at lower levels; a pattern of ongoing "de-industrialization" that some have characterized as a "catabolic" process, inevitably resulting in ever greater political, social, technological, and demographic "simplification" over an extended period (i.e. centuries).

3   *A much more rapid breakdown,* with little advance warning and/or prior preparation, as modern agricultural/industrial/technological civilization rather quickly (and unexpect-edly) crosses over the edge of a partly unforeseen precipice—most likely a "finite energy and resources" threshold—with severe-to-chaotic political, economic, social, and demographic consequences; a "hard landing" collapse that develops over a few years to at most a few decades.

4   *A sudden and total systemic collapse,* most likely resulting from an all-encompassing and rapidly expanding global "territorial and resource war" involving the use of nuclear, chemical, and/or biological weapons of mass destruction; complete devastation and unimaginable social chaos, with deaths probably in the billions; an "irreversible" political, economic, and societal collapse occurring within a few days to at most a few weeks.

It goes without saying that each of the above collapse scenarios would be characterized by—indeed, would undoubtedly necessitate—a very significant decrease in global human numbers, almost certainly numbering in the hundreds of millions (if not several billions). This would happen irrespective of whether such a reduction would be sudden (a catastrophic mass "die-off") or develop somewhat more gradually (and, one hopes, rather more humanely).

For a more detailed discussion and analysis of the causes and consequences of civilizational collapse, as well as providing several points of entry into the literature describing a broad range of collapse scenarios (both historical and contemporary), the interested reader may wish to consult the following: Catton 1980, 2009; Tainter 1988; Hardin 1993; Smith *et al.* 1998; Meadows *et al.* 2004; Diamond 2005; Grant 2005; Heinberg 2005, 2007; Kunstler 2005; Homer-Dixon 2006; Ponting 2007; Greer 2008, 2011; Orlov 2008; Ahmed 2010; Dilworth 2010; Ophuls 2012; Ehrlich and Ehrlich 2013; Oreskes and Conway 2014.

In sum, the *synergistic combination* of the previously-mentioned "critical challenges," when considered together with any of the just-described "collapse scenarios," surely represents a toxic brew. Succinctly stated in the language of systems theory, Ophuls argues that:

In fact, the potential for catastrophe is ever present in chaotic systems. The gradual accumulation of small changes can push a system over an unseen threshold and thereby precipitate rapid and radical change . . . (and) the very fact that complex systems [civilizations] have key links and nodes connected by multiple feedback loops means that they are vulnerable to a cascade of failure. To put it another way, systems that are too tightly coupled or too efficient are fragile; they lack resilience. . . . When formerly separate problems coalesce into a problematique, [a civilization] does not face one or two discrete challenges, as in simpler times, but instead a swarm of simultaneous challenges that can overwhelm its capacity to respond, thereby provoking a general collapse (i.e., a catastrophe that propagates rapidly across a globe that is ever more tightly coupled).

(Ophuls 2012: 39)

Civilizations are (thus) trapped in a vicious circle. They must keep solving the problems of complexity, for that is the price of civilized existence, but every solution creates new, ever more difficult problems, which then require new, ever more demanding solutions. Thus, complexity breeds more of the same, and each increase in complexity makes it harder to cope, while at the same time escalating the penalty for failure. In effect, civilizations enact a tragedy in which their raison d'être—the use of energy to foster the complexity that has raised them above the hunter-gatherer level of subsistence—becomes the agent of their ultimate downfall (Ophuls 2012: 36).

And it certainly doesn't help that our current deteriorating state of affairs—with a few notable exceptions—has been further exacerbated by a generalized lack of political, economic, social, and moral foresight and cooperation on both a national and global level, not to mention a recalcitrant human nature all too prone to both individual and collective denial. Nevertheless, to the extent that humans universally share a deep-rooted and powerful "investment in immortality," however we might individually or collectively choose to define it, it is essential that we keep trying to bias the future in a positive direction.

Consumption and equity concerns

Even though I have previously referred to the significance of global (and per capita) energy and resource consumption, this matter undoubtedly deserves further discussion and elaboration. To a certain extent, the quantitative importance of consumption to the population/environment dynamic can easily be demonstrated by the following manipulation of variables in the well-known I = PCT equation: *Impact = Population × Consumption × Technology* (Holdren and Ehrlich 1974). Even if considerably enhanced technological and other conservation-oriented efficiencies (T) could reduce global energy usage and "waste and pollution" by as much as 50 percent, these gains would quickly be cancelled out by a doubling of population (P). To many observers, this suggests that the most effective short-term means of reducing humankind's "total impact" (I) on the global environment would be to focus on significantly reducing per capita consumption (C). This not only could, but undoubtedly should, include efforts to reduce (or minimize) as much as possible the very large (and in some instances, growing) "affluence differentials" between the developed and less-developed worlds.

Put another way, this suggests that the developed world also has a population problem of significant proportions, particularly when one considers that per capita consumption rates (and corresponding ecosystem impacts) in so-called "rich" nations may be 5, 10, 25, 50, or even 100 times greater than in those nations designated as materially "poor." Therefore, it should not be surprising to anyone that the less-developed world's typical response to suggestions that they significantly curtail their "rampant" population growth is an equally emphatic call for developed nations to greatly reduce their "profligate" consumption levels, or population, or both!

Given this current impasse, let me make a few additional observations on matters pertaining to population growth, per capita consumption levels, and ongoing attempts to minimize as much as possible the above-mentioned "disparities" between rich and poor. Certainly, if greater fairness or balance in the distribution and utilization of the Earth's finite resources (i.e. enhanced global equity) is to be coupled with a considerably enhanced standard of living (quality of life) for the mildly-to-severely "disadvantaged 80 percent" of the world's peoples, something has simply "got to give." For example, according to Myers:

> Per capita consumption worldwide has increased by 3% per year during the past quarter century, so it is reasonable to suppose that people in the future will want it to increase by at least 2% per year (provided it can be sustainable). Per capita consumption would then double in 35 years, quadruple in 70 years and increase eightfold by 2100. . . . Were global population to reach 11 billion people by 2100, total consumption would (then) expand 15 times—an amount surely unsustainable given available stocks of nonrenewable natural resources and given the Earth's limited capacity to absorb pollution among other forms of waste. Even a low-variant projection for global population, 6.0 billion by 2100 (albeit after a mid-century peak of 8.0 billion) would leave consumption soaring 8.4 times.
>
> *(Myers 1997: 212)*

In short, it seems increasingly evident that even greatly enhanced technological efficiencies (on a worldwide scale) and considerably reduced per capita consumption (by nations in the developed world) *will not be enough by themselves* to bring about the oft-articulated, and presumably desirable, goals of greater equity and justice, particularly in a world that seems destined to add another 3 billion people within the next two or three generations. And if one further argues that humanity's fundamental goal—indeed, ethical first principle—must necessarily be to preserve the stability and resilience of the Earth's integrated ecosystem(s), the logical (and pragmatic) consequence seems both obvious and irrefutable: *only a global human population "optimized" at a considerably reduced size will provide the opportunity to build a much better quality of life for everyone.*

Finally, a few closing comments about equity concerns may also be relevant. I fully agree that a cooperative global effort to resolve humanity's current crises, in terms of population and otherwise, will require both the perception and the reality of an honest movement toward equity of all kinds (gender, class, ethnic, religious, economic, educational, etc.). But it is important to note that in addition to enhanced equity for those currently alive (what might be defined as *intra-generational* or "spatial" equity), there is also the equally important matter of equity for future generations (*inter-generational* or "temporal" equity), and to recognize further that these two imperatives may frequently come into conflict.

In fact, given the inevitability of increasing tensions in the ongoing dynamic between present and future generations, so much in evidence already, it is of crucial importance that we develop the political and moral courage *now* to make the kinds of decisions that will maintain or enhance an acceptable quality of life *later on* (for our descendants). Suffice it to say that none of these decisions will be easy, especially those concerned with matters pertaining to the beginnings of life (e.g. encouraging voluntary and equitable limits on fertility) or those concerned with issues at life's end (e.g. developing ethically acceptable limits on the use of "extraordinary measures" to marginally prolong life).

Last, but not necessarily least, as many have eloquently described, there is yet another balance that must be maintained. For the lack of a better term, this might be described as a "geo-biological equity," establishing a balance not only between our species and numerous other life forms via biodiversity and wilderness preservation, but also with the Earth itself via conservation of the varied components of the geosphere (Cafaro and Crist 2012). Simply stated, humanity will surely be better able to confront these issues if we can collectively come to regard ourselves more as the Earth's long-term stewards rather than its absolute masters (Wilson 1992).

Ongoing uncertainties

I fully realize that population projections are not predictions and, as mentioned earlier, I very much hope that continuation of recent worldwide declines in fertility suggests that global human numbers could "peak" (stabilize) somewhere in the range of 9 to 10 billion during the mid-/late twenty-first century, and then begin a slow but steady decline. Much of this guarded optimism is based on the assumption—but not the assurance—that certain inferences based on the demographic transition model are empirically justified, particularly the claim that there is a strong positive correlation between increased economic, social, physical, and sexual well-being, and steadily decreasing fertility levels. But it is entirely possible that these assumptions and correlations are also "projections" rather than "predictions," leaving at least three possibilities insufficiently addressed.

First, what sorts of unpredictable and potentially deleterious instabilities might be introduced in the meantime, as both the Earth and humanity attempt to cope with the increasingly severe twenty-first-century political, economic, environmental, sociocultural, and moral "difficulties and discontinuities" discussed earlier? And what effect, if any, will the "dislocations" stimulated by these problems, most likely resulting in a *decrease* in economic, social, and physical well-being, have on the above-mentioned declining fertility rates, or for that matter on mortality rates?

Second, even if the demographic transition model does have predictive value, will global fertility rates necessarily keep on declining to levels below ZPG (zero population growth), as any attempt at significant population reduction requires? Or might they stabilize at levels that are considerably smaller than at present, yet still modestly positive (perhaps in the 2.2 to 2.5 fertility range)? In other words, will the demographic trajectories observed in the developed world over the past century necessarily be the case for nations in the developing world over the next half-century?

Third, just how large a "shrinkage" (population reduction) should there be, assuming we are indeed fortunate enough to reach that critical turning point? This of course is a matter which has very much to do with a set of even more difficult projections, not so much about changes in population size, but rather about the Earth's long-term optimal and sustainable carrying capacity. Until convincing evidence is presented to the contrary, it would seem prudent to adhere to the rather conservative "global optimum" of 1 to 2 billion articulated throughout this chapter.

Coordinating the effort

This leads to a crucial final point—the ineluctable fact that in our multinational and politically fragmented world, solutions cannot be imposed from without. Ultimately, both individually and collectively, the people of each sovereign state must come to terms with, and subsequently resolve, their own unique demographic and consumption problems, motivated, it is hoped, not only by an increasing awareness of global realities, but even more by their local consequences. In this regard, given the limited time available and the excruciatingly difficult decisions that must be made, it is daunting to realize that population problems are often the most pronounced in areas of the world where national sovereignty—and the requisite political, economic, and social stability—is most tenuous (Connelly and Kennedy 1994; Kaplan 1994; Weisman 2013).

However, at no point do I make the case—nor do I recommend—that the political means toward the goal of significantly reduced global human numbers necessarily involve collective, interventionist, centrally administered, rigidly target-oriented, or draconian top-down measures implemented by some sort of supra-national world government. Rather, such measures as are employed should be essentially voluntary, broadly equitable, flexibly designed, locally focused (bottom-up), primarily educational, and appropriately sensitive to various cultural, ethnic, gender, and religious considerations (as well as the strong likelihood of deeply-rooted biological inclinations and propensities).

To be sure, these measures would need to be coordinated over a lengthy period of time (several generations) by some sort of international clearing house whose primary function would be to provide all relevant political and other "entities"—including, and most especially, various non-governmental organizations (NGOs) and public-interest groups—with accurate, internally coherent, and consistent information, both scientific and sociopolitical. Such information would be designed to address each entity's particular and unique demographic situation, all within the broader context (generalized goal) of moving toward a considerably smaller and increasingly optimal world population that might provide a better quality of life for all.

I do not at this time see the likelihood of going much beyond this level of international cooperation and coordination, the basic framework of which already exists. Whether this sort of structure and/or strategy will be sufficient for the enormity of the task, however, I am not prepared to answer. What I do know is that humanity does not need any further delay in educating itself about—and subsequently confronting—these critically important issues. Our "window of opportunity" may not be open much longer.

Because of these (and other) difficulties, it remains to be seen whether humanity will be capable of mounting a unified and lasting effort toward population limitation and subsequent reduction. Clearly this will be an unprecedented undertaking, a broad-ranging effort that must be conducted on a species-wide scale, and an endeavor that by its very nature must be sustained for a century or more. While posterity demands that we be successful, I am only cautiously optimistic that such success can be achieved by rational human forethought, or by means compatible with contemporary social, political, and ethical norms. One can only hope that these ongoing doubts about our capacity to confront these problems successfully will somehow serve to strengthen our resolve.

Final thoughts

And so, the crucial question: is it naïve to suggest that the evidence is now sufficiently convincing to encourage a "critical mass" of knowledgeable, concerned, and motivated investigators to quickly begin to put together a serious, legitimate, and empirically well-documented case for averting what appears to be a rapidly emerging global catastrophe? If so, it would certainly become much easier—or more "palatable"—for still other scientists, as well as environmentalists, politicians, economists, moralists, and other concerned citizens of the planet, to speak forthrightly and with ever greater confidence about humanity's responsibility to rapidly and resolutely address this burgeoning existential crisis.

Surely it is essential that elected public officials, civil servants at all levels of government, academics from a broad range of disciplines, representatives of the news media, religious leaders from all the major faith traditions, and spokespersons for national and international environmental organizations, should not feel as though they are committing political, professional, or moral suicide by bringing these matters to public attention. For time is becoming increasingly precious, and the above-mentioned "window of opportunity" for effective remedial action may shortly be closing, if it has not already done so.

I very much hope that this all-too-brief and partly hortatory chapter has helped to clarify an important and often underappreciated point: that ongoing population growth has a significant influence on, or connection with, nearly every other critical issue that humanity currently faces. I hope it is also obvious that this influence is both reciprocal and mutually reinforcing, resulting in numerous and interconnected positive feedback (or deviation amplifying) systems and subsystems, many of which are imperfectly understood. It may thus be entirely appropriate to characterize the twentieth and early twenty-first centuries' rapid and continuing population expansion as *the* critical factor that not only undergirds—but also reinforces—many, if not most, of our species' growing political, economic, social, environmental, and moral difficulties.

Until demonstrated otherwise, *I would therefore suggest that unchecked or "insufficiently restrained" population growth should be considered the single most important feature in an admittedly complex (and synergistic) physical, ecological, biocultural, and sociopolitical landscape.* More than two centuries after the publication of *An Essay on the Principle of Population*, it is surely worth remembering that, except for not fully anticipating the subsequent human capacity to overcome—if only temporarily—certain "checks" on population expansion, the analysis by the Reverend Thomas Malthus (2004 [1798]: 20) of the "strong and constantly operating check on population [emerging] from the difficulty of subsistence" may have been right on target!

In any event, it should by now be unassailable that the limitation of human population size, and subsequently confronting the numerous problems that will be engendered by its eventual and inevitable contraction, should occupy a central position within the "modern problematique," and as such should be dealt with much more forthrightly, and much more promptly, than has heretofore been the case.

More than half a century ago, at the dawn of the nuclear age, Albert Einstein suggested that we shall require a new manner of thinking, if humankind is to survive. Even though the aptly named "population explosion" is neither as instantaneous nor as spectacular as its nuclear counterpart, its ultimate consequences may be just as real (and potentially just as devastating) as the so-called "nuclear winter" scenarios promulgated in the early 1980s (Turco *et al.* 1983).

That there will be a large-scale reduction in global human numbers over the next two or more centuries appears to be inevitable. The primary issue may well be whether this lengthy and difficult process will be moderately benign or unpredictably chaotic. More specifically, is modern humanity capable of a comprehensive organized effort to compassionately reduce global human numbers, or will brutal self-interest prevail—either haphazardly or selectively—resulting in an unprecedented toll of human lives, not to mention the growing likelihood of a global civilizational collapse? Clearly we must begin our "new manner of thinking" about this critically important issue now, so that Einstein's prescient and very legitimate concerns about human and civilizational survival into the twenty-first century and beyond may be addressed as rapidly, as fully, and as humanely as possible.

Assuming then, my postulata as granted, I say that the power of population is indefinitely greater than the power in the earth to produce subsistence for man.

(*Thomas Malthus 2004[1798]*)

References

Ahmed N M 2010. *A User's Guide to the Crisis of Civilization (and How to Save it)*. London: Pluto Press.

Bartlett A A 1998. Reflections in 1998 on the twentieth anniversary of the publication of the paper: "Forgotten fundamentals of the energy crisis." *NPG Special Reports*. Teaneck, NJ: Negative Population Growth.

Beck R and Kolankiewicz L 2000. The environmental movement's retreat from advocating US population stabilization (1970–1988): A first draft of history. *Journal of Policy History* 12(1): 123–151.

Brown L R, Gardner G and Halweil B 1999. *Beyond Malthus: Nineteen Dimensions of the Population Challenge*. New York: W. W. Norton & Company.

Cafaro P and Crist E 2012. *Life on the Brink: Environmentalists Confront Overpopulation*. Athens: The University of Georgia Press.

Catton W R 1980. *Overshoot: The Ecological Basis of Revolutionary Change*. Urbana: University of Illinois Press.

Catton W R 2009. *Bottleneck: Humanity's Impending Impasse*. Bloomington, IN: Xlibris Corporation. www.Xlibris.com

Cohen J E 1995. *How Many People Can the Earth Support?* New York: W. W. Norton & Company.

Connelly M and Kennedy P 1994. Must it be the West against the rest? *The Atlantic Monthly* 274(6), pp. 61–84.

Diamond J 2005. *Collapse: How Societies Choose to Fail or Succeed*. New York: Viking Penguin.

Dilworth C 2010. *Too Smart for our Own Good: The Ecological Predicament of Humankind*. Cambridge, UK: Cambridge University Press.

Ehrlich P R and Ehrlich A H 2013. Can a collapse of global civilization be avoided? *Proceedings of the Royal Society B: Biological Sciences* 280(1754). http://rspb.royalsocietypublishing.org/content/280/1754/20122845 (accessed 4 November 2013).

Grant L 1996. *Juggernaut: Growth on a Finite Planet*. Santa Ana, CA: Seven Locks Press.

Grant L 2005. *The Collapsing Bubble: Growth and Fossil Energy*. Santa Ana, CA: Seven Locks Press.

Greer J M 2008. *The Long Descent: A User's Guide to the End of the Industrial Age*. Gabriola Island, BC: New Society Publishers.

Greer J M 2011. *The Wealth of Nature: Economics as if Survival Mattered*. Gabriola Island, BC: New Society Publishers.

Gregg A 1955. A medical aspect of the population problem. *Science* 121(3150): 681–682.

Hardin G 1993. *Living within Limits: Ecology, Economics, and Population Taboos*. New York: Oxford University Press.

Hardin G 1999. *The Ostrich Factor: Our Population Myopia*. New York: Oxford University Press.

Hartmann T 2004. *The Last Hours of Ancient Sunlight: The Fate of the World and what we Can Do before it's Too Late*. New York: Three Rivers Press.

Heinberg R 2005. *The Party's Over: Oil, War and the Fate of Industrial Societies*. Gabriola Island, BC: New Society Publishers.

Heinberg R 2007. *Peak Everything: Waking Up to the Century of Declines*. Gabriola Island, BC: New Society Publishers.

Hern W A 1993. Is human culture carcinogenic for uncontrollable population growth and ecological destruction? *Bioscience* 43(11): 768–773.

Hern W A 1999. How many times has the human population doubled? Comparisons with cancer. *Population and Environment* 21(1): 59–80.

Holdren J P and Ehrlich P R 1974. Human population and the global environment. *American Scientist* 62(3): 282–292.

Homer-Dixon T 2006. *The Upside of Down: Catastrophe, Creativity, and the Renewal of Civilization.* Washington, DC: Island Press.

Kaplan R D 1994. The Coming Anarchy. *The Atlantic Monthly* 273(2), pp. 44–76.

Klare M T 2012. *The Race for What's Left: The Global Scramble for the World's Last Resources.* New York: Henry Holt and Co.

Kunstler J H 2005. *The Long Emergency: Surviving the Converging Catastrophes of the Twenty-First Century.* New York: Atlantic Monthly Press.

Malthus T R 2004 [1798]. *An Essay on the Principle of Population* (edited by P Appleman). Norton Critical Editions. 2nd edn. New York: W. W. Norton & Company.

Meadows D, Randers J and Meadows D 2004. *Limits to Growth: The 30-Year Update.* White River Junction, VT: Chelsea Green Publishing Co.

Myers N 1997. The population/environment predicament: Even more urgent than supposed. *Politics and the Life Sciences* 16(2): 211–213.

Ophuls W 2012. *Immoderate Greatness: Why Civilizations Fail.* North Charleston, SC: CreateSpace Independent Publishing Platform.

Oreskes N and Conway E M 2014. *The Collapse of Western Civilization: A View from the Future.* New York: Columbia University Press.

Orlov D 2008. *Reinventing Collapse: The Soviet Example and American Prospects.* Gabriola Island, BC: New Society Publishers.

Ponting C 2007. *A New Green History of the World: The Environment and the Collapse of Great Civilizations.* New York: Penguin Books.

Smail J K 1995. Confronting the 21st century's hidden crisis: Reducing human numbers by 80%. *NPG Forum Series.* Teaneck, NJ: Negative Population Growth.

Smail J K 1997a. Averting the 21st century's demographic crisis: Can human numbers be reduced by 75%? *Population and Environment* 18(6): 565–580.

Smail J K 1997b. Beyond population stabilization: The case for dramatically reducing global human numbers. *Politics and the Life Sciences* 16(2): 183–192. [*Note*: This "Roundtable Article" was accompanied by 16 "Commentaries" contributed by an international group of scholars and public policy analysts (*Politics and the Life Sciences* 16(2): 193–230).]

Smail, J K 1997c. Population growth seems to affect everything but is seldom held responsible for anything. *Politics and the Life Sciences* 16(2): 231–236. [*Note*: Author's "Response" to the 16 "Commentaries" mentioned in Smail 1997b.]

Smail J K 2002a. Confronting a surfeit of people: Reducing global human numbers to sustainable levels (an essay on population two centuries after Malthus). *Environment, Development and Sustainability* 4(1): 21–50.

Smail J K 2002b. Remembering Malthus: A preliminary argument for a significant reduction in global human numbers. *American Journal of Physical Anthropology* 118(3): 292–297.

Smail J K 2003a. Remembering Malthus II: Establishing sustainable population optimums. *American Journal of Physical Anthropology* 122(3): 287–294.

Smail J K 2003b. Remembering Malthus III: Implementing a global population reduction. *American Journal of Physical Anthropology* 122(3): 295–300.

Smail J K 2004. Global population reduction: Confronting the inevitable. *World-Watch Magazine* 17(5), pp. 58–59.

Smail J K 2008. Acknowledging and confronting the inevitable: A significant shrinkage in global human numbers and other inconvenient truths. *Culture Change*, posted 5 May. www.culturechange.org/cms/index.php?option=com_content&task=view&id=168dItamid=1 (accessed 12 May 2008).

Smith J W, Lyons G and Moore E 1998. *Global Meltdown: Immigration, Multiculturalism, and National Breakdown in the New World Disorder.* Westport, CT: Praeger.

Tainter J A 1988. *The Collapse of Complex Societies.* Cambridge, UK: Cambridge University Press.

Turco R P, Toon O B, Ackerman T P, Pollack J P and Sagan C 1983. Nuclear winter: Global consequences of multiple nuclear explosions. *Science* 222(4630): 1283–1292.

Weisman A 2013. *Countdown: Our Last Best Hope for a Future on Earth?* New York: Little, Brown and Company.

Wilson E O 1992. *The Diversity of Life.* Cambridge, MA: Harvard University Press.

PART VII

Environment and education

31

CHILDREN'S LANGUAGE ABOUT THE ENVIRONMENT

Bryan Wee and Hillary Mason

Introduction

The environment, for all its intended simplicity, is framed by cultural perceptions and preferences that underlie environmental decision-making. Put another way, the environment means different things to different people. In a world that is increasingly subject to a wide range of global environmental impacts, there is a need for anthropological research that elucidates how the environment is interpreted and valued by different cultures. Culture refers to the ways by which landscapes are interpreted as text, one that is inscribed in social patterns and learned behaviors over time (Balée and Erickson 2006). Specific to our chapter, we recognize the environment as a social construct that is made intelligible through the use of cultural norms such as language, thereby giving form to what Matthews (1995: 285) calls "the raw materials of our social and material existence." Similarly, Balée and Erickson (2006: 9) use the term ecological *episteme* to describe "a way of knowing the environment that has its origins in the particular relationship it has had over time to local landscapes and to their metamorphosis at human hands." These socially constructed realities, or *epistemes*, are conditioned by our interactions with the environment and manifested in our language about the environment. Language structures our understanding of ourselves and of the landscapes we make an impact on. Without language, there would be neither common values nor a shared sense of responsibility, both of which are at the center of efforts to protect conditions that support life (Stibbe 2014). This chapter provides an expanded understanding of language as the encoding of particular social realities (Stibbe 2012), and how it shapes individual as well as collective perspectives about the environment.

In the first part of our chapter, we integrate the dual concepts of sense of place and linguistic relativity in explaining how language constitutes the cognitive and social fabric of our everyday lives. Understanding that language operates within a set of culturally bounded rules offers critical insight into how people inhabit and shape environments (Stables 2001). To highlight this point, the second part of this chapter offers a unique case study of children's language about the environment in China, a nation where human and natural landscapes are being irreversibly altered. Few studies have sought to understand children's language about the environment even though children are, like adults, people whose agency (or lack thereof) plays an important role in the development of their worldviews (Wee and Anthamatten

2014). We elaborate on the primary themes that emerged from this case study; namely, children's language about the environment as *affective expression, linguistic assimilation,* and *discursive practice.* A synthesis of our findings contributes to the 'linguistic turn' in research (Stibbe 2014) by addressing how language, particularly Chinese, constructs social realities. Our chapter concludes with broad considerations for attending to language and the discourse surrounding notions of equity and sustainability.

Language about the environment

From an anthropological standpoint, a study of language about the environment attends to how human societies express and situate themselves in the world. Concurrently, it supports a deeper appreciation of cultural relativism in linguistic communities. We gain a better understanding of "the ways in which a particular population purposefully or unintentionally shapes its environment, and the ways in which its relations with the environment shape its culture and its social, economic and political life" (Shoreman-Ouimet and Kopnina 2011: 5).

Sense of place

Sense of place, defined as a way of being in the world, validates the importance of inferred meanings across diverse landscapes (Cresswell 2009). People do not simply occupy physical spaces; they endow spaces with meanings through shared experiences as well as cultural expectations and actions. For example, asking people what it means to 'live in a city' is to consider spatial and social factors such as where they live and what they do for a living. Likewise, language is simultaneously spatial and social. Physical spaces are transformed into cultural places through social interactions that are constantly mediated and reinforced by language, turning our perceptions into reality (Lucy 1997). Language is also a form of social discourse, where a system of symbols is used so frequently that shared meanings are linguistically encoded and employed as cultural resources. Metaphors such as 'going green' make little sense in a literal translation. However, a cultural translation of its intended meaning in North America yields a reference to how people might think about and engage in environmental sustainability. Like all words, the 'environment' relates to something outside itself. Yet there is a danger that for a concept as ubiquitous as the environment, its meanings are assumed (erroneously) to be independent of context.

Linguistic relativity

Linguistic relativity explains how language contributes to cultural features of thought and behavior (Whorf 1956). For example, Sapir and Whorf describe how the Yupik and Inuit have more than 40 different words for snow, while the Hopi have one noun covering everything that flies (insect, bird, and airplane are the same word) in their Native American language (Whorf 1956). Likewise, the Ka'apor Indians of eastern Amazonia used local names to symbolize indigenous forestry practices that resulted in a distinctive ecological landscape, referred to as *taper* in their native language (Balée 1998). Importantly, Balée (1998) contends that the endemic tree species in this region would never have existed without indigenous forestry, and that the projection of culture (language) onto nature (forests) developed unique relationships between the Ka'apor and the environment. Chomsky (1995: 14) has noted that while the neurological processing of language is universally linked to how our brains function, the resulting perceptions and cognitive associations "may or may not directly relate to these locutions." Thus the environment becomes something familiar to us because we have named it, and "cast a linguistic net" over the places we inhabit (Tuan 1991: 686).

Children and visual narratives

In addition to language about the environment, this chapter pursues a deeper discussion of the discursive processes by which meanings are shaped and conveyed through the social realities of children. Our focus on children is intentional because their views of the environment are shaped, intentionally or otherwise, by adults (Wee 2012). To communicate effectively in linguistic communities, children will use words with shared meanings that are available to them through learned behaviors. Thus their language provides a window into broader ideas and discursive practices about the environment. For the purposes of this chapter, we were not concerned with the analysis of relationships between different variables and linguistic structures used by children to describe the environment. Instead, we sought to understand what children's stories, or visual narratives, revealed in terms of their language about the environment. Children tend to express their observations in the form of symbols and stories rather than a set of instructions for others to learn or follow (Spencer and Darvizeh 1983). Visual narratives explore children's environmental views in ways that encourage creativity while retaining authenticity (Rose 2007). An ability to 'see' through the eyes of a child refers not only to visual perception, but to how meanings specific to places and experiences are socially constructed. Visual narratives have been validated in prior research related to children's views of the environment (Wee 2012) and children's perceptions of play in urban environments (Wee and Anthamatten 2014). Importantly, the use of visual narratives allowed us to engage in research with children on more equal terms by validating their perspectives, language, and culture.

Case study: Children's stories about the environment in Chinese

According to Hajer (1995: 13–14), "[contemporary] environmental conflict has changed. It no longer focuses on the question of whether there is an environmental crisis; it is essentially about its *interpretation* [italics added]." If we are to effectively address environmental challenges, there is a need to reveal these interpretations; that is, meanings about the environment that are continually produced and reinforced across diverse human societies. We contend that these processes do not occur in a vacuum; instead, social norms legitimize thoughts, language, and behaviors. To exemplify this point, we sought to understand how the Chinese language, as one example of a social norm, produces meanings about the environment for a subset of children in China. Chinese, instead of Mandarin, is used in this chapter because it subsumes the common/standard Chinese language in China, as well as other variants of the language that are used in nations like Taiwan, Singapore, and Malaysia.

China is still the world's most populous country (India is a close second), and a nation undergoing rapid urbanization fueled by unprecedented economic development. As a result, 1.4 billion people are experiencing extreme environmental and social impacts, ranging from intensified climatic events (e.g. severe droughts and floods) to demographic instabilities (e.g. an aging and gender-imbalanced population) (Campanella 2008). Shoreman-Ouimet and Kopnina (2011: 1) note that "understanding the [environmental] damage being done by communities is of vital importance . . . environmental anthropology today is arguably more critical than ever before." Widespread environmental changes on a global scale also signal a need for anthropological research where the focus is no longer on either environmental or social problems, but rather on the links between physical change, social settings, and specific cultural practices such as language.

Nanjing, our study site, is the capital of Jiangsu province in eastern China. It is home to approximately 8 million people, and like many other Chinese cities today, has undergone economic revitalization. Nanjing is where I (Bryan Wee) had been engaged in research collaborations with a local university related to environmental curricula reform. To appreciate decisions about curricula is to understand the cultural contexts within which those decisions are made; thus, I spent considerable time 'on the streets' exploring the city and its inhabitants. The following image (Figure 31.1) intentionally juxtaposes modernity (advertisement) and tradition (cyclist) as a reminder that tensions between the forces of globalization and culture underlie environmental as well as educational challenges in China.

Figure 31.1 Downtown Nanjing, outside a large shopping mall.

Source: Photo by Bryan Wee.

Connections or *guanxi* in Chinese culture are crucial not only for successful business ventures, but also the development of trust and relationships. In this case, university administrators in Nanjing leveraged prior *guanxi* with an urban elementary school principal and teachers. My role was presented as 'educational consultant' rather than researcher to minimize concern among the teachers that they were being evaluated, and also to encourage more student participation. Ideally, this would also de-emphasize a 'right' answer from children. A total of 74 children aged 11–12 years agreed to participate in our case study, comprising 53 males and 21 females. This was not surprising given the demographic outcomes of China's population control measures, which until recently, maintained a one-child policy favoring male heirs. We embraced the use of complementary approaches to data collection suggested by Gu (2004), cited in Wu (2011: 578), who writes, "to fully express ideas, nothing is more effective than images; to fully convey an image nothing can excel language. Language is born of images; images are born of thought." As a result, we asked children (in Mandarin) to "Draw a picture of the environment," and "Write a story that describes your picture." Children's drawings were used to corroborate our interpretations of each story. With assistance from a translator, the stories were qualitatively coded using core linguistic structures in contemporary written Chinese (Chen 1993; You 2005) to generate emergent themes underlying children's language about the environment. These themes are detailed in the following section.

Case study findings

Children in this study commonly used descriptive language to write a story about the environment. For example, one child provided the following narrative (all excerpts have been translated from Chinese to English): *"Two friends saw some trees cut down and cars along the road giving out smoke harmful to humans, so they were determined to protect the environment. On the roadside on a patch of grass they planted trees and flowers."*

In these instances, children typically gave their drawings some degree of character development and contextualized their images with more detail. Uniquely, however, children would also express feelings toward nature, life, and/or society. Another child wrote the following story for her drawing (Figure 31.2): *"In a beautiful forest, the animals are happily playing, butterflies are flying about freely, the flowers and grasses are dancing in the wind, birds are in the apple tree eating fruits."*

Embedded within this child's narrative and her drawing are the use of descriptive words that convey positive emotions and a particular feeling about the environment. Not only is there an explicit reference to affect, the movements of plants, animals, and insects portray an environment that is alive. The following is another example of a story and drawing that exemplifies the presence of affect in a child's descriptions of the environment using the Chinese language (Figure 31.3): *"On a bright and sunny morning, in a meadow filled with bird songs and fragrant flowers lived a rabbit and family. Early one day, the rabbit goes out collecting food while the birds are in the trees."*

A) 请画出你认为的"环境"的景象。
B) 请以简单的几个句子写出图画中的故事。

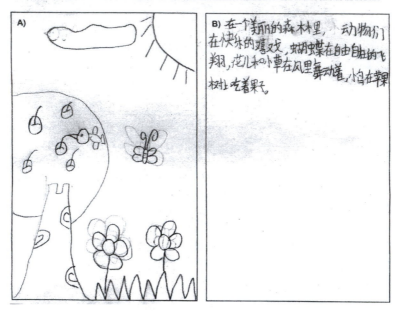

Figure 31.2 Story and drawing of the environment, female student.

A) 请画出你认为的"环境"的景象。
B) 请以简单的几个句子写出图画中的故事。

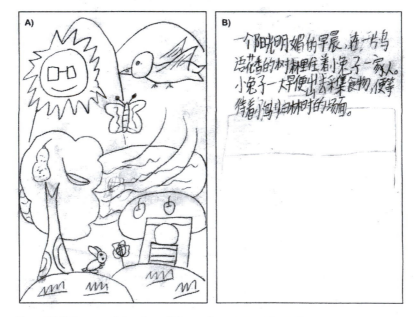

Figure 31.3 Story and drawing of the environment, male student.

Themes and reflections

Language about the environment as affective expression

Children's language about the environment draws attention to the epistemic foundations of linguistic communities (Bowers 2001). For example, there is no direct translation for 'environment' in Chinese. The word 'environment' or its closest equivalent 环境 literally means 'surroundings,' whereas in English, the 'environment' refers to external conditions that 'surround' organisms. That may explain why Wee (2012) found that Chinese students residing in the USA who were bilingual (English and Chinese) held environmental views similar to their peers in the USA, but different from students in China who spoke only Chinese. Rolston (1997) makes the point that the use of the word 'environment,' in English, objectifies the environment, turning it into an external entity that can be categorized and managed. This 'nature-as-object' perspective is reinforced when 'environment' falls within the language of the natural sciences, which is often the case in English-speaking countries such as the USA and the UK (Bonnett 1999).

According to Tuan (1991: 686), "Plants and animals become a part of the human socioeconomic order when they appear in a classificatory scheme. At a more affective level, storytelling converts objects out there into *real presences* [italics added]." While the use of stories in the case study may explain why children's language about the environment demonstrated affective expression, it is also possible that culture-specific thought patterns and linguistic rules embedded in language systems favored affective phrases over systematic categorizations. The Chinese language, unlike English, involves affect and cognition. For example, the word 'heart' is translated into 心 in Chinese, and it refers to the source of feelings as well as ideas. Excerpts from children's stories also highlight the reliance on phrases that are key linguistic structures in Chinese. For example, the use of phrases such as 'birds and butterflies are happily living together' supports the use of active verbs. By contrast, the English language which tends to be noun-heavy, emphasizes a logical order in which places or items are named; for example, 'there are birds and butterflies.' For these reasons, Liu (1992) contends that native English speakers struggle with phonological similarities between words in Chinese and also experience difficulties with Chinese compounds that involve emotions or attitudes.

Numerous writers have emphasized affect as a critical factor in developing human–environment relationships. Rachel Carson (2004) wrote that:

> [For the child] . . . it is not half so important to know as to feel. If facts are the seeds that produce knowledge and wisdom, then the emotions and the impressions of the senses are the fertile soil in which the seeds must grow.
>
> *(Carson 2004: 56)*

Steven Jay Gould (1991: 14) adds, "we cannot win this battle to save species and environments without forging an emotional bond between ourselves and nature, for we will not fight to save what we do not love." Is there room for affect in the languages that we use to describe, under-stand, and protect the environment? Research by Reis and Roth (2010) suggests that we have a long road ahead. For example, they attribute the gap in research on environmental language and pedagogy to educational approaches that strive to provide objective measures of learning. Chomsky (1965, cited in Di Vesta and Palermo 1974) declared that the study of language is about understanding the human mind and its cognitive components. Perhaps in this context, the study of language is about understanding the human heart and its affective capacity to describe the environment as something to be felt, instead of a static object to be labeled.

Language about the environment as linguistic assimilation

According to Tochon (2009: 658), "globalization and the spread of English [language] have raised concerns about the economic, political, cultural and linguistic hegemony of the West over the rest of the world." Chinese, for example, is a historic amalgamation of traditional (e.g. Confucian classics) and 'borrowed' vocabulary from Western nations (You 2005). Furthermore, Tuan (1991) describes how exploration and colonialism involved the use of words to differentiate places that were suited to the purposes of the explorer or colonizer. He notes, for example, how Asia was once upon a time "defined negatively as all that was not Europe . . . in order to serve as the backward, yet glamorous and exotic, Other" (1991: 689).

Another example of linguistic assimilation is found in environmental impact assessments, which are typically written in a technical form devoid of feelings because dominant Western worldviews continue to present environmental phenomena in scientific language that is value-free in order to preserve the notion of universal knowledge (Mühlhäusler 2001). This suggests that the use of 'environment' in the language of science may similarly lead to a loss of meanings, in particular the parts of languages that are associated with affect. As noted earlier, Chinese as a language involves affect and cognition, and that makes us wonder if children's written responses would have differed had they been asked to define the environment, which is often the case in science. The irony here is that while scientific language is intended to be objective, the design and use of language in human societies reflect a constant negotiation of meanings that is entirely subjective.

In linguistic assimilation, the imposition of a particular way of knowing shifts the meanings attached to words (Tochon 2009). For example, Walsh (2005: 303) describes how the Hopi term, *kachina*, after being translated into English, now refers to "the kind of doll in tourist shops in the American southwest, thus losing the constellation of meanings associated with spiritual values among the Hopi." Similarly, language used in sustainable development (SD) and education for sustainable development (ESD) has resulted in concern about the environment rather than concern for the environment, where words end up as slogans or as unquestioned directions for environmental behaviors that conceal hidden agendas (Jickling and Spork 1998). Ultimately, language determines what can be known, and "speech – the right to speak and be heard, the right to name and have that name 'stick' – is empowerment" (Tuan 1991: 685). It sensitizes us to the power of words and their meanings that are either subjugated or promoted to the point where they simply *belong*.

Language about the environment as discursive practice

Placing linguistic assimilation in a discursive context raises further issues of epistemology and power. Discourse refers to rules that "govern the ways that a topic can be meaningfully talked about . . . influences how ideas are put into practice and regulates the conduct of others" (Hall 1997: 44). For example, Kopnina (2012) notes that even well-intentioned efforts to conserve resources can be grounded in anthropocentric worldviews reflecting both social discourses and material realities that privilege one set of imperatives over others. Wee (2013: 267) highlights the discursive nature of schooling whereby environmental education finds itself "embedded within the disciplinary framework [of science] that pursues a singular, objective reality." Bonnett (1999: 316) extends the argument by calling into question the suitability of traditional subjects like science for environmental learning when "historically many of the central motives were shaped in a cultural milieu preoccupied with subordinating and exploiting nature." Discourse, therefore, explains how human–environment relationships are encoded in language that supports, intentionally or otherwise, the (re)production of environmental knowledge.

Di Vesta and Palermo (1974) explain how, by the age of eight, children are already adept at participating in society. Thus, learning a new language is not only about the comprehension of linguistic rules, it also requires the acquisition of culture-specific discourses. In schools in the USA, children from different cultural and linguistic backgrounds are expected to perform at 'academically proficient' levels after only a brief period of English language instruction. Children who struggle to understand the discourses required for schooling can end up being marginalized, rejecting their mother tongue, and with it their identities and cultures that are so closely tied to language (Tochon 2009).

In regard to an environmental education curriculum, ProjectWILD has an international component where materials are adapted to "suit the wildlife and ecosystems of the country and are translated [from English] in most cases" (Council for Environmental Education 2013). While this approach may provide some answers to the environmental challenges that countries like China are facing, it may not equitably represent meanings about the environment that are uniquely shaped by different languages, such as Chinese. According to Bonnett (2013), the real environmental catastrophe lies in the subjugation of words, such as the environment, by dominant discourses. This results in default modes of thinking and acting that are no longer appropriate, perhaps even counterproductive, to solving environmental problems.

Conclusion

On the one hand, the environment has become an umbrella concept driving ecological, social, and economic agendas across the world. Yet on the other hand, as a cultural and linguistic construct, it represents multiple social realities that inevitably resist a standardized account of the term. It is a paradox that is accentuated by our inabilities to fully understand it. While we are increasingly familiar with the 'what' of children's environmental ideas, our knowledge of the 'why' is lacking. This is particularly true for words like 'environment' and 'science' that are rooted in orthodoxy – words we take for granted in our everyday lives, their meanings all but assured to remain unquestioned by virtue of their epistemological positions in linguistic communities. It is not our intent to risk descriptive romanticism and oversimplify language about the environment as reflecting either shortcomings or virtues of different cultures. At the same time, however, language is more than just the sum of its parts. It is embedded with social norms and linguistic codes. If we are to embrace cultural pluralism in environmental anthropology, it is imperative that research continues to value language about the environment – specifically, how cultural and linguistic referents construct distinctive meanings for different groups of people. These will be crucial to revealing the unique and enduring elements of human–environment relationships across cultures. These are also the social realities that will eventually drive consumer actions, decisions about resource allocation, and educational policies. Ultimately, children's language about the environment sensitizes us to the ways in which communities think and act in relation to the environment. If indeed language has the power to shape how the environment is interpreted, and in so doing enables or hinders efforts to mitigate environmental impacts, then language about the environment ought to be integrated into our discourses and practices in environmental anthropology.

References

Balée W 1998. Historical Ecology: Premises and Postulates. In W Balée (ed.) *Advances in Historical Ecology*. New York: Columbia University Press, pp. 13–29.

Balée W L and Erickson C L 2006. *Time and Complexity in Historical Ecology: Studies in the Neotropical Lowlands*. New York: Columbia University Press.

Bonnett M 1999. Education for Sustainable Development: A Coherent Philosophy for Environmental Education. *Cambridge Journal of Education* 29(3): 313–324.

Bonnett M 2013. Normalizing Catastrophe: Sustainability and Scientism. *Environmental Education Research* 19(2): 187–197.

Bowers C 2001. How Language Limits our Understanding of Environmental Education. *Environmental Education Research* 7(2): 141–151.

Campanella T 2008. *The Concrete Dragon*. New York: Princeton Architectural Press.

Carson R 2004. *Sense of Wonder*. New York: HarperCollins.

Chen P 1993. Modern Written Chinese in Development. *Language in Society* 22(4): 505–537.

Chomsky N 1965. *Aspects of the Theory of Syntax*. MIT Research Laboratory of Electronics Special Technical Report 11. Cambridge, MA: The MIT Press.

Chomsky N 1995. Language and Nature. *Mind* 104(413): 1–61.

Council for Environmental Education 2013. ProjectWILD International. www.projectwild.org/InternationalSponsors.htm (accessed 31 March 2013).

Cresswell T 2009. Place. In N Thrift and R Kitchen (eds) *International Encyclopedia of Human Geography*, Volume 8. Oxford: Elsevier, pp. 69–177.

Di Vesta F and Palermo D 1974. Language Development. *Review of Research in Education* 2(1): 55–107.

Gould S J 1991. Enchanted Evening. *Natural History* 100: 4–14.

Gu M D 2004. Elucidation of Images in the *Book of Changes*: Ancient Insights into Modern Language Philosophy and Hermeneutics. *Journal of Chinese Philosophy* 31(4): 469–488.

Hajer M 1995. *The Politics of Environmental Discourse: Ecological Modernization and the Policy Process*. New York: Oxford University Press.

Hall S 1997. *Representation: Cultural Representations and Signifying Practices*. Thousand Oaks, CA and London: Sage.

Jickling B and Spork H 1998. Education for the Environment: A Critique. *Environmental Education Research* 4(3): 309–327.

Liu J 1992. Bridging Language and Culture: A Cognitive Approach to the Study of Chinese Compounds. *Journal of the Chinese Language Teachers Association* 27(3): 1–19.

Lucy J 1997. Linguistic Relativity. *Annual Review of Anthropology* 26: 291–312.

Kopnina H 2012. Education for Sustainable Development ESD: The Turn away from 'Environment' in Environmental Education? *Environmental Education Research* 18(5): 699–717.

Matthews H 1995. Culture, Environmental Experience and Environmental Awareness: Making Sense of Young Kenyan Children's Views of Place. *The Geographical Journal* 161(3): 285–295.

Mühlhäusler P 2001. Talking about Environmental Issues. In A Fill and P Mühlhäusler (eds) *The Ecolinguistics Reader*. New York: Continuum, pp. 31–42.

Reis G and Roth W M 2010. A Feeling for the Environment: Emotion Talk in/for the Pedagogy of Public Environmental Education. *Journal of Environmental Education* 41(2): 71–87.

Rolston III H 1997. Nature for Real: Is Nature a Social Construct? In T D J Chappell (ed.) *The Philosophy of the Environment*. Edinburgh: University of Edinburgh Press, pp. 38–64.

Rose G 2007. *Visual Methodologies: An Introduction to the Interpretation of Visual Materials*. London and Thousand Oaks, CA: Sage Publications.

Shoreman–Ouimet E and Kopnina H 2011. Environmental Anthropology of Yesterday and Today. In Eleanor Shoreman-Ouimet and Helen Kopnina (eds) *Environmental Anthropology Today*. London and New York: Routledge, pp. 1–33.

Spencer C and Darvizeh Z 1983. Young Children's Place Descriptions: Maps and Route Finding: A Comparison of Nursery School Children in Iran and Britain. *International Journal of Early Childhood* 15(1): 26–31.

Stables A 2001. Language and Meaning in Environmental Education: An Overview. *Environmental Education Research* 7(2): 21–128.

Stibbe A 2012. *Animals Erased: Discourse, Ecology, and Reconnection with the Natural World*. Middletown, CT: Wesleyan University Press.

Stibbe A 2014. An Ecolinguistic Approach to Critical Discourse Studies. *Critical Discourse Studies* 11(1): 117–128.

Tochon F 2009. The Key to Global Understanding: World Languages Education – Why Schools Need to Adapt. *Review of Educational Research* 79(2): 650–681.

Tuan Y 1991. Language and the Making of Place: A Narrative-Descriptive Approach. *Annals of the Association of American Geographers* 81(4): 684–696.

Walsh M 2005. Will Indigenous Languages Survive? *Annual Review of Anthropology* 34: 293–315.

Wee B 2012. A Cross-Cultural Exploration of Children's Everyday Ideas: Implications for Science Teaching and Learning. *International Journal of Science Education* 34(4): 609–627.

Wee B 2013. On Agendas and Perspectives in Environmental Education: Revisiting Kopnina, Disciplinary Imperatives and the Paradoxes of (Multi)cultures. *Environmental Education Research* 19(2): 266–268.

Wee B and Anthamatten P 2014. Using Photography to Visualize Children's Culture of Play: A Socio-Spatial Perspective. *Geographical Review* 104(1): 87–100.

Whorf B 1956. *Language, Thought and Reality*. Cambridge, MA: The MIT Press,

Wu Z 2011. Interpretation, Autonomy, and Transformation: Chinese Pedagogic Discourse in a Cross-Cultural Perspective. *Journal of Curriculum Studies* 43(5): 569–590.

You X 2005. Conflation of Rhetorical Traditions: The Formation of Modern Chinese Writing Instruction. *Rhetoric Review* 24(2): 150–169.

32

"YOU HAVE TO *DO* IT"

Creating agency for environmental sustainability through experiential education, transformative learning, and kincentricity

Brenda R. Beckwith, Tania Halber, and Nancy J. Turner

You don't learn from reading it in books; you have to do *it.*

Gitga'ata Elder (Thompson 2004: 88)

Introduction

How can we humans, in our increasingly urbanized society, reconnect ourselves with the natural world and rekindle our relationships with place and with other species, relationships still held by some people, but widely forgotten by those in mainstream society? This question is critically important as we face major challenges at a global scale, from erosion of the earth's biodiversity and productivity to the mounting perils of climate change. Increasingly, academic institutions are focusing on human-centered pursuits, including economics, business, technology, and health, mostly taught in artificial environments such as classrooms and labs. Yet, to develop the "eco-friendly" relationships we need to support environmental sustainability well into the future, different learning styles, methods, and models are necessary. Developing opportunities that open our eyes to multiple "ways of knowing" and a more compassionate "way of being" is critical to creating life-long learners who will become tomorrow's change agents. In this chapter we synthesize and discuss the role of experiential education in creating agency for transformative learning and methods of inquiry that foster and promote environmental sustainability.

We first provide some background and context relating to experiential education, transformative learning, and kincentricity, as a distinctive worldview. We emphasize the academic trends and environmental failings that indicate an urgent need for us to alter our approach, at a societal level, to how we relate to other species and the places that support us. We then present three case studies to highlight a range of personal engagement and structural coordination in experiential education. All three case examples include components of what we call "transformative kincentric learning and living," an educational model that is adaptive, dynamic, and holistic, and involves the whole learner, their community, and the natural learning environment. The learning experience in this model includes mindfulness, relational and personal growth, and embodied and situated engagement. The intent is not to evaluate whether or not transformative learning has occurred, but rather to focus on the process of experiential learning and the associated environments as contexts within which transformative learning can, and often does, take place.

We define experiential learning as: "the process of learning through active participation and 'hands-on' experience: 'learning by doing'." Transformative learning is education that results in a shift or change in the perspective of self, the world within which we live, and our role within it. The term "worldview" reflects the principles we require to make sense of the world around us, including values, traditions, and customs. They are part of the teachings within a culture, guiding children, youth, and adults alike in their actions, developing culturally appropriate behavior toward each other and toward the broader community of living beings and environments on which we all depend. Kincentricity is a worldview in which our close relationship – *kinship* – is acknowledged, not only to other humans, but also to all other life-forms (see Salmón 2000). These kinship relationships emphasize our responsibilities to other species and a requirement to care for them and their habitats as we would our human relations and their homes (Turner 2005).

As the earth becomes more developed and people flock into urban centers, our collective disconnection from nature continues to grow; many of us no longer see ourselves as part of the natural world. Our general sense of environmental apathy has resulted in an accelerated rate of environmental deterioration and continued destruction of species and habitats worldwide (WWF 2014; see also Millennium Ecosystem Assessment 2005). A positive role for people is difficult to realize. If the current trajectory is to be slowed, we will require not only novel applications of technology and innovation, but also a fundamental and unyielding change in societal attitudes and values. We need a paradigm shift away from the consumerist and neoliberal values that have created our current bleak environmental situation.

Historically, there are examples of how broad-scale collective thinking can shift; for instance, in our changed attitudes regarding gendered roles and racial stereotypes in the global North. Societal changes have occurred in large part because key leaders and educators demonstrated different ways of being (e.g. Martin Luther King, Jr); people actively gathered and participated in focal, inspiring experiences; and these pivotal lessons were promoted through educational experiences and the media. Change was shown to be possible and people embodied it. People became transformed and active contributors within a greater interconnected movement for positive change.

It is now widely thought that environmental education, and similar alternative approaches to education – some recently being introduced and some millennia old – that focus on deep relationships with the natural world can help to foster a more just and sustainable society (see Kopnina 2014). This new arena of contemplative pedagogy has emerged since the mid-1990s with the vision of fostering education that encourages deep inquiry, critical reflection, and mindfulness in post-secondary institutions (see Barbezat and Bush 2014). Indigenous teaching and learning traditions differ significantly from standard Western academic notions of education (Berkes 2012; Davidson-Hunt and Berkes 2003; Turner and Berkes 2006). Through their experiences and teachings, Indigenous peoples in many parts of the world have developed close ties with their homelands and with other beings, in relationships of kincentricity with other species and environmental entities like mountains, rivers, and rocks (Turner 2005). Such perspectives foster attitudes of respect, responsibility, and reciprocity toward other species, as conveyed and reflected through their stories, ceremonies, institutions, and both formal and informal modes of knowledge transmission (Atleo 2011; Turner 2014).

For Indigenous scholars, kincentric learning has the ultimate goal of transformation of the self/ego to help us to become complete people, achievable only by being open to different perspectives and values (Battiste 2002; Atleo and Fitznor 2008).

Good leadership, shared learning, and experiential education are pivotal in creating stronger relationships with nature that reflect empathy and values more conducive to sustainability and biocultural conservation. Our own sustenance and well-being depend directly on the integrity of environmental processes and the flourishing of other life-forms. We need educational experiences that enhance our environmental awareness and provide us with new perspectives that motivate us to change our behavior toward the environment (Halber 2012), as well as help us to find deeper meaning about, and confidence within, ourselves. We need to strive for learning that results in a transformative experience for the learner. To date, research on transformative learning by Western scholars (Snyder 2008; Taylor 2008; Illeris 2009), has been largely confined to examining the process in formal education settings (e.g. post-secondary educational institutions).

Despite all our high-tech, scientific, and economic expertise, we seem incapable of developing educational models that will produce empowered leaders well-voiced in environmental sustainability. We propose here that informal settings outside the standard classroom may be equally, or even more, important venues for transformative kincentric learning and living for all of us. Some of the most profound educational experiences take place in the outdoors, using our imaginations and natural human capacities for inquiry and curiosity, away from the complicated technologies that many of us both take for granted and rely on heavily today.

Case studies in experiential education

In this section, we describe three case examples of educational initiatives and programs that we believe are representative of transformative kincentric learning and living opportunities that can lead to, and in many demonstrable ways have resulted in, transformative changes within learners and participants. Case 1, the *Pit-cooking class* experience, describes an all-day annual university field trip based on a time-honored collaborative Indigenous food-preparation method in which food is cooked in an "earth oven" using hot rocks. Pit-cooking has been learned and honed by Nancy Turner in classes and with Indigenous communities over the last 35 years. The *Redfish* field experience, Case 2, is a 5–6-week university- and community-based field school, teaching and supporting students to become environmental and social justice leaders in their home communities. In 2008, Nadine Raynolds had a vision to create a field school for post-secondary students that would provide them with the knowledge and skills required to be tomorrow's change agents. Brenda Beckwith has remained involved with the field school, as a developer, facilitator, and instructor, since its beginning. The third case, the *Tribal Journeys* experience, describes the life-changing experiences of participants canoeing Indigenous ancestral routes in the waters of the Pacific Northwest Coast, an annual event researched and recorded by Tania Halber for her doctoral dissertation.

In the following case studies (see Figure 32.1), we identify commonalities across experiences, and discuss how these common elements and themes might be applied more widely to foster transformative learning, offering approaches that can lead to more sustainable living in North America and beyond. By examining both Western and Indigenous teaching and learning wisdom, the cases offer methods that are outside more "formal" conventional approaches to education. Together they provide a spectrum of experiential and transformative learning opportunities as a way to expand boundaries and add to the environmental sustainability conversation.

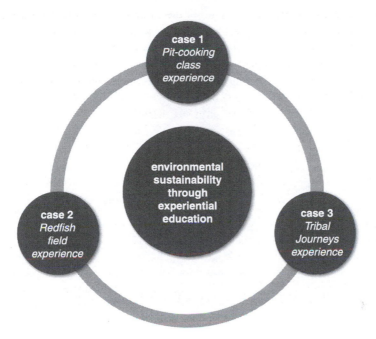

Figure 32.1 Case studies of experiential education and opportunities for transformative learning to help achieve environmental sustainability.

Case 1: "Down to earth cooking": the Pit-cooking class experience

Communal cooking in underground pits is practiced in many parts of the world. Far more than just a cooking technique, it is a time-honored and place-based activity that integrates knowledge, practice, and belief in a way that honors the food and those who have harvested and prepared it. It is highly participatory, requiring many participants working in concert, to successfully cook the food. Pit-cooked food has a special flavor, and the serving of steaming-hot freshly cooked seafood or vegetables is a festive, shared occasion – a celebration that, once experienced, is not easily forgotten. In short, participating in a communal cooking experience, such as pit-cooking, can be enjoyable, informative, and transformative in its effects.

Nancy Turner first experienced pit-cooking in 1980 when, with her colleagues John Thomas (Ditidaht cultural specialist), Harriet Kuhnlein (ethnonutritionist), and colleagues, she visited John's mother, Ida Jones, at her home in the Pacheedaht First Nation community of Port Renfrew on Vancouver Island. They wanted to learn about a traditional cooking method that Mrs Jones, at that time in her eighties, had experienced as a young woman (Kuhnlein *et al.* 1982; Turner *et al.* 1983). Mrs Jones described the pit-cooking process in detail, then attended and witnessed their attempts to reconstruct and reproduce the technique, widely used over past millennia for cooking and preparing immense quantities of food, including camas bulbs, silverwood roots, and springbank clover roots, as well as clams and other types of Indigenous foods. It took them a number of trials before they were able to produce well-cooked and flavored food that was neither undercooked nor burned. Nancy also learned pit-cooking as practiced in the Interior Plateau region of British Columbia from Secwepemc Elder Mary Thomas. She adapted these methods to cook other kinds of foods, such as

415

small potatoes of different varieties, beets, onions, and other root vegetables, and experimented with many other foods like salmon wrapped in thimbleberry leaves, deer meat, and shellfish.

Using Mrs Jones' recipe, and with armloads of salal branches and sword-fern fronds to surround the food and protect it from the red-hot rocks while allowing the steam to circulate, Nancy and her colleagues started to include a pit-cooking field trip in her Environmental Studies "Plants and Human Cultures" courses at the University of Victoria, BC. These field trips were held at local First Nations' communities (e.g. Tsawout on the Saanich Peninsula) or at special locales (e.g. Sandcut Beach, north of Sooke, Vancouver Island). The day-long pit-cooking experience often included the participation of other teachers, including Indigenous knowledge holders and respected experts in traditional practices. Students participated in the entire process, from digging the pit, building the fire and selecting and heating the rocks, to preparing the food and surrounding vegetation and putting it in the pit. While the food cooked, students learned about and practiced other plant-based skills such as basketry and cordage making.

Case 2: Change agents for the future: the Redfish field experience

The Redfish School of Change is "a non-profit program developed through a shared recognition that the world is in a troubled state, and that it deeply needs people, in their own communities and bioregions, to facilitate positive change" (Redfish School of Change 2015). Initially a partnership among GreenLearning Canada (at the time part of the Pembina Institute), the University of Victoria, BC, and Pearson College UWC, the Redfish School of Change was born in 2008. Brenda Beckwith helped to develop this program in the School of Environmental Studies at the University of Victoria, BC, and has taught a course based on ethnoecology and sustenance ecology since the beginning of the program in 2009. The six-week field school provided 16 students with university credits for three Environmental Studies courses, moving the students and three instructors through several bioregions from the West Kootenay region to southern Vancouver Island, BC. The Redfish School director provides post-program guidance and mentoring for each student as they attempt to navigate and organize their projects once they are back in their respective life realities.

The one assignment that sets this field school apart is the Community Action Project (CAP). Every student comes into the program with a project in mind that focuses on environmental sustainability or social justice. Themes of past projects include community and school gardens, environmental and outdoor education, food security and urban food alternatives, environmental awareness and activism, media promotions (print and video), and multigenerational learning. After completing the Redfish program, they develop, coordinate, and facilitate the CAP in their home community. During Redfish, the instructors ensure that the students are developing their competencies through direct instruction, group discussion, personal reflection, one-to-one meetings, consultation with local community environmental and social justice leaders, and assessment. As leadership is a key program component of Redfish, students are first taught and then expected to administer important aspects of the field school, including organizing and preparing meals, facilitating daily "check-ins," and coordinating responsibilities and roles of fellow participants while traveling.

Redfish is designed to support student success in becoming leaders in environmental issues including ecological stewardship, sustainability, and social justice. Students "learn by doing," integrating content learning and skill development as a united educational process that is first modeled, then expressed. They reflect on their learning and deepen an understanding about themselves within multiple contexts as capable and important leaders, thereby finding their unique purpose, building confidence, and seeing themselves and each other on a positive life trajectory for making meaningful change in the world.

Case 3: The pull of transformative learning: the Tribal Journeys experience

Canoe journeys, a traditional form of transport amongst Indigenous Peoples on the coast in many parts of the world, are both a practice of embodied and spiritual connection to culturally specific ways of knowing and being and a method of transforming many of the challenges faced by participants in the modern world. Tania Halber Suarez (2012), drawing on the work of both Indigenous scholars (e.g. Battiste 2002; Atleo and Fitznor 2008) and Western scholars (Snyder 2008; Taylor 2008) has documented the role of organized canoe journeys on the Pacific Northwest Coast of North America as informal and non-academic learning events that have developed transformative learning among most participating individuals, their families, and their communities. *Tribal Journeys* is a convergence of annual ocean voyages in traditional cedar dugout canoes by Indigenous Peoples from Western Washington and British Columbia to a host destination. Tracing ancestral trading routes, *Tribal Journeys* recreates a long-standing traditional practice of human-powered transportation as a process for both formal and informal experiential learning. *Tribal Journeys* was inspired in British Columbia by a young Heiltsuk man who had experienced a personal transformation through rigorous training on a remote island as an alternative justice process imposed on him as a young offender and lawbreaker.

Participants, with family members and sometimes friends, are organized into a family system for the duration of the journey. "Canoe families" are cross-generational and vary in number depending on the size of the canoe. A canoe will typically have from 8 to 14 pullers (paddlers). Larger canoes have crews of 20 or more. Depending on the distance to be traveled, the journey takes anywhere from 2 to 4 weeks to complete. As participants land at each stop, they follow traditional formal protocols, with Elders announcing who their people are, and where they come from, and asking permission of the hosting nation to land their canoe. Canoe families wait to be invited on land by the hosts, who greet them with ceremonies, gifts, dance, storytelling, and feasting – a process that is bound by deep meaning, respect, and ritual recreation of the ways of their ancestors.

Case study analysis

The three case studies represent a spectrum of experiential and transformative education. From a university field-trip experience, to a field school, to a field ("ocean" in this case) journey, all three incorporate the fundamental learning components that can lead directly to kincentric learning and the fostering of an environmental sustainability ethic. In much the same way that the Slow Food Movement (www.slowfood.com) reminded us that meals are more than just the food we consume, these examples demonstrate that meaningful learning is much more than the material we deliver as educators. This is *Slow Learning,* an academic process that blurs the lines between learning and living because it is embodied and situated, and participants find a deeper resonance through experiences that are both personal and relational. Table 32.1 provides an inventory and comparison of the features of the three case studies, showing areas of commonality and divergence.

Table 32.1 Case study analysis for the features and themes of transformative kincentric learning and living.

CASE STUDY	Pit-cooking class experience	Redfish field experience	Tribal Journeys experience
Feature 1: *Time Period*	1 day (with annual repetition).	5–6 weeks.	2–4 weeks (with annual repetition).
Feature 2: *Participants*	University class, including instructor, teaching assistant, students (30+), and possibly special guests (e.g. traditional skills experts, First Nations representatives, organic farmers).	University field program, including 2–3 instructors, program assistant(s), students (16–18), multiple multigenerational community members, local experts.	Multigenerational, multicultural Indigenous "canoe families," including 8–20 pullers (paddlers). Tribal Councils, Elders, hosting communities, and guests.
Feature 3: *Locale*	Multiple locations outdoors depending on year and instructor: wilderness beach, organic farm, First Nations reserve lands, parks.	Multiple locations depending on program director and development: usually lodges and hostels, camping, in West Kootenay, Okanagan, lower mainland, southern Vancouver Island and Gulf Islands.	Canoe journey within the waters and coast of the Pacific Northwest and stopping at host communities along the way.
Feature 4: *Physicality*	Day spent outside, collecting materials, preparing food and pit, learning traditional skills, service learning opportunities, cleaning up site.	Much time spent outside, traveling (e.g. canoeing, hiking, backpacking, cycling), camping, service learning, interpretive tours and discussions, conducting fieldwork, participating in group activities and personal reflection (e.g. overnight solo).	Most time spent with ground crew on land, in support boats, and in canoe with 7–10 hours per day of "pulling," and multiple stops in hosting communities along the journey.
Feature 5: *Key Components*	• TEK • situated learning • multicultural • multigenerational • experiential • time in nature • group learning • worldview integrated into daily life • enacted, taught, and learned through storytelling, cooking • somatic and embodied knowing	• TEK and scientific • situated learning • multicultural • multigenerational • experiential • time in nature • group learning • worldview integrated into daily life • enacted, taught, and learned through living and learning in community • embodied leadership	• TEK • situated learning • multicultural • multigenerational • experiential • time in nature • group learning • worldview integrated into daily life • enacted, taught, and learned through drumming, dancing, storytelling, paddling, ceremony

Theme			
Theme 1: *Learning about values and worldview* "mindful"	• university code of conduct • ancestral cultural memory. Transmission of TEK by learning hands-on traditional food preparation and associated skills, lessons in storytelling, interpretive ecological walks, or service learning, such as ecological restoration activities.	• community code of conduct • social justice and activism. Understanding of the complexity, scale and interdependence of ecological, social, and economic systems. Appreciation for plurality in ways of knowing and among scientific and cultural perspectives toward creating social change.	• somatic and embodied knowing • cultural code of conduct • ancestral cultural memory • individual and community transformation. Deepening understanding of differing approaches to cultural knowledge and TEK. Learning one's culture and appropriate behavioral protocols through dancing, drumming, paddling, singing, storytelling, and sharing circles.
Theme 2: *Learning about oneself* "personal"	Students are encouraged to explore, share stories, observe nature, and wait in anticipation for the food to be revealed.	Capacity to develop effective strategies for a broad range of social and environmental challenges. Appreciation for and reflection on the ways to maintain balance and sustain a life dedicated to creating change.	The nature of *Tribal Journeys* provides learners with time to self-reflect and a safe environment within "canoe families" to talk about what they are learning in a sharing circle to help process the experience and learn about self.
Theme 3: *Learning about others* "relational"	Communal time-honored activity that is highly participatory, requiring many pairs of hands, working together in concert, to successfully prepare and cook the food.	Capacity and confidence to employ leadership skills for effective community action. Ability to participate collaboratively in finding solutions for social and environmental challenges.	Build relationships and a shared community among participants. Time with Elders and other family members, including the non-human other. Time in larger community (e.g. protocol).
Theme 4: *Learning with the senses* "embodied"	The process of pit-cooking requires learning with the senses, including selecting and preparing appropriate vegetation for the pit, suitable rocks for optimal cooking density, and the food to be eaten.	Although not expressed as a learning objective of the program, the operation of the field school is whole–bodied and widely kinetic.	Experiential and sensory learning plays a key role; participants often report life-changing experiences using their senses beyond the primary ones, including emotions ("feelings") and energy.
Theme 5: *Learning across space and time* "situated"	Pit-cooking is dependent on TEK specific to the place where it occurs; and time in terms of optimal conditions, cooking time, learning time, time in nature.	Appreciation of the relevance of place and the features that distinguish regional and local contexts and landscape dynamics.	The place and time (season, length of journey) provide the context and conditions for transformative learning.

These cases collectively provide opportunities for transformative kincentric learning and living through activities and experiences within applied and situated environments. We argue that, like a nautilus, experiential education reflects a spiraling process; participants – *both students and teachers* – work together as co-creators to build an enriching and meaningful educational experience that is adaptive, holistic, and interconnected. Education cannot be separated out from life; it is kincentric (based on relationships) and weaves together multiple ways of knowing and approaches to learning. Concepts, experiences, and skills are initiated, revisited, and reinforced, in each case going deeper and deeper, increasing in complexity, in connectivity, in understanding, and in creating an integrated "whole." It is through these experiences that transformation can occur.

Transformative, kincentric learning, and living discussion

In order to develop and foster transformative learning that can, in turn, lead to global sustainable living, we use the learning themes drawn from the case studies to construct a "transformative kincentric learning and living model" (see Figure 32.2) and to develop guiding principles for future transformative kincentric learning and living curricula. Our model integrates a learner's whole being into the transformative learning cycle, encouraging each participant to develop their own somatic ways of knowing, embodying their values, worldview, and cultural memory from their families – back to a time when we were all directly dependent on the natural environment for our survival. By expanding the boundaries of how transformation can take place, this approach makes it possible for contemporary generations of learners to *re/construct* their unique identities as an important component of their learning and development.

As learning becomes more embodied and more *lived*, students deepen their personal self-awareness and understanding of their own being. The process can be a natural and organic one, completely enjoyable and captivating, combining quick lessons and "ah-ha!" moments with a deeper, more gradual *coming into knowing*. Transformational learning emerges from providing the student or the participant with the content, context, and connections to generate an open learning environment empowering the student to find their unique way within it. Students can be transformed when they find the "words that best represent [their] lived experience"; an experience most often lacking words previously (Mah y Busch 2014: 120). The learning can involve the whole body, the senses, the emotions, and a learner's personal and cultural history. The rhythm of the paddle in canoe journeys, the sense of empowerment that comes with connections to community in the Redfish experience, the special fragrance of the food in the cooking pit – each has a place in changing the way we regard ourselves, our sense of self, and our role in the environment and in our lives. Many of these experiences cannot be taught *per se*, but as educators, we create the learning opportunity through situations and environments that facilitate the natural stimulation of the students' imagination, and release of their creativity and curiosity. Individual transformation comes through the act of being in an experience of deeply engaged learning.

To guide this transformative learning process, mentorship is an important element, exemplified in all three case studies. The mentor/apprentice paradigm is an invaluable source of learning and personal growth, not only for those being mentored, but for the mentors as well. Through an intentional and focused educational experience, the instructor teaches by example, modeling how to do a skilled activity and creating a situation for the learner to take ownership of their own learning experience. One-on-one mentorship is not often experienced, and not possible, in the classroom of a large academic institution. However, it is exactly this kind of educational relationship that is needed for students to come into a richer understanding of the nuances and complexities of people's connectedness with ancestors, non-living relatives, creator/spirit, animals, and the natural environment. It is where the self finds its role within a community of others and its role within its landscape, and comes to express its deeper responsibility to and resonance for environmental sustainability.

Overarching kincentric learning and living model themes

The five interconnected themes of experiential learning identified in Figure 32.2, taken together, make up kincentric learning and living, recognizing the connections and relationships with all things: *Hishuk ish ts'awalk'* ("everything is one" in Nuu-chah-nulth). Thus, "education is not separated out of life." When all these teaching themes are considered and supported, and become subsequently embodied and made a part of their own self-identity and worldview by students/participants, the outcome for many individuals can be profound.

The first theme, students/participants *learning about values and worldview* (their own and others), is indeed the most important, and is often disregarded or shied away from in post-secondary classrooms. This is where participants become more perceptive, reflective, and "mindful," and learn about the importance of respect, gratitude, empathy, ritual, and interconnectedness within a dominant learning culture that seldom provides space for these values. This learning theme can result from lessons embedded in many stories that portray generosity and kindness, in ceremony, such as the First Salmon Ceremony of many First Nations. Empathy – a feeling of responsibility, love, appreciation, and connection with others, including other life-forms – is a key element of this learning. It is learned through positive relationships and is what motivates us to change our behaviors and to take action.

In the *Pit-cooking class* case study, transformative kincentric learning is not forced, but comes through living the experience. Taught in an embodied way, the learning is inseparable from the values and worldview steeped in tradition, community, and ceremony from

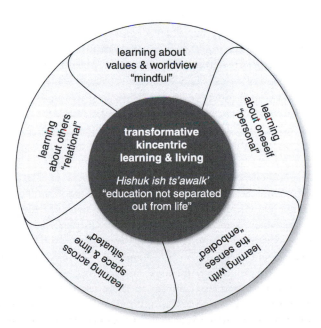

Figure 32.2 Experiential education expressed as a model for transformative kincentric learning and living.

generations of ancestors who used such cooking methods long before their contemporary counterparts. It takes many participants to make pit-cooking a success; each learner has an individual responsibility and is part of a larger interconnected community relying on each other and the natural elements. Celebrating with delicious, flavorful food, prepared together in an outdoor setting, is also part of this special learning experience. *Redfish* field participants learn about values and develop worldview through a number of ways, including course assignments (e.g. creative eco-writing and reflective journals), designed to challenge students to develop learning modules that are then shared back with the group. Students work alone, with each other, in groups and with communities, both Indigenous and non-Indigenous. Participants team with community members to develop a service-learning project, bringing opportunities for exposure to multiple perspectives and values which act as sites to examine one's own belief systems alongside others. The *Tribal Journeys* experience is deeply rooted in Indigenous cultures, worldviews, and history. Like the *Pit-cooking class* experience, the canoe journey incorporates the wisdom, knowledge, and experience of Elders, which they pass on experientially to participants. Respect, responsibility, and reciprocity are embedded within vital ecological and logistical knowledge, such as how to make Western red cedar (*Thuja plicata*) dugout canoes, navigate tides and currents, and locate ancestral trading routes. Important cultural lessons are shared, including learning what ceremonies are appropriate, how to teach each other, and stories of the close relationships between humans and nature.

Learning about oneself, the second theme, is essential to making an experiential learning opportunity transformational. The student/participant needs to find profound meaning in their learning experience, to make it "personal," and to be able to see themselves in a new role or identity, with greater self-confidence and empowerment, and a new capacity for critical reflection and awareness. Encouraging students to take on roles of leadership and action, and reinforcing their efforts to do so can lead to a realization of personal potential and abilities that might not have manifested themselves in conventional educational settings. The *Pit-cooking class* experience provides a rich opportunity for participants to interact with others in a collaborative way, encouraging both leadership and teamwork. The experience conveys how our food is connected to eco-cultural knowledge systems and to each individual, and how sharing food brings people together in mutual rewarding ways. It is an experience that can change peoples' perspectives about the role that food plays in their lives, and in the wider context of environmental and social well-being. Students who had experienced pit-cooking, and then continued with similar community-engaged work post-graduation, started to promote and use this cooking method on their own. The *Redfish* field experience also helps students to gain self-knowledge and learning about others by developing applicable skills, as well as more non-tangible skills in leadership, mentoring, group work, decision-making, and critical reflection. The ultimate goal of Indigenous teaching and wisdom is to transform oneself by finding one's true self in order to become a complete person. To do so one must learn from and with their community, and help others to discover their leader, or follower, roles within their own learning cycles. The pulling of the paddle in the *Tribal Journeys* experience builds confidence and competencies that are built simultaneously, strengthened, and refined the more they are applied. Participants are assessed for their own innate talents and abilities, and these are nurtured and magnified throughout the learning process. Learning about self is a process toward personal ownership of the learning experience, where the student/participant is a co-creator of their own transformation, and the transformation of their canoe families and communities.

Learning about others and one's relationship to them – even if those "others" are not fully realized at the time, such as others found in a forest, or on the ocean – is vital to kincentric learning and living. The experience, or realization, of interconnections – for example, with culture and heritage, family and friends, and human and non-human communities – provides powerful and deeply meaningful stimuli for learning. Through experiential learning within a situated context, the student/participant learns intimately about the "relational" nature of the experience. Group learning, where everyone in the group plays an important part in the learning success of the collective, is facilitated through feelings of belonging and critical reflection, positive reinforcement and sharing, and inclusive experiences. Both the *Pit-cooking class* and *Tribal Journeys* experiences offer participants the opportunity to witness first-hand ancestral ceremonies, community interactions, and kincentric ways in the world. In all three case examples, group learning allows all participants to learn about and rely on each other. The very nature of *Tribal Journeys*, where large and heavy dugout canoes must be maneuvered through ocean currents and tides without capsizing, demands collaboration and teamwork; learning about others is essential for survival. Participants undergo an intensive learning cycle about themselves, each other, and their communities by supporting and honoring each person's way of being and doing. *Redfish* students learn through a diversity of pedagogical approaches; they live *in community*, learn directly *from community*, and come to appreciate natural and personal kincentric relationships *through community engagement*, all impossible without learning about others.

Sensory learning is another theme often overlooked at the post-secondary level, but is an essential ingredient for transformative kincentric learning and living. Whereas conventional pedagogy tends to be linear – professor speaks, students listen – applied learning opens up opportunities for the individual to be more engaged and the learning experience more fully "embodied." Learning is intensified through kinesis (movement or "doing"), and through engaging all the senses, as well as a range of emotions, felt, and observed in others. Keen perceptions, feelings, and the personal awareness that arise through these experiences help one to find balance and a mindful presence in one's life. Experiential learning that provides opportunities for participants to overcome their self-doubt and fears and develop this state for themselves is a strong catalyst for transformative learning. The senses – tasting, smelling, touching, listening, and seeing – are awoken in each of these learning venues. For example, when the pit is opened, during the *Pit-cooking class* experience, all of the senses take over, and many have said that food never smelled or tasted so good. Students in the *Redfish* experience engage their senses in both formal and informal ways, both in a variety of "classrooms" and in different natural settings. *Tribal Journeys* is an experiential process that relies heavily on the senses for learning. Traditional knowledge is embodied by listening, observing, doing, smelling, and touching through paddling, dancing, singing, storytelling, and drumming; through all of these experiences, participants connect deeply with the natural environment and with other life-forms.

Learning across space and time is a significant element of transformative, kincentric learning and living that emphasizes the local or "situated" aspects. The three case studies presented here are each deeply situated in place and occur over a relatively long time interval, given the objectives of the experience. Although the *Pit-cooking class* field trip takes place over just one day, the time it takes to collectively prepare the pit, heat the rocks, gather the cooking vegetation, and assemble the food (about three hours), to cook the food (about two–three hours), and then to open the pit and enjoy tasting the food, makes the importance of *taking time* clear to students. Obtaining the desired results requires extensive traditional ecological knowledge (TEK), ranging from where to build the pit and how to select the best rocks and vegetation to how to assemble a proper pit for cooking food. This knowledge relies heavily on familiarity with place and a sense of timing. The intervals of intense activity, focused in one location, interspersed with a more relaxed pace of interacting – learning about plant materials and other applications – over a broader area provide students with an additional appreciation of situated learning.

For both the *Redfish* and *Tribal Journeys* experiences, much of the movement occurs by human-powered means; the students/participants are contributing simultaneously to the well-being of the group and their own personal sense of confidence and accomplishment by helping to transport themselves and others. In the *Redfish* field school, students, instructors, program assistants, and sometimes guests move themselves across the landscape (e.g. paddling canoes on a river, hiking the back country, cycling a dedicated rail trail) from learning place to learning place. The role of space and time in their learning is a constant consideration, as is overcoming the inherent bodily and mental challenges associated with regular physical exertion. The *Tribal Journeys* experience is physically and mentally grueling, requiring patience and persistence as participants "pull" for many hours, facing at times treacherous ocean conditions, ever changing, that they must become familiar with over a journey of several weeks. In their negotiations across time and space, participants are required to follow ten canoe rules, emphasizing community, collaboration, reciprocity, connectivity, and accountability for each other and the natural environment. These rules reinforce participant commitment to deep meaningful engagement with themselves, each other, and their non-human kin, through their experiences as dictated by time and space.

Creating agency through environmental curricula

The students/participants in the three case studies presented here all experience learning approaches that are largely place-based, integrative, and holistic, with learners spending a significant period of time in nature. The intent of transformative kincentric learning and living is for the participants to learn in a multicultural, multigenerational, and multispecies context, exemplified during *Tribal Journeys*. In the cases of the *Pit-cooking class* field trip and the *Redfish* field school, the somewhat homogeneous group of university students (in terms of background, ethnicity) learn from, and alongside, community members, knowledge holders, specialists, and experts, as well as from each other. In all three cases, the majority of the lessons learned come from knowledge generated and transmitted through multifaceted and experiential means.

While all three cases converge in terms of their transformational kincentric themes, they do differ in their learning approaches. These range from using a traditional, informal, and largely Indigenous approach, based on cultural and TEK wisdom and skills, to the integration of formal conventional university learning activities, such as scientific fieldwork and earning credit for university courses, but with an appreciation for plurality in ways of knowing. The three case studies highlight the importance of learning experientially in nature, learning about one's self, interconnected group learning, learning with the senses, and learning in place and time. While transformative learning is the ultimate goal, we argue that conventional Western learning contexts can inhibit learner transformation and kincentric thinking, in which connections and relationships with all species are accentuated. The objectives of the activities analyzed here differ on a spectrum from bridging traditional university learning environments to focusing solely on the growth, and indeed transformation, of the individual and community. What *is* possible within a conventional Western educational context is a focus on and encouragement of doing what we can, within and outside conventional educational structural norms, to create hybrid educational environments, like the Redfish School of Change program which incorporates experiential learning about and within community (all communities), with the ultimate purpose of creating an appetite for life-long learning and leaders for the future. Another possibility is to have learners engage in all three of the programs reviewed here for strongly transformative learning to strengthen the conditions within which the likelihood of transformative learning can occur. Ultimately, some participants may develop into skilled *change agents* for bringing about the permanent long-term environmental sustainability of our world, for ourselves, and our non-human relations.

Drawing from our analysis, we suggest eight guiding principles that can be applied in developing more integrative and inclusive environmental curricula at the post-secondary level, with a goal to create and sustain learning opportunities that encourage deeply meaningful and transformative experiences and create agency for environmental sustainability.

1   Allow time for reflection and processing of learning.
2   Promote learning in place (situated and place-based).
3   Provide opportunities for personal growth, and an exploration and critical reflection of self.
4   Develop group learning opportunities that are collaborative and inclusive, embracing multicultural, multigenerational, and multispecies participants and knowledge holders.
5   Incorporate kinetic, somatic, and embodied learning.
6   Create opportunities for learning connected to culture, community, and the natural environment.
7   Emphasize that the well-being of the natural environment is a critical component to the well-being and transformation of the learner.
8   Integrate perspectives and values of kincentricity, reciprocity, responsibility, and sustainability into each learning activity and demonstrate how these are connected to the learners' daily life.

Conclusions

To promote transformative kincentric learning and living at a societal level, we need to find ways of knowledge transmission that promote a desire for life-long learning and sustained environmental engagement. There is great complexity in the array of human–environment relationships around the world, far more than we will ever be able to understand. This complexity is daunting, but it is also inspiring, awesome, and humbling. Through teaching methods that aim to shift our attitudes and values in a holistic way, to stimulate curiosity and a sense of wonder, and foster empathy, we can, collectively, make a difference and see a positive way forward.

The trail blazed by Rachel Carson and more recently David Suzuki, Naomi Klein, Wangari Maathai, and Vandana Shiva give us renewed hope and vision for the future and leaders across the globe to take us into a more sustainable future. Furthermore, numerous writings (see Cajete 1994; Turner *et al.* 2008; Atleo 2011; Tuhiwai-Smith 2012) and the findings of the Truth and Reconciliation Commission of Canada (please see http://nctr.ca/reports.php) emphasize the need to recognize and support Indigenous ways of knowing and approaches to learning. All of these inspire the kinds of educational program that we exemplify here.

Economic considerations, rather than cultural values and ethics, have driven much development in the world. As a consequence we have caused tremendous damage to the earth (e.g. loss of biodiversity, environmental contamination) and face intensive Indigenous social justice issues (e.g. loss of biocultural resources, suppression of traditional practices).

Climate change is an immediate and growing concern, affecting the productivity and health of the earth's landscapes and the livelihoods of all peoples around the globe. Can the current model of post-secondary education provide the inspired and innovative leaders we need? We argue in this chapter that transformative kincentric learning and living can arise through experience within applied and situated learning opportunities. Through these educational approaches, students/participants can, and often do, become transformed in their values and worldviews. The realized transformation of self continues, and it is often these inspired individuals who, subsequently, have the capability, confidence, and knowledge to tackle the environmental and sustainability issues of tomorrow. These people are changed by their transformative experience and are empowered to step into the role of leader or educator for others.

The case studies described in this chapter (*Pit-cooking class* experience, *Redfish* field experience, and *Tribal Journeys* experience) present stories of life-affirming and transformative educational experiences for participants, along with direct and tangible ways of connecting with and engaging in the world around them. Through the embodiment of this learning, students develop personal strategies for enhancing environmental sustainability, and personal and communal well-being. The approaches analyzed above allow for a holistic learning environment to be realized, where learners teach and teachers continue their learning experiences, adapting and growing as educators, and in which humans are seen as active players and positive contributors across an evolving interconnected landscape. From our analysis, we have identified core overarching themes: learning new values and worldviews; learning about ourselves; learning about others, both human and non-human; learning with the full spectrum of senses and emotions; and learning in time and place. These themes combine to create a transformative, kincentric teaching and learning model. We have developed guiding principles to assist in developing curricula that are kincentrically based and transformative in their effects.

Acknowledgments

We are grateful to our friends, colleagues, and teachers from First Nations, university, and local communities for their contributions to our work. In particular, we thank the Tula Foundation – Hakai Institute, the Social Sciences and Humanities Research Council of Canada, the Redfish School of Change, Canoe Journey Family, and the University of Victoria, BC, for their support. Thank you to Valerie Huff for your insightful editorial comments.

References

Atleo E R (Chief Umeek) 2011. *Principles of Tsawalk: An Indigenous Approach to Global Crisis*. Vancouver: University of British Columbia Press.

Atleo M R and L Fitznor 2008. Aboriginal educators discuss recognizing, reclaiming and revitalizing their multicompetences in heritage/English language usage to promote aboriginal students' success in formal education. Paper presented at Celebrating the Local, Negotiating the School: Symposium on Language and Literacy in Aboriginal Communities, 7–8 November, Saskatoon, Saskatchewan. http://words. usask.ca/aerc/research-projects/past-projects (accessed 9 November 2008).

Barbezat D P and M Bush 2014. *Contemplative Practices in Higher Education: Powerful Methods to Transform Teaching and Learning*. San Francisco, CA: Jossey-Bass.

Battiste M 2002. Indigenous knowledge and pedagogy in Indigenous education: Literature review with recommendations. In *Our Children: Keepers of the Sacred Knowledge*. Report commissioned for the Minister's National Working Group on Education. www.afn.ca/uploads/files/education/

24._2002_oct_marie_battiste_indigenousknowledgeandpedagogy_lit_review_for_min_working_group.pdf (accessed October 2015).

Berkes F 2012. *Sacred Ecology: Traditional Ecological Knowledge and Resource Management.* 3rd edn. Philadelphia, PA: Taylor & Francis.

Cajete G 1994. *Look to the Mountain: An Ecology of Indigenous Education.* Skyland, Buncombe, NC: Kivaki Press.

Davidson-Hunt I and F Berkes 2003. Learning as you journey: Anishinaabe perception of social-ecological environments and adaptive learning. *Conservation Ecology* 8(1): article 5. www.consecol.org/vol8/iss1/art5/ (accessed 12 February 2015).

Halber Suarez T 2012. Tribal Journeys: An Integrated Voice Approach towards Transformative Learning. Unpublished PhD thesis, Department of Education, University of Victoria, British Columbia, pp. 1–256.

Illeris K 2009. An overview on transformative learning. In K Illeris (ed.) *Contemporary Theories of Learning: Learning Theorists . . . in their Own Words.* London and New York: Routledge, pp. 90–105.

Kopnina H 2014. Revisiting education for sustainable development (ESD): Examining anthropogenic bias through the transition of environmental education to ESD. *Sustainable Development* 22(2): 73–83.

Kuhnlein H V, N J Turner and D Kluckner 1982. Nutritional significance of two important root foods use by Native People of the coast of British Columbia. *Ecology of Food and Nutrition* 12(2): 89–95.

Mah y Busch J D 2014. A pedagogical heartbeat: The integration of critical and contemplative pedagogies for transformative education. *The Journal of Contemplative Inquiry* 1(1): 113–133.

Millennium Ecosystem Assessment 2005. *Ecosystems and Human Well-being: Synthesis.* Washington, DC: Island Press.

Redfish School of Change 2015. www.schoolofchange.ca/ (accessed 13 February 2015).

Salmón E 2000. Kincentric ecology: Indigenous perceptions of the human–nature relationship. *Ecological Applications* 10(5): 1327–1332.

Snyder C 2008. Grabbing hold of a moving target: Identifying and measuring the transformative learning process. *Journal of Transformative Education* 6: 159–181.

Taylor E W 2008. Transformative learning theory. *New Directions for Adult and Continuing Education* 119: 5–15.

Thompson J 2004. Gitga'at Plant Project: The Intergenerational Transmission of Traditional Ecological Knowledge Using School Science Curricula. Unpublished MSc thesis, Department of Environmental Studies, University of Victoria, British Columbia.

Tuhiwai-Smith L 2012. *Decolonizing Methodologies: Research and Indigenous Peoples.* 2nd edn. New York: Zed Books.

Turner N J 2005. *The Earth's Blanket: Traditional Teachings for Sustainable Living.* Seattle: University of Washington Press.

Turner N J 2014. *Ancient Pathways, Ancestral Knowledge: Ethnobotany and Ecological Wisdom of Indigenous Peoples of Northwestern North America.* McGill–Queen's Native and Northern Series. Montreal, QC: McGill–Queen's University Press.

Turner N J and F Berkes 2006. Coming to understanding: Developing conservation through incremental learning in the Pacific Northwest. *Human Ecology* 34: 495–513.

Turner N J, J Thomas (Tl'iishal), B F Carlson and R T Ogilvie 1983. *Ethnobotany of the Nitinaht Indians of Vancouver Island.* Victoria: British Columbia Provincial Museum (now Royal BC Museum).

Turner N J, A Marshall, J C Thompson (Edōsdi), R J Hood, C Hill and E A Hill 2008. "Ebb and flow": Transmitting environmental knowledge in a contemporary Aboriginal community. In J S Lutz and B Neis (eds) *Making and Moving Knowledge: Interdisciplinary and Community-based Research in a World on the Edge.* Montreal, QC: McGill–Queen's University Press, pp. 45–63.

WWF (World Wide Fund for Nature) 2014. *Living Planet Report 2014.* www.worldwildlife.org/pages/living-planet-report-2014 (accessed 23 November 2014).

33

COGNITION AND CULTURAL MODELING

Kimberly Kirner

Introduction: culture, cognition, and the environment

Intuitively, we know that for human beings, culture and the physical world are inseparably entwined. Every person is connected to the environment through cultural channels of economy, politics, and other dimensions of the social life. Fundamentally, humans adapt to their physical world through the medium of culture, and at the same time, their physical world is constructed by it. This cultural construction of the environment is both literal (through domestication, the built environment, and anthropogenic environmental change) and figurative (the mind, which is in constant relationship with culture, and shapes our very sensory perception). The significance of differences in various groups' cultural constructions of the physical world has only recently widely infiltrated environmental management, conservation biology, and other fields that were historically less inclined to consider perspectives outside Western scientific epistemology.

When we take a cross-cultural approach to how humans think, feel, and behave toward the physical world, we find that there are both relatively universal cognitive patterns (such as generating rules of thumb and taxonomies in order to conceptually organize nature and make decisions about how to interact with it) and very divergent culturally-constructed details (such as various ways to understand interactions between humans and non-humans) (Anderson 1996). Worldview and values, including and perhaps especially those integrated with religious identity and practice, impact the ways in which people view themselves in the non-human world, and this in turn affects how they structure environmental knowledge and resource management (Anderson 1996; Berkes 1999). Indigenous worldviews can have radically different ontologies and epistemologies from mainstream Euro-centric assumptions of nature/ human dichotomy, objectivity, and materialism (Bird-David 1999; Descola 2013; Viveiros de Castro 1998). In addition, different groups (and different individuals within any group) will have different experiences with the physical world, including the relative immediacy of their economic dependence, power in management processes, educational training, and childhood interactions – and these varied experiences with the physical world shape divergent patterns in affect, cognition, and behavior (Bang *et al.* 2007; Milton 2002; Nabhan and Trimble 1994).

Patterns in behavior toward non-humans and the physical world in general are therefore intimately tied to emotion, perception, and cognition, both at individual and collective levels. The relationship of individual cognition, culture, and the human–environment relationship has been variously theorized, both within environmental anthropology and in the interdisciplinary discourse around human cognition (see, for example, Dove and Carpenter [2007] for an overview of the history of environmental anthropological thought). Cognitive psychology has often avoided or disregarded the cultural dimension of cognition based on assumptions that arise from a Euro-centric worldview: that cognition is an internal process (the primacy of the individual), that the content of cognition can be separated from the process of cognition (dichotomous thinking); and that the process of cognition is not strongly impacted by cultural difference (universalist orientation) (Bender and Beller 2013). Given the underlying assumption in cultural anthropology of the enduring and significant impact of culture on human thought and behavior, sometimes to the near-exclusion of universalist thinking in contemporary theory, this has meant that psychology and anthropology have made sometimes strange and uncomfortable partners in the study of cognition – and that researchers have debated the fruitfulness of such a partnership (for example, see the discussion by Le Guen; Shweder; and Unsworth, all in the special volume [2012] of *Topics in Cognitive Science*).

In part, the significant differences in approach between anthropology and psychology may be traced to divergent goals among those who study cognition. In cultural anthropology, the focus is most frequently on the details of a particular group's knowledge and behavior, which tends to highlight the cross-cultural differences between groups of people. While some anthropologists have broken with this trend (particularly those trained in biological anthropology or the hard sciences, such as Konner's 2003 work), most have provided detailed case studies of particular cultures' ways of shaping knowledge about and behavior toward nature, rather than the universal constraints and mechanisms that underlie these variations. In cognitive psychology, the goal is often to find brain-based universals that underlie human thought and behavior, which is paired with the use of quantitative analysis geared to focus on common patterns rather than outliers or "noise."

The problematic assumption for quite some time has been that psychology would address "how" people think (process) and anthropology the "what" that is thought (content). Increasingly, it has become apparent that it is a false dichotomy to separate the "what" of cognition from the "how" of cognition: these are inseparable as parts of one process. Works in both social psychology (e.g. Nisbett 2003) and cultural anthropology (e.g. Shweder 1991) have pointed toward a more unified understanding of culture and cognition: process and content are emergent as integrated parts of one whole, which are both embodied by the individual mind and constructed by social context. Knowledge and ideas about nature, the content of cognition, is shaped by the process of thinking – and both content and process are embedded in a social learning experience contextualized by place (see also, for example, the cross-cultural comparison by Bang *et al.* [2007] of Native American and European-American ways of relating to and thinking about nature in Wisconsin). If, for example, an individual is raised in a culture with a relational epistemology – in which the physical world is full of conscious beings with whom one is in relationship – this also tends to impact the content of his/her cognition (say, knowledge of plants and animals) and how it is organized.

Cognition and its development arise both from universally shared biological structures and ecological constraints; and from culturally (and situationally) dependent interactions and experiences (Rogoff 2003). It is neither the case that our cognition is entirely culturally programmed, as if we were computers networked in a system; nor is it the case that our cognition is an individual process that simply gives rise to emergent patterns of cultural information (both are common misunderstandings among students in psychology and anthropology, though most of the literature is more nuanced). Furthermore, it is not true that all differences are cultural and all similarities are biological (Rogoff 2003). Rather, there are complex feedback mechanisms at work in which our social and physical environments shape adaptable cognitive structures in ways about which we are variously self-aware, and therefore have varying degrees of agency and manipulation (ranging from Bourdieu's [1977] concept of *habitus* as largely beneath self-awareness and conscious decision-making to Kronenfeld's [2008] work that suggests greater individual awareness and agency). At the same time, these adaptable structures vary somewhat person to person, as does our social and physical environment. No matter how seemingly homogeneous "a" cultural group may appear to be to the outside researcher, it has internal variance, making every individual slightly different in their cognition and emotion. Furthermore, cognition is not a one-way street to behavior, nor is it the result of passive acquisition of information from one's environment, but rather arises from and is integrated with interaction itself. The relationship between cognition, perception, behavior (practice, or "doing"), and situational context has been particularly addressed by embodied cognition (from philosophy, see Rosch *et al.* [1991]) and situated cognition (see, for example, the pioneering work of an interdisciplinary team conducting research on education in Brown *et al.* [1989]). Cognition concerning human–environment interaction, therefore, is a dense web of relationships between human and physical worlds, individual and group, biology and culture, in ways that we are only beginning to understand.

The high degree of variability of (a) individual experience of the social and physical environment, (b) underlying neurology, and (c) self-awareness in the interactive process that gives rise to cognition means that schemas (that is, constructions our minds develop and use in order to interpret our social and physical environments, generate initial feelings and associations, assess our options, and select appropriate behaviors) can differ substantially between groups and between individuals within a group, even if they are in the same physical environment and engaged in similar activities (Atran *et al.* 2005). We cannot assume that any geographic area's population, or even individuals within self-identified subcultures within that population, will share the same cognitive patterns with regard to environmental knowledge and interaction. Earlier theories about the formation and transmission of culture often treated culture as a literal thing: for example, the Durkheimian concept of social facts (1936) posited that unintended cultural forces arose from human behavior in a group, and these acted with their own power on individuals, compelling them to feel, think, and behave in particular ways. In more recent social theory, however, culture does not reside in shared norms or rules so much as it is a concept that describes the distribution of mutually constitutive representations of reality across individual minds. Culture and cognition are therefore process, not merely content – a constantly shifting (even if slightly) interrelationship of emergent individuals and emergent patterns in which those individuals are embedded and to which they contribute.

Cognitive patterns (epistemologies, schemas, cultural models – both in terms of "what" is thought and "how" to think it) become widely held (and therefore culturally significant) when they work in unison with the common underlying limitations and brain-based mechanisms shared among humans as a species – that is, when they are "core-compatible" and aligned with human "habits of mind" (Atran *et al.* 2005). This more or less harmonious pairing of the way of thinking and the thought itself with how many humans' minds work leads to more enduring and easily transmissible ways of knowing and knowledge. Yet how the human mind works gives a rather broad swath of territory for innovation, so there can (and often does) arise a great deal of diversity in environmental knowledge (both in content and epistemology) about the same physical environment. This can mean that cognition changes not only person to person, but also in a single individual across time. Cognition is contextual and situational; it happens as interactions occur, reaching into vague abstractions but crystallizing the details as the scenario unfolds (see, for example, the many case studies in D'Andrade and Strauss [1992]; Holland and Quinn [1987]; and Kronenfeld [2008]). When we think of cognition and culture in this way – as dynamic, situational, and emergent – we can recognize that what is often treated statistically as "noise" or outliers in behavior and thought may be, in fact, variation that is important for environmental decision-making and should not be dismissed. Such "noise" (divergence from statistically common patterns) may point toward differing situational contexts that are important for understanding how a physical environment might be differently experienced and conceptualized.

There are many ways to approach understanding and the representation of this variation in cognition and its relationship to human–environment interaction, including a focus on emergent behavior (agent-based models – see, for example, the literature on modeling land-use change, such as Tsai *et al.* [2015]); rules or norms that govern choices (decision trees – see, for example, Gladwin and Butler's [1984] article on modeling decisions that become adaptive strategies over time); or cultural frameworks that help orient our perceptions, feelings, interpretations of our surroundings, and actions (cultural models, the focus of this chapter). The benefits of utilizing cultural models extend to environmental modeling as a whole: aside from providing a mechanism for epistemic justice (ensuring that minority or margin-alized worldviews and epistemologies are taken into account in environmental policy and management), such methods improve the researcher's understanding of the issue at hand, improve the reception of the research process and findings among diverse stakeholder groups, and often result in better outcomes for policy or management strategies (Jakeman *et al.* 2006). Such models can provide a means for researchers to develop more complex, rich knowledge around an environmental issue or resource, productively challenging the prevailing Western scientific assumptions to ensure that data, analysis, and policy or management recommendations are optimal (Gagnon and Berteaux 2009; Moller *et al.* 2004). They can also form useful representations of divergent ways to understand the same environmental domain in order to assist in communication and cultural brokering between diverse stakeholder groups (Gagnon and Berteaux 2009; Olsson *et al.* 2004). When an organization, such as a governmental agency or nonprofit, is engaged in attempting to change human behavior (such as encouraging water conservation or recycling), the learning process that both researchers and participants go through in the iterative work of model development, feedback, and refinement – which affords an opportunity for bringing to awareness assumptions and potential consequences of models – is itself frequently part of the desired outcome (Jakeman *et al.* 2006). Cultural modeling as a methodology can therefore not only contribute to policy or management decision-making through providing representations of emergent patterns in how people think and act in a certain domain, but can also feed into the process of changing these thoughts and actions.

Cultural models and applications to environmental management

Frake (1980) was instrumental in conceptualizing a theory of culture as a "theory of codes" that described shared knowledge, and argued for an anthropology that found these cultural codes which allow for successful navigation of the social and physical environment. He conceptualized the task of doing anthropology as not only describing behavioral events, but explaining why the events occur, with a particular emphasis on one's capacity to predict other people's behavior and select appropriate actions to take in various contexts. As someone who was both cultural ecologist and cognitive anthropologist, Frake paved the way in his work for later iterations and refinements of theory about cultural frameworks, including cultural model theory. On an individual level, cultural models organize complex information into a flexible abstract mental object that can be held in working memory and filled in with appropriate specifics; they provide frameworks with which we can understand what is happening around us, assess others as belonging within or outside our social groups, and determine appropriate courses of action (D'Andrade 1995; D'Andrade and Strauss 1992; Holland and Quinn 1987). For any given domain (such as water management) there may be one, several, or many cultural models (each made up of many distinct but associated schemas). These cultural models may conflict or work together, as well as be subconsciously held or provide a thought-library from which the individual consciously selects a model to instantiate in interpreting others or selecting actions (Kronenfeld 2008).

As a basic illustrative example, consider the domain of gardening. "Gardening" as a cultural model would involve many flexible schemas, or constitutive elements, organized in domains, such as "seed acquisition and use," "purposes of gardening," "types of people who garden," and "the annual garden cycle." Alternative schemas may involve visual, script-based, or other mental representations of the domain at hand – such as scripts about why gardening is worthwhile or images of what a garden looks like at various times of the year. Some of these schemas may follow a prototype-extension format, in which the gardener considers a particular image or script to be the quintessential option by which interpretations of less obvious contexts are made. An example is how, for many Americans, "vegetable gardens" bring to mind tidy rows of peas, carrots, and beans, yet the schema for "vegetable garden" is flexible enough to allow them to use it when faced with raised beds or an intercropped garden. Other schemas may be held like a library in the mind, with the gardener able to self-consciously select from equally valid options, though sociocultural pressures often still impact that selection process. For example, an American gardener may have a schema for "type of garden" that includes vegetable, cottage, traditional suburban American (lawn with hedges) as equally valid options to select, but may feel pressure from neighbors to select a particular type. So too with cultural models: the emergent pattern that arises from all those schemas as a particular type of human activity related to the land and plants.

Cultural models give individuals "skeletal principles for meaning making" (Bang *et al.* 2007: 13868), including foundational cognitive processes such as salience (how much attention to give) and attribution of causality (not only in terms of causal relationships, but what in the environment is worthy of explanation). Cultural models that govern interactions with the physical environment are often embedded in religion, uniting traditional ecological knowledge with sacred ecology. These representations of domains of culture are not merely useful to humans in navigating social and physical environments, but are linked to the emotional and psychological meanings one attaches to one's own actions and interpretations of others' actions, and therefore are interrelated with one's identity and sense of self in interpersonal interactions. The interrelationship of cognition with identity is at the heart of understanding the often emotionally charged political conflict that arises in environmental management and policy. In land use policy-making for the public lands of the American West, for example, there are often passionate debates about the purpose of nature and the optimal way in which humans should relate to and appreciate the physical world (Hedrick 2007). Those who live in suburban or urban locations frequently have very different ways of knowing (and resulting knowledge) about their environments from those who live agrarian lives in rural locations. Identities that feature prominently in debates about land use in the American West (for example, environmentalists and cattle ranchers) are often strongly held and integrated with these different ways of knowing, which can result in significant conflict in the policy-making process (including litigation).

Conflict occurs not only because of differences in diverse stakeholders' cultural models, but also because the models may be associated with deeply internalized senses of self and "other," as well as embedded in an ontology fundamental to one's identity. Cognition is not only about managing cattle, a dooryard garden, or water; cognition is also about constructing a sense of what defines our species within the physical world, the "right" relationships to have with non-human beings, and making meaning of human life and experience. Cognition, as has been discussed, is not only about "what" one knows, but "how" one knows it. Relational epistemologies, for example, posit that non-human beings are persons with whom one relates. The "right" relationship of humans to nature, in this case, is therefore not manager-to-resource, but person-to-person (or person-to-community). Sustainable management may result from a variety of epistemologies and resulting knowledge, but the ethics may vary considerably (even when the outcomes do not): "right" relationship may be defined not only in terms of policy and management decisions, but also in terms of ritual obligations, social interactions, and other culturally constructed ways of integrating knowing-about-nature and interacting-with-nature.

Cultural modeling therefore affords the researcher the ability to describe, within one framework, both the content and process of cognition, as well as how this relates to emotion and action. In environmental management and policy work, such models are useful for addressing stakeholder differences, articulating core issues and ideas to policy-makers, and rallying communities for engagement in environmental issues. Cultural models have been applied to many different environmental domains, including stakeholder assessment of environmental conditions (Kronenfeld and Hedrick 2005); resource management (Paolisso 2002; Pfeffer *et al.* 2001) and restoration (Paolisso and Dery 2010); environmental planning (Christel *et al.* 2001); toxic phytoplankton impacts (Falk *et al.* 2000; Kempton and Falk 2000); and climate change (e.g. Kempton *et al.* 1996). Cultural modeling, as an iterative, inter-active process that directly engages participants from stakeholder groups is appealing as a methodology both in its capacity to deliver predictive models that are accessible to policy-makers and environmental managers, and to ensure such models represent the diverse perspectives and knowledge of people on the ground. In this way, they capture variance in a population rather than treating outliers as statistical "noise"; the variance is reflective of diversity within and between cultural groups that is significant in environmental policy, resource management, and conservation. The implications of cultural models for environmental decision-making are significant. Content bias and core values, which impact perception and interpretation of the physical world, are integral to how people interact with nature (Atran *et al.* 2005). These differing core values afford different frameworks for calculating who or what has interests in decision-making about the environment, with some cultural frameworks including nature as a non-person person or a collective of non-human persons with interests. Ultimately, people may vary in how useful they find a given cultural framework.

Methods in cultural modeling of environmental domains

It is important to be attentive to broad areas of culture that commonly impact individual cognition and behavior (Atran *et al.* 2005):

1 folk ecology (cognition of ecological relations among species);
2 cultural epidemiology (mapping levels of agreement and variation among participants, as well as social networks that provide pathways for information to flow); and

3   spiritual values (operationalizing supernatural beings or forces in the context of ecological understanding and decision-making).

Such research often involves mixed methods, using both qualitative data and quantitative data to refine models over several iterations or to triangulate data in one iteration. Alternatively, cultural model research may quantify qualitative data such that cluster analysis or latent class analysis can be performed on it. These are analytical frameworks that start with qualitative analysis (usually grounded theory) to assign codes to data and then apply statistical methods which allow exploration of how a domain is categorized across respondents, with certain concepts "clustering" more closely together (as they are more tightly associated) and others having less in common (for more information, see Bernard 2011; Glaser 2003).

For example, the first stage of identifying and describing cultural models may be entirely qualitative (for example, having a number of participants free-list in response to a given word such as "conservation" or a photo that represents a key environmental domain of interest such as a high desert landscape). The qualitative analysis, frequently conducted using grounded theory in order to build models from "the data up," may then produce one or more cultural models. The second stage of cultural model research may then test and refine the models using quantitative research. For example, core themes that run through the cultural model may be turned into statements suitable for surveys that ask for a Likert-scaled or yes/no quantification of agreement, which can then be analyzed for degree of consensus among a given population or community or between different stakeholder groups. Researchers' selection of methods, as in much of anthropology, depends on a confluence of factors that include the researcher's expertise, time and monetary constraints, sample size and participant willingness, and appropriateness of method to the domain and research questions at hand.

Cultural model studies may vary considerably in terms of the type of data they collect, the way they analyze that data, the number of participants in the sample, and how participants are identified and recruited. Qualitative data may be elicited through interviews, life histories, participant observation, open-ended questionnaires, free-listing, or pile-sorting, among others. There may be only a couple of dozen participants, particularly if the method of data collection is extensive (life history, for example) or there may be hundreds or thousands of participants, particularly if using questionnaires. Participants may be a select pool of folk experts, professional experts, representatives of a specific stakeholder group, or draw from the public at large – all dependent on the research question at hand.

A study of farmer land conservation in Maryland, for example, used farmer discourse in semi-structured interviews to generate cultural models of how to conserve rural lands (Paolisso et al. 2013). Through looking for "expository, explanatory, and/or argumentative discourse" (2013: 16) in the interview data in an iterative, mixed deductive and inductive coding process, the researchers built a model of the tenets farmers held for successful land conservation. Paolisso et al. (2013) noted that some of these tenets diverge from those of many land conservation organizations (such as farmers' overall agreement that the "best use" of land is for food production under active management), and that these tenets inform farmers' aesthetic assessment of land itself (that is, they would find a "well-managed farm" more beautiful than wilderness). The study, which was conducted in much the same way as Kronenfeld and Hedrick's (2005) study of ranchers' cultural models of environmental condition and Hedrick's (2007) work on ranchers' decision models regarding conservation easements, generated similar results – that "best use" is active management, and aesthetically pleasing land is well-managed land. Such studies have significant implications for collective actions for land conservation that bring together farmers or ranchers and land conservation organizations. Divergent cultural models of land conservation and environmental condition do not mean that fruitful mutual engagement cannot be had between stakeholder groups, but they point toward potential barriers to such engagement that can be addressed through activities and processes which encourage cross-stakeholder group understanding, identification of common goals (as opposed to values or views), and collaboration in problem-solving in order to meet agreed-upon goals.

Studies may triangulate qualitative data in order to strengthen the validity of findings. Wagner-Tsukamoto and Tadajewski (2006) investigated the problem-solving behavior of green consumers by using observation of consumer behavior, archival research, and interviewing that prompted participants to describe how they assessed the environmental friendliness of products (see also Tadajewski and Wagner-Tsukamoto 2006). They also used cross-cultural comparison of British and German participants, finding that those who self-consciously used cultural models when faced with specific products had better outcomes in accurately assessing products for environmental impact, as opposed to those participants who assessed products in fixed, abstract terms. For example, a consumer who contemplated the total environmental impact of a specific product they were looking at in the store, inclusive of imagined production, transport, consumption, and discard costs, would more accurately assess environmental impact than a consumer who categorically looked for products labeled "environmentally friendly." In this way, cultural models can reveal important cognitive glitches in conservation behaviors: while high motivation to conserve resources is necessary for improving sustainability-oriented actions in individuals, it is not sufficient to produce such behavior on its own (Wagner-Tsukamoto and Tadajewski 2006). Individuals may be highly motivated to conserve resources, but without sufficient knowledge or a complex model for how to assess resources embedded in consumer products. Falling back on labels may hide the real environmental costs of a product under vague platitudes, yet produce feelings in individuals of having been supportive of conservation without actually assessing the environmental impact of their decisions.

Decisions and behavior occur in the meeting place of emotion and knowledge, and how these different aspects of the mental process affect patterns in human–environment interactions can be crucial for the successful development and dissemination of conservation programs. Cognitive-Affective Mapping (CAM, first developed by philosopher Paul Thagard [2006]) focuses primarily on affect, which frequently arises as an important dimension to cultural models, along with key concepts or beliefs. CAM codes qualitative data (such as interviews or historic documents) for themes, very much like cultural modeling, but then assigns a positive, negative, or neutral designation to associated affective values as well as an intensity or strength of the emotion. This produces a graphical display of how concepts are related to emotional response in a given stakeholder population. Because it produces a graphical product, CAM can be used not only for data collection and analysis, but also for communication to policy-makers or in cultural brokering among stakeholders (Wolfe 2012). CAM can assist in understanding conflict among stakeholders and in helping stakeholders to become aware of their emotional differences in ways that can lead to resolving such conflicts (Homer–Dixon et al. 2014), leading to greater collaboration for solving problems in conservation or sustainable management.

Wolfe (2012) used CAM to analyze interview data in order to investigate values and associated emotions in a community of water users. Such research explained the mixed results of water efficiency programs more thoroughly than the usual discussion of obstacles to implementation, affording a better understanding of why some water conservation strategies work and others do not in a given community, given the distribution of values, assumptions, knowledge, and the emotional associations to these. The study revealed strongly divergent beliefs about residential consumers' roles in water efficiency on the part of two distinctly different groups of water management practitioners. Wolfe's study points to yet more utility for cultural modeling: addressing policy or program inefficiency not only in terms of its fit to the public, but also in terms of potentially problematic divergent models among professional practitioners (and their organizations), which could negatively impact development and implementation of such programs. Additionally, because CAM (and cultural modeling more broadly) can be conducted using qualitative data over time and scale (through the collection of archival material), the researcher can explore how models diverged over time and space (Wolfe 2012).

Cultural consensus modeling (CCM) is a form of analysis that allows a researcher to see "graded patterns of variation" within and between populations at various scales and explore behavioral consequences of such variation (the method and theory were first developed by Romney *et al.* [1986] and is described in detail by Weller [2007]). Unlike CAM and purely qualitative cultural modeling methods, CCM is uniquely suited to fixed-format questionnaires or sorting tasks that can be quantified, though it can be done in a qualitative manner as well (or can use both approaches simultaneously). In conducting CCM research in the lowland rainforest in Guatemala, Atran *et al.* (2005) found that consensus may not be apparent even among people who share the same environment and similar activities within it. Cultural and historical differences, including at the individual level, can yield a lack of consensus even in the face of similar environmental contexts.

By contrast, Miller *et al.* (2004) used CCM to explore yellowfin tuna fishery management in Hawaii, sampling among both fishermen and fishery scientists. Questions with yes/no answers (dichotomous questions) were developed from conversations with the study populations and a literature review, designed to assess answers to fishery knowledge questions. Participants could also provide additional information to researchers after finishing the structured interview portion. The study revealed that despite belonging to different stakeholder communities, fishermen and fishery scientists had overall consensus, but had sharply divergent responses on a few questions, indicating a shared "cultural code" but with differing knowledge (Miller *et al.* 2004). Overall, CCM can be extremely useful in identifying patterns of consensus and divergence within and between groups who are utilizing or managing the same environment, but may best be designed through prior qualitative studies, even if informal.

It can often be useful to use both qualitative and quantitative data in a single study. Convergent mixed-methods cultural modeling may collect both types of data and simultaneously conduct analysis on them. Mixed methods can also be formally used in an iterative fashion: exploratory mixed-methods studies begin with qualitative data for developing models that can then be tested and refined using quantitative methods. Explanatory models begin with quantitative data analysis to identify patterns of consensus, which can then be further explained through subsequent qualitative feedback. In a study of cognitive models of forest ecology among forest managers in various institutions, researchers interviewed informants using domain analysis, collected questionnaires, and used free-listing and card-sorting in order to capture a rich set of data that could speak to potential patterns of consensus and divergence among forest management institutions (Richardson *et al.* 1996). The study revealed that surprisingly, management institutions did not homogenize managers' cultural models of ecology to nearly the degree that had been previously assumed. Such information is helpful, as it indicates that a substantial portion of the causality behind a manager's individual cognition of forest ecology will have been influenced by a confluence of factors that occurred prior to his/her existing management position, including cultural background, childhood experience of the physical environment, career path, and economic relationship to the land (Richardson *et al.* 1996). High levels of intra-agency diversity in cultural models of the ecology of the environment under management has implications for how to handle divergent perspectives and knowledge in the workplace in ways that productively capitalize on such diversity, rather than rendering it a source of conflict.

Recent critique in environmental anthropology has pointed out that even as the field has more impact on environmental policy, the use of quantitative and environmental data has been in decline (Charnley and Durham 2010). This is particularly problematic for situations in which the goal is to influence policy-making or programs by providing a comprehensive understanding of how potential regulatory or other structures may impact and provoke certain responses in populations. In reviewing several large samples of recent literature in environmental anthropology to make the critique, and then providing an extended case study of a problematic large-scale development project in the Brazilian Amazon, Charnley and Durham (2010) made a compelling case for the importance of incorporating quantitative data in environmental anthropological research.

Conclusion

Culture is at the center of both human cognition and the human–nature relationship. It is messy and its boundaries are permeable, a complex set of emergent patterns in which individuals themselves are both agents and recipients. The emergent quality of culture and cognition makes it challenging to characterize, particularly for policy-makers and environmental managers, who rarely have the capacity to use ethnographic literature as a basis for assessing management and policy alternatives, communicating with stakeholder groups, or managing stakeholder conflict. Yet it is incredibly important to find ways to communicate cultural and cognitive diversity, and its impact on social conflict and human behavior in the physical world, to decision-makers at all levels – ranging from helping households become more aware of their underlying assumptions to assisting nations in crafting environmental policy that is equitable and likely to work. Cultural modeling bridges the gap between detailed ethnographic studies focused on accuracy and the politics of representation and macro-scale quantitative models designed to be useful for decision-makers. By studying culture as a set of social networks, processes grounded in interaction, and distributed cognition, it is possible for anthropologists to create models ranging from micro-scale to macro-scale that speak to the real diversity of people's values, knowledge, perceived needs, and behaviors in ways that are easily communicated to decision-makers.

Cultural modeling as a methodology is not one method, but an approach to integrating many methods. These methods might use a variety of qualitative and quantitative data, which may or may not be formally integrated in a mixed-methods design. Across all cultural model studies, however, are a few key features:

1   data is collected on a specific domain, then primarily analyzed in ways that build models inductively;
2   variation and outliers in the data are viewed as meaningful; and
3   models are often refined through an iterative process that engages stakeholders at multiple stages in the research.

In all cases, cultural models integrate knowledge, values, and emotion as well as linking cognition to behavior. In so doing, they have a great deal of capacity to explain behavioral patterns in ways that meaningfully speak to problems in environmental management and policy-making: understanding stakeholder conflicts, garnering greater consensus and support, handling divergent views within institutions, ensuring cultural competency in programs and policies, and (certainly not the least) providing for greater epistemic justice.

References

Anderson, E. N. 1996. *Ecologies of the Heart: Emotion, Belief, and the Environment*. Oxford: Oxford University Press.

Atran, Scott, Douglas L. Medin and Norbert O. Ross. 2005. The Cultural Mind: Environmental Decision-Making and Cultural Modeling within and across Populations. *Psychological Review* 112(4): 744–776.

Bang, Megan, Douglas L. Medin and Scott Atran. 2007. Cultural Mosaics and Mental Models of Nature. *Proceedings of the National Academy of Sciences of the United States of America* 104(35): 13868–13874.

Bender, Andrea and Sieghard Beller. 2013. Cognition Is . . . Fundamentally Cultural. *Behavioral Science* 3(1): 42–54.

Berkes, Fikret. 1999. *Sacred Ecology: Traditional Ecological Knowledge and Resource Management*. Philadelphia, PA: Taylor & Francis.

Bernard, H. Russell. 2011. *Research Methods in Anthropology: Qualitative and Quantitative Approaches*. 5th edn. Lanham, MD: AltaMira Press.

Bird-David, Nurit. 1999. "Animism" Revisited: Personhood, Environment, and Relational Epistemology. *Current Anthropology* 40(S1): S67–S91.

Bourdieu, Pierre. 1977. *Outline of a Theory of Practice*. Cambridge, UK: Cambridge University Press.

Brown, John S., Allan Collins and Paul Duguid. 1989. Situated Cognition and the Culture of Learning. *Educational Researcher* 18(1): 32–42.

Charnley, Susan and William H. Durham. 2010. Anthropology and Environmental Policy: What Counts? *American Anthropologist* 112(3): 397–415.

Christel, Douglas, Willett D. Kempton and Jennifer Harris. 2001. *The Effects of Values and Cultural Models on Policy: An Anthropological Approach to Environmental Policy in Tampa Bay*. Newark: College of Marine Studies, University of Delaware.

D'Andrade, Roy. 1995. *The Development of Cognitive Anthropology*. Cambridge, UK: Cambridge University Press.

D'Andrade, Roy G. and Claudia Strauss (eds) 1992. *Human Motives and Cultural Models*. Cambridge, UK: Cambridge University Press.

Descola, Philippe. 2013. *Beyond Nature and Culture* (transl. Janet Lloyd). Chicago, IL: University of Chicago Press.

Dove, Michael R. and Carol Carpenter (eds) 2007. *Environmental Anthropology: A Historical Reader*. Chichester, UK: Wiley–Blackwell.

Durkheim, Émile. 1936. *The Rules of Sociological Method*. New York: The Free Press.

Falk, James M., Forbes L. Darby and Willett Kempton. 2000. *Understanding Mid-Atlantic Residents' Concerns, Attitudes, and Perceptions about Harmful Algal Blooms – Pfiesteria piscicida*. Newark: University of Delaware Sea Grant College Program.

Frake, Charles O. 1980. *Language and Cultural Description*. Stanford, CA: Stanford University Press.

Gagnon, Catherine A. and Dominique Berteaux. 2009. Integrating Traditional Ecological Knowledge and Ecological Science: A Question of Scale. *Ecology and Society* 14(2): 19.

Gladwin, Christina H. and John Butler. 1984. Is Gardening an Adaptive Strategy for Florida Family Farmers? *Human Organization* 43(3): 208–216.

Glaser, Barney G. 2003. *The Grounded Theory Perspective II: Description's Remodeling of Grounded Theory Methodology*. Mill Valley, CA: Sociology Press.

Hedrick, Kimberly. 2007. Our Way of Life: Identity, Landscape, and Conflict. Unpublished PhD dissertation, Department of Anthropology, University of California, Riverside.

Holland, Dorothy and Naomi Quinn (eds) 1987. *Cultural Models in Language and Thought*. Cambridge, UK: Cambridge University Press.

Homer-Dixon, Thomas, Manjana Milkoreit, Steven J. Mock, Tobias Schröder and Paul Thagard. 2014. The Conceptual Structure of Social Disputes: Cognitive-Affective Maps as a Tool for Conflict Analysis and Resolution. *SAGE Open* 4(1). doi: 10.1177/2158244014526210

Jakeman, A. J., R. A. Letcher and J. P. Norton. 2006. Ten Iterative Steps in Development and Evaluation of Environmental Models. *Environmental Modelling and Software* 21(5): 602–614.

Kempton, Willett M. and James Falk. 2000. Cultural Models of *Pfiesteria*: Toward Cultivating More Appropriate Risk Perceptions. *Coastal Management* 28(4): 273–285.

Kempton, Willett M., James S. Boster and Jennifer A. Hartley. 1996. *Environmental Values in American Culture*. Cambridge, MA: The MIT Press.

Konner, Melvin. 2003. *The Tangled Wing: Biological Constraints on the Human Spirit*. 2nd edn. Chicago, IL: Holt Paperbacks.

Kronenfeld, David B. 2008. *Culture, Society, and Cognition: Collective Goals, Values, Action, and Knowledge*. Berlin: Mouton de Gruyter.

Kronenfeld, David B. and Kimberly D. Hedrick. 2005. Culture, Cultural Models, and the Division of Labor. *Cybernetics and Systems* 36(8): 817–845.

Le Guen, Olivier. 2012. Cognitive Anthropological Fieldwork. *Topics in Cognitive Science* 4(3): 445–452.

Miller, Marc L., John Kaneko, Paul Bartram, Joe Marks and Devon Brewer. 2004. Cultural Consensus Analysis and Environmental Anthropology: Yellowfin Tuna Fishery Management in Hawaii. *Cross-Cultural Research* 38(3): 289–314.

Milton, Kay. 2002. *Loving Nature: Towards an Ecology of Emotion*. London and New York: Routledge.

Moller, Henrik, Fikret Berkes, P. O. B. Lyver and M. Kislalioglu. 2004. Combining Scientific and Traditional Ecological Knowledge: Monitoring Populations for Co-Management. *Ecology and Society* 9(3): 2.

Nabhan, Gary P. and Stephen Trimble (eds) 1994. *The Geography of Childhood: Why Children Need Wild Places*. Boston, MA: Beacon Press.

Nisbett, Richard E. 2003. *The Geography of Thought*. New York: Simon and Schuster.

Olsson, Per, Carl Folke and Fikret Berkes. 2004. Adaptive Comanagement for Building Resilience in Social-Ecological Systems. *Environmental Management* 34(1): 75–90.

Paolisso, Michael. 2002. Blue Crabs and Controversy on the Chesapeake Bay: A Cultural Model for Understanding Watermen's Reasoning about Blue Crab Management. *Human Organization* 61(3): 226–239.

Paolisso, Michael and Nicole Dery. 2010. A Cultural Model Assessment of Oyster Restoration Alternatives for the Chesapeake Bay. *Human Organization* 69(2): 169–179.

Paolisso, Michael, Priscilla Weeks and Jane Packard. 2013. A Cultural Model of Farmer Land Conservation. *Human Organization* 72(1): 12–22.

Pfeffer, Max J., John W. Schelhas and Leyla Ann Day. 2001. Forest Conservation, Value Conflict, and Interest Formation in a Honduran National Park. *Rural Sociology* 66(3): 382–402.

Richardson, Catherine Woods, Robert G. Lee and Marc L. Miller. 1996. Thinking about Ecology: Cognition of Pacific Northwest Forest Managers across Diverse Institutions. *Human Organization* 55(3): 314–323.

Rogoff, Barbara. 2003. *The Cultural Nature of Human Development*. Oxford: Oxford University Press.

Romney, A. Kimball, Susan C. Weller and William H. Batchelder. 1986. Culture as Consensus: A Theory of Culture and Informant Accuracy. *American Anthropologist* 88(2): 313–338.

Rosch, Eleanor, Evan Thompson and Francisco J. Varela. 1991. *The Embodied Mind: Cognitive Science and Human Experience*. Cambridge, MA: The MIT Press.

Shweder, Richard A. 1991. *Thinking through Culture: Expeditions in Cultural Psychology*. Cambridge, MA: Harvard University Press.

Shweder, Richard A. 2012. Anthropology's Disenchantment with the Cognitive Revolution. *Topics in Cognitive Science* 4(3): 354–361.

Tadajewski, Mark and Sigmund Wagner-Tsukamoto. 2006. Anthropology and Consumer Research: Qualitative Insights into Green Consumer Behavior. *Qualitative Market Research* 9(1): 8–25.

Thagard, Paul. 2006. *Hot Thought: Mechanisms and Applications of Emotional Cognition*. Cambridge, MA: The MIT Press.

Tsai, Yushiou, Asim Zia, Christopher Koliba, Gabriela Bucini, Justin Guilbert and Brian Beckage. 2015. An Interactive Land Use Transition Agent-Based Model (ILUTABM): Endogenizing Human–Environment Interactions in the Western Missisquoi Watershed. *Land Use Policy* 49: 161–176.

Unsworth, Sara J. 2012. Anthropology in the Cognitive Sciences: The Value of Diversity. *Topics in Cognitive Science* 4(3): 429–436.

Viveiros de Castro, Eduardo. 1998. Cosmological Deixis and Amerindian Perspectivism. *Journal of the Royal Anthropological Institute* 4(3): 469–488.

Wagner-Tsukamoto, Sigmund and Mark Tadajewski. 2006. Cognitive Anthropology and the Problem-Solving Behaviour of Green Consumers. *Journal of Consumer Behaviour* 5(3): 235–244.

Weller, Susan. 2007. Cultural Consensus Theory: Applications and Frequently Asked Questions. *Field Methods* 19(4): 339–368.

Wolfe, S. E. 2012. Water Cognition and Cognitive Affect Mapping: Identifying Priority Clusters within a Canadian Water Efficiency Community. *Water Resource Management* 26(10): 2991–3004.

34

PERCEIVING NATURE'S PERSONHOOD

Anthropological enhancements to environmental education

Rob Efird

Introduction

Li Bo was born in the ancient city of Dali, in China's southwestern province of Yunnan. Though Li's father was not a farmer, he enjoyed growing food and tended a large garden. One day, when Li was a child, his father took him out into the garden and helped him to plant a pumpkin seed. What happened next changed the course of Li's life: when the seed responded by bursting from the earth and growing into a pumpkin, Li was filled with surprise and delight. "That," he recalls, "was when I became an environmentalist."

Li shared this story many years later while leading Friends of Nature (*Ziran zhi you*), China's most prominent environmental non-governmental organization (NGO). For Li, it seems, a pleasurable childhood experience of interacting with the non-human world appears to have fostered a lifelong commitment to environmental care. Anthropologist Kay Milton (2002: 72) has described this transformation as one in which "a nature lover has emerged from a process of learning reinforced by enjoyment." Given the typically lengthy and intimate relationships that ethnographers form with the people and places they study, this is a dynamic that anthropologists such as Milton are well-positioned to both observe and assess.[1] It is also a transformation sought by practitioners of environmental education (EE), an international and interdisciplinary effort to address environmental degradation by fostering stewardship and ecological sustainability. Yet the potential contributions of anthropologists to environmental education theory and practice have yet to be widely appreciated.[2] This is a major loss, for as Milton has persuasively argued (1996), the key role that culture plays in environmental protection demonstrates anthropology's direct relevance to environmentalism and its analysis.

A case in point is Milton's own research, which helps us to gain a better understanding of why people care for and protect the non-human world. Milton's work on this question deserves a wider appreciation among scholars, practitioners, citizens and policy-makers who are interested in environmental education, because although active environmental care—or "pro-environmental behavior"—is often seen as the ultimate goal of EE, there is no clear consensus on how to foster it. Milton suggests that active environmental care is the product of an emotional process wherein people perceive in nature qualities of "personhood," qualities such as individuality, capacity for emotion, and volition. This perception of personhood emerges from interactions such as those enjoyed by Li Bo, during which humans experience a "responsive relatedness" (Milton 2002: 48) with the non-human world: Li Bo planted a seed, and the seed responded by transforming into a pumpkin plant—thereby transforming Li Bo in the process.

This chapter explores Milton's approach to personhood and its implications for environmental education theory and practice. Following a brief introduction to environmental education and the challenges that researchers have faced in assessing the development of pro-environmental behavior, I discuss how Milton's sophisticated analysis of emotion and environmental care helps us to understand this process more clearly. I conclude by suggesting how Milton's ideas can be applied to enhance the practice of environmental education.

Environmental education: knowledge, emotion, and action

Huanjing baohu, jiaoyu wei ben. [Education is the foundation of environmental protetion.]
(Ministry of Education of the People's Republic of China 2003)

In response to mounting environmental challenges at both local and global scales, an international movement led by the United Nations (UN) began promoting environmental education and, later, Education for Sustainable Development (ESD) in the early 1970s. Subsequently, a growing number of governments, including those of the United States, China, Taiwan, and Japan, have enacted laws or adopted government policies that mandate some form of environmental education for their citizens. These initiatives have precipitated a sharp increase in the number and diversity of formal and informal opportunities for environmental learning, and they have helped to feed a dramatic growth in research on environmental education that had begun in the 1960s. Despite these encouraging developments, the effectiveness of environmental education remains uncertain, and researchers remain unclear about the precise combination of experiences that motivate environmental care.

Environmental education is conventionally defined with reference to its goals, which typically include some combination of knowledge, attitudes, abilities, and behavior. In the *Journal of Environmental Education*'s inaugural issue, for example, environmental education is defined on the basis of its aim to produce "a citizenry that is knowledgeable concerning the biophysical environment and its associated problems, aware of how to help solve these problems, and motivated to work towards their solution" (Stapp *et al.* 1969: 31). This combination of goals is roughly similar to the emphases of UN policy, the mandatory guidelines for environmental education issued by China's Ministry of Education, and the government policies of Japan, the United States, and Taiwan, all of which seek to motivate action to resolve environmental problems. However, while there is broad agreement on the importance of these core goals, there remains considerable uncertainty on how to achieve them. In particular, while methods of knowledge transfer have long constituted the focus of formal education, methods of motivating action "which maintains or improves conditions necessary for ecosystem stability, biological diversity, and abundance" (Short 2010: 18) remain poorly understood. This is a serious failing, since, as noted above, informed action on behalf of the environment—so-called "responsible environmental behavior"—is widely acknowledged as the preeminent objective of environmental education.

Initially, many researchers assumed that the acquisition of knowledge concerning the environment would lead to pro-environmental attitudes that would in turn motivate the desired behaviors. This hypothetical process was referred to as the K-A-B (Knowledge →Attitudes→ Behavior) model. Since formal educational systems are premised on the value of knowledge and its transformative potential, it is easy to understand why such an approach might be appealing and persuasive to professional educators. But beginning in the 1980s, a series of studies undermined this model's credibility and showed that the possession of environmental knowledge and problem-solving skills, while important, did not automatically result in environmentally responsible behavior (see, for example, Hungerford and Volk 1990; Marcinkowski 1998). As Wals (2012: 633) concluded: "just providing information, raising awareness, and changing attitudes apparently is not enough to change people's behavior. People's environmental behaviors are far too complex and contextual to be captured by a simple causal model." Nevertheless, a knowledge-based approach to environmental education remains dominant in most schools, nature centers, and public education campaigns, and knowledge remains the focus of program assessment (Stern *et al.* 2014). This state of affairs adds an extra urgency to the question: if knowledge is not the key, then what *does* foster people's motivation to behave sustainably and solve environmental problems?

Despite decades of effort by a vibrant and growing international network of environmental education researchers, this gap between knowledge and action has yet to be sufficiently explained (Efird 2014; Kollmuss and Agyeman 2002). In part, this is due to weaknesses in program assessments: a recent meta-review of more than 20 years of environmental education assessments concludes (Stern *et al.* 2014: 602) that although there is "broad evidence that EE programs can lead to positive changes in student knowledge, awareness, skills, attentions, intentions, and behavior . . . we found only circumstantial evidence related to how or why these programs produce these results." This empirical weakness may be partially explained by imperfections in the assessment measures, but the effort to gather better evidence and draw stronger causal connections is further complicated by a number of inherent difficulties, including the multiplicity of factors contributing to desired behavioral outcomes, the complexity of their interaction, and the difficulty of conducting longitudinal studies to assess long-term impact.

One effort to overcome these challenges has developed into a large, multicultural body of scholarship on the "significant life experiences" (SLE) that form adult environmentalists. More than three decades of this research on the link between childhood experience and responsible environmental behavior in North America, Central America, Europe, Africa, East Asia, and Australia has yielded broadly consistent conclusions: according to Chawla and Cushing (2007: 440), "from half to more than 80% of the respondents identify childhood experiences of nature as a significant experience [and] they mention influential family members or other role models equally often or second in importance." In other words,

> these findings suggest that nature activities in childhood and youth, as well as examples of parents, teachers and other role models who show an interest in nature, are key "entry-level variables" that predispose people to take an interest in nature themselves and later work for its protection.
>
> *(Chawla and Cushing 2007: 440)*[3]

Of course, this observed correlation between environmentally responsible behavior and certain "significant life experiences" does not constitute a causal explanation.[4] In order to explain how experiences of nature and the social influence of role models actually result in action on behalf of the environment, SLE researchers have posited the existence of "environmental sensitivity" as a causal variable. Described as the consequence of "an individual's contact with the outdoors in relatively pristine environments either alone or with close personal friends or relatives" (Hungerford and Volk 1990: 264), environmental sensitivity has been defined by Peterson (1982: 5) as "a set of affective attributes which result in an individual viewing the environment from an empathetic perspective." It is this empathetic perspective that motivates people to act. In other words, it is not your experiences of nature or people *per se*, but the affective state of empathy ("environmental sensitivity") that such experiences foster which in turn motivates your environmentally responsible behavior. Since the 1980s, environmental sensitivity has been repeatedly affirmed as a key precursor (Hungerford and Volk 1990) and even a prerequisite (Peterson 1982) for such pro-environmental behavior, and the concept is now firmly entrenched in mainstream research and assessment.[5]

Surprisingly, however, this embrace has largely ignored a key unanswered question: how exactly do experiences such as contact with the outdoors and the presence of role models actually foster an empathetic perspective? Clearly, not all individuals respond to such experiences in the same way. Some people end up with feelings of fear or revulsion. What makes the difference? This question is raised in an incisive overview of SLE research by one of its foremost practitioners:

> The experiences that people remember as significant in motivating their care and concern for the natural world may be characterized as exchanges between an external and internal environment: an external environment composed of the qualities of physical surroundings, and social mediators of the physical world's meaning; and an internal environment of the child's needs, abilities, emotions, and interests. Almost all of the categories of analysis in the existing research refer to the external environment of natural areas and altered habitats, or social mediators such as friends and relatives, teachers, and books. Very few categories even begin to address the "silent side" of these experiences, which is the internal environment of the child who receptively responds to these places and people . . . In future interviews and surveys, and in observations of children's own environmental behavior, more attention needs to be given to articulating the characteristics of the person who ultimately gives external events their significance . . . *the ultimate target of research about significant life experiences is not merely to know the experiences that people have had, but how significance becomes constructed.*
>
> (Chawla 1998: 380; emphasis added)

In order to understand how experience motivates care and concern for the environment, we need to first understand how experience is given meaning in our individual internal environments. In the first place, as Chawla points out, this would help us to explain why the same experiences produce different emotions and outcomes in different people. Thus far, this type of research has been lacking.

In over a decade of work with nature conservationists in the UK and Ireland, anthropologist Kay Milton has focused on the question of what motivates care and concern for the environment.[6] The ecological model of emotion that Milton has developed gives voice to the "silent side" that Chawla mentions, and helps us to gain a better understanding of this vital internal link between experience and action. Milton explains how emotion is this link: emotions motivate action by identifying what matters to us (2002: 149), and indeed are fundamental to all learning. In this emotional process, Milton found that environmental care and commitment are often associated with the perception of what she terms "personhood" in nature. Specifically, this perception of personhood involves the discovery of characteristics like individuality, volition, and emotion in non-human beings, attributes that characterize humans but are not unique to them. This finding suggests a number of possible refinements to environmental education theory and practice.

Perceiving personhood: enhancing theories of environmental learning

People called him the "birdwatching cop" (*guanniao jingcha*). While pursuing graduate studies at Shanghai Normal University, Wang Ximin was taken birdwatching by a fellow student— and was immediately smitten. "It was so fascinating!" he recalls. "All along, each of those birds had a different name! I never knew that." As a child, Wang's rural upbringing gave him plenty of opportunities to directly experience nature and the outdoors, "but no one ever told me what this thing was called, or what that thing was called." However, as soon as he was introduced by name to the living things around him—when he could put names to faces—he perceived them in a new light, and his relationship with the non-human world underwent a powerful change.

Wang's passion for birding and his outrage at bird poaching prompted him to enlist in the Jiangsu Province Public Security Bureau for several years, where he worked to enforce anti-poaching laws while writing essays on birding that were published in the local media. Nowadays Wang relies on education to promote conservation: as Head of the Environmental Education Team for China's largest botanical garden—the Chinese Academy of Sciences' Xishuangbanna Tropical Botanical Garden—Wang and his staff educate thousands of Chinese visitors every year, and the garden is a major center for environmental education graduate training and practice.

What motivates people like Wang Ximin to devote their careers to care for the non-human world? As noted above, the significant life experience studies of Chawla and others consistently find that direct contact with nature is a key factor. Yet as Chawla points out, we are missing a link: although we have identified patterns, apparent correlations of influences and outcomes, we only vaguely understand how a particular experience is internally made meaningful such that it inspires environmental care. Anthropologist Kay Milton offers a persuasive answer: care for nature may be motivated by the perception of nature's "personhood."

How does this happen? In the first place, argues Milton, the perception of personhood in nature occurs in a process of learning and experience that is fundamentally emotional. Recall Chawla's question regarding children's inner, "silent side" where experiences are made meaningful, and childhood experience of nature comes to motivate care for the non-human world. Milton would characterize this as an emotional process of learning (2002, 2005a, 2007) in which biological and socio-cultural influences combine to connect us to our surroundings. Emotions, writes Milton, identify what matters to us, and thereby motivate us to particular ends. In particular, the environmentalists she spoke with often empathized or identified with non-human animals and other living beings. This sentiment closely resembles the "environmental sensitivity" invoked by EE researchers. Indeed, like the SLE researchers, Milton finds that childhood experience of direct nature contact and the influence of an older companion are common themes among the environmentalists with whom she worked (2002: 63–70). But she takes the analysis further: she explains how "significance is constructed" and nature made meaningful through the perception of personhood in the non-human world.

Personhood, for Milton, is represented by such qualities as volition, capacity for emotion, responsiveness . . . and individuality: that unique combination of name, appearance, and behavior that kindled Wang Ximin's passion for birds. Humans can and do perceive these attributes in non-human animals (such as pets), which relate to each other and to us in ways that seem to demonstrate these qualities. But, as Milton says (2002: 78), we can also perceive them in other natural entities, including "ecosystems, Mother Earth and nature as a whole, because these things can also relate to us, and/or appear to do so, in responsive ways."

Our predisposition to discover personhood in the non-human world is most vividly and elaborately evidenced by the beliefs and practices of many hunter-gatherer societies, in which humans live in an intimately interactive and often directly dependent relationship with the non-human world. Bird-David (1999) describes this as a "relational epistemology." But this propensity is far from unique to hunter-gatherers: Milton holds that it is characteristic of all humans. Following Bird-David, she argues (2002: 86) that "we can perceive personhood in anything that appears actively to relate to us, that engages our attention in ways that suggest the possibility of interaction." It is simply that the "intensity" of this responsive relationship is greater in societies such as those of hunter-gatherers, due to the quantity and quality of contact between humans and nature.

Milton is careful to distinguish the perception of personhood from anthropomorphism, describing it instead as "egomorphism," since

> our understanding of non-human animals as persons—that is, as beings with emotions, purposes and personalities—is based on our perceptions of them as 'like me', as distinct from 'like us', or human-like. These perceptions arise in our interactions with them, and in our observations of their interaction with each other, in which intersubjectivity is self-evidently generated. They are no different, in essence, from our perception of our fellow human beings as persons.
>
> *(Milton 2005a: 263)*

Milton's well-reasoned choice of terminology also highlights the connection between perceptions of personhood and care, for it is the perceived similarity between non-human beings and ourselves that enables us to identify with them, and it is this identification that forms the basis for care. As Milton (2002: 79) puts it, "the quality of personhood, which we perceive in ourselves, in other human beings and in non-human entities, is the similarity which most effectively, in western cultures, induces identification with other things." This identification serves in turn as the foundation for empathy, the seed from which active care often grows.

In addition to fostering identification and empathy, the perception of another being's personhood may also serve as evidence of its autonomy and hence the moral (as well as perhaps legal) basis for its entitlement to protection. Whales are an illustrative example of the dramatic change in public sentiment that can result from the perception of personhood and its moral implications. As Milton (2002: 30) notes, recent opposition to whaling has been framed in terms of "moral arguments [that] stress the personhood of whales, drawing attention to the similarities between whales and human beings, in their intelligences, their social organization, their capacity for emotional experience, and so on." The successful campaign to change people's attitudes and behavior toward whales suggests the role that perceptions of personhood can play in formal environmental learning.

Personhood in practice: applications to environmental learning

How can Milton's insights be applied in the practice of environmental education? First, her research offers strong evidence for the centrality of emotion to environmental learning.[7] In fact, learning of all kinds is fundamentally an emotional process: Milton notes that the acquisition, retention, and recall of knowledge are all mediated by emotion. To contrast reason and emotion, therefore, is a basic misunderstanding of how emotion (in the form of "interest" or "attention") directs, conditions, and motivates all thought processes. One of Milton's signal contributions to the study of environmentalism is her demonstration that the oft-invoked contrast between "rational" and "emotional" views of nature—frequently used to denigrate "irrational" or "sentimental" environmentalists—is a false one. So-called "rational" views of animals as resources are no less emotionally motivated than the perception of animals as persons.

Yet if care is the desired outcome (rather than fear, or revulsion, for example) what is vital is not simply an emotional relationship *per se* but one of pleasure, affection, or compassion. This can be decisive, for as Milton (2002: 115) observes, there is no reason to assume that the personalization of non-human entities will result in sympathy, "especially when they are assumed to cause harm (like foxes who steal chickens and spirits who cause damaging storms)." For environmental educators, therefore, cultivating a pleasurable perception of nature's personhood is critical.

Here it is necessary to note (but impossible to faithfully reproduce) Milton's sophisticated argument that emotion is neither exclusively biological nor socio-cultural, but the product of both influences (2002, 2005b, 2007). For the environmental educator, however, the implication is that the emotional valence of an experience cannot be solely determined by the meaning it is consciously given through social influences, such as teaching or modeling. In SLE research and other EE scholarship, much is made of the influence of role models. This influence is undeniable; but it is not the only influence, only one of the most easily identified. Milton's characterization of emotion shows that we need to give greater attention to the *pre*-social roots of emotion, and pleasure in particular. Following Damasio (1999) and James (1890), Milton sees the process of "feeling" to be one in which a physical stimulus precedes its characterization as a particular emotion (e.g. we cry and *then* "feel sad"—not the opposite). This suggests that environmental educators ought to pay special attention to the sensory context of learning, in order to maximize the possibility that an experience of nature will be "felt" as pleasurable. Environmental learning centers often prioritize physical comfort (keeping children warm and dry, for example) for this very reason.

But if feelings and emotion are so important, where does that leave knowledge? As noted above, the past half-century of environmental education research has been characterized by an ongoing and unresolved debate regarding the relative importance of knowledge in fostering stewardship and "pro-environmental behavior." Milton's work shows us how this preoccupation with knowledge overlooks how learning is essentially emotional in the first place: once we recognize that interest and attention are emotions, then it becomes clear that learning (the basis of "knowledge") is fundamentally emotional. What is important is the valence of this emotional process—is it frightening? Boring? Pleasurable?—and the particular characteristics of one's environment that are perceived in the process: are non-human beings perceived as possessing or lacking emotion, volition, individuality, or responsiveness?

However, this is not to say that scientific knowledge is irrelevant to the cultivation of environmental care. While Milton points out that science has tended to de-personalize nature in a way that "serves capitalism very well by making the exploitation of nature morally acceptable" (2002: 53), science has also provided detailed knowledge of an organism's or environment's characteristics and fostered a heightened awareness of nature's "responsive relatedness" to human action. The examples that Milton offers of this responsive relationship are negative (such as climate change and species extinctions), but science also offers us evidence of symbiotic or potentially benevolent interactions. One example is provided by the recent scholarship on plant sensing and communication (Karban 2015) and plant "intelligence" (Mancuso and Viola 2015), which reveals the complexity, sensitivity, and responsiveness of plants to humans and other organisms. Similarly, empirically-based popular studies of bird–human relationships (e.g. Marzluff and Angell 2005; Young 2013) can help readers perceive the personhood of their non-human neighbors.

As Li Bo's experience with gardening shows, however, scientific knowledge is no prerequisite: direct experience often suffices. In fact, simple introductions can effect profound transformations, as we know from human interactions. Think of how the brief, interactive experience of a personal introduction transforms a generic stranger into a "somebody" and thereby alters our attitude and behavior toward them. As Wang Ximin discovered when he was introduced to birding, a similar dynamic is possible with non-human animals.

As noted above in the discussion of hunter-gatherers, Milton (2002: 50) argues that our sensitivity to personhood in non-human animals depends on "the intensity with which they engage our attention and respond to what we do." While direct, intense interaction is not necessary for the perception of personhood, the greater the frequency and diversity of direct interaction, the more opportunities there are for personhood to be perceived. Widespread evidence of hunter-gatherer societies perceiving personhood in the non-human world—including elements like the sun, the wind, the rain, and the earth—reflect an intimate coexistence with, and even dependence upon, those elements. The problem for environmental educators is a familiar one: children in contemporary urbanized societies have fewer opportunities for direct contact with nature than ever before (Louv 2008). Milton's research offers additional testimony to the need for such contact, while demonstrating that this contact should take place in pleasurable ways that involve an interactive, "responsive relatedness" to the non-human beings in our environments. In general, the greater the number and variety of such contacts, the more likely we are to discover the personhood of these beings. If we're hoping that the outcome will be empathy and active care, then these engagements need to be facilitated in ways that make perceiving personhood satisfying and fun.

Conclusion: sustainable pleasures

Milton makes a persuasive case that emotion shapes learning, and this chapter has argued that emotion therefore deserves a greater role in environmental education theory and practice. But if emotion shapes learning, then—Milton reminds us—the opposite is also true: learning shapes emotion (2005b: 36). That is, what we learn can condition the emotions we experience in subsequent, similar contexts. To illustrate this, Milton recalls learning to fear snakes during fieldwork in Africa, such that her leg muscles tightened when walking through tall grass even after returning to Ireland (where there are no snakes). While this is an example of a fear response, a learned pleasurable response is equally conceivable. Once we learn to enjoy interacting with a non-human person, we are more likely to experience a similar feeling during subsequent encounters, a "sustainable pleasure."

Sustainable pleasures represent one of the best justifications for environmental education. In the first place, every child is arguably entitled to these enduring, healthy, and accessible sources of emotional well-being. Beyond this birthright, however, sustainable pleasures are likely to have a broader appeal than the instrumentalist perspective that sees environmental education as a means of fostering a set of predetermined behaviors. If, as some argue (Jickling and Wals 2008; Wals 2012), the instrumental approach ought to be supplanted by an emancipatory perspective that emphasizes capacity-building and critical thinking, the capacity to perceive (and enjoy) nature's personhood deserves nurturing as well.

Notes

1 See Kopnina (2012, 2013) concerning the advantages of anthropological methodology in environmental education (EE) research.

2 Among the 100+ contributors in the 2013 *International Handbook of Research on Environmental Education*, for example, there does not appear to be a single anthropologist. By contrast, children's environmental learning is the focus of one chapter in a recent collection of anthropological research on children's learning (Zarger 2010). The author's extensive research on the topic (e.g. Zarger 2002; Zarger and Stepp 2004; Baines and Zarger 2012) appears to be little known in the field of environmental education research.

3 In the wake of these studies, the importance of children's direct contact with nature has become a focus of popular concern, as shown in North America by Richard Louv's (2008) best-selling book *Last Child in the Woods* (as well as the civic organization Children & Nature Network) and proposed legislation (No Child Left Inside Act; US Congress 2013) that the book has inspired. However, the equal importance of social experiences—such as the presence of role models—has received far less attention.

4 For a detailed discussion of the strengths and potential weaknesses of significant life experience research, see Chawla and Derr (2012).

5 For example, "environmental sensitivity" is a key component of the North American National Environmental Literacy Assessment (in which it is defined as "having positive feelings for the environment"). As Marcinkowski correctly notes, however:

> What remains most difficult about environmental sensitivity is its assessment (e.g. the method and timing of data collection, the sensitivity of measures and/or analyses). From post hoc research with adults, it is believed that this 'sense of empathy' toward the natural world develops over time (Tanner 1980; Peterson 1982), though little is currently known about its development over time, in part due to these assessment difficulties.
>
> *(Marcinkowski 1998: 30–31)*

6 Milton's writings include the book *Loving Nature* (2002) and a series of book chapters that focus on, and elaborate, that book's core themes (2005a, 2005b, 2007).

7 The key role of emotion in environmental learning is also explored by prominent environmental education scholars such as Sobel (1996).

References

Baines K and Zarger R 2012. Circles of value: Integrating Maya environmental knowledge into Belizean schools. In H Kopnina (ed.) *Anthropology of Environmental Education*. New York: Nova Science Publishers, pp. 65–86.

Bird-David N 1999. Animism revisited: Personhood, environment and relational epistemology. *Current Anthropology* 40 (Supplement, February): 67–91.

Chawla L 1998. Significant life experiences revisited: A review of research on sources of environmental sensitivity. *Environmental Education Research* 4(4): 369–382.

Chawla L and Cushing D F 2007. Education for strategic behavior. *Environmental Education Research* 13(4): 427–452.

Chawla L and Derr V 2012. The development of conservation behaviors in childhood and youth. In S Clayton (ed.) *The Oxford Handbook of Environmental and Conservation Psychology*. Oxford: Oxford University Press, pp. 527–555.

Damasio A R 1999. *The Feeling of What Happens: Body and Emotion in the Making of Consciousness*. London: Heinemann.

Efird R 2014. Closing the green gap: Policy and practice in Chinese environmental education. In R Efird and J C-K Lee (eds) *Schooling for Sustainable Development across the Pacific*. Dordrecht, the Netherlands: Springer, pp. 279–292.

Hungerford H and Volk T 1990. Changing learner behavior through environmental education. *Journal of Environmental Education* 21(3): 8–21.

James W 1890. *Principles of Psychology*. New York: Holt.

Jickling B and Wals A E J 2008. Globalization and environmental education: Looking beyond sustainable development. *Journal of Curriculum Studies* 40(1): 1–21.

Karban R 2015. *Plant Sensing and Communication*. Chicago, IL: Chicago University Press.

Kollmuss A and Agyeman J 2002. Mind the gap: Why do people act environmentally and what are the barriers to pro-environmental behavior? *Environmental Education Research* 8(3): 239–260.

Kopnina H 2012. Introduction: Ethnography of environmental education. In H Kopnina (ed.) *Anthropology of Environmental Education*. New York: Nova Science Publishers.

Kopnina H 2013. Future directions in environmental anthropology: Incorporating ethnography of environmental education. In H Kopnina and E Shoreman-Ouimet (eds) *Environmental Anthropology: Future Directions*. New York: Routledge, pp. 77–97.

Louv R 2008. *Last Child in the Woods: Saving our Children from Nature-deficit Disorder*. Chapel Hill, NC: Algonquin.

Mancuso S and Viola A 2015. *Brilliant Green: The Surprising History and Science of Plant Intelligence*. Washington, DC: Island Press.

Marcinkowski T 1998. Predictors of responsible environmental behavior: A review of three dissertation studies. In H Hungerford, W Bluhm, T Volk and J Ramsey (eds) *Essential Readings in Environmental Education*. Champaign, IL: Stipes Publishing Co., pp. 227–256.

Marzluff J and Angell T 2005. *In the Company of Crows and Ravens*. New Haven, CT: Yale University Press.

Milton K 1996. *Environmentalism and Cultural Theory: Exploring the Role of Anthropology in Environmental Discourse*. London: Routledge.

Milton K 2002. *Loving Nature: Towards an Ecology of Emotion*. London and New York: Routledge.

Milton K 2005a. Anthropomorphism or egomorphism? The perception of non-human animals by human ones. In J Knight (ed.) *Animals in Person*. Oxford: Berg, pp. 255–271.

Milton K 2005b. Meanings, feelings and human ecology. In K Milton and M Svasek (eds) *Mixed Emotions: Anthropological Studies of Feeling*. Oxford: Berg, pp. 25–41.

Milton K 2007. Emotion (or life, the universe, everything). In H Wulff (ed.) *The Emotions: A Cultural Reader*. Oxford: Berg, pp. 61–76.

Ministry of Education of the People's Republic of China 2003. Notice concerning the Ministry of Education's promulgation of the "Guidelines for implementing primary and secondary environmental education (trial)," 9 October 2003. Beijing: Ministry of Education of the People's Republic of China.

Peterson N 1982. Developmental Variables Affecting Environmental Sensitivity in Professional Environmental Educators. Unpublished Master's thesis, Southern Illinois University, Carbondale.

Short P 2010. Responsible environmental action: Its role and status in environmental education and environmental quality. *The Journal of Environmental Education* 41(1): 7–21.

Sobel D 1996. *Beyond Ecophobia: Reclaiming the Heart in Nature Education*. Great Barrington, MA: Orion Society.

Stapp W B *et al.* 1969. The concept of environmental education. *The Journal of Environmental Education* 1(1): 30–31.

Stern M J, Powell R B and Hill D 2014. Environmental education program evaluation in the new millennium: What do we measure and what have we learned? *Environmental Education Research* 20(5): 581–611.

Tanner T 1980. Significant life experiences. *The Journal of Environmental Education* 11(4): 20–24.

US Congress 2013. S.1306—No Child Left Inside Act of 2013. 113th Congress (2013–2014).

Wals A E J 2012. Learning our way out of unsustainability: The role of environmental education. In S D Clayton (ed.) *The Oxford Handbook of Environmental and Conservation Psychology*. Oxford: Oxford University Press, pp. 628–644.

Young J 2013. *What the Robin Knows: How Birds Reveal the Secrets of the Natural World*. New York: Mariner.

Zarger R K 2002. Acquisition and transmission of subsistence knowledge by Q'eqchi' Maya in Belize. In J R Stepp, F S Wyndham and R K Zarger (eds) *Ethnobiology and Biocultural Diversity*. Athens: University of Georgia Press, pp. 593–603.

Zarger R K 2010. Learning the environment. In D Lancy, J Bock and S Gaskins (eds) *The Anthropology of Learning in Childhood*. Walnut Creek, CA: AltaMira Press, pp. 341–370.

Zarger R K and Stepp J R 2004. Persistence of botanical knowledge among Tzeltal Maya children. *Current Anthropology* 45(3): 413–418.

35

SCHOOLING THE WORLD

Land-based pedagogies and the culture of schooling

Carol Black

"See that Milky Way: that Wanjina lying down. 'E got his foot in the water. Wanjina come right down to the ground at night-time. We in that water right now; only this fire keep us dry! Spirits floating around all the time, night-time, in that water. We nearly all water ourselves. That's why we all joined together; trees, animals, plants, humans, heavens, waterholes. We all joined in water."

Paddy Neowarra, Ngarinyin lawman (Bell 2010, 24)

"In an epistemological-ontological frame, Indigenous cosmologies would be examples of a symbolic interconnectedness – an abstraction of a moral code. It would be a way in which to view the world – the basis for an epistemological stance. From a Haudenosaunee worldview, this is what happened."

Vanessa Watts, Anishnaabe-Haudenosaunee scholar (2013, 26)

"The medium is the message."

Marshall McLuhan (1994, 7)

Introduction

At its deepest level anthropology raises questions that are epistemological in nature: how do we know the things we think we know about the world and our place in it, and how is that knowledge conditioned by culture rather than absolute? After centuries of being dismissed as "mythology" or "folklore" by Euro-Western scientists, the ecological knowledge of small-scale Indigenous societies is now increasingly valued by natural scientists, conservation organizations, and international agencies. Unfortunately, however, there tends to be only superficial recognition of this value in the current global movement for universal schooling, which has arguably become the most powerful vector worldwide for the destruction of traditional ecological knowledge and the Indigenous pedagogies through which it is transmitted to future generations (Barnhardt and Kawagley 2005; Ohmagari and Berkes 1997; Rival 2000; Simpson 2014).

Institutional schooling as the primary venue for children's learning is a very recent historical phenomenon; as Sutton (2000: 107) points out, "the worldwide institutionalization of children in schools may rank among the most profound forces of global cultural change of the twentieth century." Historically, advocates of universal schooling have shared several key assumptions and attitudes with Christian missionaries:

1   that the new knowledge and systems they are bringing are an unalloyed good;
2   that all people worldwide should adopt these systems in essentially the same form; and
3   that nothing of importance is lost when old understandings and practices are abandoned and replaced with the new.

Just as non-Christian societies have been seen by missionaries as "heathen" rather than as having different but valid spiritual beliefs, societies that lack schools are often seen not as having different but valid modes of knowledge and learning, but as "uneducated" and "illiterate." And just as the "salvation" of Indigenous people has often historically been the companion of conquest, the "education" of Indigenous people is often an integral part of planned programs of economic development and resource extraction on Indigenous lands (Pandya 2005; Rival 2000; Sutton 2000).

Marie Battiste has coined the term "cognitive imperialism" to describe the process through which schools function to validate certain forms of cognition and to devalue other forms of human perception, intellect, art, and spiritual understanding which for millennia have guided human relationship to the natural world in material ways (Battiste 1998: 19). Proponents of universal education view the teaching of environmental science in the classroom as the appropriate way to educate students about natural systems and conservation; Indigenous knowledge is generally given at best a secondary epistemological status within the school system, often viewed as superstition or mythology, as something which may have value as part of students' cultural heritage, but not as "real" knowledge that will frame their understanding of reality and guide their decisions in the future (Canessa 2004; Watts 2013; Zarger 2010).

Because of the widespread tendency to see "education" as a universal good, even as a universal "human right," the complex cascade of direct and indirect changes that occur when societies move from Indigenous pedagogies to institutional schooling have not received adequate study, and even radical critics of Eurocentric education often accept as inevitable that school itself is now the universal vehicle for human learning (Rival 2000; Zarger 2010). Efforts may be made to hire Indigenous teachers, to incorporate traditional knowledge and practices into the classroom, or to implement "two-way" or "both-ways" education, which attempt to provide "the best of both" Indigenous and Eurocentric intellectual traditions. But as Marshall McLuhan (1994: 7) famously said about television, *"the medium is the message"*; in other words, it is essential to closely examine school itself as a Eurocentric cultural construct. The structures, rituals, and assumptions of modern schooling both embed and rapidly propagate the epistemologies, values, and economic ideologies of Euro-Western societies, and may alter Indigenous cultures, livelihoods, and environments in radical and sometimes irrevocable ways. It is likewise essential to recognize that this phenomenon is not just curricular but deeply structural, and its impacts are not easily mitigated at a superficial level.

The culture of schooling

Henrich *et al.* (2010: 1) have pointed out the disconnect between anthropology and the other behavioral sciences—including cognitive science, educational psychology, and child development studies—which frequently make universal statements about human nature, cognition, development, and behavior based on observations limited to "Western, Educated, Industrialized, Rich, and Democratic (WEIRD)" societies. But the ethnographic record makes it clear that "WEIRD" societies are not at all typical of human societies in the ways they approach learning; far from being the "norm" against which other societies should be measured, they represent a radical departure from previous approaches to child development.

"Indigenous" societies are extraordinarily diverse, dynamic, and constantly evolving; the boundaries between the "traditional" and the "modern" are indistinct, complex, and constantly shifting; as Barnhardt and Kawagley (2005: 12) caution, any generalizations should be recognized as "indicative and not definitive." But in our anxiety not to essentialize or idealize cultures, it is equally important that we do not overlook what Zarger (2010: 356) has called a "remarkable degree of overlap in broad findings" about the ways the culture of modern institutional schooling differs from Indigenous land-based pedagogies all over the world (Anderson 2012; Gaskins and Paradise 2010; Jain and Jain 2015; Ohmagari and Berkes 1997; Pandya 2005; Rival 2000; Rogoff 2003; Sarangapani 2003; Simpson 2014; Sorenson 1976; Stairs 1995; Teasdale 1990). These differences may include:

1   *Physical separation of children from nature:* It is in itself a radical disruption of the relationship between human beings and the natural environment to physically confine children indoors for most of the day. Children in small-scale societies typically spend most of their time outdoors immersed in the natural environment, and develop an intimate knowledge of their local ecosystems through long hours of whole-body play, independent exploration and experimentation, and active participation in land-based subsistence activities.

2   *Physical segregation of children from the community:* In almost all small-scale societies (including European societies until very recently), children have grown up embedded in the adult community and in mixed-age groups of children. Learning through emulation of older children, through the care and guidance of younger children, and through observation of and participation in adult livelihoods, all primary modes of learning in small-scale societies, is thus profoundly disrupted by full-time attendance in age-segregated institutions.

3   *Authority, hierarchy, and coercion:* Modern education is normally organized in hierarchical authority structures that extend from child to teacher to district to state to national government. Learning is understood as compulsory, and children in a classroom are generally not permitted to move or speak without explicit permission from an authority figure, with the threat of punishment to enforce control. This stands in stark contrast to many small-scale societies, in which learning is non-coerced, based on voluntary observation, participation, and free play, and where even very young children may have a high degree of autonomy and freedom from direct control of their moment-to-moment choices and activities.

4   *Individualism, competition, and ranking:* In most modern schools, learning is constructed as a competition between individuals, and students are ranked publicly by their performance in ways that have lifelong consequences. Many Indigenous cultures consider overt competition, ranking, or boasting to be undesirable, and may have significant social sanctions against individuals who set themselves above others (Boehm 1999). Within an egalitarian cultural ethos, being identified as a "star student" may cause children such discomfort that they intentionally lower their performance in order to avoid this unwanted designation (Gibson and Vialle 2007).

5   *Standardization and the construction of "failure":* Modern schooling creates universalized standards of learning tied to chronological age and then speaks in terms of "failure" or "disability" if children are unable to meet those standards. Indigenous societies often have a more flexible approach to child development, assuming that a child will learn when he or she is ready, that not all children will learn the same things in the same ways, and that natural variations in the timing of learning have little importance.

6   *Abstracted, text-based learning:* Most learning in schools is based on de-contextualized knowledge encoded in written form. School activities generally have no immediate purpose, but are seen as a preparation for future life. In most small-scale cultures, learning is contextualized in daily survival activities; children learn most of what they know through hands-on experience and participation in community life. There may be few activities whose specific purpose is "to learn"; learning is a natural by-product of doing, not a separate activity.

7   *Explicit instruction and evaluation:* School learning relies heavily on direct teacher-controlled instruction and explicit evaluation. Adult involvement in Indigenous learning is more often based on example or demonstration, or in indirect modes such as storytelling or ceremony rather than in explicit instruction. Adults often assume it is best to let the child observe, experiment, and participate rather than to instruct him/her directly. It is often not assumed that learning will be immediately visible or measurable, but that understanding and competence will emerge over time. Recent studies in child cognitive development indicate that young children exposed to direct instruction may focus their attention more on the teacher than on the subject at hand, becoming less exploratory and experimental in their interaction with the environment, suggesting that changes in the social construction of learning may have impacts on how children learn about the environment (Bonawitz *et al.* 2011).

8   *Narrowly focused attentional state:* Gaskins and Paradise (2010: 98) have suggested that there are significant cultural differences in attentional stance, and that children in cultures where learning is largely non-coerced and observational spend much of their time in a state of "open attention," where attention is broadly focused but alert over prolonged periods of time, enabling children to pick up on small changes in their environment and attend in a sustained way to activities or events of interest. Children in school, by contrast, are asked to narrowly focus their attention on tasks that the teacher assigns, to switch their attention on command, and to tune out other information from the environment, which is seen as a "distraction." A child in a classroom in a state of "open attention" would probably be seen as having an attention "disorder"; conversely, a child in the state of narrowed attention fostered in schools may be less able to learn from observation of the environment.

9   *Analytic, secular, "objective" knowledge:* Schools promote an analytic approach to knowledge, which is compartmentalized into separate "subjects," with the secular realm clearly segregated from the spiritual. Scientific knowledge is understood as "objective," with human beings as the "subject" and the natural world as the "object" of human examination. Indigenous cultures generally construe knowledge in a holistic way, with, for example, botanical knowledge inseparable from both spiritual beliefs and pragmatic survival skills. The natural world is often understood as existing in a reciprocal relationship with human beings; other species and land may be understood as having agency, part of a web of reciprocal obligations, rather than as merely the passive object of human study. This perspective often includes the understanding that "the land teaches us" (Deloria and Wildcat 2001: 121; Watts 2013; Pawu-Kurlpurlurnu *et al.* 2008).

Figure 35.1 Ladakhi children play in a multi-age group as their parents work at the harvest nearby. From time to time they join the work to watch or participate. Both work and play are collaborative and non-competitive, and learning occurs incrementally and contextually.

Source: Photo by Jim Hurst, from the film *Schooling the World* (Black 2010).

Figure 35.2 In school, children's learning is largely abstracted from their environment, and has little utility in rural settings. Learning is socially constructed as competitive and individualistic, with large numbers of children designated as "failures."

Source: Photo by Jim Hurst, from the film *Schooling the World* (Black 2010).

Environmental impacts of schooling

This "culture of schooling" impacts small-scale cultures and environments at multiple levels. The institutionalization of children may sever crucial links in the web of relationships between human beings, knowledge, and land found in many Indigenous societies, altering how children perceive, interact with, and understand their natural environment. Rival (2000: 150) has observed that among the Huaorani of Ecuador, "schools introduce a new type of spatiotemporal organization, de-skill children in relation to their indigenous knowledge, alter the forest environment, and modify traditional social relationships." For agricultural or pastoral societies, the loss of children's participation and skill development in farming, herding, and childcare can negatively impact the long-term economic viability of land-based livelihoods (Norberg-Hodge 2009; Rival 2000). For Ongee hunter-gatherers in the Andaman Islands or the Huaorani in Ecuador (where schools are often privately funded by oil companies), schooling has been introduced as part of planned resource development on tribal lands, and dovetails with an agenda of concentrating widely dispersed populations, shifting children off the land into cash-based livelihoods, and training more cooperative partners in resource extraction (Pandya 2005; Rival 2000). This underlying agenda is often amplified by overt messages in the school curriculum about "progress," "development," "good jobs," and "higher" standards of living which lead to the stigmatization of land-based livelihoods as "backward" or "primitive" and of traditional elders as "ignorant" and "illiterate" (Canessa 2004; Norberg-Hodge 2009; Rival 2000).

The structural format of school generally imposes a gradual de-skilling of children from land-based livelihoods. Young people who are in school all day do not have the opportunity to attain the depth and breadth of perception and insight into plant and animal life, weather patterns, and interaction among species and elements in ecosystems that their elders had, and the result can be a steady loss of detailed knowledge in successive generations (Ohmagari and Berkes 1997; Pandya 2005; Rival 2000). Both Zarger (2010) and Rival (2000: 154) found that first-generation schooled children could still name many plant and animal species, but Rival found significant losses among Huaorani children in the practical skills involved in hunting, climbing trees to gather fruits, and making household objects such as hammocks and clay pots, and found (2000: 155) that "only nonschooled children could successfully associate names and wild specimens collected from the forest." Ohmagari and Berkes (1997) found that along with losses in material skills such as hunting, fur preparation, and food processing were losses in culturally significant attitudes and practices such as patience, self-reliance, and food sharing. Gikuyu parents in Ngecha, Kenya and Quechua parents in the Peruvian Andes reported increased selfishness and decreased respect for elders among children as they absorb the competitive, individualistic values inculcated in school (Edwards and Whiting 2004; Tillman Salas 2005). Chavajay and Rogoff (2002: 55) have found that the hierarchical construction of learning in school may "contribute to the reshaping of traditional collaborative social organization among indigenous Mayan people."

"The education trap"

As students lose knowledge, skills, and attitudes for land-based survival, they frequently fail to gain the promised benefits of modern schools. As Barnhardt and Kawagley (2005) point out, Indigenous students in many parts of the world have

> demonstrated a distinct lack of enthusiasm for the experience of schooling in its conventional form—an aversion that is most often attributable to an alien institutional

457

culture, rather than any lack of innate intelligence, ingenuity, or problem-solving skills on the part of the students.

(Barnhardt and Kawagley 2005: 10)

Students in oppressed or colonized societies may be actively resistant to the agendas of educators; as Hampton (1995: 7) puts it, "the failure of non-Native education of Natives can be read as the success of native resistance to cultural, spiritual, and psychological genocide" (see also Ogbu 2000; Teasdale 1990). But whether caused by cultural incompatibility, active resistance to colonialism, poor school quality, discrimination, or a combination of factors, the result may be extraordinarily high failure rates among Indigenous students (Canessa 2004; Munroe and Gauvain 2010; Rival 2000; Wilson 2014).

For many students, the long-term consequence is what Martyn Namarong of Papua New Guinea has called "the education trap" (Romanes 2011: 1)—the global phenomenon of Indigenous children who no longer learn land-based survival skills, but who fail to achieve a level of success in school that has any real personal or market value (Black 2010; Canessa 2004; Lancy 2010; Pandya 2005; Romanes 2011). Schooling tends to accelerate a general trend toward the urbanization of land-based peoples; school training has little value in traditional rural environments, and qualifies one at best for jobs in an urban cash economy; unsuccessful students often migrate into unskilled low-wage labor and unemployment in urban fringe areas or slums. Those who do remain on the land experience increased pressure to accept resource extraction on their territories, as mining, oil drilling, plantations, and timber operations offer jobs for those who are no longer competent in land-based subsistence livelihoods. And as traditional livelihoods are disrupted or abandoned, traditional methods of waste, resource, and water quality management may go along with them, often leading to increases in pollution and resource degradation on Indigenous lands. Nutritional status and health may deteriorate as traditional foods are replaced with cheap processed foods high in sugar and salt and low in nutrients; mental health problems, substance abuse, and suicide often increase sharply as traditional belief systems and social structures break down without adequate replacement. Poverty statistics that measure only changes in cash income rather than painting a more detailed ecological picture may thus conceal significant degradation of physical environments and quality of life. At the end of this cascade of changes, Indigenous people often find traditional hunting, fishing, and plant use outlawed in the name of environmental "conservation," making a revival of sustainable traditional livelihoods difficult or impossible (Black 2010; Norberg-Hodge 2009; Ohmagari and Berkes 1997; Survival International 2007).

Proposed solutions

A number of reforms are typically proposed to mitigate the negative impacts of schooling on Indigenous children: these include hiring Indigenous teachers, including Indigenous knowledge in the curriculum, and the creation of Indigenous-run schools with a philosophy of "two-way" or "both ways" education. While all of these reforms may have positive impacts for students, where they leave the Eurocentric structure of institutional school intact—with its underlying culture, epistemology, power structure, and systems of evaluation—they may be severely limited in their power to effect significant change.

Few would question that hiring Indigenous teachers is beneficial, but Battiste (2002: 8) emphasizes that "an Indigenous people's heritage can be fully learned or understood only by means of the pedagogy traditionally employed by these peoples themselves." Indigenous

Figure 35.3 These "uneducated" Ladakhi women are highly skilled in sustainable food and textile production, animal care, sustainable building, and water and waste management. Here they are laughing about the helplessness of young people who have gone away to school: "They just stand around with their hands in their pockets. They don't know how to do anything."

Source: Photo by Jim Hurst, from the film *Schooling the World* (Black 2010).

Figure 35.4 "The education trap": millions of young people who fail in school find themselves without the skills to live on the land, but without the skills to succeed in the cash economy.

Source: Photo by Jim Hurst, from the film *Schooling the World* (Black 2010).

teachers have generally had to leave their communities and ecosystems to succeed in a modern university system; they have had to accept the validity of a culture of individualism, competition, ranking, and credentials which may be alien to their own cultural norms; and they have had to accept the standards of evidence required by academia, where a peer-reviewed study is considered a valid knowledge source, but the words of an Indigenous elder are not (Simpson 2014). Their position as teacher requires them in turn to impose the same values and standards on their students. Credentialed teachers may find it challenging to unpack the impacts of their professional indoctrination; as Battiste (1998: 24) asks, "[W]here are Indigenous people to find experts who can rise above the value contamination of their own education?"

Canessa's (2004) research in Bolivia shows that Aymara teachers working in their own communities of origin may in some cases be so assimilated to a mainstream neoliberal paradigm of "development" and "progress" that they transmit racist conceptions of inferiority to Aymara children. The teacher's status in the community often derives from his having "succeeded" in "escaping" the "poor" "underdeveloped" village of his youth (schoolteachers in small, remote communities are almost always men). He exhorts the children to work hard to "succeed" as he did, while at the same time rebuking them for being "dirty" and "backward." A teacher from Pocobaya, Bolivia portrays his own community as shameful to his students:

> We were poor and backward in 1825 and look at us! We are poor and backward now. We are poorly dressed and poorly fed . . . Who has an adequate house here? No one . . . [O]ur houses are like the houses of animals.
>
> *(Canessa 2004: 191)*

As Canessa points out, the adobe houses in Pocobaya are solidly built and warm, and the traditional local diet is more nutritious than many urban people's diets. But the constant repetition of the terms "progress" and "civilization" in the classroom successfully instills in children a belief in their own inferiority.

Another frequent reform involves "including" Indigenous knowledge in the curriculum. Often it is assumed that this is a simple matter of dedicating a small percentage of total class time to Indigenous subject matter. Activities may be approached in what Canessa (2004) calls a "folkloric" manner; students may dress in traditional costume and perform traditional songs or dances on special holidays; "legends" and "myths" may be read aloud or illustrated, or traditional arts and crafts may be taught in the classroom. Another approach is what Leanne Simpson has called the "extractive" approach, where Indigenous botanical or ecological knowledge that satisfies the criteria of modern science is "extracted" from its Indigenous context (Klein 2013). These approaches can tend to trivialize, distort, or amputate the complex meanings that Indigenous people bring to their understanding of human relationship to the natural world (Battiste 2002; Sarangapani 2003). As Watts explains:

> [H]abitats and ecosystems are better understood as societies from an Indigenous point of view; meaning that they have ethical structures, inter-species treaties and agreements . . . When an Indigenous cosmology is translated through a Euro-Western process, it necessitates a distinction between place and thought. The result of this distinction is a colonized interpretation of both place and thought, where land is simply dirt and thought is only possessed by humans.
>
> *(Watts 2013: 23, 32)*

Seemingly straightforward efforts to integrate Indigenous knowledge into the school curriculum may be stubbornly unsuccessful, raising more questions than they answer. Baines and Zarger (2012: 76–80) provide a detailed account of their effort to create a school science curriculum based on the traditional botanical knowledge of a Mayan community in Belize. With the support and consultation of the local community, they designed a lesson plan for students aged 8–13 that attempted to connect local plant knowledge with an understanding of the scientific method. Students were first taught in class about the five senses and about how scientists, as well as traditional Mayans, use their senses to gain knowledge about the natural world. They were then sent outside with a worksheet and asked to list "two ways that each sense can help you find out something about a plant that is important to you in the bush, the farm or around the house." Responses regarding the sense of sight included:

"Mango tree that have a dark green leaf"
"The *jom* (calabash) tree with my round eyes"
"The *mox* (waha leaf) to wrap tamales"
"Trees"
"White truck outside"
"The angry animal"
"Like dead things"
"Things"

Given the extensive knowledge and competence the children demonstrated outside school, the researchers were surprised to find that they seemed to find this exercise "challenging." Any effort to interpret these results should consider the impacts of the social construction of institutional school on children's cognitive and emotional experience of the activity. How do the power relationships and the reward-and-punishment framework of the classroom affect their thinking strategies? How does the analytical, abstracted emphasis of school science intersect with their contextualized way of thinking about plants? How does the time-pressured, competitive, coerced framework of school assignments intersect with knowledge gained in non-coercive, non-competitive situations like helping elders with daily tasks, or playing and exploring with multi-age groups of children?

As Chavajay and Rogoff (2002) have pointed out, the social construction of Indigenous learning has potential benefits for all children, and in fact many proposals for reform of mainstream education systems involve facilitating learning in ways that look more like Indigenous pedagogies than like the "culture of schooling" which has been dominant throughout the twentieth century and beyond. In the United States, despite extensive state-mandated science curricula, rates of science knowledge are surprisingly low, with one recent study indicating that one in four Americans does not understand that the Earth revolves around the sun (National Science Foundation 2014: Appendix 7, Table 7–9). Western scientists as well as researchers in science education have suggested that freedom, curiosity, observation, experimentation, and horizontal collaboration—precisely the conditions of learning in most Indigenous societies—may be more effective conditions for deep science learning than the teacher-directed, textbook-based instruction found in most classrooms (Vedder-Weiss and Fortus 2011).

In any case, it must be recognized that efforts to "Indigenize the curriculum" may have unforeseen complexities and pitfalls. Ultimately each community must answer for itself whether it is in fact a net benefit to make the attempt to bring Indigenous environmental knowledge into the "culture of schooling," or whether, as Anderson (2012) and Sarangapani (2003) suggest, in some cases, Indigenous knowledge can best be kept alive by keeping it *out* of the classroom.

The reform trap

More comprehensive initiatives such as Indigenous-run charter schools in the United States or "two-way" education in Australia's Northern Territory have often achieved strong support in local communities, with many students and families reporting greatly improved experiences. In the effort to develop satisfying programs for Indigenous students, however, these schools may find themselves moving farther from the structures and content of conventional schools; instead of bringing elders into the classroom, for example, they may bring students out into the bush with elders, and they may reduce emphasis on quantitative measures such as standardized testing (Mandel and Teamey 2015; Teasdale 1990).

In some regions, Indigenous parents go beyond these partial solutions and choose not to send children to school at all, or to send some children and keep others at home (Lynch and Judd 2009; Rival 2000; Sarangapani 2003). Governments and NGOs often portray these parents as negligent or oppressive, and the children as truant or deprived, but families may in fact be making well-reasoned decisions about how to maintain their cultural integrity while still accessing some of the positive returns of schooling. In rare cases, there has been recognition by governments or NGOs that instruction in basic academic skills can be offered in ways that do not require the disruption of culture and environment that occurs with the full-time institutionalization of children. Lessons in literacy, arithmetic, health, governance, and land rights can be conducted at flexible times, for example, so that traditional culture and skill development remain in the foreground, and they can include adults rather than excluding them, in order to reduce disruption to family relationships and respect for elders (Lynch and Judd 2009).

Unfortunately, however, as long as the success or failure of these initiatives is measured by mainstream educational metrics, even the best projects can fall victim to a predictable cycle of partial reform, partial success (as measured by the community), partial "failure" (as measured by mainstream metrics), followed by defunding and a return to conventional education. After a 25-year initiative in "two-way" education in Australia's Northern Territory, a new government report shows fewer than 10 percent of children achieving the government minimum educational standards, and actually recommends abandoning bilingual education and sending Aboriginal children from remote areas to English-only boarding schools—essentially a return to nineteenth- and early twentieth-century educational policy (Wilson 2014). Unless both the goals and the social and epistemological construction of modern institutional schooling are examined at a deeper structural level, this process can tend to repeat itself, becoming a kind of "reform trap." Sustainable solutions will not come, according to Nishnaabeg scholar Leanne Betasamosake Simpson (2014: 22) until Indigenous people "stop looking for legitimacy within the colonizer's education system and return to valuing and recognizing our individual and collective intelligence on its own merits and on our own terms."

Learning the land

The Kaluli people of Bosavi in Papua New Guinea are master ornithologists; Steven Feld has estimated that a typical Kaluli adult may be able to identify 60 species of birds by their songs (Feld: personal communication), with the ability to distinguish between contact, alarm, and social calls, along with extensive knowledge of habitat, ecology, and migratory patterns (Feld 2012). How is this remarkable level of knowledge passed along to children?

The Kaluli believe that birds are the spirits of their dead, and they hear birdsongs as rich with the human emotions of sorrow and longing; the call of the spotted fruitdove is heard as "the cry of a young child, hungry and calling for its mother" (Feld 2012: 30). The Kaluli have an extensive poetic tradition of song and story involving the voices of birds, which map familiar places in the forest: "Since the spirits of the dead, the 'gone reflections' (*ane mama*), typically reappear in the treetops as birds, songs follow forest paths from a bird's flight perspective" (Feld 2001: 47).

During his initial research on this musical tradition, Feld worked closely with a Kaluli man, Jubi, in an attempt to cross-reference Kaluli bird knowledge with scientific taxonomy. He describes how he came face to face with the limitations of his approach rather suddenly one day:

> We came to an impasse trying to specify the zoological content of closely related Kaluli taxa. With characteristic patience, Jubi was imitating calls, behavior, and nesting. Suddenly something snapped; I asked a question and Jubi blurted back, "Listen—to you they are birds, to me they are voices in the forest."
>
> *(Feld 2012: 44–45)*

Feld realized that he had been "forcing a method of knowledge construction—isolation and reduction—onto a domain of experience that Kaluli do not isolate or reduce." His severing of "mythology" from "science" was a violation of fundamental Kaluli beliefs about the nature of reality; "that things have a visible and invisible aspect; that sounds and behaviors have an outside, an inside, and an underneath; or that human relationships are reflected in the ecology and natural order of the forest" (Feld 2012: 45)

This complex context for natural observations may in fact be what enables children to absorb large amounts of information about their environment. Feld recorded two women singing as they rested after scraping sago pith. Papuan women are commonly accompanied by their children as they go about such tasks; children may be playing nearby, older children may be helping with the work or caring for babies and toddlers, and younger children may be imitating adults with improvised tools (Sorenson 1976). As the two women rested, they began to sing a song about the call of the Golden Whistler (*doloso:k*, *Pachycephala pectoralis*). The song names the bird, its characteristic sound, and locates the bird in local places and trees; as Feld says (2001: 47), "the progression of named places creates a textual path of familiar lands, evocative of deeply held feelings and memories." As the women sing, the husband of one begins to scrape sago pith in a rhythm that accompanies their song, and then begins to mimic the bird's whistle in the same rhythm. The rich layers of sound created by the combination of natural sounds of the forest, the women singing, the sago being rhythmically scraped, and the imitated birdsong would simply be washing over the children playing nearby.

The result is that a repetitive physical task becomes rich with poetry, spirit, and knowledge of the natural world. The children are in a comfortable, relaxed family setting; immersed in the sounds and sights of nature; able to observe and absorb their parents' techniques for physical subsistence and at the same time absorb the stories, songs, and spiritual understanding of their people. The name and call of the bird, in this rich context, enters the memory as easily and permanently as the refrain of a favorite song. Context, emotion, repetition, relaxation, and "open attention" are all factors, as is identification with the community the song arises from (Gaskins and Paradise 2010). Unlike school learning, where the laborious "learning curve" of intentional memorization is often followed by an equally steep "forgetting curve," this type of learning is permanent (Smith 1998: 31–33). And just as it would be impossible to memorize the lyrics of a song as a random list of words out of order, there may be no way to memorize the calls of 60 bird species without the rich layering of spirit, story, emotion, family, place, and survival in which they are embedded for the Kaluli. By Western epistemological standards, the Kaluli are anthropomorphizing the birds, making a rather childish cognitive error. And yet the Kaluli know the birds and their environment in a way that would take a scientist a lifetime to master.

Blackfoot educator Narcisse Blood explains that it is Euro-Western educators who are making a cognitive error when they assume Indigenous knowledge to be a relatively small body of folklore and ecological information that can be treated as ancillary to a Euro-Western education. Indigenous land-based knowledge systems, Blood says, are in fact entire knowledge paradigms as extensive and as complex as the Euro-Western paradigm (Mandel and Teamey 2015). The solution to the conflict between Indigenous land-based pedagogies and modern schooling, Simpson (2014) maintains, is for Indigenous peoples to take back control of the education of their children, to rethink its goals from the ground up, to decide what knowledge they want to prioritize and how they want to teach it, and to refuse to be evaluated and defined as "failures" by the metrics of their colonizers. As Simpson puts it:

> In order to foster expertise within Nishinaabeg intelligence, we need people engaged with land as curriculum and engaged in our languages for decades, not weeks. Shouldn't we, as communities, support and nurture children that choose to only educate themselves within Nishnaabewin? Wouldn't this create a strong generation of Elders? Don't we deserve learning spaces where we do not have to address state learning objectives, curriculum, credentialism and careerism, where our only concern for recognition comes from within?
>
> *(Simpson 2014: 23)*

One of the Kaluli songs recorded by Feld refers to "a small Ornate Fruitdove (*iya:u, Ptilinopus ornatus*) that hovers at a creek" repeating the call, *"I won't be coming back"* (Feld 2001: 48). The song compares

> the children of Bosavi to fruitdoves flying away to the new school opened in the early 1970s by missionaries at the first Bosavi airstrip. The birds stop at each village on the way, calling back to their mothers, fathers, sisters, and brothers to say "I won't be coming back."
>
> *(Feld 2001: 49)*

This song, Feld says, is one of the most memorable in all of Bosavi because of the intensity of the emotions of longing and loss it conveys.

The two women singing it refused to send their children to school.

References

Anderson E N 2012. Tales Best Told Out of School: Traditional Life-skills Education Meets Modern Science Education. In H Kopnina (ed.) *Anthropology of Environmental Education: Education in a Competitive and Globalizing World.* New York: Nova Science Publishers, Inc., pp. 41–64.

Baines K and Zarger R 2012. Circles of Value: Integrating Maya Environmental Knowledge into Belizean Schools. In H Kopnina (ed.) *Anthropology of Environmental Education: Education in a Competitive and Globalizing World*. New York: Nova Science Publishers, Inc., pp. 65–86.

Barnhardt R and Kawagley A O 2005. Indigenous Knowledge Systems and Alaska Native Ways of Knowing. *Anthropology & Education Quarterly* 36(1): 8–23.

Battiste M 1998. Enabling the Autumn Seed: Toward a Decolonized Approach to Aboriginal Knowledge, Language, and Education. *Canadian Journal of Native Education* 22(1): 16–27.

——— 2002. *Indigenous Knowledge and Pedagogy in First Nations Education: A Literature Review with Recommendations*. Prepared for the National Working Group on Education and the Minister of Indian Affairs. Ottawa, ON: Indian and Northern Affairs Canada (INAC).

Black C 2010. *Schooling the World*. Documentary film. Los Angeles, CA: Lost People Films.

Boehm C 1999. *Hierarchy in the Forest: The Evolution of Egalitarian Behavior*. Cambridge, MA: Harvard University Press.

Bonawitz E, Shafto P, Gweon H, Goodman N D, Spelke E and Schulz L 2011. The Double-edged Sword of Pedagogy: Instruction Limits Spontaneous Exploration and Discovery. *Cognition* 120(3): 322–330.

Canessa A 2004. Reproducing Racism: Schooling and Race in Highland Bolivia. *Race Ethnicity and Education* 7(2): 185–204.

Chavajay P and Rogoff B 2002. Schooling and Traditional Collaborative Social Organization of Problem Solving by Mayan Mothers and Children. *Developmental Psychology* 38(1): 55–66.

Deloria Jr V and Wildcat D R 2001. *Power and Place: Indian Education in America*. Golden, CO: Fulcrum.

Edwards C P and Whiting B (eds) 2004. *Ngecha: A Kenyan Village in a Time of Rapid Social Change*. Lincoln, NE and London: University of Nebraska Press.

Feld S 2001. *Bosavi: Rainforest Music from Papua New Guinea*. Recorded and annotated by Steven Feld. A collaborative production of Smithsonian Folkways Recordings and the Institute of Papua New Guinea Studies. Washington, DC: Smithsonian Folkways Recordings.

———2012. *Sound and Sentiment: Birds, Weeping, Poetics, and Song in Kaluli Expression*. 3rd edn. Durham, NC and London: Duke University Press.

Gaskins S and Paradise R 2010. Learning through Observation in Daily Life. In D F Lancy, J Bock and S Gaskins (eds) *The Anthropology of Learning in Childhood*. Lanham, MD: Altamira Press, pp. 85–117.

Gibson K and Vialle W J 2007. The Australian Aboriginal View of Giftedness. In S N Phillipson and M McCann (eds) *Conceptions of Giftedness*. Mahwah, NJ: Lawrence Erlbaum Associates, pp. 197–224.

Hampton E 1995. Towards a Redefinition of Indian Education. In M Battiste and J Barman (eds) *First Nations Education in Canada: The Circle Unfolds*. Vancouver: University of British Columbia Press, pp. 5–46.

Henrich J, Heine S J and Norenzayan A 2010. The Weirdest People in the World? *Behavioral and Brain Sciences* 33(2–3): 61–83.

Jain M and Jain S 2015. The Culture of Schooling. Shikshantar: The Peoples' Institute for Education and Development. http://shikshantar.org (accessed 22 April 2016).

Klein N 2013. Dancing the World into Being: A Conversation with Idle No More's Leanne Simpson. *YES! Magazine*, posted 5 March. www.yesmagazine.org/peace-justice/dancing-the-world-into-being-a-conversation-with-idle-no-more-leanne-simpson (accessed 10 September 2015).

Lancy D 2010. Children's Learning in New Settings. In D F Lancy, J Bock and S Gaskins (eds) *The Anthropology of Learning in Childhood*. Lanham, MD: AltaMira Press, pp. 443–463.

Lynch K and Judd A 2009. *The School of Life: Education in a Pastoralist Community*. Bristol, UK: Taylor Brothers. http://issuu.com/kelleyslynch/docs/sol_final_issuu/1 (accessed 10 September 2015).

McLuhan M 1994. *Understanding Media*. Cambridge, MA: The MIT Press.

Mandel U and Teamey K 2015. *Re-learning the Land: A Story of Red Crow College*. Documentary film. Enlivened Learning Films, Oregon, USA.

Munroe R L and Gauvain M 2010. The Cross-cultural Study of Children's Learning and Socialization: A Short History. In D F Lancy, J Bock and S Gaskins (eds) *The Anthropology of Learning in Childhood*. Lanham, MD: AltaMira Press, pp. 35–63.

National Science Foundation 2014. Chapter 7: Science and Technology: Public Attitudes and Understanding. Appendix 7, Table 7–9. In *National Science Board Science and Engineering Indicators 2014*. Arlington, VA: NSF. (www.nsf.gov/statistics/seind14/index.cfm/chapter-7/c7h.htm (accessed 31 January 2015).

Norberg-Hodge H 2009. *Ancient Futures: Learning from Ladakh for a Globalizing World*. San Francisco, CA: Sierra Club Books.

Ogbu J U 2000. Understanding Cultural Diversity and Learning. In B A U Levinson (ed.) *Schooling the Symbolic Animal*. Lanham, MD: Rowman & Littlefield, pp. 248–266.

Ohmagari K and Berkes F 1997. Transmission of Indigenous Knowledge and Bush Skills among the Western James Bay Cree Women of Subarctic Canada. *Human Ecology* 25(2): 197–222.

Pandya V 2005. Deforesting among Andamanese Children: Political Economy and History of Schooling. In B S Hewlett and M E Lamb (eds) *Hunter-Gatherer Childhoods: Evolutionary, Developmental, & Cultural Perspectives*. New Brunswick, NJ: Transaction Publishers, pp. 385–406.

Pawu-Kurlpurlurnu W J, Holmes M and Box L 2008. *Ngurra-kurlu: A Way of Working with Warlpiri People*. DKCRC Report No. 41. Alice Springs, NT: Desert Knowledge CRC.

Rival L 2000. Formal Schooling and the Production of Modern Citizens in the Ecuadorian Amazon. In B A U Levinson (ed.) *Schooling the Symbolic Animal*. Lanham, MD: Rowman & Littlefield, pp. 146–165.

Rogoff B 2003. *The Cultural Nature of Human Development*. New York: Oxford University Press.

Romanes D 2011. Development: A Misplaced Emphasis on Education? *The Interpreter*, posted 16 November. www.lowyinterpreter.org/post/2011/11/16/Development-Misplaced-emphasis-on-education.aspx?COLLCC=1766281335& (accessed 10 September 2015).

Sarangapani P 2003. Indigenising Curriculum: Questions Posed by Baiga *Vidya*. *Comparative Education* 39(2): 199–209.

Simpson L B 2014. Land as Pedagogy: Nishnaabeg Intelligence and Rebellious Transformation. *Decolonization: Indigeneity, Education, & Society* 3(3): 1–25.

Smith F 1998. *The Book of Learning and Forgetting*. New York: Teachers College Press.

Sorenson E R 1976. *The Edge of the Forest: Land, Childhood and Change in a New Guinea Protoagricultural Society*. Washington, DC: Smithsonian Institution Press.

Stairs A 1995. Learning and Teaching in Native Education. In M Battiste and J Barman (eds) *First Nations Education in Canada: The Circle Unfolds*. Vancouver: University of British Columbia Press, pp. 139–153.

Survival International 2007. *Progress Can Kill*. http://assets.survival-international.org/static/lib/downloads/source/progresscankill/full_report.pdf (accessed 10 September 2015).

Sutton M 2000. Culture, Modernization, and Formal Education. In B A U Levinson (ed.) *Schooling the Symbolic Animal*. Lanham MD: Rowman & Littlefield, pp. 107–115.

Teasdale G R 1990. Interactions between "Traditional" and "Western" Systems of Learning: The Australian Experience. Appendix in A Little (ed.) *Understanding Culture: A Precondition for Effective Learning*. Paris: UNESCO. http://unesdoc.unesco.org/images/0008/000862/086254EB.pdf (accessed 10 September 2015).

Tillman Salas M 2005. *Iskay Yachay: Two Kinds of Knowledge*. Documentary film. Lima, Peru: Proyecto Andino de Tecnologías Campesinas.

Vedder-Weiss D and Fortus D 2011. Adolescents' Declining Motivation to Learn Science: Inevitable or Not? *Journal of Research in Science Teaching* 48(2): 199–216.

Watts V 2013. Indigenous Place-thought and Agency amongst Humans and Non-humans (First Woman and Sky Woman Go on a European World Tour!). *Decolonization: Indigeneity, Education & Society* 2(1): 20–34.

Wilson B 2014. *A Share in the Future: Review of Indigenous Education in the Northern Territory*. Darwin: Northern Territory Department of Education. www.education.nt.gov.au/__data/assets/pdf_file/0007/37294/A-Share-in-the-Future-The-Review-of-Indigenous-Education-in-the-Northern-Territory.pdf (accessed 10 September 2015).

Zarger R 2010. Learning the Environment. In D F Lancy, J Bock and S Gaskins (eds) *The Anthropology of Learning in Childhood*. Lanham, MD: AltaMira Press, pp. 341–369.

INDEX